MACRO

Economics *for* Life

Smart Choices for All?

SECOND EDITION

Avi J. Cohen

York University
University of Toronto

Toronto

Vice-President, CMPS: Gary Bennett
Editorial Director: Claudine O'Donnell
Marketing Manager: Claire Varley
Program Manager: Joel Gladstone
Project Manager: Richard di Santo
Developmental Editor: Suzanne Simpson Millar
Developmental Team Lead: Suzanne Schaan
Media Editor: Victoria Naik
Production Services: Mohinder Singh, Aptara®, Inc.
Permissions Project Manager: Joanne Tang
Photo Permissions Research: Jamey O'Quinn, Lumina Datamatics, Inc.
Text Permissions Research: Tom Wilcox, Lumina Datamatics, Inc.
Cover Designer: Anthony Leung
Interior Designer: Anthony Leung, Pearson/Cenveo Publishing Services
Cover Image: Deryk Ouseley/derykouseley.com

Original edition published by Pearson Education, Inc., Upper Saddle River, New Jersey, USA. Copyright © 2013 Pearson Education, Inc. This edition is authorized for sale only in Canada.

Library and Archives Canada Cataloguing in Publication

Cohen, Avi J., author
    Macroeconomics for life : smart choices for all? / Avi J. Cohen. — Second edition.

Includes index.
ISBN 978-0-13-313584-8 (bound)

    1. Macroeconomics.   I. Title.

HB172.5.C63 2014   339   C2014-907484-0

ISBN: 978-0-13-313584-8

To Susan — for encouraging me to find my voice.

A.J.C.

About the Author

Avi J. Cohen

Avi J. Cohen is Professor of Economics at York University and at the University of Toronto. He has a PhD from Stanford University; is a Life Fellow of Clare Hall, University of Cambridge; and is past Co-Chair of the Canadian Economics Association Education Committee.

Professor Cohen has been President of the History of Economics Society, a Senior Research Fellow at the Center for the History of Political Economy at Duke University, and has research interests in the history of economics, economic history, and economic education. He has published in *Journal of Economic Perspectives, Journal of Economic Education, History of Political Economy, Journal of the History of Economic Thought, Cambridge Journal of Economics, Journal of Economic History,* and *Explorations in Economic History,* among other journals and books.

Professor Cohen is co-author of the best-selling *Study Guide* that accompanied the first eight editions of Parkin/Bade's *Economics.* He is the winner of numerous teaching awards, including Canada's most prestigious national award for educational leadership, the 3M Teaching Fellowship.

Brief Contents

Table of Contents

Preface to Students xv
Preface to Instructors xxi
Acknowledgments xxvii

Are Sweatshops All Bad?
Globalization and
Trade Policy 386

Preface to Students

I wrote *Macroeconomics for Life: Smart Choices for All?* to show you how to use economic ideas to make smart choices in life. I focus on the core concepts that you can use regularly to make smart choices in your life as a consumer, as a businessperson, and as an informed citizen.

The question in this book's subtitle—Smart Choices for All?—comes from the question, "Do markets coordinate smart individual choices to produce the products and services we want, or do markets produce undesirable outcomes like unemployment, falling living standards, bankruptcies, financial bubbles, and inflation?"

Economists ask this fundamental macroeconomic question this way:

If left alone by government, do the price mechanisms of market economies adjust quickly to maintain steady growth in living standards, full employment, and stable prices?

There is no single right answer. Economists, politicians, and citizens fall into two main camps in answering this question.

The "Yes—Markets Self-Adjust" camp believes that our market economy generally performs well and that government will only make it worse. They argue government should keep its hands off the economy: the hands-off camp.

The "No—Markets Fail Often" camp has less faith in the market economy's ability to perform consistently well and believes that government must get involved to improve the market's performance. They argue for a hands-on role for government: the hands-on camp.

Your vote helps elect a government whose policy decisions influence our economy's performance—living standards, unemployment, and inflation. Those policies can make the difference between steady growth in living standards or a prolonged recession when jobs are hard to find—in other words, your economic well-being. Do you think policies based on a hands-off or hands-on view of the market economy will make you, and Canada, better off? Learning the core concepts of macroeconomics enables you to make an informed choice about the fundamental macroeconomic question. My goal is to provide you the tools for answering that question in a way that makes most sense *to you*.

The only way for me to know how close I've come to achieving my goal is to hear from you. Let me know what works for you in this book—and, more importantly, what doesn't. You can write to me at **avicohen@yorku.ca**. In future editions, I will acknowledge by name all students who help improve *Economics for Life*.

Professor Avi J. Cohen
Department of Economics
York University
University of Toronto

Whenever you see this icon, the ideas of the hands-off camp are being discussed.

Whenever you see this icon, the ideas of the hands-on camp are being discussed.

Features of This Book

Welcome to *Macroeconomics for Life: Smart Choices for All?* This tour of your textbook is designed to help you use this book effectively and complete your course successfully.

Chapter Opener

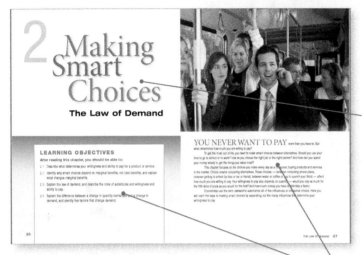

Every chapter begins with a two-page spread. These two pages set the theme for the chapter. Like a trailer for a movie, this opening spread gives you a preview of what is coming and prepares you for the "feature presentation."

Every chapter has a title and a subtitle. The main title summarizes the content of the chapter in plain language. The subtitle for the chapter is in the language economists use when referring to the concepts.

Every chapter is divided into main sections, and each of these sections is accompanied by a learning objective. The learning objective describes what you will have learned after reading each section. Once you have read the chapter, you can review these learning objectives to test your understanding of the chapter material.

Every chapter begins with an overview that introduces you to the main ideas and themes in the chapter. This introduction connects the economic principles discussed in the chapter to the choices and decisions you make in your everyday life.

Learning Objectives

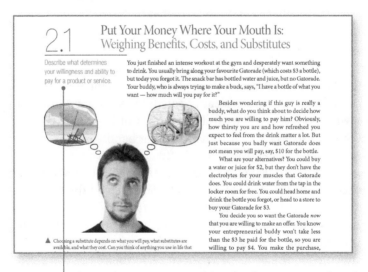

Learning objectives are repeated at the beginning of each main section of every chapter and provide an important reminder of what you will learn in each section.

Special Features

badly you want it plays a role. But just as important is what your alternative choices are. There are substitutes for everything — water for Gatorade, a yoga class for a gym workout, long underwear or a move to Florida for winter coats. Substitutes need not be exactly the same product or service. Substitutes just have to basically satisfy the same want. For any choice, what you are willing and able to pay, or to give up, depends on what substitutes are available, and what they cost.

The final factor determining how much you are willing and able to give up is how much you can afford. Are you able to pay the price of the product or service you want? Can you afford to take the time to relax all evening when you have a test tomorrow?

The list of things we want is endless. But the choices we actually make reflect our willingness — and ability — to give up something in exchange. Economists use the term **demand** to describe consumers' willingness and ability to pay for a particular product or service. Demand is *not* just what consumers want. You must put your money (or time) where your mouth is in order to demand a product or service. And those demands, or choices, are smart choices only when expected benefits are greater than opportunity costs.

> **demand** consumers' willingness and ability to pay for a particular product or service

Refresh 2.1

1. What is the difference between wants and demands?
2. What is the key factor that would make you choose to download a song for free rather than pay for it on iTunes? Explain your choice.
3. You have just started at a school that is a 30-minute drive from home or a 90-minute transit ride. Which is your smart choice, taking the transit or buying a car? Justify your choice.

MyEconLab
For answers to these Refresh Questions, visit MyEconLab.

Refresh

The Refresh feature provides three questions that require you to review and apply the concepts in the preceding section. These questions give you the opportunity to assess your understanding of the principles developed in the section. Answers to these questions are located on MyEconLab (www.myeconlab.com) that accompanies this book.

---

headphones (listening pleasure and blocking out the world) is greater than the additional cost (the $200 price tag). You are willing and able to pay $200. Sold! An economist would say that, at the price of $200, your *quantity demanded* of Beats Solo headphones is one.

Quantity demanded, as we will see, is not the same as *demand*. **Quantity demanded** is the amount you actually plan to buy at a given price, taking into account everything that affects your willingness and ability to pay.

We saw in the previous section that if circumstances change the additional benefit, your choice may change. The second bottle of Gatorade wasn't worth as much as the first, and the value of the headphones would change if you were driving to school in a car with a good sound system instead of riding the bus. But our focus here is not on benefits. Our focus is on *what happens to your buying decision when the price — the additional cost you pay — changes*. In order to focus on the relationship between price and quantity demanded, we will keep all other influences on demand the same.

> **quantity demanded** amount you actually plan to buy at a given price

Key Terms

Key terms are bolded in the text where they first appear, and definitions for key terms are in the margin. A complete list of all key terms and definitions are in the glossary at the end of the book.

Your willingness to pay, determined at the margin by changing circumstances including quantity, is important in determining prices, ranging from low prices for water to high prices for diamonds.

Economics *Out There*

Coke's Automatic Price Gouging

In the late 1990s, Coca-Cola Co. worked on technology to automatically raise prices in soft-drink vending machines on hot days. Critics — calling the plan "shameful" and a "cynical ploy" to exploit consumers "when they are most susceptible to price gouging" — suggested Coca-Cola should abandon the plan. The company claimed it was fair that the price should rise with demand, and that the machines simply automate that process. Unconvinced, critics warned that the plan would alienate customers, with the reminder that "archrival Pepsi is out there, and you can hardly tell the difference."

- The public reaction to these variable-price vending machines was so negative that Coca-Cola never introduced them.

- However, the strategy is based on the correct observation that willingness to pay changes with circumstances — the principle of marginal benefit.
- The strategy failed not because the economics were wrong, but because the idea of paying different prices for the same product seemed so unfair — "price gouging." (However, in Chapter 9 we will look at examples where consumers accept businesses charging different consumers different prices for the same product — cellphone minutes cost providers the same, whether daytime, evening, or weekend. Why are prices different? [*Hint:* Consumer willingness to pay.])
- Notice the line about Pepsi — substitutes are always available, which limits willingness to pay for any product, regardless of the marginal benefit.

Source: "Coke's Automatic Price Gouging," *San Francisco Chronicle*, October 29, 1999, p. A22.

Economics Out There

These feature boxes provide real-world examples of the economic principle being discussed. The stories told in Economics Out There help you make connections between the concepts in the chapter and everyday life.

Notes

In the margin, you will see notes that provide a quick explanation of the idea, concept, or principle being discussed in the narrative.

NOTE
Rising prices create two incentives for increased quantity supplied — higher profits and covering higher marginal opportunity costs of production.

quantity supplied the quantity you actually plan to supply at a given price

As your eye goes down the columns in Figure 3.1, note that as the price rises, the quantity supplied increases. (What happens to quantity demanded as price rises?) In general, when prices rise, individuals and businesses devote more of their time or resources to producing or supplying — more money stimulates more quantity supplied. The two reasons for this are the desire for profits (higher prices usually mean higher profits) and the need for a higher price to cover higher marginal opportunity costs — your weekend time is worth more to you than your *World of Warcraft* time.

Quantity supplied, as we will see, is not the same as supply. **Quantity supplied** is a more limited concept — the quantity you actually plan to supply at a given price, taking into account everything that affects your willingness to supply work hours.

Let's take the economist's idea of supply and apply it to Paola's willingness to supply a particular quantity of piercings at a particular price.

Body Piercings or Nail Sets?

Businesses, like consumers, make smart choices based on Key 1 — Choose only when additional benefits are greater than additional *opportunity costs*.

Paola's first choice is *what to produce* with her resources — the labour and equipment she has in her shop. She can do body piercing, and she can also paint fingernails. Let's limit her choices to full body piercings and full sets of fingernails to allow the simple, made-up numbers below.

Paola's Parlour has special tools for piercing and for nail painting. There are four people working (including Paola). All four are equally skilled at piercing (the business started with just piercing), but their fingernail skills differ from expert (Paola) to beginner (Parminder). The table in Figure 3.2 shows the different combinations of fingernail sets and piercings that Paola's Parlour can produce in a day.

Three Keys Icon

In keeping with the theme of making smart choices, you will also find an icon in the margin beside text that discusses the Three Keys to Smart Choices. The key (or keys) being discussed is indicated by the number on the key icon.

Study Guide

CHAPTER 2 SUMMARY

2.1 Put Your Money Where Your Mouth Is: Weighing Benefits, Costs, and Substitutes

Your willingness to buy a product or service depends on your ability to pay, comparative benefits and costs, and the availability of substitutes.

- **Preferences** — your wants and their intensities.
- **Demand** — consumers' willingness and ability to pay for a particular product or service.
- For any choice, what you are willing to pay or give up depends on the cost and availability of substitutes.

2.2 Living on the Edge: Smart Choices Are Marginal Choices

Key 2 states, "Count only *additional* benefits and *additional* costs." Additional benefits mean marginal benefits — not total benefits — and marginal benefits change with circumstances.

- **Marginal benefit** — the additional benefit from a choice, changing with circumstances.
- Marginal benefit explains the diamond/water paradox. Why do diamonds cost more than water, when water is more valuable for survival? Willingness to pay depends on marginal benefit, not total benefit. Because water is abundant, marginal benefit is low. Because diamonds are scarce, marginal benefit is high.

2.3 Move On When the Price Isn't Right: The Law of Demand

The demand curve combines two forces — switch to substitutes; willingness and ability to pay — determining quantity demanded, and can be read as a demand curve and as a marginal benefit curve.

- **Quantity demanded** — the amount you actually plan to buy at a given price.
- **Market demand** — the sum of demands of all individuals willing and able to buy a particular product or service.

- **Law of demand** — if the price of a product or service rises, quantity demanded decreases, other things remaining the same.
- **Demand curve** — shows the relationship between price and quantity demanded, other things remaining the same.

2.4 Moving the Margins: What Can Change Demand?

Quantity demanded changes only with a change in price. All other influences on consumer choice change demand.

- Demand is a catch-all term summarizing all possible influences on consumers' willingness and ability to pay for a particular product or service.
  - **Increase in demand** — increase in consumers' willingness and ability to pay. Rightward shift of demand curve.
  - **Decrease in demand** — decrease in consumers' willingness and ability to pay. Leftward shift of demand curve.
- Demand changes with changes in preferences, prices of related goods, income, expected future price, and number of consumers. For example, demand increases with:
  - increase in preferences.
  - rise in price of a **substitute** — products or services used in place of each other to satisfy the same want.
  - fall in price of a **complement** — products or services used together to satisfy the same want.
  - increase in income for **normal goods** — products or services you buy more of when your income increases.
  - decrease in income for **inferior goods** — products or services you buy less of when your income increases.
  - rise in expected future prices.
  - increase in number of consumers.

Study Guide

At the end of each chapter you will find a study guide designed to assist you in reviewing and testing your understanding of the material in the chapter. The study guide for each chapter includes:

- Chapter Summary
- 15 True/False Questions
- 15 Multiple Choice Questions

Chapter Summary

Organized by section, the summary recaps the main ideas in each chapter. The first item (in red) under each section head is the most important point in that section. All key terms are in bold.

TRUE/FALSE

Circle the correct answer. Solutions to these questions are available at the end of the book and on MyEconLab. You can also visit the MyEconLab Study Plan to access additional questions that will help you master the concepts covered in this chapter.

2.1 Weighing Benefits, Costs, and Substitutes

1. Demand is the same as wants.   T   F

2. Your willingness to pay for a product depends on what substitutes are available, and what they cost.   T   F

3. What you can afford is just about money.   T   F

2.2 Smart Choices Are Marginal Choices

4. Marginal cost is the same as additional cost.   T   F

5. The flat fee charged at an all-you-can-eat restaurant should not influence how much food you eat once you are seated.   T   F

6. Marginal benefit always equals average benefit.   T   F

7. Willingness to pay depends on marginal benefit, not total benefit.   T   F

2.3 The Law of Demand

8. Quantity demanded is the same as demand.   T   F

9. If the price of a product or service changes, quantity demanded changes.   T   F

10. Market demand is the sum of the demands of all individuals.   T   F

11. Demand curves may be straight lines or curves, but always slope downward to the left.   T   F

2.4 What Can Change Demand?

12. If your willingness to pay decreases, demand decreases.   T   F

13. If your ability to pay decreases, demand increases.   T   F

14. Throughout the month of December, the quantity of video game consoles purchased increases even as the price rises. This violates the law of demand.   T   F

15. A decrease in income always shifts the demand curve leftward.   T   F

True/False Questions

There are 15 true/false questions, organized by learning objective. The heading next to each learning objective number gives you the topic of the questions that follow. Each question is answered at the end of the book, with a brief explanation.

MULTIPLE CHOICE

Circle the best answer. Solutions to these questions are available at the end of the book and on MyEconLab. You can also visit the MyEconLab Study Plan to access similar questions that will help you master the concepts covered in this chapter.

2.1 Weighing Benefits, Costs, and Substitutes

1. Economists describe the list of your wants and their intensities as
   a) demand.
   b) supply.
   c) benefit.
   d) preferences.

2. Costs are
   a) worth money.
   b) whatever we are willing to give up.
   c) the answer to the question "What do we want?"
   d) whatever we are willing to get.

3. Your preferences measure
   a) the availability of substitutes.
   b) how limited your time is.
   c) the price of a product.
   d) how badly you want something.

2.2 Smart Choices Are Marginal Choices

4. All-you-can-eat buffet restaurants charge a fixed fee for eating. With each plate that Anna eats, she experiences
   a) decreasing marginal costs.
   b) increasing marginal costs.
   c) decreasing marginal benefits.
   d) increasing marginal benefits.

5. Thinking like economists, a dating couple should break up when the
   a) total benefits of dating are greater than the total costs of dating.
   b) total costs of dating are greater than the total benefits of dating.
   c) additional benefits of dating are greater than the additional costs of dating.
   d) additional costs of dating are greater than the additional benefits of dating.

48   CHAPTER 2   MAKING SMART CHOICES

Multiple Choice Questions

There are 15 multiple choice questions organized by learning objective. The heading next to each learning objective number gives you the topic of the questions that follow. Each question is answered at the end of the book, with a brief explanation.

Using Your Textbook to Achieve Success in Your Course

This textbook is set up for your success. Each element is designed to help you organize, understand, and learn the material efficiently and easily. Here is a four-step guide to being successful in this course.

1: Fully understand the learning objectives

The learning objectives in each chapter are presented in the chapter opener and repeated in the margin at the beginning of each section of the chapter. If you can do what each learning objective asks, you will understand what is most important in each section. These learning objectives are the core of the course. Master these and you have mastered the course. The most important point in each section — a one- to two-sentence summary of what each learning objective asks — appears in red after each section head in the Study Guide's Chapter Summary.

2: Check your understanding of the learning objectives

At the end of each complete section, there are three questions titled Refresh. When you complete a section, take the 5 to 10 minutes required to answer the Refresh questions. These questions are designed for you to assess how well you have mastered the learning objective. They will help you make sure you understand what is important.

Research shows that small quizzes help students get higher grades and retain more of what they learn than spending the same amount of time highlighting and rereading material.

3: Complete the Study Guide material

After finishing the chapter, complete the Study Guide pages — it will save you study time and reinforce what you have mastered. The Study Guide is divided into two main sections, a chapter summary and a set of exam-like questions.

Chapter Summary The Chapter Summary contains the key points you need to know. It is organized using the same major sections as the chapter. The first item in red under each section head is the most important point in that section. The Chapter Summary is an excellent study aid for the night before a test. It's a final check of the ideas — the learning objectives — you have studied.

Exam-Like Questions Do the true/false and multiple-choice questions *without looking at the answers*. This is the single most important tip for profitably using the Study Guide. Struggling for the answers to questions you find challenging is one of the most effective ways to learn. The athletic saying of "No pain, no gain" applies equally to studying. You will learn the most from right answers you have had to struggle for and from your wrong answers and mistakes. Look at the answers only *after* you have attempted all the questions. When you finally do check the answers, be sure to understand where you went wrong and why your right answers are right.

4: Know it before you go on

Master each chapter by taking the above actions *before* moving on. Feel confident that you understand the chapter's objectives. By following this simple four-point plan you will be making a smart choice for learning, and you will do well in the course.

Preface to Instructors

When people ask me what I do, I say, "I teach Economics." While I am a full professor at two universities, a productive academic with an active research program (past president of the History of Economics Society) and honourable service commitments to my schools, my professional identity is largely tied to my teaching.

As a young assistant professor, the immortality of publishing articles in journals that would forever be in libraries was an important goal. But over time, I came to realize how few people would read those articles, let alone be affected by them. Most of my, and I suspect your, "academic footprint" on this earth will be through our students. Over a career, we teach tens of thousands students.

As economists and teachers, what do we want our lasting "economic footprint" to be? There is a wonderful old *Saturday Night Live* skit by Father Guido Sarducci called "The Five Minute University" (**http://www.youtube.com/watch?v=kO8x8eoU3L4**). Watch it. His premise is to teach in five minutes what an average college or university graduate remembers five years after graduating. For economics, he states it's the two words "supply and demand." That's it.

The serious question behind the skit, the one that motivates this book, is "What do we really want our students to remember of what we teach them in an introductory economics class?"

The vast, vast majority of students in introductory economics never take another economics course. *Economics for Life* is designed to help those students learn what they need to know to be economically literate citizens. If we can teach students the fundamentals of thinking like an economist, they will be equipped to make smarter choices in their lives as consumers, as businesspeople, and as citizens evaluating policies proposed by politicians.

For microeconomics, the essentials are grounded in the Three Keys to Smart Choices, which form the core of *Microeconomics for Life: Smart Choices for You.*

Key 1: Choose only when additional benefits are greater than additional *opportunity costs*.

ADDITIONAL BENEFITS VS. OPPORTUNITY COSTS

Key 2: Count only *additional* benefits and *additional* opportunity costs.

ADDITIONAL BENEFITS & COSTS

Key 3: Be sure to count *all* additional benefits and costs, including *implicit costs* and *externalities*.

IMPLICIT COSTS & EXTERNALITIES

We can teach all topics in micro with those three keys.

Because economists disagree far more about macroeconomics than microeconomics, I incorporated that disagreement into the core of the macro textbook as **"the fundamental macroeconomic question."**

If left alone by government, do the price mechanisms of market economies adjust quickly to maintain steady growth in living standards, full employment, and stable prices?

Not only do economists disagree over the answer to this question, so do the politicians our students will be voting for, for the rest of their lives. I believe the essential macroeconomic concepts students must know in order to answer that question for themselves — the macroeconomics they need to know *as citizens* — are included in *Macroeconomics for Life: Smart Choices for All*?

Focusing on essential concepts means letting go of many of the more technical concepts and tools that most introductory courses include to prepare students to become economics majors. I consider these exclusions to be a major strength of the textbooks. The excluded concepts detract from the student's accepting the value of the basic economic analysis that will enhance her decision-making throughout her life. As one strays beyond the core concepts and stories set out in *Economics for Life*, diminishing returns set in rapidly.

It is far more valuable, I believe, for students to understand and apply the core economic concepts well than to be exposed to a wide range of concepts they will not master and therefore will likely soon forget.

Economics for Life is also designed to get students **interested** in economics as a way of thinking that will help them make smarter choices in their lives. Concepts are not presented as theoretical ideas that must be learned in isolation, or as formulas for a set of problems. Instead, each chapter begins with a scenario, and the concepts emerge logically as the narrative unfolds.

Vision (and Graphs) for the Second Edition

The first edition had narratives based on tables of numbers — implicit graphs — but very few graphs. The second edition makes these implicit graphs explicit. The addition of simple demand and supply graphs and production possibilities frontiers fits smoothly into the existing flow of the book's narrative, providing the students an additional powerful tool for their understanding of the material. Graphs now appear in chapters on demand and supply, rent controls and minimum wages, explanation of choosing output where marginal revenue equals marginal cost, externalities, labour-hiring decisions, and in the macro text, in chapters on aggregate demand and aggregate supply (complete with output gaps and shocks), and the money, loanable funds and foreign exchange markets.

The vision of focusing on the core economic concepts remains the foundation of the second edition. There are still no indifference curves or detailed models of market structure in micro. Although I believe that the many detailed firm cost curves are not core concepts (once students master marginal cost and marginal revenue), for those who want to teach the complete model of perfect competition, there is a concise treatment in the new Appendix to Chapter 9. (Contact me if you would like to discuss my reasons for excising cost curves beyond marginal cost.) In macro there are no derivations of aggregate demand from the aggregate expenditure model, detailed multiplier formulas (whether spending, tax, transfer, or money) or aggregate production functions.

Micro still focuses on the Three Keys for Smart Choices, and the macro narrative focuses on using the expanded circular flow diagram and simple aggregate demand and aggregate supply graphs to explore the question: "How well do markets adjust to provide steady growth in living standards, full employment, and stable prices?" Students are asked throughout the macro text, "Should the government keep it's hands off of the economy, or does it need to be hands on?" I try to present sympathetically the strongest case for both the hands-off and hands-on positions.

ADDITIONAL
BENEFITS
VS.
OPPORTUNITY
COSTS

Join Me!

The second edition of *Economics for Life* retains the focus on the question "What do we really want our students to remember of what we teach them in an introductory economics class?" The focus is on essential economic concepts students need to know to become economically literate citizens, delivered in an engaging, narrative style. **Those concepts are now illustrated with the core graphs that are at the heart of thinking like an economist.** Because fewer topics are covered in more depth, this literacy-targeted approach allows instructors to spend more time in the classroom helping students master the core concepts, supported by active learning exercises, group work, economic experiments, and other forms of engagement that are integrated into both the student exercises and the Instructor's Manual. Have a look for more details.

What I find exciting about these books is the possibility of helping far more students "get" the benefit of thinking like an economist. If these books succeed in doing what they set out to do — and you and your students will be the judges of that — then your students will be more actively engaged with the material. Students will learn economics in a way that will stay with them — even five years after leaving your classroom.

This brings us back to the question of your "economic footprint." You will cover fewer topics using *Economics for Life* (the 12 micro or 9 macro chapters can be covered in a semester, with room for discussion), but your students will retain more. If we do our jobs well, after five years, your students will actually be *ahead* of students who were exposed to the full range of topics. Your economic footprint will be larger. You will have produced more students who have better learned the fundamentals of thinking like an economist, and who are making smarter choices in their lives as consumers, as businesspeople, and as citizens evaluating policies proposed by politicians.

You will have succeeded in helping your students learn how to use economics in life.

Avi Cohen
Toronto

Supplements

This textbook is supported by many supplemental materials designed to help instructors quickly customize their courses and enhance student learning.

All of the supplements have been developed and edited by Professor Avi Cohen, the author of the text. Professor Cohen has over 30 years of experience teaching introductory economics, is an award-winning teacher, and is a 3M National Teaching Fellow. He is the author of the *Study Guide* accompanying the first eight editions of Michael Parkin's and Robin Bade's *Economics: Canada in the Global Environment*. He served for many years at York University as Dean's Advisor on Technology Enhanced Learning (TEL), where he developed and ran *do TEL*, a faculty development program for instructors interested in transforming their face-to face courses to blended or fully online formats.

The following support materials developed by Professor Cohen are available for instructors.

Instructor's Manual

The Instructor's Manual (IM) will assist you in preparing for and teaching this course, whether you are a neophyte teaching the course for the first time, or an experienced instructor looking for ways to enliven your classroom or to adapt to the growing world of fully or partially online courses. The IM is organized by chapter, paralleling the textbook organization.

To make it easy and efficient for you to customize your lectures, each chapter includes an overview and concise summary of the main ideas, concepts and key graphs. You will find class discussion questions and answers to the student Refresh questions for each chapter.

Whether you are teaching 30 students or 500, we provide proven strategies for enhancing the interactivity of your classroom or online environment. Strategies, current discussion topics, economic data, and media stories will be updated regularly on Professor Cohen's teaching blog. See the Instructor's Manual for details.

PowerPoint Presentations

The PowerPoint® slides are a set of lectures based on the textbook content, paralleling the Chapter Summary found in the end-of-chapter Study Guide material. Professor Cohen selected, developed, and edited all of the content in the slides to allow you to be able to prepare and present a focused and manageable lecture without having to wade through an excessive number of slides. You can, of course, still elaborate on each slide's material. The parallels between the slides and the Study Guide's Chapter Summary make it easier for students to connect the textbook material, your classroom presentation, and the Study Guide exercises.

The design of the slides matches the textbook design so students connect more easily the material they have read and the content of your classroom presentation. The font sizes of the slides have been tested for readability from the back of a 500-seat lecture hall as well as on mobile devices. The graphs' slides are dynamic — as you click through them, curves shift and new equilibrium points appear.

Narrated Dynamic Graphs

The PowerPoint graphs, built from the textbook graphic files, are the basis of the Narrated Dynamic Graphs. For each analytical graph in the textbook, there is a short MP4 video. In a voice-over, Professor Cohen talks the student through the meaning of the graph, and traces shifts of curves and changes in outcomes. There is a moving cursor directing students' attention to the portion of the graph being discussed in the narration. These MP4 files, which tell the story of each graph, can be viewed online or downloaded to a student's computer or mobile device.

Pearson TestGen

Professor Cohen created or edited all multiple choice and true/false questions in the testbank. Multiple choice questions have five good choices. "None of the above" and "All of the above" are actually used as correct answers, and sometimes the fifth choice is humorous. Questions are classified by level of difficulty (1 – 3) and as recall or analytical.

This computerized test item file enables instructors to view and edit existing test questions, add questions, generate tests, and print tests in a variety of formats. Powerful search and sort functions make it easy to locate questions and arrange them in any order desired. TestGen also enables instructors to administer tests on a local area network, have the tests graded electronically, and have the results prepared in electronic or printed reports. These questions are also available in MyTest, which is available through MyEconLab at www.myeconlab.com.

MyEconLab

Pearson Canada's online resource, MyEconLab, offers instructors and students all of their resources in one place, written and designed to accompany this text. MyEconLab creates a perfect pedagogical loop that provides not only text-specific assessment and practice problems, but also tutorial support to make sure students learn from their mistakes.

At the core of MyEconLab are the following features:

NEW Dynamic Study Modules: Canadian study modules allow students to work through groups of question and check their understanding of foundational Economics topics. As students work through questions, the Dynamic Study Modules assess their knowledge and only show questions that still require practice. Dynamic Study Modules can be completed online using your computer, tablet, or mobile device.

NEW Learning Catalytics: Learning Catalytics is a "bring your own device" student engagement, assessment, and classroom intelligence system. It allows instructors to engage students in class with a variety of questions types designed to gauge student understanding.

Study Plan: As students work through the Study Plan, they can clearly see which topics they have mastered — and, more importantly, which they need to work on. Each question has been carefully written to match the concepts, language, and focus of the text, so students can get an accurate sense of how well they've understood the chapter content.

Adaptive Assessment: Integrated directly into the MyEconLab Study Plan, Pearson's adaptive assessment is the latest technology for individualized learning and mastery. As students work through each question, they are provided with a custom learning path tailored specifically to the concepts they need to practise and master.

Unlimited Practice: Most Study Plan exercises contain algorithmically generated values to ensure that students get as much practice as they need. Every problem links students to learning resources that further reinforce the concepts they need to master.

Auto-Graded Tests and Assignments: MyEconLab comes with two preloaded Sample Tests for each chapter. Students can use these tests for self-assessment and obtain immediate feedback. Instructors can assign the Sample Tests or use them along with Test Bank questions or their own exercises to create tests or quizzes.

Economics Video Questions: Instructors also have access to a series of video questions that tie current events to key concepts from the text.

Learning Resources: Each assessment contains a link to the eText page that discusses the concept being applied. Students also have access to guided solutions, dynamic narrated graphs, news feeds, and glossary flash cards.

Experiments in MyEconLab: Experiments are a fun and engaging way to promote active learning and mastery of important economic concepts. Pearson's Experiments program is flexible and easy for instructors and students to use. They include single-player experiments that allow students to play against virtual players from anywhere at any time and multiplayer experiments allow you to assign and manage a real-time experiment with your class.

Acknowledgments

Joseph Gladstone, Project Developer, had the original vision for this book. While we have developed that vision collaboratively, Joseph has been the guiding force and, in all but title, a co-author. Without his counsel, wisdom, and vast experience in teaching and publishing, this book would not have come to life.

Ian Howe wrote the Study Guide for the first edition and helped polish all of the original textbook chapters. His humour and vast knowledge of StatsCan data and policy issues continue to enliven many questions at the end of each chapter and in the Instructor's Manual. Andrew Dickens searched out and compiled most data for tables and charts. Deryk Ouseley drew the marvelous illustrations on the covers and others inside that capture the spirit of the *Economics for Life* books.

Much of what is good (I think; you judge) in this book comes from my long association with Robin Bade and Michael Parkin. During more than 20 years as an author to the Study Guide accompanying their *Economics: Canada in the Global Environment*, I have learned so much from their skills as teachers, writers, and economists. Their commitment to clarity, conciseness, and helping students learn has made them both an inspiration and role models. Although this textbook is intended for a slightly different audience, I hope that it will be judged to be in their league.

Many students in both my York and University of Toronto classes caught typos, ambiguities, and offered suggestions for improving the text, including Zaid Faiz, Harpal Hothi, Catherine Huntley, Vadim Slukovich, and Mia Viswanathan. Lior Krimus and Mahsa Nasseri plastered a first edition textbook with dozens of sticky notes containing detailed suggestions for better explaining concepts in ways students would "get it." The time-machine analogy for explaining marginal revenue and pricing decisions with the one-price rule in Chapter 9 is their idea.

Thanks to Dwayne Benjamin, who invited me to teach the ECO105Y course at the St. George campus, and has steadfastly supported giving the many science, public policy, and international relations students at the University of Toronto a different way to learn introductory economics, while retaining the option to become Economics majors and minors.

The team Pearson assembled — Susan Bindernagel, Richard di Santo, Joel Gladstone, Leigh-Ann Graham, Jurek Konieczny, Suzanne Simpson Millar, Victoria Naik, Mohinder Singh, Karen Townsend, Nurlan Turdaliev, and Claire Varley — have shown me how much hard work and skill go into transforming a manuscript into a product for the now-digital marketplace. I have learned that I am not simply an author, but a "digital content creator!" Thank you all.

Claudine O'Donnell deserves pride-of-place thanks for this second edition, as did Gary Bennett and Allan Reynolds for the first. It is because of their abiding faith and support that the *Economics for Life* books are before you.

Avi J. Cohen
Toronto
September 2014

The author and the publisher thank the reviewers and consultants for their time, ideas, and suggestions that have helped make this textbook better. Their input has been extremely positive and their expertise invaluable in making this new economics book more accessible and useful to both professors and students.

Aurelia Best, Centennial College
Darren Chapman, Fanshawe College
Carol Derksen, Red River College
Paritosh Ghosh, Red Deer College
Jamal Hejazi, University of Ottawa
Randy Hull, Fanshawe College
Sacha Des Rosiers, Dawson College
Gail English, New Brunswick Community College
Agostino Menna, Niagara College of Applied Arts & Technology
John O'Laney, New Brunswick Community College
Stephanie Powers, Red Deer College
Geoffrey Prince, Centennial College
Charles Ramsay, Dawson College
Sheila Ross, Southern Alberta Institute of Technology
John Saba, Champlain Regional College
Patrick Sherlock, Nova Scotia Community College
Sarah Stevens, Georgian College
Nurlan Turdaliev, University of Windsor
Franc A. Weissenhorn, Nova Scotia Community College
Carl Weston, Mohawk College

MACRO

Economics *for* Life

Smart Choices for All?

1 What's in Economics for You?

Scarcity, Opportunity Cost, Trade, and Models

LEARNING OBJECTIVES

After reading this chapter, you should be able to:

1.1 Explain scarcity and describe why you must make smart choices among your wants.

1.2 Define and describe opportunity cost.

1.3 Describe how comparative advantage, specialization, and trade make us all better off.

1.4 Explain how models like the circular flow of economic life make smart choices easier.

1.5 Differentiate microeconomic and macroeconomic choices, and explain the Three Keys model for smart choices.

WHAT DO YOU WANT OUT OF LIFE?

Riches? Fame? Love? Adventure? A successful career? To make the world a better place? To live a life that respects the environment? To express your creativity? Happiness? Children? A long and healthy life? All of the above?

Many people believe economics is just about money and business, but economics can help you get what you want out of life.

The title of this book comes from a quote by Nobel Prize–winning author George Bernard Shaw: "Economy is the art of making the most of life." Economics is partly about getting the most for your money, but it is also about making smart choices generally. I wrote this book because I believe that if you learn a little economics, it will help you make the most of your life, whatever you are after. That same knowledge will also help you better understand the world around you and the choices you face as a citizen.

You don't need to be trained as an economist to lead a productive and satisfying life. But if you can learn *to think like an economist,* you can get more out of whatever life you choose to lead, and the world will be better for it.

1.1 Are You Getting Enough?
Scarcity and Choice

Explain scarcity and describe why you must make smart choices among your wants.

Can you afford to buy everything you want? If not, every dollar you spend involves a choice. If you buy the Xbox One, you might not be able to afford your English textbook. If you treat your friends to a movie, you might have to work an extra shift at your job or give up your weekend camping trip.

It would be great to have enough money to buy everything you want, but it would not eliminate the need to make smart choices. Imagine winning the biggest lottery in the world. You can buy whatever you want for yourself, your family, and your friends. But you still have only 80-some years on this planet (if you are lucky and healthy), only 24 hours in a day, and a limited amount of energy. Do you want to spend the week boarding in Whistler or surfing in Australia? Do you want to spend time raising your kids or exploring the world? Will you go to that third party on New Year's Eve or give in to sleep? Do you want to spend money on yourself, or set up a charitable foundation to help others? Bill Gates, one of the richest people on Earth, has chosen to set up the Bill and Melinda Gates Foundation. With billions of dollars in assets, the Foundation still receives more requests for worthy causes than it has dollars. How does it choose which requests to fund?

Economists call this inability to satisfy all of our wants the problem of **scarcity**. Scarcity arises from our limited money, time, and energy. All mortals, even billionaires, face the problem of scarcity. We all have to make choices about what we will get and what we will give up. Businesses with limited capital must choose between spending more on research or on marketing. Governments must make similar choices in facing the problem of scarcity. Spending more on colleges and universities leaves less to spend on health care. Or if governments try to spend more on all social programs, the higher taxes to pay for them mean less take-home pay for all of us.

Because none of us — individuals, businesses, governments — can ever satisfy all of our wants, smart choices are essential to making the most of our lives.

Economics is about how individuals, businesses, and governments make the best possible choices to get what they want, and how those choices interact in markets.

scarcity the problem that arises from our limited money, time, and energy

economics how individuals, businesses, and governments make the best possible choices to get what they want, and how those choices interact in markets

Refresh 1.1

MyEconLab

For answers to these Refresh Questions, visit MyEconLab.

1. Define scarcity and give one example from your own experience.

2. Write a definition of economics in your own words that includes the word *scarcity*.

3. Social activists argue that materialism is one of the biggest problems with society: If we all wanted less, instead of always wanting more, there would be plenty to go around for everyone. Do you agree with this statement? Why or why not?

Give It Up for Opportunity Cost! Opportunity Cost

Scarcity means you must choose, and if you want the most out of what limited money and time you have, you need to make smart choices. A choice is like a fork in the road. You have to compare the alternatives — where does each path take you — and then pick one. You make a smart choice by weighing benefits and costs.

Choose to Snooze?

What are you going to do with the next hour? Since you are reading this, you must be considering studying as one choice. If you were out far too late last night, or up taking care of a crying baby, sleep might be your alternative choice. If those are your top choices, let's compare benefits of the two paths from this fork. For studying, the benefits are higher marks on your next test, learning something, and (if I have done my job well) perhaps enjoying reading this chapter. For sleep, the benefits are being more alert, more productive, less grumpy, and (if I have done my job poorly) avoiding the pain of reading this chapter.

If you choose the studying path, what is *the cost of your decision*? It is the hour of sleep you give up (with the benefits of rest). And if you choose sleep, the cost is the studying you give up (leading to lower marks).

In weighing the benefits and costs of any decision, we compare what we get from each path with what we give up from the other. For any choice (what we get), its true cost is what we have to give up to get it. The true cost of any choice is what economists call **opportunity cost**: the cost of the best alternative given up.

▲ The true cost of any choice you make is what you must give up to get it.

opportunity cost the cost of the best alternative given up

Opportunity Cost Beats Money Cost

For smart decisions, it turns out that opportunity cost is more important than money cost. Suppose you win a free trip for one to Bermuda that has to be taken the first week in December. What is the money cost of the trip? (This is not a trick question.) Zero — it's free.

But imagine you have a business client in Saskatoon who can meet to sign a million-dollar contract *only* during the first week in December. What is the opportunity cost of your "free" trip to Bermuda? $1 million. A smart decision to take or not take the trip depends on opportunity cost, not money cost.

Or what if your current significant other lives out of town, and the only time you can get together is during the first week in December? What is the opportunity cost of taking your "free" trip for one? Besides losing out on the benefits of time together, you may be kissing that relationship goodbye.

All choices are forks in the road, and the cost of any path taken is the value of the path you must give up. Because of scarcity, every choice involves a trade-off — to get something, you must give up something else. *To make a smart choice, the value of what you get must be greater than the value of what you give up.* The benefits of a smart choice must outweigh the opportunity costs.

NOTE
Scarcity means every choice involves a trade-off.

Economics *Out There*

Where Have All the Men Gone?

Women make up 60 percent of undergraduate college and university students. Why do women so outnumber men? There are many explanations, from women's liberation to schools rewarding girls' more obedient behaviour and punishing boys' ADD (attention deficit disorder). There is also a simple economic explanation based on opportunity cost.

- Think of going or not going to college or university as a fork in the road.
- Weigh the costs and benefits of each choice. Everyone pays the same tuition and fees, but the benefits given up with each choice are different for women and men.
- More women than men go to college and university because the cost of *not* going is higher for women — men's alternative is higher-paying blue-collar jobs. Women's alternative tends to be lower-paying clerical or retail jobs.

Women with post-secondary education earn 50 to 80 percent more a year than women with only a high-school diploma. Men with the same post-secondary education earn only 25 to 30 percent more a year than men with only a high-school diploma. *The gap in pay* between high-school and post-secondary women is larger than the same gap for men.

Because of the differences in opportunity cost — women who don't go to college or university *give up* a bigger income gain than men do — the rate of return for a college diploma or university degree is 9 percent for women, and only around 6 percent for men. Incentives matter, and people respond to the incentives. For women, it pays more to get a post-secondary education.

---

incentives rewards and penalties for choices

Incentives Work Since smart choices compare costs and benefits, your decisions will change with changes in costs or benefits. We all respond to **incentives** — rewards and penalties for choices. You are more likely to choose a path that leads to a reward, and avoid one with a penalty. A change in incentives causes a change in choices. If your Saskatoon business deal is worth only $100 instead of $1 000 000, you might take the trip to Bermuda. If you were up most of last night, you are more likely to sleep than to study. If you have a test tomorrow instead of next week, you are more likely to study than to sleep.

To make the most out of life and make smart decisions, you must always ask the questions, "What is the opportunity cost of my choice?" and "Do the benefits outweigh the opportunity costs?"

Refresh 1.2

MyEconLab

For answers to these Refresh Questions, visit MyEconLab.

1. What is the opportunity cost of any choice?

2. This weekend, your top choices are going camping with your friends or working extra hours at your part-time job. List three facts (think rewards and penalties) that, if they changed, would influence your decision.

3. Your sister is trying to decide whether to go to college or get a job after high school. What would you advise her to do based only on the money cost of attending college? Based on the opportunity cost of her attending college?

Why Don't You Cook Breakfast?
Gains from Trade

What did you have for breakfast today? Did you have cereal and orange juice at home, or did you buy coffee and a bagel at Tim Hortons on the way to school? Either way, you made a choice — to make breakfast for yourself, or to buy it from a business. This is the most basic choice you and everyone else makes in trying to do the best you can: Do you yourself produce the products and services you want, or do you earn money at a job and then buy (or trade money for) products and services made by others?

These days, that basic choice sounds crazy. We all work (or hope to) at jobs, earning money by specializing in a particular occupation. We use that money to buy what we want. Even a "homemade" breakfast uses cereal and juice bought at a grocery store. But if you go back only a few hundred years in Canadian history, most Aboriginal peoples and pioneers were largely self-sufficient, making for themselves most of what they needed — hunting and growing their own food, making clothes from animal hides, and building shelters from available resources.

Voluntary Trade

What happened to lead us all away from self-sufficiency toward specializing and trading? The historical answer to that question is complex, but the simple economic answer is that specializing and trading make us better off, so of course people made that basic choice. It's simple self-interest at work.

Our standard of living, in terms of material products and services, is much higher than it was hundreds of years ago in Canada. (What we have done to the environment, which in the past was better than in the present, is another story that I will also explain in terms of self-interest in Chapter 11.) The irony is that *as individuals,* we are hopeless at supporting ourselves compared to our ancestors. Yet *collectively,* our standard of living is much better.

Trade is the key to our prosperity. Trade makes all of us better off. Why? Trade is voluntary. Any time two people make a voluntary trade, each person feels that what they get is of greater value than what they give up. If there weren't mutual benefits, the trade wouldn't happen. But how does trade make us better off?

NOTE
When you "trade" money for coffee at Tim Hortons, that is a voluntary exchange. If you thought you would be better off keeping the money instead of the coffee, you wouldn't pay. If Tims weren't better off with your money instead of the coffee, it wouldn't sell.

Bake or Chop?   Again, opportunity cost is the key to the mutual benefits from trade. To illustrate, let's take a simple imaginary example of two early Canadians who are each self-sufficient in producing food and shelter.

Jill grows her own wheat to make bread, and chops her own wood for fire and shelter. If she spends an entire month producing only bread, she can make 50 loaves. Alternatively, if she spends all her time chopping wood, she can cut 100 logs. Her monthly choice of how to spend her time looks like the picture in the margin.

Since Jill is self-sufficient, that means she can consume only what she produces herself, so she must divide her time and produce some bread and some wood. The table in Figure 1.1 shows different possible combinations (*A – F*) of bread and wood she can produce, depending on how she divides up her time during the month. From these production possibilities, Jill chooses to produce possibility *D*, 20 loaves of bread and 60 logs of wood. We will get to the graph in a moment.

▲ Since she's self-sufficient, Jill must choose how much bread to bake and wood to chop in order to survive.

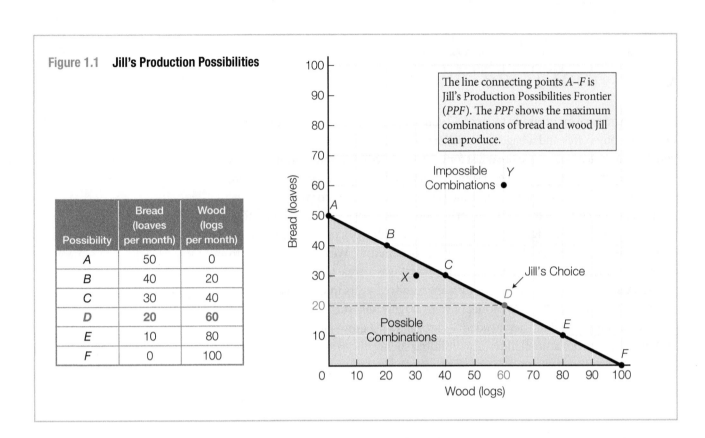

Figure 1.1   Jill's Production Possibilities

Possibility	Bread (loaves per month)	Wood (logs per month)
A	50	0
B	40	20
C	30	40
D	20	60
E	10	80
F	0	100

The line connecting points A–F is Jill's Production Possibilities Frontier (PPF). The PPF shows the maximum combinations of bread and wood Jill can produce.

Marie, Jill's nearest neighbour, also grows her own wheat to make bread, and chops her own wood for fire and shelter. The table in Figure 1.2 shows the possible monthly combinations of bread and wood she can produce, depending on how she divides up her time.

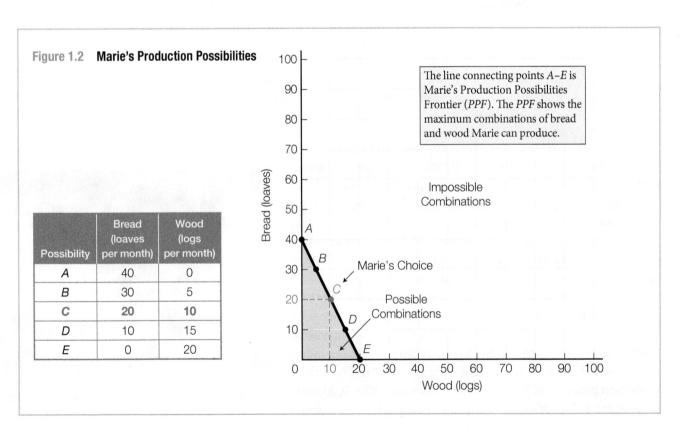

Figure 1.2   Marie's Production Possibilities

Possibility	Bread (loaves per month)	Wood (logs per month)
A	40	0
B	30	5
C	20	10
D	10	15
E	0	20

The line connecting points A–E is Marie's Production Possibilities Frontier (PPF). The PPF shows the maximum combinations of bread and wood Marie can produce.

Marie is weaker than Jill, so if Marie spends an entire month producing only bread, she can make 40 loaves (possibility *A* in Figure 1.2). Alternatively, if she spends all her time chopping wood, she can cut only 20 logs (possibility *E*). Since Marie is also self-sufficient, and can consume only what she produces herself, she divides her time and produces some bread and some wood. From these production possibilities, Marie chooses to produce possibility *C*, 20 loaves of bread and 10 logs of wood.

Production Possibilities Frontier   A **production possibilities frontier** — *PPF* for short — shows the maximum combinations of products or services that can be produced with existing inputs. The graphs in Figures 1.1 and 1.2 show the production possibilities of our two pioneers.

production possibilities frontier   maximum combinations of products or services that can be produced with existing inputs

Look first at Jill's *PPF* in the Figure 1.1 graph. The monthly quantity of wood she can produce is measured on the horizontal axis. The monthly quantity of bread is measured on the vertical axis. When you connect the points representing her possible combinations of wood and bread (*A* – *F* from the Figure 1.1 table), you get the straight black line that is Jill's production possibilities frontier. The points on Jill's *PPF* show the *maximum* combinations of bread and wood she can produce if she uses all of her time, tools, and other inputs. Jill chose combination *D, 20 loaves and 60 logs*.

Jill could also choose not to work so hard and produce less. She could choose to produce any combination of bread and wood *inside* her production possibilities frontier. For example, she could decide to produce the combination of 30 loaves and 30 logs (possibility *X*). The shaded area inside her *PPF* represents all of her "possible combinations." These combinations are possible, but are not maximum.

Combinations of bread and wood *outside* of Jill's *PPF* are impossible for her to produce. Jill, like all of us, faces the problem of scarcity. She has limited time and energy, and can't produce everything she might want. A combination of 60 loaves of bread and 60 logs of wood (possibility *Y*) might make Jill happier and more comfortable, but that combination is impossible for her to produce.

Similarly, Marie's *PPF* in the Figure 1.2 graph shows the maximum possible combinations of bread and wood she can produce. Marie chose combination *C*. Her other possible production combinations are inside her *PPF*. Impossible combinations are outside her *PPF*. Marie has fewer possible combinations of bread and wood production than Jill.

Deal or No Deal? Do the Numbers

Can trade make both Jill and Marie better off? It doesn't look promising, especially for Jill. She is a better bread maker than Marie (50 loaves versus 40 loaves) *and* a better wood chopper (100 logs versus 20 logs). An economist would describe Jill as having an **absolute advantage** — the ability to produce a product or service at a *lower absolute cost* than another producer — over Marie in both bread production and wood production. That is, Jill is more productive as a bread maker and as a wood chopper. If we were to measure dollar costs (which I have left out to keep the example as simple as possible), absolute advantage would mean Jill could produce both bread and wood at lower absolute dollar costs than Marie could.

absolute advantage   the ability to produce a product or service at a lower absolute cost than another producer

If you are not keen on history, then in place of Jill and Marie, think China and Canada. If China can produce everything at lower cost than Canada, can there be mutually beneficial gains from trade for both countries? What's the benefit for China? Won't all Canadians end up unemployed?

comparative advantage the ability to produce a product or service at a lower opportunity cost than another producer

Comparative Advantage But mutually beneficial gains from trade do not depend on absolute advantage. They depend on what economists call **comparative advantage** — the ability to produce a product or service at a *lower opportunity cost* than another producer. To figure out comparative advantage, we need to calculate *opportunity costs* for Jill and Marie.

Opportunity costs are always calculated by comparing two alternative possibilities — two choices. Comparing possibilities *A* and *F* in the Figure 1.1 table or graph, Jill can produce 50 loaves of bread and zero wood or 100 logs of wood and zero bread. If she chooses to bake 50 loaves of bread, the opportunity cost is 100 logs of wood. If she instead chooses to chop 100 logs of wood, the opportunity cost is 50 loaves of bread. Opportunity cost is the value of the path — the choice — *not taken.*

To compare opportunity costs, it is easier if we measure them per unit of the product chosen. Here is a simple, useful formula for finding opportunity cost:

$$\text{Opportunity cost} = \frac{\text{Give Up}}{\text{Get}}$$

So Jill's opportunity cost of producing more bread is

$$\text{Opportunity cost of additional bread} = \frac{\text{100 logs of wood}}{\text{50 loaves of bread}} = \frac{\text{2 logs of wood}}{\text{1 loaf of bread}}$$

Jill must give up 2 logs of wood to get each additional loaf of bread.

What is Jill's opportunity cost of producing more wood?

$$\text{Opportunity cost of additional wood} = \frac{\text{50 loaves of bread}}{\text{100 logs of wood}} = \frac{\tfrac{1}{2}\text{ loaf of bread}}{\text{1 log of wood}}$$

Jill must give up ½ loaf of bread to get each additional log of wood.

If you calculate opportunity costs for Marie (compare possibilities *A* and *E* in Figure 1.2), her opportunity cost of getting an additional loaf of bread is giving up ½ log of wood, and her opportunity cost of getting an additional log of wood is giving up 2 loaves of bread. These opportunity cost calculations are summarized in Figure 1.3. Since comparative advantage is defined as lowest opportunity cost (not lowest absolute cost), you can see that Marie has a comparative advantage in bread-making (give up ½ log of wood versus Jill's 2 logs of wood), while Jill has a comparative advantage in wood-chopping (give up ½ loaf of bread versus Marie's 2 loaves of bread).

Figure 1.3 Opportunity Costs for Jill and Marie

	Opportunity Cost of 1 Additional	
	Loaf of Bread	Log of Wood
Jill	Gives up 2 logs of wood	Gives up ½ loaf of bread
Marie	Gives up ½ log of wood	Gives up 2 loaves of bread
Comparative Advantage	Marie has comparative advantage (lower opportunity cost) in bread-making	Jill has comparative advantage (lower opportunity cost) in wood-chopping

Smart Deals

Here's the payoff to these calculations. Instead of each pioneer being self-sufficient, and producing everything she needs herself, look what happens if our pioneers specialize in producing what each is best at, and then trading.

According to comparative advantage, Jill should specialize in only chopping wood, and Marie should specialize in only making bread. In this way, Jill will produce 100 logs of wood and no bread, and Marie will produce 40 loaves of bread and no wood. If they then trade 20 logs of wood for 20 loaves of bread:

- Jill ends up with 20 loaves of bread (0 produced plus 20 traded for) and 80 logs of wood (100 produced minus 20 traded away);

- Marie ends up with 20 loaves of bread (40 produced minus 20 traded away) and 20 logs of wood (0 produced plus 20 traded for).

Figure 1.4 tells the story of Jill and Marie's specialization and trade.

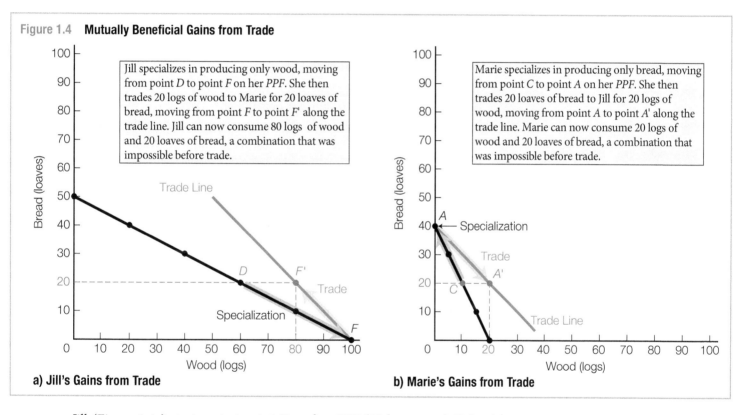

Figure 1.4   Mutually Beneficial Gains from Trade

a) Jill's Gains from Trade

Jill specializes in producing only wood, moving from point D to point F on her PPF. She then trades 20 logs of wood to Marie for 20 loaves of bread, moving from point F to point F' along the trade line. Jill can now consume 80 logs of wood and 20 loaves of bread, a combination that was impossible before trade.

b) Marie's Gains from Trade

Marie specializes in producing only bread, moving from point C to point A on her PPF. She then trades 20 loaves of bread to Jill for 20 logs of wood, moving from point A to point A' along the trade line. Marie can now consume 20 logs of wood and 20 loaves of bread, a combination that was impossible before trade.

Jill (Figure 1.4a) starts out at point D on her PPF (20 loaves and 60 logs). Choosing to specialize in only chopping wood, she moves down along her production possibilities frontier to point F, producing 100 logs of wood and no bread.

Marie (Figure 1.4b) starts out at point C on her PPF (20 loaves and 10 logs). Choosing to specialize in only baking bread, she moves up along her production possibilities frontier to point A, producing 40 loaves of bread and no wood.

Trade occurs along the blue trade lines. As either Jill or Marie moves along the trade lines to exchange wood for bread, 1 log of wood trades for 1 loaf of bread.

Jill moves from her point F (100 logs, 0 loaves) to the new point F' along the trade line, trading 20 logs of wood for 20 loaves of bread. She ends up with 80 logs of wood and 20 loaves of bread.

Marie moves from her point A (40 loaves, 0 logs) along the trade line to the new point A', trading 20 loaves of bread for 20 logs of wood. She ends up with 20 loaves and 20 logs.

Achieving the Impossible   Check it out. *After trading, Jill and Marie are both better off than when they were each self-sufficient.* Before trade, the best Jill could produce with 20 loaves of bread was 60 logs of wood (point *D*). After trade, Jill has the same amount of bread and more wood. Before trade, the best Marie could produce with 20 loaves of bread was just 10 logs of wood (point *C*). After trade, Marie has the same amount of bread and more wood.

Jill and Marie each reach a combination of wood and bread that was impossible before trade. After specialization and trade, each can now consume a combination of wood and bread that is outside of her production possibilities frontier. Voluntary trade is not a zero-sum game, where one person's gain is the other's loss. Both traders gain.

What is remarkable is that these *gains from trade*, which improve both Jill's and Marie's standards of living (with more wood they can stay warmer or build better houses), *happen without anyone working harder, or without any improvement in technology or new inputs.* Both are better off because they have made smart decisions to specialize and trade, rather than each trying to produce only what each will consume. Both can have toast for breakfast (bread roasted over a fire), even though each produced only part of what was necessary to make the breakfast.

Notice also that there are gains for both Jill and Marie, even though Jill can produce more bread and wood than Marie can. Despite Jill's absolute advantage in producing everything at lower cost, there are still differences in opportunity costs, or comparative advantage. *Comparative advantage is the key to mutually beneficial gains from trade.* The trade can be between individuals, or between countries. That is why China trades with Canada, even though China can produce most things more cheaply than Canada can. There are still differences in comparative advantage based on opportunity costs. Trade allows us all to work smarter and live better.

So the next time you buy breakfast, don't feel guilty about spending the money when you could have cooked it yourself — feel smart about specializing and trading — a smart choice that makes you better off!

NOTE
Specialization according to comparative advantage is the key to mutually beneficial gains from trade. All arguments you will ever hear for freer trade are based on comparative advantage.

Refresh 1.3

MyEconLab

For answers to these Refresh Questions, visit MyEconLab.

1. Explain the difference between absolute advantage and comparative advantage.

2. If you spend the next hour working at Canadian Tire, you will earn $10. If instead you spend the next hour studying economics, your next test score will improve by five marks. Calculate the opportunity cost of studying in terms of dollars given up per mark. Calculate the opportunity cost of working in terms of marks given up per dollar.

3. The best auto mechanic in town (who charges $120/hour) is also a better typist than her office manager (who earns $20/hour). The mechanic decides to do her own typing. Is this a smart choice for her to make? Explain your answer.
    [*Hint:* The best alternative employment for the office manager is another office job that also pays $20/hour.]

Economists as Mapmakers and Scientists: Thinking Like an Economist

Explain how models like the circular flow of economic life make smart choices easier.

Canada is a very large country, the second largest in the world in terms of geographical area. Have you ever had the urge to follow in the footsteps of our ancestors and explore the land — perhaps a trip to the northernmost tip of the Northwest Territories, or a cross-country trip from Newfoundland to British Columbia?

Why Maps (and Economists) Are Useful

How do you start planning your trip? The satellite photo of Canada below, while amazing to look at, is not very useful. It contains too much information and too little information. How can that be? The photo captures every aspect of Canada that can be seen from space — lakes, rivers, mountains, and forests. But the photo doesn't reveal smaller details that are important for your trip — most importantly, roads, railways, or ferry services.

Economics is the study of mankind in the ordinary business of life.

— Alfred Marshall (1890)

A map of the same area shows you the auto route along the Trans-Canada Highway (you've decided it's too cold to go up north). Why is the map so much more useful than the satellite photo? Because it focuses your attention on the information that is most relevant for your task, and leaves all other information in the background.

Learning to think like an economist allows the key "roads" to making smart choices stand out — like looking at life on the map. This kind of thinking makes difficult decisions and understanding the complex world around you easier.

There are an almost infinite number of choices we could look at, so to keep things manageable, let's limit ourselves to the opening definition of economics: *Economics is about how individuals, businesses, and governments make the best possible choices to get what they want, and about how those choices interact in markets.* (We will look at markets more closely in Chapter 4, but for the moment, think of a market as the interaction of buyers and sellers.)

Another good definition of economics was presented in 1890 by Alfred Marshall, a legendary professor who first created economics as a separate subject at the University of Cambridge. Marshall said: "Economics is the study of mankind in the ordinary business of life."

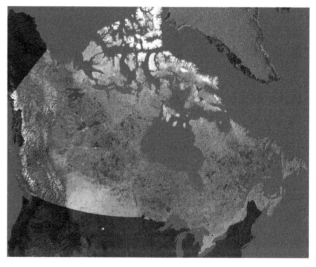

▲ Satellite photo of Canada — not useful for trip planning.

Elvele Images Ltd/Alamy

▲ Map of Canada with the Trans-Canada Highway — useful for trip planning.

Vladislav Gajic/Fotolia

The Circular Flow of Economic Life

Even limiting ourselves to these definitions of economics, the choices are still overwhelming. Imagine 35 million people spread out over 10 million square kilometres, engaged in the "ordinary business of life," earning a living, specializing in producing products and services, selling, and buying. Instead of trying to capture every detail of every action and choice (like the satellite photo), Figure 1.5 shows a map version of the same economic activity.

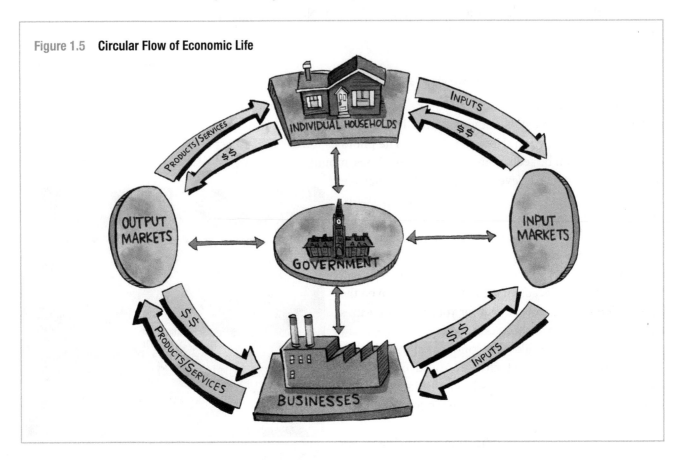

Figure 1.5   Circular Flow of Economic Life

Economic Models   The maps that economists use are called economic models. A **model** is a simplified representation of the real world, focusing attention on what's important for understanding a specific idea or concept.

Figure 1.5 is an economic model called the "circular flow of economic life." It shows you the simplest big picture of how an economist thinks about economic choices. All the complexity of the Canadian economy is reduced to three sets of players: households, businesses, and governments. Individuals in households ultimately own all of the **inputs** of an economy — the productive resources used to produce products and services. The four types of inputs are labour (the ability to work), natural resources, capital equipment, and entrepreneurial ability. Even the assets of the largest corporations, such as Imperial Oil, Ford, or BlackBerry, are ultimately owned by individual shareholders.

Households and businesses interact in two sets of markets — input markets (where businesses buy the inputs they need to produce products and services), and output markets (where businesses sell their products and services). Governments (in the middle) set the rules of the game and can choose to interact, or not, in almost any aspect of the economy.

model   a simplified representation of the real world, focusing attention on what's important for understanding

inputs   the productive resources — labour, natural resources, capital equipment, and entrepreneurial ability — used to produce products and services

Follow the Flow Clockwise   Follow the circle, starting at the top. Individuals in households sell or rent to businesses the labour, resources, capital, and entrepreneurial abilities they own. This is the outer blue flow on the right-hand side of the circle, from top to bottom. In exchange, businesses pay wages and other money rewards to households. This is the inner green flow on the right-hand side of the circle, from bottom to top. These exchanges, or trades, happen in input markets, where households are the sellers and businesses are the buyers. When Mr. Sub hires you to work in its stores, that interaction happens in an input market — the labour market.

Businesses then use those inputs to produce products and services, which they sell to households. This is the outer blue flow on the left-hand side of the circle, from bottom to top. In exchange, households use the money they have earned in input markets to pay businesses for these purchases. This is the inner green flow on the left-hand side of the circle, from top to bottom. These exchanges, or trades, happen in output markets, where households are the buyers and businesses are the sellers. These are markets where you buy your breakfast from a store or supermarket, your cars from Ford or Toyota, your piercings from a neighbourhood piercing parlour, and so on.

At the end of the trip around the circle, households have the products and services they need to live, and businesses end up with the money. That sets the stage for the next trip around the circle, where businesses again buy inputs from individuals in households, and the flow goes on.

So there you have it — an economic model, a sort of map, to guide you on your economics road trip toward understanding and making smart choices.

Models as the Economist's Laboratory

An economic model, like a map, is useful because it is focused and leaves out unnecessary information. But how do you know if the information your model leaves out is important, preventing you from making a smart choice? The test of a good map is if it gets you quickly and safely to where you want to go, without your getting lost. What is the test of a good economic model?

A good economic model helps you make smart choices, or helps you better understand the observed facts of the economic world around you. The test is in comparing the simplified picture of the model with the facts. If the model helps you understand or predict the facts, it's a good model.

But testing an economic model is difficult because the facts we observe are affected by many factors, including factors the model leaves out. For example, the circular flow model in Figure 1.5 leaves out economic factors like international trade between Canada and other countries, the value of the Canadian dollar, and competition between specific banks like RBC or TD Bank. The model also leaves out non-economic factors like the weather, global warming, and military conflicts. Yet all of those factors affect the Canadian economy. Is the simple model still useful even though it ignores those complicating factors?

All Other Things Unchanged   To test models against the facts, economists do what natural scientists do. We assume that "other things are unchanged," to remove the influence of the factors left out of the simplified model. Here is a natural science example.

NOTE
Economic models, which assume all other things not in the model are unchanged, are the mental equivalent of controlled experiments in a laboratory.

The law of gravity predicts that, all other factors unchanged, objects fall at the same rate regardless of their mass. So if we drop a bowling ball and a feather from a tall building, and find the bowling ball hits the ground first, does that disprove the law of gravity? No, because we are not controlling for air resistance, which changes the path of the feather more than the bowling ball. To accurately test the law of gravity, we must perform the same experiment in a laboratory vacuum, so that we eliminate, or control for, the influence of air resistance as an "other factor." We need to keep all other factors unchanged.

A good economic example is the model of demand and supply. In Chapter 2 you will learn about the "law of demand," which predicts that, all other factors unchanged, as the price of a product rises, the quantity demanded by consumers decreases. If the price of wine rises, and consumers buy more wine, does that disprove the law of demand? Not necessarily, because we are not controlling for changes in other factors, like increasing income, which could lead consumers to buy more wine even as the price rises. To accurately test the "law of demand," we need to keep all other factors, like income, unchanged.

Economists, and citizens like you, have it much tougher than scientists. We can't pause everything in the world while focusing only on the factors we are interested in. Instead, we have to use economic models to isolate the factors we think are important. The economic models you will learn here focus attention on what is important by assuming that all other things not in the model are unchanged. Thinking like an economist and using economic models is the mental equivalent of the controlled experiments of the laboratory!

Economics *Out There*

Do You Want to Be an Online Gamer Economist?

More and more online gaming businesses are hiring economists. As an academic economist, Yanis Varoufakis was well aware of economists'

> "inability to run experiments on a macroeconomy such as rewinding time to, say, 1932, in order to see whether the US would have rebounded [from the Great Depression] without the New Deal [a policy of massive government spending] . . . . Even at the level of the microeconomy, keeping faith with the *ceteris paribus* assumption (. . . keeping all other things equal [unchanged] in order to measure, e.g., the relationship between the price of and the demand for milk) is impossible."

Varfoufakis signed on to work with Valve, a major video game company behind hits like *Half-Life*, *Portal*, *Team Fortress*, and *Dota*. The attraction was

> "In sharp contrast to our incapacity to perform truly scientific tests in 'normal' economic settings, Valve's digital economies are a marvelous test-bed for meaningful experimentation. . . . we can change the economy's underlying values, rules and settings, and then sit back to observe how the community responds, how relative prices change, the new behavioural patterns that evolve. An economist's paradise indeed . . ."

Online gaming businesses aren't limited to creating models of the economy. They have complete digital gaming economies and can literally change one factor at a time and digitally capture all of the resulting changes.

If you like gaming, perhaps economics is for you — or better still, if you love economics, maybe online gaming is for you!

Source: Yanis Varoufakis, "It All Began with a Strange Email," *Valve Economics*, June 14, 2012, http://blogs.valvesoftware.com/economics/it-all-began-with-a-strange-email/.

Positive and Normative Statements In trying to explain the facts of the world, economists, like other scientists, distinguish facts from opinions.

Positive statements are about what is; about things that can be checked. "Toronto is closer to Vancouver than to St. John's, Newfoundland" is a positive statement. It can be evaluated as true or false by checking the facts. (False. Vancouver is 3354 kilometres away from Toronto; St. John's is 2112 kilometres away.)

Normative statements involve value judgments or opinions; things that cannot be factually checked. "You should go to Vancouver for your holiday instead of St. John's" is a normative statement. A normative statement is based on personal values, which differ among individuals. Normative statements cannot be tested or shown to be true or false.

The distinction between positive statements and normative statements will also help you make smart choices. To make smart choices in life, you first have to decide on your goals — What do you value? Should you spend your life getting rich or helping others? Those are normative questions. Once you choose your goals, thinking like an economist and using economic models and positive statements will help you effectively achieve them, and get you to where you want to go.

positive statements about what is; can be evaluated as true or false by checking the facts

normative statements about what you believe should be; involve value judgments

Refresh 1.4

1. Who are the three sets of players in the circular flow model of economic life?

2. Write a positive statement linking increasing government taxes on tobacco and smoking habits. Now rewrite it as a normative statement.

3. If you are trying to decide whether to buy a car, what are the most important factors to focus on when making your decision? What are some of the factors that you ignore, or leave out of your decision? Explain how your thinking resembles an economic model.

MyEconLab

For answers to these Refresh Questions, visit MyEconLab.

Where and How to Look:
Models for Microeconomics and Macroeconomics

1.5

Differentiate microeconomic and macroeconomic choices, and explain the Three Keys model for smart choices.

"One size fits all" does not apply to maps or to models. The map of Canada with the highlighted Trans-Canada Highway may be fine for planning the big picture of your trip, but when you are trying to get to a hostel in downtown Fredricton, New Brunswick, from the Trans-Canada, a detailed city map is far more useful. Different needs require different kinds of maps. Depending on the task, economists also use different kinds of models.

The economic way of thinking, while always concerned with smart choices and their interactions in markets, can be applied on different scales to understand microeconomics and macroeconomics.

It's All Greek to Me:
Microeconomics or Macroeconomics?

Microeconomics "Micro" comes from the Greek word *mikros*, meaning "little" or "small." A microscope lets us see little details of an object. A micromanager supervises every tiny detail of an employee's work (ever had a boss like that?). A detailed city map has a micro scale. **Microeconomics** analyzes the choices made by individuals in households, individual businesses, and governments, and how those choices interact in markets.

Microeconomic choices for individuals include whether to go to college or to get a job, whether to be self-sufficient or to specialize and trade, whether to take out a bank loan or to run up a credit card balance, and whether to get married or to stay single. (Yes, there is even a microeconomic analysis comparing the benefits and costs of marriage!)

Microeconomic choices for businesses include what product or service to produce, how much to spend on research and development of new products, which technology to use, which marketing strategy to use, and whether to outsource manufacturing to China or produce in Canada.

Microeconomic choices for governments focus on individual industries. For example, should the government step in and regulate the wireless phone industry (including Bell, Telus, Rogers, and smaller providers), or let competition determine the winners and losers? How would a carbon tax affect car sales?

Macroeconomics When we step back from individual details and look at the big picture, we are taking a "macro" view. Macro comes from the Greek word *makros*, meaning "large." The macrocosm is the cosmos, or the whole of a complex structure. A macrobiotic diet consists of whole, pure foods based on Taoist principles of the overall balance of yin and yang. **Macroeconomics** analyzes the performance of the whole Canadian economy and the global economy, the combined outcomes of all individual microeconomic choices. For the circular flow model in Figure 1.5, instead of focusing on the individual exchanges in markets, macroeconomics focuses on the whole circle, the combined outcomes of all of the individual interactions in markets.

Macroeconomics focuses on overall outcomes of market interactions, including Canadian unemployment, inflation rates, government deficits and surpluses, interest rates set by the Bank of Canada, the value of the Canadian dollar, and international trade. Macroeconomics also examines the policy choices governments make that affect the whole economy — for example, whether to play an active economic role by spending and taxing (more likely for New Democrats or Liberals) or to leave the economy alone (more likely for Conservatives), whether to raise or lower taxes, whether to raise or lower interest rates, and whether to defend the value of the Canadian dollar or let it be determined by economic forces. Since government macroeconomic policy choices will affect your personal economic fortunes, as a citizen you have a personal incentive to learn some macroeconomics so you can make more informed choices when voting for politicians.

microeconomics analyzes choices that individuals in households, individual businesses, and governments make, and how those choices interact in markets

macroeconomics analyzes performance of the whole Canadian economy and global economy, the combined outcomes of all individual microeconomic choices

Looking at the Trees or the Forest? The difference between micro and macro views is reflected in the subtitle of these books — *Microeconomics for Life: Smart Choices for You* and *Macroeconomics for Life: Smart Choices for All?* The microeconomics book, with the subtitle *Smart Choices for You,* is about individual choices. The macroeconomic book, with the subtitle *Smart Choices for All?,* is about the combined market outcomes of all choices. Micro looks at the individual trees, while macro looks at the forest.

Three Keys to Smart Choices: Weigh Marginal Benefits and Marginal Costs

Whether you are taking a course in microeconomics, macroeconomics, or both, all roads to smart choices begin with microeconomic choices.

Good road maps make travel easier, and economic models make smart choices easier. Figure 1.6 shows a second economic model to help guide all of your microeconomic choices toward being smart choices. This model consists of three keys to consider when standing at any fork in the road, when making any choice. While this model doesn't look like a traditional map (no cities, roads, or lines), it serves the same function as all maps and models do — focusing your attention on the information that is most useful for making a smart choice, and leaving all other information in the background.

For each key, pay special attention to the words in **BOLDED CAPS** in the explanations.

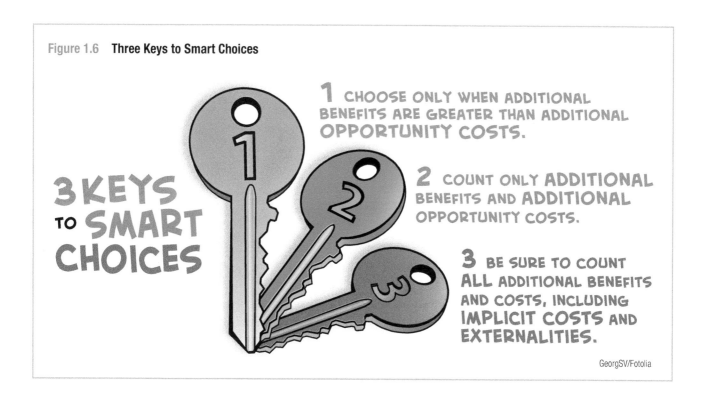

Figure 1.6 **Three Keys to Smart Choices**

3 KEYS TO SMART CHOICES

1 CHOOSE ONLY WHEN ADDITIONAL BENEFITS ARE GREATER THAN ADDITIONAL OPPORTUNITY COSTS.

2 COUNT ONLY ADDITIONAL BENEFITS AND ADDITIONAL OPPORTUNITY COSTS.

3 BE SURE TO COUNT ALL ADDITIONAL BENEFITS AND COSTS, INCLUDING IMPLICIT COSTS AND EXTERNALITIES.

GeorgSV/Fotolia

ADDITIONAL
BENEFITS
VS.
OPPORTUNITY
COSTS

Key 1: Opportunity Costs Rule To make a smart choice, when you weigh benefits against costs, additional benefits must be greater than additional *opportunity costs*. When counting costs, people who make dumb decisions usually count only money costs, rather than including opportunity costs as well. Remember the "free" trip to Bermuda? The money cost was zero, but the opportunity cost was the $1-million deal you would have given up. Or think about your decision to go to college. For that fork in the road, the additional benefits include the higher lifetime income you will earn from your education. The additional costs are the money you spend on tuition and books (these money costs are also opportunity costs, as you could have spent the same money to buy other things), as well as the income you give up by not working full time. The additional benefits must be greater than all additional opportunity costs (and the data show that they are — so congratulations on making a smart choice!).

ADDITIONAL
BENEFITS
& COSTS

Key 2: Look Forward Only to Additional Benefits and Opportunity Costs If you are deciding whether or not to study for the next hour, the tuition you paid for this course is irrelevant. You can't get it back whether you choose to study or not. When standing at a fork in the road, don't look back, only look forward. Your previous decisions or the money you already spent are history and can't be undone. The past is the same no matter which fork you choose now, so it shouldn't influence your choice.

Your choices should weigh the *additional* benefit from the next hour of studying against the *additional* cost (giving up sleep, or perhaps working an extra hour at your part-time job). It's not the total benefit of all hours spent studying or the average benefit of an hour of studying that matters, only the additional benefit. Economists use the word "marginal" instead of "additional," so you can also read Key 2 as "Count only **marginal benefits** — additional benefits from your next choice — and **marginal opportunity costs** — additional opportunity costs from your next choice." Chapter 2 will explain marginal benefits, and Chapter 3 will explain marginal costs. Thinking like an economist means thinking at the margin.

marginal benefits additional benefits from the next choice

marginal opportunity costs additional opportunity costs from the next choice

IMPLICIT
COSTS &
EXTERNALITIES

Key 3: Implicit Costs and Externalities Count, Too If you invest $1000 in your own business, and expect to get $1100 back in a year, is that a smart choice? You can't know until you compare the best alternative use of your money. If the best your bank pays is $1050 in a year, invest in your business. But if the bank is paying 20 percent interest, paying $1200 in a year, your business investment is not a smart choice. Economists use the term **implicit costs** to describe the opportunity costs of investing your own money or time. These *implicit costs* will not show up on the books your accountant would prepare, as we will see in Chapter 7. But smart choices must incorporate implicit costs.

implicit costs opportunity costs of investing your own money or time

Negative Externalities   Driving a car is expensive. Think of the gas bill alone for driving clear across Canada! But your costs also include car payments, insurance, repairs, licence fees, tolls, and parking. What's more, as expensive as those costs are, they don't cover the total cost of driving a car. Your car also emits pollution, but you don't pay for the costs of damage to the environment from acid rain, or for the increased medical costs to treat patients suffering from asthma and other pollution-related illnesses. Economists call these costs that you create, but don't pay for directly, **negative externalities**. They are costs that affect others who are external to a choice or trade. But from an environmentalist's or economist's point of view, *external costs* should be included in making smart decisions.

> **negative (or positive) externalities**   costs (or benefits) that affect others external to a choice or a trade

Positive Externalities   There are also **positive externalities**, benefits that affect others who are external to a choice or trade. If you plant a beautiful garden in your front lawn, you certainly benefit, but so do all of your neighbours who take in the colours and smells. Again, from an economist's point of view, *positive externalities* should be included in making smart decisions, but they are not.

As we will see in Microeconomics Chapter 11, market economies like ours in Canada tend to produce too many products and services that have negative externalities, and too few products and services that have positive externalities. Government policy can play an important role in adjusting for external costs and benefits to result in smart decisions for society.

Moving On

The Three Keys will guide all of your microeconomic choices. If you go on to study macroeconomics, they and the circular flow model of economic life will continue to guide you.

Now that you have been introduced to the economic models, let's get on with the journey. You will use the Three Keys model to make smart decisions many times over the coming chapters. Don't worry if they seem a bit sketchy for now. Each time we use them, we will fill in some of the details that might seem to be missing.

The models in Figures 1.5 and 1.6 will help you learn to think like an economist, which will help you get more out of whatever life you choose to lead, as well as help you make better decisions as a citizen.

Refresh 1.5

1. List the three keys to smart choices, and highlight the most important words in each key.

2. Find one story in today's news that you think is about microeconomics, and one that is about macroeconomics. How did you decide whether the story was about micro or macro economics?

3. Highway 407 ETR in Toronto is a toll road that uses transponders to keep track of how many kilometres you drive on it, and then sends you a monthly bill. Highway 401 runs parallel to Highway 407 and is free. Why do drivers voluntarily pay the tolls? (Use opportunity cost in your answer.) Suppose the government could calculate the cost per kilometre of the pollution damage from your driving, and send you a similar monthly bill. How might that additional cost affect your decision to drive?

MyEconLab

For answers to these Refresh Questions, visit MyEconLab.

Study Guide

1.1 Are You Getting Enough? Scarcity and Choice

Because you can never satisfy all of your wants, making the most out of your life requires smart choices about what to go after, and what to give up.

- The problem of **scarcity** arises because of limited money, time, and energy.
- **Economics** is how individuals, businesses, and governments make the best possible choices to get what they want, and how those choices interact in markets.

1.2 Give It Up for Opportunity Cost! Opportunity Cost

Opportunity cost is the single most important concept both in economics and for making smart choices in life.

- Because of scarcity, every choice involves a trade-off — you have to give up something to get something else.
- The true cost of any choice is the **opportunity cost** — the cost of the best alternative given up.
- For a smart choice, the value of what you get must be greater than value of what you give up.
- **Incentives** — rewards and penalties for choices.
- You are more likely to choose actions with rewards (positive incentives), and avoid actions with penalties (negative incentives).

1.3 Why Don't You Cook Breakfast? Gains from Trade

Opportunity cost and comparative advantage are key to understanding why specializing and trading make us all better off.

- With voluntary trade, each person feels that what they get is of greater value than what they give up.
- **Production possibilities frontier** (*PPF*) — graph showing the maximum combinations of products or services that can be produced with existing inputs.
- **Absolute advantage** — the ability to produce a product or service at a lower absolute cost than another producer.

- **Comparative advantage** — the ability to produce a product or service at a lower opportunity cost than another producer.
- Trade makes individuals better off when each specializes in the product or service where they have a comparative advantage (lower opportunity cost) and then trades for the other product or service.
- Specialization according to comparative advantage and trade allows each trader to consume outside her *PPF*, a combination that was impossible without trade. All arguments you will ever hear for freer trade are based on comparative advantage.
- Even if one individual has an absolute advantage in producing everything at lower cost, as long as there are differences in comparative advantage, there are mutually beneficial gains from specializing and trading.

1.4 Economists as Mapmakers and Scientists: Thinking Like an Economist

The circular-flow model, like all economic models, focuses attention on what's important for understanding and shows how smart choices by households, businesses, and governments interact in markets.

- An economic **model** is a simplified representation of the real world, focusing attention on what's important for understanding.
- The circular flow model of economic life reduces the complexity of the Canadian economy to three sets of players who interact in markets — households, businesses, and governments.
  - In input markets, households are sellers and businesses are buyers.
  - In output markets, households are buyers and businesses are sellers.
  - Governments set rules of the game and can choose to interact in any aspect of the economy.
  - **Inputs** are the productive resources — labour, natural resources, capital equipment, and entrepreneurial ability — used to produce products and services.
- Economic models, which assume all other things not in the model are unchanged, are the mental equivalent of controlled experiments in a laboratory.

- **Positive statements** — about what is; can be evaluated as true or false by checking the facts.

- **Normative statements** — about what you believe *should* be; involve value judgments.
  - Cannot be factually checked.

1.5 Where and How to Look: Models for Microeconomics and Macroeconomics

The Three Keys model summarizes the core of microeconomics, providing the basis for smart choices in all areas of your life.

- **Microeconomics** analyzes choices that individuals in households, individual businesses, and governments make, and how those choices interact in markets.

- **Macroeconomics** analyzes performance of the whole Canadian economy and global economy, the combined outcomes of all individual microeconomic choices.

- The Three Keys Model to Smart Choices:
  1. Choose only when additional benefits are greater than additional *opportunity costs*.
  2. Count only *additional* benefits and *additional* opportunity costs.
  3. Be sure to count *all* additional benefits and costs, including *implicit costs* and *externalities*.

- Important concepts in the Three Keys model:
  - Marginal = "additional"
  - **Marginal benefits** — additional benefits from the next choice.
  - **Marginal opportunity costs** — additional opportunity costs from the next choice.
  - **Implicit costs** — opportunity costs of investing your own money or time.
  - **Negative** (or **positive**) **externalities** — costs (or benefits) that affect others external to a choice or a trade.

TRUE/FALSE

Circle the correct answer. Solutions to these questions are available at the end of the book and on MyEconLab. You can also visit the MyEconLab Study Plan to access additional questions that will help you master the concepts covered in this chapter.

1.1 Scarcity and Choice

1. Economics is about how individuals, businesses, and governments make the best possible choices to get what they want, and how those choices interact in markets. T F

2. People who win the lottery don't have to make smart choices. T F

1.2 Opportunity Cost

3. Opportunity cost equals money cost. T F

4. The Government of Canada announced a $1000 Apprenticeship Incentive Grant to pay for tuition, travel, and tools for apprentices in the sealing trades. This will eliminate the opportunity cost of being an apprentice. T F

5. According to Economics Out There on p. 6, men have a larger incentive to get a post-secondary education because *not* getting a post-secondary education results in a relatively worse outcome compared to women. T F

1.3 Gains from Trade

6. Traditionally, women specialized in unpaid work at home and men specialized in paid work outside the house. One possible explanation is that men have a comparative advantage in performing housework (for example, cooking, cleaning, and child care). T F

7. Combinations of products inside a production possibilities frontier are impossible to produce. T F

8. Comparative advantage is the ability to produce at a lower absolute cost, compared to another producer. T F

9. Voluntary trade is a zero-sum game, where one person's gain is the other's loss. T F

1.4 Thinking Like an Economist

10. In input markets, households are sellers and businesses are buyers; in output markets, households are buyers and businesses are sellers. T F

11. Economists can perform controlled experiments just like natural scientists. T F

12. The statement "Tuition fees should be reduced" is a normative statement. T F

1.5 Models for Microeconomics and Macroeconomics

13. Decisions to go to college or take out a loan are macroeconomic choices. T F

14. Microeconomics analyzes choices that individuals in households, individual businesses, and governments make, and how those choices interact in markets. T F

15. Negative externalities are benefits that affect others external to a choice or a trade. T F

MULTIPLE CHOICE

Circle the best answer. Solutions to these questions are available at the end of the book and on MyEconLab. You can also visit the MyEconLab Study Plan to access similar questions that will help you master the concepts covered in this chapter.

1.1 Scarcity and Choice

1. You can't get everything you want because you are limited by
   a) time.
   b) money.
   c) energy.
   d) all of the above.

2. Scarcity is
   a) not a challenge for governments.
   b) not a challenge for celebrities.
   c) not a challenge for people who win the lottery.
   d) a challenge for everyone.

3. Economics does *not* focus on
   a) individuals.
   b) animals.
   c) businesses.
   d) government.

1.2 Opportunity Cost

4. Opportunity cost includes
   a) time you give up.
   b) energy you spend.
   c) money you spend.
   d) all of the above.

5. In deciding whether to study or sleep for the next hour, you should consider all of the following *except*
   a) how much tuition you paid.
   b) how tired you are.
   c) how productive you will be in that hour.
   d) how much value you place on sleeping in that hour.

6. Recently, the proportion of 25- to 29-year-old women with university degrees rose from 21 percent to 34 percent, while the proportion of 25- to 29-year-old men with degrees rose from 16 percent to 21 percent. There is a similar trend for college diplomas. More woman than men are getting post-secondary education because
   a) the gap in pay between post-secondary and high-school graduates is higher for women.
   b) the cost of not going to post-secondary education is higher for women.
   c) the opportunity cost of going to post-secondary education is lower for women.
   d) all of the above.

7. If the resource-rich sector of Alberta's economy slows down,
   a) opportunity costs of upgrading to a college diploma increase.
   b) opportunity costs of upgrading to a college diploma decrease.
   c) incentives to drop out of college increase.
   d) all of the above.

1.3 Gains from Trade

8. Mutually beneficial gains from trade come from
   a) absolute advantage.
   b) comparative advantage.
   c) self-sufficiency.
   d) China.

9. The easiest way to calculate opportunity cost is
   a) $\dfrac{\text{give up}}{\text{get}}$
   b) $\dfrac{\text{get}}{\text{give up}}$
   c) give up – get
   d) get – give up

10. In one hour, Chloe can bake 24 cookies or 12 muffins. Zabeen can bake 6 cookies or 2 muffins. For mutually beneficial trade, Chloe should
    a) bake cookies because she has a comparative advantage.
    b) bake cookies because she has an absolute advantage.
    c) bake muffins because she has a comparative advantage.
    d) bake muffins because she has an absolute advantage.

1.4 Thinking Like an Economist

11. Which of the following statements is normative?
    a) Economists should not make normative statements.
    b) Warts are caused by handling toads.
    c) As smartphone prices fall, people will buy more of them.
    d) As test dates get closer, students study more hours.

12. In the circular-flow model,
    a) households ultimately own all inputs of an economy.
    b) governments set the rules of the game.
    c) businesses are sellers and households are buyers in output markets.
    d) all of the above.

13. Which of the following is *not* a microeconomic choice for businesses?
    a) what interest rate to set
    b) what products to supply
    c) what quantity of output to produce
    d) how many workers to hire

14. Which of the following is *not* a microeconomic choice for governments?
    a) increasing tuition rates
    b) taxing automobile emissions
    c) increasing the exchange rate of the Canadian dollar
    d) increasing the number of taxi licences

15. All of the following should be considered when making smart choices, *except*
    a) external costs and benefits.
    b) past costs and benefits.
    c) implicit costs.
    d) additional costs and additional benefits.

2 Making Smart Choices

The Law of Demand

LEARNING OBJECTIVES

After reading this chapter, you should be able to:

2.1 Describe what determines your willingness and ability to pay for a product or service.

2.2 Identify why smart choices depend on marginal benefits, not total benefits, and explain what changes marginal benefits.

2.3 Explain the law of demand, and describe the roles of substitutes and willingness and ability to pay.

2.4 Explain the difference between a change in quantity demanded and a change in demand, and identify five factors that change demand.

YOU NEVER WANT TO PAY more than you have to. But

what determines how much you are willing to pay?

To get the most out of life, you need to make smart choices between alternatives. Should you use your time to go to school or to work? How do you choose the right job or the right partner? And how can you spend your money wisely to get the things you value most?

This chapter focuses on the choices you make every day as a consumer, buying products and services in the market. Choice means comparing alternatives. Those choices — between competing phone plans, between getting to school by bike or car or transit, between water or coffee or pop to quench your thirst — affect how much you are willing to pay. Your willingness to pay also depends on quantity — would you pay as much for the fifth slice of pizza as you would for the first? And how much money you have is definitely a factor.

Economists use the term *demand* to summarize all of the influences on consumer choice. Here you will learn the keys to making smart choices by separating out the many influences that determine your willingness to pay.

2.1 Put Your Money Where Your Mouth Is: Weighing Benefits, Costs, and Substitutes

Describe what determines your willingness and ability to pay for a product or service.

You just finished an intense workout at the gym and desperately want something to drink. You usually bring along your favourite Gatorade (which costs $3 a bottle), but today you forgot it. The snack bar has bottled water and juice, but no Gatorade. Your buddy, who is always trying to make a buck, says, "I have a bottle of what you want — how much will you pay for it?"

sellingpix/Shutterstock

EBFoto/Shutterstock

makeitdouble/Shutterstock

▲ Choosing a substitute depends on what you will pay, what substitutes are available, and what they cost. Can you think of anything you use in life that doesn't have a substitute?

Besides wondering if this guy is really a buddy, what do you think about to decide how much you are willing to pay him? Obviously, how thirsty you are and how refreshed you expect to feel from the drink matter a lot. But just because you badly want Gatorade does not mean you will pay, say, $10 for the bottle.

What are your alternatives? You could buy a water or juice for $2, but they don't have the electrolytes for your muscles that Gatorade does. You could drink water from the tap in the locker room for free. You could head home and drink the bottle you forgot, or head to a store to buy your Gatorade for $3.

You decide you so want the Gatorade *now* that you are willing to make an offer. You know your entrepreneurial buddy won't take less than the $3 he paid for the bottle, so you are willing to pay $4. You make the purchase, quench your thirst — and then ditch the buddy.

ADDITIONAL BENEFITS VS. OPPORTUNITY COSTS

We all make hundreds of choices a day that are similar — what to eat; what to wear; what to buy; whether to spend time studying, working, working out, or relaxing; whom to vote for. . . . All these choices are based (consciously or unconsciously) on a comparison of expected benefits and costs. This is Key 1 of the Three Keys to Smart Choices from Chapter 1: Choose only when additional benefits are greater than additional *opportunity costs*.

How Badly Do You Want It?

The first part of the comparison requires you to have a sense of the expected benefits from your choice. The expected benefit question is, "How badly do you want it?" What satisfaction do you expect to get from this choice? The want and the satisfaction might be quite logical — I want a warm coat so I won't freeze during the winter in Regina. I want water because I am thirsty. I want to spend the evening studying because I have a test tomorrow. Or your desire for the latest, biggest-screen phone may be based on more emotional reasons — wanting to look cool, or to impress others, or just because, well, you want it. Businesses spend money on advertising, in part, to convince you to want their product. Economists describe all of your wants — and how intense each want is — as your **preferences**.

preferences your wants and their intensities

What Will You Give Up?

For the second part of the comparison, the cost question is, "How much are you willing and able to give up for it?" I purposely chose the words *give up* when you might have expected me to say, "How much are you willing and able to *pay* for it?" There's a reason for this choice, just as there are reasons for all of your choices. Many things we want — Gatorade or phones — we have to pay for with money. But for many other things we want, what we have to give up is our time or our effort. Spending the evening studying means not seeing your friends, playing with your kids, or working at your part-time job. Cost always means *opportunity cost* — what you are willing to give up.

What determines *how much* you are willing to give up? Certainly, how badly you want it plays a role. But just as important is what your alternative choices are. There are substitutes for everything — water for Gatorade, a yoga class for a gym workout, long underwear or a move to Florida for winter coats. Substitutes need not be exactly the same product or service. Substitutes just have to basically satisfy the same want. For any choice, what you are willing and able to pay, or to give up, depends on what substitutes are available, and what they cost.

The final factor determining how much you are willing and able to give up is how much you can afford. Are you able to pay the price of the product or service you want? Can you afford to take the time to relax all evening when you have a test tomorrow?

The list of things we want is endless. But the choices we actually make reflect our willingness — and ability — to give up something in exchange. Economists use the term **demand** to describe consumers' willingness and ability to pay for a particular product or service. Demand is *not* just what consumers want. You must put your money (or time) where your mouth is in order to demand a product or service. And those demands, or choices, are smart choices only when expected benefits are greater than opportunity costs.

demand consumers' willingness and ability to pay for a particular product or service

Refresh 2.1

1. What is the difference between wants and demands?

2. What is the key factor that would make you choose to download a song for free rather than pay for it on iTunes? Explain your choice.

3. You have just started at a school that is a 30-minute drive from home or a 90-minute transit ride. Which is your smart choice, taking the transit or buying a car? Justify your choice.

MyEconLab

For answers to these Refresh Questions, visit MyEconLab.

2.2 Living on the Edge: Smart Choices Are Marginal Choices

Identify why smart choices depend on marginal benefits, not total benefits, and explain what changes marginal benefits.

You make a smart choice only when expected benefits are greater than opportunity costs. But the benefits or satisfaction you expect to get depend on the circumstances.

Marginal Benefits Change with Circumstances

To see how benefits change with circumstances, let's return to the Gatorade example. Suppose you remembered to bring a bottle to the gym, and gulped it all after your workout. If your greedy buddy then asked you how much you were willing to pay for another bottle, chances are it would be much less than the $4 you were willing to pay when you had few convenient Gatorade alternatives. The *additional* benefit you will get from his second bottle is less than the benefit you got from your thirst-quenching first bottle. So your willingness to pay is less for the second bottle.

What if you have a test tomorrow, and you have to choose between spending the evening studying or going out with a friend? If you have been studying like mad for days already, the *additional* benefit of a few more hours might not help much, so you choose to visit. But if you have been busy working at your job all week and haven't cracked a book, the *additional* benefit of studying will be large, and you give up the friend time.

In both cases, the *additional* benefit you expect, and your willingness to pay (either in money or giving up friend time you value), depends on the circumstances. The economist's term for *additional* benefit is **marginal benefit**. Marginal means "on or at the edge," just like the margins of these textbook pages are at the edges of the pages.

marginal benefit the additional benefit from a choice, changing with circumstances

Key 2 of the Three Keys to Smart Choices says that when you compare expected benefits and costs, count only *additional* benefits and *additional* costs, or marginal benefits and marginal costs. Here we are explaining marginal benefits; in Chapter 3 we will explain marginal costs.

A smart decision to study (or not) does not depend on the total value of all hours spent studying, or the average value of an hour spent studying, but only on the *marginal* value of the additional time spent studying (compared with the additional cost of giving up those hours).

What if you choose to spend the evening studying, and your friend gets angry and shouts, "Is your stupid economics course more important than I am?" At the margin, the answer is yes. Your choice to study tonight doesn't necessarily mean that, overall, you value the course more than the friend (well, depending on the friend, you might). What your choice means is that tonight, at the margin, you value the next few hours spent studying more than you value spending the next few hours with your friend.

▲ The difference between total growth and marginal growth is the difference between "How tall are you?" and "How much have you grown?" The *difference* between the second-highest mark and the highest represents your *marginal*, or *additional*, growth during the past year.

But margins, and circumstances, change. Your choice would be different if you had another week before the test, or if you hadn't seen your friend for months. The value you place on an activity or thing depends on the margin, and *that* additional value is marginal benefit.

Your friend's angry accusation comes from the common mistake (not smart) of looking at choices as all or nothing — friend versus economics. That's not the (smart) choice you made at the margin — the marginal benefit of the time spent studying tonight was greater than the value, or marginal benefit, of the same time spent with your friend.

Marginal Benefits Decrease with Quantity

The Gatorade and studying examples share a common circumstance that regularly changes marginal benefit — quantity. The first Gatorade after a workout is very satisfying — it has a high marginal benefit. The second Gatorade is less satisfying, and a third or fourth might make you sick. Your first hour studying might raise your test mark by 40 marks. But as you spend more hours studying, each additional hour provides fewer additional marks. Additional quantities consumed give you decreasing marginal benefit.

Since marginal benefit is the key to how much you are willing to pay, decreasing marginal benefit means decreasing willingness to pay for additional quantities of the same product or service.

Your willingness to pay, determined at the margin by changing circumstances including quantity, is important in determining prices, ranging from low prices for water to high prices for diamonds.

NOTE
Additional quantities consumed of the same product or service give decreasing marginal benefit.

Economics *Out There*

Coke's Automatic Price Gouging

In the late 1990s, Coca-Cola Co. worked on technology to automatically raise prices in soft-drink vending machines on hot days. Critics — calling the plan "shameful" and a "cynical ploy" to exploit consumers "when they are most susceptible to price gouging" — suggested Coca-Cola should abandon the plan. The company claimed it was fair that the price should rise with demand, and that the machines simply automate that process. Unconvinced, critics warned that the plan would alienate customers, with the reminder that "archrival Pepsi is out there, and you can hardly tell the difference."

- The public reaction to these variable-price vending machines was so negative that Coca-Cola never introduced them.

- However, the strategy is based on the correct observation that willingness to pay changes with circumstances — the principle of marginal benefit.

- The strategy failed not because the economics were wrong, but because the idea of paying different prices for the same product seemed so unfair — "price gouging." (However, in Chapter 9 we will look at examples where consumers accept businesses charging different consumers different prices for the same product — cellphone minutes cost providers the same, whether daytime, evening, or weekend. Why are prices different? [*Hint:* Consumer willingness to pay.])

- Notice the line about Pepsi — substitutes are always available, which limits willingness to pay for any product, regardless of the marginal benefit.

Source: "Coke's Automatic Price Gouging," *San Francisco Chronicle*, October 29, 1999, p. A22.

The Diamond/Water Paradox

NOTE

Willingness to pay, a key part of demand, depends on marginal benefits, not total benefits. If you think about total benefits you will get confused in section 2.3. Think marginal!

The distinction between looking at choices at the margin (smart) instead of as "all or nothing" or total-value choices helps make sense of the diamond/water paradox you may have heard about. What's more valuable in providing benefit or satisfaction — diamonds or water? One answer is water. Water is essential for survival, while diamonds are an unnecessary frill. But then why do diamonds cost far more than water?

You can solve the paradox by distinguishing marginal benefit from total benefit. You would die without any water, so you would be willing to pay everything you can for the first drink. But when water is abundant and cheap, and you are not dying of thirst, what would you be willing to pay, at the margin, for your next drink today? Not much. Marginal benefit is low, even though the total benefit of all water consumed (including the first, life-saving drink) is high.

Diamonds won't keep you alive, but they are relatively scarce, and desirable for that very reason. What would you pay for what is likely your first diamond? A lot. *Marginal benefit* is high. Because diamonds are scarce, there aren't many out there (compared to drinks of water), so *total benefit* is low. But willingness to pay depends on marginal benefit, not total benefit, so people are generally willing to pay more for a diamond (high marginal benefit) than for a glass of water (low marginal benefit).

Marginal benefit, as we will see in Chapter 4, is important not only for making smart choices, but also for explaining how prices are determined in the real world.

Refresh 2.2

MyEconLab

For answers to these Refresh Questions, visit MyEconLab.

1. In your own words, define *marginal benefit*.

2. Explain why we are willing to pay more for a diamond than a glass of water even though water is essential for survival and diamonds are an unnecessary luxury.

3. You and your entrepreneurial buddy have a concession stand on the beach. It is a hot, sunny, crowded day, and you are selling a few $5 collapsible umbrellas as sun shades. The skies suddenly darken, rain begins to pour, and your buddy quickly switches the umbrella price sign to $10. Will you sell more or fewer umbrellas? Explain your thinking, including your analysis of the customer's decision.

Move On When the Price Isn't Right: The Law of Demand

After weeks of boring bus rides to school and overhearing too many other riders' personal phone conversations, you finally decide to buy a good pair of headphones. You research the alternatives and decide to buy the Beats Solo model in green. You would have loved the Beats Pro model, or Bose Quiet Comfort headphones, but decided you couldn't afford those.

Explain the law of demand, and describe the roles of substitutes and willingness and ability to pay.

Quantity Demanded

Let's presume you made a smart choice, so the additional benefit of these headphones (listening pleasure and blocking out the world) is greater than the additional cost (the $200 price tag). You are willing and able to pay $200. Sold! An economist would say that, at the price of $200, your *quantity demanded* of Beats Solo headphones is one.

Quantity demanded, as we will see, is not the same as *demand.* **Quantity demanded** is the amount you actually plan to buy at a given price, taking into account everything that affects your willingness and ability to pay.

quantity demanded amount you actually plan to buy at a given price

We saw in the previous section that if circumstances change the additional benefit, your choice may change. The second bottle of Gatorade wasn't worth as much as the first, and the value of the headphones would change if you were driving to school in a car with a good sound system instead of riding the bus. But our focus here is not on benefits. Our focus is on *what happens to your buying decision when the price — the additional cost you pay — changes.* In order to focus on the relationship between price and quantity demanded, we will keep all other influences on demand the same.

Changing Prices Change Quantity Demanded What if this Beats model were priced at $225 instead of $200? How might that change your decision to buy? You might want these headphones so badly that you would be willing to pay $225, judging that the additional benefit is still greater than the $200 cost. (That means that at $200, you felt you were getting a bargain!) But since you are a smart shopper and have limited income, you would still be thinking carefully about alternatives. There are substitutes for everything. For listening to music and sound-blocking there are cheaper headphones, and the not-so-great earbuds that came with your phone. The extra $25 cost might be enough to change your choice from the Beats Solo headphones to one of these substitutes. And if the price were $250, you, along with many more consumers out there, would definitely change your smart choice away from these specific headphones to a substitute. At a price of $250, your quantity demanded is zero.

What if Apple puts these headphones on sale for $150 instead of $200? Given your willingness and ability to pay, this is such a bargain that you decide to buy two — one for you, and one as a gift for your boyfriend or girlfriend. At a price of $150, your quantity demanded is two.

If we put your combinations of prices (willing and able to pay) and quantities demanded into a table, it looks like Figure 2.1.

NOTE
When the price of a product rises, consumers switch to cheaper substitutes. The quantity demanded of the original product, at the now higher price, decreases.

Figure 2.1 Your Demand for Beats Headphones

Price (willing and able to pay)	Quantity Demanded
$150	2
$200	1
$250	0

As your eye goes down the two columns, notice that as the price rises, the quantity demanded decreases. In general, when prices rise, consumers look for substitutes. When something becomes more expensive, people economize on its use.

Philip Harvey/CORBIS

▲ A change to a new behaviour is often encouraged by an increase in the cost of an old behaviour. What might make this man change from using a hose and water to using a broom to clean his walk?

Water or Brooms?   Households in the City of Toronto used to pay a fixed monthly price for water that didn't change with the quantity of water used. So the *additional* cost of using more water was zero. With "free" marginal water, many residents would "sweep" their sidewalks and driveways with a hose. But when water became metered, so that users paid for each additional cubic metre (m^3), many gave up this practice and started sweeping with a broom. (Only economics teaches you that water and brooms are substitutes!) Other reactions to higher water prices included placing flow regulators on showers, taking showers instead of baths, installing water-saving dual flush toilets, and planting ground cover that consumes less water than grass. With a higher price for water, the quantity demanded decreased.

The Law of Demand

The market for any product or service consists of millions of potential customers, each trying to make a smart choice about what to buy. **Market demand** is the sum of the demands of all individuals willing and able to buy a particular product or service.

Whether it is the market for headphones, water, or anything else, substitutes exist, so that consumers buy a smaller quantity at higher prices, and a larger quantity at lower prices. This inverse relationship (when one goes up, the other goes down) between price and quantity demanded is so universal that economists call it (somewhat grandiosely) the **law of demand**: If the price of a product or service rises, the quantity demanded of the product or service decreases. If the price falls, the quantity demanded increases. The law of demand works as long as other influences on demand besides price do not change. The next section will explore what happens when other influences do change. Will the law of demand then fail? Stay tuned.

market demand   sum of demands of all individuals willing and able to buy a particular product or service

law of demand   if the price of a product or service rises, quantity demanded decreases, other things remaining the same

Market Demand Curve for Water   The table of numbers in Figure 2.2 illustrates the inverse relationship between price and quantity demanded for the market demand for water. If you graph the combinations of prices and quantity demanded, you get the *market demand curve* in Figure 2.2.

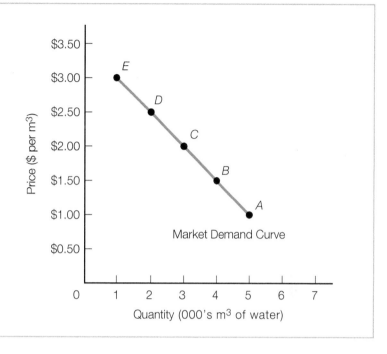

Figure 2.2   **Market Demand for Water**

Row	Price ($ per m³)	Quantity Demanded (000's of m³ per month)
A	$1.00	5
B	$1.50	4
C	$2.00	3
D	$2.50	2
E	$3.00	1

A **demand curve** shows the relationship between price and quantity demanded, when all other influences on demand besides price do not change.

For example, the table in Figure 2.2 shows that when the price of a cubic metre (m³) of water is $1, the quantity demanded is 5000 m³ per month (row *A*). When the price is $3, the quantity demanded is 1000 m³ (row *E*). The other rows in the table show the quantities demanded for prices in between $1 and $3.

We can draw the market demand curve for water by plotting these combinations on a graph that has *quantity* on the horizontal axis and *price* on the vertical axis. The points on the demand curve labelled *A* to *E* correspond to the rows of the table.

Economizing Decisions   The law of demand, represented by a demand curve, is yet another way of saying that when something becomes more expensive, people economize on its use. This law helps explain many decisions beyond shopping decisions or how to sweep a sidewalk.

Mother Teresa's charity wanted to open a shelter for the homeless in New York City. When city bureaucrats insisted on expensive but unnecessary renovations to the building, the charity abandoned the project. Mother Teresa didn't abandon her commitment to the poor. When the cost of helping the poor in New York went up, she decided that, at the margin, her efforts would do more good elsewhere. For her charity, a shelter elsewhere was a substitute for a New York shelter.

Because there are substitutes for everything, higher prices create incentives for smart consumers to reduce their purchases of more expensive products or services and look for alternatives.

demand curve shows the relationship between price and quantity demanded, other things remaining the same

NOTE
Demand curves can be straight lines (like this simple one) or curves, but they all slope downward to the right — as the price falls, quantity demanded increases.

Two Ways to Read a Demand Curve

The demand curve shows graphically the relationship between price and quantity demanded, when all other influences on demand do not change. The demand curve is a simple yet powerful tool summarizing the two forces that determine quantity demanded — the switch to substitutes and willingness and ability to pay.

Because there are two forces determining quantity demanded, there are two ways to "read" a demand curve — as a demand curve and as a marginal benefit curve. Both readings are correct, but each highlights a different force. You can see the two readings in Figure 2.3.

Figure 2.3 **Two Ways to Read a Demand Curve**

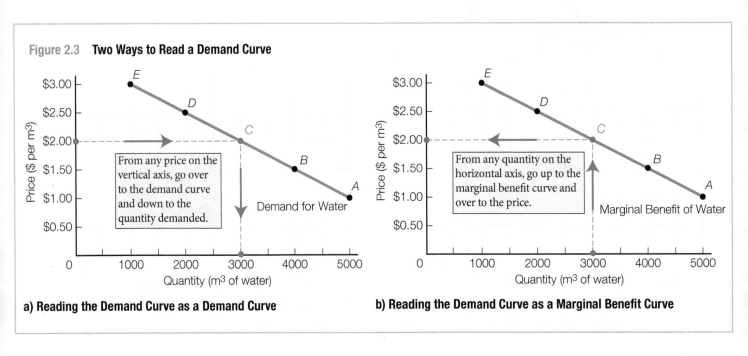

a) **Reading the Demand Curve as a Demand Curve**

b) **Reading the Demand Curve as a Marginal Benefit Curve**

Demand Curve To read Figure 2.3a as a demand curve, start with price. For any given price, the demand curve tells you the quantity demanded. For example, start with the price of $2 on the vertical axis (Price). To find quantity demanded at $2, you trace a line from the $2 price over to the demand curve and then down to the horizontal axis (Quantity) to read the quantity demanded, which is 3000 m³ of water per month. You can do the same for any price — from any chosen price, go over to the demand curve and then down to read the corresponding quantity demanded.

To see how a price rise from $2 to $3 causes a switch to substitutes, and a decrease in quantity demanded, for each price go over to the demand curve and then down to the quantity demanded. The rise in price of $1 causes a decrease in quantity demanded of 2000 m³ of water per month (3000 – 1000).

Marginal Benefit Curve   To read Figure 2.3b as a marginal benefit curve, start with quantity. For a given quantity, the marginal benefit curve tells you the maximum price people are willing and able to pay for the last unit available. Start with the quantity 3000 m^3 of water on the horizontal axis (Quantity). To find the maximum price people are willing and able to pay for the 3000th cubic metre of water, you trace a line up to the marginal benefit curve and over to the vertical (Price) axis to read the price, which is $2. You can do the same for any quantity — from any chosen quantity, go up to the marginal benefit curve and then over to read the corresponding price, which is the maximum price people are willing and able to pay for that last available unit of water.

To see how an increase in quantity from 3000 to 4000 m^3 causes a decreased marginal benefit and decreases willingness and ability to pay, for each quantity go up to the marginal benefit curve and then over to the price. $2 is the most someone is willing and able to pay for the 3000th cubic metre of water, and $1.50 is the most someone is willing and able to pay for the 4000th cubic metre of water. The 4000th m^3 of water, compared to the 3000th m^3 of water, provides a decreased marginal benefit. The increase in quantity of 1000 m^3 causes a decrease in marginal benefit of $0.50 ($2.00 − $1.50).

The Demand Curve Is Also a Marginal Benefit Curve   You read a demand curve over and down. You read a marginal benefit curve up and over. While the demand curve has a double identity both as a demand curve and as a marginal benefit curve, we generally refer to it as a demand curve. Sometimes, though, the marginal benefit reading will make it easier to understand smart choices.

Both readings are movements along an unchanged demand curve. But what about the other influences on demand that we have been keeping constant? What happens if they change? The two ways to read a demand curve will help you answer that question.

NOTE
You read a demand curve over and down. You read a marginal benefit curve up and over.

Refresh 2.3

1. In just a couple of sentences, explain the law of demand to a friend who is not taking this economics course.

2. You own a car and work at a job that you cannot get to by public transit. If the price of gasoline goes up dramatically, does the law of demand apply to you? Explain the choices you might make in responding to this price rise.

3. You have tickets for a concert tonight that you have been looking forward to. Your mother, who is helping you pay your tuition, phones and says that it's very important to her that you come to Grandma's birthday party tonight. Using the law of demand, explain your decision — the concert or Grandma's party? [*Hint:* Think about opportunity cost.]

MyEconLab

For answers to these Refresh Questions, visit MyEconLab.

2.4

Moving the Margins: What Can Change Demand?

Explain the difference between a change in quantity demanded and a change in demand, and identify five factors that change demand.

The price of gasoline in Halifax rose from $0.99 per litre to $1.39 per litre between 2010 and 2012. But the quantity of gasoline motorists bought actually *increased*. Does that disprove the "law of demand"?

If nothing else changed except the price of gasoline, the answer would be yes — and I'd have to quit this job as an economist and do something more socially useful, like being a trash collector.

But I, and other economists, have enough confidence in the law of demand that if we observe a rise in price leading to an *increase* in purchases, we take it as a signal that something else must have changed at the same time.

Economists use the concept of *demand* to summarize all the influences on consumer choice. Your demand for any product or service reflects your willingness and ability to pay. In the examples of Gatorade, headphones, and water, we have seen that your willingness to pay depends on things like your preferences, what substitutes are available, and marginal benefit. Your ability to pay depends on your income.

As long as all these factors (and a few more) do not change, the law of demand holds true: If the price of a product or service rises, the quantity demanded decreases.

But when change happens, economists distinguish between two kinds of change:

- If the price of a product or service changes, that affects *quantity demanded*. This is represented graphically by a movement along an unchanged demand curve.

- If anything else changes, that affects *demand*. This is represented graphically by a shift of the entire demand curve.

Quantity demanded is a much more limited term than *demand*. Only a change in price changes quantity demanded. A change in any other influence on consumer choice changes demand. This may sound like semantic hair-splitting — quantity demanded versus demand — but it is important for avoiding not-smart thinking.

Why Bother Distinguishing between Quantity Demanded and Demand?

Suppose you observe a witch placing a curse on some poor young man, who dies a month later. The apparent conclusion is that the curse was fatal. But if the witch had been secretly poisoning his food with arsenic all along, what was the real cause of death? Something else changed that was really behind the observed result.

What if a gasoline supplier decides to raise his prices to increase his sales, based on the observed result that when gasoline prices rose between 2010 and 2012, motorists bought more gasoline. What do you think would happen? Would this be a smart choice?

We live in a complicated world, where everything depends on everything else. There are obvious connections between events like a lottery win increasing your spending, or high ticket prices increasing movie downloads. But non-economic events like the weather can affect coffee prices, and a whiff of a terrorist threat can sink airline stock prices. So when you observe a change in the economy like increased gasoline purchases, how do you decide what caused it when so many interdependent things can change at the same time? (Was the young man's death caused by curse, arsenic, or natural causes?)

Controlled Experiments   Scientists deal with this interdependence problem by performing controlled experiments in a laboratory. The law of gravity claims that, all other factors unchanged, objects fall at the same rate regardless of their mass. So if we drop a bowling ball and a feather from a tall building, and find the bowling ball hits the ground first, does that disprove the law of gravity? No, because we are not controlling for air resistance, which changes the path of the feather more than the bowling ball. To accurately test the law of gravity, we must perform the same experiment in a laboratory vacuum, so that we eliminate, or control for, the influence of air resistance as an "other factor." We need to keep all other factors unchanged.

Economists, and citizens like you, have it much tougher than scientists. We can't pause everything in the world while changing only the factors we are interested in. Instead, we have to use economic thinking to make sense of the changes. The distinction between a change in quantity demanded and a change in demand is the economist's way of trying to mentally imitate a controlled experiment.

The law of demand is the simplest of all the interdependent relationships. *If nothing else changes,* a rise in the price of gasoline will cause a decrease in the quantity demanded of gasoline.

Let's look at the more complicated parts (like air resistance for the law of gravity) — all the important "other things" that can cause a change in demand.

NOTE
It is difficult to distinguish an event's actual causes from apparent causes. Scientists use controlled laboratory experiments to isolate one cause while keeping all other factors unchanged. Economists use distinctions like change in quantity demanded versus change in demand to mentally imitate controlled experiments.

Five Ways to Change Demand and Shift the Demand Curve

Only a change in the price of a product or service itself changes *quantity demanded* of that product or service. But there are five important other factors that can change market demand — the willingness and ability to pay for a product or service. They are:

- Preferences
- Prices of related products
- Income
- Expected future prices
- Number of consumers

A change in any of these five factors shifts the demand curve.

Preferences   There are many reasons why businesses advertise, but ultimately they are trying to get you to want their product, to persuade you that you need what they sell. Remember that economists use the term "preferences" to describe your wants and their intensities — so, for an economist, advertising is about increasing your preferences for a product or service.

Most car commercials are not about information but about showing you a fabulous, fun driving experience that the manufacturer wants you to believe will be yours only if you buy its car.

All businesses want to increase your preferences, because if they succeed in increasing the intensity of your want or desire for their product you will be willing to pay more for it. If Apple runs a successful ad campaign that makes you and many other consumers feel you can't live (and be cool) without Beats headphones, what would happen to your willingness and ability to pay, according to our earlier example? Look at Figure 2.4 on the next page.

Figure 2.4 An Increase in Demand for Beats Headphones

Price	Quantity Demanded (originally)	Quantity Demanded (after advertising)
$150	2	3
$200	1	2
$250	0	1
$300	0	0

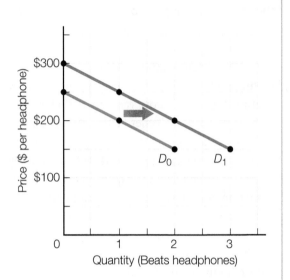

Look first at demand curve D_0, which shows your original plans, before advertising, to buy no headphones if the price is $250, one if the price is $200, and two headphones if the price is $150. Reading the demand curve as a marginal benefit curve — up and over — makes most sense here. For the first set of headphones, go up to demand curve D_0 and over to the price axis. You were willing and able to pay $200. For the second set, go up to demand curve D_0 and over to the price axis. You were willing and able to pay $150. Connecting those points yields the demand curve D_0.

After the successful ad campaign, your willingness and ability to pay has increased, represented by demand curve D_1. For each set of headphones, your willingness and ability to pay is now described by the points on demand curve D_1. Going up to D_1 and over, for the first set, you are now willing and able to pay $250 instead of $200. For the second set, you are now willing and able to pay $200 instead of $150. Before advertising, you were not willing to pay anything for a third set of headphones. Now you are willing and able to pay $150.

Your ability to pay has not changed, it's just that you are willing to give up more of your unchanged income because the intensity of your wants increased. Advertising succeeded in moving the margin, increasing both the marginal benefit you expect to get from the Beats headphones and your willingness to pay. Economists call any increase in consumers' willingness and ability to pay an **increase in demand**. Consumers are now willing to pay a higher price for the same quantity of a product.

Changes in preferences can also cause a decrease in demand. What if a Health Canada study shows conclusively that regular listening with Beats headphones causes serious hearing loss and mushrooms to grow out of your ears? If you and other consumers believe the study, consumers' willingness and ability to pay decreases, resulting in a **decrease in demand** for headphones. Consumers are now willing to pay only a lower price for the same quantity of a product.

increase in demand increase in consumers' willingness and ability to pay

decrease in demand decrease in consumers' willingness and ability to pay

In January 2014, the National Hockey League held its once-a-year outdoor hockey game in Ann Arbor, Michigan, at the University of Michigan football stadium. Ann Arbor has a population of 115 000, and the Michigan stadium, the largest in North America, holds 110 000 people. What happened to the demand for hotel rooms in Ann Arbor? The large number of fans attending the game increased the willingness to pay and *increased the demand* for hotel rooms. On the other hand, think of the demand by tourists for hotel rooms in Toronto before and after a 2012 outbreak of bedbugs. The fear of bug bites decreased tourists' preferences for Toronto hotel bookings. With decreased willingness to pay, there was a decrease in demand for Toronto hotel rooms.

NOTE
An increase in preferences causes an increase in demand, not a change in quantity demanded.

Any change in preferences causes a change in demand. An increase in preferences causes an increase in demand. A decrease in preferences causes a decrease in demand.

Prices of Related Products Many products or services you choose to buy are related. Changes in price of a different, related product or service will affect your demand for the original product or service. There are two main types of related products: substitutes and complements.

Substitutes are products or services that can be used in place of each other to satisfy the same want. Examples of substitutes are headphones and earbuds for listening to music, or water and Gatorade for quenching thirst.

substitutes products or services used in place of each other to satisfy the same want

What happens to your demand for Beats headphones when the price of other headphones falls drastically? You are not willing to pay as much for the Beats, as your smart choice now involves much cheaper alternatives. A fall in the price of a substitute decreases the demand for the related product.

If the price of water skyrockets because of a drought, your willingness to pay for Gatorade increases. A rise in the price of a substitute increases demand for the related product.

Economics *Out There*

Diamond Engagement Rings Were Not Forever

More than 80 percent of North American brides receive a diamond engagement ring, at an average cost of over $3000.

It wasn't always that way. The tradition of diamond engagement rings only began in the late 1800s when the discovery of diamond mines in South Africa drove down the price of diamonds. Then, in 1919, diamond sales plunged and didn't recover for over 20 years! But diamond prices and demand changed forever when the De Beers diamond company hired the firm N. W. Ayers to create a national advertising campaign, which included paying Hollywood actresses to wear diamond rings in public.

Sales rose over 50 percent in three years. In 1947, a female copywriter at Ayers created the tag line "A diamond is forever." De Beers used that line with a steady stream of photos showing happy newlyweds with the brides all wearing diamond engagement rings. Sales rose all through the 1950s, and by 1965, 80 percent of brides had diamond engagement rings. The advertising campaign also introduced the guideline for how much grooms should spend on a diamond ring — it started at one month's salary, quickly doubled to two months' salary, and most recently stood at three months' salary.

This was perhaps one of the most successful ad campaigns ever for increasing preferences, willingness to pay, and demand.

Source: Meghan O'Rourke, "Diamonds Are a Girl's Worst Friend," *Slate*, June 11, 2007, http://www.slate.com/articles/news_and_politics/weddings/2007/06/diamonds_are_a_girls_worst_friend.html.

complements   products or services used together to satisfy the same want

Complements are products or services that are used together to satisfy the same want. Music players and headphones are complementary products, as are hot dogs and hot dog buns, or cars and gasoline.

If music player prices fall, that makes owning headphones more attractive, and will increase your willingness to pay for Beats headphones. A fall in the price of a complement increases demand for the related product because the cost of using both products together decreases.

When gasoline prices rose significantly in 2012, gas-guzzling eight-cylinder SUVs became much more expensive to operate. The rise in gas prices decreased the demand for eight-cylinder SUVs. A rise in the price of a complement decreases demand for the related product because the cost of using both products together increases.

Income   Winning a million dollars in a lottery would have a large effect on your demand for products and services. Demand reflects your willingness and ability to pay. With more money, or more income, you are more able (and still willing) to pay for things and not worry about it. But not always.

Take your demand for Beats headphones from Figure 2.4, before any advertising (demand curve D_0). If your income increases, the effect on your willingness and ability to pay is similar to the effect of an increase in preferences (demand curve D_1). At each quantity you are still willing and now *able to pay more,* so the increase in income increases demand. The intensity of your wants doesn't change with a change in income, but what you have to *give up in other products or services* decreases. With more income, you can spend more on headphones and still have lots of extra cash to buy other things. Higher income lowers your real opportunity cost of spending. There is more "get" and less "give up."

If unfortunately your income falls, so does your ability to pay, and your demand for headphones decreases.

normal goods   products or services you buy more of when your income increases

Economists call products like headphones **normal goods** — products and services that you buy more of when your income increases. For a normal good, an increase in income increases demand, and a decrease in income decreases demand.

But not all products are normal goods. Can you think of products or services you buy as a poor student that you will buy *less of* when your income goes up? If you have been living on Kraft Dinner, you may never want to eat it again once you can afford real food. And what about those endless bus rides? If you could afford a car, what would happen to your demand for public transit?

inferior goods   products or services you buy less of when your income increases

Economists call these products and services, for which an increase in income *decreases* demand, **inferior goods** — products and services that you buy less of when your income increases. Similarly, a decrease in income increases demand for inferior goods.

Businesses care about the distinction between normal and inferior goods. If incomes are rising and your business sells a normal good, the increase in demand increases sales. But if you sell an inferior good, prepare for a possible drop in sales and reduce inventory so you don't get stuck with unsold goods. The demand for inferior goods is more likely to increase during a downturn in the economy, where unemployed people economize on their food budget and buy more Kraft Dinner and Hamburger Helper.

Expected Future Prices   Smart choices depend not only on prices and incomes today, but also on our expectation of future prices. Consumers choose between substitutes, and one of many possible substitutions is a purchase tomorrow for a purchase today. We do this all the time with gasoline. If it's the weekend and you decide to wait until mid-week to buy gas because you expect the price to fall, that decreases your demand for gasoline today. Likewise, if you are expecting prices to rise, you fill up now, increasing your demand for gasoline today. Notice that your decision is not determined by the current price (that would be a quantity demanded decision), but by whether you expect the current price (whatever it may be) to fall or rise in the future.

An expected future price fall decreases demand today. An expected future price rise increases demand today.

NOTE
A rise in expected future price causes an increase in demand today.

Number of Consumers   So far, the explanation for all the factors that change demand are the same for an individual as for all consumers whose combined willingness and ability to pay make up market demand. Looking at willingness and ability to pay, it makes more sense to look at the demand curve as a marginal benefit curve. For any quantity, we examine how a change in each factor affects the price the consumer is willing and able to pay. Each such change in demand changes marginal benefit and moves the margin. As marginal benefits increase or decrease, demand increases or decreases.

For the last factor, the number of consumers, the explanation makes more sense if we read the demand curve as a demand curve. Start with any price, and examine how a change in consumer numbers affects quantity demanded. For each price, if the number of consumers increases, we need to add together all the quantities demanded by all consumers at that price.

Let's take our earlier table of the market demand for water, and add a third column showing the quantity demanded after many new households move into the city and start using water. Look at Figure 2.5 on the next page.

Figure 2.5 More Consumers Increase the Market Demand for Water

Price ($ per m³)	Quantity Demanded (000's of m³ per month)	Quantity Demanded with More Households (000's of m³ per month)
$1.00	5	10
$1.50	4	9
$2.00	3	8
$2.50	2	7
$3.00	1	6

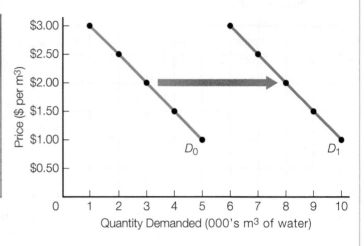

NOTE
An increased number of consumers increases demand.

At any price (first column), it is no surprise that with additional households (last column), quantity demanded is greater than it was originally (middle column). The increased number of consumers increases demand, just as an increase in preferences or an increase in income (for normal goods) increases demand. A decrease in the number of consumers decreases demand, just as a decrease in the price of a substitute product or service or a decrease in expected future prices decreases demand.

Moving Along or Shifting the Demand Curve   Any increase (or decrease) in demand caused by the five factors can be described in alternative ways. For the first four factors, the description for an increase in demand is:

- At any given quantity, consumers are willing and able to pay a higher price. This is the marginal benefit reading of the demand curve.

For the fifth factor, number of consumers, the description for an increase in demand is:

- At any given price, consumers plan to buy a larger quantity. This is the demand curve reading of the demand curve.

While the marginal benefit reading of the demand curve provides the best intuition behind changes in demand, the demand curve reading will be most useful for understanding the economic world around you, and is used most often.

NOTE
An increase in demand is a rightward shift of the demand curve. A decrease in demand is a leftward shift of the demand curve.

In the demand curve reading, an increase in demand is also called a rightward shift of the demand curve. A decrease in demand is a leftward shift of the demand curve. We will always call an increase in demand a rightward shift, and a decrease in demand a leftward shift of the demand curve.

When none of the five factors change, we can focus on the relationship between price and quantity demanded. That is represented in Figure 2.6a as a movement along the demand curve D_0. If the price rises, and all other things do not change, that is a movement up along the demand curve to a smaller quantity demanded. If the price falls, all other things unchanged, that is a movement down along the demand curve to a larger quantity demanded.

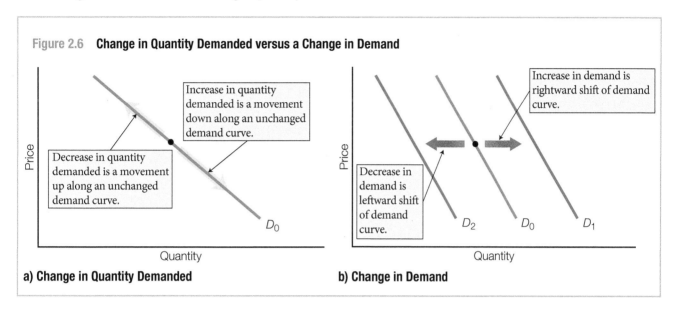

Figure 2.6 **Change in Quantity Demanded versus a Change in Demand**

a) Change in Quantity Demanded

b) Change in Demand

Figure 2.6b shows an increase in demand as the rightward shift from D_0 to D_1. The leftward shift from D_0 to D_2 is a decrease in demand. These shifts in demand are caused by changes in any of the five factors — preferences, prices of related products, income, expected future prices, and number of consumers.

Saving the Law of Demand

You have learned to distinguish between a change in quantity demanded (caused by a change in the price of the product) and a change in demand (caused by changes in preferences, prices of related products, income, expected future prices, and number of consumers). Can we now explain why, when gasoline prices increased from $0.99 per litre to $1.39 per litre between 2010 and 2012, the quantity of gasoline motorists bought actually increased? Can we save the law of demand?

According to the law of demand, if the price of a product rises, the quantity demanded of the product decreases (as long as other factors besides price do not change). The rise in gas prices alone would have decreased the quantity demanded, *but other things also changed.*

While a complete explanation is more complex (involving supply factors from Chapter 3 as well as demand), a major change was the increased number of drivers and cars on the road. This increase in the number of consumers increased demand for gasoline. The effect of the increase in demand outweighed the price effect of the decrease in quantity demanded.

To conclusively explain whether the witch's curse or the arsenic killed the poor young man, you need a controlled experiment. And without the economist's equivalent of a controlled experiment — the mental distinction between quantity demanded and demand — you never would have been able to explain what happened in the gasoline market.

Figure 2.7 is a good study device for reviewing the difference between the law of demand (focusing on quantity demanded and movements along the demand curve) and the factors that change demand (and shift the demand curve).

Figure 2.7   Law of Demand and Changes in Demand

The Law of Demand *The quantity demanded of a product or service*	
Decreases if:	*Increases if:*
• price of the product or service rises	• price of the product or service falls

Changes in Demand *The demand for a product or service*	
Decreases if:	*Increases if:*
• preferences decrease	• preferences increase
• price of a substitute falls	• price of a substitute rises
• price of a complement rises	• price of a complement falls
• income decreases (normal good)	• income increases (normal good)
• income increases (inferior good)	• income decreases (inferior good)
• expected future price falls	• expected future price rises
• number of consumers decreases	• number of consumers increases

Refresh 2.4

MyEconLab

For answers to these Refresh Questions, visit MyEconLab.

1. Explain the difference between a change in quantity demanded and a change in demand. Identify the five factors that can change demand.

2. Roses sell for about $40 a bouquet most of the year, and at that price, worldwide sales are 6 million bouquets per month. Every February, the price of roses doubles to $80 a bouquet, but the quantity of roses demanded and sold also increases, to 24 million bouquets per month. The cost of producing roses doesn't change throughout the year. Explain what else is going on that saves the law of demand.

3. There are some "status goods," like Rolex watches, that people want to own *because* they are expensive. In contradiction to the law of demand, if Rolex watches were less expensive, fewer "status-seeking" consumers would demand them. Reconcile status products or services with the law of demand. How does the existence of cheap "knock-off" imitations of Rolex watches fit with the law of demand?

Study Guide

2.1 Put Your Money Where Your Mouth Is: Weighing Benefits, Costs, and Substitutes

Your willingness to buy a product or service depends on your ability to pay, comparative benefits and costs, and the availability of substitutes.

- **Preferences** — your wants and their intensities.

- **Demand** — consumers' willingness and ability to pay for a particular product or service.

- For any choice, what you are willing to pay or give up depends on the cost and availability of substitutes.

2.2 Living on the Edge: Smart Choices Are Marginal Choices

Key 2 states, "Count only *additional* benefits and *additional* costs." Additional benefits mean marginal benefits — not total benefits — and marginal benefits change with circumstances.

- **Marginal benefit** — the additional benefit from a choice, changing with circumstances.

- Marginal benefit explains the diamond/water paradox. Why do diamonds cost more than water, when water is more valuable for survival? Willingness to pay depends on marginal benefit, not total benefit. Because water is abundant, marginal benefit is low. Because diamonds are scarce, marginal benefit is high.

2.3 Move On When the Price Isn't Right: The Law of Demand

The demand curve combines two forces — switch to substitutes; willingness and ability to pay — determining quantity demanded, and can be read as a demand curve and as a marginal benefit curve.

- **Quantity demanded** — the amount you actually plan to buy at a given price.

- **Market demand** — the sum of demands of all individuals willing and able to buy a particular product or service.

- **Law of demand** — if the price of a product or service rises, quantity demanded decreases, other things remaining the same.

- **Demand curve** — shows the relationship between price and quantity demanded, other things remaining the same.

2.4 Moving the Margins: What Can Change Demand?

Quantity demanded changes only with a change in price. All other influences on consumer choice change demand.

- Demand is a catch-all term summarizing all possible influences on consumers' willingness and ability to pay for a particular product or service.
  - **Increase in demand** — increase in consumers' willingness and ability to pay. Rightward shift of demand curve.
  - **Decrease in demand** — decrease in consumers' willingness and ability to pay. Leftward shift of demand curve.

- Demand changes with changes in preferences, prices of related goods, income, expected future price, and number of consumers. For example, demand increases with:
  - increase in preferences.
  - rise in price of a **substitute** — products or services used in place of each other to satisfy the same want.
  - fall in price of a **complement** — products or services used together to satisfy the same want.
  - increase in income for **normal goods** — products or services you buy more of when your income increases.
  - decrease in income for **inferior goods** — products or services you buy less of when your income increases.
  - rise in expected future prices.
  - increase in number of consumers.

TRUE/FALSE

Circle the correct answer. Solutions to these questions are available at the end of the book and on MyEconLab. You can also visit the MyEconLab Study Plan to access additional questions that will help you master the concepts covered in this chapter.

2.1 Weighing Benefits, Costs, and Substitutes

1. Demand is the same as wants.   T   F

2. Your willingness to pay for a product depends on what substitutes are available, and what they cost.   T   F

3. What you can afford is just about money.   T   F

2.2 Smart Choices Are Marginal Choices

4. Marginal cost is the same as additional cost.   T   F

5. The flat fee charged at an all-you-can-eat restaurant should not influence how much food you eat once you are seated.   T   F

6. Marginal benefit always equals average benefit.   T   F

7. Willingness to pay depends on marginal benefit, not total benefit.   T   F

2.3 The Law of Demand

8. Quantity demanded is the same as demand.   T   F

9. If the price of a product or service changes, quantity demanded changes.   T   F

10. Market demand is the sum of the demands of all individuals.   T   F

11. Demand curves may be straight lines or curves, but always slope downward to the left.   T   F

2.4 What Can Change Demand?

12. If your willingness to pay decreases, demand decreases.   T   F

13. If your ability to pay decreases, demand increases.   T   F

14. Throughout the month of December, the quantity of video game consoles purchased increases even as the price rises. This violates the law of demand.   T   F

15. A decrease in income always shifts the demand curve leftward.   T   F

MULTIPLE CHOICE

Circle the best answer. Solutions to these questions are available at the end of the book and on MyEconLab. You can also visit the MyEconLab Study Plan to access similar questions that will help you master the concepts covered in this chapter.

2.1 Weighing Benefits, Costs, and Substitutes

1. Economists describe the list of your wants and their intensities as
   a) demand.
   b) supply.
   c) benefit.
   d) preferences.

2. Costs are
   a) worth money.
   b) whatever we are willing to give up.
   c) the answer to the question "What do we want?"
   d) whatever we are willing to get.

3. Your preferences measure
   a) the availability of substitutes.
   b) how limited your time is.
   c) the price of a product.
   d) how badly you want something.

2.2 Smart Choices Are Marginal Choices

4. All-you-can-eat buffet restaurants charge a fixed fee for eating. With each plate that Anna eats, she experiences
   a) decreasing marginal costs.
   b) increasing marginal costs.
   c) decreasing marginal benefits.
   d) increasing marginal benefits.

5. Thinking like economists, a dating couple should break up when the
   a) total benefits of dating are greater than the total costs of dating.
   b) total costs of dating are greater than the total benefits of dating.
   c) additional benefits of dating are greater than the additional costs of dating.
   d) additional costs of dating are greater than the additional benefits of dating.

6. Peter wants two cars, one for everyday and the other for special occasions. He has only $15 000, so he buys only one car. His quantity demanded of cars is
   a) 1.
   b) 2.
   c) 15 000.
   d) 30 000.

7. The price of diamonds is higher than the price of water because
   a) total benefits from water are relatively low.
   b) total benefits from diamonds are relatively high.
   c) marginal benefits from water are relatively high.
   d) marginal benefits from diamonds are relatively high.

2.3 The Law of Demand

8. When the price of a product rises,
   a) consumers look for more expensive substitutes.
   b) quantity demanded increases.
   c) consumers look for cheaper substitutes.
   d) consumers use more of the product.

9. If homeowners were charged for garbage collection by the number of garbage bags used, there would be a(n)
   a) increase in demand for garbage collection.
   b) decrease in demand for garbage collection.
   c) increase in quantity demanded of garbage collection.
   d) decrease in quantity demanded of garbage collection.

10. A sociology class is a substitute for an economics class if
    a) attending the two classes has the same opportunity cost.
    b) the two classes satisfy the same want.
    c) both classes are at the same time.
    d) both classes are taught by the same instructor.

2.4 What Can Change Demand?

11. What is most likely to be an inferior good?
    a) fast food
    b) antique furniture
    c) school bags
    d) textbooks

12. Demand
    a) increases with a rise in price.
    b) is the same as quantity demanded.
    c) changes with income.
    d) decreases with a rise in price.

13. If the price of cars rises, the demand for tires
    a) increases.
    b) decreases.
    c) stay the same.
    d) depend on the price of tires.

14. Which of the following could cause a leftward shift of the demand curve for a product?
    a) increase in income
    b) decrease in income
    c) increase in the price of a substitute
    d) all of the above

15. If Kraft Dinner is an inferior good, a rise in the price of Kraft Dinner
    a) decreases demand for Kraft Dinner.
    b) increases demand for Kraft Dinner.
    c) increases the quantity demanded of Kraft Dinner.
    d) decreases the quantity demanded of Kraft Dinner.

3 Show Me the Money

The Law of Supply

LEARNING OBJECTIVES

After reading this chapter, you should be able to:

3.1 Explain why marginal costs are ultimately opportunity costs.

3.2 Define sunk costs and explain why they do not influence smart, forward-looking decisions.

3.3 Explain the law of supply and describe the roles of higher profits and higher marginal opportunity costs of production.

3.4 Explain the difference between a change in quantity supplied and a change in supply, and list six factors that change supply.

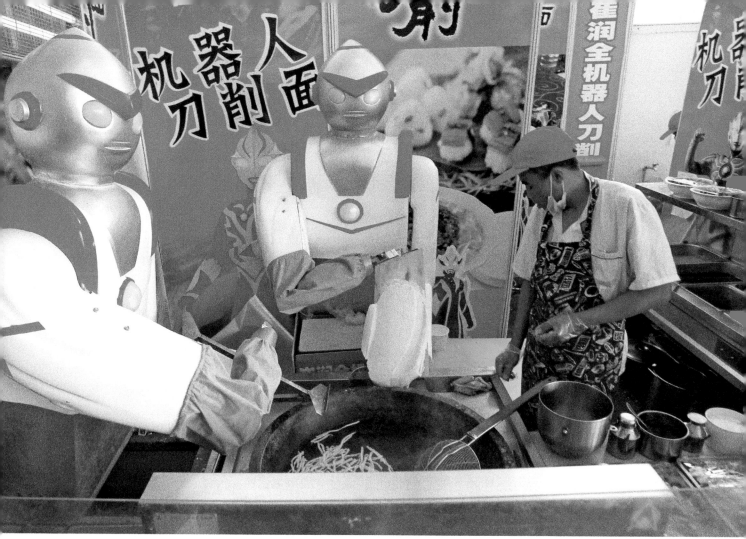

MONEY IS THE MARKET'S REWARD

to individuals or businesses who give up something of value. Your boss rewards you with an hourly wage for supplying labour services. A business producing a top-selling product is rewarded with profits (as long as revenues are greater than costs).

What goes into decisions to sell or supply services or products to the market? What price do you need to get to be willing to work? How much money does it take before a business is willing to supply?

This chapter focuses on choices businesses make every day in producing and selling. Economists use the term *supply* to summarize all of the influences on business decisions. You will learn about influences that change business supply, which include new technologies like noodle-slicing robots!

Business decisions seem more "objective" than consumer decisions that seem to be based on "subjective" desires and preferences. After all, there is a bottom line in business with prices, costs, and profits. But business supply decisions are not as straightforward or objective as you might think.

3.1 What Does It Really Cost? Costs Are Opportunity Costs

Explain why marginal costs are ultimately opportunity costs.

ADDITIONAL BENEFITS VS. OPPORTUNITY COSTS

Supply, like demand, starts with decision makers choosing among alternative opportunities by comparing expected benefits and costs at the margin.

How Much to Work?

It's Sunday night and your boss calls in a panic, begging you to work as many hours as possible next week. You normally work 10 hours a week, but the extra money would come in handy. The timing, however, couldn't be worse. You have two midterms the following week, and your out-of-town best friend is coming in next weekend for the only visit you will have in six months. How many hours then are you willing to work?

Of course you will make a smart choice, weighing the additional benefits and costs of working extra hours. The additional, or marginal, benefits are the $15 per hour you earn. The additional costs are opportunity costs — the alternative uses of the time you have to give up.

You want to attend all your classes, keep time for studying for midterms, and definitely keep the weekend free. You are willing to give up the 10 hours a week you spend playing *World of Warcraft*. When your boss hears you are willing to work only a total of 20 hours, while she is hoping for 60 hours, she instantly replies, "What if I pay you double time for all your hours next week?"

Well, that changes things. At $30 per hour, you will willingly give up your game time, skip a few classes where you are not having a test, but still keep the weekend free. You are up to 35 hours of work, but your boss is totally desperate and asks again, "What if I pay you triple time?"

At that price, you will also cut back on your sleep, reduce your study time, and try to reschedule your weekend visit. (Is the visit worth giving up $700 for a weekend's work?) Your boss relaxes a bit when you promise 55 hours.

Notice that the quantity of work or time that you are willing to supply to your boss increases as the price she is willing to pay you rises. In order to get you to switch more of your time from alternative uses, she has to offer you more money (which increases her costs).

For your supply decision, there are always alternative uses of your time, and each use has a different cost to you. Your game time is worth the least to you, the weekend time the most. Your willingness to work changes with circumstances, depending on the price offered and the opportunity cost — the value you place on alternative uses of your time.

NOTE
Your willingness to work depends on the price offered and on the opportunity costs of alternative uses of your time.

marginal cost additional opportunity cost of increasing quantity supplied, changing with circumstances

Marginal Cost The economist's term for the additional opportunity cost of alternative uses of your time is **marginal cost** — the additional opportunity cost of increasing the quantity of whatever is being supplied. For you, the opportunity cost, or marginal cost, of an hour of game time is less than the opportunity cost, or marginal cost, of an hour of weekend time. As you shift your time away from alternative uses to work, *the marginal cost of your time increases*. You give up the least valuable time first, and continue giving up increasingly valuable time as the price you are offered rises.

How Demand and Supply Choices Are Similar There are similarities between the demand choices from Chapter 2 and your supply choices.

As a demander, think about products or services you might buy. There are always substitutes available, which is why consumers buy less of a product or service as the price rises — we all switch to cheaper alternatives. Willingness to pay depends on available substitutes and changes with circumstances — the marginal benefit of the first bottle of Gatorade is greater than the marginal benefit of the second bottle.

As a supplier, think about the number of hours you might work. There are always alternative uses of your time, with different values to you. Willingness to supply hours depends on those alternatives and changes with circumstances — the opportunity cost of giving up your gaming hours is less than the opportunity cost of giving up your weekend hours with your best friend. That is one reason why suppliers supply more as the price rises — higher prices are necessary to compensate for the higher opportunity costs as you give up additional time (or other resources).

How Demand and Supply Choices Are Different There are also important differences between smart demand and smart supply choices.

As a demander buying products and services, marginal benefit — the maximum you are willing to pay — decreases as you buy more. As a supplier of labour hours or other resources, marginal cost — the minimum you need to be paid — increases as you supply more.

For demand and supply, the comparison of benefits and costs is also reversed. As a demander of products and services, marginal benefit is your subjective satisfaction, and marginal cost is measured in dollars — the price you must pay. As a supplier of labour, marginal benefit is measured in dollars — the hourly wage rate you earn — and marginal cost is an opportunity cost, the value of alternative uses of the time that you must give up.

What Do Inputs *Really* Cost?

Any business supply decision involves the same smart choice between marginal benefit and marginal cost as your work decision. The marginal benefit or reward from selling is measured in the dollar price you receive, and all marginal costs are ultimately opportunity costs.

Let's look at a business: Paola's Parlour for Piercing and Nails. To supply her services to the market, Paola, like any businessperson, has to buy inputs (studs, tools, polish), pay rent to her landlord, and pay wages to her employees. What do those hard dollar actual costs have to do with opportunity costs? Which costs are *real* costs?

Take the nickel studs Paola buys for $1 each from a stud supplier. If the world price of nickel rises because of increasing demand from China for the metal, Paola has to pay more for her studs. The stud supplier will sell to Paola only as long as she pays as much as the best price he can get from another customer, whether in China or Canada. Paola's stud cost has to cover the opportunity cost of the stud supplier.

The same goes for Paola's rent or the wages she pays to her employees. If Paola's landlord finds another tenant willing to pay more for the shop space, then once Paola's lease is up, she has to pay that higher amount or the landlord will rent to the other tenant. If Paola's employees, like you, have alternative uses of their time that they value more than what she pays, or if they can get job offers elsewhere at higher wages, Paola has to match the offers or start advertising for help wanted.

Zach Weiner

▲ There are always alternative uses of your time. You must decide how much your game time is worth to you.

▲ Paola's inputs include studs, polish and labour, Like all businesspeople, Paola must pay an input owners at least the best alternative price the input owner can get.

Marginal Costs Are Ultimately Opportunity Costs To hire or buy inputs, a business must pay a price matching the best opportunity cost of the input owner. The real cost of any input is determined by the best alternative use of that input. All marginal costs are ultimately opportunity costs. Marginal costs can be measured in dollars, but they are an opportunity cost — the value of the best alternative use of that input.

As we will see in the next section, Paola's smart business supply decisions depend on whether the price (the marginal benefit) she receives for a piercing is greater than her marginal opportunity costs.

Refresh 3.1

MyEconLab

For answers to these Refresh Questions, visit MyEconLab.

1. Explain why marginal costs are ultimately opportunity costs.

2. In 2013, Microsoft released a limited supply of Xbox Ones with a list price of $500 The units immediately started selling on eBay and other online auction websites for far more than $500. What factors determined that increase in price of an Xbox One?

3. During a recession, it is much harder for workers to find better-paying jobs. Explain how a recession might affect Paola's labour costs.

3.2 Forget It, It's History: Sunk Costs Don't Matter for Future Choices

Define sunk costs and explain why they do not influence smart, forward-looking decisions.

Paola bases her business supply decisions on her costs, which are ultimately opportunity costs. But some expenses are not opportunity costs. This is another part of supply decisions that is not as straightforward as you might think.

Past expenses that cannot be reversed or recovered are *not* opportunity costs. If Paola has signed a year's lease for her rent that she cannot get out of, then her rent becomes irrelevant for her future decisions. How can that be?

NOTE
Past expenses are not marginal opportunity costs and have no influence on smart choices.

Paola's or your decisions are always forward looking. A smart decision about which fork in the road to take compares the expected future benefits and the expected future costs of each path. When Paola has to decide whether to supply more piercings or fingernail sets, or to choose between buying new tools or hiring more employees, the rent expense is the same, so its influence cancels out. The past expense of rent paid (or legally contracted for) is the same for either fork Paola chooses, so it shouldn't influence her decision.

sunk costs past expenses that cannot be recovered

These irreversible costs are called **sunk costs** — past, already-paid expenses that cannot be recovered. In other words, they are history — they can't be changed. Decisions that have already been made and can't be changed don't matter for forward-looking economic decisions.

Suppose you paid your tuition for this semester, and the refund date has passed. Your boss's request for extra hours comes at a time when you are finding it hard to balance work and school, and you are considering dropping out.

Your decision to drop out and work full-time (making your boss very happy), versus staying in school, depends on how you evaluate the expected benefits and costs of each fork in your career road. Dropping out and working more means more income right away, while staying in school means less income now but probably more in the future. (We will look at data connecting education and income in Chapter 12.) The tuition you paid is history. You can't get it back no matter which fork you choose — staying in school or dropping out — so it is not part of the opportunity costs of either choice.

ADDITIONAL
BENEFITS
& COSTS

Refresh 3.2

1. Why aren't sunk costs part of the opportunity costs of forward-looking decisions?

2. If you bought a $100 textbook for a course, and then dropped out after the tuition refund date, is that $100 a sunk cost? Explain your answer.

3. Suppose you have just paid your bus fare. A friend in a car pulls up and offers you a ride. Explain how you would decide between staying on the bus or taking the ride, and the influence of the paid fare on your choice.

MyEconLab

For answers to these Refresh Questions, visit MyEconLab.

More for More Money: The Law of Supply

3.3

Explain the law of supply, and describe the roles of higher profits and higher marginal opportunity costs of production.

Demand is not just what you want. It is your willingness and ability to pay for a product or service — putting your money where your mouth is. Similarly, the economist's idea of supply is not just offering things for sale. **Supply** is the overall willingness of businesses (or individuals) to sell a particular product or service because the price covers all opportunity costs of production.

Quantity Supplied

Let's look at how an economist would describe your supply decision about how many hours to work at your part-time job. Figure 3.1 combines price information — the lowest wage you are willing to accept — and the quantity of work you will supply at each wage.

supply businesses' willingness to produce a particular product or service because price covers all opportunity costs

Figure 3.1   Your Supply of Hours Worked

Price (minimum willing to accept per hour)	Quantity Supplied (hours of work at that price)
$15	10 – 20
$30	35
$45	55

At a price of $15 per hour, your quantity supplied of work could be anywhere between 10 and 20 hours. At $30 per hour, your quantity supplied of work is 35 hours, and at $45 per hour, your quantity supplied is 55 hours.

quantity supplied   the quantity you actually plan to supply at a given price

As your eye goes down the columns in Figure 3.1, note that as the price rises, the quantity supplied increases. (What happens to quantity demanded as price rises?) In general, when prices rise, individuals and businesses devote more of their time or resources to producing or supplying — more money stimulates more quantity supplied. The two reasons for this are the desire for profits (higher prices usually mean higher profits) and the need for a higher price to cover higher marginal opportunity costs — your weekend time is worth more to you than your *World of Warcraft* time.

Quantity supplied, as we will see, is not the same as supply. **Quantity supplied** is a more limited concept — the quantity you actually plan to supply at a given price, taking into account everything that affects your willingness to supply work hours.

Let's take the economist's idea of supply and apply it to Paola's willingness to supply a particular quantity of piercings at a particular price.

Body Piercings or Nail Sets?

Businesses, like consumers, make smart choices based on Key 1 — Choose only when additional benefits are greater than additional *opportunity costs*.

Paola's first choice is *what to produce* with her resources — the labour and equipment she has in her shop. She can do body piercing, and she can also paint fingernails. Let's limit her choices to full body piercings and full sets of fingernails to allow the simple, made-up numbers below.

Paola's Parlour has special tools for piercing and for nail painting. There are four people working (including Paola). All four are equally skilled at piercing (the business started with just piercing), but their fingernail skills differ from expert (Paola) to beginner (Parminder). The table in Figure 3.2 shows the different combinations of fingernail sets and piercings that Paola's Parlour can produce in a day.

Figure 3.2   Paola's Parlour Production Possibilities Frontier

Combination	Fingernails (full sets)	Piercings (full body)
A	15	0
B	14	1
C	12	2
D	9	3
E	5	4
F	0	5

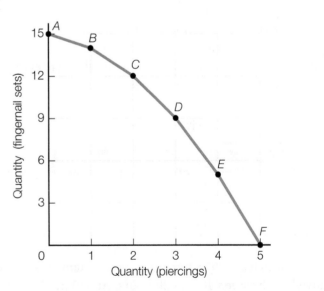

At one extreme (combination *A*) all four workers do fingernails only, so they produce 15 fingernail sets and no piercings. If Paola starts shifting some staff from fingernails to piercings, she moves to combination *B* (14 fingernail sets and 1 full body piercing). Shifting more staff and equipment out of fingernails and into piercing gives combination *C* (12 fingernail sets and 2 piercings), and then combinations *D* (9 fingernail sets and 3 piercings) and *E* (5 fingernail sets and 4 piercings). Combination *F* is the other extreme, where the Paola's Parlour produces only piercings — 5 piercings and 0 fingernail sets. As you will see, the pattern of numbers in the table in Figure 3.2 has a lot to do with differences in fingernail painting skills.

Paola's Parlour's Production Possibilities Frontier   We can graph the table of numbers in Figure 3.2 as Paola's production possibilities frontier (*PPF*). The graph in Figure 3.2 shows Paola's Parlour's *PPF*, with daily output of piercings measured on the horizontal axis, and daily output of fingernail sets measured on the vertical axis. Each point (*A* – *F*) on the frontier corresponds to a combination in the table.

Increasing Marginal Opportunity Costs

The numbers and graph in Figure 3.2 don't make much business sense — they are just maximum possible combinations of piercings and nail sets that Paola's Parlour can produce. To use the numbers for Paola's business supply decisions, we must translate them into marginal costs. (And eventually into profits in Chapter 8.)

Remember that costs are ultimately opportunity costs. The cost of acquiring or producing products or services is the value of the best alternative opportunity we must give up to get them. To get more piercings, Paola gives up doing nail sets. Opportunity cost is what we give up divided by what we get:

$$\text{Opportunity Cost} = \frac{\text{Give Up}}{\text{Get}}$$

Figure 3.3 (on the next page) shows, in the last column, the marginal opportunity costs to Paola of producing more piercings.

Figure 3.3 Paola's Parlour's Marginal Opportunity Costs

Combination	Fingernails (full sets)	Piercings (full body)	Marginal Opportunity Cost of Producing More Piercings (fingernail sets given up)
A	15	0	
			$\frac{(15 - 14)}{1} = 1$
B	14	1	
			$\frac{(14 - 12)}{1} = 2$
C	12	2	
			$\frac{(12 - 9)}{1} = 3$
D	9	3	
			$\frac{(9 - 5)}{1} = 4$
E	5	4	
			$\frac{(5 - 0)}{1} = 5$
F	0	5	

What is the marginal opportunity cost of producing the first piercing? To move from 0 to 1 piercing (from combination *A* to *B*), Paola gives up 1 fingernail set, because fingernail production drops from 15 to 14 sets as some staff time switches from fingernails to piercing. In exchange, she gets 1 piercing. So substituting into the formula, the marginal opportunity cost of the first piercing is

$$\frac{1 \text{ fingernail set}}{1 \text{ piercing}} = 1 \text{ fingernail set per piercing}$$

To produce a second piercing (moving from combination *B* to *C*), Paola gives up 2 fingernail sets (14 – 12 sets). The marginal opportunity cost of the second additional piercing is 2 fingernail sets given up per piercing. The third piercing (moving from combination *C* to *D*) has a marginal opportunity cost of 3 fingernail sets given up (12 – 9 sets) per piercing. In moving the last of her staff to piercing, for the fifth piercing she gives up 5 fingernail sets (5 – 0 sets). The marginal opportunity cost of the last additional piercing — the fifth — is 5 fingernail sets given up per piercing.

Opportunity Costs Are Marginal Costs If you are wondering what the difference is between opportunity cost, marginal cost, and marginal opportunity cost — since they seem like the same thing — good for you! You are not confused, you're right. *All opportunity costs are marginal costs, and all marginal costs are opportunity costs.*

Opportunity cost and marginal cost are two sides of the same coin. Opportunity cost focuses on the value of the opportunity *given up* when you make a decision. On the flip side, marginal cost focuses on the *additional cost* of that decision. Paola must give up 5 fingernail sets in deciding to produce the fifth piercing. So the marginal opportunity cost of the fifth piercing is 5 fingernail sets. **Marginal opportunity cost** is the complete term for any cost relevant to a smart decision. We will usually use the shorter name — *marginal cost* — when describing supply decisions.

Figure 3.4a begins to illustrate the economic sense of these numbers. The numbers in the table for marginal opportunity costs and quantity of piercings come from Figure 3.3 (columns 4 and 3). Each point on the graph in Figure 3.4a shows the marginal opportunity cost measured in fingernail sets given up per piercing (along the vertical axis) for each quantity of piercings supplied (along the horizontal axis).

marginal opportunity cost
complete term for any cost relevant to a smart decision

Figure 3.4   Increasing Marginal Opportunity Cost

Marginal Opportunity Cost of Additional Piercings (fingernail sets given up)	Quantity Supplied (piercings)
1	1
2	2
3	3
4	4
5	5

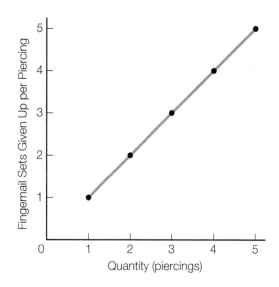

a) Marginal Opportunity Cost of Additional Piercings Measured in Fingernail Sets

Price (marginal opportunity cost or minimum willing to accept per piercing)	Quantity Supplied (piercings)
$ 20	1
$ 40	2
$ 60	3
$ 80	4
$100	5

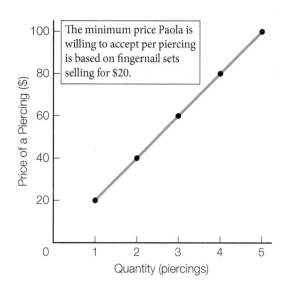

b) Marginal Opportunity Cost of Additional Piercings Measured in $

Note in Figure 3.4a that as Paola increases her quantity supplied of piercings, her marginal opportunity costs increase, from 1 fingernail set given up for the first piercing to 5 fingernail sets given up for the fifth piercing. This is the same pattern in the decision to shift your time away from alternative uses to work more hours — the marginal cost of additional time given up increases as you give up increasingly more valuable uses of your time.

Paying for Opportunity Costs   So far, the numbers in Paola's example are measured in piercings or fingernail sets. But Paola, as a profit-seeking entrepreneur, wants to make a smart supply decision based on dollar prices. Luckily, it is easy to convert body decorations to dollars. Suppose that fingernail full sets sell for $20. Then the marginal opportunity costs for supplying additional piercings appear in the table in Figure 3.4b on the previous page.

The marginal opportunity cost of producing and supplying the first piercing is $20 (the cost of 1 nail set given up); of the second piercing, $40 (2 nail sets given up); all the way up to $100 for the fifth piercing. So for Paola to be willing to supply 1 piercing, she needs to receive a price of at least $20 to cover the costs of the alternative use of her inputs. To continue to supply more piercings, she needs to receive higher prices to cover her higher marginal opportunity costs. Paola won't supply the fifth piercing unless she receives at least $100 for it, because that is what she would be giving up from the best alternative use of her inputs (5 fingernail sets at $20 each).

The graph in Figure 3.4b shows, for each quantity of piercings supplied (along the horizontal axis), the minimum price Paola will accept to cover her increasing marginal opportunity costs (along the vertical axis). Because of increasing marginal opportunity costs, the minimum price rises as Paola's quantity supplied increases.

Why Marginal Opportunity Costs Increase   Are the reasons for Paola's increasing marginal opportunity costs the same as for your work decision? And is there a connection between the increasing marginal opportunity costs of Paola's curved-shaped *PPF*, compared to the straight-line *PPF*s in Chapter 1 for Jill and Marie making bread and wood?

The answers to these important questions come from differences among inputs to production. Paola's increasing marginal opportunity costs arise because her staff and equipment are not equally good at piercing and painting. Paola is better (more productive) at doing fingernails than is Parminder, and the tools can't be easily switched between tasks — nail-polish brushes and emery boards aren't much help in piercing.

These differences in productivity cause increasing marginal opportunity costs. Think about Paola as she decides to reduce fingernail output and produce the first piercing. Remember that all staff are equally skilled at piercing. Who will she switch first to piercing? As an economizer, she will switch the person who is least productive for fingernails — Parminder. So her given up, or forgone, fingernail production is small (1 set). To increase piercing output more, she has to then switch staff who are slightly better at doing fingernails, so the opportunity cost is higher (2 fingernail sets). And who is the last person she switches when moving entirely to piercing? Of course, it is Paola herself — the best nail painter — so the opportunity cost of that fifth piercing is the highest, at 5 fingernail sets given up.

Increasing marginal opportunity costs arise because inputs are not equally productive in all activities. There are always opportunity costs in switching between activities because time spent on piercing can no longer be spent on fingernails. But *increasing* opportunity costs arise because of the differing skill levels of the staff being switched.

The reasons for Paola's increasing marginal opportunity costs are not quite the same as the reasons for your decision to supply more work hours as the price rises, but there is much in common. For your work decision, increasing marginal opportunity costs arise from differences in the value of alternative uses of your time (from gaming to weekend fun). For Paola's decision to supply additional piercings, increasing marginal opportunity costs arise from differences in employee skill levels and equipment in producing alternative services. The common reason is alternative uses (of time or inputs) with increasing opportunity costs.

When Marginal Opportunity Costs Are Constant If all of Paola's staff and equipment were equally good at piercing and fingernail painting, the opportunity costs would always be the same, no matter what combinations of piercings and fingernails she produced.

NOTE
Marginal opportunity costs are constant when inputs are equally productive in all activities.

The *PPF* examples of Jill and Marie in Chapter 1 have such constant marginal opportunity costs. Jill's straight line *PPF* means that as she switches between combinations of bread and wood, her marginal opportunity costs do not change. Jill's skills don't change as she switches between making bread and chopping wood. All that changes is the amount of time she spends on each task. The same is true for Marie. While Marie's skills and abilities differ from Jill's, Marie's skills don't change as she switches her time between tasks. For each person, marginal opportunity costs are constant as she switches between combinations of bread and wood.

In the real world, marginal opportunity costs may be increasing or constant. We will examine both cases in Chapter 9. Most businesses have inputs that are *not* equally productive in all activities, and so have increasing marginal opportunity costs. That is the case we will focus on here.

The Law of Supply

Just as you are willing to supply more hours of work only if the price you are paid rises, Paola's business must receive a higher price to be willing to supply a greater quantity to the market. She needs the higher price to cover her increasing marginal opportunity costs as she increases production.

Market supply is the sum of the supplies of all businesses willing to produce a particular product or service. Suppose there are 100 piercing businesses just like Paola's. The market supply of piercings is the sum of the supplies of all piercing businesses, and looks like the table in Figure 3.5.

market supply sum of supplies of all businesses willing to produce a particular product or service

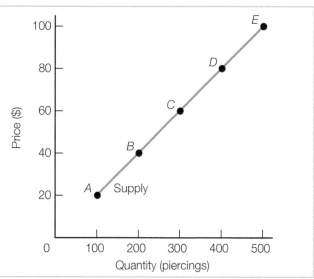

Figure 3.5   Market Supply of Piercings

Row	Price (marginal opportunity cost or minimum willing to accept per piercings)	Quantity Supplied (piercings)
A	$ 20	100
B	$ 40	200
C	$ 60	300
D	$ 80	400
E	$100	500

law of supply if the price of a product or service rises, quantity supplied increases

The positive relationship between price and quantity supplied (both go up together) is so universal that economists call it the **law of supply**: If the price of a product or service rises, the quantity supplied increases. Higher prices create incentives for increased production through higher profits and by covering higher marginal opportunity costs of production.

The law of supply works as long as other factors besides price do not change. Section 3.4 explores what happens when other factors do change.

Supply Curve of Piercings In Figure 3.5 on the previous page, if you take the combinations of prices and quantity supplied from the table and graph them, you get the upward-sloping supply curve.

For example, when the price of a piercing is $20, the quantity supplied by all businesses is 100 piercings (point *A*). When the price is $100, the quantity supplied is 500 (point *E*). Other points on the supply curve show the quantities supplied for prices between $20 and $100.

We draw the market supply curve for piercings by plotting these combinations on a graph that has *quantity* on the horizontal axis and *price* on the vertical axis. The points labelled *A* to *E* correspond to the rows of the table.

supply curve shows relationship between price and quantity supplied, other things remaining the same

A **supply curve** shows the relationship between price and quantity supplied, when all other influences on supply besides price do not change.

Two Ways to Read a Supply Curve

The supply curve shows graphically the relationship between price and quantity supplied, when all other influences on supply do not change. The supply curve is a simple yet powerful tool summarizing the two forces determining quantity supplied — the desire for higher profits and the need to cover increasing marginal opportunity costs of production.

Because there are two forces determining quantity supplied, there are two ways to "read" a supply curve — as a supply curve and as a marginal cost curve. Both readings are correct, but each highlights a different force. You can see the two readings in Figures 3.6a and 3.6b.

Figure 3.6 Two Ways to Read a Supply Curve

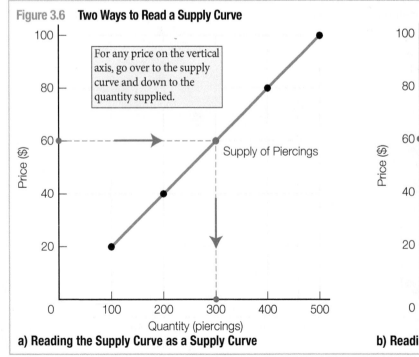

For any price on the vertical axis, go over to the supply curve and down to the quantity supplied.

Supply of Piercings

a) Reading the Supply Curve as a Supply Curve

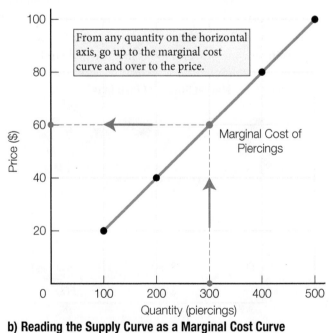

From any quantity on the horizontal axis, go up to the marginal cost curve and over to the price.

Marginal Cost of Piercings

b) Reading the Supply Curve as a Marginal Cost Curve

Supply Curve   To read Figure 3.6a as a supply curve, start with price. For any price, the supply curve tells you the quantity businesses are willing to supply. For example, start with the price of $60 on the vertical axis (Price). To find quantity supplied at $60, trace a line from the $60 price over to the supply curve and then down to the horizontal axis (Quantity) to read the quantity supplied, which is 300 piercings per day. You can do the same for any price — from any price, go over to the supply curve and then down to read the corresponding quantity supplied.

To think about how a price rise from $60 to $80 increases the quantity businesses are willing to supply, for each price, go over to the supply curve and then down to the quantity supplied. The rise in price of $20 increases quantity supplied by 100 piercings per day (400 – 300).

Marginal Cost Curve   To read Figure 3.6b as a marginal cost curve, start with quantity. For any quantity, the marginal cost curve tells you the minimum price businesses will accept that covers all marginal opportunity costs of production. Start with the quantity 300 piercings on the horizontal axis (Quantity). To find the minimum price businesses will accept to produce the 300th piercing, trace a line up to the marginal cost curve and over to the vertical (Price) axis to read the price, which is $60. You can do the same for any quantity — from any quantity, go up to the marginal cost curve and then over to read the corresponding price, which is the minimum price businesses will accept for that last piercing.

To think about how an increase in quantity supplied from 300 to 400 piercings increases marginal opportunity cost and the minimum price businesses will accept, for each quantity, go up to the marginal cost curve and then over to the price. Sixty dollars is the lowest price a business will accept for the 300th piercing, and $80 is the lowest price someone will accept for the 400th piercing. The increase in quantity of 100 units causes an increase in marginal opportunity cost of $20 per unit ($80 – $60).

The Supply Curve Is Also a Marginal Cost Curve   You read a supply curve over and down. You read a marginal cost curve up and over. While the supply curve has a double identity both as a supply curve and as a marginal cost curve, we generally refer to it as a supply curve. Sometimes, though, the marginal cost reading makes it easier to understand smart choices.

Both readings are movements along an unchanged supply curve. But what about the other influences on supply that we have been keeping constant? What happens if they change? The two ways to read a supply curve will help you answer that question.

Refresh 3.3

1. Explain why Paola needs a higher price to be willing to supply more piercings.

2. If you could spend the next hour studying economics or working at your part-time job, which pays $11 an hour, what is your personal opportunity cost, in dollars, of studying?

3. Suppose Paola's Parlour was producing only piercings and no fingernail sets. If Paola wanted to start producing some fingernail sets, which staff person should she switch to fingernails first? Who should she switch last? Explain your answers.

MyEconLab

For answers to these Refresh Questions, visit MyEconLab.

3.4 Changing the Bottom Line: What Can Change Supply?

Explain the difference between a change in quantity supplied and a change in supply, and list five factors that change supply.

The average price of an ultrabook computer in Canada fell from around $2000 in 2010 to under $800 in 2013. But the quantity of ultrabook computers businesses sold *increased*.

Does that contradict the "law of supply"?

If nothing else changed except the price of ultrabooks, the answer would be yes. Why would ultrabook producers be willing to supply more ultrabooks at lower prices? Something is not right. But like evidence that appears to disprove the law of demand, a fall in price that increases quantity supplied is a signal that something else must have changed at the same time.

Economists use the term *supply* to summarize all of the influences on business decisions. In the examples of your work decision or Paola's piercings, that willingness to supply depends on the value of alternative uses of time or inputs and on marginal opportunity costs.

As long as these factors (and some others that we are about to look at) do not change, the law of supply holds true: If the price of a product or service rises, quantity supplied increases.

But change happens, and economists distinguish two kinds of change:

- If the price of a product or service changes, that affects *quantity supplied*. This is represented graphically by moving along an unchanged supply curve.

- If anything else changes, that affects *supply*. This is represented graphically by a shift of the entire supply curve.

This distinction is the same as the distinction in Chapter 2 between quantity demanded and demand.

Economics *Out There*

Uncorking the Okanagan

In the Okanagan region of British Columbia. — an area known for its fruit production — large excavation machines are ripping out apple trees to make way for a new crop: grapes. Local landowners hope the switch will allow them to make more profits from their property by jumping into the province's booming wine industry. Landowner Bryan Hardman says that in the past he has been a price taker, but is setting up his own winery because he "wants to be a price maker, and believes the wine business is the place to do it."

- This story beautifully illustrates the law of supply. Higher prices and profits are creating incentives to increase quantity supplied of grapes and wine.

- It also illustrates how all inputs must be paid their opportunity costs. Even though the Okanagan Valley is a world-class area for apple-growing, landowners can make more money switching to grapes — more than covering their opportunity costs — so they do.

- If land is not equally productive for grape-growing, which apple orchards would you expect to be dug up and replanted with grapes first? Which would be replanted last?

- Consider Mr. Hardman's comment about wanting to be a price maker instead of a price taker. We will use those exact terms in Chapter 8 when we discuss competition among businesses in an industry.

Source: Wendy Stueck, "Uncorking the Okanagan," *The Globe and Mail*, October 7, 2006, p. B4.

Six Ways to Change Supply and Shift the Supply Curve

Only a change in the price of a product or service itself changes *quantity supplied* of that product or service. There are six other important factors that change market supply — the willingness to produce a product or service. They are:

- Technology
- Environment
- Prices of inputs
- Prices of related products or services produced
- Expected future prices
- Number of businesses

A change in any of these six factors shifts the supply curve.

Technology   Paola is overjoyed because she just bought a new piercing gun that allows her employees to do more piercings in a day. This increase in productivity from the new technology reduces her costs. Word spreads quickly, and all of the other piercing parlour owners realize that to stay competitive, they also must adopt the new technology. The result is an increase in market supply, which is shown in Figure 3.7 and can be described either by reading the supply curve as a supply curve or as a marginal cost curve.

Figure 3.7   Increase in Market Supply of Piercings

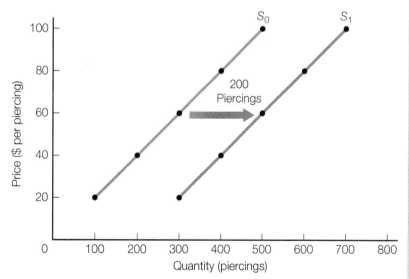

Price (marginal opportunity cost or minimum willing to accept per piercing)	Quantity Supplied (before technology improvement)	Quantity Supplied (after technology improvement)
$ 20	100	300
$ 40	200	400
$ 60	300	500
$ 80	400	600
$100	500	700

Let's start with the supply curve reading, which begins with price and goes over and down to the quantity supplied. At a price of \$20 (the first row in the table), before the new technology, businesses were willing to supply 100 piercings (column 2). On the graph, from the price of \$20 on the vertical axis, go over to supply curve S_0 and down to the quantity of 100 piercings.

Still in the first row of the table, at the unchanged price of \$20, with the new technology, businesses will now supply 300 piercings (column 3). On the graph, from the price of \$20, go over to the new supply curve S_1 and down to the quantity of 300 piercings. That is an increase in supply of 200 piercings (300 – 100).

As you look down the rest of the rows of the table, at every price businesses will supply 200 more piercings with the new technology. Economists call this an **increase in supply** — an increase in business's willingness to supply at any price. This increase in supply is represented on the graph by a rightward shift of the supply curve, from S_0 to S_1. The horizontal distance between S_0 and S_1 is 200 piercings.

The increase in supply can also be described by reading the supply curve as a marginal cost curve — up and over from quantity supplied to price. Before the new technology, to supply 300 piercings, businesses needed a minimum price of \$60 per piercing to cover marginal opportunity costs. On the graph, from the quantity 300 on the horizontal axis, go up to supply curve S_0 and over to the price of \$60. After the new technology, to supply 300 piercings businesses now need a price of only \$20 per piercing — from the quantity 300, go up to supply curve S_1 and over to the price of \$20.

The new technology lowers Paola's and other piercers' marginal opportunity costs, so they can accept a lower price while still covering all costs. For any quantity supplied, after the new technology, the minimum price businesses are willing to accept falls because marginal costs are lower.

Either way, whether you read the supply curve as a supply curve or a marginal cost curve, the result is an increase in supply — a rightward shift of supply curve.

increase in supply   increase in businesses' willingness to supply; rightward shift of supply curve

NOTE
An improvement in technology increases supply, and does not change quantity supplied.

Economics *Out There*

Army of Noodle-Shaving Robots Invades Restaurants

Chinese restaurant owner and entrepreneur Cui Runguan developed a robot (see photo on page 51) that hand-slices noodles into a pot of boiling water.

The robots "can slice noodles better than human chefs, they never get tired or bored, and it is much cheaper than a real human chef" says Liu Maohu, a noodle shop owner. Each robot costs under \$2000, but replaces a chef costing \$4700 per year.

- This technological change decreases costs and increases supply.
- If I am a restaurant owner, noodle robots "show me more money," so I increase supply.

Source: Paula Forbes, "China Is Building an Army of Noodle-Making Robots," *Eater*, August 17, 2012, http://eater.com/archives/2012/08/17/china-is-building-an-army-of-noodle-making-robots.php; Raymond Wong, "Army of Noodle-Shaving Robots Invade Restaurants in China," *Dvice*, August 20, 2013, http://www.dvice.com/archives/2012/08/noodle_shaving.php.

Environment   Extreme weather — droughts, storms, tornadoes, earthquakes — can have a powerful effect on supply. Extreme environmental events can reduce or destroy wheat crops, decreasing market supply, and shifting the supply curve for wheat leftward. The reverse is also true. Good weather conditions produce bumper crops, increasing wheat supply and shifting the market supply curve for wheat rightward.

Water temperature can affect fish stocks. A change in the temperature of water may lower reproduction rates, fewer fish are born, market supply decreases, and the supply curve for fish shifts leftward. If the change in water temperature encourages reproduction, fish supply increases, and the supply curve for fish shifts rightward.

Price of Inputs   Paola and other businesses must pay a price for inputs matching the best opportunity cost of the input owner. If those opportunity costs and input prices fall, Paola's costs decrease. At any price for piercings, lower costs for studs or electricity mean Paola earns higher profits, so she will want to supply more. The effect of lower input prices on market supply is the same as a technology improvement. Lower input prices increase market supply and shift the supply curve rightward.

The reverse is also true: Higher input prices mean higher costs for Paola and, at any price, lower profits. Therefore, market supply decreases. The supply curve shifts leftward.

Prices of Related Products and Services   Paola's Parlour produces both piercings and fingernail sets. What happens to Paola's supply of piercings when the price of fingernail sets falls from $20 to $10 per set? Since Paola wants to earn maximum profits, which service will she supply more of, and which less, when the price of fingernail sets falls? Take a minute to see if you can answer that question before reading on.

When the price of fingernail sets falls, Paola will supply more piercings and fewer fingernail sets. You probably reasoned that when the price of fingernail sets falls, they are less profitable to produce, so Paola will shift more of her resources to producing piercings. You are correct. A fall in the price of fingernail sets increases the supply of piercings. The supply curve of piercings shifts rightward.

You can also reason out the answer to the question of what happens to Paola's supply of piercings when the price of fingernail sets falls by thinking of the supply curve as a marginal cost curve. The lower price of fingernail sets lowers Paola's marginal opportunity cost of producing piercings. The real opportunity cost of producing more piercings is the fingernail sets Paola must give up. When those fingernail sets fall in price, Paola's marginal opportunity cost for producing piercings decreases. So the minimum price Paola will accept to supply any quantity of piercings falls. The supply curve of piercings shifts rightward.

In reverse, a rise in the price of fingernail sets decreases the supply of piercings. The supply curve of piercings shifts leftward. This is a **decrease in supply** — a decrease in business's willingness to produce.

A change in the price of related products or services supplied leads a business to reconsider its most profitable choices. A business will supply more of one product or service when alternative products or services it produces fall in price, and supply less when alternative products or services it produces rise in price.

Expected Future Prices   What happens to the supply of a product or service when the expected future price of the product or service changes? In Chapter 2, you learned that consumer demand changes if consumers expect lower or higher prices in the future. The same is true for businesses. If Paola expects falling piercing prices in the future, she will try to supply more now, while the price is relatively high. When future prices are expected to fall, supply increases in the present. The supply curve shifts rightward.

If Paola expects future prices to rise, she may reduce her current supply and increase her supply when prices and profits are higher. When future prices are expected to rise, supply decreases in the present. The supply curve shifts leftward.

Number of Businesses   An increase in the number of businesses increases market supply and shifts the supply curve rightward. It is no surprise that at any price, more businesses will supply a greater quantity. The increased number of businesses increases supply, just as an improvement in technology or a fall in input prices increases supply. A decrease in the number of businesses decreases supply, just as a rise in the price of a related product or service or an increase in expected future prices decreases supply.

Why would businesses enter (increase supply) or exit (decrease supply) a market? Usually, when profits are high, new competitors enter a market, increasing market supply. If profits are lower than elsewhere in the economy, competitors exit from the market, decreasing market supply. Those exiting businesses search for more profitable uses of their resources. You will learn more about these entry and exit stories in Chapter 7.

decrease in supply   decrease in business's willingness to produce; leftward shift of supply curve

NOTE
A fall in expected future price increases supply today.

NOTE
An increased number of businesses increases supply.

Moving Along or Shifting the Supply Curve Any increase (or decrease) in supply caused by changes in any of the six factors discussed can be described in alternative ways. You can read the supply curve either as a supply curve or as a marginal cost curve.

- At any price, businesses will supply a larger quantity. This is the supply curve reading of an increase in supply.

- At any quantity supplied, businesses will accept a lower price because their marginal opportunity costs of production are lower. This is the marginal cost reading of an increase in supply.

Figure 3.8   **Change in Quantity Supplied versus a Change in Supply**

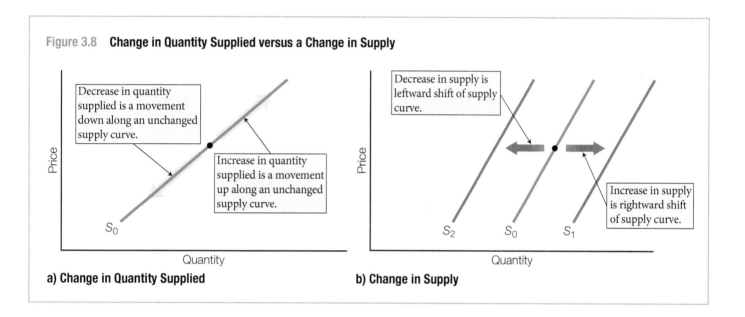

a) Change in Quantity Supplied

b) Change in Supply

In both readings, an increase in supply is also called a rightward shift of the supply curve. A decrease in supply is called a leftward shift of the supply curve.

When none of the six factors change to shift the supply curve, we can focus on the relationship between price and quantity supplied. That is represented in Figure 3.8a as moving along the supply curve S_0. If the price rises, and all other things do not change, that is a movement up along the supply curve to a larger quantity supplied. If the price falls, all other things unchanged, that is a movement down along the supply curve to a smaller quantity supplied.

Figure 3.8b shows an increase in supply, as the rightward shift from S_0 to S_1. The leftward shift from S_0 to S_2 is a decrease in supply. These shifts in supply are caused by changes in any of the six factors — technology, environment, prices of inputs, prices of related products or services produced, expected future prices, or number of businesses.

NOTE
An increase in supply is a rightward shift of the supply curve. A decrease in supply is a leftward shift of the supply curve.

Saving the Law of Supply

A change in quantity supplied (caused by a change in the price of the product or service itself) differs from a change in supply (caused by changes in technology, environment, prices of inputs, prices of related products or services produced, expected future prices, or the number of businesses). Can you now see why, when ultrabook computer prices fell from $2000 to under $800, the quantity of ultrabooks sold actually *increased*? Is the "law of supply" really a law?

If the price of a product or service falls, the quantity supplied decreases, *as long as other factors do not change*. The fall in ultrabook prices alone would *decrease* quantity supplied, not increase it. But other things changed. While a complete explanation involves demand factors as well as supply, major changes included technological improvements in computer chips and falling input prices. These *increased the supply* of ultrabook computers. Using the marginal cost reading of an increase in supply, at any quantity supplied, businesses were willing to accept a lower price because marginal opportunity costs of production were lower. The effect of the increase in supply outweighed the lower prices decreasing quantity supplied.

Figure 3.9 is a good study device for reviewing the difference between the law of supply and the factors that change supply.

Figure 3.9   Law of Supply and Changes in Supply

The Law of Supply *The quantity supplied of a product or service*	
Decreases if:	*Increases if:*
• price of the product or service falls	• price of the product or service rises

Changes in Supply *The supply for a product or service*	
Decreases if:	*Increases if:*
• _____	• technology improves
• environmental change harms production	• environment change helps production
• price of an input rises	• price of an input falls
• price of a related product or service rises	• price of a related product or service falls
• expected future price rises	• expected future price falls
• number of businesses decreases	• number of businesses increases

---

Refresh 3.4

MyEconLab

For answers to these Refresh Questions, visit MyEconLab.

1. Explain the difference between a change in quantity supplied and a change in supply. In your answer, distinguish the six factors that can change supply.

2. Suppose you have two part-time jobs, babysitting and pizza delivery. After younger babysitters start working for less, babysitting clients pay only $8 instead of $10 per hour. What happens to your supply of hours for delivering pizzas? Explain.

3. When the price of nail sets falls, Paola's hard dollar costs do not change. Will the quantity of piercings Paola supplies increase or decrease? Explain.

Study Guide

3.1 What Does It Really Cost? Costs Are Opportunity Costs

Businesses must pay higher prices to obtain more of an input because opportunity costs change with circumstances. The marginal costs of additional inputs (like labour) are ultimately opportunity costs — the best alternative use of the input.

- **Marginal cost** — additional opportunity cost of increasing quantity supplied, changing with circumstances.
  - For the working example, you are supplying time, and the marginal cost of your time increases as you increase the quantity of hours supplied.

- Differences between smart supply choices and smart demand choices:
  - For supply, marginal cost increases as you supply more.
  - For demand, marginal benefit decreases as you buy more.
  - For supply, marginal benefit is measured in $ (wages you earn); marginal cost is the opportunity cost of time.
  - For demand, marginal benefit is the satisfaction you get; marginal cost is measured in $ (the price you pay).

3.2 Forget It, It's History: Sunk Costs Don't Matter for Future Choices

Sunk costs that cannot be reversed are not part of opportunity costs. Sunk costs do not influence smart, forward-looking decisions.

- **Sunk costs** — past expenses that cannot be recovered.

- Sunk costs are the same no matter which fork in the road you take, so they have no influence on smart choices.

3.3 More for More Money: The Law of Supply

If the price of a product or service rises, quantity supplied increases. Businesses increase production when higher prices either create higher profits or cover higher marginal opportunity costs of production.

- **Supply** — businesses' willingness to produce a particular product or service because price covers all opportunity costs.

- **Quantity supplied** — quantity you actually plan to supply at a given price.

- **Marginal opportunity cost** — complete term for any cost relevant to a smart decision.
  - All opportunity costs are marginal costs; all marginal costs are opportunity costs.

- Increasing marginal opportunity costs arise because inputs are not equally productive in all activities.
  - Where inputs are equally productive in all activities, marginal opportunity costs are constant.

- **Market supply** — sum of supplies of all businesses willing to produce a particular product or service.

- **Law of supply** — if the price of a product or service rises, quantity supplied increases.

- **Supply curve** — shows the relationship between price and quantity supplied, other things remaining the same.
  - There are two ways to read a supply curve.
  - As a supply curve, read over and down from price to quantity supplied.
  - As a marginal cost curve, read up and over from quantity supplied to price. A marginal cost curve shows the minimum price businesses will accept that covers all marginal opportunity costs of production.

3.4 Changing the Bottom Line: What Can Change Supply?

Quantity supplied is changed only by a change in price. Supply is changed by all other influences on business decisions.

- Supply is a catch-all term summarizing all possible influences on businesses' willingness to produce a particular product or service.

- Supply changes with changes in technology, environment, prices of inputs, prices of related products or services produced, expected future prices, and number of businesses. For example, supply increases with:
  - improvement in technology
  - environmental change helping production
  - fall in price of an input
  - fall in price of a related product or service
  - fall in expected future price
  - increase in number of businesses

- **Increase in supply** — increase in businesses' willingness to supply. Can be described in two ways:
  - At any unchanged price, businesses are now willing to supply a greater quantity.
  - For producing any unchanged quantity, businesses are now willing to accept a lower price.

- **Decrease in supply** — decrease in business's willingness to supply.

TRUE/FALSE

Circle the correct answer. Solutions to these questions are available at the end of the book and on MyEconLab. You can also visit the MyEconLab Study Plan to access additional questions that will help you master the concepts covered in this chapter.

3.1 Costs Are Opportunity Costs

1. When higher-paying jobs are harder to find for workers, a business will pay more to hire labour.   T   F

2. Any smart business supply decision involves a choice between a business's marginal benefit (or reward) from supplying (or selling) its product and the business's marginal opportunity cost of producing the product.   T   F

3. Any smart worker supply decision involves a choice between a worker's marginal benefit (or reward) from supplying (or selling) her work and the worker's marginal opportunity cost of working.   T   F

4. Gordie's marginal opportunity cost of spending an extra hour on Facebook increases if he suddenly has the opportunity to go on a date with his high school crush.   T   F

3.2 Sunk Costs Don't Matter for Future Choices

5. Businesses should consider the monthly rent when deciding whether to produce more of a product or service.   T   F

6. Sunk costs are part of opportunity costs.   T   F

3.3 The Law of Supply

7. Businesses must receive higher prices as output increases to compensate for increasing marginal opportunity costs.   T   F

8. Opportunity cost equals what you get divided by what you give up.   T   F

9. As you shift time *away* from watching TV to working more hours, the marginal opportunity cost of working decreases.   T   F

10. All opportunity costs are marginal costs, and all marginal costs are opportunity costs.   T   F

11. To read a supply curve as a marginal cost curve, you start with price and go over and down to quantity supplied.   T   F

3.4 What Can Change Supply?

12. A rise in the price of inputs used by businesses decreases market supply.   T   F

13. A rise in the price of a related product a business produces increases market supply of the other product.   T   F

14. A rise in expected future prices shifts today's supply curve leftward.   T   F

15. Moving up along a supply curve is an increase in supply.   T   F

MULTIPLE CHOICE

Circle the best answer. Solutions to these questions are available at the end of the book and on MyEconLab. You can also visit the MyEconLab Study Plan to access similar questions that will help you master the concepts covered in this chapter.

3.1 Costs Are Opportunity Costs

1. Your opportunity cost of watching *The Big Bang Theory* increases if
   a) it is your favourite TV show.
   b) you have an expensive television.
   c) you have an exam the next day.
   d) all of the above.

2. The opportunity cost of going to school is highest for someone who
   a) has to give up a job paying $10 an hour.
   b) has to give up a job paying $15 an hour.
   c) loves school.
   d) has to give up a volunteer opportunity.

3. Which statement is *false*?
   a) Marginal costs are opportunity costs.
   b) Opportunity costs are marginal costs.
   c) Sunk costs are marginal costs.
   d) Marginal opportunity costs increase as quantity supplied increases.

3.2 Sunk Costs Don't Matter for Future Choices

4. Gamblers on slot machines often believe that the more they lose, the greater are their chances of winning on the next turn. However, the chances of winning on any turn are actually random — they do not depend on past turns. Therefore, the money lost on the previous turn is a(n)
   a) total cost.
   b) sunk cost.
   c) smart cost.
   d) opportunity cost.

5. Your friend Larry is deciding whether to break up with his current girlfriend, Lucy. He tells you that his number-one reason for staying with her is his tattoo, which says "I love Lucy." Based on economic thinking, you advise him to ignore his tattoo because it is a(n)
   a) opportunity cost.
   b) marginal cost.
   c) sunk cost.
   d) total cost.

3.3 The Law of Supply

6. If all workers and equipment are equally productive in all activities, the opportunity cost of increasing output is always
   a) increasing.
   b) decreasing.
   c) the same.
   d) low.

7. The law of supply applies to an individual's decision to work because
   a) as the wage rises, the quantity of hours a worker is willing to supply increases.
   b) as the price workers receive rises, the quantity of hours a worker is willing to supply increases.
   c) workers need to be compensated with higher wages to work more hours to cover increasing marginal opportunity costs.
   d) all of the above.

8. When a fall in price causes businesses to decrease the quantity supplied of a product, this illustrates
   a) the law of supply.
   b) the law of demand.
   c) a decrease in supply.
   d) an increase in supply.

9. Suppose that all inputs in a business are equally productive at all activities. As the business increases its output, marginal opportunity cost
   a) increases.
   b) decreases.
   c) is constant.
   d) is zero.

3.4 What Can Change Supply?

10. Which factor below does *not* change supply?
    a) prices of inputs
    b) expected future prices
    c) price of the supplied product or service
    d) number of businesses

11. The supply of a product or service increases with a(n)
    a) improvement in technology producing it.
    b) rise in the price a related product or service produced.
    c) rise in the price of an input.
    d) rise in the future price of the product or service.

12. The market supply of tires decreases if
    a) the price of oil — a major input used to produce tires — rises.
    b) tire-making technology improves.
    c) the expected future price of tires falls.
    d) new tire businesses enter the market.

13. The furniture industry shifts to using particleboard (glued wood chips), rather than real wood, which reduces costs. This
    a) increases supply.
    b) decreases supply.
    c) leaves furniture supply unchanged.
    d) effect on supply depends on demand.

14. Which factor below can change supply?
    a) income
    b) environmental change
    c) number of consumers
    d) price of a complement

15. Popeye's Parlour supplies both piercing and tattoo services. Higher prices for piercings will cause Popeye's
    a) quantity supplied of tattoos to increase.
    b) quantity supplied of tattoos to decrease.
    c) supply of tattoos to increase.
    d) supply of tattoos to decrease.

4

Coordinating Smart Choices

Demand and Supply

LEARNING OBJECTIVES

After reading this chapter, you should be able to:

4.1 Describe what a market is and the necessary rules for voluntary exchange.

4.2 Explain how shortages and surpluses affect prices.

4.3 Identify how market-clearing or equilibrium prices equalize quantity demanded and quantity supplied.

4.4 Predict how changes in demand and supply affect equilibrium prices and quantities.

4.5 Explain the efficiency of markets using the concepts of consumer surplus and producer surplus.

HAVE YOU EVER organized a milestone birthday party (20th, 50th, 80th?)

and felt like it was a miracle everything worked out? There are so many details to coordinate — who's helping with the food, who's decorating the cake, who's tending bar, and what about toilet paper? Now imagine organizing one day in the life of a small town — or, if your imagination is up to it, in Toronto. Think about the millions of consumers who each make hundreds of decisions about what to eat or which headphones to buy. Now think about the thousands of businesses that decide what to produce, where to find inputs, who to hire. Somehow, businesses produce just about everything consumers want to buy — for a price. With no one in charge, it seems miraculous. How are all those billions of decisions coordinated so that you (and everyone else) can find the food you want for breakfast and the headphones you want at the electronics store, let alone places to live, water, jobs, and gas?

If all that doesn't seem enough of a miracle, consider that the coordination problem is a fast-moving target. Japanese food becomes fashionable, condos replace houses, new immigrants arrive with different tastes — and yet businesses adjust, and we all continue to find the changing items we are looking for.

Markets and prices are the keys to these apparent miracles. As consumers, we each make smart choices in our own interests. Businesses make smart choices in pursuit of profits. Markets, when they work well, create incentives that coordinate the right products and services being produced in the right quantities and at the right locations to satisfy our wants. This chapter explains how markets form prices, which provide signals and incentives that coordinate the smart choices of consumers and businesses.

4.1 What's a Market?

market the interactions between buyers and sellers

Rolling Stone magazine named Jimi Hendrix the number-one rock guitarist of all time. Suppose you really want a vinyl copy of his first album, *Are You Experienced*? You can check out the local used record stores, you can prowl garage sales for 60-something-year-olds cleaning out their basement album collections, or you can go online to eBay. These are all markets. A **market** is not a place (physical or virtual) or a thing: It's a process — the interactions between buyers and sellers. Markets exist wherever there is a process of competing bids (from buyers or demanders) and offers (from sellers or suppliers). What is common to all markets is a negotiation between a buyer and a seller that results in an exchange.

Markets Mix Competition and Cooperation

Markets are an unlikely mix of competition and cooperation. There is competition between buyers trying to get the same product. This is most obvious in auction markets like eBay, where you bid against other buyers and the highest bid wins. But even in a store with fixed prices or at a garage sale, you are competing with other potential buyers on a first-come, first-gets basis.

Sellers also compete with each other for customers. Whether offering an album or artichokes, sellers try to get customers to buy from them by offering a lower price, better service, or higher quality than their competitors.

It is harder to see the cooperation in markets between buyers and sellers. Because any purchase or sale is voluntary, an exchange between a buyer and seller happens only when both sides end up better off. If you paid $100 for that rare Jimi Hendrix album, you must have felt that the benefit or satisfaction you would get is worth at least $100 (or you wouldn't have bought it). If the seller accepted $100, she felt that was at least the minimum she wanted to receive to give up the album (or she wouldn't have sold it).

ADDITIONAL
BENEFITS
VS.
OPPORTUNITY
COSTS

Using the economist's terms for smart choices from Chapters 2 and 3, for you, the buyer, the marginal benefit of the album is at least as great as its price (your marginal opportunity cost). For the seller, the price is at least as great as her estimate of marginal opportunity cost (the next best offer for the album). As long as the album — or any other product — sells voluntarily in a market, both sides are better off. Both buyer and seller have made smart choices.

Sure, you would have loved to pay less than $100, and the seller would have preferred to get $200. "Better off" doesn't require the buyer to get the lowest possible price or the seller to get the highest possible price. Both participants in the exchange are better off just as long each one has made a smart choice.

Voluntary exchange is essentially cooperative, and both sides win. Businesses want satisfied customers who will return, and businesses make money when they supply products or services that consumers want to buy. Consumers are better off when businesses supply products or services that provide satisfaction that is worth (or of greater value than) the price.

The Rules of the Game

For markets to work and voluntary exchanges to happen, some basic rules of the game are necessary. Through laws, government must define and protect property rights and enforce contracts between buyers and sellers. **Property rights** are rules that ensure that when you own something, no one can take it away from you by force. Property can be physical property (land, buildings, cars), financial property (stocks, bonds, savings), and intellectual property (music, books, or software resulting from creative effort, and protected by copyright and patents).

Without property rights, there would be no incentive to produce anything for exchange. Imagine that you operate a car-detailing business and have just finished a beautiful and time-consuming job on a 2015 Honda Acura. The owner of the car comes along, says thanks, and drives away without paying. If no laws protected you against theft, what incentive would you have to continue your business? While this example may sound outrageous, it's not much different from the case of a band that produces an album for sale, only to have it downloaded for free without the band or the record company being paid. Without property rights, most of our time and energy would have to go into protecting our property, rather than producing products or services.

While property rights are a prerequisite for anything to be produced, governments must also enforce agreements between buyers and sellers. For a successful exchange, both buyer and seller must deliver what they agreed to, and there must be some legal "referee" to settle disagreements.

property rights legally enforceable guarantees of ownership of physical, financial, and intellectual property

Can I Trust You ? Consider the enormous amount of trust involved when you make an online purchase on eBay. The seller trusts you will pay. You trust the product will be delivered. This trust does not happen accidentally.

Part of the reason eBay has been successful is that it has implemented rules that promote the necessary trust. The PayPal system guarantees that payments made by the buyer are received by the seller. And the ability of buyers to give anonymous and public feedback about their experiences with a seller creates enormous incentives for sellers to "produce" happy customers. If these informal rules don't work, the legal system is still the ultimate referee. This enormous trust between complete strangers is the foundation for the billions of voluntary exchanges that happen every day in all markets. Even passionate supporters of "free markets" acknowledge that there is an important role for government in defining and enforcing property rights so that free and voluntary exchanges can happen in markets.

Refresh 4.1

1. In your own words, define what a market is.

2. You are negotiating over the price of a new car with a car dealer. Explain how this process contains both cooperation and competition.

3. The Recording Industry Association of America's (RIAA) mission is "to foster a business and legal climate that supports and promotes our members' . . . intellectual property rights worldwide." Have you ever downloaded music? Write a short argument (three or four sentences) defending people's right to download music for free. Now, write a short argument against that position, including the concept of property rights. Which do you agree with? Explain why.

MyEconLab

For answers to these Refresh Questions, visit MyEconLab.

Where Do Prices Come From?
Price Signals from Combining Demand and Supply

Explain how shortages and surpluses affect prices.

Why do most stores sell Gatorade for $3 a bottle, and doughnuts for 99 cents? Think back to the smart choices that consumers (Chapter 2) and businesses (Chapter 3) make: Prices play a central role. Consumers compare prices and marginal benefits *(buy if the marginal benefit is greater than the price)*, while businesses compare prices and marginal opportunity costs *(sell if the price is greater than the marginal opportunity costs)*. Where do these prices come from?

Prices are the outcome of a market process of competing bids and offers. These negotiations between buyers and sellers may be obvious on eBay or at garage sales, but when you buy Gatorade at the corner store or a coffee and bagel at Tim Hortons, the store has set the price and there is no negotiation. The only "process" seems to be the cashier tapping your debit card or making change. For most purchases we make as consumers, the answer to the question "Where do prices come from?" seems to be "Businesses set prices." What gives?

It's true that in a market economy, businesses are free to set any price they choose. But no one can force consumers to buy at any price, and competing businesses may set lower or higher prices. So why do prices settle at particular numbers?

The economist's short answer to these questions about where prices come from is . . . (drum roll) . . . the interaction of demand and supply in markets with appropriate property rights! But that answer, while true, is pretty useless. We can point to anything that happens in an economy and say, in our best educated voice, "It is all determined by the laws of demand and supply." The longer and more useful answer exposes the hidden interactions between buyers and sellers, and also explains the miracles of markets in providing the products and services we want.

▲ This Canadian women's soccer team plays by the same rules as other soccer teams. Consistent rules make the game safe, fair, predictable, and understandable — features also needed for a well-functioning market.

Economics *Out There*

Rules of the Game Are Necessary for All Games, Not Just Markets

The game of football can be considered a model for how markets have developed. The earliest version, folk football, was played in medieval England — there were few rules, and the ones that were in place came about spontaneously and based on custom. There was "little skill . . . just muscle." The sport continued this way for centuries, until folk football morphed into soccer and rugby, and official rules were adopted. Skill started to matter, and the new forms of football were embraced the world over.

Typical markets grow in the way folk football did — evolving spontaneously, driven by participants, unstructured to

the point when rules begin to develop. Only when the rules become formal does a market reach its full potential. "An absolutely free market is like folk football, a free-for-all brawl. A real market is like American football, an ordered brawl."

Like other markets, eBay is not a free-for-all brawl because of the rules and procedures that have evolved to ensure trust and enforce contracts. Instead of competition between two football teams, there is competition between thousands of buyers, and between thousands of sellers. But the rules allow cooperative deals to be struck.

Source: John McMillan, *Reinventing the Bazaar*, Norton, 2002, pp. 12–13.

Prices in Action

Paradoxically, the best way to understand why prices settle at particular numbers is to look at what happens in markets when prices have not settled. Let's begin the story of "Where do prices come from?" by looking at what happens when markets are *not* working to coordinate smart choices, leaving frustrated consumers and producers.

NOTE
Prices come from the interaction of demand and supply, in markets with appropriate property rights.

Since the story has to explain particular numbers, it will be helpful to have . . . particular numbers! Let's use a simple set of made-up numbers for the market for piercings (recall our example of Paola's Parlour for Piercing and Nails introduced in Chapter 3).

Figure 4.1 Market Demand and Supply for Piercings

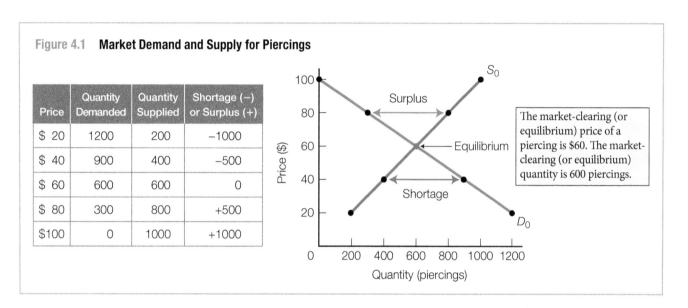

Price	Quantity Demanded	Quantity Supplied	Shortage (−) or Surplus (+)
$ 20	1200	200	−1000
$ 40	900	400	−500
$ 60	600	600	0
$ 80	300	800	+500
$100	0	1000	+1000

The market-clearing (or equilibrium) price of a piercing is $60. The market-clearing (or equilibrium) quantity is 600 piercings.

Demand Meets Supply   Figure 4.1 combines the market demand and market supply for piercings. The graph of the demand and supply curves is based on the numbers in the table. Let's look at the table first.

The three columns in the table in Figure 4.1 show alternative market prices for piercings (column 1), and, for each price, the quantity of piercings demanded (column 2) and supplied (column 3). If you look down columns 1 and 2 together, you see that as the price rises, the quantity demanded decreases. This is the law of demand. As a product becomes more expensive, consumers economize on its use and search for cheaper substitutes. If you look down columns 1 and 3 together, you see that as the price rises, the quantity supplied increases. This is the law of supply. Higher prices increase business's willingness to supply, because higher prices mean higher profits and the ability to profitably cover higher marginal opportunity costs. Higher prices generally lead to decreased quantity demanded and to increased quantity supplied in almost all markets.

Plotting those combinations of price and quantity demanded, and then price and quantity supplied, gives us the downward-sloping demand curve (D_0) and the upward-sloping supply curve (S_0) in the graph. (We will get to the surplus and shortage arrows soon.) In answering the question "Where do prices come from?" we will read the curves as demand and supply curves. For example, for a price of $20, we go over to the demand curve, and down to the quantity demanded of 1200 piercings. For that same $20 price, we go over to the supply curve and down to the quantity supplied of 200 piercings. For both the table of numbers and the graph, we read from price to quantity.

We know from the law of demand that consumers prefer lower prices, and we know from the law of supply that businesses prefer higher prices. How do prices get set in a way that reconciles these opposing goals?

Frustrated Buyers   What if the market price of piercings were $40 in parlours all around town? You might think that this relatively low price would make for happy consumers, but the numbers in Figure 4.1 tell another story. Look at row 2 of the table, where the price of a piercing is $40. Consumers want to buy 900 piercings, but Paola and her competitors are willing to supply only 400 piercings. While the 400 people who are able to buy a piercing for $40 will be happy, there are 500 frustrated buyers (900 − 400 = 500) who are willing and able to pay $40 but who can't get a parlour to do the piercing. This is a **shortage**, where quantity demanded exceeds quantity supplied. In markets with shortages, or **excess demand**, consumers experience long lineups and out-of-stock items at stores. Businesses experience products flying off the shelves and any inventories quickly dropping to zero.

On the graph, the horizontal distance between the supply and demand curves at the price of $40 represents that shortage of 500 piercings. This is the red arrow labelled *shortage*.

Shortages encourage competition among buyers. The consumers who most want the piercing will be willing to pay a bit more than $40, rather than being left with nothing. Buyers may bid for the scarce piercings (just like on eBay), driving up the price. Even if buyers don't actively bid up prices (when was the last time you offered to pay extra at Tim Hortons in hopes that they would find one more glazed doughnut for you?), sellers find that they can raise prices and still sell everything they have produced. Either way, shortages create pressure for prices to rise.

Rising prices provide signals and incentives, which are the key to how markets meet our wants. For businesses, higher prices are a signal, like a hand waving persistently in a classroom, saying, "Higher profits over here!" Higher prices and higher profits create an incentive for businesses to produce more and increase their quantity supplied. For consumers, higher prices mean we must revisit our smart choices. As prices go up, some consumers will give up on buying piercings and switch their planned purchases to some cheaper form of body decoration, like henna tattoos or costume jewellery. Quantity demanded decreases with higher prices.

Both adjustments — the increase in quantity supplied, and the decrease in quantity demanded — work to eliminate the shortage.

shortage or excess demand   quantity demanded exceeds quantity supplied

NOTE
Shortages create pressure for prices to rise.
Rising prices provide signals and incentives for businesses to increase quantity supplied and for consumers to decrease quantity demanded, eliminating the shortage.

Frustrated Sellers Instead of $40, what if the market price of piercings were $80? Look at row 4 of the table in Figure 4.1. At the relatively high price of $80, consumers want to buy only 300 piercings, but piercing parlours are eagerly willing to supply 800 piercings. So, all over town, parlours are expecting customers who don't show up, and idle piercers are sitting and checking Facebook. Parlours happily sell 300 piercings at $80, but are frustrated to the tune of 500 unsold piercings (800 − 300 = 500) they were willing to supply at that price. This is a **surplus**, where quantity supplied exceeds quantity demanded. In markets with surpluses, or **excess supply**, businesses experience underemployed resources, unsold products sitting on shelves, or rising inventories in warehouses. Those consumers willing and able to buy at the high price experience their choice of where to buy and sellers who are eager to please.

On the graph, the horizontal distance between the demand and supply curves at the price of $80 represents that surplus of 500 piercings. This is the blue arrow labelled *surplus*.

Surpluses encourage competition among sellers. The businesses that are most efficient or desperate for sales will cut their prices rather than be faced with empty piercing beds or unsold products. Some businesses will hold sales, or offer extras in trying to woo customers (free nail set with any piercing!). As discounts appear, consumers will be less willing to pay the $80 price. Surpluses create pressure for prices to fall.

Falling prices also provide signals and incentives, but in the opposite direction to rising prices. For consumers, falling prices are an incentive to buy more of now less expensive products or services, switching from substitutes whose prices have not changed. And as prices fall, more people can afford to buy. More smart decisions result in buying products or services with lower prices. Quantity demanded increases.

For businesses, falling prices are bad news — a warning signal of "lower profits ahead." They will decrease the quantities they are willing to supply, and switch inputs to more profitable opportunities. Paola will move some of her staff from piercings to fingernails. Quantity supplied decreases.

Both adjustments — increased quantity demanded, and decreased quantity supplied — work to eliminate the surplus.

Adjusting Prices and Quantities When there are shortages and surpluses, price adjustments play the key role. You may be thinking that the prices you observe in most markets don't adjust continuously and, in fact, settle for long times at particular values. Even the question I posed — "Why do prices settle at particular numbers?" — seems inconsistent with the stories about prices rising or falling in reaction to shortages and surpluses — but there is a reconciliation.

Most businesses have some *market power* (a concept coming in Chapter 8), which means they have some control over setting prices. Businesses pick a price point that they expect will make the most profits, taking into account all cooperative and competitive forces. For a mutually beneficial exchange with a cooperating customer, price must be less than the customer's marginal benefit but also must profitably cover the business's marginal opportunity costs. The price point also must be competitive with what other similar businesses charge. Once a business picks a price point, it may turn out to be too low (shortages develop and products sell out quickly) or too high (resulting in surpluses, underemployed resources, and rising inventories). But over time, especially in the face of competition, businesses react to market conditions of shortages or surpluses and adjust price points.

ADDITIONAL
BENEFITS
VS.
OPPORTUNITY
COSTS

Quantity adjustments also play an important role in the stories of how markets react to shortages or surpluses. When your local electronics store is always selling out of Beats headphones and frustrated customers come to the desk looking for them, the store orders more. Shortages lead to step-by-step increases in quantity supplied. If your local corner store regularly orders one case of Gatorade a week, but finds not all of the bottles are selling, it cuts back to ordering one case every other week. Surpluses lead to step-by-step decreases in quantity supplied. In response to excess demand or excess supply, businesses adjust quantities continuously, and can do so in small steps to match changing market conditions. When your boss asks you to work an extra shift next week, or your neighbourhood Tim Hortons bakes 10 dozen chocolate doughnuts a day instead of 13 dozen, those are quantity adjustments.

Self-Interest at Work   What is remarkable about all of these price adjustments (not so frequent) and quantity adjustments (frequent) is that no consumer or business needs to know anything about anyone's personal wants or production capabilities. Prices (and quantities) serve as signals to consumers and businesses, and all anyone has to do is consider his or her own self-interest. As long as there is an imbalance between quantity demanded and quantity supplied, prices will eventually adjust and send signals for consumers and businesses to change their smart decisions.

Consumers and businesses take all of these signals, and each makes self-interested smart decisions based on the price. As a byproduct of all these individual decisions made by complete strangers, markets provide the products and services we want.

NOTE
Even when prices don't change, shortages and surpluses create incentives for frequent quantity adjustments to better coordinate smart choices of businesses and consumers.

> *It is not from the benevolence of the butcher, the brewer, or the baker that we expect our dinner, but from their regard to their own interest.*
> —*Adam Smith,*
> The Wealth of Nations, *1776*

Refresh 4.2

MyEconLab

For answers to these Refresh Questions, visit MyEconLab.

1. In your own words, define what a shortage is. Explain who competes and what happens to prices when there is a shortage.

2. Old Navy decides to price a new line of jeans at $95, which covers all marginal opportunity costs as well as a healthy profit margin. If Old Navy has priced the jeans too high, what signals will the company receive? Based on those signals, what actions might Old Navy take next?

3. Most provincial parks charge a fixed price for a camping permit, and allow you to reserve specific campsites in advance. By the time the summer holiday weekends arrive, all the permits are usually taken. There is excess demand but no price adjustment. Suggest a pricing system for provincial parks that allows them to take advantage of the higher demand for campsites on holiday weekends. Your system should explain who is competing and who is cooperating.

When Prices Sit Still: Market-Clearing or Equilibrium Prices

So, after reading stories of rising prices (from shortages) and falling prices (from surpluses), you may be wondering, "When do prices finally sit still, and settle at particular values?" Look at row 3 of Figure 4.1 on page 81, where the price of a piercing is $60. At $60, consumers want to buy 600 piercings, and all of the piercing parlours combined want to supply 600 piercings. At last, quantity demanded equals quantity supplied. On the graph in Figure 4.1, this is point where the demand curve and the supply curve intersect. With no shortages or surpluses, there are no competitive forces pushing prices up or down. Consumers are happy because every person who is willing and able to pay $60 gets a piercing. Businesses are happy because the $60 price profitably covers their marginal opportunity costs for the 600 piercings they supply.

There are consumers out there who would demand a piercing at $20, but think $60 is outrageous. They don't get pierced. But they made a smart decision: For them, a piercing isn't worth $60, or $60 is more than they can reasonably afford. They make a smart choice to spend their money elsewhere, and thus are not putting pressure on piercing prices. Likewise, there are parlours out there that would supply more piercings if the price were $80, but $60 doesn't cover their marginal opportunity costs so they use their resources to produce something else (nail sets? pedicures?) that they can sell at a price that profitably covers marginal opportunity costs.

The price that coordinates quantity demanded and quantity supplied is so important that economists have two names for it. (Don't you have a few names — nicknames — for people who are important to you?)

Market-Clearing Price

Market-clearing price is one name for the price equalizes quantity demanded and quantity supplied. At the market-clearing price, there are no longer frustrated buyers or sellers. There is a match for every buyer and seller, and all go home happy. Everyone who volunteers to exchange $60 for a piercing (both consumers buying and parlours selling) is better off, or they wouldn't have bought and sold.

market-clearing price the price that equalizes quantity demanded and quantity supplied

Equilibrium Price

The second name for the price that equalizes quantity demanded and quantity supplied is **equilibrium price**. *Equilibrium* is a term from physics that means a balance of forces resulting in an unchanging outcome. The equilibrium price exactly balances forces of competition and cooperation to coordinate the smart choices of consumers and businesses. At the equilibrium price, there is no tendency for change (until some new event occurs to disturb the balance, as we will see) and no incentives for anyone — consumers or businesses — to change their own, self-interested, smart decisions. No one is kicking himself for making a mistaken purchase or missing a better opportunity. Everyone has done the best they can in their exchanges, given the wants and resources they started with.

equilibrium price the price that equalizes quantity demanded and quantity supplied, balancing the forces of competition and cooperation, so that there is no tendency for change

Why is this particular "price that sits still" so important that it gets two names? It is the culmination of the forces of cooperation and competition that explains the miracle of markets. Ironically, when markets are functioning well and clearing, we don't pay much attention to this miracle. We find what we want for breakfast at Tim Hortons, the headphones we like are on the shelf at the electronics store, and we find jobs, gas for our cars, and all the other products and services that satisfy our wants. And businesses find customers for all the products and services they want to profitably supply. Often, it's only when something goes wrong — perhaps a labour dispute or a natural disaster that disrupts supplies — that we realize how conveniently we usually find what we want to buy.

The fact that consumers find that businesses have produced just about everything they want to buy, and with no one in charge, and that billions of decisions get coordinated is due to . . . (drum roll reprise) . . . the interaction of demand and supply, in markets with appropriate property rights! The law of demand is shorthand for the smart choices of consumers. The law of supply is shorthand for the smart choices of businesses. Market-clearing prices (and quantities) result when smart choices are coordinated. The forces of competition (between consumers, and between businesses) are balanced with the forces of cooperation (voluntary, mutually beneficial exchanges between consumers and businesses). The key to this outcome is that price signals in markets create incentives so that while each person acts only in her own self-interest, the unintended consequence is the coordinated production of all the products and services we want.

NOTE

Price signals in markets create incentives so that while each person acts only in her own self-interest, the unintended consequence is the production of all the products and services we want.

The Invisible Hand   Perhaps the most famous phrase in economics that describes this outcome is Adam Smith's "invisible hand" in his 1776 book, *The Wealth of Nations*:

> When an individual makes choices, "he intends only his own gain, and he is in this . . . led by an invisible hand to promote an end which was no part of his intention. . . . By pursuing his own interest he frequently promotes that of the society more effectually than when he really intends to promote it."

The miracle is that markets channel self-interest, as though "by an invisible hand," so that society produces the products and services we want, without the government doing anything beyond setting the rules of the game.

Refresh 4.3

MyEconLab

For answers to these Refresh Questions, visit MyEconLab.

1. List and define the two other names for "prices that sit still."

2. In an attempt to promote the social good of energy conservation, Toronto Hydro introduced the Peaksaver Program. Participating households received a $25 reward for allowing a "peaksaver" switch to be installed on their central air conditioners, which briefly turns off the air conditioner during peak demand times on hot summer days. Do you think the program would work without the $25 reward? Why or why not?

3. Explain the idea of Adam Smith's "invisible hand." Your explanation should illustrate the balance between the forces of competition and cooperation at "prices that sit still." (I can't give away the answer to question 1, can I?)

Moving Targets:
What Happens When Demand and Supply Change?

We live in a fast-paced society where change happens regularly. Food and clothing go in and out of style, technology is constantly changing, and businesses may boom in Alberta and bust in New Brunswick. Even if markets succeed in temporarily coordinating the plans of consumers and businesses and settle at equilibrium prices, what happens when something changes? Will markets still be efficient — coordinating the right products and services being produced in the right quantities at the right locations to satisfy our wants when the "right" target keeps moving?

Believe it or not, all stories about shortages, surpluses, mutually beneficial trades, and adjusting prices and quantities we've looked at so far actually had very limited change. Yes, prices and quantities changed, and smart decisions changed — but in the background, I was holding almost everything else constant.

All the stories began with the numbers in Figure 4.1 on page 81, which illustrate the law of demand (when price rises, quantity demanded decreases) and the law of supply (when price rises, quantity supplied increases). We could focus carefully on those price-quantity relationships because *we were holding all other influences on consumers' choices and on businesses' choices constant.*

Recall the Chapter 2 distinction between a change in quantity demanded and a change in demand. Five factors can cause a change in demand. Name at least three and win a prize! Answer: changes in preferences, prices of related products, income, expected future prices, and number of consumers. All of those are unchanged in the numbers in Figure 4.1. And remember that Chapter 3 distinction between a change in quantity supplied and a change in supply? The six factors that can cause a change in supply (changes in technology, environment, prices of inputs, prices of related products produced, expected future prices, number of businesses) also are all unchanged in Figure 4.1.

Don't give up on this chapter because you fear I plan to slog through changes in all 11 factors. I won't. I have combined the explanations into groups: what happens to equilibrium prices and quantities when there are increases or decreases in demand, increases or decreases in supply, and combinations where demand and supply both change. As a bonus, I will let you in on the secret to thinking like an economist and making smart choices in this ever-changing world.

Changes in Demand

NOTE

For an increase in demand, the equilibrium price rises, and quantity supplied increases.

Increase in Demand   When the Japanese food craze hit years ago, there was an increase in demand for sushi, triggered by this change in preferences. The demand curve for sushi shifted rightward. Increased demand drives up the market price, and restaurants responded to that signal of higher profits by increasing the quantity supplied of sushi. Any factor that increases demand causes a rise in the equilibrium price and an increase in the quantity supplied.

Figure 4.2 shows a similar *increase in demand* for the piercing market. The demand curve shifts rightward from D_0 to D_1. The equilibrium price rises from P_0 to P_1 and the equilibrium quantity increases from Q_0 to Q_1.

Figure 4.2   Increase in Demand

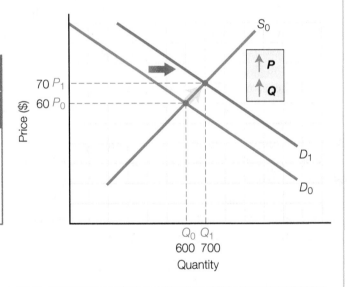

| Price | Quantity Demanded | | Quantity Supplied |
	Original (D_0)	New (D_1)	(S_0)
$40	900 $\rightarrow$	1150	400
$50	750 $\rightarrow$	900	500
$60	600 $\rightarrow$	850	600
$70	450 $\rightarrow$	700	700
$80	300 $\rightarrow$	550	800

In the table in Figure 4.2, start with the original equilibrium in the piercing market, where the price (P_0) is $60. At that price, quantity demanded (D_0) equals quantity supplied (S_0), which is 600 piercings.

When demand increases (from D_0 to D_1), at every price, the new quantity demanded is now 250 piercings more than the original quantity demanded. At the price of $60, the original quantity demanded was 600. Then the new quantity demanded increases by 250 to 850 piercings. There is no change in supply — the supply curve and the numbers for quantity supplied (S_0) remain the same.

After the increase in demand, the new equilibrium price (P_1) is $70. At that price, the new quantity demanded (Q_1) equals quantity supplied (Q_1), which is 700 piercings.

The increase in demand raises the equilibrium price ($\uparrow$ P) and increases the equilibrium quantity ($\uparrow$ Q).

Decrease in Demand When business boomed in Alberta from oil revenues, many people moved out west from New Brunswick. What did this decrease in population do to the real estate market in New Brunswick? There was a decrease in demand. The demand curve for housing shifts leftward, driving down the market price, and decreasing the quantity supplied of houses for sale. Any factor that decreases demand causes a fall in the equilibrium price and a decrease in the quantity supplied.

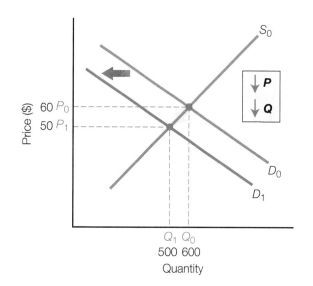

Figure 4.3 shows a similar *decrease in demand* for the piercing market. The demand curve shifts leftward from D_0 to D_1. The equilibrium price falls from P_0 to P_1 and the equilibrium quantity decreases from Q_0 to Q_1.

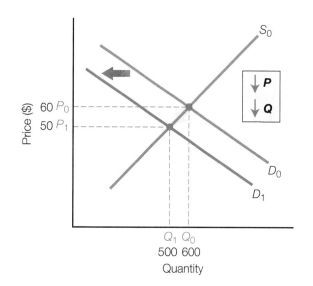

NOTE
For a decrease in demand, the equilibrium price falls, and quantity supplied decreases.

Figure 4.3 Decrease in Demand

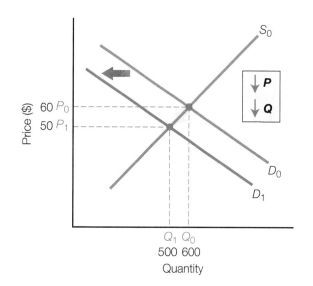

| Price | Quantity Demanded | | Quantity Supplied |
	Original (D_0)	New (D_1)	(S_0)
$40	900 →	650	400
$50	750 →	500	500
$60	600 →	350	600
$70	450 →	200	700
$80	300 →	50	800

In the table in Figure 4.3, start with the original equilibrium in the piercing market, where the price (P_0) is $60. At that price, quantity demanded (D_0) equals quantity supplied (S_0), which is 600 piercings.

When demand decreases (from D_0 to D_1), at every price, the new quantity demanded is now 250 piercings less than the original quantity demanded. At the price of $60, the original quantity demanded was 600. Then the new quantity demanded decreases by 250 to 350 piercings. There is no change in supply — the supply curve and the numbers for quantity supplied (S_0) remain the same.

After the decrease in demand, the new equilibrium price (P_1) is $50. At that price, the new quantity demanded (Q_1) equals quantity supplied (Q_1), which is 500 piercings.

The decrease in demand lowers the equilibrium price (⬇ P) and decreases the equilibrium quantity (⬇ Q).

Changes in Supply

NOTE

For an increase in supply, the equilibrium price falls, and quantity demanded increases.

Increase in Supply   The continuous improvement in semiconductor technology makes it cheaper to produce tablets and increases their supply. The supply curve for tablets shifts rightward. Market price falls as Amazon, Samsung, and Apple compete for customers by lowering prices to reflect their lower costs of production. Consumers respond to lower prices by increasing their quantity demanded of tablets. Any factor that increases supply causes a fall in the equilibrium price and an increase in the quantity demanded.

Figure 4.4 shows a similar *increase in supply* for the piercing market. The supply curve shifts rightward from S_0 to S_1. The equilibrium price falls from P_0 to P_1 and the equilibrium quantity increases from Q_0 to Q_1.

Figure 4.4   Increase in Supply

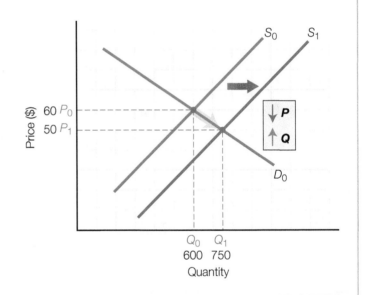

Price	Quantity Demanded (D_0)	Quantity Supplied Original (S_0)	Quantity Supplied New (S_1)
$40	900	400 →	650
$50	750	500 →	750
$60	600	600 →	850
$70	450	700 →	950
$80	300	800 →	1050

In the table in Figure 4.4, start with the original equilibrium in the piercing market, where the price (P_0) is $60. At that price, quantity demanded (D_0) equals quantity supplied (S_0) which is 600 piercings.

When supply increases (from S_0 to S_1), at every price, the new quantity supplied is now 250 piercings more than the original quantity supplied. For example, at the price of $60, the original quantity supplied was 600. Then the new quantity supplied increases by 250 to 850 piercings. There is no change in demand — the demand curve and the numbers for quantity demanded (D_0) remain the same.

After the increase in supply, the new equilibrium price (P_1) is $50. At that price, the new quantity demanded (Q_1) equals quantity supplied (Q_1), which is 750 piercings.

The increase in supply lowers the equilibrium price (↓ P) and increases the equilibrium quantity (↑ Q).

NOTE

For a decrease in supply, the equilibrium price rises, and quantity demanded decreases.

Decrease in Supply   The business boom in Alberta drove up wages, as businesses competed for scarce workers. The average hourly wage, even at fast-food restaurants, rose from $10 to $15. This rise in inputs costs decreases supply. The supply curve of fast food shifts leftward from S_0 to S_1. Restaurants are only willing to supply meals at higher prices, and the market price of meals rises. Rising prices cause customers to rethink their smart food choices, and quantity demanded of restaurant meals decreases. Any factor that decreases supply causes a rise in the equilibrium price and a decrease in the quantity demanded.

Figure 4.5 shows a similar *decrease in supply* for the piercing market. The supply curve shifts leftward from S_0 to S_1. The equilibrium price rises from P_0 to P_1 and the equilibrium quantity decreases from Q_0 to Q_1.

Figure 4.5 Decrease in Supply

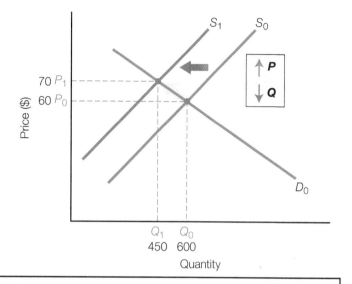

Price	Quantity Demanded (D_0)	Quantity Supplied		
		Original (S_0)		New (S_1)
$40	900	400	→	150
$50	750	500	→	250
$60	600	600	→	350
$70	450	700	→	450
$80	300	800	→	550

In the table in Figure 4.5, start with the original equilibrium in the piercing market, where the price (P_0) is $60. At that price, quantity demanded (D_0) equals quantity supplied (S_0), which is 600 piercings.

When supply decreases (from S_0 to S_1), at every price, the new quantity supplied is now 250 piercings less than the original quantity supplied. For example, at the price of $60, the original quantity supplied was 600. Now the new quantity supplied has decreased by 250 to 350 piercings. There is no change in demand — the demand curve and the numbers for quantity demanded (D_0) remain the same.

After the decrease in supply, the new equilibrium price (P_1) is $70. At that price, the new quantity demanded (Q_1) equals quantity supplied (Q_1), which is 450 piercings.

The decrease in supply raises the equilibrium price (⬆ P) and decreases the equilibrium quantity (⬇ Q).

Economics *Out There*

Lobsters Galore!

Unusually warm ocean temperatures near the Atlantic coast in the spring of 2013 dramatically increased the supply of lobsters. A Nova Scotia lobster broker predicted that "If the price [of lobster] doesn't drop, I'll eat my shirt."

He was spared from having his shirt for lunch because, sure enough, lobster prices dropped from $10 a pound in the winter to $5 a pound in May. As catches continued to increase during the spring, the price dropped to a low of $3 a pound.

- This is a classic case of an environmental change increasing supply. With no change in demand, the price falls and lobster lovers get to eat more. The fall in price increases quantity demanded to bring supply and demand back into equilibrium.

Source: Chris Lambie, "Lobster prices set to drop as volume increases," *The Chronicle Herald*, May 3, 2013, http://thechronicleherald.ca/business/1127543-lobster-prices-set-to-drop-as-volume-increases

Combining Changes in Demand and Supply

Once you allow both demand and supply to change at the same time, the effects on the equilibrium price and quantity are a bit more complicated. If demand and supply change together, for any of the reasons above, the effects are illustrated in Figure 4.6. P_0 and Q_0 are the original equilibrium price and quantity before the change. P_1 and Q_1 are the new equilibrium price and quantity after the changes in both demand and supply.

Increase in Both Demand and Supply

An increase in demand alone (D_0 to D_1) raises the equilibrium price and increases the equilibrium quantity. An increase in supply alone (S_0 to S_1) lowers the equilibrium price and increases the equilibrium quantity. Figure 4.6a combines these effects. Because both the increase in demand and the increase in supply increase the quantity, we know for sure that the equilibrium quantity increases (Q_0 to Q_1).

But the effect on the price is not so clear because price is being pushed in opposite directions. The increase in demand puts pressure on the price to rise, while the increase in supply puts pressure on the price to fall. I have drawn the shifts of the demand and supply curves so that these pressures cancel out, and the equilibrium price does not change — it remains at P_0. But a slightly larger or smaller shift in either the demand curve or the supply curve could cause the price to rise (if the rightward shift in demand is larger than the rightward shift in supply) or to fall (if the rightward shift in demand is smaller than the rightward shift in supply). Without more precise information, we cannot predict what will happen to the equilibrium price.

Decrease in Both Demand and Supply

A decrease in demand alone (D_0 to D_1) lowers the equilibrium price and decreases the equilibrium quantity. A decrease in supply alone (S_0 to S_1) raises the equilibrium price and decreases the equilibrium quantity. Figure 4.6b combines these effects. Because both the decrease in demand and the decrease in supply decrease the quantity, we know for sure that the equilibrium quantity decreases (Q_0 to Q_1).

Again, the effect on the price is not clear because price is being pushed in opposite directions. Without more precise information about how large or small are the (leftward) shifts of demand and supply, we cannot predict what will happen to the equilibrium price.

Increase in Demand and Decrease in Supply

An increase in demand alone (D_0 to D_1) raises the equilibrium price and increases the equilibrium quantity. A decrease in supply alone (S_0 to S_1) raises the equilibrium price and decreases the equilibrium quantity. Figure 4.6c combines these effects. Because both the increase in demand and the decrease in supply increase the price, we know for sure that the equilibrium price rises (P_0 to P_1).

But in this case the effect on the quantity is not so clear because quantity is being pushed in opposite directions. The increase in demand puts pressure on the quantity to increase, while the decrease in supply puts pressure on the quantity to decrease. Without more precise information about how large or small are the shifts of demand (rightward) and supply (leftward), we cannot accurately predict what will happen to the equilibrium quantity.

Decrease in Demand and Increase in Supply A decrease in demand alone (D_0 to D_1) lowers the equilibrium price and decreases the equilibrium quantity. An increase in supply alone (S_0 to S_1) lowers the equilibrium price and increases the equilibrium quantity. Figure 4.6d combines these effects. Because both the decrease in demand and the increase in supply decrease the price, we know for sure that the equilibrium price falls.

Again, the effect on the quantity is not clear because quantity is being pushed in opposite directions. Without more precise information about how large or small are the shifts of demand (leftward) and supply (rightward), we cannot predict what will happen to the equilibrium quantity.

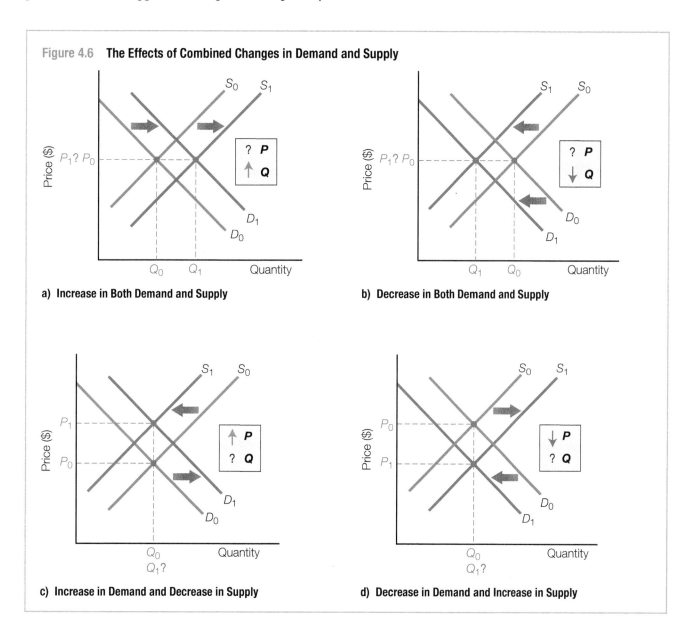

Figure 4.6   The Effects of Combined Changes in Demand and Supply

a) **Increase in Both Demand and Supply**

b) **Decrease in Both Demand and Supply**

c) **Increase in Demand and Decrease in Supply**

d) **Decrease in Demand and Increase in Supply**

Putting It All Together

Figure 4.7 is a good study device for reviewing all of the effects on price and quantity of any changes in demand and supply.

Figure 4.7 Effects of Changes in Demand or Supply

Change	Shifts of Curves	Effect on Equilibrium Price	Effect on Equilibrium Quantity
Increase in Demand	Demand shifts rightward	↑	↑
Decrease in Demand	Demand shifts leftward	↓	↓
Increase in Supply	Supply shifts rightward	↓	↑
Decrease in Supply	Supply shifts leftward	↑	↓
Increase in Demand and Increase in Supply	Demand shifts rightward; Supply shifts rightward	Need exact numbers to predict outcome	↑
Decrease in Demand and Decrease in Supply	Demand shifts leftward; Supply shifts leftward	Need exact numbers to predict outcome	↓
Increase in Demand and Decrease in Supply	Demand shifts rightward; Supply shifts leftward	↑	Need exact numbers to predict outcome
Decrease in Demand and Increase in Supply	Demand shifts leftward; Supply shifts rightward	↓	Need exact numbers to predict outcome

Economists Do It with Models

Think of all the simple demand and supply graphs in this chapter as models. They focus our attention on the reasons why mutually beneficial trades happen in a market, and select just enough information to predict where market-clearing prices and quantities will end up. As well, the models tell us when we do not have enough information to make those predictions.

In the real world, all 11 factors that influence consumers' and businesses' choices are changing constantly. Demand and supply graphs are like controlled laboratory experiments. They hold all influences constant except one (or two), so we can see the effect of that one influence alone. Let me explain.

Start in Equilibrium When I draw a demand curve and a supply curve that intersect at price P_0 and quantity Q_0, I am holding constant all 11 factors that can shift the demand or supply curves and influence consumers' and businesses' choices. Once prices sit still at the market-clearing price there is no tendency for change. This is our starting point — the original equilibrium outcome.

One Change at a Time   In each "thought experiment" in Figures 4.2 through 4.5, I change one factor that affects demand or supply, while continuing to hold all other influences constant. That change is modelled as the shift of the demand or supply curve.

The results of these controlled thought experiments are the new market-clearing prices of P_1 and Q_1. When prices sit still at the new market-clearing price P_1 and quantity Q_1, once is again no further tendency for change. This is the new equilibrium outcome.

Even in Figure 4.6, when two factors change, we are still comparing an original equilibrium outcome (P_0 and Q_0) with a second equilibrium outcome (P_1 and Q_1), while continuing to hold all other influences constant.

This simplified way of using a model to isolate the impact of one (or two) factors in the economy is called **comparative statics** — the comparison of two equilibrium outcomes. Static means unchanging. Each equilibrium is static — there is no tendency for change. We start with one equilibrium outcome, change a single factor that affects demand or supply, and then compare it to the new equilibrium outcome. We compare two static, equilibrium outcomes. That simplified comparison allows us to predict changes in price and quantity, despite all of the complexities in the real world.

My favourite saying for this way of thinking is "Economists do it with models."

comparative statics   comparing two equilibrium outcomes to isolate the effect of changing one factor at a time

NOTE
"Economists do it with models" describes the economic way of thinking

Refresh 4.4

1. What happens to the market-clearing price and quantity of a product or service when demand increases? When demand decreases? When supply increases? When supply decreases?

2. Predicting changes in market-clearing prices and quantities is harder when *both* demand *and* supply change at the same time. You run a halal butcher shop in Ottawa. There is expected to be an increase in the number of practising Muslims in Ottawa who prefer halal meat. Rents for retail space are also falling all over town. Predict what will happen to the market-clearing price for halal meat. Predict what will happen to the market-clearing quantity. Explain your predictions.

3. In response to the business boom in Alberta, the city of Edmonton offered $200-per-month rent subsidies to low-income families so they could afford to live and work in the city. If you were asked to advise the city on this policy, what would you tell them about the impact it will have on rents? Will the rents go up or down? Explain your reasoning to the city officials.

MyEconLab

For answers to these Refresh Questions, visit MyEconLab.

4.5 Getting More Than You Bargained For: Consumer Surplus, Producer Surplus, and Efficiency

Explain the efficiency of markets using the concepts of consumer surplus and producer surplus.

When markets clear at equilibrium prices, lots of good things happen. There are no frustrated buyers or sellers. There is a balance between the forces of competition and cooperation, and quantity demanded equals quantity supplied. Mutually beneficial trades result in the miracle of markets — the right products and services being produced in the right quantities and at the right locations to satisfy our wants.

But wait, the results are even better than that! With an efficient market outcome, consumers get more benefits than they pay for, and businesses receive more money than they need to cover their opportunity costs. To see how this happens, we need to read demand and supply curves as marginal benefit and marginal cost curves.

Consumer Surplus

The market demand curve in Figure 4.1 on page 81 is also a marginal benefit curve. Figure 4.8 reproduces that demand curve and labels it also as a marginal benefit (*MB*) curve. A *market* demand curve combines the willingness and ability to pay of *all* consumers in this market. Some consumers, with a high willingness and ability to pay, are located up at the top left of the demand curve. Others, with less willingness and ability to pay, are located further down along the demand curve. Let me explain.

To read this demand curve as a marginal benefit curve, start with a quantity and go up and over to see the maximum price someone is willing and able to pay for that unit. For the 150th piercing, going up to the marginal benefit curve and over to the vertical axis tells us that someone is willing and able to pay $90 for that 150th piercing.

When the market-clearing price settles at $60, every consumer pays the same price — $60 per piercing. So the consumer who buys the 150th piercing gets an extra $30 worth of benefit ($90 − $60 = $30) — money that she was willing to pay but doesn't have to. On the graph in Figure 4.8, that extra benefit is the vertical distance between the marginal benefit curve and the market price.

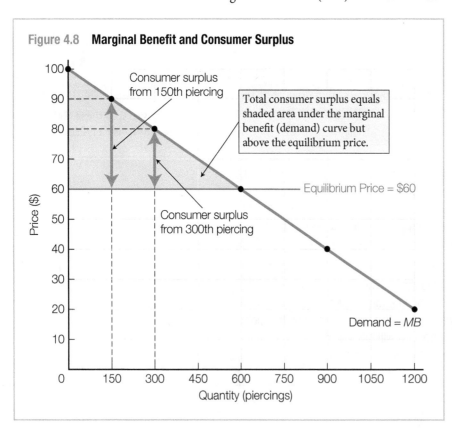

Figure 4.8 Marginal Benefit and Consumer Surplus

Consumer surplus from 150th piercing

Total consumer surplus equals shaded area under the marginal benefit (demand) curve but above the equilibrium price.

Consumer surplus from 300th piercing

Equilibrium Price = $60

Demand = *MB*

Price ($) / Quantity (piercings)

Economists call this extra benefit **consumer surplus** — the difference between the amount a consumer is willing and able to pay, and the price actually paid. If we combine the consumer surplus for every piercing sold, from 1 to 600 piercings, the consumer surplus equals the green shaded area under the marginal benefit (demand) curve, but above the market price.

Did you ever go to a store where the receipt shows the total amount that you saved — the difference between the regular price and the sale price, added up for all of your purchases? Consumer surplus is like that total "saving." The green area under the marginal benefit curve but above the equilibrium price is total consumer surplus — the extra money all consumers were willing and able to pay for piercings but didn't have to. A bargain!

Producer Surplus

The market supply curve in Figure 4.1 on page 81 is also a marginal cost curve. Figure 4.9 reproduces the market supply curve in Figure 4.1 and labels it as a marginal cost (*MC*) curve. A *market* supply curve combines the supply decisions of *all* businesses in a market — the minimum prices businesses are willing to

accept, covering all marginal opportunity costs of production, in order to supply piercings in this market. Businesses, with low marginal opportunity costs of production, are located down at the bottom of the supply curve. Others, with higher marginal opportunity costs of production, are located further up the supply curve.

To read the supply curve in Figure 4.9 as a marginal cost curve, start with a quantity and go up and over to see the minimum price a business is willing to accept for producing that unit. For the 300th piercing, going up to the marginal cost curve and over to the vertical axis tells us that some business is willing to accept $30 for supplying that 300th piercing.

But when the market-clearing price settles at $60, every business receives

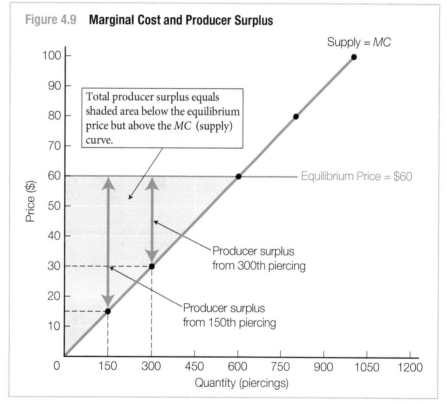

Figure 4.9   **Marginal Cost and Producer Surplus**

$60 per piercing. So the business that was willing to sell the 300th piercing at $20 is getting an extra $40 worth of revenue ($60 − $20 = $40) over its marginal costs. On the graph, that extra revenue above marginal cost is the vertical distance between the marginal cost curve and the market price.

Economists call this extra revenue **producer surplus** — the difference between the amount a producer is willing to accept, and the price actually received. If we combine the producer surplus for every piercing sold, from 1 to 600 piercings, the producer surplus equals the shaded blue area below the market price but above the marginal cost (supply) curve.

Producer surplus represents the revenues that are greater than marginal opportunity costs of production when selling at the equilibrium price.

Economic Efficiency

When markets work well, producing the right products and services that consumers want, at competitive prices that are profitable for businesses, everyone is happy. This outcome is the miracle of markets.

But happiness is relative. How do we know there isn't a better outcome out there? *Consumer surplus* and *producer surplus* are useful measures for comparing outcomes.

Figure 4.10 combines the demand (marginal benefit) and the supply (marginal cost) curves from Figures 4.8 and 4.9.

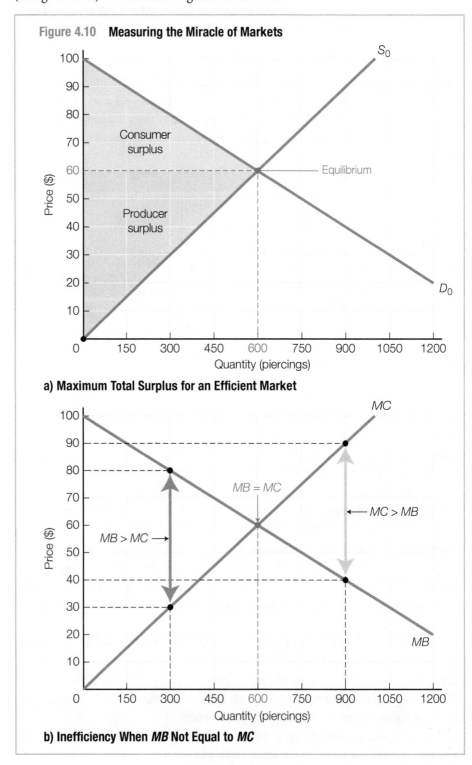

Figure 4.10   Measuring the Miracle of Markets

a) Maximum Total Surplus for an Efficient Market

b) Inefficiency When *MB* Not Equal to *MC*

Combining the green area of consumer surplus and the blue area of producer surplus — the total shaded area in Figure 4.10a — gives us the **total surplus**. The quantity of piercings that results in the "best" outcome is the quantity with the largest total surplus.

The invisible hand leads smart consumers and businesses to the outcome with the largest total surplus. This comes from following Key 1: Choose only when additional benefits are greater than additional *opportunity costs*. Figure 4.10b is key for understanding why.

ADDITIONAL BENEFITS VS. OPPORTUNITY COSTS

Marginal Benefit Greater Than Marginal Cost   In Figure 4.10b, look at the quantity of 300 piercings and compare marginal benefits and marginal costs. Go up to the marginal benefit curve and over to price. Some consumer is willing and able to pay $80 for that 300th piercing. Now go up to the marginal cost curve and over to price. A business is willing to produce that 300th piercing for a price of $30. Marginal benefit ($80) is greater than marginal cost ($30) for the 300th piercing.

Will this 300th piercing be produced and sold? Yes, because there is a mutually beneficial trade. With a consumer willing and able to pay $80, and a business willing to accept $30, an exchange takes place. The consumer and the business are both better off. For every quantity between 1 and 600 piercings, marginal benefit is greater than marginal cost, and it is smart for both consumers and businesses to trade dollars for piercings. The self-interest of consumers and producers increases output and sales until the quantity reaches 600 piercings and the price settles at $60 per piercing.

Marginal Cost Greater Than Marginal Benefit   The story is reversed for any quantities greater than 600 piercings. Again, look at Figure 4.10b. Start at the quantity of 900 piercings, go up to the marginal benefit curve and over to price. Some consumer is willing and able to pay $40 for that 900th piercing. Now go up to the marginal cost curve and over to price. A business will only produce that 900th piercing for a price of $90. Marginal cost ($90) is greater than marginal benefit ($40) for the 900th piercing.

Will this 900th piercing be produced and sold? Not if consumers and businesses are making smart choices. A consumer is willing and able to pay only $40 for that piercing, but a business needs at least $90 for it. No mutually beneficial trade is possible. There will *not* be an exchange.

For every quantity greater than 600 piercings, marginal cost is greater than marginal benefit. There are no mutually beneficial trades. If output was more than 600 piercings, people would *not* be making smart choices. Self-interest reduces output and sales until the quantity decreases to 600 piercings, and the price settles at $60 per piercing.

Comparing Total Surplus Figure 4.11 shows the total surplus for these examples of outputs of 300 piercings (Figure 4.11a) and 900 piercings (Figure 4.11b).

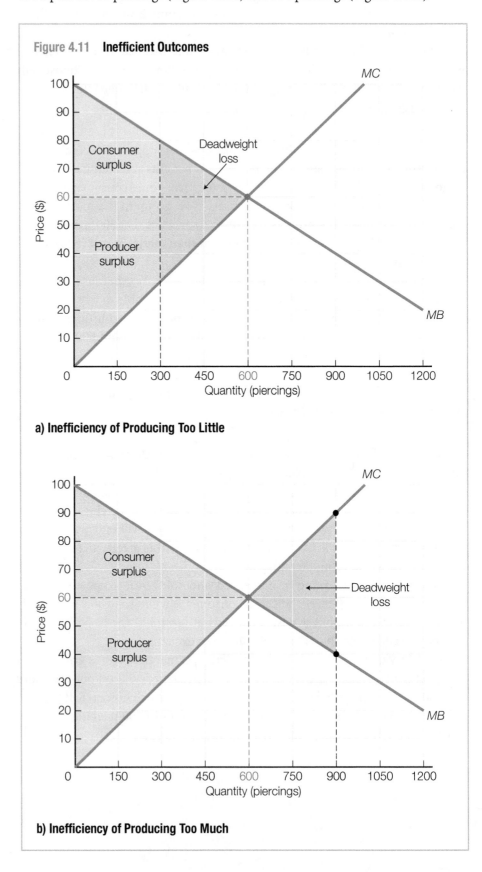

Figure 4.11 **Inefficient Outcomes**

a) **Inefficiency of Producing Too Little**

b) **Inefficiency of Producing Too Much**

The total surplus for 300 piercings (Figure 4.11a) is the areas of consumer surplus (green) plus producer surplus (blue). That total area is less than total surplus for 600 piercings in Figure 4.10a. The difference between the two areas of total surplus is the grey triangle in Figure 4.11a labelled **deadweight loss**. The output of 300 piercings is *inefficient* because there are mutually beneficial trades that are *not* happening. Producing and selling all piercings between 300 and 600 would make both consumers and producers better off because marginal benefits are greater than marginal costs. A society that stopped producing at 300 piercings would not be making the best use of its scarce resources. This inefficiency is *deadweight loss* — the decrease in total surplus compared to an efficient market outcome.

The output of 900 piercings (Figure 4.11b) also results in a deadweight loss, but from producing too *many* piercings relative to the economically efficient outcome. The grey deadweight loss triangle represents the not-smart use of resources, which cost more than the benefits they provide. This deadweight loss must be subtracted from the green consumer and blue producer surplus areas. Again, the total surplus is less than the total surplus for 600 piercings.

Efficient Market Outcome   An **efficient market outcome** does more than just coordinate smart choices of businesses and consumers to produce the miracle of markets. Consumers buy only products and services where marginal benefit is greater than price. These products and services are produced at the lowest cost, and their price just covers all opportunity costs of production. This is the outcome where the demand (marginal benefit) curve and supply (marginal cost) curve intersect.

Marginal benefit equals marginal cost at the quantity of an efficient market outcome. The benefit that consumers get from the last unit bought just equals the marginal cost of producing that unit. For all units up to the last unit, there is consumer surplus because marginal benefit is greater than marginal cost. For all units up to the last unit, there is producer surplus because price is greater than marginal cost. Total surplus = consumer surplus plus producer surplus — at the equilibrium quantity is greater than for any other outcome.

Too Good to Be True?   If the efficient market outcome seems too good to always be true, you are right. Sometimes markets fail to produce such desirable, efficient outcomes. Some inefficiencies result from unintended consequences of government policies like rent controls (see Chapter 6). Other inefficiencies result from monopoly power (see Chapters 9 and 10) or externalities (see Chapter 11). We will use the concepts of consumer surplus and producer surplus in those chapters to measure inefficiencies from market failures.

Refresh 4.5

1. "At the quantity of an efficient market outcome, marginal benefit equals marginal cost." Explain this statement in your own words.

2. In the market for e-readers, at the prices of $40, $60, $80, $100, and $120, the following quantities are demanded: 2000, 1600, 1200, 800, and 600 units. The quantities supplied at those prices are 400, 800, 1200, 1600, and 2000 units. Draw a graph of this market. For the 800th unit, what is the consumer surplus? What is the producer surplus ?

3. For the e-reader market above, explain the reduction in total surplus that happens if the quantity of output increases beyond the efficient market outcome.

Study Guide

CHAPTER 4 SUMMARY

4.1 What's a Market?

Markets connect competition between buyers, competition between sellers, and cooperation between buyers and sellers. Government guarantees of property rights allow markets to function.

- **Market** — the interactions between buyers and sellers.

- Because any purchase or sale is voluntary, an exchange between a buyer and seller happens only when both sides end up better off.
  - Buyers are better off when businesses supply products or services that provide satisfaction (marginal benefit) that is at least as great as the price paid.
  - Sellers are better off when the price received is at least as great as marginal opportunity costs.

- **Property rights** — legally enforceable guarantees of ownership of physical, financial, and intellectual property.

4.2 Where Do Prices Come From?
Price Signals from Combining Demand and Supply

When there are shortages, competition between buyers drives prices up. When there are surpluses, competition between sellers drives prices down.

- Prices are the outcome of a market process of competing bids (from buyers) and offers (from sellers).

- When the market price turns out to be too low:
  - **shortage, or excess demand** — quantity demanded exceeds quantity supplied.
  - shortages create pressure for prices to rise.
  - rising prices provide signals and incentives for businesses to increase quantity supplied and for consumers to decrease quantity demanded, eliminating the shortage.

- When the market price turns out to be too high:
  - **surplus, or excess supply** — quantity supplied exceeds quantity demanded.
  - surpluses create pressure for prices to fall.
  - falling prices provide signals and incentives for businesses to decrease quantity supplied and for consumers to increase quantity demanded, eliminating the surplus.

- Even when prices don't change, shortages and surpluses also create incentives for frequent *quantity adjustments* to better coordinate smart choices of businesses and consumers.

4.3 When Prices Sit Still:
Market-Clearing or Equilibrium Prices

Market-clearing or equilibrium prices balance quantity demanded and quantity supplied, coordinating the smart choices of consumers and businesses.

- The price that coordinates the smart choices of consumers and businesses has two names:
  - **market-clearing price** — the price that equalizes quantity demanded and quantity supplied.
  - **equilibrium price** — the price that balances forces of competition and cooperation, so that there is no tendency for change.

- Price signals in markets create incentives, so that while each person acts only in her own self-interest, the result (coordinated through Adam Smith's invisible hand of competition) is the miracle of continuous, ever-changing production of the products and services we want.

4.4 Moving Targets: What Happens When Demand and Supply Change?

When demand or supply change, equilibrium prices and quantities change. The price changes cause businesses and consumers to adjust their smart choices. Well-functioning markets supply the changed products and services demanded.

- For a change in demand (changes in preferences, prices of related products, income, expected future prices, number of consumers)
  - an increase in demand (rightward shift of demand curve) causes a rise in the equilibrium price, and an increase in quantity supplied.
  - a decrease in demand (leftward shift of demand curve) causes a fall in the equilibrium price, and a decrease in quantity supplied.
- For a change in supply (changes in technology, environment, prices of inputs, prices of related products produced, expected future prices, number of businesses)
  - an increase in supply (rightward shift of supply curve) causes a fall in the equilibrium price and an increase in quantity demanded.
  - a decrease in supply (leftward shift of supply curve) causes a rise in the equilibrium price and a decrease in quantity demanded.
- When both demand and supply change at the same time, we can predict the change in either the equilibrium price or in the equilibrium quantity. But without information about the relative size of the shifts of the demand and supply curves, we cannot predict what will happen to the other equilibrium outcome.
  - when both demand and supply increase, the equilibrium price may rise/fall/remain constant, and the equilibrium quantity increases.
  - when both demand and supply decrease, the equilibrium price may rise/fall/remain constant, and the equilibrium quantity decreases.
  - when demand increases and supply decreases, the equilibrium price rises and the equilibrium quantity may rise/fall/remain constant.
  - when demand decreases and supply increases, the equilibrium price falls, and the equilibrium quantity may rise/fall/remain constant.
- **Comparative statics** — comparing two equilibrium outcomes to isolate the effect of changing one factor at a time.

4.5 Getting More Than You Bargained For: Consumer Surplus, Producer Surplus, and Efficiency

An efficient market outcome has the largest total surplus, prices just cover all opportunity costs of production and consumers' marginal benefit equals businesses' marginal cost.

- Reading demand and supply curves as marginal benefit and marginal cost curves reveals the concepts of:
  - **consumer surplus** — the difference between the amount a consumer is willing and able to pay, and the price actually paid. The area under the marginal benefit curve but above the market price.
  - **producer surplus** — the difference between the amount a producer is willing to accept, and the price actually received. The area below the market price but above the marginal cost curve.
  - **total surplus** — consumer surplus plus producer surplus.
  - **deadweight loss** — decrease in total surplus compared to an economically efficient outcome.
- **Efficient market outcome** — coordinates smart choices of businesses and consumers so
  - consumers buy only products and services where marginal benefit is greater than price.
  - product and services are produced at lowest cost, with prices just covering all opportunity costs of production.
  - at the quantity of an efficient market outcome, marginal benefit equals marginal cost ($MB = MC$).

Circle the correct answer. Solutions to these questions are available at the end of the book and on MyEconLab. You can also visit the MyEconLab Study Plan to access additional questions that will help you master the concepts covered in this chapter.

Apu Nahasapeemapetilon opens an outdoor iced cappuccino stand on his street in order to sell coffee to neighbours during peak hours of the day. Apu's product is unique enough that it allows him some choice in what price to charge. Use this scenario to answer questions 1 to 6.

4.1 What's a Market?

1. If customers are allowed to steal the iced   **T F**
cappuccinos without paying, this would
still be a market.

2. The price should cover what it costs to   **T F**
make the iced cappuccinos, but not the
cost of Apu's time.

4.2 Price Signals from Combining Demand and Supply

3. In order for price and quantity adjustments   **T F**
to occur in this market, Apu needs to be
aware of the personal wants of his neighbours.

4. If Apu prices above the maximum price   **T F**
that consumers are willing to pay,
he will end up with excess supply.

5. If Apu prices below the maximum price   **T F**
that consumers are willing to pay,
he will lose out on potential profits.

4.3 Market-Clearing or Equilibrium Prices

6. If Apu sets a price that leaves him with   **T F**
no excess demand and no excess supply,
he has found the equilibrium price.

7. When a market is in equilibrium, consumers   **T F**
who are not willing to pay the market-clearing
price have made a smart choice.

8. When a market is in equilibrium, the   **T F**
market-clearing quantity equals the
quantity demanded at the equilibrium price.

4.4 What Happens When Demand and Supply Change?

9. If new businesses enter the steel market,   **T F**
the equilibrium price of steel falls and the
equilibrium quantity decreases.

10. Suppose the demand for earbuds increases   **T F**
while the cost of producing them decreases.
The market-clearing quantity of earbuds
increases and the price always falls.

11. Durham University researchers report   **T F**
Scottish grey seals are having more sex
thanks to global warming. This is
because, as drinking water becomes
scarce, the females must travel farther
distances and other males are able to
seduce them. The market price for seal coat
fur will likely increase.

12. Ontario recently had a ratio of 27 students   **T F**
for each full-time professor, while other
provinces had a ratio of 18-to-one. It is estimated
that Ontario needs 11 000 more professors by
the end of the decade. If universities reduced
qualification requirements to allow students with
college degrees to teach introductory university
courses, this would help reduce the shortage.

4.5 Consumer Surplus, Producer Surplus, and Efficiency

13. Producer surplus is the marginal cost of   **T F**
producing a product minus the price of
the product.

14. Deadweight loss is the difference between   **T F**
consumer surplus and producer surplus at
the economically efficient outcome.

15. The economically efficient outcome has   **T F**
the smallest deadweight loss.

Circle the best answer. Solutions to these questions are available at the end of the book and on MyEconLab. You can also visit the MyEconLab Study Plan to access similar questions that will help you master the concepts covered in this chapter.

4.1 What's a Market?

1. The place where buyers and sellers meet is called a(n)
   a) store.
   b) economy.
   c) party.
   d) market.

2. Voluntary exchange happens in a market as long as the
   a) price is less than the marginal opportunity cost of the seller.
   b) marginal benefit for the buyer is less than the price.
   c) price equals or exceeds the marginal opportunity cost of the buyer.
   d) marginal benefit for the buyer exceeds the price.

3. For markets to work,
   a) governments must establish fair market prices.
   b) governments must establish an online trading system.
   c) governments must define and protect property rights.
   d) all of the above are true.

4.2 Price Signals from Combining Demand and Supply

4. **If a market is not at the market-clearing price,**
   a) prices adjust.
   b) prices send signals for consumers and businesses to change their smart decisions.
   c) quantities adjust.
   d) all of the above.

5. **Which of the following is *not* a quantity adjustment?**
   a) Tim Hortons asking its workers to work overtime
   b) bookstores ordering extra copies of *The Hunger Games*
   c) Leon's Furniture eliminating sales tax on all patio furniture
   d) a fish processing plant laying off 10 percent of its workers

6. **When the price is too low we see**
   a) unsold products.
   b) excess supply.
   c) shortages.
   d) frustrated sellers.

4.3 Market-Clearing or Equilibrium Prices

7. **A price at which there are no shortages and no surpluses is a**
   a) maximum price.
   b) minimum price.
   c) affordable price.
   d) market-clearing price.

8. **In equilibrium,**
   a) the price consumers are willing to pay equals the prices suppliers are willing to accept.
   b) consumers would like to buy more at the current price.
   c) producers would like to sell more at the current price.
   d) all of the above.

4.4 What Happens When Demand and Supply Change?

9. **If demand increases and supply decreases, this leads to**
   a) higher prices.
   b) lower prices.
   c) chaos.
   d) a shortage in the market.

10. **Which will cause prices to fall?**
    a) demand increases and supply decreases
    b) demand increases and supply increases
    c) demand decreases and supply decreases
    d) demand decreases and supply increases

11. **A surplus can be eliminated by**
    a) increasing supply.
    b) decreasing the quantity demanded.
    c) allowing the price to fall.
    d) allowing the market-clearing quantity to fall.

12. **The Children's Fitness Tax Credit was introduced by the Government of Canada to provide parents with a tax credit (benefit) of up to $500 to register a child under the age of 16 in a program of physical activity. Therefore,**
    a) demand for *The Hunger Games* novels may increase.
    b) demand for *The Hunger Games* novels may decrease.
    c) supply of *The Hunger Games* novels may increase.
    d) supply of *The Hunger Games* novels may decrease.

4.5 Consumer Surplus, Producer Surplus, and Efficiency

13. **Consumer surplus is the**
    a) difference between the amount a consumer is willing to accept and the price actually received.
    b) difference between the amount a consumer is willing and able to pay and the price actually paid.
    c) difference between the amount a consumer is willing and able to pay and the amount a producer is willing to accept.
    d) area under the marginal benefit curve.

14. **For any quantity produced, total surplus is the**
    a) deadweight loss.
    b) area under the marginal benefit curve but above the marginal cost curve.
    c) area above the marginal cost curve but below the market price.
    d) area under the marginal benefit curve but above the market price.

15. **If the quantity produced is more than the efficient market outcome,**
    a) deadweight loss is eliminated.
    b) total surplus is greater than total surplus for the efficient market outcome.
    c) marginal cost is greater than marginal benefit.
    d) marginal benefit is greater than marginal cost.

5 Are Your Smart Choices Smart for All?

Macroeconomics and Microeconomics

WE ARE SHIFTING OUR GAZE from individual trees

(microeconomics) to the whole forest (macroeconomics). Microeconomics looks at smart choices of individual consumers and businesses, while macroeconomics looks at the combined market outcomes of all of those individual choices.

According to Adam Smith's invisible hand, price signals in markets create incentives so that while each person (a focus on each tree) acts only in his self-interest, the unintended consequence is the production of all of the products and services we want (a healthy, growing forest).

Macroeconomics questions how well Smith's invisible hand works in a wider context. When all the smart choices of individuals are combined, is the result the best outcome for the economy as a whole?

Consider this example. During tough economic times, many people are unemployed — they can't find jobs, aren't earning incomes, and cut back on their spending. Businesses aren't selling enough because consumers aren't buying — products sit on shelves and profits are down. But if only businesses would hire the people looking for work, those new employees would earn incomes and buy the unsold products. It seems everyone (workers and businesses) could be better off, yet those mutually beneficial exchanges don't happen. Why?

This is the core question for macroeconomics. Do smart choices by consumers and businesses imply that smart choices are being made for the economy as a whole? What does the answer to this question mean for government economic policy; for you as a consumer, a businessperson, and an investor; and for your choices as a voter? This chapter examines macroeconomics by questioning whether microeconomic lessons extend to the economy as a whole.

5.1 Is the Whole Greater Than the Sum of the Parts? Reconciling Macroeconomics and Microeconomics

Explain how macroeconomics differs from microeconomics.

Most years since the 2008 Global Financial Crisis have been dismal for the economies of Canada, the United States, and Europe. Unemployment has remained persistently higher than normal. Over 7 percent of the workforce has been unable to find jobs in Canada and the United States. The situation is even worse in Europe, where the unemployment rate averages over 12 percent, and is higher than 25 percent in Greece and Spain. The unemployment numbers are much worse for people under the age of 25 — see Economics Out There on p. 109.

The Global Financial Crisis and the Great Depression

To understand how we got to where we were in 2014 (as I wrote this) we have to go back a few years. The story of the Global Financial Crisis begins with constantly rising, or inflating, housing prices in the United States (and Canada) between 1996 and 2006. This housing price bubble (you inflate soap bubbles with air; you inflate housing price bubbles with demand) led homeowners, real estate investors, mortgage lenders (a mortgage is a loan to buy a house), and financial institutions to take bigger and bigger risks. It seemed that house prices could only go up, and there was easy money to be made. Banks issued mortgages with no down payments to borrowers who really couldn't afford them (called "sub-prime" mortgages), assuming that even if a borrower couldn't make his payments, the bank could sell the house at an ever-rising price to recover the loan. Banks and other financial institutions bundled these mortgages together and sold them to investors. The investors who bought the bundled mortgages received the mortgage payments. The sale of these bundled mortgages provided more money for the financial institutions to provide even more mortgages, making it easier for house buyers to demand houses, which further inflated housing prices (the bubble just kept getting bigger).

The Global Financial Crisis When housing prices began to fall, the bubble burst, and the value of all of those mortgages plunged. Investors and banks holding now almost worthless assets were forced to sell other assets to meet their obligations, and panicked selling led to broadly falling asset prices and the failure of banks and other financial institutions. Stock market values plunged 40 percent, housing prices kept falling, and in the United States borrowers walked away from houses that were worth less than what they owed on their mortgages. Businesses went bankrupt, the Canadian auto industry was in danger of collapse, and unemployment in Canada in 2009 peaked at 8.7 percent.

The economic downturn that started in 2008 has also been named the "Great Recession" in comparison with the even more severe economic downturn between 1929 and 1933 called the "Great Depression." (Chapter 6 explains that a recession is a milder and shorter downturn than a depression.)

INVEST IN REAL ESTATE

No cash?
No credit?
No previous experience?
No problem!

▲ Ads like this one encouraged people to believe that the price of real estate would go up and up forever. You would be rich tomorrow with no risk by going into debt today. There is a saying that if something seems too good to be true, it probably is. Did this housing market fit that saying?

HOUSING

PERSONAL INCOME

Mike Keefe THE DENVER POST 2005

www.CartoonStock.com.

Anthony Leung/Shutterstock (TV); David Buffington/Photodisc/Getty Images (house); Creatas/Jupiter Images (woman)

Mike Keefe/InToon.com

The Great Depression   As bad as things were in Canada in 2009, they were nowhere near as terrible as the hardships people suffered during the Great Depression. Triggered by a stock market bubble that burst in 1929, economic activity collapsed. By 1933, 20 percent of the Canadian and U.S. workforce was unemployed, and output of products and services fell by more than 30 percent. There were 30 percent fewer products, including food, to sustain a population that kept increasing. The prices consumers paid for products and services fell by over 20 percent. While falling prices sound good to those of us used to rising prices, because of unemployment, wages were falling even faster. And falling prices for businesses are a disaster, as falling revenues make it harder to pay off existing debts, so there is less money to invest in expanding output or improving productivity. To make things worse, there were no government programs like employment insurance, welfare, health care, or the Canada Pension Plan to ease the suffering. The effects of the Great Depression lasted over a decade. It took until 1941, when the government began spending heavily on military production for World War II, for standards of living to return to 1929 levels.

Government Blunders   Governments tried to counteract the downturn, but they took almost all of the *wrong* policy actions, making the downturn worse, not better. Britain's decision to base the value of its currency on the value of gold (the gold standard) raised the value of the British pound relative to other currencies, making British exports more expensive and slowing their sales, contributing to the downturn in Britain and elsewhere. (We will discuss exchange rates between currencies in Chapter 10.) Central banks, especially the Federal Reserve in the United States, implemented monetary policy (coming in Chapter 11) that allowed banks to fail, reduced the supply of money, and made it more difficult for consumers and businesses to restore the spending necessary to turn around the economy. Governments, faced with falling tax revenues, tried to balance their budgets and avoid deficits by reducing spending and increasing taxes (fiscal policy, coming in Chapter 12), which pushed economies further into recession. And governments, attempting to protect their domestic industries from foreign competitors during difficult business conditions, put up tariffs (taxes on imports) that caused international trade to break down, reducing the gains from trade. (We will discuss trade policy in Chapter 13.)

Economics *Out There*

The Youth Jobless Recovery

In a story on youth unemployment, *The Economist* magazine reported that the number of young people out of work globally is almost as large as the entire population of the United States. Youth unemployment rates in countries like Greece and Spain reached levels of 40–50 percent! Around the world, the slow recovery from the Global Financial Crisis has not improved employment possibilities for those under 25 years old.

   Employment for Canadians under 25 was 2.68 million in September 2008 when the financial crisis hit. At the end of December 2013, more than five years later, that number had still not recovered to pre-crisis levels. Only 2.42 million under-25s were employed, and the youth unemployment rate has stayed around 14 percent, about twice as high as the overall unemployment rate.

▲ Youth unemployment worldwide was the cover story in the British edition of April 27, 2013 of the influential *Economist* magazine.

Courtesy of The Economist Magazine

Sources: Based on "Generation Jobless," *Economist,* April 27, 2013, U.K. print edition; "The Youth Jobless Recovery: Good News in Canada, At Last?," Glen Hodgson, *The Globe and Mail,* July 3, 2013.

▲ Unemployed men like those pictured here had to line up at soup kitchens for a meal during the Great Depression. Are food banks today like these soup kitchens?

Toronto Star Syndicate/CP Images

Macroeconomics These topics — business cycle bubbles and recessions; unemployment and inflation; money and the financial system; exchange rates between currencies; government fiscal, monetary, and trade policies — are all part of macroeconomics. *Macroeconomics* analyzes the performance of the whole Canadian economy and the global economy — the combined outcomes of all individual microeconomic choices.

What Happened to the Miracle of Markets?

Believe it or not, I hope you are feeling a bit puzzled by this discussion of macroeconomics, because it should sound very contradictory to what you learned about microeconomics.

Microeconomics *Microeconomics* analyzes the choices made by individuals in households, businesses, and governments, and how those choices interact in markets. We looked at the interaction of those choices (in Chapter 4) and found that markets react quickly to shortages, surpluses, or changes in demand or supply because prices adjust smart choices. Price signals in markets create incentives so that while each person acts only in her own self-interest, the result (coordinated through Adam Smith's invisible hand of competition) is the miracle of continuous, ever-changing production of the products and services we want.

So how does market coordination of smart choices produce not-smart outcomes like mass unemployment, falling living standards, bankruptcies, financial bubbles, and deflation or inflation?

We will spend the rest of this book finding answers to those questions, but let's start with a basic reason why smart individual microeconomic choices may not always add up to smart macroeconomic outcomes.

Fallacy of Composition Sometimes a choice made by one person produces a different outcome from when the same choice is made by many people. Let's look at two examples.

Suppose an individual farmer in Saskatchewan plants more wheat than usual. Prairie weather is perfect for growing, and he harvests a bumper crop. The small farmer's increase in supply has almost no impact on the world price for wheat. The farmer's income goes up with a greater quantity and a constant price of wheat. But if *all* farmers plant more wheat and weather is good around the world, the great increase in supply drives down the world price of wheat so much that all farmers end up with less income than before.

This is an example of the **fallacy of composition** — what is true for one (micro) is not necessarily true for all (macro). Or in other words, "the whole is greater than the sum of the individual parts."

◀ This farmer is harvesting a bumper crop. He hopes to make a huge profit on such a good crop, but his profit will depend on world prices, which depend upon the choices made by other wheat farmers in Canada and the rest of the world.

Paradox of Thrift   This second example is about your decision to save. A paradox is a statement that seems to contradict itself, like "Saving your money might lower your savings." If you save more from your income, your savings will increase and your spending will decrease. But if many people save more and spend less, businesses experience falling sales, cut back production, and lay off workers so that incomes fall. Paradoxically, the result may be *less* saving, because without employment income, people have to withdraw their savings from banks rather than increase them. Economists call this the **paradox of thrift**. Again, what is true for one is not necessarily true for all.

NOTE
"Thrift" means being very careful in managing your money.

paradox of thrift   attempts to increase saving cause total savings to decrease because of falling employment and incomes

Connections between Input and Output Markets

Another way the whole economy is greater than the sum of the individual parts comes from connections between input and output markets. The circular flow model of economic life, Figure 5.1, explains the microeconomic miracle of markets. It also plays an important role in macroeconomics. The model reduces the complexity of the Canadian economy to three players — households, businesses, and governments. Households and businesses interact in two sets of markets — input markets, where businesses buy from households the inputs they need to produce products and services, and output markets, where businesses sell their products and services to households. Government sets the rules of the game and can choose to interact, or not, in almost any aspect of the economy. When markets work well, self-interest and the invisible hand of competition coordinate the smart choices of households and businesses in both sets of markets.

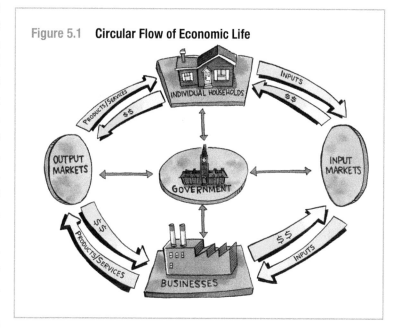

Figure 5.1   **Circular Flow of Economic Life**

Before we look at the macroeconomic connection between input markets and output markets, here's a review of the basics of the circular flow. Beginning at the top, individuals in households sell or rent out their inputs — labour, capital, land, and entrepreneurial abilities — to businesses. In exchange, businesses pay households wages, interest, rent, and other financial rewards. These exchanges happen in input markets and determine your income. Businesses use those inputs to produce products and services to sell to households. In exchange, households use the income earned in input markets to pay businesses for their purchases. These exchanges happen in output markets and determine the value of all of products and services sold.

At the end of the trip around the circle, households have the products and services they need, and businesses end up with the money. That sets the stage for the next trip around the circle, where businesses again buy inputs from individuals in households in exchange for income, then produce outputs that households buy — and the circular flow goes on.

The Macroeconomic Connection   Microeconomics focuses on the interaction of demand and supply *in input markets alone* or *in output markets alone.*

Suppose wages in the labour market — an input market — are higher than the equilibrium wage. Workers are eager to supply labour, but businesses are unwilling to hire workers at the higher wage. There is a surplus of labour. In the labour market alone, wages fall, restoring the balance between demand and supply, and coordinating the smart choices of households supplying labour with the smart choices of businesses demanding labour.

In output markets alone, price adjustments also coordinate the smart choices of consumers and businesses, balancing consumer demand with business supply of products and services.

Macroeconomics focuses on the *connections* between input and output markets and how those connections can break. Falling wages mean falling incomes. If you work 40 hours per week, and your wage falls from $20 per hour to $15 per hour, your weekly income falls from $800 to $600. Ouch! So your demand for products and services in output markets decreases. With decreased demand, businesses experience falling prices of outputs and, in turn, hire fewer workers.

The *connections* between input and output markets can block the coordination of smart choices. In the economy as a whole, income and spending depend on each other. Consumer spending is business income. Business spending is consumer income. If consumers and businesses both cut spending (as happened in the Global Financial Crisis), everyone's income falls and unemployment increases. The smooth trips around the circular flow break.

Money, Banks, and Expectations   As the stories of the Global Financial Crisis and the Great Depression show, money, banks, and expectations play major roles in speculative bubbles that inflate, burst, and trigger the downturns. Microeconomics does not focus on any of these factors. They are part of a macroeconomic focus on the whole economy. Money serves the whole economy, as do the banking system and Canada's central bank, the Bank of Canada. Expectations, like believing that housing prices would continue to rise, are judgment-based and also depend on the state of the whole economy.

Do Market Economies Quickly Self-Adjust?

So which focus is "right?" Do markets coordinate smart individual choices to produce the miracle of the continuous, ever-changing production of the products and services we want (microeconomic focus), or do markets often fail and produce undesirable outcomes like unemployment, falling living standards, bankruptcies, financial bubbles, and deflation or inflation (macroeconomic focus)?

As you probably guessed, there is no single right answer to the question. Sometimes markets work well and quickly in coordinating individual choices, sometimes not. Economists call the periodic ups and downs of overall economic activity *business cycles* (a concept defined in Chapter 6). The following more precise rewording of the question will guide everything we discuss in the rest of this book.

The Fundamental Macroeconomic Question

If left alone by government, do the price mechanisms
of market economies adjust quickly to maintain steady growth
in living standards, full employment, and stable prices?

More simply, if left alone, do markets quickly self-adjust?

Say's Law   Most economists in 1929, at the start of the Great Depression,
believed only the "Yes — Markets Self-Adjust" answer: the microeconomic focus
on the miracle of markets. The belief that market economies would always
quickly self-adjust was based on work by Jean-Baptiste Say (1767–1832), a
French economist and supporter of Adam Smith's views on free trade and
markets. **Say's Law** claims that "supply creates its own demand."

We can illustrate Say's Law using the circular flow model in Figure 5.1
on page 111. Starting at the top, households *supply* inputs to businesses in
exchange for money. Households sell their inputs in input markets because they
want the money to *demand* products and services in output markets. When
households spend all of the money earned in input markets to buy products and
services in output markets, supply does create its own demand. The flow
continues smoothly around the circle.

In the middle of the Great Depression, economists who believed in Say's
Law started to look pretty silly. Economic events were crying out for a better
explanation of the ups and downs of business cycles, especially the "downs" of
decreasing spending, output, and living standards, combined with unemployment
and deflation.

Keynesian Revolution   John Maynard Keynes (1883–1946) rescued
economists' reputations. Keynes, one of the most brilliant and influential minds
of the twentieth century, created the subject of macroeconomics.

In his famous 1936 book, *The General Theory of Employment, Interest and
Money*, Keynes rejected Say's Law as a "special theory" that sometimes holds
true but usually does not. He agreed that given enough time, the self-adjusting
mechanisms might bring market economies back to steady growth, full
employment, and stable prices. But Keynes also believed it could take decades,
during which time there would be serious and needless human suffering. He
believed proper government policy could correct the problems more quickly in
the short run, which was his focus. He is famously quoted as saying, "In the long
run, we are all dead."

Keynes rejected Say's Law as a general truth, and explained the Great
Depression by emphasizing the roles of money, banks, and expectations in
connecting input markets and output markets. Households earning incomes in
input markets are paid in money. If households save the money rather than
spend it, businesses will not find the demand they expect for their products and
services in output markets. This is the paradox of thrift: businesses cut back
production, lay off workers, and the economy goes into a downturn.

Say's Law   supply creates
its own demand

*The long run is a misleading
guide to current affairs. In
the long run we are all dead.
Economists set themselves
too easy, too useless a task if
in tempestuous seasons they
can only tell us when the
storm is long past, the ocean
will be flat again.*

—*John Maynard Keynes, 1923*

▶

John Maynard Keynes, shown here in his study, was chosen as Man of the Year by *Time*
magazine in 1965. He was chosen because his principles helped countries "avoid the violent
cycles . . . to produce a phenomenal economic growth and to achieve remarkably stable prices."

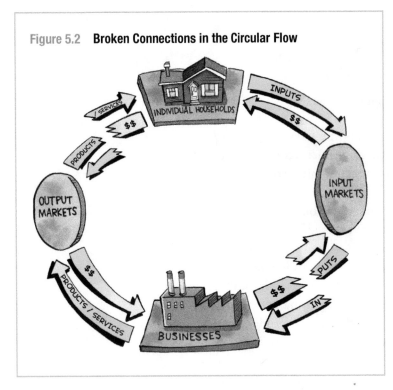

Figure 5.2 **Broken Connections in the Circular Flow**

Figure 5.2 shows possible breaks in connections between input markets and output markets.

With these broken connections between input markets and output markets, Keynes's answer to the fundamental macroeconomic question is "No — Markets Fail Often."

Expectations Expectations can also interfere with the self-adjusting mechanisms of market economies. In the stock market bubble of 1929, or the housing price bubble of 1996–2006, people began to *expect* that prices would continue to rise. Expectations can be self-fulfilling, as long as most people share them. If investors expect housing prices to continue rising, they will buy (and then sell, or "flip") more houses to make profits, and that demand causes housing prices to rise. But when rising prices are based only on expectations, not on economic fundamentals, a change in expectations can quickly burst a bubble. If investors start expecting prices to fall, they sell quickly to avoid losses before prices fall further. That increase in selling causes housing prices to fall faster, leading more people to expect prices to fall, leading to more selling, and a rapid collapse in prices. Expectations, which can shift quickly because they are guesses about an uncertain future, help explain the cycles of boom and bust in market economies.

Introducing Macroeconomics Keynes's work created the field of macroeconomics. If you had been studying economics before 1936, there were no macroeconomic textbooks like the one you are reading. Now that macroeconomics exists, in the next section we will look at modern economists' views on whether market economies quickly self-adjust or not, and what that means for government macroeconomic policy and your living standards.

"I believe myself to be writing a book on economic theory which will largely revolutionise . . . the way the world thinks about economic problems."

—*John Maynard Keynes, 1935*

Refresh 5.1

MyEconLab

For answers to these Refresh Questions, visit MyEconLab.

1. Explain, in your own words, the *fallacy of composition* or the *paradox of thrift*. Give an example of the concept you choose.

2. Use the circular flow model to explain how supply can create its own demand. Who are the suppliers and the demanders in your explanation?

3. Give an example of how the *connections* between input and output markets can block the coordination of smart choices. Explain how you think markets could eventually restore the coordination.

Should Government Be Hands-Off or Hands-On? Economics and Politics

Since the time of Keynes, macroeconomics has made great gains in understanding how the economy works. Economists have learned from past experiences and have developed more sophisticated mathematical tools for extending Keynes's insights about macroeconomic ups and downs. Economists have also developed sophisticated tools for extending Say's insights, and for understanding the conditions under which markets adjust quickly and well and produce the miracle of the continuous, ever-changing production of the products and services we want. Luckily for you, since you are not trying to become an economist, you don't have to master those mathematical tools.

While economists have learned much since the Great Depression, they still disagree — and so do politicians — about macroeconomics. The disagreements between the followers of Say and those of Keynes about the fundamental macroeconomic questions continue today.

Because there is no agreement, you will have to decide which answers make most sense to you. The answers are important because they could make the difference between economic prosperity and recession. Your personal economic success will be affected by the macroeconomic performance of the economy, and that performance is affected by government policies that will be put in place by the politicians you elect.

Let me describe the differences between the two major camps in terms of "Yes — Markets Self-Adjust" and "No — Markets Fail Often" answers to the fundamental macroeconomic question. The answers use the concepts of market failure and government failure from microeconomics.

"Oh, I'm just riding out the cycle."

Charles Barsotti

Market Failure versus Government Failure

Since the Great Depression and Global Financial Crisis happened, you might think that the only reasonable answer to the fundamental macroeconomic question is, "No — Markets Fail Often." Despite these long-lasting business cycles, the answer "Yes — Markets Self-Adjust" is also possible because of the importance of the initial, qualifying phrase, "if left alone by government." Markets can fail, but so can governments.

Market Failure   All economists agree that sometimes markets fail to produce outcomes in the public interest. This can happen because of externalities (section 1.5) or economies of scale that allow large businesses to monopolize a market. In these instances, markets may produce outcomes that are inefficient or inequitable and not in society's best interests. When there is **market failure**, government policy that acts in the public interest can improve market outcomes.

market failure   market outcomes are inefficient or inequitable and fail to serve the public interest

Government Failure   It is also possible that government policy may *not* act in the public interest. Lobbying, campaign contributions, and political pressure can cause governments to act in the interests of businesses, labour organizations, or other special interest groups. Even when aiming for the public interest, government policymakers often lack timely and accurate information for making smart policy decisions. The complexity of the economy, the banking system, changeable expectations, and connections to the global economy make it easy for government policymakers to make "honest mistakes" when trying to solve complex, interconnected macroeconomic problems. When government policy fails to serve the public interest, it is called **government failure**.

government failure   government policy fails to serve the public interest

It is possible that the problems of business cycles or unemployment are caused by government failure — bad policy — not by the market economy. Government failure certainly contributed to the severity of the Great Depression. So even when we see the ups and downs of economic activity, the answer to the question, "If left alone by government, do markets quickly self-adjust?" may still be "Yes" if bad government policies *caused* the failure.

Economists often disagree. There is a joke that if you ask three macroeconomists a question, you will get five answers. So in sorting economists (and politicians) into only two camps — "Yes — Markets Self-Adjust" and "No — Markets Fail Often" answers to the fundamental macroeconomic question — I am simplifying their many differences. Let's look at the two camps, and how their economics connect to politics.

Economics *Out There*

Government as the Problem, Markets as the Solution

The pictured book — *The Financial Crisis and the Free Market Cure: Why Pure Capitalism is the World Economy's Only Hope,* by John Allison (McGraw-Hill, 2012) — is a good example of the view that government failures are the cause of business cycles. The author argues that "It is impossible to have a systemic failure of the financial markets without mistakes by government policy makers being the primary cause." He goes on to claim that the Global Financial Crisis was not due to financial causes but was caused by faulty government policies. One approving quote on the book cover by Charles Koch — a billionaire supporter of the Republican Tea Party in the United States — says "our economic crisis was a failure not of the free market, but of the government." The cure is for the government to keeps its hands off, and let markets self-adjust.

"Yes — Left Alone, Markets Self-Adjust"

Following in the footsteps of Adam Smith, Jean-Baptiste Say, and Friedrich von Hayek (see Economics Out There, p. 118), the "Yes" camp of economists argues that, if left alone by government, the price mechanisms of market economies adjust quickly to maintain steady growth in living standards, full employment, and stable prices.

The "Yes — Markets Self-Adjust" camp allows for some ups and downs in economic activity, and occasional unemployment and inflation, but believes those economic problems are caused by events outside the economy (like natural disasters or wars) or by government policies. The "Yes" camp argues that markets are the most flexible way for the economy to adjust to changes, even if those adjustments take some time. These economists believe that money, banks, and expectations don't significantly affect the exchanges of physical products and services around the circular flow, or block coordination between input and output markets. Through the invisible hand of competition, the "Yes" camp believes markets direct self-interest to promote efficiency and rising living standards.

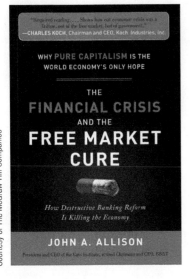

Hands-Off   Believers that markets will self-adjust — usually quickly, always in the long run — see little role for government policy that interferes with markets. Furthermore, this camp believes that even when markets temporarily fail, government policy will likely make things worse, not better. Government failure is more likely than market failure. This camp also sees government policy as a source of economic problems, not a solution to the problems. Therefore, the "Yes — Markets Self-Adjust" camp argues for a hands-off role for government.

Politicians on the right of the political spectrum — Conservatives and Libertarians in Canada, Republicans in the United States — fit into this camp, supporting a hands-off role for government. They believe that, if left alone by government, markets will produce the miracle of the continuous, ever-changing production of the products and services we want, producing rising standards of living, full employment, and stable prices.

As this drawing illustrates, the "Yes — Markets Self-Adjust" camp believes government should take a hands-off approach to markets and let them adjust on their own.

"No — Left Alone, Markets Fail Often"

Following in the footsteps of John Maynard Keynes, the "No" camp of economists argues that, if left alone by government, the self-adjusting mechanisms of market economies are often slow and weak. As a result, business cycles, long periods of unemployment that reduce living standards, and rising or falling prices happen often.

The "No — Markets Fail Often" camp believes that most economic problems are caused internally as unintended by-products of normally functioning markets. This camp emphasizes that money, banks, and expectations can block the connections between input and output markets. While they prefer the flexibility of market economies to any other economic system, these economists see self-interest and greed promoting speculative bubbles that inevitably cause cycles of boom and bust.

Hands-On   Believers that markets create economic problems on their own and often fail see an important role for government policy. This camp believes government polices mostly serve the public interest. Market failure problems can be serious, and market failure is more likely than government failure for this camp. Therefore, the "No — Markets Fail Often" camp argues for a hands-on role for government.

Politicians on the left of the political spectrum — federal Liberals, New Democrats, and the Bloc Québécois in Canada, Democrats in the United States — fit into this camp, supporting a hands-on role for government. They believe that if left alone, markets will produce inequality in living standards, with much economic insecurity and hardship for those who do not possess skills that markets value. Government has a responsibility to maintain a social safety net to support the economic welfare of citizens left behind by markets, especially labour markets.

As this drawing illustrates, the "No — Markets Fail Often" camp believes government should take a hands-on approach because markets do not adjust quickly enough to avoid pain for many people. Broken connections between input and output markets cause markets to fail.

Economics *Out There*

Courtesy of econstories.tv

▲ This photo is from "Fear the Boom and Bust," which presents a rap debate between Hayek and Keynes.

"Fear the Boom and Bust" — A Hayek vs. Keynes Rap Anthem

Friedrich von Hayek was an Austrian economist, a contemporary of Keynes, and an important leader of the "Yes — Markets Self-Adjust — Hands-Off" camp. Although not well-recognized during much of his lifetime, Hayek became famous when

winning the 1974 Nobel Prize in Economics at a time when Say's ideas of self-adjusting markets were being developed by economists in the "Yes" camp.

This video of an imaginary meeting between Keynes and Hayek was produced at George Mason University, which is home to many economists of the "Austrian School" who follow Hayek's ideas. Unlike many online videos, this video is historically accurate about both Keynes's and Hayek's ideas.

The chorus of this "rap anthem" beautifully illustrates the differences between the "No — Markets Fail Often — Hands-On" position of Keynes and the "Yes — Markets Self-Adjust — Hands-Off" position of Hayek:

"We've been going back and forth for a century,

[Keynes] I want to steer markets,

[Hayek] I want them set free."

In the video, listen also for the "paradox of thrift" and concepts coming in Chapter 6 — "$C + I + G$" and "animal spirits." Econstories.tv has many other informative and fun economics videos.

Source: http://econstories.tv/fear-the-boom-and-bust/. Music and lyrics by John Papola and Russ Roberts.

Are "Yes" and "No" the Only Answers? Macroeconomic Agreements

There are important differences between the "Yes — Markets Self-Adjust — Hands-Off" and "No — Markets Fail Often — Hands-On" camps. I focus on these differences to make it easier for you to understand different views of the macro economy. But, as in most things in life, it's not always a question of yes or no. There are also agreements between the camps, so the actual differences are not as extreme as I have described them.

For example, all macroeconomists agree that:

- there is some role for government (setting the rules of the game), but differ on how big a role there should be for fiscal and monetary policy
- prices and markets adjust, but differ on how long the adjustments take (how quick is "quickly"?)
- business cycles happen even without government failure, but differ in focusing on the relatively steady growth of market economies in the *long run* ("Yes"), or focusing on correcting the ups and downs of business cycles in the *short run* ("No")

When you add the agreements to the disagreements, the differences between the camps are more subtle than a simple yes or no. The difference are more a matter of emphasis, not black and white but shades of grey.

Nonetheless, there are real disagreements between the camps, and I focus on them to help you better understand the issues involved. When you read the "Yes — Markets Self-Adjust — Hands-Off" and "No — Markets Fail Often — Hands-On" answers to the fundamental macroeconomic question, don't think about the answers as right or wrong. Think about them as exposing two distinct ways of looking at the macro economy, and as helping you decide how *you* are going to answer that fundamental macro question.

If my goal were to help you to become an economist, I would focus more on the agreements between macroeconomists. But my goal is to help you make smarter choices as a citizen. For that, you need to focus on the differences to be able to vote *yes* for one political party's economic policies and *no* to the others' policies.

The Fundamental Macroeconomic Question: Comparing Camps

Figure 5.3 is a good study device for reviewing the differences between the two camps. We will be revisiting these differences throughout the textbook. By the time you finish this course, you should be able to decide which camp makes the most sense to how you see the world — and maybe even decide that both camps have valuable insights for different macroeconomic events.

Figure 5.3   The Fundamental Macroeconomic Question

Answer	If left alone by government, do the price mechanisms of market economies adjust quickly to maintain steady growth in living standards, full employment, and stable prices?	
	Yes — Left Alone, Markets Self-Adjust	No — Left Alone, Markets Fail Often
Fallacy of Composition	Macroeconomic and microeconomic outcomes the same	Macroeconomic and microeconomic outcomes different
Origins of Business Cycles	Causes external to markets; government policy	Causes internal to markets; connection failures between input and output markets; money, banking, expectations
Which Failure Is More Likely?	Government failure	Market failure
Role for Government	Hands-off	Hands-on
Political Spectrum	Right—Conservative Party of Canada, Libertarian	Left—Liberal Party of Canada, New Democrats, Bloc Québécois, Green

Refresh 5.2

1. What is the fundamental macroeconomic question?

2. In your own words, list the key arguments for each side of the hands-off versus hands-on debate.

3. From your own current experience and economic understanding, which side of the macroeconomic debate do you tend to support? Explain why. What might make you change your mind?

MyEconLab

For answers to these Refresh Questions, visit MyEconLab.

5.3 Adding Up Everyone's Choices: Macroeconomic Outcomes and Players

Identify three key economic outcomes and five macroeconomic players whose choices produce those outcomes.

By the time you finish this book, if I have done my job well, you will better understand the world around you, see more clearly the connections between your personal choices and outcomes for Canada, and be able to use your knowledge to support politicians and policies that you think best for your future. But right now, I'll bet your brain hurts from reading abstract, fundamental questions about markets adjustments and failures.

You will be relieved to hear that this section presents more basic topics — living standards, unemployment, and inflation — topics in the media all of the time.

These topics are the outcomes of the choices made by all of the macroeconomic players. Look again at the definition of macroeconomics, but notice the words now in italics — macroeconomics analyzes the *performance* of the whole Canadian economy and the global economy, the combined *outcomes* of all individual microeconomic choices.

How do we evaluate the performance of the Canadian economy? You guessed it — by measuring the key outcomes: living standards, unemployment, and inflation. And who makes those individual choices that combine to produce these outcomes — the macroeconomics players you are about to meet.

Three Key Macroeconomic Outcomes

Gross Domestic Product   The most important concept for understanding your standard of living, and perhaps the most basic macroeconomic concept, is *gross domestic product* or GDP. GDP is the value of all final products and services produced annually in a country. Chapter 6 defines GDP and explains in detail how it is measured. In general, the higher the GDP, the more products and services there are to satisfy our wants. More products and services per person means higher living standards.

Unemployment   In a market economy, to be able to buy products and services in output markets, you usually must earn income by selling something you own in input markets. For most households, that means finding a job — selling your labour to a business in input markets.

According to the Beatles, "money can't buy you love," but it buys just about everything else in a market economy. That is why being unemployed, and not earning money, is a serious problem. Chapter 7 defines unemployment and explains in detail how it is measured. In general though, more unemployment is bad and less unemployment is good.

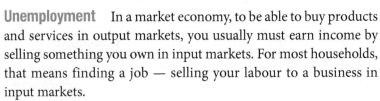

Oscar F. Chuyn/Shutterstock

Inflation   In microeconomics, the price of any one product or service rises or falls with changes in demand and supply. In macroeconomics, *inflation* is a rise in the average level of *all* prices in an economy. Chapter 6 defines inflation and explains how it is measured using the Consumer Price Index. In general though, higher and unpredictable inflation is bad and lower and predictable inflation is good.

Overview   These three concepts — GDP, unemployment, inflation — are important performance indicators for almost every part of macroeconomics. Once you can measure these three key outcomes, you will be better able to evaluate the claims of the two camps of economists — whether or not market economies maintain steady growth in living standards, full employment, and stable prices.

▲ This worker needed millions of dollars to buy a few groceries in Zimbabwe in 2008. While this level of inflation is not common, it happens when a country's currency loses its value. If money is losing its value at this rate, how can a business price its products?

Can't Tell the Players without a Scorecard: Macroeconomic Players

How do we connect macroeconomic outcomes such as GDP, unemployment, and inflation to smart individual microeconomic choices? One way we will move from a microeconomic single tree focus to seeing the macroeconomic forest is to organize individuals into groups. We have already used groups in the circular flow model of economic life. The circular flow model groups individuals into households, businesses, and government.

But the circular flow model needs more information to fully explain macroeconomic outcomes. To get the missing macroeconomic information to make our model — map — more useful for this trip, we must add two more players — banks and other countries with whom we trade.

Here are each of the five players, whose combined choices produce macroeconomic outcomes.

Households as Consumers   Individuals in households supply labour and other inputs in input markets, and use the income they earn to buy products and services in output markets. For our macroeconomic model, we will focus on the choices households make about spending (or saving) the money they earn. Because of this focus on spending, we will rename these players *consumers*.

You have two major choices as a consumer. You can spend or save your money, and you can buy products and services produced in Canada or imported from other countries. With our focus on the forest instead of the trees, we will not look at microeconomic choices like your buying a Samsung or Apple phone, or eating out in a restaurant instead of cooking at home.

Businesses   Businesses hire labour and other inputs from consumers in input markets, and sell the products and services produced with those inputs in output markets. Businesses also make decisions about increasing their output by building new factories and buying new machinery. Economists call business purchases of new factories and any new equipment **investment spending**.

Business input choices include hiring labour or not, and buying inputs domestically or importing from other countries. In selling output, businesses can choose to sell products and services domestically or to export them to other countries — wherever profits are highest. We will not look at microeconomic business choices such as whether a dairy produces more milk or more cream, or whether Ford produces more cars than trucks.

investment spending   business purchases of new factories and equipment

Government

Government   Government, besides setting the legal rules of the game for all economic activity, can choose to interact, or not, in any aspect of the economy. We use *government* to represent all levels of government — federal, provincial, and municipal. But our explanation of government choices will focus largely on the federal government, the Government of Canada.

Government Choices   Of the many possible government choices, we will focus on just two: government buying products and services, and government taxes and transfer payments (such as Employment Assistance payments and Canada Pension Plan payments).

Government policy decisions to leave the economy alone or influence it — hands-off or hands-on — take two forms — fiscal policy and monetary policy.

Fiscal policy (discussed in Chapter 12) uses government purchases, taxes, and transfers to achieve the macroeconomic outcomes of steady growth, full employment, and stable prices.

fiscal policy   government purchases, and taxes/transfers to achieve macroeconomic outcomes of steady growth, full employment, and stable prices

Bank of Canada and the Banking System   The Bank of Canada, together with the banking system it oversees, is a new macroeconomic player we will add to the circular flow model. The banking system takes deposits of money and makes loans to consumers and businesses. The key choice for banks is whether to make loans or not.

The Bank of Canada is Canada's central bank, responsible for supervising the banking system, financial markets, and conducting **monetary policy** (discussed in Chapter 11) — changing interest rates and the supply of money to achieve the macroeconomic outcomes of steady growth, full employment, and stable prices.

monetary policy   the Bank of Canada changes interest rates and the supply of money to achieve the macroeconomic outcomes of steady growth, full employment, and stable prices

Rest of the World (R.O.W.)   Our main focus is on the Canadian economy. But Canada is a relatively small player in the global economy and has trading relationships with many countries, especially the United States. (It is said, "When the United States sneezes, Canada catches a cold.") What goes on in other countries affects macroeconomic outcomes in Canada. After the Global Financial Crisis started in the United States, Americans bought fewer Canadian exports, which helped push Canada into a recession.

Countries in the rest of the world can choose to buy Canadian products and services (exports from Canada) or not, and sell their products and services to us (imports to Canada) or to other countries. There are similar choices about investing money. Canadians can invest money in banks and financial assets in other countries, and the R.O.W. can invest money in Canadian banks and financial assets. Exchanges of exports, imports, and money all require exchanges between the Canadian dollar and other currencies. These choices affect the value of the Canadian dollar, which has an impact on our macroeconomy, the topic of Chapter 10.

Refresh 5.3

MyEconLab

For answers to these Refresh Questions, visit MyEconLab.

1.   List the five key macroeconomic players and the macro-related choices they make.

2.   Use the three key macroeconomic outcomes to describe what a healthy economy looks like. Explain how each aspect of your description helps the economy as a whole become healthy.

3.   Create a simple cause-and-effect diagram that illustrates how a decision of one macroeconomic player could affect you directly.

Focusing on Your Future: Why You Should Think Like a Macroeconomist

If I haven't yet convinced you that your future success in life will be affected by macroeconomics, this last section should do it. What makes macroeconomics personally important for you, long beyond passing this course? Here are the top two reasons.

Your Economic Future:
Reason 1 for Thinking Like a Macroeconomist

Reason number one: Your personal economic success is affected by the macroeconomic performance of the economy — GDP, unemployment, and inflation.

GDP The higher the GDP per person, the more products and services there are to satisfy your wants, and everyone else's, too. GDP affects your standard of living.

Unemployment Unemployment affects the odds of your finding a well-paying job that you also enjoy. When unemployment is high, jobs are hard to find, and you compete against many others eager for the same job you are after. Employers have the advantage in bargaining over wages and working conditions. If you are an employer hiring during periods of high unemployment, you can choose your new employee from a large number of qualified applicants.

When unemployment is low, jobs are more plentiful, and employers are the ones competing against each other for the relatively scarce number of workers available. Workers get their pick among jobs, and gain an advantage in bargaining.

Unemployment tends to be inversely related (when one goes up, the other goes down) to growth in GDP. As GDP goes up, unemployment goes down. When the economy is growing, increasing the quantity of products and services produced, unemployment decreases.

Inflation Inflation affects your standard of living. When prices are rising, the same amount of money buys fewer products and services. If your income is not rising as fast as the prices of what you buy, your income will buy less. Similarly, inflation reduces what your savings can buy — those saved, unchanging dollars buy fewer products and services.

These three key macroeconomic outcomes are closely tied to your material well-being. If you need more convincing about how your self-interest is affected by macroeconomics, here are a few more examples.

Even More Macroeconomics in Your Life Monetary policy and interest rates affect how easy or hard it is to get a loan, how much your monthly car lease rates will be, and how much you will pay for a mortgage or line of credit. Understanding how interest rates are determined will help you decide what a good mortgage interest rate is and which type of mortgage is best for you.

The value of the Canadian dollar affects prices of exports and imports, which in turn affect over a third of all jobs in Canada. A fall in the value of the Canadian dollar makes Canadian exports cheaper for foreign buyers, increasing the production of Canadian exports, increasing Canadian GDP, and creating new jobs in export businesses. A rise in the value of the Canadian dollar makes cross-border shopping a better bargain for Canadians, makes imports like Hyundai cars or Samsung phones less expensive, and creates jobs in Canadian businesses that distribute imports. But the rising value of the Canadian dollar may eliminate the manufacturing jobs you may be training for.

Fiscal policy changes taxes and transfers, which affects how much the government takes out of your paycheque and adds on at the cash register as sales taxes, as well as the benefits you receive if you are unemployed, disabled, or retired.

Macroeconomics affects most parts of your economic well-being during your entire lifetime. Understanding the fundamentals of macroeconomics will help you make smart choices throughout your life.

Your Vote Matters:
Reason 2 for Thinking Like a Macroeconomist

Reason number two: As a citizen, you vote for governments whose policy decisions influence our economy's performance — GDP, unemployment, and inflation. Those policies could make the difference between boom or bust, between steady growth in living standards or a long-lasting recession — in other words, your economic future. Politicians will ask you to support policies based on either a "Yes — Markets Self-Adjust — Hands-Off" or a "No — Markets Fail Often — Hands-On" view of the economy. You can make an informed choice by understanding macroeconomics and using that knowledge to decide on your own answer to the fundamental macroeconomic question. This course (and this book) provides you with the tools you need to choose between politicians' economic policies and therefore your well-being.

You, Too, Can Think Enough Like a Macroeconomist

This course provides the basic information for you to think enough like a macroeconomist — without actually having to become one — to be better able to understand the world around you and make smarter choices for your personal success.

Circular Flow Connections Macroeconomics is not about individual choices, but about the *combined outcome* of those choices. The key to thinking like a macroeconomist, to understand how the economy as a whole works, and how well it is performing, is to focus on *connections* inside the economy and out to the rest of the world. The Canadian economy, with all of its complexities and connections to the banking system, to changeable expectations, and to the global economy, can appear overwhelming. But the circular flow model of the economy, like a good map, helps you focus on the most important connections and information for understanding the answers to the fundamental macroeconomic question:

If left alone by government, do the price mechanisms of market economies adjust quickly to maintain steady growth in living standards, full employment, and stable prices?

Hands-Off or Hands-On? Whenever I present the "Yes — Markets Self-Adjust — Hands-Off" answer, you will see the icon with its arms crossed.

The "No — Markets Fail Often — Hands-On" answer will have the icon with its arms open.

Notice that in the "No — Markets Fail Often — Hands-On" icon, the hands of government hold the broken connection between input markets and output markets, the broken connection between income and spending in the example of tough economic times starting the chapter. Because macroeconomic problems usually arise from broken connections, from *combining* the choices of the five macro players — households, businesses, R.O.W., the banking system, government — the icon reminds you that to think like a macroeconomist means focusing on connections.

Economics does not furnish a body of settled conclusions immediately applicable to policy. It is a method rather than a doctrine, an apparatus of the mind, a technique of thinking which helps its possessor to draw correct conclusions.

—*John Maynard Keynes, 1922*

Refresh 5.4

1. List the three key macroeconomic performance outcomes. In a sentence for each, explain how understanding them could help you make smarter choices for your own future.

2. Explain how a rise in the value of the Canadian dollar could benefit some Canadians but cause problems for others. Would you want the government to control the value of the Canadian dollar? Explain your answer.

3. Over the next week, make a note each time you hear or read about any one of the macroeconomic performance outcomes. Include where it occurred and to what it was referring. Add a note explaining how it might affect you directly.

MyEconLab

For answers to these Refresh Questions, visit MyEconLab.

Study Guide

5.1 Is the Whole Greater Than the Sum of the Parts? Reconciling Macroeconomics and Microeconomics

Macroeconomics examines if smart microeconomic choices by individuals add up to smart macroeconomic outcomes for the economy as a whole.

- The Global Financial Crisis of 2008–2009 and the Great Depression of 1929–1933 involved financial bubbles that burst, high unemployment, falling living standards, bankruptcies, as well as government policy mistakes.

- **Macroeconomics** analyzes the performance of the whole Canadian economy and global economy — the combined outcomes of all individual microeconomic choices.

- **Microeconomics** analyzes choices that individuals in households, businesses, and governments make, and how those choices interact in markets.

- **Fallacy of composition** — what is true for one is not true for all; the whole is greater than the sum of the individual parts.

  - **Paradox of thrift** — attempts to increase saving cause total savings to decrease because of falling employment and incomes.

- The circular flow model reduces the complexity of the Canadian economy to three players — households, businesses, and governments.

  - Input markets determine incomes.

  - Output markets determine the value of all products and services sold.

  - Macroeconomics focuses on *connections* between input and output markets.

- The fundamental macroeconomic question: "If left alone by government, do the price mechanisms of market economies adjust quickly to maintain steady growth in living standards, full employment, and stable prices?"

  - "Yes — Markets Self-Adjust" answer is based on **Say's Law** — supply creates its own demand.

  - "No — Markets Fail Often" answer is from J. M. Keynes, founder of macroeconomics in the 1930s.

5.2 Should Government Be Hands-Off or Hands-On? Economics and Politics

The "Yes" and "No" answers to the question "If left alone, do markets quickly self-adjust?" differ on the fallacy of composition, causes of business cycles, risk of government failure versus market failure, role for government, and political positions.

- Like J. B. Say and J. M. Keynes, economists and politicians today disagree about the fundamental macroeconomic question.

- **Market failure** — market outcomes are inefficient or inequitable and fail to serve the public interest.

- **Government failure** — government policy fails to serve the public interest.

- "Yes — Left Alone, Markets Self-Adjust — Hands Off" camp believes

  - macroeconomic and microeconomic outcomes are the same.

  - external events or government policy cause business cycles.

  - government failure is more likely than market failure.

  - government should be hands-off.

- "No — Left Alone, Markets Fail Often — Hands On" camp believes

  - fallacy of composition — macroeconomic and microeconomic outcomes are different.

  - markets cause business cycles through connection failures between input and output markets, roles of money, banking, and expectations.

  - market failure is more likely than government failure.

  - government should be hands-on.

- There are also agreements between camps.

- Politicians on the political right tend to be in "Yes — Markets Self-Adjust" camp, so government hands-off.

- Politicians on the political left tend to be in "No — Markets Fail Often" camp, so government hands-on.

5.3 Adding Up Everyone's Choices: Macroeconomic Outcomes and Players

Three key performance outcomes of the Canadian economy are GDP, unemployment, and inflation; produced by the choices of five macroeconomic players — consumers, businesses, government, Bank of Canada and the banking system, and the rest of the world.

- Good outcomes are higher *gross domestic product* (GDP), lower unemployment, and low and predictable inflation.

- Consumer choices:
  - spend income or save
  - buy Canadian products and services, or imports

- Business choices:
  - **investment spending** — business purchases of new factories and equipment
  - hiring workers or not
  - buying inputs domestically or importing
  - selling outputs domestically or exporting

- Government choices:
  - buying products and services
  - **fiscal policy** — government purchases, taxes/transfers to achieve the macroeconomic outcomes of steady growth, full employment, and stable prices

- Bank of Canada and banking system choices:
  - making loans or not
  - **monetary policy** — Bank of Canada changes interest rates and the supply of money to achieve the macroeconomic outcomes of steady growth, full employment, and stable prices.

- Rest of World (R.O.W.) choices:
  - buying Canadian exports or not, selling imports to Canada or not
  - investing money in Canada or not, accepting Canadian investments or not

5.4 Focusing on Your Future: Why You Should Think Like a Macroeconomist

Macroeconomics affects your future — GDP affects living standards, unemployment affects the odds of your finding a job, and inflation can reduce your living standards. Macroeconomics also informs your vote for politicians and policies influencing economic performance, and illuminates the important parts of complex economies.

- Your personal economic success is affected by
  - GDP — higher GDP per person allows higher living standards
  - unemployment — affects odds of finding a job
  - inflation — reduces living standards if income does not rise as fast as the prices of what you buy
  - interest rates, exchange rates, and government taxes and transfer payments

- Understanding macroeconomics helps you make smart choices and informs your vote for politicians whose economic policies influence economic performance and therefore your economic success.

- Thinking like a macroeconomist means using the circular flow model to focus on *connections* inside the economy and out to the rest of the world.

TRUE/FALSE

Circle the correct answer. Solutions to these questions are available at the end of the book and on MyEconLab. You can also visit the MyEconLab Study Plan to access additional questions that will help you master the concepts covered in this chapter.

A tall man wearing an expensive suit and tinted sunglasses walks into the coffee shop where you are studying. He notices your textbook and says:

> *"I have a top-secret mission for you. We've detected aliens on the Planet of Plutonomics. Some of these aliens look like Klingons from the Star Trek movies and some look like Yoda from the Star Wars movies. We need you to verify whether our findings about their economy — based on satellite images — are true or false."*

Use this scenario to answer questions 1–15.

5.1 Reconciling Macro and Micro

1. Klingon look-alikes are working for money, and paying money to buy products and services. This evidence suggests input and output markets.   T   F

2. Yoda look-alikes are paying taxes, and some are receiving transfer payments from the government. This evidence suggests that government is part of the circular flow of economic life.   T   F

3. Every government worker on Plutonomics   T   F
is a superstar at solving microeconomic
problems. Therefore, the government of
Plutonomics must be a superstar at solving
macroeconomic problems.

4. Everyone on Plutonomics is a superstar at   T   F
saving. Therefore, the Planet of Plutonomics
must be a superstar at saving.

5.2 Hands-Off or Hands-On?

5. Government policies on Plutonomics were   T   F
based on the special interests of female Yoda
look-alikes rather than on the public interest,
resulting in a high level of unemployment for
men. This suggests that the high unemployment
level for men could have been caused by
government failure.

6. A political party on Plutonomics called the   T   F
Laissez-Faire-Isn't-Fair Party believes that
government policy can improve market
outcomes by acting in the public interest.
This suggests the political party prefers a
hands-on approach.

7. A political party on Plutonomics called the   T   F
Lazy Far Right Party believes that an invisible
hand promotes efficiency and raises living
standards. This suggests that this political
party prefers a hands-on approach.

8. A political party on Plutonomics called the   T   F
Hazy Far Left Party believes that the whole of
Plutonomics is greater than the sum of the
parts. This suggests that this political party
prefers a hands-on approach.

5.3 Macroeconomic Outcomes and Players

9. The GDP per person on Plutonomics steadily   T   F
declined in recent years. This suggests that
their standard of living is increasing.

10. Unemployment on Plutonomics increased in   T   F
recent years. This suggests that their situation
is improving.

11. The prices of iPads, Bridgestone tires,   T   F
slim-fitting jeans, Dippity-Do hair gel,
piercings, and tattoos are all rising on
Plutonomics. This suggests that there is
inflation in their economy.

12. The Planet of Plutonomics does not use   T   F
Canadian dollars. This suggests that they
would never be able to buy Canadian exports.

5.4 Focusing on Your Future

13. Home buyers on Plutonomics will be affected   T   F
by their government's monetary policy.

14. The high level of unemployment on   T   F
Plutonomics suggests that workers have the
advantage in bargaining with employers.

15. The best understanding of the macroeconomy   T   F
of Plutonomics comes from studying the input
markets alone and the output markets alone.

MULTIPLE CHOICE

Circle the best answer. Solutions to these questions are available at the end of the book and on MyEconLab. You can also visit the MyEconLab Study Plan to access similar questions that will help you master the concepts covered in this chapter.

5.1 Reconciling Macro and Micro

1. **What do the Great Depression and Global Financial Crisis have in common?**
   a) Both were great for depression.
   b) Both had a stock market crash.
   c) Both had rising prices.
   d) Both had government programs like employment insurance.

2. **Who is to blame for inflating the housing price bubble?**
   a) Homeowners
   b) Mortgage lenders
   c) Banks and other financial institutions
   d) All of the above

3. **During the Global Financial Crisis, all of these indicators fell *except***
   a) stock market values.
   b) unemployment.
   c) housing prices.
   d) asset prices.

4. **When everyone saves their money, total savings decrease. This is an example of**
   a) the Zero Sum Scenario.
   b) the Fallacy of Combination.
   c) Say's Law.
   d) the Paradox of Thrift.

5. Say's Law claims that
   a) supply is greater than demand.
   b) demand is greater than supply.
   c) supply creates its own demand.
   d) demand creates its own supply.

5.2 Hands-Off or Hands-On?

6. Those favouring a government hands-off approach argue that markets will
   a) self-adjust.
   b) quickly self-adjust.
   c) not quickly self-adjust.
   d) quickly-self adjust if left alone by government.

7. Which political party supports a hands-off approach by government?
   a) Liberal Party of Canada
   b) Conservative Party of Canada
   c) NDP
   d) Bloc Québécois

5.3 Macroeconomic Outcomes and Players

8. The performance of the Canadian economy is measured by the key outcome(s) of
   a) GDP.
   b) unemployment.
   c) inflation.
   d) all of the above.

9. Purchases of new factories and equipment by businesses are called
   a) stock investments.
   b) investment spending.
   c) labour costs.
   d) exports.

10. Transfer payments by governments to consumers include
    a) Employment Insurance for the unemployed.
    b) Old Age Security payments to seniors.
    c) Canadian Child Tax Benefit payments to low-income families.
    d) all of the above.

11. Monetary policy is the responsibility of the
    a) Bank of Montreal.
    b) Bank of Nova Scotia.
    c) Bank of Canada.
    d) Government of Canada.

5.4 Focusing on Your Future

12. Unemployment matters to your personal economic success because it affects your ability to
    a) find a job.
    b) bargain for higher wages.
    c) bargain for better working conditions.
    d) do all of the above.

13. When unemployment increases,
    a) the chance of finding a job decreases.
    b) GDP increases.
    c) the economy is growing.
    d) all of the above.

14. Inflation is a rise in the
    a) average price level in the economy.
    b) value of money.
    c) quantity of products and services in the economy.
    d) standard of living in the economy.

15. Which connection is *not* important for thinking like a macroeconomist?
    a) Connection between households and consumers
    b) Connection between input and output markets
    c) Connection between Canada and the rest of the world
    d) Connection between money/banks/expectations and input and output markets

6 Up Around the Circular Flow

GDP, Economic Growth, and Business Cycles

WHY WAS MY GRANDPARENTS' standard of
living so different from ours? My grandfather and grandmother were born in the 1890s, "courted" on horseback, and lived through the Great Depression. They took in boarders to make ends meet, and their apartment had few closets since, like many people, they had only a few changes of clothing. Although the prices they paid for products seem unimaginably low (10 cents for a silent movie, 15 cents for a pound of sausages), wages were also low. In 1935, the average wage for a Canadian factory worker, working 44 hours per week, was $870 a year. That's about 38 cents per hour!

What determined my grandparents' standard of living, and our much higher standard of living today? The answer has everything to do with GDP — gross domestic product. In this chapter, we will explore the challenges of measuring GDP and comparing Canadian GDP over different years. Changes in technology, productivity, quantities, and prices all affect GDP and our standard of living. Which changes increase living standards, and which cause ups and downs around a rising trend of living standards that allows us to enjoy walk-in closets, 3-D movies, and highly specialized products and services? And what changes in our living standards does GDP totally miss?

While the term "GDP" sounds awfully boring, it is the stuff of the stories you may tell to your grandchildren about what life was like when you were young, during the Global Financial Crisis of 2008–2009, or before driverless cars.

Higher Prices, More Stuff, or Both? Nominal GDP and Real GDP

The "gross" in gross domestic product is not the "gross" you use talking with friends. The dictionary definition of "gross" is "total, aggregate, overall, or combined." Those are definitely macroeconomic words, concerned with the *economy as a whole*. When we measure GDP — the value of *all* final products and services produced annually in a country — we measure the total, or combined, output of the economy.

Many of the individual parts of GDP (products, quantities, prices) can and do change over time, making it hard to compare GDP in different years. To sort out the influence of the changing different parts, economists have developed more precise measures of GDP — nominal GDP, real GDP, and real GDP per person.

Nominal GDP

nominal GDP value at current prices of all final products and services produced annually in a country

Nominal GDP is the value *at current prices* of all final products and services produced annually in a country. Let's examine the key words in this definition using the Canadian economy as an example.

Value The worth, in Canadian dollars, of all the products and services produced.

Current Prices To add together the value of all automobiles, piercings, movies, and every other final product and service, take the price of each and multiply by the quantity produced. Nominal GDP uses current prices, which means that to calculate nominal GDP for 1935, we use the prices and quantities current in 1935. To calculate nominal GDP for 2013, we use the prices and quantities current in 2013.

We can reduce this huge, macro-size addition problem to a single line by using abbreviations. The superscript letters A, B, C, . . . Z represent the different products and services. For each product or service, *P* stands for its price, and *Q* stands for its quantity. Each price (*P*) and quantity (*Q*) is for a specific year.

NOTE
In equations, two letters together indicates multiplication.
So *PQ* means $P \times Q$.

Here's what the calculation of nominal GDP for 1935 looks like.

$$\text{Nominal GDP}_{1935} = P^A_{1935}\, Q^A_{1935} + P^B_{1935}\, Q^B_{1935} + P^C_{1935}\, Q^C_{1935} + \ldots + P^Z_{1935}\, Q^Z_{1935}$$

The nominal GDP calculation for 2013 is

$$\text{Nominal GDP}_{2013} = P^A_{2013}\, Q^A_{2013} + P^B_{2013}\, Q^B_{2013} + P^C_{2013}\, Q^C_{2013} + \ldots + P^Z_{2013}\, Q^Z_{2013}$$

This Ford, a fancy car in its time, cost $580 in 1935. A similar car in 2013 cost over $27 000. Price increases cause increases in nominal GDP. What other factors increase nominal GDP?

Nominal GDP for Canada in 1935 was $4.3 billion. Nominal GDP for 2013 was $1778 billion. That's 400 times greater than 1935! But, before you conclude that we were 400 times better off in 2013 than we were in 1935, look again at the two formulas above. In comparing nominal GDPs, notice that the increase from 1935 to 2013 could have been due to changes in prices (for example, if P^A_{2013} is greater than P^A_{1935} — in 1935, gas was 5 cents a litre), or changes in quantities of products or services (if Q^A_{2013} is greater than Q^A_{1935}), or a combination of price and quantity changes.

The source of the increase in nominal GDP makes a big difference. If all of the increase were due to increased prices, then the higher nominal GDP in 2013 would have the same quantities of products and services as in 1935. We would be no better off. If all of the increase were due to increased quantities, then in 2013 we truly would have 400 times as much "stuff" to satisfy our wants compared to 1935.

Final Products and Services   A final product or service is consumed directly by consumers. A loaf of bread you buy at the bakery, or your new Honda Civic, are final products. The flour that the bakery purchases as an input to make the bread or the steel Honda purchases to make the car are called *intermediate products* and are not included in nominal GDP. Why? The value of the intermediate products is already included in the value of the final products, so to add the value of the flour to the value of the bread would be double counting. This double-counting problem is important, and we will come back to it in section 6.2.

Produced Annually   Nominal GDP for any year counts only the products and services produced in that year. Nominal GDP for 2013, for example, would include only products and services that were actually produced in 2013. Used products, or products produced in previous years but resold later, are not counted as part of nominal GDP. If you resell your 2013 Honda Civic in 2016, its value does not count towards nominal GDP in 2016.

Nominal GDP is measured as a **flow** — an amount per unit of time. Nominal GDP is usually calculated for a period of one year. But economists calculate GDP continuously in order to track how the economy is doing. They provide estimates for each quarter (three months) of a year's economic activity. These quarterly estimates are then added together at the end of the year to measure nominal GDP for that year.

flow   amount per unit of time

In a Country Nominal GDP for Canada includes all final products and services produced within the borders of Canada, no matter what the nationality of the business doing the producing. Honda Civics produced in Alliston, Ontario, are part of Canadian GDP even if the factory is owned and operated by the Japanese head office of Honda. Similarly, Tim Hortons stores in the United States contribute to U.S. GDP, even though the corporation is based in Canada.

Graphing GDP The clearest way to see how nominal GDP changes over time is to put the data into a graph. Figure 6.1 shows nominal GDP (measured in billions of dollars) on the vertical axis, for each year on the horizontal axis. Nominal GDP is the blue line, and you can see the dramatic increases over time. (The red line is for real GDP, coming next.)

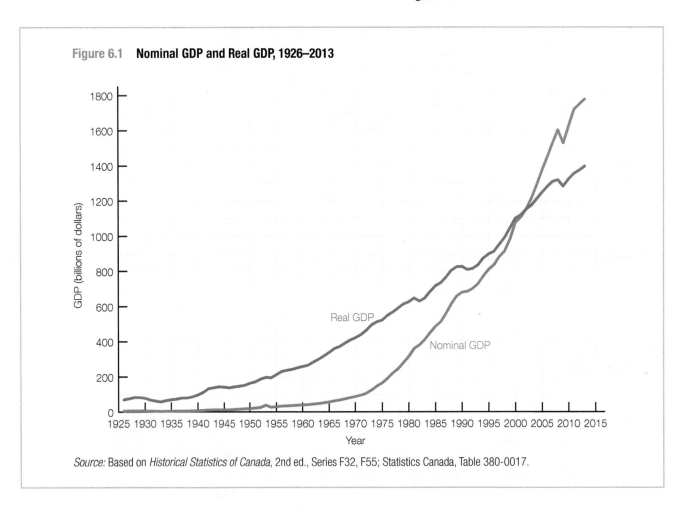

Figure 6.1 **Nominal GDP and Real GDP, 1926–2013**

Source: Based on *Historical Statistics of Canada*, 2nd ed., Series F32, F55; Statistics Canada, Table 380-0017.

You will often see numbers and graphs of nominal GDP in the media. But we are most interested in how GDP affects us — our standard of living. So how do we sort out how much of the increase in nominal GDP is due to price increases, and how much represents increases in quantities of products and services that make us better off?

Real GDP

Real GDP is the value *at constant prices* of all final products and services produced annually in a country. The only word that is different from the nominal GDP definition is *constant* in place of *current*. By holding prices constant, any differences in real GDP between years must be due to differences in quantities of products and services.

real GDP value at constant prices of all final products and services produced annually in a country

The red line in Figure 6.1 uses 2002 prices to calculate real GDP for every year. If we do calculations for 1935 and 2013 like those for nominal GDP but keep prices constant at 2002 levels, then this time for real GDP, we get

$$\text{Real GDP}_{1935} = P^A_{2002}\, Q^A_{1935} + P^B_{2002}\, Q^B_{1935} + P^C_{2002}\, Q^C_{1935} + \ldots + P^Z_{2002}\, Q^Z_{1935}$$

and

$$\text{Real GDP}_{2013} = P^A_{2002}\, Q^A_{2013} + P^B_{2002}\, Q^B_{2013} + P^C_{2002}\, Q^C_{2013} + \ldots + P^Z_{2002}\, Q^Z_{2013}$$

By holding prices constant at the 2002 level, real GDP comparisons eliminate the effects of inflation (or deflation) and isolate changes in physical quantities of products and services only. The red line in Figure 6.1 represents real GDP for each year between 1926 and 2013. Real GDP doesn't rise as steeply as does the blue line for nominal GDP. Real GDP in 1935 was $69 billion and in 2013 was $1778 billion. We had about 25 times as much stuff in 2013 as in 1935, much less than 400 times!

To further highlight the difference between nominal GDP and real GDP, Figure 6.2 focuses on just the most recent years, 2002–2013. Because 2002 is the year we use as a standard for constant prices, by definition nominal GDP in 2002 equals real GDP in 2002. The increases after 2002 in nominal GDP are greater than the increases in real GDP, because nominal GDP includes both price and quantity increases, while real GDP holds prices constant at the 2002 level and only changes quantities.

For measuring the macroeconomic performance outcome of steady growth in living standards, real GDP provides much more useful information than nominal GDP. For that reason, we will focus on real GDP for the rest of the book, just as economists do.

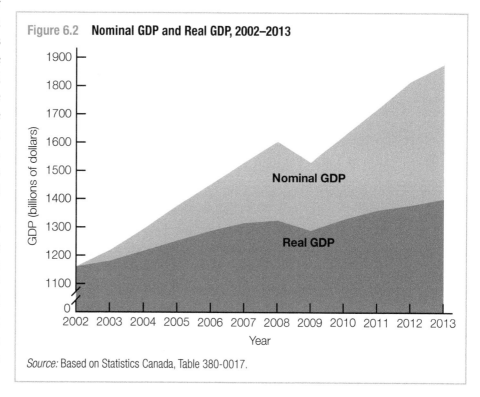

Figure 6.2 **Nominal GDP and Real GDP, 2002–2013**

Source: Based on Statistics Canada, Table 380-0017.

Real GDP per Person

real GDP per person real GDP divided by population

Real GDP is a better measure than nominal GDP for judging living standards, but there is an even more accurate measurement. **Real GDP per person** equals real GDP divided by the population of a country.

Consider the following question. Measured in constant 2002 U.S. dollars, India's real GDP in 2011 was $427 billion and Israel's was $97 billion. Which country was better off? Israel by far. India has almost a billion people, while Israel has about 6 million. If we calculate GDP per person it is only $440 in India, but over $16 100 in Israel.

Real GDP per person is the best measure of a country's ability to meet the material needs of its citizens. Real GDP per person in Canada rose from $7200 in 1926 to $39 748 in 2013. If we graph that trend as a line (coming in Figure 6.3), it rises even more slowly than real GDP because while real GDP was growing, so was the population of Canada, from about 9.6 million in 1926 to 35.2 million in 2013. Each measure of GDP gives us some information about what changes over time — prices or quantities or population. But there are still challenges to overcome in measuring GDP before we can accurately judge the performance of a country's economy in maintaining steady growth in living standards.

Refresh 6.1

MyEconLab

For answers to these Refresh Questions, visit MyEconLab.

1. What is the definition of nominal GDP? What one word is different in the definition of real GDP? How does that word change affect the accuracy of the measurement?

2. In Figure 6.1, explain why the graphs of nominal GDP and real GDP intersect at the year 2002.

3. In your own words, explain why real GDP per person is a more accurate measure of standard of living than nominal GDP. List two factors that could increase real GDP per person and explain why.

6.2   How to Measure GDP: Value Added and the Enlarged Circular Flow

Explain how to measure GDP using value added, and the equality of aggregate spending and aggregate income.

Real GDP is calculated by adding up the value of all *final* products and services produced annually in a country. It includes only final products and services — consumed directly by consumers — and excludes intermediate products and services to avoid double counting.

How do GDP statisticians decide which products and services are final, and which are intermediate, since often the same product could be either? The loaf of bread you buy at the bakery is a final product. But when Second Cup buys that same loaf of bread to make sandwiches to sell, it is an intermediate product. The same problem applies to the tablet computer you buy for school (final product) and the tablet computers Goldcorp buys for its geologists exploring for new gold deposits (intermediate product). So statisticians can't calculate GDP by simply adding up all the bread or tablet computers sold.

You are probably not all that interested in the statisticians' problem, but the solution will help you think like a macroeconomist, achieve personal success, and allow you to make more informed choices as a citizen.

Value Added without Double Counting

The solution to the double counting problem comes from the important business concept of value added. **Value added** is the value of a business's outputs minus the value of intermediate products and services bought from other businesses.

value added   value of output minus the value of intermediate products and services bought from other businesses

Let's look at a simple example, with made-up numbers and only one final product — bread. Going from left to right in Figure 6.3, a farmer grows wheat, which she sells to the miller, who grinds it into flour and then sells the flour to the baker. The baker turns the flour into bread, and sells it to you, the consumer. We will assume the farmer rents her land and pays herself wages, but uses her own seeds and doesn't buy any intermediate products or services from anyone else, so that the example doesn't have to go back in time forever.

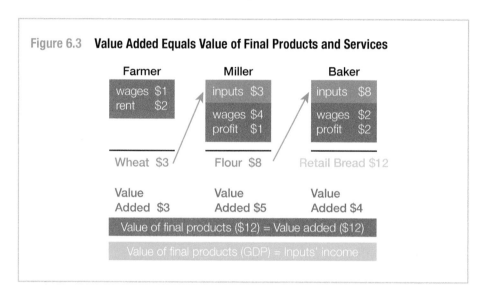

Figure 6.3   Value Added Equals Value of Final Products and Services

Farmer	Miller	Baker
wages $1 rent $2	inputs $3 wages $4 profit $1	inputs $8 wages $2 profit $2
Wheat $3	Flour $8	Retail Bread $12
Value Added $3	Value Added $5	Value Added $4

Value of final products ($12) = Value added ($12)

Value of final products (GDP) = Inputs' income

Here's how the story goes. The farmer pays herself wages of $1 and pays rent of $2 to the landowner. She sells the wheat for $3 to the miller. The farmer's value added is

$3 = $3 (output) − $0 (intermediate products)

Because the farmer doesn't buy intermediate products or services, her value added (in red) equals the value of her wheat output.

The miller buys the wheat as an intermediate product (in blue), pays his workers wages of $4, earns a profit of $1, and sells the flour for $8. The miller's value added is

$5 = $8 (output) − $3 (intermediate products)

The baker buys the flour as an intermediate product (in blue), pays wages of $2, earns a profit of $2, and sells the organic, locally grown, artisanal bread to the final consumer for $12. The baker's value added is

$4 = $12 (output) − $8 (intermediate products)

The end. (Aren't you glad we didn't go even further back in time?)

▲ These consumers are paying the retail price for these final products. The retail price includes all the value added by the various businesses and people who brought the products to market.

Double Counting   There are three payoffs to slogging through these numbers. First, you can see clearly the double-counting problem. If we add up the value of all intermediate products (wheat, flour) as well as the final product (bread) in Figure 6.3, we get $23 ($3 + $8 + $12). The $23 number is not an accurate measure of what this simple economy produces because it includes the value of the wheat and flour multiple times. The accurate measure of GDP is the value of the only final product produced — one $12 loaf of bread.

Value Added Equals Value of Final Products and Services   The second payoff comes from looking at the red value-added numbers in the middle of Figure 6.3. Summing the value added by each of the three businesses, $3 (farmer) + $5 (miller) + $4 (baker), we get $12. That number is the same as the value of the (only) final product or service produced. So to calculate GDP, we don't have to sort out intermediate from final products or services. All we have to do is to sum the value added by each business. Businesses keep good accounting records of their value added in order to make smart business decisions, and because the Canada Revenue Agency (the tax collector) requires such records.

Value Added Equals Inputs' Incomes   The third payoff is important because it helps you think like a macroeconomist. Value added is the sum of all wages paid to workers, rent paid to landowners, and profits paid to business entrepreneurs. (Our simple example doesn't have interest paid on capital.) Value added not only equals the value of final outputs, it also equals the value of all incomes earned by owners of inputs ($12), shown at the bottom of Figure 6.3.

Does this equality between the value of outputs and the value of inputs remind you of anything? [*Hint:* It is circular.]

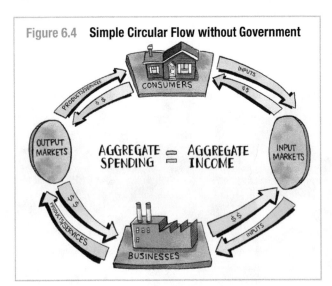

Figure 6.4   Simple Circular Flow without Government

Circular Flow of Income and Spending

Travelling clockwise around the circular flow diagram in Figure 6.4, consumers (households) sell inputs to businesses in input markets in exchange for wages, interest, rent, and profits. The value of all transactions in input markets equals value added, and equals aggregate (total) income in the economy as a whole. The right side of the circle represents aggregate income.

Businesses use the inputs to produce products and services, which are sold in output markets. Consumers use their income to buy those outputs. The value of all final products and services sold in output markets equals the aggregate spending in the economy as a whole. The left side of the circle represents aggregate spending.

The equality between the two sides of the circle, between aggregate income and aggregate spending, is a reflection of Say's Law — supply creates its own demand. Consumers supply inputs because they want to spend the income they earn to demand outputs.

Because the two halves of the circular flow are equal in value, GDP can be calculated using either half. For GDP,

aggregate spending = aggregate income

spending on final products and services = payments to input owners

Enlarging the Circular Flow: Adding R.O.W.

Our final tasks in measuring GDP are connecting aggregate spending to the five macroeconomic players introduced in Chapter 5 — consumers, businesses, government, R.O.W. (the rest of the world), and banks. To do so, we must enlarge the circular flow diagram to include the rest of the world, and then the Bank of Canada and the banking system.

With more players, the diagram gets more complicated, so to help you follow the flows, let's first simplify what is included, and then add the new players one at a time.

Figure 6.5 is a simple circular flow of income and spending focusing on consumers and businesses. Government has been removed from the middle, and the diagram only shows money flows. The key simplification on both sides of the circle is to "follow the money ($)."

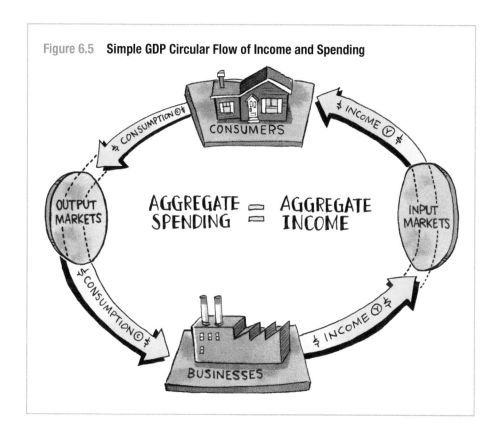

Figure 6.5 **Simple GDP Circular Flow of Income and Spending**

Income and Consumer Spending   On the right side, consumers earn income by selling inputs to businesses. The flow of physical inputs is left out, leaving only the dollar flow of income to consumers. Economists use the letter Y for income. On the left side, consumers use their income to buy products and services from businesses. The flow of physical products and services is left out, leaving only the dollar flow of consumer spending going to businesses. Economists use the letter C for *consumption* spending by consumers.

Sticking with the simplified money flows, Figure 6.6

- adds business spending
- moves government out to the side
- adds the rest of the world to the flow of spending on the left side of the circle

Let's discuss the flows of spending by the new macroeconomic players.

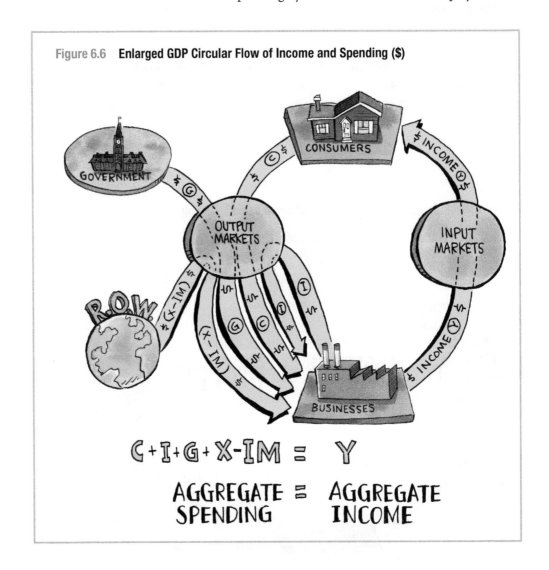

Figure 6.6   Enlarged GDP Circular Flow of Income and Spending ($)

Business Investment Spending   Consumers are not the only ones who spend money buying products and services. When businesses build new factories or buy new machinery, that is called investment spending. Economists use the letter *I* to represent *business investment spending*. Businesses are spending on products or services produced by other businesses, which is why the arrow representing investment spending goes from businesses, to output markets, and back to businesses.

Government Spending on Products and Services   When governments build highways or hire the services of accounting firms, those are purchases of products and services in output markets. Economists use the letter *G* to represent *government spending on products and services*.

R.O.W. Exports and Imports

Other countries around the globe spend money on Canadian products and services. When Ontario ice wine or Prince Edward Island oysters are sold in the United States, those are Canadian exports. Other countries also produce products and services that we import into Canada. Your purchase of an Xbox One or a Montreal hockey rink's purchase of a Zamboni ice-cleaning machine (made in California) are imports, where spending flows out of Canada to businesses in R.O.W.

Economists use the letter X to represent *exports* and the letters IM to represent *imports* (I was already taken for investment). Combining the flows of exports and imports give us *net exports*, represented as $X - IM$. Net exports takes the spending by R.O.W. on Canadian exports and subtracts Canadian spending on imports from R.O.W. That net flow of spending on Canadian products and services is represented by the arrow from R.O.W. through output markets to Canadian businesses.

Aggregate Spending Equals Aggregate Income

The expanded circular flow in Figure 6.6 still has aggregate income (Y) on the right side, and aggregate spending on the left side, but with more details about the different kinds of spending by the macroeconomic players. Aggregate spending consists of consumption spending by consumers (C), business investment spending (I), government spending on products and services (G), and net exports ($X - IM$).

This connection between input markets and output markets, between aggregate income and aggregate spending, is so important that economists have what I call a mantra about it. You need to learn this mantra by heart, and I promise that you will because we use it so often to explain macroeconomic events. The mantra is

$$C + I + G + X - IM = Y$$

This economist is using his own special mantra to gain peace. It's the mantra you should also learn by heart.

Repeat that until you can say it with your eyes closed. It is part of your training to think like a macroeconomist.

Why Subtract Imports?

Since our mantra adds up spending, why do we *subtract* imports? Remember, the circular flow shows how to measure Canadian **GDP** — the value of all final products and services produced annually in Canada. We can measure Canadian GDP either by aggregate spending on Canadian final products and services or by aggregate income (value added). We do not count imports since they are produced outside of Canada. But why not just ignore imports? Why do we subtract them?

The answer has to do with how the other spending flows, C, I, and G, are measured. Some consumption spending (C) is on imports, and some business investment spending (I) is on imported machinery, and even governments (G) buy from other countries. Imports are included in those spending measurements, so we have to subtract them out at the end to get an accurate measure of Canadian GDP.

gross domestic product (GDP)
value of all final products and services produced annually in Canada

Enlarging the Circular Flow: Adding Banks

The last player to add to the circular flow is the banking system. Figure 6.7 illustrates all money flows of all players, and will help us investigate whether individual smart choices add up to smart choices for the economy as a whole.

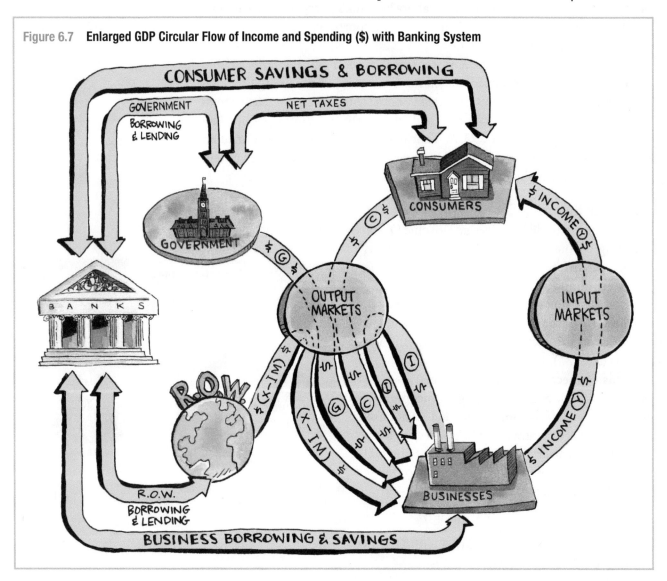

Figure 6.7   Enlarged GDP Circular Flow of Income and Spending ($) with Banking System

Let's look at the individual choices, including those from the banking system, in the order that the players appear in our mantra $C + I + G + X - IM = Y$.

Consumer Choices   Consumers can choose to spend their income or to save it. The green line with arrows pointing both ways between consumers and banks is the flow of consumer savings into, or loans out of, the banking system.

The income that consumers can spend or save is called **disposable income** — income after net taxes have been paid to government. **Net taxes**, represented by the letter T, equal taxes paid to government minus transfer payments (Employment Assistance, Old Age Security) consumers receive from government. The green line with arrows pointing both ways between consumers and government is the flow of net taxes paid by consumers to government.

disposable income   aggregate income minus net taxes

net taxes   taxes minus transfer payments

Business Choices   Besides hiring inputs and producing outputs, businesses make investment spending choices. Long before production can begin and before receiving revenues from sales, businesses must invest in building factories and buying the equipment necessary to start production. Because of the time lag between when businesses build factories and when sales revenues start to flow in, businesses usually need to borrow money for investment spending. In Figure 6.7, the green line with arrows pointing both ways between businesses and banks is business borrowing and savings.

Government Choices   Government collects taxes, makes transfer payments, and spends to buy products and services in output markets. Government also borrows money from the banking system, and can deposit, or lend, money to the banking system. In Figure 6.7, the green line with arrows both ways between government and banks is government borrowing and lending.

Government policy choices are not yet part of this diagram. They are discussed in Chapter 12.

R.O.W. Choices   The rest of the world can choose to buy Canadian exports (or buy from their own or other countries) and sell their own products and services to us as Canadian imports. R.O.W. can also choose to invest money in Canada or borrow money from Canada. The green line with arrows pointing both ways between R.O.W. and banks is R.O.W. borrowing and lending.

Banks   Banks take deposits from consumers, businesses, government, and R.O.W., and make loans to all of the players.

Say's Law with Banks   Say's Law seems to break down if consumers save their income instead of spending it. But if banks take those savings and lend them to businesses who increase their investment spending, it is still possible for all income earned in input markets to create equal demand for products and services in output markets. These banking transactions take place in the *loanable funds markets*, which you will learn about in Chapter 8.

Enough Measuring   The enlarged circular flow diagram of Figure 6.7 allows us to think about all measurements of GDP, as well as the choices of the macroeconomic players. But it is not enough just to measure GDP and how it changes. We have to understand what the GDP number means. Is there a "good" number for GDP, and what causes economic output and incomes to grow? Those are our next topics.

Refresh 6.2

1. Explain value added and how it solves the double-counting problem in calculating GDP.

2. Make a list of the imported products or services you bought last month. Of all of the money you spend in a year, what percentage of it do you think you spend on imported products or services?

3. Explain to a friend who is not taking an economics course why understanding GDP and how to measure it is important in her life.

MyEconLab

For answers to these Refresh Questions, visit MyEconLab.

When Macroeconomic Dreams Come True: Potential GDP and Economic Growth

Explain how economic growth occurs and how it is measured.

Have you ever been lectured by a parent, teacher, or guidance counsellor about not living up to your potential? Haven't we all? Well, if the economy always lived up to its potential, there would be no lectures from economists or policymakers about how to improve performance. This would be the fairy tale version (where dreams come true) of macroeconomic performance — the ideal hands-off scenario from Chapter 5.

No economist — hands-off or hands-on — believes this dream always comes true. But all recognize potential GDP as a key goal that economic performance should aim for in the short run.

A key long-run goal of economic performance is to *increase* the economy's potential for producing products and services. This is the subject of economic growth — how to increase potential GDP over time in a fast and sustainable way. The best economic dreams are of a growing economy.

Potential GDP

potential GDP real GDP when all inputs — labour, capital, land/resources, and entrepreneurial ability — are fully employed

Potential GDP is a reference point for a well-functioning market economy, the outcome if Adam Smith's invisible hand works perfectly. Potential GDP is real GDP when all inputs — labour, capital, land (and other resources), and entrepreneurial ability — are fully employed. When real GDP equals potential GDP, the outcome for the economy as a whole is the same as when smart choices of households and of businesses are coordinated in each separate market. Everyone is getting the most bang per buck for their choices. The whole is equal to the sum of the well-functioning parts.

potential GDP per person potential GDP divided by the population

Potential GDP per Person Just as real GDP per person is a better measure of living standards than is real GDP, potential GDP per person is a better measure of maximum living standards than is potential GDP. **Potential GDP per person** equals potential GDP divided by the population. Potential GDP per person is the highest material standard of living the economy is normally capable of producing if all existing inputs are fully employed.

Look at Figures 6.8 and 6.9.

Figure 6.8 adds the data for potential GDP per person (the black line) to previous data for real GDP per person.

Figure 6.9 focuses on a more recent period of time for potential and real GDP per person for the years 1980–2011.

Notice two similarities between the two figures. First, potential GDP per person increases over time. This is economic growth. Second, real GDP per person fluctuates around potential GDP per person. In some years (2009), real GDP per person is less than potential GDP per person, while in other years (1989), real GDP per person is greater than potential GDP per person.

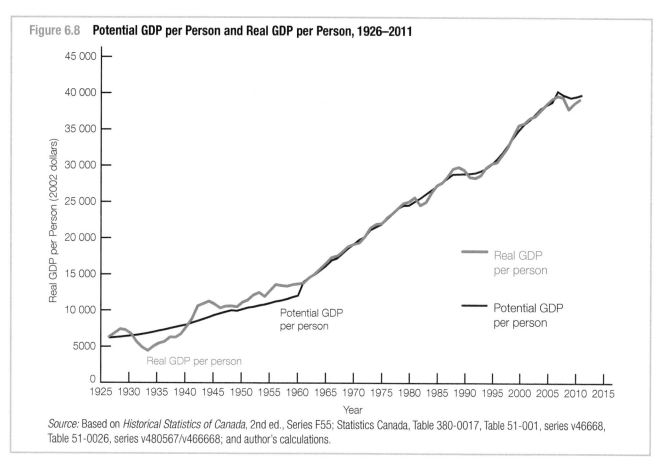

Figure 6.8 Potential GDP per Person and Real GDP per Person, 1926–2011

Source: Based on *Historical Statistics of Canada*, 2nd ed., Series F55; Statistics Canada, Table 380-0017, Table 51-001, series v46668, Table 51-0026, series v480567/v466668; and author's calculations.

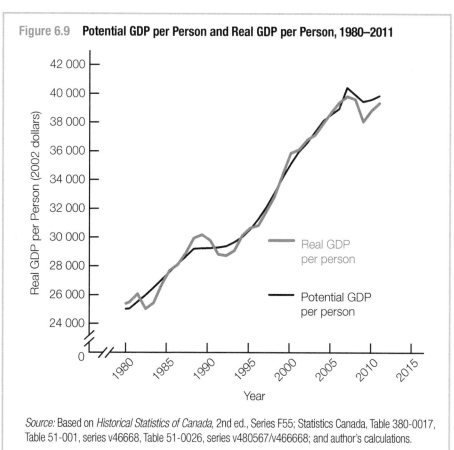

Figure 6.9 Potential GDP per Person and Real GDP per Person, 1980–2011

Source: Based on *Historical Statistics of Canada*, 2nd ed., Series F55; Statistics Canada, Table 380-0017, Table 51-001, series v46668, Table 51-0026, series v480567/v466668; and author's calculations.

Economic Growth

Economic growth is the expansion of the economy's capacity to produce products and services.

Economic growth is caused by increases in the quantity or quality of a country's inputs — its labour, capital, land/resources, and entrepreneurship. These increases enhance the economy's capacity to produce more stuff, increasing potential GDP.

Economic Growth and Production Possibilities Frontier We can illustrate increases in potential GDP per person — economic growth — using Chapter 1's *production possibilities frontier* (*PPF*). Potential GDP per person is like a *PPF*, showing the maximum combinations of outputs that can be produced with existing inputs. Chapter 1, with its micro focus, describes the *PPF*s for individuals — Jill and Marie. With our macro focus, we can also describe a *PPF* for a whole country. The maximum combinations of products and services that a country can produce is the same as the output when all existing inputs are fully employed.

Figure 6.10a shows a macro production possibilities frontier for a whole country. The macro *PPF aggregates* all of the products and services in the economy into two groups. Consumer goods (per person) are on the horizontal axis, and business factories and equipment, also called capital goods (per person), are on the vertical axis.

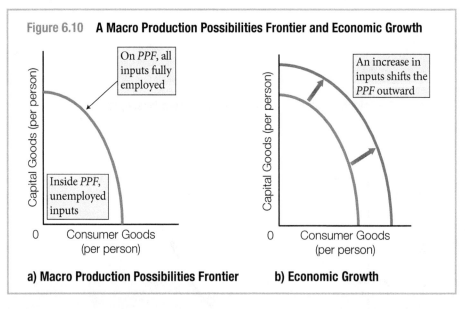

Figure 6.10 A Macro Production Possibilities Frontier and Economic Growth

On *PPF*, all inputs fully employed

Inside *PPF*, unemployed inputs

An increase in inputs shifts the *PPF* outward

a) Macro Production Possibilities Frontier

b) Economic Growth

The *PPF* in Figure 6.10a is the economy's potential GDP per person. An economy that realizes its potential GDP is at a point *on* the *PPF*. Points inside the frontier (possible but not maximum) represent unemployed inputs — labourers without jobs, factories not operating, farmland not producing crops. The economy has not lived up to its potential. Notice that inputs do not appear on the graph. The *PPF* takes the quantity and quality of all existing inputs as given in order to focus on the maximum combinations of outputs that the inputs can produce.

Figure 6.10b shows what happens to the macro *PPF* — potential GDP per person — when the quantity or quality of inputs increases. Think of economic growth as an outward shift of a country's macro *PPF*. With increased inputs, the country can produce more products and services.

Let's look at how changes in quantity and quality for each input contribute to economic growth.

Labour The quantity of labour in a country increases from a growing domestic population (caused by more births, a lower death rate) or from immigration. Even for an unchanging population, the quantity of labour inputs supplied to input markets can increase from increases in the percentage of the population that works. Economists call this the *labour force participation rate*.

Female labour force participation has increased dramatically, as you can see in Figure 6.11. Since World War II, more women have been working for many reasons, including having fewer children to raise; labour-saving household appliances like washing machines and dishwashers; and changing social attitudes about the role of women. At one time, women lost their jobs if they got married. More women now work because they can.

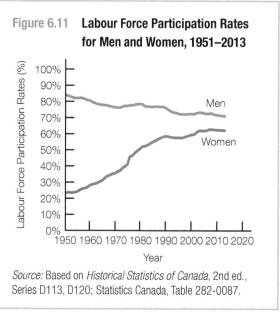

Figure 6.11 **Labour Force Participation Rates for Men and Women, 1951–2013**

Source: Based on *Historical Statistics of Canada*, 2nd ed., Series D113, D120; Statistics Canada, Table 282-0087.

If you have ever taken care of children or been responsible for cooking and housekeeping, you may be thinking, "what do you mean 'more women working'? It's just working outside the household as opposed to inside!" You are anticipating what measurements of GDP miss, which we will discuss in the last section of this chapter.

The quality of labour inputs can increase through training and education. Economists call such quality increases improvements in **human capital** — increased earning potential from work experience, on-the-job training, and education.

human capital increased earning potential from work experience, on-the-job training, and education

Capital Capital is the factories and equipment businesses use to produce products and services. When businesses invest in more equipment to produce output, they increase the quantity of capital. More capital allows workers to produce more. A chef with a food processor can prepare more meals than a chef with only a knife.

When Paola, the owner of Paola's Parlour for Piercing and Nails, replaces her old equipment with newly invented piercing guns doubling the number of piercings her employees do, that is an increase in the quality of capital. Economists call improvements in the quality of capital **technological change**.

technological change improvements in the quality of capital

There are many sources of technological change. Scientists and engineers invent new and better ways of making existing products and services, or new and better products and services. Because new technologies are usually incorporated in new capital equipment, it is hard to separate increases in the quantity of capital from increases in the quality of capital. But both increase potential GDP.

▶

This piercing specialist at Paola's Parlour for Piercing and Nails is using one of the new piercing guns Paola purchased. This technological change allows him to do more piercings in a day. By investing in better equipment, Paola increases the quality of her capital.

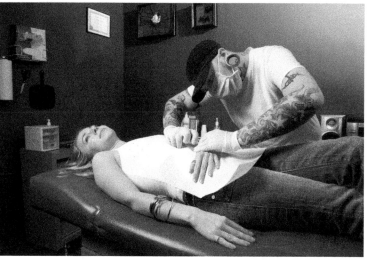

Land and Other Natural Resources Since the national boundaries of Canada are set, you may be wondering, "How can you increase the quantity of land?" Good question. Potential GDP increases with an increase in the quantity of land *that can contribute to production*. Building the railways in the nineteenth century connected markets in eastern and western Canada with the Prairies. With new markets, it became profitable for prairie farmers to bring previously undeveloped land into production. Just as an increase in labour force participation increases the quantity of labour even when population is unchanged, the quantity of land can increase even when national boundaries don't change. Potential GDP increases by *bringing new inputs into the circular flow of markets*.

The discovery of the Hibernia oil fields off the coast of Newfoundland and the discovery of new diamond deposits in Nunavut are examples of increases in the quantity of land and resources that increase potential GDP. These discoveries don't just happen. They are the result of competitive efforts by businesses and entrepreneurs to find new ways to make profits. Government also plays a role by building railways and supporting scientific research.

What appear to be increases in the quality of land and resources are usually due to other factors. When farmers increase the productivity of their land by using fertilizers, the real source of increased output is not better quality land, but better farming techniques using fertilizer as a capital input. Technological change also contributes to increases in the quantity and productivity of land and resources. The invention of new extraction technologies is helping to make Alberta's oil sands a profitable "new" resource.

Improvements in the "quality" of land and resources are due to applications of capital or technological change.

▶ Huge trucks and heavy equipment move earth from this open pit mine in the Alberta oil sands. By finding new ways to separate the oil from the sands, such as using super-heated water under extreme pressure, oil companies increase the quality of their resources.

Todd Korol/Aurora Photos/Corbis

Entrepreneurship When entrepreneurs improve management techniques, corporate organization, or worker/management relations that increase productivity, they also increase potential GDP. Quantity and quality are so interrelated for entrepreneurship that we don't ever try to differentiate them. See Economics Out There for the story of how the CEO of Goldcorp used crowd-sourcing tactics and an online competition to help discover rich new gold deposits.

Expanding the Circular Flow   Economic growth happens when increases in the quantity and quality of inputs expand the circular flow. If we choose a moment in time to start the growth story, there is a fixed quantity (and quality) of inputs in an economy. Economists call this a **stock** — an amount at a moment in time. Think of a stock as a snapshot.

The stock of inputs has labour (including human capital), capital (including the current state of technology), land/resources, and entrepreneurship. With these inputs, households, businesses, and government make their best smart choices. Those choices include, for example, going to school (a household choice), investing in new and technologically improved capital equipment (a business choice), or supporting scientific research (a government choice). As a result of those choices, at the end of the flow around the circle, the stock of inputs has changed in quantity and quality, and so has the economy's potential to produce products and services.

The next year starts with that newly expanded stock of inputs. Households, businesses, and government again make their best smart choices. This process where inputs serve as a basis for choices, and choices then transform the stock of inputs, continues in an ever-expanding circle when economic growth progresses smoothly. When Say's Law holds true, market economies have steady growth in living standards, as well as full employment and stable prices (coming in Chapter 7).

stock   fixed amount at a moment in time

NOTE
Economic growth is caused by increases in the quantity or quality of a country's inputs — its labour, capital, land, and entrepreneurship.

Economics *Out There*

Wikinomics

In 1999, a small, struggling Toronto gold-mining firm was headed for bankruptcy.

Its 50-year-old mine in Red Lake, Ontario, seemed to have run dry. Even with a $10-million exploration budget, Goldcorp geologists couldn't locate new gold deposits that they were almost certain were buried on the Red Lake property.

Goldcorp's CEO, Rob McEwan, made a bold and unconventional decision to make public all the secret and valuable geological data the company had collected going back to 1948. His plan was to use the Internet to "open source" the exploration process.

The "Goldcorp Challenge" offered rewards of over $500 000 to anyone suggesting methods and location estimates for new gold discoveries. Contestants identified 60 targets on the property that company geologists had missed. More than 80 percent of new targets submitted yielded significant quantities of gold — over 8 million ounces! The untried collaborative process saved two to three years of exploration time, dramatically increased productivity, and saved the company. Thanks to Rob McEwan's entrepreneurial decision, the value of Goldcorp's stock increased 300 percent, and he became a wealthy philanthropist.

Source: Don Tapscott and Anthony D. Williams, *Wikinomics: How Mass Collaboration Changes Everything* (New York: Portfolio, 2006).

Measuring Economic Growth Rates

Potential GDP is the dream goal for an economy. But dreams don't always come true, so macroeconomists judge improvements in an economy's actual performance by measuring actual increases in real GDP per person.

There is economic growth when real GDP increases over time. The statistic for evaluating economic growth is the **economic growth rate**, the annual percentage change in real GDP per person. The formula is

economic growth rate annual percentage change in real GDP per person

$$\text{Real GDP per person growth rate (percent)} = \frac{\text{Real GDP per person this year} - \text{Real GDP per person last year}}{\text{Real GDP per person last year}} \times 100$$

For example, if real GDP per person this year is $42 000, and real GDP per person last year was $40 000, then

$$\text{Real GDP per person growth rate} = \frac{\$42\,000 - \$40\,000}{\$40\,000} \times 100 = 5 \text{ percent}$$

The total output per person the economy actually produced increased by 5 percent over the year.

Figure 6.12 shows annual growth rates of Canadian real GDP per person since 1926.

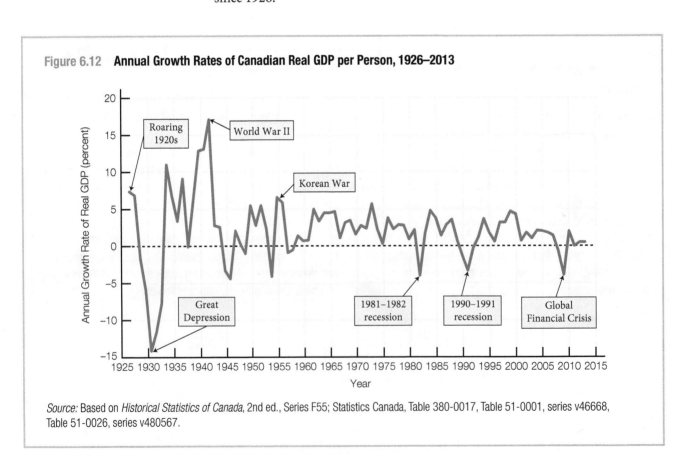

Figure 6.12 Annual Growth Rates of Canadian Real GDP per Person, 1926–2013

Source: Based on *Historical Statistics of Canada*, 2nd ed., Series F55; Statistics Canada, Table 380-0017, Table 51-0001, series v46668, Table 51-0026, series v480567.

Historical Growth Rates The highest positive rates of annual economic growth occurred in the 1920s (7.4 percent in 1927 — one reason they were called the "Roaring '20s"), during World War II wartime production (17.1 percent in 1942), during the U.S. Korean War (5.5 percent in 1952), during the 1960s (4.6 percent from 1964 to 1966), and in the early 1970s (5.7 percent in 1973). Negative growth rates, when real GDP per person actually fell from the previous year, occurred in the Great Depression (−14.1 percent in 1931), in 1982 (−4.0 percent) and 1991 (−3.3 percent), and in the Global Financial Crisis of 2008/2009 (−3.9 percent for 2009).

Over the entire 1926–2013 period, the average annual rate of economic growth of real GDP per person in Canada was 2.1 percent.

Since the purpose of these numbers is to judge economic performance, it is important to understand what the numbers mean. Is 2 percent a "good" number? How much better a number is the 7.4 percent of the Roaring '20s?

What's in a Number? Growth rates for individual years regularly go up and down as a result of business cycles. For long-run changes in living standards, growth rates over longer time spans, like the 2.1 percent over the past 87 years, are more important. Over decades, a market economy whose GDP per person grows at an annual rate of 2.5 to 3 percent is doing very well.

Figure 6.13 shows average annual growth rates in real GDP per person for the industrialized market economies of North America, Europe, Japan, and Australia going back to 1870. Each bar represents a 20-year time span. For most of these 20-year bars, annual growth rates were between 1.2 percent and 2.2 percent. The period of exceptional growth was 1950–1970, with an annual growth rate of almost 4 percent. The average for Canada, of (roughly) the four most recent bars on Figure 6.13 gives the 2.1 percent growth rate.

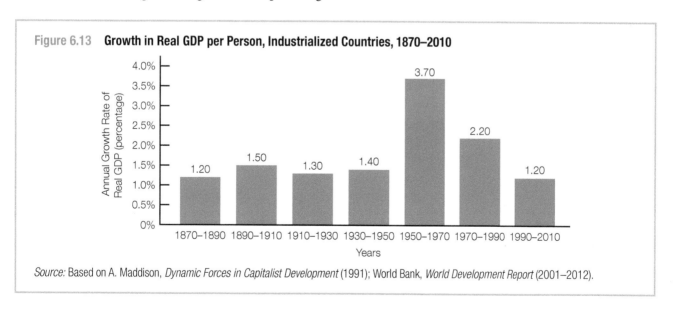

Figure 6.13 **Growth in Real GDP per Person, Industrialized Countries, 1870–2010**

Source: Based on A. Maddison, *Dynamic Forces in Capitalist Development* (1991); World Bank, *World Development Report* (2001–2012).

To take a different historical perspective, the growth rate of real GDP per person in Europe between the years 500 and 1500 was effectively zero! This is one of the reasons this 10-century time span was called the "Dark Ages."

I once thought these small differences in growth rates — 1, 2, 4 percent — didn't make much difference. Boy, was I wrong!

Compounding and the Rule of 70 What makes small differences so important and powerful is the wonder of compounding.

If you put $100 in a savings account that pays 3 percent interest per year, at the end of the year you have $103. If you leave the money in the account, the second year you earn 3 percent again, but this time on the original $100 plus the $3 in interest from the previous year. In year three, you earn 3 percent interest on $106.09, and the compounding continues as long as you leave your money in the account. How long does it take to double your money?

Don't worry — this is not a dreaded word problem from math class. There is a simple rule that answers the question and illustrates the compounded impact of small differences in growth rates. According to the **Rule of 70**, the number of years it takes for an initial amount to double is roughly 70 divided by the annual percentage growth rate of the amount. For our $100 at 3 percent example, 70 divided by 3 equals 23.3 years to double — to reach $200. Figure 6.14 shows the Rule of 70 for growth rates of 1 to 10 percent.

Rule of 70 number of years it takes for the initial amount to double is roughly 70 divided by annual percentage growth rate

Figure 6.14 Rule of 70

Growth Rate (% per year)	1	2	3	4	5	6	7	8	9	10
Years to Double	70	35	23.3	17.5	14	11.7	10	8.8	7.8	7

The Rule of 70 tells us that, with an average annual growth rate of 2.1 percent (see page 151) between 1926 and 2013, Canadian GDP per person doubles roughly every 35 years (actually, 70 divided by 2.1 equals 33.3 years). That means that over the 87 years, real GDP per person increased somewhere between four and eight times. The actual number, which requires a bit more calculation, shows Canadian real GDP per person increased over 5.5 times between 1926 and 2013. We now have over 5.5 times more stuff per person than my grandparents had.

If the growth rate over this entire time span had been 3 percent instead of 2.1 percent, real GDP per person would have increased over 10 times instead of 5.5. In other words, with a 3 percent growth rate, we would be almost twice as well off today as we are currently with our 2.1 percent growth rate. That's almost double the material standard of living for a 0.9 percent difference in annual growth rates! The wonder of compounding comes from the long number of years the compounding is allowed to work. Compounding is the secret to the slogan many banks use: "You work hard for your money; make your money work hard for you."

Productivity, Growth, and Living Standards

Our standard of living has improved over time because of increases in the quantity and quality of inputs, including technological change. Just as real GDP per person is the key measure of our standard of living, productivity is the key *source* of our improving standard of living. **Productivity** is usually measured as the quantity of real GDP produced by an hour of labour. Increases in the quantity and quality of inputs increase labour productivity. Increased productivity allows an economy to produce more stuff, and allows us to work fewer hours to be able to afford the same stuff.

productivity   measured as quantity of real GDP produced by an hour of labour

Work Time per Purchase   Here are some examples going back to my grandparents' time about how much time at work it takes to buy a product. A pair of women's stockings cost just 25 cents in 1897, but workers typically earned about 15 cents per hour. So it took 1 hour and 41 minutes of work to "buy" a pair of stockings. In 1997, a pair of stockings (of far superior quality) cost $4, but because of higher wages, the work time required for purchase was only 18 minutes!

A pound of sausages "cost" 70 minutes of work in 1919, but only 12 minutes in 1997. An electric clothes washing machine cost $110 in 1911, and took 553 hours of work to earn. In 1997, a washing machine (again of far superior quality), cost $338 but took only 26 hours of work to buy.

Two more examples are movies and cell phones. In 1926, a silent movie cost 17 cents and took 19 minutes of work to earn. In 1997, a movie cost $4.25, but took the same 19 minutes of work to earn. There was no change in the real cost of going to the movies (although modern movie technology is better). The first cellular phone, the Motorola DynaTAC 8000X, which looked like a brick and weighed just as much, cost $4195 and took 456 hours of work to earn in 1984. In 1997, a Motorola cell phone cost $120 and only 9 hours of work.

▲ Martin Cooper, a former Motorola researcher, made the first-ever wireless call from a busy New York street corner in April 1973. Cell phones, though, did not become available to the public until 1984. Can you imagine a world without wireless communications?

◀ These two washing machines, one from 1937 and the other from 2012, show how everyday items improve. Changes in technology often decrease the work time per purchase. As well, the newer items are often of much higher quality and capability.

Productivity Is Everything Without gains from trade, there are only two sustainable ways to increase real GDP per person. The first is to put a larger fraction of the population to work — increase the labour force participation rate — as has happened in Canada since World War II. But labour force participation reaches a limit once most people capable of working are working. The second is to increase productivity so that each worker produces more. Sustainable increases in real GDP per person are caused essentially by increases in productivity.

Paul Krugman, a Nobel Prize–winning economist who teaches at Princeton University and writes for *The New York Times*, put it this way:

> Productivity isn't everything, but in the long run it is almost everything. A country's ability to improve its standard of living over time depends almost entirely on its ability to raise its output per worker.

Competition and Creative Destruction Rising living standards come from increases in the quantity and quality of inputs, which increase productivity and decrease the amount of work it takes to buy products and services. As a result, we are much better off than our grandparents and great-grandparents.

What causes the increases in the quantity and quality of inputs? Competition — the same competitive forces of Adam Smith's invisible hand! Business competition is about figuring out new ways to beat your rivals in the market. In the short run, businesses can earn profits by cutting costs, developing new technologies of production, inventing new products, exploiting economies of large-scale production, or finding new or cheaper sources of raw materials and resources.

Over longer periods of time, these competitive actions, which result from the endless quest for profits, make businesses and labour more productive and improve living standards and product choices for consumers. Joseph Schumpeter (1883–1950) was a Harvard economist who saw that competitive actions of business "revolutionize the economic structure from within, incessantly destroying the old one, incessantly creating a new one. This process of **creative destruction** is the essential fact about capitalism." These competitive smart choices of businesses expand and transform the stock of inputs as we move around the circular flow from one year to the next.

creative destruction competitive business innovations generate profits for winners, improving living standards for all, but destroy less productive or less desirable products and production methods

▶

These 1960s high school students are in a typing class using — for them — modern electric typewriters. Typewriters were the victims of creative destruction from newer computer technology. What do you use today that you think will be the victim of creative destruction within the next five years?

The increases in the quantity and quality of inputs, which improve productivity and standards of living, also have an opportunity cost — the destruction of less productive and less desirable businesses and products. Computers destroyed typewriters, online streaming destroyed DVDs and video stores, and robotic assembly lines destroyed the jobs of many workers.

A Government of Canada report entitled "Compete to Win" concludes that

> to raise Canadians' standard of living . . . the key will be to encourage more competition at home and more exposure to competition from abroad. Competition drives the productivity that ultimately sustains our incomes, jobs, and quality of life.

The technological innovations and investments that businesses make to compete have opportunity costs beyond the obsolete businesses that fail and workers who lose jobs. All economists agree that another unintended macroeconomic consequence of these productivity-improving smart choices are the ups and downs of the business cycles.

Refresh 6.3

1. In your own words, define potential GDP per person.

2. In your own words, explain how economic growth occurs and how it is measured.

3. A country can increase labour force participation, which increases potential GDP, by allowing child labour and reducing vacation time. Do you think such choices should be allowed? Explain why or why not. What questions do such choices raise about the quest for profits and improved standards of living?

MyEconLab

For answers to these Refresh Questions, visit MyEconLab.

Boom and Bust: Business Cycles

6.4

When the economy lives up to its potential, real GDP equals potential GDP, and all inputs — labour, capital, land/resources, and entrepreneurship — are fully employed. Since short-run dreams of potential GDP do not always come true, economists and the media have developed a language to describe situations where real GDP does not equal potential GDP.

Describe business cycles in terms of real GDP and output gaps as a target for policymakers.

How to Speak Business Cycles

Chapter 5 described business cycles as ups and downs of overall economic activity. But now that you know about real GDP and potential GDP, you are ready for a precise definition. **Business cycles** are fluctuations of real GDP around potential GDP.

To illustrate the language of business cycles, let's look at the last complete Canadian business cycle around the Global Financial Crisis. Figure 6.15 is similar to Figure 6.9, but focuses only on the business cycle surrounding the 2008–2009 recession.

business cycles up and down fluctuations of real GDP around potential GDP

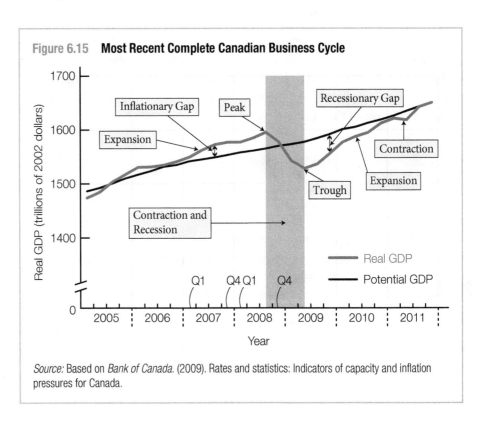

Figure 6.15 **Most Recent Complete Canadian Business Cycle**

Source: Based on *Bank of Canada.* (2009). Rates and statistics: Indicators of capacity and inflation pressures for Canada.

Phases of a Business Cycle The "boom and bust" of business cycles usually begins with the "boom." An **expansion** is any period (measured in quarters, or three-month blocks) during which real GDP increases. Real GDP expanded from 2005 to 2008. The expansion reached its peak in the third quarter of 2008. Just as when you reach the peak of a mountain you start down the other side, real GDP started decreasing after the peak. A **contraction** (the "bust") is any period during which real GDP decreases. Real GDP decreased throughout the rest of 2008 and the second quarter of 2009. Real GDP then started increasing again. The second quarter of 2009 is called the *trough* of the contraction, the lowest point of the cycle.

expansion period during which real GDP increases

contraction period during which real GDP decreases

Notice, in Figure 6.15, the shaded orange area labelled "Contraction and Recession." This nine-month time span (quarter four of 2008 and quarters one and two of 2009) is called a *recession*. The exact definition of **recession** is two or more successive quarters of contraction in real GDP. A short one-quarter long contraction, like the one in the second quarter of 2011, is a contraction but not a recession.

You might be wondering about the definition of a depression — a word that was much used in discussing the 2008–2009 contraction, comparing it to the Great Depression of 1929. There is no agreed-upon, precise economic definition of a depression. Since macroeconomics was invented after the Great Depression, there has not been any downturn approaching that severity. In plain language, the definition of a depression might be "a really, really bad recession." Economists still have work to do on their language skills.

Output Gaps, Unemployment, and Inflation

The language of business cycles focuses on the ups and downs, highs and lows, of fluctuations in real GDP. There are two other important definitions that focus on fluctuations *around* potential GDP — the differences between real GDP and potential GDP.

Look again at Figure 6.15. When real GDP is below potential GDP, as it was for all of 2009, 2010, and the first two quarters of 2011, there are unemployed inputs. Labour, capital, land/resources, or entrepreneurship are not fully utilized, which is why actual GDP is less than potential GDP. Workers are unemployed, factories are sitting idle, and land is not being used. Economists call this a **recessionary gap** — when real GDP is below potential GDP. For any time period, we can measure the size of the recessionary gap as the vertical distance between potential GDP and real GDP. Figure 6.15 labels the recessionary gap for the fourth quarter of 2009, but a recessionary gap exists for every quarter when real GDP is less than potential GDP.

There is an **inflationary gap** when real GDP is above potential GDP. From the expansion of the third quarter of 2005 to the fourth quarter of 2008, there was an inflationary gap. Figure 6.15 labels the inflationary gap for the third quarter of 2007. Not only are all inputs fully employed, the economy is working overtime. As you will learn, this overheated economic activity can cause inflation, hence the term *inflationary gap*. (You might be wondering, how can real GDP be above potential GDP when potential GDP is full employment? If so, good for you! The answer comes in the next chapter. But here is a hint — it depends on the precise definition of *full employment*.)

Both recessionary gaps and inflationary gaps measure the difference between actual output (real GDP) and the full employment output of an economy (potential GDP). Economists refer to both as **output gaps**, which are calculated as real GDP minus potential GDP. For recessionary gaps, the output gap is negative (real GDP less than potential GDP). For inflationary gaps, the output gap is positive (real GDP greater than potential GDP).

Refresh 6.4

MyEconLab

For answers to these Refresh Questions, visit MyEconLab.

1. Describe the sequence of a typical business cycle, beginning with an expansion and ending with an expansion.

2. In the first quarter of 2009, real GDP was $1292 billion and potential GDP was $1331 billion. What kind of gap existed and what was its size?

3. Go to www.statcan.gc.ca to find the quarterly data for real GDP starting with 2012. Do the data show a contraction or a recession since 2012? If so, identify the quarters involved.

6.5   My GDP Is Bigger Than Yours: What's Wrong with GDP as a Measure of Well-Being?

Identify five limitations of real GDP per person as a measure of well-being.

GDP, especially real GDP per person, is the single best measure of economic performance and of material standards of living. Real GDP per person is "the tool" for comparing our standard of living with that of our grandparents or grandchildren. But that does not mean that the country with the highest real GDP per person has the highest quality of life or is the "best" country in which to live.

What's Missing from Real GDP?

Here are five limitations of real GDP per person as a measure of well-being, or quality of life.

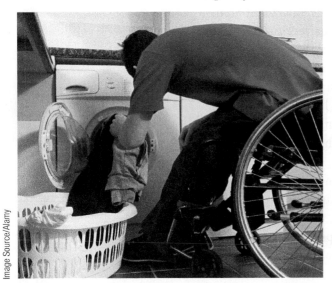

Image Source/Alamy

▲ Working in the home for no salary does not get included in the calculation of GDP. This husband, doing the family's laundry, is certainly working and contributing to the well-being of the family and therefore the country. This is just one example of what is missed from real GDP. What do you do that is not counted in real GDP?

Non-Market Production   Productive activities that are counted as part of GDP must be bought and sold in the input or output markets of an economy. Yet many productive activities that contribute to our well-being happen outside of markets. All household activities like cooking, cleaning, and child care are not counted in GDP statistics. Because women provide the majority of household services, women's contributions to economic well-being are under-represented. In addition, all volunteer services, such as at food banks, in hospitals, and in homeless shelters, are not counted in GDP.

Here's an example of how GDP misses such activities. A high-powered business executive has a chauffeur hired by her corporation. If she falls in love with him, gets married, and he continues to drive for her, but now as a husband rather than a hired chauffeur, real GDP falls. There is no change in the actual service that contributes to well-being; the service simply moved from a market transaction to an outside market transaction.

Underground Economy Activities in the *underground economy* are purposefully hidden from government, either because they are illegal, or are legal but avoid taxes (which is also illegal). Imagine the response Statistics Canada would get from asking a drug dealer, "Would you please tell me the value of final products and services your business produced in 2014?"

Unreported legal productive activities include cash payments for home renovations or repairs (that avoid income tax for the renovator and HST for the consumer), and unreported tips earned by servers, taxi drivers, and other workers.

Economists estimate the size of the underground economy in Canada is between 5 and 15 percent of GDP.

Environmental Damage Productive economic activity often produces undesirable negative externalities like pollution, climate change, and resource depletion. The costs of environmental damage are not included in GDP. Higher GDP is often associated with greater environmental damage. Similarly, when economic activity uses up non-renewable resources like oil, GDP goes up, but there is no subtraction for the fewer resources that are left for your grandchildren.

Leisure When people work more, real GDP increases. But don't you like your holiday time? The more leisure time people take, the lower real GDP will be.

Most European countries have a lower GDP per person than Canada, but have more vacation time. By law, Canadians get 10 paid vacation days and another 8 paid statutory holidays. European Union countries like Germany, Italy, and Spain have 20 paid vacation days, and 10–13 paid statutory holidays. Would you sacrifice some material standard of living in exchange for almost three more weeks of vacation a year? Many Europeans look at how hard we work with pity and feel that they know how to live better. These are personal choices, but regardless of the choice you or Europeans make, GDP per person does not capture the value of leisure.

This woman is paying cash for the work she had done. Activities like this are part of the underground economy. Why might this woman and man participate in illegal transactions?

These women enjoying a coffee in a Parisian café are not adding to real GDP, beyond the value of the coffees. Should we be worried that leisure time does not increase real GDP?

Political Freedoms and Social Justice There is no necessary connection between higher real GDP per person and the benefits of democracy and political freedom. There are countries, often rich with oil or other natural resources, that have high real GDP per person, but limited political freedom.

In such countries, as well as in democratic countries like Canada with market economies, a high real GDP per person does not guarantee an equitable distribution of income. Real GDP per person is a statistical average for the country as a whole. Even in Canada, the richest 20 percent of households had an average income of $135 500 in 2010 (after taxes and transfer payments) while the poorest 20 percent of households had an average income of $14 600.

Growth Rates of Real GDP per Person are Better These limitations of GDP mean that higher real GDP per person does not always means a better quality of life. But economists are still comfortable using a country's *growth rate of real GDP per person* to judge economic *progress* over time. As long as there are no significant changes over time in the extent of non-market production, the underground economy, environmental damage, leisure, political freedom, and social justice, the growth of real GDP per person is still the best measure of *increases* in the standard of living and well-being for a country.

Where Would You Rather Live?

Because of the limitations of real GDP per person as a measure of the quality of life, the United Nations Development Programme developed a broader measure of well-being called the Human Development Index (HDI). The HDI weights equally life expectancy, educational achievement, and income.

In the most recent HDI report, the top five countries are Norway, Australia, United States, Netherlands, and Germany. Canada ranks eleventh. The bottom five countries, out of 186 ranked, are Burkina Faso, Chad, Mozambique, Congo, and Niger.

Refresh 6.5

MyEconLab

For answers to these Refresh Questions, visit MyEconLab.

1. In your own words, explain what the underground economy is. Why is it not included in GDP?

2. More and more people are eating their meals in restaurants instead of cooking at home. Explain how this social trend affects real GDP. How might it affect their quality of life?

3. Of the five factors not included in real GDP as a measure of well-being, which makes the most difference to your personal quality of life? Explain why.

Study Guide

CHAPTER 6 SUMMARY

6.1 Higher Prices, More Stuff, or Both? Nominal GDP and Real GDP

GDP concepts measure the value of all final products and services produced annually in a country; nominal GDP combines changes in prices and quantities, real GDP measure only changes in quantities, and real GDP per person is the best measure of material standard of living.

- **Nominal GDP** — value *at current prices* of all final products and services produced annually in a country. To calculate nominal GDP:
  - $\text{Nominal GDP}_{1935} = P^A{}_{1935}\, Q^A{}_{1935} + P^B{}_{1935}\, Q^B{}_{1935} + P^C{}_{1935}\, Q^C{}_{1935} + \ldots + P^Z{}_{1935}\, Q^Z{}_{1935}$
  - $\text{Nominal GDP}_{2013} = P^A{}_{2013}\, Q^A{}_{2013} + P^B{}_{2013}\, Q^B{}_{2013} + P^C{}_{2013}\, Q^C{}_{2013} + \ldots + P^Z{}_{2013}\, Q^Z{}_{2013}$

- Differences in nominal GDP between years are due to either price changes or quantity changes.

- **Flow** — amount per unit of time.

- GDP includes products and services produced within a country's borders, no matter what the nationality of the business doing the producing.

- **Real GDP** — value *at constant prices* of all final products and services produced annually in a country. To calculate real GDP using 2002 constant prices:
  - $\text{Real GDP}_{1935} = P^A{}_{2002}\, Q^A{}_{1935} + P^B{}_{2002}\, Q^B{}_{1935} + P^C{}_{2002}\, Q^C{}_{1935} + \ldots + P^Z{}_{2002}\, Q^Z{}_{1935}$
  - $\text{Real GDP}_{2013} = P^A{}_{2002}\, Q^A{}_{2013} + P^B{}_{2002}\, Q^B{}_{2013} + P^C{}_{2002}\, Q^C{}_{2013} + \ldots + P^Z{}_{2002}\, Q^Z{}_{2013}$
  - Real GDP uses constant prices for a single year to value the quantities of products and services produced in different years. Differences in real GDP between years show only changes in quantities.

- **Real GDP per person** — real GDP divided by population.
  - Real GDP per person is the best measure of material standard of living.

6.2 How to Measure GDP: Value Added and the Enlarged Circular Flow

Value added solves the problems of double counting and distinguishing final and intermediate products and services, and shows how aggregate spending equals aggregate income in circular flow diagrams.

- **Value added** — value of output minus the value of intermediate products and services bought from other businesses.

- Value added solves the problems of double counting and of distinguishing between final and intermediate products and services.
  - value of final products and services = value added
  - value of final products and services (GDP) = input's income

- GDP can be calculated using either half of the circular flow.
  - aggregate spending (GDP) = aggregate income (Y)
  - spending on final products and services = payments to input owners

- Flows of spending on the enlarged circular flow:
  - C — consumption spending by consumers.
  - I — business investment spending on factories and machines made by businesses.
  - G — government spending on products and services.
  - X — spending by the rest of the world (R.O.W.) on Canadian exports of products and services.
  - IM — Canadian spending on imports of products and services produced by the rest of the world.

- Aggregate spending equals aggregate income (Y)
  - $C + I + G + X - IM = Y$
  - Only products and services produced in Canada count toward Canadian GDP. Because some consumption, investment, and government spending is on imports, imports must be subtracted to accurately measure GDP.

- Figure 6.7 — Enlarged GDP Circular Flow of Income and Spending with Banking System — will be key for answering all macroeconomic questions.

- Consumer choices:
  - spend or save
  - **disposable income** — aggregate income minus net taxes
  - **net taxes** — taxes minus transfer payments
- Business choices:
  - hiring inputs and producing products and services
  - investment spending (often financed by borrowing)
- Government choices:
  - collect taxes, make transfer payments
  - spending on products and services
  - policy choices in Chapter 12
- R.O.W. choices:
  - buy Canadian exports or products and services from elsewhere
  - sell imports to Canada or elsewhere
  - invest and borrow money in Canada or elsewhere
- Bank choices:
  - take deposits and make loans

6.3 When Macroeconomic Dreams Come True: Potential GDP and Economic Growth

By increasing the quantity and quality of inputs, economic growth increases productivity and potential GDP per person, raising maximum possible living standards.

- **Potential GDP** — real GDP when all inputs — labour, capital, land/resources, and entrepreneurship — are fully employed. Short-run goal for economic performance if Adam Smith's invisible hand works perfectly.
- **Potential GDP per person** — potential GDP divided by the population. Short-run maximum possible living standards for an economy.
- **Economic growth** — expansion of economy's capacity to produce products and services; increase in potential GDP (per person).
- A macro production possibilities frontier (*PPF*) shows maximum combinations of products and services that a country can produce, the output when all inputs — labour, capital, land/resources, and entrepreneurship — are fully employed.
  - On the macro *PPF*, all inputs are fully employed; economy producing at potential GDP.
  - Inside the macro *PPF*, some inputs are unemployed; economy producing below potential GDP.
- Economic growth increases potential GDP (per person) and shifts the macro *PPF* outward.

- Economic growth is caused by increases in the quantity or quality of a country's inputs, including technological change — labour, capital, land/resources, and entrepreneurship.
- Increases in labour:
  - *quantity* — from population growth; immigration; increase in labour force participation rate
  - *quality* — from increases in **human capital** — increased earning potential from work experience, on-the-job training, and education
- Increases in capital:
  - *quantity* — from more factories and equipment
  - *quality* — from **technological change** — improvements in quality of capital through innovation, research, and development
- Increases in land and resources:
  - *quantity* — by bringing land and resources not connected to markets into the circular flow
  - *quality* — increases usually due to increases in capital used with land
- Increases in entrepreneurship:
  - *quantity* and *quality* interrelated; improvements from better management techniques, organization, and worker/management relations
- When economic growth progresses smoothly, the stock of inputs serves as a basis for choices, and choices then transform the stock of inputs, continuing in an ever-expanding circle.
  - **stock** — fixed amount at a moment in time
- **Economic growth rate** — annual percentage change in real GDP per person.

$$\begin{array}{l} \text{Real GDP} \\ \text{per person} \\ \text{growth rate} \\ \text{(percent)} \end{array} = \frac{\begin{array}{l}\text{Real GDP per} \\ \text{person this year}\end{array} - \begin{array}{l}\text{Real GDP per} \\ \text{person last year}\end{array}}{\text{Real GDP per person last year}} \times 100$$

- **Rule of 70** — number of years it takes for initial amount to double is roughly 70 divided by annual percentage growth rate.
  - Because of *compounding*, small differences in annual growth rates have large consequences over time.
- **Productivity** — measured as quantity of real GDP produced by an hour of labour.
  - Increases in productivity increase living standards; more can be produced, and amount of work time required to buy products and services is reduced.
- **Creative destruction** — competitive business innovations generate profits for winners, improving living standards for all, but destroy less productive or less desirable products and production methods.

6.4 Boom and Bust: Business Cycles

Business cycles — fluctuations of real GDP around potential GDP — are periods of real GDP expansion and contraction. Output gaps measure the difference between real GDP and potential GDP, and "closing the gap" is an important target for policymakers.

- **Business cycles** — up and down fluctuations of real GDP around potential GDP.

- Language of business cycles:
    - **expansion** — period during which real GDP increases
    - *peak* — highest point of an expansion; the turning point beginning a contraction
    - **contraction** — period during which real GDP decreases
    - *trough* — lowest point of a contraction; the turning point beginning an expansion
    - **recession** — two or more successive quarters of contraction of real GDP

- **Output gap** — real GDP minus potential GDP.
    - **recessionary gap** — real GDP below potential GDP; gap is a negative number
    - **inflationary gap** — real GDP above potential GDP; gap is a positive number

6.5 My GDP Is Bigger Than Yours: What's Wrong with GDP as a Measure of Well-Being?

Real GDP per person is a limited measure of well-being because it excludes non-market production, underground economy, environmental damage, leisure, and political freedoms and social justice.

- Real GDP per person is a limited measure of well-being; does not include:
    - non-market production — household production is not counted but improves the quality of life
    - *underground economy* — hides activities that are illegal, or legal but avoiding taxes (cash payments for services, unreported tips)
    - environmental damage — real GDP does not subtract costs of environmental damage and resource depletion
    - leisure — more leisure lowers real GDP, but leisure may be desirable
    - political freedoms and social justice — countries with high real GDP per person can have limited political freedoms, unequal distributions of income

- Growth rates of real GDP per person are still useful for judging economic progress if there are no significant changes over time in the limitations.

- United Nations Human Development Index (HDI) measures quality of life by combining life expectancy, educational achievement, and income.

TRUE/FALSE

Circle the correct answer. Solutions to these questions are available at the end of the book and on MyEconLab. You can also visit the MyEconLab Study Plan to access additional questions that will help you master the concepts covered in this chapter.

An old man wearing a sweater vest and thick-rimmed glasses walks into the coffee shop that you're relaxing in. He notices that you're reading *The Economist* magazine and says:

> *"Hello, youngster. Back in the year 1935, our economy was going through some tough times. I've lived through the Great Depression, the Global Financial Crisis, and other recessions. Let me tell you a few stories."*

Use this scenario to answer questions 1–15.

6.1 Nominal GDP and Real GDP

1. In 1935, Canada's nominal GDP was about $5 billion. In 2013, it was about $1800 billion. That means that the average Canadian is about 360 times better off today compared to 1935.   T   F

2. In 1935, Canada's real GDP was about $70 billion. In 2013, it was about $1400 billion. That means that the average Canadian is about 20 times better off today compared to 1935.   T   F

3. In 1935, Canada's real GDP per person was about $7000. In 2013, it was about $40 000. That means that the average Canadian is about 6 times better off today compared to 1935.   T   F

4. During the 1990s, real GDP rose faster than nominal GDP.   T   F

6.2   Value Added and the Enlarged Circular Flow

5. Back in 2012, I contributed to nominal GDP by selling my used 2009 Ford truck to my friend.   T   F

6. My rich neighbour, Pablo, purchased a new Ferrari made in Italy, increasing Canadian GDP.   T   F

6.3   Potential GDP and Economic Growth

7. Back in 1911, it took more hours of work to earn enough money to buy sausages than it takes today.   T   F

8. Back in the 1970s, the cell phone was invented. This increased the quality of labour.   T   F

9. An old friend of mine, Farmer Fred, started using fertilizer back in 1941. This increased the quality of the land.   T   F

10. My sister put $1000 in a savings account in 1935 with a fixed annual interest rate of 1 percent per year, then left the account alone. With compound interest, the savings account balance reached $2000 in 2005.   T   F

6.4   Business Cycles

11. The economy expanded in the early 2000s and hit a peak in 2008.   T   F

12. Back in my youth, I remember a three quarter contraction in real GDP. This was a recession.   T   F

6.5   What's Wrong with GDP as a Measure of Well-Being?

13. If underground economic activity were included in GDP calculations, measured GDP levels would be higher.   T   F

14. Real GDP per person in the United States is much higher than in Canada. Americans are therefore better off than Canadians.   T   F

15. If two economies have the same real GDP per person, then the overall well-being must be the same in each economy.   T   F

MULTIPLE CHOICE

Circle the best answer. Solutions to these questions are available at the end of the book and on MyEconLab. You can also visit the MyEconLab Study Plan to access similar questions that will help you master the concepts covered in this chapter.

6.1   Nominal GDP and Real GDP

1. Gross Domestic Product (GDP) is the value of all products and services
  a) that are gross-looking.
  b) produced in domestic households.
  c) produced in a country, including gross-looking products and services.
  d) produced in a country, excluding gross-looking products and services.

2. To calculate nominal GDP for 1935, we use the prices in
  a) 1935 and quantities in 1935.
  b) 1935 and quantities in 2002.
  c) 2002 and quantities in 1935.
  d) 2002 and quantities in 2002.

3. You observe that nominal GDP increases between 2013 and 2014, and the population also increases. If the entire increase in nominal GDP was due to rising prices, then
  a) nominal GDP remains unchanged.
  b) real GDP remains unchanged.
  c) real GDP per person remains unchanged.
  d) living standards remain unchanged.

6.2   Value Added and the Enlarged Circular Flow

4. GDP equals the value of
  a) spending on final products and services.
  b) business's outputs minus the value of intermediate products and services bought from other businesses.
  c) incomes earned by owners of inputs.
  d) all of the above.

5. In the "mantra" for calculating GDP, imports are subtracted because
   a) some consumption spending is on imports.
   b) some business investment spending is on imports.
   c) some government spending is on imports.
   d) all of the above.

6. Which of the following increases investment spending (*I*) by $200?
   a) You are hired by the government to shuffle paper uselessly for $200.
   b) You are hired by Dunder-Mifflin, the business on the television show *The Office*, to shuffle paper uselessly for $200.
   c) You hire your significant other to shuffle paper uselessly for $200.
   d) You lose your job because your employer replaces you with a paper shuffler machine that costs $200.

6.3 Potential GDP and Economic Growth

7. When real GDP equals potential GDP,
   a) all inputs are fully employed.
   b) everyone is getting the most bang per buck for their choices.
   c) the whole is equal to the sum of the well-functioning parts.
   d) all of the above.

8. If real GDP per person this year is $41 000, and real GDP per person last year was $40 000, then the economic growth rate is
   a) −5.0 percent.
   b) 2.5 percent.
   c) −2.5 percent.
   d) 5.0 percent.

9. Which is *not* a source of economic growth?
   a) More workers
   b) Better educated workers
   c) Higher stock market prices
   d) Growing quantities of capital equipment

10. Our long-run standard of living depends most on increases in
    a) population growth.
    b) employment growth.
    c) productivity.
    d) land.

6.4 Business Cycles

11. A recession occurs when real GDP
    a) is negative.
    b) growth is negative.
    c) growth is negative for two quarters in a row.
    d) growth is negative for two years in a row.

12. An output gap is
    a) negative if real GDP is above potential GDP.
    b) negative for an inflationary gap.
    c) positive if real GDP equals potential GDP.
    d) positive for an inflationary gap.

6.5 What's Wrong with GDP as a Measure of Well-Being?

13. Maud and her three sons belong to a church in their hometown of Springfield. The church provides benefits to the community, such as counselling, worship services, and distribution of food and clothing to the poor. Suppose that Maud's New Year's resolution for 2015 is to give up her $50 000 a year job to devote all of her time to fundraising for the church. As a result, GDP in 2015
    a) increases by $150 000.
    b) increases by $200 000.
    c) decreases by $50 000.
    d) decreases by $150 000.

14. Economists estimate the size of the underground economy in Canada to be between 5 and 15 percent of GDP. Which activities are part of the underground economy?
    a) Ecstasy sales
    b) Bartender tips
    c) Taxi driver tips
    d) All of the above

15. Moby goes from a stay-at-home father to a paid worker. He now earns $200 a week but pays $100 a week for day care and $100 a week for a housekeeper. Moby is better off by
    a) $0 and GDP increases by $0.
    b) $0 and GDP increases by $400.
    c) $200 and GDP increases by $0.
    d) $200 and GDP increases by $400.

7

Costs of (Not) Working and Living

Unemployment and Inflation

LEARNING OBJECTIVES

After reading this chapter, you should be able to:

7.1 Explain what the unemployment rate measures and misses, and identify four types of unemployment.

7.2 Define the natural rate of unemployment and explain its connection to recessionary and inflationary output gaps.

7.3 Explain how the inflation rate is calculated, what it misses, and three problems inflation creates.

7.4 Use the quantity theory of money to explain where inflation comes from.

7.5 Describe the Phillips Curve and its connections to demand-pull and cost-push inflations.

JOBS IN CANADA between 2009 and 2011 were extremely hard to find.

The unemployment rate hit a high of 8.3 percent in 2009 and has only been decreasing slowly, to around 7 percent in 2014. These average Canadian unemployment rates hide big regional differences, with higher rates in the Atlantic provinces (10 percent in New Brunswick during 2014) and much lower rates in the prairies (3.2 percent in Saskatchewan). Youth (ages 15 to 24) unemployment has been much worse, sticking around 14 percent through 2014.

While the unemployment rate in Canada was decreasing, the inflation rate was rising. In 2009, the inflation rate in Canada — the average increase in all prices over a year — was almost zero. The inflation rate rose to a high of 3.7 percent in 2011.

But what do these numbers actually mean? In judging the performance of the economy, what are "good" numbers for unemployment and inflation, what are "bad" numbers, and why are the numbers different in different parts of the country? And what do these numbers mean for you personally? Your job prospects? Your standard of living? Your smart financial choices?

In this chapter you will learn how unemployment and inflation are measured, how they are connected to each other and to GDP, and how to find useful information to aid your job searches. As a bonus, you will learn how to calculate how much higher the cost of living is now compared to the prices your grandparents or great-grandparents paid.

7.1 Who Is Unemployed? Healthy and Unhealthy Types of Unemployment

Explain what the unemployment rate measures and misses, and identify four types of unemployment.

Unemployment is something nearly everyone worries about. Not having a paying job, and not earning money in input markets, creates serious hardship — you can't afford to buy the necessities of life in output markets. Unemployment is not good for society as a whole either, because when people are not working, there are fewer products and services in output markets to meet everyone's needs.

Out of Work Is Not Enough

Government pays close attention to the number of unemployed. Each month, Statistics Canada surveys 54 000 households about their employment status, placing everyone in the working-age population (age 15 and over) into one of three categories:

- employed
- unemployed
- not in the labour force

unemployed not employed and actively seeking work

Calculating the Unemployment Rate   You are *employed* if you are working either full-time or part-time at a paid job. You are ***unemployed*** if you are not doing paid work and are actively searching for a job, as well as if you are on temporary layoff or about to start a new job.

If you do not fit into the employed or unemployed categories — if you are, for example, a full-time student, homemaker, or retiree — you are *not in the labour force*. Simply not working does not officially mean you are unemployed.

Figure 7.1 shows the number of Canadians in each of the three categories for July 2014.

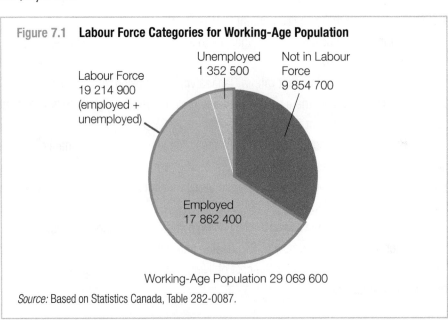

Figure 7.1   Labour Force Categories for Working-Age Population

Unemployed 1 352 500

Not in Labour Force 9 854 700

Labour Force 19 214 900 (employed + unemployed)

Employed 17 862 400

Working-Age Population 29 069 600

Source: Based on Statistics Canada, Table 282-0087.

In order to calculate the unemployment rate, Statistics Canada first calculates the labour force. The **labour force** is the sum of the employed and the unemployed.

$$\text{Labour Force} = \text{Employed} + \text{Unemployed}$$

The **unemployment rate** is the percentage of the people in the labour force who are unemployed — without work and actively seeking a job.

$$\text{Unemployment Rate} = \frac{\text{Unemployed}}{\text{Labour Force}} \times 100$$

Plugging in the (rounded) numbers from Figure 7.1 shows how the 7.0 percent unemployment rate for July 2014 was calculated.

$$\text{Unemployment Rate} = \frac{1\ 352\ 500}{19\ 214\ 900} \times 100 = 7.0 \text{ percent}$$

The size of the labour force is also used to calculate the **labour force participation rate** — the percentage of the working-age population who are in the labour force (employed or unemployed):

$$\text{Labour Force Participation Rate} = \frac{\text{Labour Force}}{\text{Working-Age Population}} \times 100$$

In July 2014, the working-age population was 29 069 600, so the labour force participation rate was

$$\text{Labour Force Participation Rate} = \frac{19\ 214\ 900}{29\ 069\ 600} \times 100 = 66.1 \text{ percent}$$

Chapter 6 showed that female labour force participation rates have increased over time and approach those for men. In July 2014, the female labour force participation rate was 61.6 percent while the rate for males was 70.7 percent.

Unemployment in Canada　Figure 7.2 shows the unemployment rate, based on the formulas above, in Canada from 1926 to 2013.

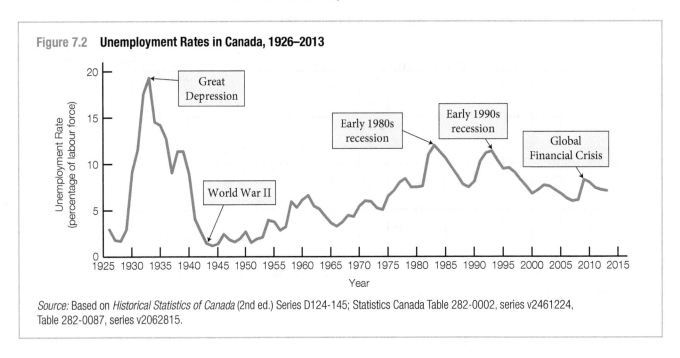

Figure 7.2　Unemployment Rates in Canada, 1926–2013

Source: Based on *Historical Statistics of Canada* (2nd ed.) Series D124-145; Statistics Canada Table 282-0002, series v2461224, Table 282-0087, series v2062815.

What stands out is the jump in unemployment during the Great Depression. The unemployment rate peaked close to 20 percent in 1933. Also notice the lowest unemployment rate, 1.2 percent, occurred during World War II.

The highest post-war unemployment rate — 11.9 percent in 1983 — occurred during the recession of the early 1980s. The unemployment rate during the early 1990s recession reached 11.4 percent in 1993. And most recently, the 2009 unemployment rate reached 8.3 percent during the Global Financial Crisis.

What the Unemployment Rate Misses

Just as the measurements of GDP have limitations, so too do the measurements of unemployment. Each of the three categories — employed, unemployed, and not in the labour force — misses some part of the full unemployment story.

Involuntary Part-Time Workers　Some workers who are employed part-time would rather have a full-time job, but can't find one. Statistics Canada calls these *involuntary part-time workers*, and keeps track of them, but they don't show up in the official unemployment rate. As the Economics Out There story on page 172 explains, during recessions businesses often try to hold on to experienced workers but cut back their hours, increasing involuntary part-time unemployment. And during expansions, involuntary part-time unemployment decreases as businesses restore full-time work before hiring new workers. These shifts between part-time and full-time work are not picked up in the unemployment rate — they are missed.

Discouraged Workers Most workers who are unemployed hope to find a job. But more than half of workers who are unemployed end up dropping out of the labour force. Workers may drop out for many reasons, including returning to school or because they have given up on finding a job.

Discouraged workers are those who want to work, but have given up actively searching for jobs. They do not show up in the unemployment rate — they are missed.

discouraged workers want to work but have given up actively searching for jobs

Instead, discouraged workers cause changes in the labour force participation rate. During recessions, when it gets harder to find jobs, there are more discouraged workers who drop out of the labour force. Ironically, this causes the official unemployment rate to *fall* when more people are actually out of work.

Consider this simple example. If 93 people are employed, and 7 people are not employed and seeking work, the official unemployment rate is 7 percent $(7 \div (93 + 7) \times 100)$. But if one of those unemployed people gets discouraged and leaves the labour force, the official unemployment rate falls to 6 percent $(6 \div (93 + 6) \times 100)$. The number of jobs has not increased but the unemployment rate goes down.

The number of discouraged workers tends to increase in recessions and decrease in expansions. Once the economy gets past the trough of a recession and begins expanding, the unemployment rate often increases even as the economy is creating more jobs, because previously discouraged workers get encouraged and re-enter the labour force actively seeking work again. The recession of the early 1990s ended in 1991, but the unemployment rate kept rising to peak in 1993 at 11.4 percent.

Figure 7.3 shows how the unemployment rate would be higher if these involuntary part-time workers and discouraged workers were counted as unemployed. Statistics Canada calls this larger percentage the measure of labour *underutilization*. For July 2014, the *labour underutilization rate* was 9.8 percent, more than the official unemployment rate of 7.3 percent.

Figure 7.3 **Unemployment and Underutilization of Labour, July 2014**

	Percentage of Labour Force
Official unemployment rate	7.3
Involuntary part-time workers	2.4
Discouraged workers	0.1
Labour Underutilization Rate	**9.8**

Source: Based on Statistics Canada, Table 282-0085.

Economics *Out There*

Regional Differences The national unemployment rate is calculated by aggregating (there is that macroeconomic word again meaning *the whole*) the statistics for all provinces. That average hides regional differences in unemployment rates across Canada. Figure 7.4 shows the unemployment rates for July 2014 by province.

Figure 7.4	**Provincial Unemployment Rates, July 2014**

Province	Unemployment Rate
Newfoundland/Labrador	12.4
Prince Edward Island	9.4
Nova Scotia	9.4
New Brunswick	10.0
Québec	8.1
Ontario	7.5
Manitoba	5.3
Saskatchewan	3.2
Alberta	4.7
British Columbia	5.9

Source: Based on Statistics Canada, Table 282-0087.

▼ The Statistics Canada homepage at www.statcan.gc.ca has the *Latest Indicators* on the left side, including population, inflation rate, unemployment rate, and growth rate of GDP. You can check the current unemployment rate at this site.

These regional differences in unemployment rates are typical. Rates in Atlantic Canada are historically higher than the average unemployment rate for all of Canada. Rates in Western Canada are historically lower than average. Central Canada, with more than 60 percent of the Canadian labour force, usually has rates close to the national average unemployment rate.

www.statcan.gc.ca/start-debut-eng.html

Source: Statistics Canada, www.statcan.gc.ca.

Healthy and Unhealthy Unemployment

What do unemployment and cholesterol have in common? Doctors tell us that there are good and bad types of cholesterol. Good cholesterol — found in foods like olive oil — improves the health of your heart. Bad cholesterol — found in fried fast foods — is unhealthy and increases your risk of heart attacks. Similarly, there are healthy types of unemployment — those that help create a more dynamic economy — and unhealthy types of unemployment — those that hurt economic production.

Economists distinguish four main types of unemployment — frictional, structural, seasonal, and cyclical. Let's look at each and see whether it is healthy or unhealthy for the economy.

Frictional Unemployment Market economies excel at reacting quickly to change. When there are surpluses or shortages, prices change and create incentives for consumers and businesses to adjust their smart choices. Those adjustments mean some businesses shrink and reduce employment, while others grow and hire additional workers. Those same changing prices and wages lead workers to move out of jobs that are disappearing (DVD factories) and into jobs that are expanding (tattoo parlours). These adjustments, where workers move between jobs, or from school to a job, are part of the normal, healthy functioning of a market economy, with its constant process of creative destruction.

Because of these continuous adjustments, at any moment in time there are workers between jobs and workers searching for jobs. This unemployment — workers between or searching for jobs — is called **frictional unemployment**.

Frictional unemployment is "healthy" unemployment, and is not a problem that policymakers need to fix.

frictional unemployment due to normal labour turnover and job search; healthy part of a changing economy

Structural Unemployment Businesses and individuals in market economies do not just react to change — they also cause change. Competitive business innovations earn profits for the winners but destroy less productive or less desirable products and production methods. This competition can come from domestic businesses or from businesses abroad in countries like India or China. Unemployment that arises because changes in technology or international competition make workers' skills obsolete is called **structural unemployment**. Robots destroyed the jobs of tool-and-die makers who used to build simpler machines for automobile production. Digital recorders have made the jobs of stenographers, who used to write notes in shorthand, obsolete.

Workers who are structurally unemployed need to retrain to find new and different jobs. There is a mismatch between the skills these workers have and the skills new jobs require. Like frictional unemployment, structural unemployment is "healthy" unemployment, part of the process of economic growth that yields rising living standards. But unlike frictional unemployment, structural unemployment is a problem that must be fixed through retraining.

structural unemployment due to technological change or international competition that makes workers' skills obsolete; there is a mismatch between the skills workers have and the skills new jobs require

seasonal unemployment   due to seasonal changes in weather

Seasonal Unemployment

Seasonal Unemployment   Jobs like fruit picking or snow shovelling are only available at certain times of the year. **Seasonal unemployment** arises because of seasonal changes in the weather and is a healthy part of an economy that adapts to the seasons. It is a function of nature. Those of us who do not live on the west coast might wish for a more California-like climate, but other than wishing, nothing else needs to be done. Seasonal unemployment is not a problem needing a policy solution.

cyclical unemployment   due to fluctuations in economic activity over the business cycle

Cyclical Unemployment

Cyclical Unemployment   Workers who lose their jobs because of contractions in economic activity suffer from cyclical unemployment. **Cyclical unemployment** arises from fluctuations over the business cycle — increasing during economic contractions and recessions and decreasing during economic expansions.

Cyclical unemployment is the one "unhealthy" unemployment — the bad, deep-fried type. Cyclical unemployment prevents the full employment part of the question: "If left alone by government, do the price mechanisms of market economies adjust quickly to maintain steady growth in living standards, *full employment,* and stable prices?" Cyclical unemployment is a problem that needs fixing, especially according to the hands-on view of market economies.

Figure 7.5 summarizes the different types of unemployment. In the next section, we will explain exactly what economists mean by "full employment."

Figure 7.5   Types of Unemployment

Type of Unemployment	Healthy/ Unhealthy	Problem That Needs Fixing?	Cause
Frictional	Healthy	No	Normal, healthy market adjustments of demand and supply
Structural	Healthy	Yes (worker retraining)	Technological change, international competition, resource depletion
Seasonal	Healthy	No	Weather and seasons
Cyclical	Unhealthy	Yes (fiscal or monetary policy)	Business cycles

Refresh 7.1

MyEconLab

For answers to these Refresh Questions, visit MyEconLab.

1. State the formula for calculating the unemployment rate, and explain what each word in the formula means. Calculate the unemployment rate when there are 1000 people in the labour force and 50 of them are unemployed.

2. Since the official unemployment rate misses several types of out-of-work people, is the measurement of any use to policymakers? Explain your answer.

3. How can your knowing the regional differences in unemployment rates help you in your job-search strategy?

How Full Is "Full Employment?"
The Natural Rate of Unemployment

Most people would say that "full employment" means everyone is employed, that the unemployment rate is zero percent. But economists define it differently.

The Natural Rate of Unemployment

Full employment for economists is the unemployment rate when all markets, including labour input markets, are working well. There still will be frictional unemployment (people between jobs), structural unemployment (people needing retraining) and seasonal unemployment (people out of work because of nature). These types of unemployment are part of the healthy functioning of market economies. The term "full employment" that Statistics Canada and the media use means that there is still unemployment, but it is frictional, structural, and seasonal. Full employment includes these types of unemployment.

The unemployment rate associated with **full employment** is called the **natural rate of unemployment** — the rate when there is only frictional, structural, and seasonal unemployment.

The natural rate of employment excludes the one "unhealthy" type of unemployment — cyclical unemployment from business cycles.

Full employment to economists — the natural rate of unemployment — is also defined as *zero percent cyclical unemployment*.

natural rate of unemployment (full employment) unemployment rate at full employment, when there is only frictional, structural, and seasonal unemployment

NOTE
Full employment is not zero percent unemployment, but zero percent cyclical unemployment.

Natural Rate of Unemployment and Potential GDP

The natural rate of unemployment — at full employment — connects to the Chapter 6 discussion of potential GDP and output gaps.

If the economy is at full employment — with no cyclical unemployment — real GDP equals potential GDP. The unemployment rate equals the natural rate and there is only frictional, structural, or seasonal unemployment.

Recessionary Gap When the economy contracts, real GDP falls below potential GDP — there is a recessionary output gap. In a recessionary gap, there are unemployed inputs — including labour — so real GDP is less than potential GDP. The additional unemployment caused by the contraction is cyclical unemployment. The unemployment rate increases above the natural rate due to cyclical unemployment.

NOTE
In a recessionary gap, the unemployment rate is above the natural rate due to cyclical unemployment.

Inflationary Gap   When the economy expands, real GDP can temporarily rise above potential GDP — there is an inflationary output gap. Not only are all inputs fully employed, the economy is working overtime. In the labour market, the unemployment rate decreases *below* the natural rate. More workers than normal are employed, so levels of frictional, structural, or seasonal unemployment drop below normal levels. The demand for labour is so great that jobs are easier to find and search times for jobs are shorter. Strong labour market demand may also draw people into the labour force who had been out of the labour force, increasing the economy's ability to produce more products and services.

The reason why real GDP can rise above potential GDP, at least for short periods of time, is that the natural rate of unemployment at full employment is not zero percent, but *zero percent cyclical unemployment.* Full employment still allows for frictional, structural, and seasonal unemployment. These types of unemployment, especially frictional unemployment, can drop below normal full employment levels. People who had been unemployed at potential GDP because of frictional, structural, or seasonal reasons are now employed. This explains the Chapter 6 question of how real GDP can be above potential GDP.

Figure 7.6 summarizes the connections between output gaps and unemployment rates.

Figure 7.6   Output Gaps and Unemployment

Real GDP and Potential GDP	Output Gap	Unemployment Rate
Real GDP equals potential GDP	None	Natural rate of unemployment — full employment (only frictional, structural, seasonal unemployment)
Real GDP below potential GDP	Recessionary gap	Unemployment rate above natural rate (cyclical unemployment)
Real GDP above potential GDP	Inflationary gap	Unemployment rate below natural rate (less than normal frictional, structural, seasonal unemployment)

What Is the Natural Rate of Unemployment?

You might be wondering, okay, so what is the natural rate of unemployment? What is the "target" rate of unemployment that a hands-off believer in Say's Law could use to show that the economy is doing fine on its own? No government involvement needed, thank you. And for a hands-on believer? What rate would signal to government that a policy is needed to reduce unemployment?

It turns out that economists disagree about the natural rate of unemployment. Most would say the natural rate is somewhere between 4 percent and 9 percent unemployment. Others would disagree and argue that whatever unemployment exists is always at the natural rate, so there is never a need for government involvement. There is also disagreement about whether the natural rate stays relatively constant over time, or changes frequently with changes in the economy that affect frictional and structural unemployment. We will explore these disagreements in Chapters 11, 12, and 13.

1. Define the natural rate of unemployment. Explain why an unemployment rate of zero does not mean that all workers have jobs.

2. Explain the connection between GDP output gaps and the unemployment rate.

3. Find a business story in the media that uses the term *unemployment*. Decide if they are using unemployment the same way an economist would. Explain any differences you discover.

MyEconLab

For answers to these Refresh Questions, visit MyEconLab.

Lightening Up Your Wallet: What Is Inflation?

7.3

Inflation is a persistent rise in the average level of all prices. You will often see a headline stating, for example: "Statistics Canada today reported that consumer prices rose 2.4 percent in the 12 months to June 2014." The 2.4 percent is the annual inflation rate in Canada. It means that the same products and services that cost $100 in June 2013 cost $102.40 one year later.

The flip side of prices rising is the value of money falling. If products that used to cost $100 now cost $102.40, your hundred dollar bill no longer buys quite as much as it did last year. Your money's buying power has fallen in value.

Where does that number of 2.4 come from, and what does it mean? Is it a "good" number or a "bad" number in evaluating the performance of the economy? And why do people and policymakers worry about inflation?

The question about worry is not as silly as it sounds. The circular flow diagram shows that your income depends on prices in input markets — the wage rate is the price of an hour of labour. If *all* prices have risen 2.4 percent, that means your wage rate has also risen 2.4 percent. Yes, products and services in output markets cost more, but your income has gone up by the same percentage. Your ability to afford those purchases is unchanged. So what's the worry?

Consumer Price Index

Every month Statistics Canada tracks the average prices urban consumers pay for a representative shopping basket of about 600 products and services. This shopping basket includes spending on housing, transportation, food, recreation, furniture, and clothing. Those prices are used to construct the **Consumer Price Index (CPI)**, the most widely used measure of average prices.

Explain how the inflation rate is calculated, what it misses, and three problems inflation creates.

inflation a persistent rise in the average price level and a fall in the value of money

Consumer Price Index (CPI) measure of the average prices of a fixed shopping basket of products and services

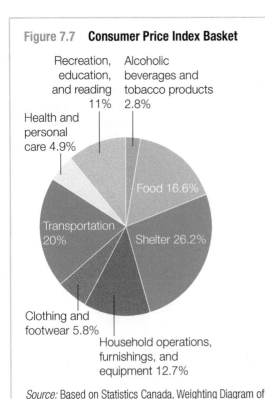

Figure 7.7   Consumer Price Index Basket

Recreation, education, and reading 11%

Alcoholic beverages and tobacco products 2.8%

Health and personal care 4.9%

Food 16.6%

Transportation 20%

Shelter 26.2%

Clothing and footwear 5.8%

Household operations, furnishings, and equipment 12.7%

Source: Based on Statistics Canada, Weighting Diagram of the Consumer Price Index - 2011 Basket at January 2013 Prices, Canada (http://www23.statcan.gc.ca/imdbbmdi/document/2301_D48_T9_V2-eng.htm)

The CPI Shopping Basket   Figure 7.7 shows the proportion of each category of spending in the CPI shopping basket. A category's proportion in the basket reflects its proportion in a typical consumer's budget. For example, housing is about 26 percent of the basket, reflecting that 26 percent of an urban consumer's spending is on housing (renting or owning). Transportation is 20 percent of spending; food is 17 percent; recreation, education and reading are 11 percent. The smallest category, at about 3 percent, is for alcoholic drinks and tobacco products.

Because consumers spend more of their budget on food than on alcohol, a change in the price of food will have a bigger impact on the CPI than a change in the price of beer.

Calculating the CPI   The CPI calculates averages prices for each of the 600 products and services and weights them by the category for each. That weighted average of prices is the Consumer Price Index.

To make it easier to compare years, prices are measured against a base year. The *base year* is currently 2002, and the cost of the basket for that year is set at 100. The CPI for 2014 takes the same basket of products and services but priced at 2014 prices, giving a value of 125.90. The same products and services that cost $100 in 2002 cost $125.90 in 2014. That's why the CPI is also called the cost of living index.

Measuring the Inflation Rate   Once we have numbers for the Consumer Price Index, we can calculate the **inflation rate**. The inflation rate is the annual percentage change in the Consumer Price Index (CPI). The general formula for the inflation rate between two years is

inflation rate   annual percentage change in the Consumer Price Index

$$\text{Inflation Rate} = \frac{\text{CPI for current year} - \text{CPI for previous year}}{\text{CPI for previous year}} \times 100$$

Look back at our original example. The CPI in June 2014 was 125.9 and the CPI a year earlier in June 2013 was 123.0. Plugging those numbers into the inflation rate formula, we get

$$\text{Inflation Rate} = \frac{125.9 - 123}{123} \times 100 = 2.4 \text{ percent}$$

◀   Statistics Canada selects a basket of products and services to track the inflation rate. In 2002, you would have paid $100 for this basket of products and services, but in 2014 the same basket cost $125.90. If your income stayed the same, it bought less.

Inflation in Canada   Figure 7.8 shows Canada's annual inflation rate, based on the formula on page 178, from 1960 to 2013.

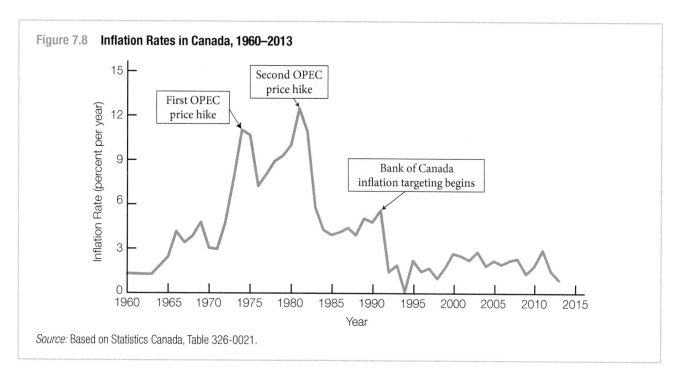

Figure 7.8   **Inflation Rates in Canada, 1960–2013**

Source: Based on Statistics Canada, Table 326-0021.

The inflation rate was under 2 percent during the early 1960s, but then increased during the Vietnam War. The dramatic increases in inflation rates that you can see in 1975 (to 10.9 percent) and 1981 (to 12.4 percent) were due to massive increases in the price of oil triggered by the Organization of Petroleum Exporting Countries (OPEC) and wars in the Middle East. Since all production requires energy, higher oil prices affected the prices of most products and services. Inflation rates fell during the recession of the early 1980s, due to deliberate actions by the Bank of Canada. They fell again during the recession of the early 1990s. Since then, the Bank of Canada, as part of its monetary policy (Chapter 11), aims to keep the inflation rate between 1 and 3 percent. The most recent June 2014 inflation rate of 2.4 percent is in the middle of the target range of the Bank of Canada.

Economics *Out There*

The Bank of Canada's Inflation Calculator

The inflation calculator allows you to see changes in the cost of living and inflation rates for any years between 1914 and today.

For example, products that cost $100 in 1980 would cost $284.39 in June 2014. That is a 184 percent increase over 34 years, which is a 3.12 percent average annual rate of inflation.

Source: Bank of Canada, http://www.bankofcanada.ca/rates/related/inflation-calculator

Core Inflation Rate   Because prices of energy and fresh foods go up and down so often, the inflation rate can change quickly from month to month. For example, due largely to changes in energy prices, the inflation rate more than doubled from 1.4 percent in March 2008 to 3.5 percent just five months later in August 2008. When oil and gasoline prices then collapsed, the inflation rate fell in just nine months almost to zero — to 0.1 percent in May 2009.

To get around these large, brief fluctuations and still provide meaningful data about inflation, the Bank of Canada also calculates the core inflation rate. The **core inflation rate** excludes the most volatile categories from the Consumer Price Index basket — fruit, vegetables, gasoline, fuel oil, natural gas, mortgage interest, intercity transportation, and tobacco products. By ignoring these products and services with large price changes from month to month, the core inflation rate provides meaningful long-run data. The core inflation rate is the percentage change in the Consumer Price Index excluding selected volatile categories.

Figure 7.9 reproduces the inflation rates from 1985–2013, and adds the core inflation rates (the red line) that have been calculated only since 1985. Over the March 2008 to May 2009 period, the core inflation rate, which removes the effects of volatile products, showed much less fluctuation, rising from 1.3 percent to a high of 2.4 percent, and back down to 2 percent. In monthly media reports of the overall inflation rate, you will usually also hear about the core inflation rate.

core inflation rate   inflation rate excluding volatile categories

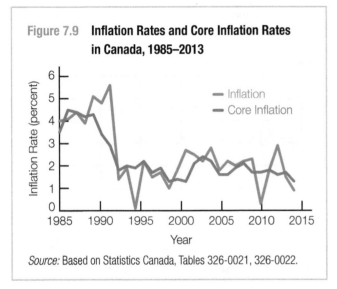

Figure 7.9   **Inflation Rates and Core Inflation Rates in Canada, 1985–2013**

Source: Based on Statistics Canada, Tables 326-0021, 326-0022.

Why Worry about Inflation?

Is inflation really a problem you should worry about? If, *on average*, all prices rise by the same percentage, including input prices that determine incomes as well as output prices, then people can afford to buy the same products and services before and after the inflation. So where's the problem? Why worry?

People and policymakers worry about inflation for three good reasons.

Falling Value of Money   A 3 percent inflation rate, for example, means that *on average*, all prices (and incomes) rise by 3 percent. But 3 percent is an *average*: some prices and incomes will rise more than 3 percent, some less, and some will not change at all. For those whose income rises at the inflation rate or faster, inflation is not a problem — no worries.

For people living on fixed incomes, like anyone with a pension that pays a fixed, unchanged dollar amount each month, inflation is a problem. Inflation reduces the purchasing power of their unchanged dollar incomes — a serious worry.

Similarly, inflation reduces the purchasing power of any savings you have. Savings account dollars do not change with the inflation rate. As prices rise, those savings account dollars buy less than before. That's a worry for most people.

Falling Value of Money and Interest Rates   The falling value of money also affects interest rates. Whether you are a lender earning interest from savings accounts or loans made to others, or a borrower paying interest on a car loan, a mortgage, or credit card balances — inflation affects the purchasing power of your loan and interest received or paid.

That interest can be measured in a number of ways. The **nominal interest rate** is the interest rate observed in the markets, paid on mortgages, and earned on savings accounts. If your savings account pays 5 percent interest per year, that is a nominal interest rate. If you kept $1000 in the account for a year, at the end of the year you would earn $50 in interest ($0.05 \times \$1000 = \$50$) added to the $1000, for a total of $1050.

But what can you buy with those $1050? If the inflation rate over the year has been zero, then the extra $50 on your original $1000 increases your purchasing power by 5 percent. But if average prices rose over the year by 3 percent — an inflation rate of 3 percent — that $50 now buys 3 percent fewer products and services than before. Your purchasing power from the earned interest has only increased by 2 percent.

The realized **real interest rate** adjusts the nominal interest rate to remove the effects of inflation.

> Real Interest Rate = Nominal Interest Rate − Inflation Rate

If the inflation rate over the year was 3 percent, then the real interest rate you received, or realized, on your savings account was

> Real Interest Rate = 5% − 3% = 2%

The nominal interest rate calculates how many extra dollars you receive or pay at the end of a loan. The realized real interest rate calculates the purchasing power you have gained or lost at the end of a loan. Real interest rates are more important than nominal interest rates for making smart saving and investing decisions.

What if the inflation rate turns out to be greater than the nominal interest rate? If the nominal interest rate you earn is 5 percent — which sounds attractive — but the inflation rate is 8 percent, your realized real rate of interest is –3 percent (5% – 8% = –3%). That means, even though you earned $50 or 5% in interest, at the end of the year you actually *lost* $30 or 3 percent of your previous purchasing power. It would have been smarter to spend the money on products or services at the beginning of the year rather than saving and earning 5 percent nominal interest. Inflation is definitely something to worry about when making a decision to spend or to save.

Your original decision to save depends on a variation of the real rate of interest called the *expected* real rate of interest, which equals the nominal interest rate minus the *expected* inflation rate. Expectations make decisions more complicated and less predictable. We will discuss these complications in Chapter 11.

nominal interest rate   observed interest rate; equal to the number of dollars received per year in interest as a percentage of the number of dollars saved

real interest rate   nominal interest rate adjusted for effects of inflation

Unpredictable Prices Discourage Planning and Investment Unpredictable prices are a serious problem for businesses. Producing for output markets takes time. Businesses must make commitments today for production that will only come to market in the future. If your business is not sure of a steady supply of inputs at predictable prices, your costs become unpredictable, and profits unstable. Unpredictability creates risk, and risk discourages business investment in future production. Business planning works best when prices are stable, or when inflation is running at a steady, predictable rate.

"HOW DO YOU WANT IT — THE CRYSTAL MUMBO-JUMBO OR STATISTICAL PROBABILITY?"

Source: www.ScienceCartoonsPlus.com.

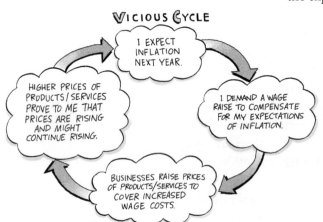

VICIOUS CYCLE

I EXPECT INFLATION NEXT YEAR.

I DEMAND A WAGE RAISE TO COMPENSATE FOR MY EXPECTATIONS OF INFLATION.

BUSINESSES RAISE PRICES OF PRODUCTS/SERVICES TO COVER INCREASED WAGE COSTS.

HIGHER PRICES OF PRODUCTS/SERVICES PROVE TO ME THAT PRICES ARE RISING AND MIGHT CONTINUE RISING.

Danger of Self-Fulfilling Expectations Imagine this scenario: You have been working on a one-year contract that pays $3000 a month. While the inflation rate this year has been zero, you expect energy prices to rise next year. Because of that, you fear the inflation rate — the cost of living — will rise by 4 percent. In negotiating a new contract, what monthly pay rate will you ask for?

If you are like most people, you will think, "The cost of living next year will be 4 percent higher. Unless I get at least a 4 percent raise, my income won't keep pace with the rising cost of living. My standard of living will go down. I'd better ask for at least $3120 a month (4 percent of $3000 is $120)."

Once expectations of inflation begin, many people think the same way. Businesses, expecting higher prices for inputs, set output prices higher to protect their profits. Banks, expecting inflation, increase nominal interest rates on loans to protect the real rate of interest they will receive. When workers, businesses, and banks expect inflation, they reasonably try and protect themselves by pushing up wages, prices of output, and interest rates. This creates self-fulfilling expectations — by reacting to the expectation of inflation we may cause inflation.

Once inflation starts, expectations of higher inflation rates can keep rising, creating a vicious cycle that, if not broken, runs the risk of spiralling out of control. Expectations of inflation helped cause the last sharp rise in inflation rates and nominal interest rates in the early 1980s. Can cycles like this be broken? What can be done? We will discuss expectations, interest rates, and monetary policy in Chapter 11.

Acceptable Inflation Most economists view a low inflation rate — under 3 percent per year — as not a serious problem, as long as the inflation rate is also predictable and steady from year to year. The Bank of Canada's target range for the inflation rate is based on this view.

Since even a low inflation rate hurts people on fixed incomes, you may be wondering why economists don't push for a zero percent inflation rate. That's a good question, and the answer will come in the last section of this chapter on trade-offs between inflation and unemployment. Every choice, including the policy choice to aim for zero inflation, has an opportunity cost.

Dangerous Downward Spirals:
If Low Inflation Is OK, Is Deflation Better?

What goes up can also go down. Prices can rise *and* fall. **Deflation** is the opposite of inflation — a persistent fall in average prices and a rise in the value of money. At first, deflation sounds attractive. As consumers, we all like lower prices, and even those on fixed incomes would seem to benefit. But a persistent fall in average prices sets up a dangerous downward spiral.

Once average prices begin falling, new attitudes begin. Consumers, believing that prices will go even lower, hold off on buying products and services, since they will get a lower price by waiting. Sales drop and businesses cut back production and employment. Wages, which also fall with falling average prices, will fall further as the economy contracts and unemployment increases. This deflationary spiral becomes the reverse image of the inflationary spiral.

Savers and Borrowers   A rise in the value of money sounds attractive. Deflation increases the purchasing power of any money you have in the bank. Deflation benefits savers — the opposite of inflation, which hurts them.

But deflation hurts borrowers. When consumers or businesses pay back loans, they are paying back more valuable dollars — in purchasing power — than the dollars they borrowed. Deflation also means consumers' incomes and businesses' revenues are falling. Consumers and businesses have less ability to pay back loans, whose dollar amounts do not change.

Falling Asset Values   During persistent deflation, the value of assets — like houses and equities — also falls. Imagine you bought a house for $300 000 with a $200 000 mortgage. Deflation sets in, and every month the value of your house falls, but your mortgage payments stay the same. Soon, your mortgage could be higher than your house's value — you actually owe more on your house than it is currently worth. During the Global Financial Crisis, many homeowners in the United States faced that unfortunate reality. Average U.S. home prices kept falling until 2012.

Falling real estate values alone are not a deflation. Deflation is a persistent fall in the average of *all* prices, not just prices in one sector of the economy. But the experience of deflation in the U.S. real estate market gives a good picture of the destructive forces of a general deflation.

deflation   persistent fall in average prices and a rise in the value of money

NOTE
Deflation benefits savers but hurts borrowers.

▲ A general deflation is like seeing price reductions on all products and services. While consumers like sale prices, deflation also decreases incomes, so consumers have less money to spend.

The Lesson of Japanese Deflation   Japan suffered from a decade of deflation after its real estate bubble burst in 1991. Partly as a result of the destructive downward spiral of deflation, the Japanese economy suffered two decades of economic stagnation, almost no growth, and significant unemployment.

Lessons learned from the Japanese experience is one reason policymakers took strong action to try to avoid deflation during the Global Financial Crisis. Deflation is much worse than low inflation.

What the Inflation Rate Misses

There are challenges in using the Consumer Price Index to measure inflation (or deflation), just as there are challenges in measuring GDP or the unemployment rate.

Standard of Living versus Cost of Living   Chapter 6 showed that changes in nominal GDP between two years can come from changes in the quantities of products and services the economy has produced, or from changes in their prices. Real GDP comparisons keep prices constant, isolating changes in quantities only. Quantities are important for measuring our standard of living.

Changes in consumer spending between two years can come from changes in the quantities of products and services consumers buy, or from changes in their prices. To isolate the impact of changing prices only, the CPI keeps the quantities of products and services in the shopping basket constant from year to year. With quantities constant, all changes in the value of the basket are due to changes in prices only. Prices are important for measuring our cost of living.

To isolate price changes, the Consumer Price Index keeps quantities constant. But in the real world, as prices change, consumers change the quantities of products and services they buy. Also, consumers eagerly buy new and improved versions of products and services. The inflation rate misses these two important trends.

Switch to Cheaper Substitutes   When the price of gasoline rises, people drive less and switch to public transit. That is the law of demand — when the price of a product rises, we tend to buy less of it. We all save money, and reduce our cost of living, by switching to cheaper substitutes. The unchanged products and services in the basket of the Consumer Price Index do not include the switch to cheaper substitutes, so the CPI *overstates* increases in the cost of living.

New and Better Products   The unchanged basket of the Consumer Price Index also misses the introduction of new products, and changes in quality of existing products. There is no easy way to compare the cost of living in a year when new products or services like the iPhone or tablet computers are introduced, to an earlier year when they didn't exist.

Many businesses upgrade the quality of their products or services while keeping the price constant. But, the CPI basket doesn't change. Even if a product in the CPI basket is improved to give more value and quality, the basket remains the same. For example, Apple's pricing strategy is to introduce a model (like the MacBook Air) and keep the price constant. But every four months or so, Apple upgrades the quality of the model with a faster processor, a bigger hard drive, or more RAM, all for the same price. Because the CPI doesn't capture these improvements in product quality, it again *overstates* increases in the cost of living.

Statistics Canada is aware of these unavoidable limitations of all price indexes, and updates the contents of the CPI shopping basket from time to time to reflect changes in consumer spending habits and changes in products. Nonetheless, the Bank of Canada estimates that the official inflation rate, based on the Consumer Price Index, *overstates* increases in the cost of living by about 0.5 percent. So an official inflation rate, for example, of 4 percent, translates into an actual increase in cost of living of 3.5 percent, but that is still just an estimate.

Refresh 7.3

1. If the CPI last year was 115.0 and it's 116.5 this year, what is the annual inflation rate?

2. Deflation lowers the cost of living. Why, then, do economists consider it worse than low inflation for the economy in general and for you in particular?

3. If you operate a small business, what problems would unpredictable inflation cause for you?

MyEconLab

For answers to these Refresh Questions, visit MyEconLab.

Inflation Starts with "*M*"
The Quantity Theory of Money

7.4

Use the quantity theory of money to explain where inflation comes from.

Where does inflation come from?

That is a macroeconomic question — dealing with the whole economy — because inflation is a persistent rise in the average of all prices in the aggregate economy.

The related microeconomics question — dealing with individual choices, individual businesses, and markets for particular products or services — is, "Where do prices come from?" (see Chapter 4.) The answer is, "Prices come from the interaction of demand and supply, in markets with appropriate property rights." Microeconomics, and the market forces of competing bids (demand) and offers (supply), explain why the price of phones or piercings rises or falls.

The explanation of why *all* prices tend to move up together (inflation) or down together (deflation) has a different source — money. Macroeconomics explains the influence of money itself.

Money and the Circular Flow

The story of inflation begins with money.

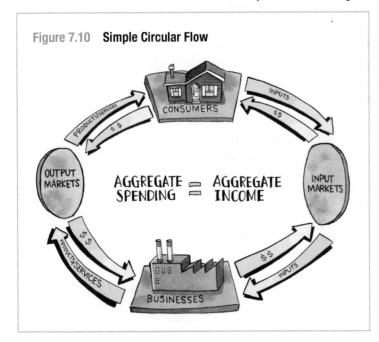

Figure 7.10   Simple Circular Flow

AGGREGATE = AGGREGATE
SPENDING = INCOME

***M* Is for Money**   Economists use the letter *M* to represent the quantity of money in the economy. Money takes many sophisticated and digital forms in the Canadian economy, as we will see in Chapter 9. But let's start with a simple story, where the only money consists of loonies, exactly 1000 of them.

The economy in our story produces $5000 worth of final products and services in a year — nominal GDP is $5000. Even though our economy is simple, it has the same circular flow of spending and income (Figure 7.10) as complicated economies. Businesses buy inputs from consumer households in input markets, paying with loonies. Businesses use the inputs to produce products and services, which they sell to consumers in output markets. Consumers use the loonie income earned in input markets to buy the products and services they want. Cash only in this simple story — no credit cards, no debit cards accepted. The $ signs on the green arrows represent loonies only.

As in Chapter 6, the value of nominal GDP ($5000 in our story) equals both the value of final products and services sold in output markets (left side), and the value-added income earned in input markets (right side). Aggregate spending equals aggregate income.

All purchases and sales, both in output markets and input markets, have to be made with loonies. Do you see a problem? I'm hoping you are wondering if I've made a mistake in my story. How can this simple economy have $5000 worth of sales with only 1000 loonies?

***V* is for Velocity**   There is no mistake. The problem disappears if each loonie changes hands more than once in a year. If each loonie were only spent (and received) once in a year, then the limit of aggregate sales in the economy would be $1000. But if each loonie changes hands five times in a year, there could be $5000 worth of purchases and sales. The number of times a unit of money changes hands during a year is called the **velocity of money**. Economists use the letter *V* to represent the velocity of money.

velocity of money (*V*)   number of times a unit of money changes hands during a year

***P* × *Q* is for Nominal GDP**   The quantity of money and its velocity have a simple relationship to nominal GDP. Nominal GDP can be represented as $P \times Q$. The nominal GDP calculation adds together price times quantity for every final product and service. $P \times Q$ is a shorthand version of that calculation.

P represents average prices — the Consumer Price Index. *Q* represents the aggregate quantity of real output, the sum of all of the physical final products and services produced. So $P \times Q$ equals nominal GDP, which also equals aggregate income. In our simple story, $P \times Q$ equals $5000.

The relationship between these four variables, *M*, *V*, *P*, and *Q*, is

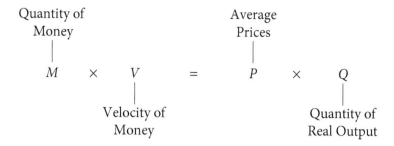

Reading from left to right, the quantity of money, multiplied by the velocity of money, equals average prices multiplied by the quantity of real output. This simple relationship — between the quantity of money and its velocity on the left side, and nominal GDP on the right side — is always true. If $5000 worth of final products and services were sold in an economy (nominal GDP is $5000 on the right side), then there had to be enough money, multiplied by the velocity of money, to allow those sales to happen (on the left side).

Fixing the Quantity Theory of Money

The payoff to using this simple relationship to explain inflation comes from fixing two of the variables, *V* and *Q*; that is, we assume that they do not change. Fixing *V*, the velocity of money, means that the number of times money changes hands stays constant from year to year. Fixing *Q*, the quantity of real output, means that the level of real GDP stays constant from year to year. Let's suppose that the quantity of real output stays constant at potential GDP.

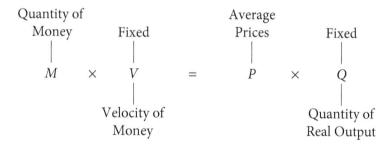

Now, plug in the numbers from our simple story — the quantity of money (*M* = $1000) and the velocity of money (*V* = 5). For average prices — the Consumer Price Index — let's pick the number 100 (*P* = 100). Since we know that *P* × *Q* = 5000, that means the number for real output must be 50 (*Q* = 5000 ÷ 100 = 50).

Plugging in those numbers, we get

$$
\begin{array}{ccccccc}
M & \times & V & = & P & \times & Q \\
1000 & \times & 5 & = & 100 & \times & 50 \\
& & 5000 & = & 5000 & &
\end{array}
$$

The two sides of this equation, just like the two halves of the circular flow, must be equal. There must be enough money, multiplied by the number of times each loonie changes hands (left side of the equation), to allow for the purchase and sale of nominal GDP (right side of the equation).

quantity theory of money increase in the quantity of money causes an equal percentage increase in the inflation rate

More Money Causes Inflation This relationship is called the **quantity theory of money**. The quantity theory states that an increase in the quantity of money causes an equal percentage increase in average prices — the inflation rate. If someone says that "printing money causes inflation," they are stating the quantity theory of money.

Here's an example of what happens when the quantity of money increases by 100 percent, doubling from 1000 loonies to 2000 loonies. Since we have fixed the velocity of money to be constant at 5 and the quantity of real output to be constant at 50, and the two sides of the equation must be equal, then average prices (P) — measured by the CPI — must also double, from 100 to 200.

$$
\begin{array}{ccccccc}
M & \times & V & = & P & \times & Q \\
2000 & \times & 5 & = & 200 & \times & 50 \\
& & 10\,000 & = & 10\,000 & &
\end{array}
$$

The increase in the quantity of money from 1000 loonies to 2000 loonies is an increase of 100 percent. The increase in the CPI, from 100 to 200, is also a 100 percent increase in the inflation rate ($(200 - 100) \div 100 \times 100 = 100$ percent).

The quantity theory of money provides an explanation for the inflation rate numbers. Our story begins with an increase in the quantity of money — the number of loonies in the economy rises from 1000 to 2000. Chapter 11 will explain how the Bank of Canada increases the quantity of money. But for now, let's say a Bank of Canada employee in a helicopter decides to play Santa Claus, and throws 1000 loonies into the air. The loonies fall to the ground and are quickly scooped up by lucky consumers.

Before the loonies fell from the sky, consumers had incomes of $1000. After, consumers have incomes of $2000 and are feeling richer. Consumers try to buy more stuff, but — and this is a big but — the quantity of real output is fixed. As consumers bid against each other trying to get more stuff, the prices of products and services rise. Prices rise, and consumers offer more money to try and get the products and not be left empty-handed — until the rise in prices matches the rise in the quantity of money.

Even when the velocity of money (V) and the quantity of real output (Q) actually do change in the real world, the basic logic of the quantity theory of money still applies. There is too much money chasing too few products and services. In the long run, there is a connection between the quantity of money and the inflation rate in an economy.

Not all inflation is directly caused by an increase in the quantity of money. The trigger that starts inflation may be somewhere else, such as a rise in the price of single product like oil. Inflation triggers are our next topic. But there cannot be inflation in the economy as a whole unless there is an accompanying increase in the quantity of money.

NOTE
Not all inflation is directly caused by increases in the quantity of money. But when there is inflation, there must be an accompanying increase in the quantity of money.

1. In your own words, explain the quantity theory of money.

2. Based on your explanation in question 1, explain how increasing the amount of money everyone has, causes prices to eventually rise.

3. The quantity theory of money assumes that the quantity of real output is at potential GDP and does not change. If, instead, the quantity of real output were below potential GDP and could change, what do you think would happen when the quantity of money increased? Explain why.

MyEconLab

For answers to these Refresh Questions, visit MyEconLab.

When Tim Hortons Pays $18 per Hour: Unemployment and Inflation Trade-offs

7.5

Describe the Phillips Curve and its connections to demand-pull and cost-push inflations.

Since 2006, Alberta has had among the lowest unemployment rates in Canada and the highest inflation rates. During the peak of the oil-driven boom in 2006, unemployment dipped as low as 3 percent, below Alberta's natural rate of unemployment (or equivalently, employment above full employment levels). The Alberta economy was growing quickly, and demand for labour was far greater than the supply. Businesses faced labour shortages. Even entry-level positions at Tim Hortons offered $18 an hour to attract scarce workers.

Demand was so great, and wages so high, that workers from as far away as the Maritimes moved to Alberta to take the higher-paying jobs. But there was a trade-off. While unemployment was low, prices were rising. The Consumer Price Index (CPI) showed an inflation rate for Alberta in 2006 of 3.9 percent, almost twice the national inflation rate of 2 percent.

The Alberta experience is not unique. There is often a trade-off between unemployment and inflation. In countries around the world, situations with low unemployment often trigger high inflation, and situations with high unemployment are often associated with low inflation.

The Phillips Curve

The trade-off between unemployment and inflation was made famous by a New Zealand–born economist named A.W. Phillips. He collected data for the United Kingdom from 1861 to 1957 that showed an inverse relation (when one goes up, the other goes down) between unemployment and inflation. In years when the unemployment rate was lower, the inflation rate was higher. In years when the unemployment rate was higher, the inflation rate was lower. The visual representation of that data took the form of a curve, which became known as the **Phillips Curve**. Most countries, including Canada, showed the same inverse relation. The Canadian numbers are shown in the Phillips Curve in Figure 7.11.

Phillips Curve graph showing an inverse relation between unemployment and inflation

Figure 7.11   Phillips Curve in Canada, 1946–1969

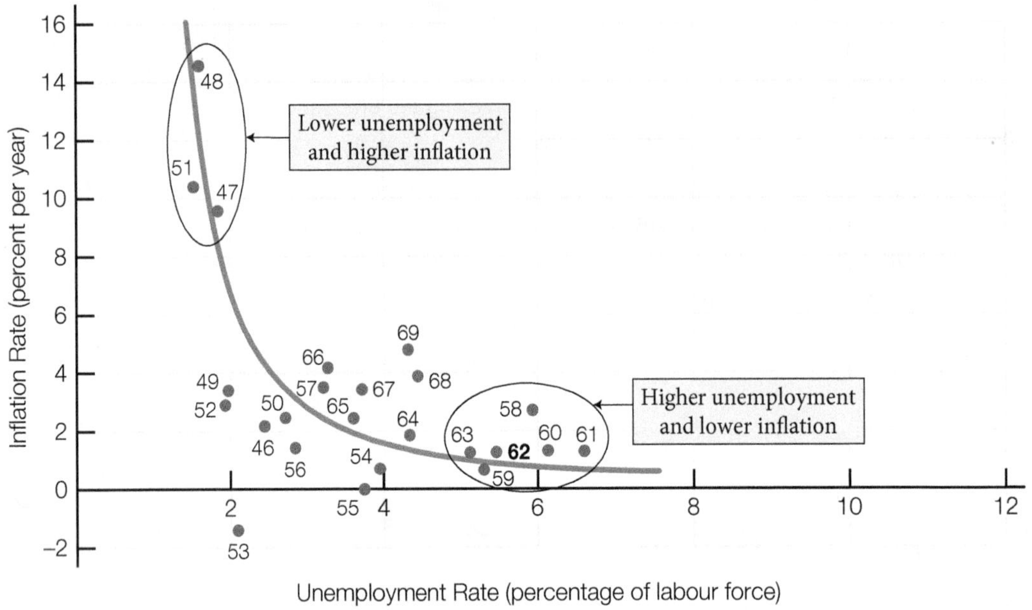

Source: Based on Leacy, F.H., ed. 1983. *Historical Statistics of Canada.* 2nd ed. Series D135-145. Ottawa: Statistics Canada; Statistics Canada CANSIM Table 326-0021, http://cansim2.statcan.gc.ca. Accessed on September 2, 2009; p. 111

The horizontal axis measures the unemployment rate. The vertical axis measures the inflation rate. Each red point on the graph represents a year between 1946 and 1969. The coordinate of a point on the horizontal axis is the unemployment rate, and the coordinate on the vertical axis is the inflation rate that year. For example, in 1962 (point **62**), the unemployment rate in Canada was 5.5 percent (from the point read down to the horizontal axis), and the inflation rate was 1.3 percent (from the point read over to the vertical axis). The blue curve drawn through the points is like the one Phillips sketched to "fit" the data points.

Notice that at the top left of the Phillips Curve, there are points with lower unemployment and higher inflation. At the bottom right of the curve are points with higher unemployment and lower inflation.

Demand-Pull Inflation   The story behind the Phillips Curve's inverse relation between unemployment and inflation is basically the Alberta story.

For years corresponding to points on the top left of the Phillips Curve, the economy was booming, with rapid growth and low unemployment. During expansion years, the economy often produces output near potential real GDP, or even slightly above potential GDP. All inputs, including labour, are fully employed. There is no cyclical unemployment, and frictional, structural, and seasonal unemployment rates may fall below normal. Demand is greater than supply in input markets — there are shortages — putting upward pressure on business costs, including wages. Since incomes are also increasing with higher wages, demand for output is strong — people have more money and are buying more things — making it easier for businesses to raise output prices to match rising costs.

Demand plays the leading role in this story, and the overall price rises are called **demand-pull inflation**. Demand is the key force causing shortages and pulling up prices. There must also be an accompanying increase in the quantity of money.

demand-pull inflation rising average prices caused by increases in demand

The story about the quantity theory of money, where a helicopter showered loonies to increase consumers' incomes, was also a demand-pull inflation story. With increased incomes, consumers demanded more products and services. But with supply fixed at potential GDP, the increased demand created shortages. Competing consumers bid up prices, just as employers in Alberta bid up starting wages to $18 an hour.

Downward Demand-Pull Deflation For years corresponding to points on the bottom right of the Phillips Curve, the demand-pull story works in reverse — decreases in demand pull prices down. During contractions, if demand for output decreases relative to supply, businesses have unsold products and services. Businesses may cut their prices to try to sell the inventory that is piling up in warehouses. Businesses will also cut back production, laying off workers. Real GDP falls, and unemployment increases. There is a recessionary gap.

It is difficult to get a raise when people all around you are out of work and eager to find a job or take yours. Increased unemployment puts downward pressure on wages, allowing businesses to cut output prices or have smaller price increases. High unemployment means consumers have less income to spend, putting more downward pressure on output prices. Decreased demand causes surpluses of unsold products and services, leading businesses to cut prices, or at least not raise them as quickly. There is a bust instead of a boom, with higher unemployment and lower inflation.

The demand-pull inflation story explains the Phillips Curve, with its trade-off between unemployment and inflation. In years with lower unemployment (strong demand), inflation is higher. In years with higher unemployment (weak demand), inflation is lower.

Economists were very confident about this idea of a trade-off between unemployment and inflation. Then the 1970s happened.

OPEC Ends the Original Phillips Curve

In 1973, the 12 members of the Organization of Petroleum Exporting Countries, OPEC, successfully agreed to restrict their combined outputs. This reduced supply of oil, together with wars in the Middle East, caused the world price of oil to skyrocket from US$3 per barrel to $12 per barrel — a 400 percent increase!

Because energy costs are a large part of the cost of most products and services, businesses around the world faced dramatically higher costs. A 400 percent increase for labour costs would see wages rise from $10 per hour to $40 per hour. Imagine the damage that would do to a business's profitability!

▲ OPEC production cutbacks in the 1970s created shortages of gasoline, causing prices to rise and triggering cost-push inflation.

While businesses raised prices to try and cover rising energy costs, consumers had far less income to spend after paying dramatically higher fuel bills for driving and home heating. Prices were rising, so there must have been an accompanying increase in the quantity of money. But demand and output decreased. While the Canadian economy didn't technically fall into a recession — two consecutive quarters of declining real GDP — the pace of economic growth slowed and unemployment increased.

These events repeated with a second oil price rise in 1979. Figure 7.12 extends Figure 7.11 to also include the years 1970 to 2013, years that include the impact of oil price rises.

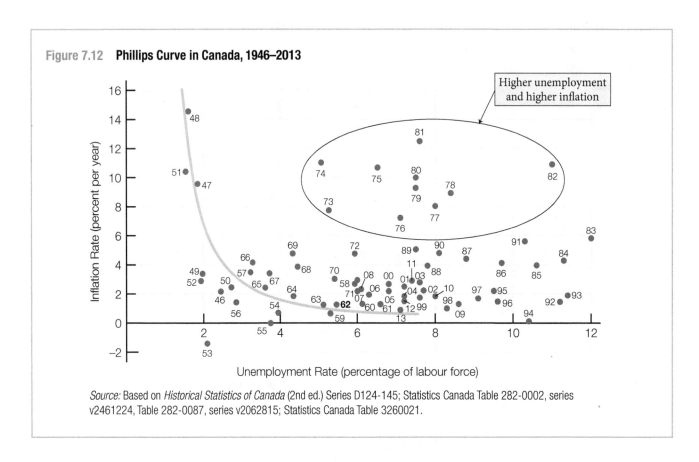

Figure 7.12   Phillips Curve in Canada, 1946–2013

Source: Based on *Historical Statistics of Canada* (2nd ed.) Series D124-145; Statistics Canada Table 282-0002, series v2461224, Table 282-0087, series v2062815; Statistics Canada Table 3260021.

The original, obvious trade-offs between inflation and unemployment — the blue Phillips Curve — disappear. There are now points on the figure, like those for 1973, 1974, and 1982, that have combinations of both higher unemployment and higher inflation. The demand-pull story of inflation failed to explain the combination of higher unemployment and higher inflation.

Supply Shocks and Cost-Push Inflation

supply shocks   events directly affecting businesses' costs, prices, and supply

Supply shocks are events that directly affect businesses' costs, prices, and supply — they are *not* caused by changes in demand. Energy price increases, droughts that reduce the supply of food, and natural disasters that destroy inputs are all examples of negative supply shocks.

Cost-Push Inflation   Supply shocks like the oil price rises do not fit the demand-pull inflation story behind the Phillips Curve's trade-off between unemployment and inflation. A new story emerged called **cost-push inflation**. Supply, not demand, plays the leading role in this story. A decrease in supply caused by increasing costs is the key force pushing up output prices. There is also an accompanying increase in the quantity of money.

cost-push inflation   rising average prices caused by decreases in supply

While average prices are rising, sales of products and services are decreasing — real GDP decreases. Since businesses are decreasing production, unemployment increases. The economy experiences a double dose of bad news — higher inflation and higher unemployment — also called **stagflation**. The word *stagflation* is a combination of *stagnation* — the economy is standing still or falling into recession with higher unemployment — and the rising prices of *inflation*.

stagflation   combination of recession (higher unemployment) and inflation (higher average prices)

The Original Phillips Curve and Beyond

When economists who believed in Say's Law could not explain the unemployment of the Great Depression, Keynes created macroeconomics. Similarly, when the demand-pull inflation story could not explain the stagflation of the 1970s and 1980s, economists developed more sophisticated explanations, including the cost-push inflation story. Just as macroeconomics did not replace microeconomics, but supplemented it, these additional explanations did not replace, but supplemented the original Phillips Curve.

Figure 7.13 summarizes the differences between the demand-pull and cost-push inflation stories. Keep in mind that all of the stories include an accompanying increase in the quantity of money.

Figure 7.13   Types of Inflation

Type of Inflation	Demand–Pull	Cost–Push
Phase of business cycle	Expansion	Contraction
Unemployment	↓ unemployment	↑ unemployment
Inflation	↑ inflation	↑ inflation
Relation between Unemployment and Inflation	Trade-off (Phillips Curve)	Combination (Stagflation) Shifting Phillips Curve

---

Long-Run Phillips Curve   There are immediate trade-offs between inflation and unemployment as the original Phillips Curve suggests. But over longer periods of time, with more years and more triggering events — including supply shocks — the trade-offs and explanations become more complicated. Two factors that complicate the original Phillips Curve are changes in the natural rate of unemployment and changes in inflation expectations.

The original Phillips Curve of Figure 7.11 is a short-run relationship assuming that inflation expectations and the natural rate of unemployment do not change over time. If the expected rate of inflation or the natural rate of unemployment change, the short-run Phillips Curve can shift. These shifts help explain the data points that do not fit on the original, unchanged Phillips Curve.

These complications are not necessary for you to think like an economist, but they make it harder for policymakers. As we will see, policies to address unemployment often make inflation worse, and policies to address inflation often make unemployment worse. And the stagflation challenges to policymakers are even more difficult.

Refresh 7.5

MyEconLab

For answers to these Refresh Questions, visit MyEconLab.

1. Explain the trade-off that the Phillips Curve illustrates.

2. Describe the difference between demand-pull inflation and cost-push inflation.

3. Would you rather have higher inflation or higher unemployment? What are the reasons behind your personal choice?

Study Guide

7.1 Who Is Unemployed?
Healthy and Unhealthy Types of Unemployment

The unemployment rate measures the percentage of the labour force who are out of work and actively searching for jobs, but misses involuntary part-time workers and discouraged workers. There are four types of unemployment — frictional, structural, seasonal, and cyclical — but only cyclical unemployment is both unhealthy and a problem.

- Statistics Canada places everyone in working-age population (age 15 and over) into one of three categories:
  - Employed — working full-time or part-time at paid job
  - Unemployed — not doing paid work and actively searching for job, or on temporary layoff, or about to start a new job
  - Not in the labour force — does not fit into employed or unemployed categories (full-time student, homemaker, retiree)
- **Labour Force** = Employed + Unemployed
- **Unemployment Rate**
  - Percentage of people in labour force who are unemployed

$$\text{Unemployment Rate} = \frac{\text{Unemployed}}{\text{Labour Force}} \times 100$$

- **Labour Force Participation Rate**
  - Percentage of working-age population in the labour force (employed or unemployed)

$$\text{Labour Force Participation Rate} = \frac{\text{Labour Force}}{\text{Working-Age Population}} \times 100$$

- Unemployment rate misses
  - *involuntary part-time workers* — employed part time, would rather have full-time job, but can't find one.
  - **discouraged workers** — want to work but have given up actively searching for jobs.

- *Labour Underutilization Rate* — unemployment rate including unemployed, involuntary part-time workers, discouraged workers.

- Healthy and unhealthy types of unemployment:
  - **Frictional unemployment** — due to normal labour turnover and job search; healthy part of a changing economy; not a problem.
  - **Structural unemployment** — due to technological change or international competition making workers' skills obsolete; there is a mismatch between the skills workers have and the skills new jobs require; healthy part of changing economy; problem requiring retraining.
  - **Seasonal unemployment** — due to seasonal changes in weather; healthy not a problem.
  - **Cyclical unemployment** — due to business cycle fluctuations in economic activity; unhealthy part of changing economy; problem needs fixing.

7.2 How Full Is "Full Employment?"
The Natural Rate of Unemployment

The natural rate of unemployment occurs at full employment, when there is only healthy frictional, structural, and seasonal unemployment. Relative to the natural rate, the unemployment rate is higher in a recessionary gap and lower in an inflationary gap.

- **Natural Rate of Unemployment** — unemployment rate at **full employment**; includes frictional, structural, seasonal unemployment.
  - Full employment is not zero percent unemployment but zero percent cyclical unemployment.
- Relation between natural rate of unemployment and potential GDP:
  - When unemployment = natural rate; real GDP = potential GDP; full employment
  - When unemployment > natural rate; real GDP < potential GDP; recessionary output gap; cyclical unemployment
  - When unemployment < natural rate; real GDP > potential GDP; inflationary output gap

7.3 Lightening Up Your Wallet: What Is Inflation?

Inflation is measured by changes in the Consumer Price Index, hurts those on fixed incomes, creates risk for business investment, and, through expectations, can create a vicious cycle of more inflation. The inflation rate overstates increases in the cost of living by missing switches to cheaper substitutes and new/improved products/services.

- **Inflation** is both a persistent rise in average prices and a fall in the value of money. When inflation occurs,
  - you must spend more to get same products and services as before.
  - your money is worth less.
- **Consumer Price Index (CPI)** — measure of average prices of fixed shopping basket of products and services.
  - CPI = 100 for the base year, currently 2002
- **Inflation rate** — annual percentage change in Consumer Price Index.

$$\text{Inflation} = \frac{\text{CPI for current year} - \text{CPI for previous year}}{\text{CPI for previous year}} \times 100$$

  - **Core inflation rate** — inflation rate excluding volatile categories.
- Inflation is a worry because of the falling value of money.
  - Inflation reduces purchasing power of people with fixed (unchanged dollar) income or savings.
  - **Nominal interest rate** — observed interest rate; equals number of dollars received per year in interest as percentage of number of dollars saved.
  - Realized **real interest rate**
    = nominal interest rate adjusted for effects of inflation
    = nominal interest rate – inflation rate.
- Inflation is a worry because unpredictable prices create risk and discourage business investment.
- Inflation is a worry because expectations of inflation can cause inflation.
- Economists view predictable inflation rates between 1 and 3 percent as acceptable.
- **Deflation** — persistent fall in average prices and a rise in value of money.
  - Falling prices can lead consumers to postpone purchases, causing economic contraction and increasing unemployment.
  - Deflation benefits savers but hurts borrowers.
  - Deflation is worse than low inflation.

- CPI fixes quantities in the shopping basket to isolate the impact of changing prices only on cost of living.
  - With fixed quantities, when prices rise the CPI misses quantity switches to cheaper substitutes and new/improved products. Inflation rate based on the CPI *overstates* increases in cost of living.

7.4 Inflation Starts with "*M*" The Quantity Theory of Money

The quantity theory of money explains inflation from an increase in the quantity of money in an economy, holding constant the velocity of money and the quantity of real output.

- For any economy with money, $M \times V = P \times Q$, where
  - M represents the quantity of money.
  - V represents the **velocity of money** — number of times a unit of money changes hands during a year.
  - P represents average prices — the Consumer Price Index.
  - Q represents the aggregate quantity of real output.
  - $P \times Q$ represents nominal GDP.
- There must be enough money, multiplied by the velocity of money, to allow sales of all final products and services produced (nominal GDP).
- **Quantity theory of money** states that an increase in the quantity of money causes an equal percentage increase in the inflation rate.
  - Quantity theory of money takes equation $M \times V = P \times Q$, fixes V and fixes Q at potential GDP.
  - Quantity theory of money is behind "printing money causes inflation."
- Not all inflation is caused by increases in quantity of money. But inflation is always accompanied by increases in quantity of money.

7.5 When Tim Hortons Pays $18 per Hour: Unemployment and Inflation Trade-offs

The Phillips Curve shows an immediate trade-off between unemployment and inflation consistent with demand-pull stories of inflation. Cost-push inflation (simultaneous unemployment and inflation) changes in expectations and changes in the natural rate of unemployment complicate the original Phillips Curve.

- **Phillips Curve** — graph showing inverse relation between unemployment and inflation.
- **Demand-pull inflation** — rising average prices caused by increases in demand — explains Phillips Curve's trade-off between unemployment and inflation.
  - During expansions, demand is key force causing shortages and pulling up prices for inputs (like wages) and for outputs.

- **Cost-push inflation** — rising average prices caused by decreases in supply — does *not* fit Phillips Curve.
  - Cost-push inflation is caused by **supply shocks** — events directly affecting businesses' costs, prices, and supply. Decrease in supply is key force pushing up output prices, while pushing economy into contraction, increasing unemployment.
  - Cost-push inflation can cause **stagflation** — combination of recession (higher unemployment) and inflation (higher average prices).

- Both demand-pull and cost-push inflation require an accompanying increase in the quantity of money.
- Over time, trade-offs between unemployment and inflation of the original Phillips Curve become complicated due to changes in
  - expectations of inflation.
  - natural rate of unemployment.

TRUE/FALSE

Circle the correct answer. Solutions to these questions are available at the end of the book and on MyEconLab. You can also visit the MyEconLab Study Plan to access additional questions that will help you master the concepts covered in this chapter.

Suppose that a group on Facebook has five people: A. J., B. J., C. J., D. J., and V. J. The group members post the following information regarding their job status:

A. J.: "I worked for BlueBerry Wireless this month and last month."

B. J.: "Last month I worked for Canwell Soup. This month I am on temporary layoff because of a temporary slowdown in the economy."

C. J.: "Last month I was not working, but I was looking for work. This month I accepted a part-time job at Burger Fling but was hoping for a full-time job."

D. J.: "I have never worked and I have never looked for work (I like to party and spin records)."

V. J.: "I was not working and looking for work last month. This month I gave up my search for work because I was discouraged."

Think of this group as a mini-economy. Use this scenario to answer questions 1–11.

7.1 Unemployment

1. B. J. would be counted as unemployed this month.   T   F

2. V. J. was unemployed in both months.   T   F

3. Between last month and this month, the number of employed persons stayed the same, but the number of unemployed decreased.   T   F

4. Between last month and this month, the unemployment rate increased.   T   F

5. If discouraged workers and involuntary part-time workers were counted in the official definition of unemployed, unemployment would have increased between last month and this month.   T   F

7.2 Natural Rate of Unemployment

6. B. J. is cyclically unemployed this month.   T   F

7. There is full employment this month.   T   F

8. If C. J. and V. J. were both structurally unemployed last month, then this economy had a recessionary gap last month.   T   F

9. V. J. is planning C. J.'s stag party (a party for a bachelor shortly before marriage). C. J. loves economics and V. J. wants to make up T-shirts for the stag that describe the current state of the economy. If average prices are rising and output is decreasing, the shirts should say *stagnation*.   T   F

7.3 Inflation

10. A. J. is a nonsmoking vegetarian who walks to work and lives with his parents. If increases in A.J.'s wage were linked to increases in the CPI — and prices of gasoline fuel, housing, meat, and tobacco were on the rise — then the wage increase would underestimate A. J.'s true cost of living increase.   T   F

11. V. J. wants to invest his savings with a bank. The bank pays an interest rate of 2 percent and the inflation rate is 2 percent. The real interest rate is 4 percent.   T   F

7.4 Quantity Theory of Money

12. According to the quantity theory, if 20 percent more money is printed, average prices increase by 20 percent.   T   F

13. If the quantity of money is $50 and nominal GDP is $100, the velocity of circulation is 0.5.　　　T　F

15. If the unemployment rate is lower when inflation is higher, this is evidence of cost-push inflation.　　　T　F

7.5 Unemployment–Inflation Trade-offs

14. If the unemployment rate is lower when inflation is higher, this evidence supports the Phillips Curve.　　　T　F

MULTIPLE CHOICE

Circle the best answer. Solutions to these questions are available at the end of the book and on MyEconLab. You can also visit the MyEconLab Study Plan to access similar questions that will help you master the concepts covered in this chapter.

7.1 Unemployment

1. **Who would be counted as unemployed?**
    a) Sirena is a college student with no job.
    b) Miguel starts a new job in a week.
    c) Reetu stopped looking for work because she was unable to find a job.
    d) Rajinder is working part-time but wishes he was working full-time.

2. **If Salma loses her job and starts looking for work, the**
    a) number of employed increases.
    b) labour force increases.
    c) labour force decreases.
    d) labour force participation rate remains unchanged.

3. **Suppose that there are 19 million people employed, 1 million unemployed, and 25 million people 15 years of age or older. Which statement is *true*?**
    a) The labour force is 19 million.
    b) The labour force participation rate is 80 percent.
    c) The unemployment rate is 4 percent.
    d) The unemployment rate is 1 percent.

4. **The summer job market for post-secondary students starts in May. In May 2009, 59 000 fewer students were employed compared to a year earlier. These students' labour force participation rate also fell over the year, from 75.2 percent to 68.6 percent. What is the correct interpretation of these results?**
    a) More students are working.
    b) More students are in the labour force.
    c) Fewer students are looking for work.
    d) Fewer students are in the labour force.

7.2 Natural Rate of Unemployment

5. **Alberta's 2.9 percent unemployment rate in June 2007 was the lowest of any province. High labour demand and wages in Alberta encouraged unemployed workers from Newfoundland and Labrador to move to Alberta, where they found jobs. This increased the**
    a) unemployment rate in Newfoundland and Labrador.
    b) labour force in Newfoundland and Labrador.
    c) unemployment rate in Alberta.
    d) labour force in Alberta.

6. **Close to 567 000 additional people became officially unemployed between October 2008 and March 2009, and another 236 000 either gave up looking because they were discouraged, expected to be called back, or were involuntary part-timers. If the 236 000 individuals were counted as unemployed, then the number of people**
    a) employed would decrease.
    b) unemployed would decrease.
    c) unemployed would increase.
    d) not in the labour force would increase.

7. **In the year grade 13 was eliminated in Ontario, grade 12 students and grade 13 students graduated at the same time. This increased the number of people leaving school to find jobs. What form of unemployment was likely to be unusually high that year?**
    a) Seasonal unemployment
    b) Frictional unemployment
    c) Structural unemployment
    d) Cyclical unemployment

8. There is a recessionary gap when the unemployment rate is
   a) below the natural rate.
   b) above the natural rate.
   c) at full employment.
   d) at the natural rate.

7.3 Inflation

9. If the CPI was 120 in 2015 and 126 in 2016, then the inflation rate was
   a) 5 percent, which is above the Bank of Canada's target range for inflation.
   b) 5 percent, which is within the Bank of Canada's target range for inflation.
   c) 20 percent, which is above the Bank of Canada's target range for inflation.
   d) 20 percent, which is within the Bank of Canada's target range for inflation.

10. What does the inflation rate miss?
    a) New products
    b) Better products
    c) Switches to cheaper substitutes
    d) All of the above

11. Inflation can harm those who
    a) are living on fixed incomes.
    b) keep money under their bed.
    c) save money in the bank.
    d) all of the above.

7.4 Quantity Theory of Money

12. The number of times a unit of money changes hands during a year is called
    a) money supply.
    b) velocity.
    c) price.
    d) real GDP.

13. Which factors are fixed in the quantity theory of money?
    a) Money and velocity
    b) Velocity and real GDP
    c) Velocity and price
    d) Price and real GDP

7.5 Unemployment–Inflation Trade-offs

14. If the Phillips Curve is true, which of the following could never happen?
    a) Invention of the Phillips screwdriver
    b) Stagflation
    c) Stagnation
    d) Inflation

15. Economists believed there was a clear trade-off between unemployment and inflation until the
    a) 1950s.
    b) 1970s.
    c) 1990s.
    d) 2000s.

8 Skating to Where the Puck Is Going

Aggregate Supply and Aggregate Demand

LEARNING OBJECTIVES

After reading this chapter, you should be able to:

8.1 Explain long-run aggregate supply and its relation to potential GDP and macroeconomic performance outcomes.

8.2 Identify how macroeconomic players choose short-run aggregate supply plans and differentiate the choices and supply shocks that change aggregate supply.

8.3 Explain the difference between a change in aggregate quantity demanded and a change in aggregate demand, and list five shocks that change aggregate demand.

8.4 Use the aggregate supply and aggregate demand model to explain the macroeconomic performance of real GDP, unemployment, and inflation.

8.5 Describe the "Yes — Markets Self-Adjust" and "No — Markets Fail Often" answers about origins, expectations, and market responses to business cycles.

WHAT MADE WAYNE GRETZKY the highest-

scoring hockey player of all time? Talent, discipline, and hard work, of course. Some say his greatness came from following this father's advice: "Skate to where the puck is going, not to where it is." By anticipating the play — seeing two steps ahead — Gretzky was able to be in the right place at the right time to score goals. Similarly, success in business depends on anticipating the market. You can get rich if you supply products or services that consumers want, when they want them, or if you correctly anticipate where stock prices or real estate values are going.

This chapter examines the choices not behind the hockey performance outcomes of goals and assists, but behind the key macroeconomic performance outcomes of real GDP, unemployment, and inflation. Macroeconomic outcomes begin two steps earlier, with supply choices made by consumers, businesses, and governments. You will examine the choices that these macroeconomic players make, and how the players' separate smart choices add up to aggregate supply and aggregate demand.

Think about how it would be if you watched a sport where you don't know the rules. Cricket? Lacrosse? Curling? The players' actions would seem incomprehensible. Aggregate supply and aggregate demand provide a framework for thinking about macroeconomics. This framework will help you understand the action in the economy — when and why it hits the targets of steady growth in living standards, full employment, and stable prices, and when it misses with business cycles, unemployment, and inflation. You may not achieve Gretzky's greatness, but understanding his father's advice will help you make smarter choices on the economic field of play and evaluate economic policies that politicians will ask you to vote for.

8.1 Macroeconomic Performance Targets: Potential GDP and Long-Run Aggregate Supply

Explain long-run aggregate supply and its relation to potential GDP and macroeconomic performance outcomes.

When hockey players perform well, they score goals and win championships. When the macro economy performs well, real GDP equals potential GDP, and there is full employment, stable prices, and steady growth in living standards. What causes the macro economy to sometimes hit these targets, and other times to miss?

From Production Possibilities Frontier to Long-Run Aggregate Supply

The aggregate supply and aggregate demand framework is a model — a simplified representation of the real word — that allows us to understand the macro economy's performance. To build this model, we return to the macro production possibilities frontier (*PPF*) from Chapter 6, reproduced in Figure 8.1a.

Figure 8.1 **Production Possibilities Frontier and Long-Run Aggregate Supply**

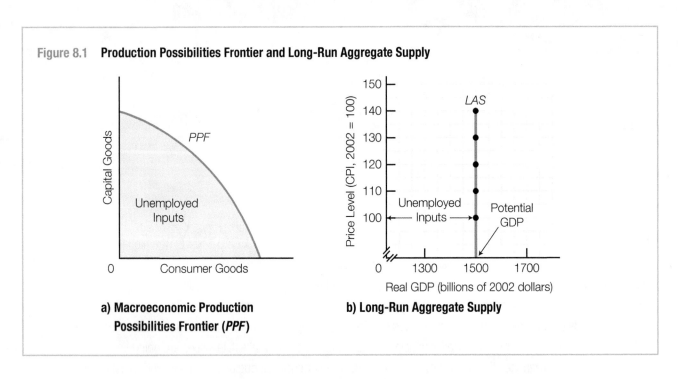

a) Macroeconomic Production Possibilities Frontier (*PPF*)

b) Long-Run Aggregate Supply

Production Possibilities Frontier The macro *PPF* shows the maximum combinations of consumer goods and capital goods that the economy can produce. At any point on the *PPF*, inputs are fully employed and the economy is producing at potential GDP. Points inside the *PPF* represent unemployed inputs — workers without jobs, factories not operating, farmland not producing crops. Notice two things about the *PPF*. First, inputs do not appear on the graph. The *PPF* takes the quantity and quality of inputs as given to focus attention on potential GDP — the outputs that those inputs can produce. Second, there are no prices on the graph, only quantities of outputs.

Long-Run Aggregate Supply   Figure 8.1b transfers the potential GDP of the *PPF* to a new graph with the economy's real GDP on the horizontal axis and price level on the vertical axis. Real GDP is measured in constant 2002 dollars. The price level is measured by the Consumer Price Index (CPI), where the price level in 2002 equals 100. Again, inputs do not directly appear on the graph.

Long-run aggregate supply is the economy's potential GDP — the quantity of real GDP supplied when all inputs are fully employed. The long-run aggregate supply curve — *LAS* — is a vertical line at potential GDP. No matter what the price level is at potential GDP, the *quantity* of real GDP does not change. If the price level rises from 100 to 140, the quantity of real GDP remains at $1500 billion.

long-run aggregate supply
potential GDP — the quantity of real GDP supplied when all inputs are fully employed

Just as all points inside the *PPF* in Figure 8.1a represent unemployed inputs, all quantities of real GDP less than potential GDP in Figure 8.1b represent unemployed inputs, including unemployed workers.

Long-run aggregate supply represents two of the macroeconomic performance targets — potential GDP and full employment. The macroeconomic targets of economic growth and stable prices will appear as we develop the rest of the aggregate supply and aggregate demand model.

Long Run versus Short Run

The aggregate supply choices of the macroeconomic players depend on the time period. That is why the words "long run" are in the definition of long-run aggregate supply.

In macroeconomics, the *long run* is a period of time long enough for all prices and wages to adjust so that Adam Smith's invisible hand works well. In the long run, prices adjust to equilibrium prices that coordinate smart choices, and the economy is producing at potential GDP. The *short run* is a period of time where some input prices do not change — they have not adjusted to clear all markets and some choices are not coordinated.

Long run and short run are *not* defined in calendar time as a number of months or years. They are defined in terms of whether all prices have adjusted to equilibrium prices (long run) or whether some prices have not adjusted (short run).

Long-run aggregate supply is the full-employment outcome of coordinated smart choices, while short-run aggregate supply, coming next, looks at the choices that consumers, businesses, and governments make two steps before.

NOTE
The *long run* is a period of time long enough for all prices and wages to adjust to equilibrium; the economy is at potential GDP.

The *short run* is a period of time when some input prices do not change; all prices have *not* adjusted to clear all markets.

Refresh 8.1

1. In your own words, explain the macroeconomic terms *long run* and *short run*.

2. Are points inside the production possibilities frontier (*PPF*) short-run or long-run points? What about points on the *PPF*? Explain.

3. What happens to the long-run aggregate supply curve (*LAS*) if the population increases? Can you predict what that will do to living standards? Explain your thinking.

MyEconLab

For answers to these Refresh Questions, visit MyEconLab.

8.2 If You Plan and Build It…
Short-Run Aggregate Supply

Identify how macroeconomic players choose short-run aggregate supply plans and differentiate the choices and supply shocks that change aggregate supply.

Businesses are the most important players for aggregate supply plans. They make supply plans in the short run. Imagine a photo of the economy at a moment in time. There are existing inputs (which determine production possibilities and long-run aggregate supply), and businesses face given input prices. They know what the wage rate is if they want to hire more labour; they know what electricity costs are if they want to use more power. Input prices do not change in the short run.

Once a business looks, Gretzky-like, two steps ahead and anticipates what consumers will demand, it starts planning its supply choices. Based on the existing inputs, the first choice is what products or services to produce and in what quantities. Those output choices, in turn, determine choices about how intensively to use inputs. A business might run a single eight-hour shift, a double shift, or even a triple shift operating 24 hours a day to produce outputs.

▲ Businesses such as the one operating this giant digger in the Alberta oil sands must plan far ahead in order to have the right machines in the right place at the right time.

JuergenBosse/iStockphoto

Short-Run Supply Plans with Existing Inputs

Macroeconomic supply plans with existing inputs are similar to microeconomic choices about *quantity supplied* (Chapter 3). Microeconomics' *law of supply* states that as the price of a product or service rises, the quantity supplied increases. Macroeconomics supply plans connecting price and quantity supplied are added together for all of the macroeconomic players. For prices, we use the average price level in the economy, as measured by the Consumer Price Index. For quantities, we use real GDP, which adds together the quantities of all final products and services produced in an economy, valued at constant prices.

short-run aggregate supply
quantity of real GDP macroeconomic players plan to supply at different price levels

Short-Run Aggregate Supply Curve   **Short-run aggregate supply** is the quantity of real GDP that macroeconomic players plan to supply at different price levels. Figure 8.2 adds a short-run aggregate supply curve (*SAS*) to the long-run aggregate supply curve of Figure 8.1b. Each point on the *SAS* curve corresponds to a row on the table in Figure 8.2. For example, look at point *A* on the *SAS* curve and row *A* of the table. If the price level is 100, short-run aggregate quantity supplied is $1300 billion of real GDP. If the price level rises to 110 (point and row *B*), short-run aggregate quantity supplied increases to $1400 billion.

The short-run aggregate supply curve is upward-sloping because input prices are fixed in the short run. When the price level rises, higher output prices with fixed input prices mean more profits, so businesses plan to increase the quantity supplied of real GDP. A fall in the price level has the opposite effect, and decreases the quantity supplied of real GDP.

The *LAS* curve and *SAS* curve intersect at point *C*, with a price level of 120 and real GDP of $1500 billion. Only at this intersection will short-run supply plans hit the target of potential GDP. The supply plans at points *A* and *B* are less than potential GDP and the supply plans at points *D* and *E* are greater than potential GDP. All of these combinations of price levels and quantities of real GDP are just *plans* — we will see whether or not the plans work out after adding information about aggregate demand.

Figure 8.2   Short-Run and Long-Run Aggregate Supply

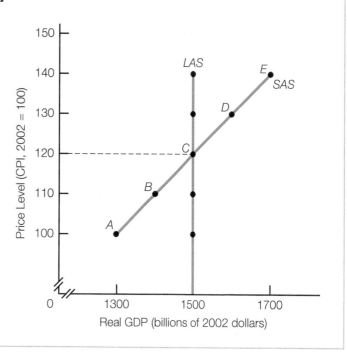

	Price Level (CPI)	Short-Run Real GDP Supplied (billions of 2002 dollars)
A	100	1300
B	110	1400
C	120	1500
D	130	1600
E	140	1700

The Law of Short-Run Aggregate Supply   The **law of short-run aggregate supply** states that as the price level rises, the aggregate quantity supplied of real GDP increases. With fixed input prices, higher output prices create incentives for increased production through higher profits and by covering higher marginal opportunity costs of production.

Supply Plans to Increase Inputs

With existing inputs, macroeconomic players make output decisions about the quantity of real GDP they plan to supply. The players also make decisions that *change* the quantities and qualities of inputs available in the future.

Increase in Potential GDP and Aggregate Supply   If you complete your post-secondary education, you add to your human capital and make yourself, and the economy, more productive. If a mining company develops a technologically advanced drilling machine, or if the government builds new transit lines that make it faster and cheaper to transport people and products, those choices increase future productivity. Any decision that increases the quantity or quality of inputs increases an economy's potential GDP. In the language of the aggregate demand and aggregate supply model, supply plans that increase input quantity or quality **increase in aggregate supply**.

law of short-run aggregate supply   as the price level rises, aggregate quantity supplied of real GDP increases

increase in aggregate supply   increase in economy's capacity to produce real GDP caused by increases in quantity or quality of inputs

Greg Balfour Evans/Alamy

◀ When government invests in building or repairing infrastructure, it is easier and less expensive for everyone to do business, thus increasing aggregate supply.

An increase in aggregate supply is economic growth — the expansion of the economy's capacity to produce products and services. Figure 8.3 shows the effects of an increase in the quantity or quality of inputs.

In Figure 8.3a, the increase in inputs shifts the production possibilities frontier to the right, from PPF_0 to PPF_1. It is now possible to produce greater combined quantities of consumer goods and capital goods. In Figure 8.3b, the increase in inputs shifts *both* the long-run aggregate supply curve (LAS_0) and the short-run aggregate supply curve (SAS_0) together rightward to LAS_1 and SAS_1. The rightward shift of *LAS* represents an increase in potential GDP. With the rightward shift in *SAS*, at any price level, businesses plan to supply more real GDP. For example, at a price level of 120, real GDP supplied with the original inputs was $1500 billion (point C on SAS_0). With additional or more productive inputs, real GDP supplied is $1700 billion (point C' on SAS_1).

Changes in the quantity or quality of inputs, including technological change, shift both *LAS* and *SAS* in the same direction. An increase in inputs shifts both *LAS* and *SAS* rightward. We will assume that after the shifts, the intersection between *LAS* and *SAS* is at a lower price level because of cost reductions — in this example, the price level falls from 120 to 110. A decrease in inputs (for example, from a natural disaster) shifts both *LAS* and *SAS* leftward.

NOTE

Changes in the quantity or quality of inputs, including technological change, shift both *LAS* and *SAS* in the same direction. An increase in inputs shifts both *LAS* and *SAS* rightward. A decrease in inputs shifts both *LAS* and *SAS* leftward.

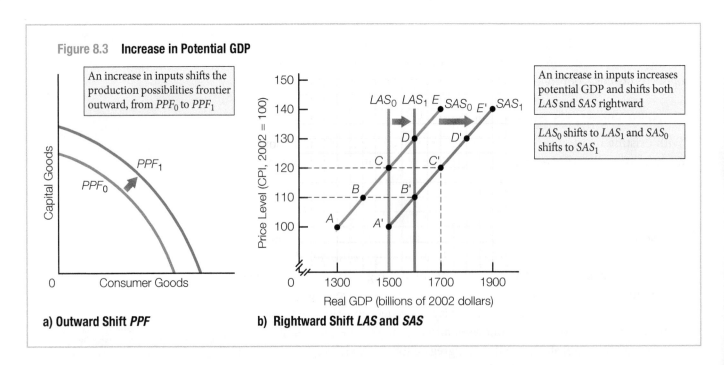

Figure 8.3   Increase in Potential GDP

An increase in inputs shifts the production possibilities frontier outward, from PPF_0 to PPF_1

An increase in inputs increases potential GDP and shifts both *LAS* snd *SAS* rightward

LAS_0 shifts to LAS_1 and SAS_0 shifts to SAS_1

a) **Outward Shift *PPF***

b) **Rightward Shift *LAS* and *SAS***

Moving Along Curves versus Shifting Curves I am hoping you notice the parallels to the microeconomic language of supply. In microeconomics, we distinguish between a change in quantity supplied (caused by a change in the price of the product or service) and a change in supply (caused by a change in any other factor). A change in quantity supplied is a movement along an unchanged supply curve. A change in supply shifts the curve.

In macroeconomics, with existing inputs and fixed input prices, a change in aggregate quantity supplied is caused by a change in the price level — a movement along an unchanged short-run aggregate supply curve (*SAS*). A change in aggregate supply — a shift of *both* the *LAS* and *SAS* curves — is caused by changes in the quantity or quality of inputs. A change in the quantity or quality of inputs changes short-run aggregate supply plans and shifts *SAS*, but also changes potential GDP and shifts *LAS* — changing the performance target for the economy. There is one more important change we haven't looked at.

Changes in Input Prices and Aggregate Supply What happens to aggregate supply if input prices change? Before I tell you, can you figure out the effect on short-run aggregate supply plans (the *SAS* curve) and long-run aggregate supply (the *LAS* curve)? Here is a hint: The effect is different on *SAS* versus *LAS*.

The short-run aggregate supply curve (*SAS*) assumes input prices are fixed. So if input prices change, the *SAS* curve shifts. Figure 8.4 shows the effect of a rise in input prices.

Originally, the short-run aggregate supply curve is SAS_0 and the long-run aggregate supply curve is *LAS*. A rise in input prices — for example, a rise in wage rates — decreases short-run aggregate supply and shifts the short-run aggregate supply curve leftward to SAS_1. With the original input prices (SAS_0), at a price level of 120, businesses plan to supply $1500 billion of real GDP. After input prices rise (SAS_1), businesses plan to supply only $1300 billion of real GDP. At any price level, rising input prices reduce profits so businesses decrease their real GDP supplied. *SAS* shifts leftward. Falling input prices have the opposite effect, increasing short-run aggregate supply and shifting *SAS* rightward.

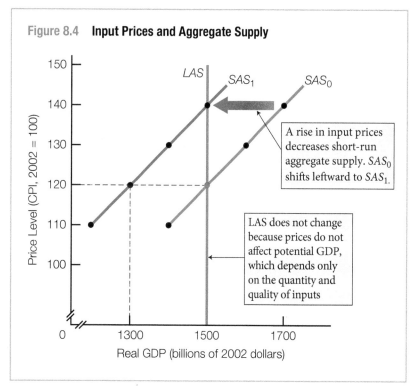

Figure 8.4   **Input Prices and Aggregate Supply**

A rise in input prices decreases short-run aggregate supply. SAS_0 shifts leftward to SAS_1.

LAS does not change because prices do not affect potential GDP, which depends only on the quantity and quality of inputs

But rising (or falling) input prices do *not* affect potential GDP, so long-run aggregate supply and the *LAS* curve do not shift. When input prices change, short-run aggregate supply changes but long-run aggregate supply does not. Changing input prices shift *SAS* but do not shift *LAS*.

NOTE

Changing input prices shift *SAS* but do not shift *LAS*. Rising input prices shift *SAS* leftward. Falling input prices shift *SAS* rightward.

Supply Shocks and Short-Run Aggregate Supply

Short-run aggregate supply is largely determined by the plans and choices that macroeconomic players — Canadian businesses, consumers, and government — make. But events beyond the players' control also affect aggregate supply.

These *supply shocks*, which you read about in Chapter 7, are events that directly affect business costs, prices, and supply. There are negative and positive supply shocks that shift the aggregate supply curves. Supply shocks can affect long-run aggregate supply and short-run aggregate supply, but we will focus on the effect on short-run aggregate supply and the *SAS* curve.

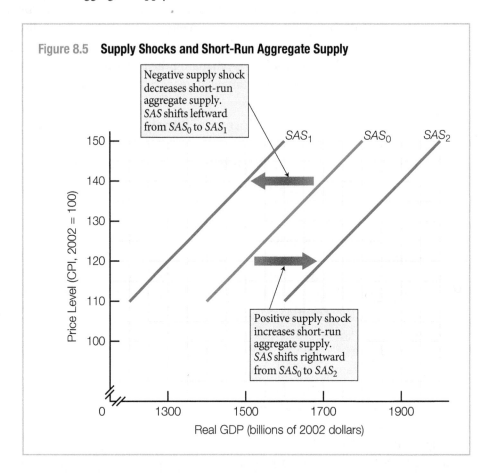

Figure 8.5 **Supply Shocks and Short-Run Aggregate Supply**

Negative supply shock decreases short-run aggregate supply. *SAS* shifts leftward from SAS_0 to SAS_1

Positive supply shock increases short-run aggregate supply. *SAS* shifts rightward from SAS_0 to SAS_2

Negative Supply Shocks Decrease Short-Run Aggregate Supply   Some negative supply shocks are caused by natural disasters, while others are created by rising input prices. Examples include droughts that decrease the supply of agricultural products, earthquakes that destroy inputs, and energy price increases. A negative supply shock in macroeconomics is similar to a decrease in supply (not quantity supplied) in microeconomics. Negative supply shocks shift *SAS* leftward.

Positive Supply Shocks Increase Short-Run Aggregate Supply   Positive supply shocks can come from new ideas and new resources or falling input prices. Examples include scientific discoveries that lead to more productive, lower-cost technologies and lower world prices for resource inputs. A positive supply shock in macroeconomics is similar to an increase in supply (not quantity supplied) in microeconomics. Positive supply shocks shift *SAS* rightward.

Figure 8.6 is a good study device for reviewing differences between the law of short-run aggregate supply (focusing on aggregate quantity supplied and movement along an unchanged *SAS* curve) and the factors that change short-run aggregate supply — negative and positive supply shocks (shifting the *SAS* curve).

Figure 8.6   Law of Short-Run Aggregate Supply and Changes in Short-Run Aggregate Supply

The Law of Short-Run Aggregate Supply *In the short run, the aggregate quantity supplied of real GDP*	
Decreases if:	*Increases if:*
• price level falls	• price level rises

Changes in Short-Run Aggregate Supply *The short-run aggregate supply of real GDP*	
Decreases if:	*Increases if:*
• businesses do not replace depreciating equipment and inputs	• businesses plan to increase quantity or quality inputs
• negative supply shock raises price for resource inputs	• positive supply shock lowers price for resource inputs
• negative supply shock destroys inputs	• positive supply shock improves technologies

Will Supply Create Its Own Demand?   The plans made by businesses, consumers, and government, together with supply shocks, combine to create short-run aggregate supply. Plans are made two Gretzky-like steps ahead, in anticipation of what demand will be. Will supply create its own demand, as Say's Law claims? Will these supply choices create enough demand so that the plans of the macroeconomic players are realized? Will the economy hit the target of potential GDP and full employment? If there are supply shocks that disrupt an economy at potential GDP, will markets quickly adjust to restore full employment, stable prices, and steady growth? To answer these questions, we must first look at aggregate demand — in the next section.

Refresh 8.2

1. Explain the difference between a change in aggregate quantity supplied and a change in aggregate supply.

2. All supply shocks shift the short-run aggregate supply curve (*SAS*). Which supply shocks also shift long-run aggregate supply? Explain their effect on *LAS*.

3. You own a pickle business and currently supply (sell) 1000 jars a month at a price of $5 per jar. Pick a specific supply shock (negative or positive) and explain your willingness — or not — to supply pickles at that same $5 price *after the shock*.

MyEconLab

For answers to these Refresh Questions, visit MyEconLab.

... Will They Come and Buy It? Aggregate Demand

Explain the difference between a change in aggregate quantity demanded and a change in aggregate demand, and list five shocks that change aggregate demand.

How much money are you planning to spend this month? We may not have Wayne Gretzky's ability to see two steps ahead, but we do still plan. As consumers, we set budgets, planning how much to spend and how much to save. Every business project has a plan — and success depends on delivering that project on time and on budget. Governments also plan. The finance minister presents a budget in Parliament outlining the government's taxing and spending plans for the year.

Of course, life happens and plans don't always work out. Your car may break down; you could lose your job; you may win the lottery. All of these events will change your actual spending from your planned spending. Before we see how plans work out, let's look at demand plans.

Demand Plans and the Circular Flow

To explain demand plans we'll use the enlarged circular flow diagram. Figure 8.7 is the same as Figure 6.7.

Figure 8.7 Enlarged GDP Circular Flow of Income and Spending ($) with Banking System

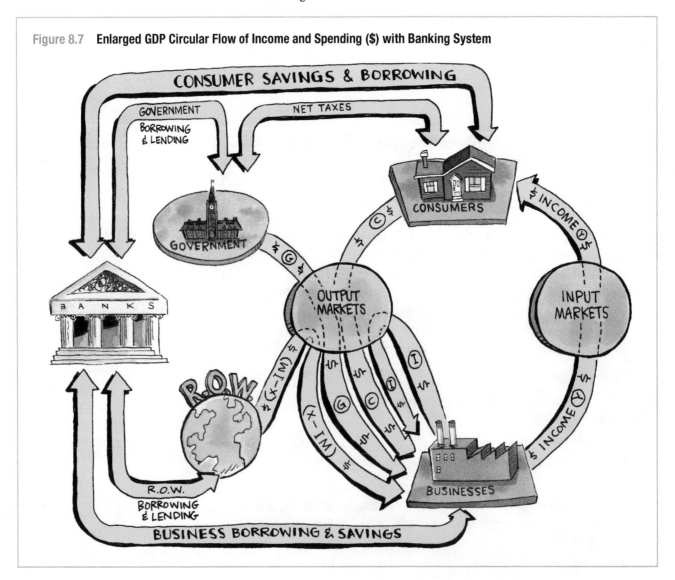

Once short-run aggregate supply decisions are made, workers have earned incomes in input markets, and products and services are available in output markets. Demand plans are mostly about buying products and services in output markets. Consumers are the most important players, but businesses, government, and the rest of the world (R.O.W.) also demand Canadian-produced products and services. The green ($) spending arrows from all of these players in Figure 8.7 flow through output markets.

Only One Aggregate Demand   All macroeconomic players make their supply plans and demand plans in the short run. For aggregate demand, there is no distinction between the long run and the short run. Long-run aggregate supply (*LAS*) is a performance target — potential GDP — where we want the economy to end up. That target is the same for aggregate supply or aggregate demand choices. So you will be happy to know that there is only one concept of aggregate demand to learn.

Aggregate Demand Curve

Macroeconomic demand plans for spending are similar to microeconomic choices about *quantity demanded* (Chapter 2). The microeconomic *law of demand* states that, as the price of a product or service rises, the quantity demanded decreases. For macroeconomics we must add together the demand plans connecting price and quantity demanded for all of the macroeconomic players. As in aggregate supply, for price we use the economy's price level as measured by the Consumer Price Index. For quantities we use real GDP.

Aggregate Demand   **Aggregate demand** is the quantity of Canadian real GDP that macroeconomic players plan to demand at different price levels. In Figure 8.8, each point on the aggregate demand curve (*AD*) corresponds to a row on the table of numbers. For example, look at point *A'* on the *AD* curve and row *A'* of the table. If the price level is 100, aggregate quantity demanded is $1700 billion of real GDP. If the price level rises to 110 (point and row *B'*), aggregate quantity demanded decreases to $1600 billion.

aggregate demand   quantity of real GDP macroeconomic players plan to demand at different price levels

Figure 8.8   **Aggregate Demand**

	Price Level (CPI)	Real GDP Demanded (billions of 2002 dollars)
A'	100	1700
B'	110	1600
C'	120	1500
D'	130	1400
E	140	1300

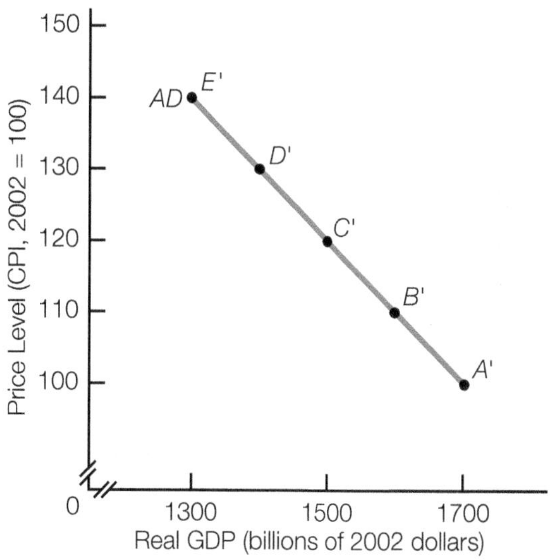

law of aggregate demand as the price level rises, aggregate quantity demanded of real GDP decreases

The Law of Aggregate Demand The **law of aggregate demand** states that as the price level rises, aggregate quantity demanded of real GDP decreases. While the macroeconomic law of aggregate demand *looks* just like the microeconomic law of demand, there is a surprising difference in the explanations behind them.

Microeconomics looks at the demand for one particular product. For example, when the price of Beats headphones rises, you switch to cheaper substitutes like other headphones, or the not-so-great earbuds that came with your phone. Macroeconomics looks at the aggregate demand for *all* products and services. When the price level rises for *all* products and services produced in Canada, there are no cheaper Canadian substitutes to switch to.

Substitutions from R.O.W. Fortunately, you can still use microeconomics' inverse relation (when one goes up, the other goes down) between price and quantity demanded. But the macroeconomic law of demand works for a different reason: Canada's connection to the rest of the world. When average prices of all Canadian products and services rise, *imported* products and services produced in other countries become relatively cheaper for Canadian consumers. And as prices of Canadian *exports* rise, the rest of the world buys less of them, switching to cheaper substitutes from other countries. When Canadians buy more imports and R.O.W. buys fewer Canadian exports, the aggregate quantity demanded of Canadian products and services decreases.

This difference in the explanations behind the microeconomic law of demand and the macroeconomic law of aggregate demand is an example of the *fallacy of composition* — what is true for one is not necessarily true for all.

Let's look at the demand plans for each of the macroeconomic players, using the letters from the mantra of *C*, *I*, *G*, *X*, and *IM*. In Chapter 6, *C*, *I*, *G*, *X*, and *IM* measured actual spending on outputs that contributed to real GDP. Here, we will look at the spending *plans* that contribute to aggregate demand, when output has been produced but not yet sold.

▲ When the prices of cars made in Canada rise, more consumers shop for imported cars, like this MINI Cooper, and fewer consumers buy Canadian-produced cars.

Consumer Demand Choices: *C* is for Consumer Spending

Consumer spending plans begin with income earned in input markets. The income that consumers can choose to spend is disposable income — income after paying net taxes. Consumers plan to save a fraction of their disposable income, and spend the rest. At the top left of Figure 8.7 on page 210, you can see the flows of consumer savings to banks, and of net taxes to government. Net taxes take about 22 percent of income. Of the disposable income left, Canadian consumers have been saving about 4 percent, and spending the other 96 percent.

For our macroeconomic focus, once consumers plan to spend, the choice between buying burgers from McDonald's or Wendy's makes no difference to Canadian real GDP as long as products and services of both businesses are made in Canada. Consumers, however, also buy imports. To measure consumers' spending plans for only Canadian products and services, we need to subtract the planned spending on imports from total consumer spending plans.

Consumer spending is by far the largest part of aggregate demand. It accounts for about 60 percent of the aggregate quantity demanded of Canadian real GDP. Consumer spending plans are also the most stable, reliable part of aggregate demand from year to year. Whether the economy is booming or busting, consumers still need to eat, have places to live, wear clothes, and use transportation. This constancy in year-to-year spending is not true for business investment spending.

Business Demand Choices: *I* is for Business Investment Spending

Business's role in aggregate demand is planned investment spending — building new factories or buying new machinery that adds inputs and increases the economy's potential to produce real GDP. New inputs increase aggregate supply (long-run and short-run), but because the machinery that businesses buy are outputs produced by other businesses, the purchases are also part of aggregate demand. That is why the arrow in Figure 8.7 for planned investment spending goes from businesses to output markets and back to businesses.

Business investment spending accounts for between 15 and 25 percent of the aggregate quantity demanded of real GDP. What is important about the business investment spending numbers is how much they can change from one year to the next. Investment spending is the most volatile, unpredictable part of aggregate demand.

Investment Can Be Postponed   One reason investment spending fluctuates so much compared to consumer spending is that it can be postponed. When a business postpones its plans to build a new factory, it can continue to operate its existing factories. Business investment is a marginal choice about adding to existing inputs. Consumers can't really postpone their plans to eat.

Government Demand Choices: *G* is for Government Spending on Products and Services

Government spending plans are set by Parliament when it passes its yearly budget. Government spending that contributes to aggregate demand under the category of *G* is plans for buying products and services in output markets. On Figure 8.7, that is the flow on the left side from government, through output markets, to businesses.

Government transfer payments (like the Canada Pension Plan and Employment Insurance) go to consumers, and show up in aggregate demand as part of planned consumer spending (*C*) from that transfer payment income. Transfer payments are *not* part of the spending category *G*.

Government spending on products and services accounts for about 20 percent of the quantity of real GDP demanded. That percentage has remained relatively stable in Canada since the 1990s.

Savage Chickens — by Doug Savage

Courtesy of www.savagechickens.com

R.O.W. Demand Choices: *X* is for R.O.W. Spending on Canadian Exports

Canadian exports are products and services produced here, but sold to the rest of the world. Italian spending plans to buy Molson Export beer fall under the category *X*. R.O.W. is the macroeconomic player (Italian or other nationalities) planning to demand our exports. On Figure 8.7, that planned spending is the flow on the bottom left side from R.O.W. through output markets to businesses.

Canada is a trading nation, and trade with the rest of the world is very important for aggregate demand. Spending by R.O.W for Canadian exports accounts for over one-third of the quantity of real GDP demanded.

Imports: *IM* Eliminates Canadian Choices from R.O.W. Spending

Imports — products and services produced in the rest of world and bought in Canada — do not contribute to Canadian planned aggregate demand or real GDP. However, imports are included in the planned spending categories of consumption, investment, and government purchases of products and services. To eliminate import purchases in output markets from aggregate demand, we must subtract imports. Rather than subtracting imports from the separate categories of *C*, *I*, and *G*, it is easier to subtract them in the single flow in Figure 8.7 from R.O.W. through output markets to businesses.

The flow from R.O.W. through output markets to businesses is labelled $X - IM$ to represent the *net* flow between R.O.W. and Canada. Spending on exports flows from R.O.W. to Canada and is part of aggregate demand for Canadian real GDP. Spending on imports flows from Canada to R.O.W. and must be subtracted to calculate the net impact of R.O.W. on aggregate demand for Canadian products and services.

NOTE
The net flow between the rest of the world (R.O.W.) and Canada is the difference between what Canada exports and what it imports.

Repeat Your Mantra: $C + I + G + X - IM = Y$

Planned spending on aggregate demand is the sum of planned consumer spending, planned business investment spending, planned government purchases of products and services, and planned net exports. For any price level, there is a planned aggregate quantity demanded. As the price level rises, the aggregate quantity demanded of Canadian real GDP decreases.

Demand Shocks and Aggregate Demand

Holding other factors constant, a change in the price level changes the aggregate *quantity demanded* of Canadian products and services, moving along an unchanged aggregate demand curve. **Demand shocks** are changes in any factor other than the price level that change aggregate demand and shift the aggregate demand curve.

Figure 8.9 illustrates how demand shocks shift the aggregate demand curve (AD). Negative demand shocks are factors that decrease aggregate demand and shift the aggregate demand curve leftward, from AD_0 to AD_1. Positive demand shocks are factors that increase aggregate demand and shift the aggregate demand curve rightward, from AD_0 to AD_2.

demand shocks changes in factors other than the price level that change aggregate demand and shift the aggregate demand curve

NOTE
Negative demand shocks decrease aggregate demand and shift AD leftward.

Positive demand shocks increase aggregate demand and shift AD rightward.

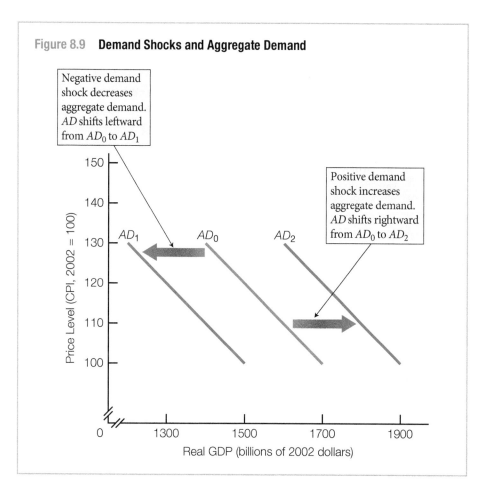

Figure 8.9 **Demand Shocks and Aggregate Demand**

Negative demand shock decreases aggregate demand. AD shifts leftward from AD_0 to AD_1

Positive demand shock increases aggregate demand. AD shifts rightward from AD_0 to AD_2

The five most important factors that cause demand shocks and change aggregate demand are expectations, interest rates, changes in government policy, GDP in R.O.W., and exchange rates between the Canadian dollar and other currencies.

Expectations Investment plans are based on expectations about an uncertain future. When an entrepreneur decides about the profitability of investing in a factory that will produce output and revenues lasting for 10 years, she must estimate costs and prices 10 years into the future. Even if she hires the best accountant in the world, those estimates are ultimately guesses, based on expectations.

Because investment plans are based on expectations, and expectations are mostly based on informed guesses, expectations can shift quickly and dramatically. That's what happened in the Global Financial Crisis, when expectations inflated about ever-rising real estate values and then all of a sudden burst — investors all began expecting values to fall. Business investment then dropped like a lead balloon. See Economics Out There for another example from the Global Financial Crisis.

More pessimistic expectations about future economic conditions are a negative demand shock — investment spending decreases and aggregate demand decreases. More optimistic expectations are a positive demand shock — investment spending increases and so does aggregate demand.

Expectations can also affect consumer spending. When consumers become more pessimistic about their economic future — expecting to lose their jobs, for example — they may decrease spending and increase savings. When consumers become more optimistic about their economic future, they increase spending and decrease savings.

Interest Rates Interest rates affect aggregate demand largely through their impact on business investment spending. Factories and machinery must be paid for before they will produce revenues for a business. Most businesses have to borrow the money to finance long-term investments, just as most consumers must borrow money to finance buying a house.

Rising interest rates are a negative demand shock. Borrowing to finance investment projects becomes more expensive and fewer investment projects are profitable. Aggregate demand decreases. Falling interest rates are a positive demand shock. Borrowing becomes cheaper and more investment projects become profitable. Aggregate demand increases.

Interest rates affect consumer spending plans for similar reasons. When interest rates on borrowed money (on your Visa bill, student loan, car loan, or mortgage, for example) rise, you borrow less and spend less. Aggregate demand decreases. When interest rates fall, you borrow more and spend more. Aggregate demand increases.

The outstanding fact is the extreme precariousness of the basis of knowledge on which our estimates of the prospective yield [of any investment] have to be made. Our knowledge of the factors that will govern the yield of an investment some years hence is usually very slight and often negligible. If we speak frankly, we have to admit that our basis of knowledge for estimating the yield ten years hence of a railway, a copper mine, a textile factory, . . . a building in the City of London amounts to little and sometimes nothing.

— John Maynard Keynes, 1937

Economics *Out There*

Putting Off Business Investment

Expenditures on machinery and equipment dropped from $254 billion in 2008 to $228 billion in 2009, a drop of $26 billion or 10.4 percent.

This is evidence of "how quickly the views and expectations changed for the worst during a period of unprecedented uncertainty," said Aron Gampel, deputy chief economist with Bank of Nova Scotia.

Yet companies have not said they are actually cancelling big projects, only shelving them for better days, said Yves Gauthier, the Statistics Canada official responsible for the survey.

"We don't want to get to the point that we are cutting off good investments, and of course there is program capital that is required to be spent, but we are cutting or delaying discretionary capital," said Vince Galifi, chief financial officer of Magna International.

Source: "Private sector spending suffers deep cutbacks," *The Globe and Mail*, Aug 2, 2009, and Statistics Canada, "Private and public investment," July 28, 2009.

Government Policy   Government policy changes affect aggregate demand. Fiscal policies involve tax and spending changes. Higher taxes are a negative demand shock. Consumers and businesses have less money to spend, decreasing aggregate demand. Decreases in government spending on products and services are also a negative demand shock. Tax cuts and more government spending are positive demand shocks, increasing aggregate demand.

Monetary policy by the Bank of Canada (coming in Chapter 10) affects interest rates and exchange rates, which in turn affect aggregate demand.

GDP in R.O.W.   R.O.W. plans to demand Canadian exports change with changes in real GDP in other countries. If China's economy is booming, it increases demand for Canadian oil, potash, Bombardier trains, and other exports. Recessions in any country that Canada trades with decrease demand for Canadian exports.

Decreases in GDP in R.O.W. are a negative demand shock, decreasing the demand for Canadian exports and decreasing Canadian aggregate demand. Increases in GDP in R.O.W. are a positive demand shock.

Exchange Rates   Exchange rates among currencies change R.O.W. planned demand for Canadian exports and Canadians' purchases of imports. When the Canadian dollar rises in value relative to the U.S. dollar or other currencies, Canadian exports become more expensive, so Americans and R.O.W. will buy fewer of them. Imports become cheaper, so Canadians buy more of them. When the Canadian dollar falls in value relative to other currencies, our exports become cheaper and R.O.W. will demand more of them. Imports become more expensive and we buy fewer of them. Exchange rates are the topic of Chapter 10.

A rise in the exchange rate is a negative demand shock, decreasing exports and increasing imports, decreasing Canadian aggregate demand. A fall in the exchange rate is a positive demand shock, increasing exports and decreasing imports, increasing Canadian aggregate demand.

Aggregate Demand Summary

You might feel overwhelmed by the choices behind aggregate supply and aggregate demand, and the lists of factors that change or "shock" aggregate supply and aggregate demand. But as we move on, I will help you absorb this information, which will be amazingly helpful for thinking about the fundamental macroeconomic question. The model of aggregate supply and aggregate demand will help you understand business cycles and government policy options — hands-off or hands-on — for responding to them.

Figure 8.10 is a good study device for reviewing the difference between the law of aggregate demand (focused on aggregate quantity demanded and movement along an unchanged *AD* curve) and the factors that change aggregate demand — negative and positive demand shocks (shifting the *AD* curve).

Figure 8.10   Law of Aggregate Demand and Changes in Aggregate Demand

The Law of Aggregate Demand *The aggregate quantity demanded of real GDP*	
Decreases if:	*Increases if:*
• price level rises	• price level falls

Changes in Aggregate Demand *The aggregate demand for real GDP*	
Decreases if negative demand shock:	*Increases if positive demand shock:*
• expectations more pessimistic	• expectations more optimistic
• interest rates rise	• interest rates fall
• government spending on products and services decreases or taxes increase	• government spending on products and services increases or taxes decrease
• GDP in R.O.W. decreases	• GDP in R.O.W. increases
• value of Canadian dollar rises	• value of Canadian dollar falls

Refresh 8.3

MyEconLab
For answers to these Refresh Questions, visit MyEconLab.

1. Explain the difference between a change in aggregate quantity demanded and a change in aggregate demand. Identify five positive demand shocks that increase aggregate demand.

2. Use the fallacy of composition to explain the difference between the law of demand (microeconomic) and the law of aggregate demand (macroeconomic).

3. How does a rise in the value of the Canadian dollar relative to the U.S. dollar change your personal consumption plans? What might you buy more of? Less of? Explain your decisions.

Hit or Miss the Macroeconomic Performance Targets?
The Aggregate Supply and Aggregate Demand Model

The model of aggregate supply and aggregate demand enables you to explain real-world macroeconomic events. For example, if there is a recession in the United States, what happens to GDP in Canada, to our unemployment, or to inflation? The aggregate supply and aggregate demand model gives you a framework for analyzing economic news and making smarter choices for your personal success.

Use the aggregate supply and aggregate demand model to explain the macroeconomic performance of real GDP, unemployment, and inflation.

Hitting the Targets:
Long-Run Macroeconomic Equilibrium

Let's start using the model to explain the best possible macroeconomic outcome — when the smart choices of all players are coordinated and the economy hits the performance targets for real GDP, unemployment, and inflation.

Equilibrium   Economists describe the outcome of *macroeconomic equilibrium* as aggregate demand matching the aggregate supply choices made two Gretzky-like steps earlier. Equilibrium means balance — there is no tendency for change. My favourite definition of equilibrium is by Joan Robinson: "In a situation which is in equilibrium, no one is kicking himself." Figure 8.11 shows an example that is both a short-run macroeconomic equilibrium and a long-run macroeconomic equilibrium.

JOAN ROBINSON

Portrait: Ramsey and Muspratt; Cover design: G. C. Harcourt and Prue Kerr, Joan Robinson, ©2009 Palgrave Macmillan. Reproduced with permission of Palgrave Macmillan.

▲ Joan Robinson (1903–1983) was a University of Cambridge economist and colleague of Keynes. Many believe she should have been the first woman to win the Nobel Prize in Economics but was unfairly denied.

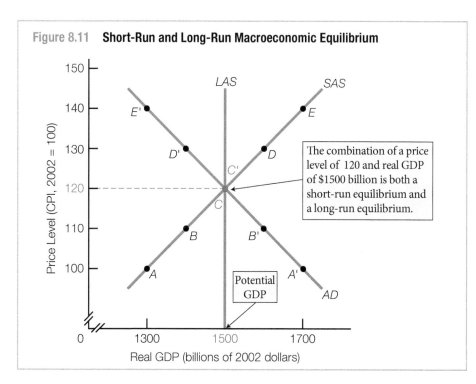

Figure 8.11   **Short-Run and Long-Run Macroeconomic Equilibrium**

The combination of a price level of 120 and real GDP of $1500 billion is both a short-run equilibrium and a long-run equilibrium.

NOTE
Short-run macroeconomic equilibrium
is where *SAS* and *AD* intersect.

Short-Run Equilibrium with Existing Inputs

Short-run equilibrium is the point where short-run aggregate supply (*SAS*) and aggregate demand (*AD*) intersect. In Figure 8.11 it is at real GDP of $1500 billion and a price level of 120.

To see why this is an equilibrium — with no tendency to change — look at what would happen if the price level were different. At a higher price level like 140, *SAS* would be $1700 billion (point *E*) while *AD* would be only $1300 billion (point *E'*). With short-run aggregate quantity supplied greater than aggregate quantity demanded, there is a surplus of products and services. Surpluses create pressure for output prices to fall. Competition between suppliers to get rid of unsold output drives down the price level, increasing aggregate quantity demanded and decreasing aggregate quantity supplied. The surplus, and the pressure for the price level to fall and real GDP to increase, only disappear when the economy reaches the equilibrium point.

At a lower price level like 110, *SAS* would be $1400 billion (point *B*) while *AD* would be $1600 billion (point *B'*). With aggregate quantity demanded greater than short-run aggregate quantity supplied, there is a shortage of products and services. Shortages create pressure for output prices to rise. Competition among consumers for scarce products and services drives up the price level, decreasing aggregate quantity demanded and increasing aggregate quantity supplied. The shortage, and the pressure for the price level to rise and real GDP to decrease, only disappear when the economy reaches the equilibrium point. At the equilibrium combination of real GDP of $1500 billion and price level of 120, there is no tendency for change.

NOTE
Long-run macroeconomic equilibrium
is the point where *SAS*, *AD*, and *LAS*
all intersect. The aggregate quantity
supplied and aggregate quantity
demanded of real GDP also
equal potential GDP.

Long-Run Equilibrium with Existing Inputs

In long-run equilibrium, the intersection of short-run aggregate supply (*SAS*) and aggregate demand (*AD*) also intersects long-run aggregate supply (*LAS*). In long-run equilibrium, the aggregate quantity supplied and aggregate quantity demanded of real GDP also equal potential GDP of $1500 billion.

The price level (120) and aggregate demand ($1500 billion) turn out to be exactly what suppliers expected when they made their production plans. Suppliers are happy because their products and services get sold at expected prices, and demanders are happy because their spending plans are realized. Consumers earned enough income in input markets to buy the products and services they planned for in output markets. Input prices, especially the wage rate, have adjusted so that all inputs — labour, capital, land/resources, and entrepreneurial ability — are fully employed. The price level is stable — there are no pressures for output prices or input prices to change. This long-run equilibrium with existing inputs is the world of Say's Law, where macroeconomic dreams come true.

Equilibrium over Time with Increasing Inputs

To fully explain the "Yes, Markets Self-Adjust" answer to the fundamental macroeconomic question — if left alone by government, do the price mechanisms of market economics quickly adjust to maintain steady growth in living standards, full employment, and stable prices? — we also must look at *changes over time in this macroeconomic equilibrium* and the role of the banking system.

Living Standards The best measure of "growth in living standards" is increasing real GDP per person. *Over time* real GDP must grow faster than the population. An increase in real GDP per person is also economic growth — an increase in potential GDP.

Stable Prices "Stable prices" means that the Consumer Price Index — the average price level — is either constant, or increasing at a low, predictable rate of inflation (1 to 3 percent per year) from year to year.

Loanable Funds Market The banking system can also be described as the **market for loanable funds**. Banks take in money (funds) in the form of savings from the macroeconomic players — consumer households, businesses, government, and R.O.W. Banks then loan out money (funds) to borrowers. Businesses do most of the borrowing in this market to finance investment spending (*I*) on new factories or new machinery. The interest rate is the price of money in the loanable funds market and is determined by the interaction between the demand for loanable funds (by borrowers) and the supply of loanable funds (from savers). Figure 8.12 is a graph of the loanable funds market.

market for loanable funds banks coordinate the supply of loanable funds (savings) with the demand for loanable funds (borrowing for investment spending). The interest rate is the price of loanable funds.

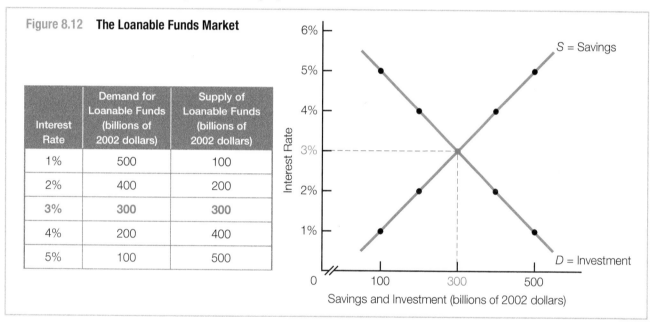

Figure 8.12 The Loanable Funds Market

Interest Rate	Demand for Loanable Funds (billions of 2002 dollars)	Supply of Loanable Funds (billions of 2002 dollars)
1%	500	100
2%	400	200
3%	300	300
4%	200	400
5%	100	500

The horizontal axis measures the quantities of money that are saved or borrowed for business investment. The interest rate is on the vertical axis. The supply curve of savings (*S*) in the loanable funds market is an upward-sloping line, like any supply curve. When rewarded with higher interest rates, people save more money. The demand curve of loanable funds for business investment spending (*I*) is a downward-sloping line, like any demand curve. Higher interest rates increase the cost of borrowing, leading businesses to borrow less and to cancel some investment projects that are no longer profitable. The interest rate is the equilibrium "price" in the loanable funds market, equalizing quantity supplied and quantity demanded. In this example, that interest rate is 3 percent and $300 billion is the quantity saved and invested.

When macroeconomic players, especially consumers, save instead of spend, Say's Law appears to be in trouble. If the income earned by supplying inputs in input markets is *not* all spent in output markets buying the products and services produced with those inputs, how does supply create its own demand?

Rescuing Say's Law over Time Banks can save the day (pun intended). Banks can loan out the saved funds to business borrowers who use the money to finance investment in new factories and equipment. That additional business investment spending (*I*), beyond what consumers spend, replaces consumer savings. Aggregate incomes earned in input markets are once again equal to aggregate spending in output markets. Aggregate supply equals aggregate demand.

Rising Living Standards Business investment spending based on borrowed funds can also explain "steady growth in living standards." As business investment increases the quantity and quality of inputs, potential GDP increases.

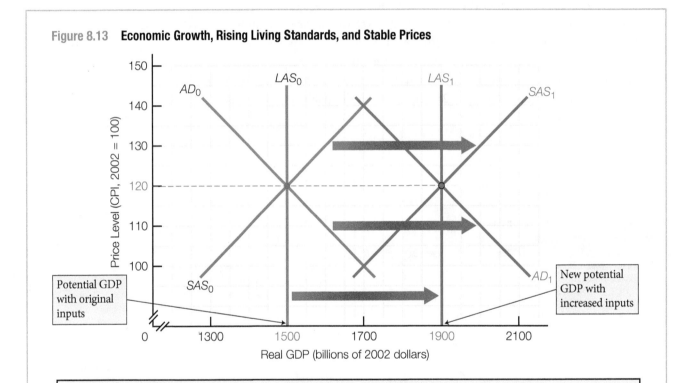

Figure 8.13 Economic Growth, Rising Living Standards, and Stable Prices

Business investment that increases the quantity and quality of inputs shifts SAS_0 and LAS_0 together rightward, to SAS_1 and LAS_1.

Potential real GDP increases.

Increased employment in new and improved factories increases incomes in input markets, so aggregate demand shifts rightward, from AD_0 to AD_1.

The new short-run and long-run equilibrium is at real GDP of $1900 billion, and a constant price level of 120.

As long as the increase in real GDP is greater than any increase in population, real GDP per person grows, and the price level is stable at 120.

The story of rising living standards in Figure 8.13 begins with long-run and short-run equilibrium at the point where SAS_0, AD_0, and LAS_0 all intersect. Real GDP is originally $1500 billion and the price level is 120. Business investment that increases the quantity and quality of inputs shifts SAS_0 and LAS_0 together rightward, to SAS_1 and LAS_1. Potential real GDP increases to $1900 billion. But will that increased aggregate supply create its own increased aggregate demand? Yes. Increased employment in new and improved factories increases incomes in input markets, so aggregate demand shifts rightward, from AD_0 to AD_1. The new long-run (and short-run) equilibrium is at real GDP of $1900 billion. The quantity supplied of real GDP equals the quantity demanded. There is no excess demand pulling up average prices; no excess supply pulling down average prices. The price level stays constant at 120.

As long as the increase in real GDP is greater than any increase in population, real GDP per person grows. Since the economy is once again at potential GDP (on the LAS_1 curve), unemployment remains at the natural rate of (full) employment and the price level is stable. When Say's Law remains true — even with savings — the circular flow of real GDP increases smoothly from year to year, producing economic growth, rising living standards, full employment, and stable prices. The equilibrium over time with expanding inputs in Figure 8.13 is the world described in Chapter 7 where bigger and better macroeconomic dreams keep coming true.

Missed Targets and Business Cycles

Business suppliers will be kicking themselves if aggregate demand does not match short-run aggregate supply at the potential GDP target (*LAS*). Maybe they produced too many products and services that are sitting unsold on shelves and the price level falls below expectations. Or business suppliers did not produce enough to satisfy unexpected consumer demand and the price level rises above expectations. Consumer household demanders will also be kicking themselves. Either businesses begin laying off workers and reducing consumer households' incomes, or consumers will be disappointed at not finding enough of the products and services they planned to buy. There is disappointment all around.

When expectations are not realized, macroeconomic outcomes do not work out as planned. What the macroeconomic players *expected* were smart choices turn out to be not-smart choices. Adjustments are necessary to get back to smart choices, and these adjustments are the stuff business cycles are made of. Recessions and expansions — the world of Keynes's business cycles — are the result of mismatches between aggregate demand and aggregate supply.

There are four mismatch cases that move an economy away from the long-run equilibrium targets: a negative demand shock, a positive demand shock, a negative supply shock, and a positive supply shock.

Negative Demand Shocks   What happens if, after macroeconomic players make short-run aggregate supply decisions in input markets, there is a negative aggregate demand shock before products and services arrive for sale in output markets?

The supply decisions result in the short-run (SAS_0) aggregate supply curve in Figure 8.14. Those decisions were based on the expectation that aggregate demand would be AD_0. AD_0 is a dotted line because the expectation did not come true. Aggregate demand turns out to be AD_1.

At the originally expected price level of 120, aggregate quantity demanded ($1300 billion) is less than aggregate quantity supplied ($1500 billion). There is a $200 billion surplus of products and services in output markets. Businesses cut output prices to get rid of unsold products. Surpluses create pressure for average prices to fall. Businesses decrease the quantity supplied of real GDP, and reduce their hiring of labour and other inputs. The short-run equilibrium, where SAS_0 and AD_1 intersect, is real GDP of $1400 billion and a price level of 110.

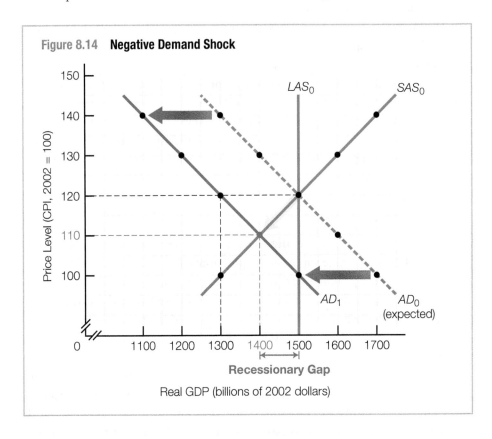

Figure 8.14   **Negative Demand Shock**

NOTE
Negative demand shocks cause a recessionary gap: falling average prices, decreased real GDP, and increased unemployment.

The results of the negative demand shock are that the price level falls (from 120 to 110), aggregate quantity supplied decreases (from $1500 billion to $1400 billion), and unemployment increases. Since real GDP is below potential GDP ($1500 billion), there is a recessionary gap.

This is the scenario of the Global Financial Crisis described in Chapter 5. The bursting U.S. housing price bubble caused expectations to fall. Because of deeply pessimistic expectations, business investment spending fell dramatically. Expectations of hard times ahead, coupled with dramatically falling values of consumers' savings invested in their houses or the stock market, caused consumers to cut back spending and increase savings. These new choices caused a negative demand shock, decreasing aggregated demand. Decreased aggregate demand put downward pressure on average prices. Aggregate quantity supplied decreased, businesses laid off workers, and the economy fell into a recessionary gap.

Positive Demand Shocks   What happens if, after macroeconomic players make short-run aggregate supply decisions, there is a positive aggregate demand shock — an increase in aggregate demand — before products and services arrive for sale in output markets?

Starting with the same supply decisions (SAS_0 and LAS_0) and expected aggregate demand (AD_0) in Figure 8.14, Figure 8.15 shows what happens when aggregate demand turns out to be AD_2.

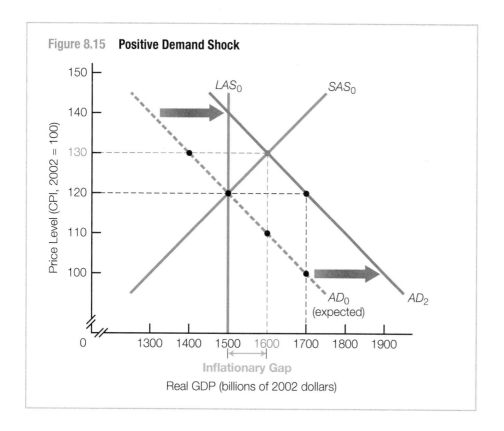

Figure 8.15   **Positive Demand Shock**

At the originally expected price level of 120, aggregate quantity demanded ($1700 billion) is greater than aggregate quantity supplied ($1500 billion). There is a $200 billion shortage of products and services in output markets. Businesses experience products flying off the shelves and inventories quickly disappear. Consumers experience long lineups and out-of-stock items at stores. In trying to get the scarce products, consumers compete against each other and bid up prices. Businesses raise prices and still sell everything they have produced. Shortages create pressure for average prices to rise. Businesses increase the quantity supplied of real GDP, and hire more labour and other inputs. The short-run equilibrium, the point where SAS_0 and AD_2 intersect, is real GDP of $1600 billion and a price level of 130.

The results of the positive demand shock are that the price level rises (from 120 to 130), aggregate quantity supplied increases (from $1500 billion to $1600 billion), and the unemployment rate decreases temporarily below the natural rate. Since real GDP is above potential GDP, there is an inflationary gap.

NOTE

Positive demand shocks cause an inflationary gap: rising average prices, increased real GDP, and decreased unemployment.

NOTE
Demand shocks cause
unemployment and inflation
to move in opposite directions,
as the Phillips Curve suggests.

Demand shocks, whether negative or positive, move unemployment and inflation in opposite directions, as the Phillips Curve suggests. Higher unemployment is associated with lower inflation, and lower unemployment is associated with higher inflation.

Negative Supply Shocks   What happens if, after macroeconomic players make short-run aggregate supply decisions, there is an unexpected negative aggregate supply shock — such as a decrease in aggregate supply caused by rising resource input prices?

In Figure 8.16, rising input prices decrease short-run aggregate supply from SAS_0 to SAS_1, but do not change potential GDP or long-run aggregate supply (LAS_0).

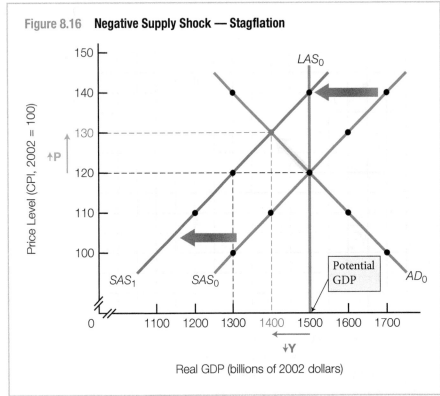

Figure 8.16   Negative Supply Shock — Stagflation

At the originally expected price level of 120, with higher input prices business are now only willing to supply $1300 billion of real GDP. Aggregate quantity demanded ($1500 billion) is greater than aggregate quantity supplied ($1300 billion). There is a $200 billion shortage of products and services in output markets. Businesses raise output prices to cover higher input costs. Rising prices lead consumers to reduce their quantity demanded of products and services. Output decreases and businesses reduce their hiring of labour and other inputs.

The result is a rise in the average price level, a decrease in real GDP and in aggregate quantity demanded, and an increase in unemployment. Real GDP falls below potential GDP. This combination of higher inflation and increased unemployment creates stagflation — inflation and recession together. The language of gaps — recessionary gaps versus inflationary gaps — does not apply to the outcomes of supply-side shocks.

The oil price shocks of the 1970s set up the classic scenario of a negative supply shock. In response to rising oil prices, businesses raised prices to cover rising energy costs. But consumers couldn't buy the same quantities of products and services as before, since they were using more of their income to pay dramatically higher gasoline and home energy bills. Quantity demanded decreased. Inflation stayed high, output decreased, and unemployment increased. Stagflation!

NOTE
Negative supply shocks
cause stagflation: rising average
prices, decreased real GDP, and
increased unemployment.

Positive Supply Shocks   Starting from long-run equilibrium, what happens if there is a positive aggregate supply shock — such as an increase in aggregate supply caused by technological improvements that increase the quality of capital and dramatically lower costs?

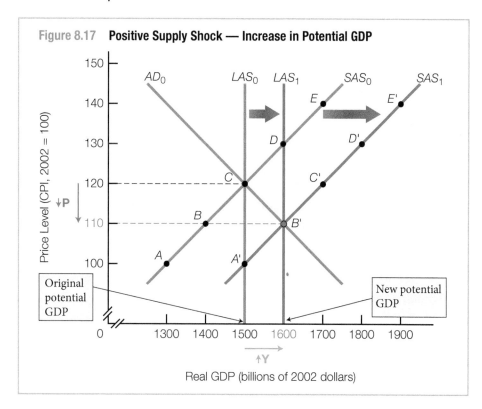

Figure 8.17   Positive Supply Shock — Increase in Potential GDP

In Figure 8.17, the economy is originally in long-run equilibrium at point C, where LAS_0, SAS_0, and AD_0 all intersect. Real GDP is $1500 billion, the price level is 120, and there is full employment since the economy is at potential GDP. Then technological change decreases costs and increases productivity, shifting *both* the long-run aggregate supply curve and the short-run aggregate supply curve together rightward to LAS_1 and SAS_1. The rightward shift of LAS is an increase in potential GDP.

The new long-run equilibrium is at point B', where LAS_1, SAS_1 and unchanged AD_0 all intersect. Real GDP increases to $1600 billion and the price level falls to 110. The economy remains at full employment at the increased potential GDP. The result is a fall in the average price level to 110, an increase in real GDP to $1600 billion, and an increase in potential GDP. With lower costs and falling output prices, aggregate quantity demanded increases from $1500 billion to $1600 billion. The economy stays at full employment, at the natural rate of unemployment. Instead of stagflation's combination of two undesirable outcomes (unemployment and inflation), the outcome of a positive supply shock is two desirable outcomes: maintaining full employment and lower inflation.

The technology boom in the late 1990s was due, in part, to a positive aggregate supply shock. Technological advances in digital information and computer technologies increased productivity and lowered costs. Although you probably can't imagine life without it, the Internet only began to operate effectively for businesses and consumers in 1995. As a result, businesses were able to lower prices, increase production, and hire more workers.

NOTE
Positive supply shocks cause falling average prices, increased real GDP, and continued full unemployment.

Economic Life Is Full of Shocks

In the real world, demand and supply shocks rarely happen one at a time — they usually happen together. For example, in the 1970s, the negative supply shock of rising oil prices combined with the negative demand shock of rising interest rates. In late 1990s, the positive supply shock of technology combined with the positive demand shock of increased exports. The North American Free Trade Agreement (NAFTA) among Canada, the United States, and Mexico allowed R.O.W. buyers in the United States and Mexico to demand more Canadian exports and increase aggregate demand.

Multiple shocks of the same type can also happen together. For example, there could be a negative demand shock of more pessimistic expectations combined with a positive demand shock of increasing GDP in R.O.W. In the late 1990s, a positive supply shock of digital technology combined with a positive supply shock of falling oil prices.

The impact on the economic performance targets of real GDP, unemployment, and inflation depends on the combined effects of the shocks. But to be able to work through these more complex scenarios, you still use the model of aggregate supply and aggregate demand. Break down the scenario into the separate effects of demand shocks and supply shocks, and then combine the results.

Agreement between Camps?　　Both camps of macroeconomists, the "Yes — Markets Self-Adjust" believers in Say's Law and the "No — Market Fail Often" followers of Keynes, largely agree in describing macroeconomic equilibrium when aggregate supply and aggregate demand match. And both camps agree in describing the effects of demand and supply shocks.

But the "Yes" and "No" camps still disagree on the fundamental macroeconomic question — if left alone by government, do the price mechanisms of market economics quickly adjust to maintain steady growth in living standards, full employment, and stable prices? Those disagreements are the topics of the last section of the chapter.

Refresh 8.4

MyEconLab
For answers to these Refresh
Questions, visit MyEconLab.

1. Explain the difference between a short-run and a long-run macroeconomic equilibrium.

2. Describe the impact of a positive demand shock on average prices, real GDP, and unemployment.

3. If consumers choose to start saving more, explain how the market for loanable funds can rescue Say's Law.

Shocking Starts and Finishes: Origins and Responses to Business Cycles

Business cycles are triggered by shocks to short-run aggregate supply and aggregate demand. Both the "Yes — Markets Self-Adjust" and the "No — Markets Fail Often" camps agree on that. The differences between the camps, and their differing hands-off and hands-on roles for government policy, have to do with the *origins* of the shocks and the *responses* of markets to the shocks.

Describe the "Yes — Markets Self-Adjust" and "No — Markets Fail Often" answers about origins, expectations, and market responses to business cycles.

Yes — Markets Self-Adjust, So Hands-Off

The "Yes" camp emphasizes the long-run, Say's Law, and the ability of the economy to hit the macroeconomic performance targets given enough time. But in the short run, this camp recognizes that business cycles do happen.

Origins of Shocks and Business Cycles — "Yes" Camp

According to the "Yes — Markets Self-Adjust" camp, shocks to aggregate supply and aggregate demand that trigger business cycles largely come from outside of the economy — aggregate supply shocks caused by nature or scientific discoveries, and aggregate demand shocks caused by mistaken government policies.

Nature-based supply shocks include natural disasters like droughts, floods, and earthquakes that destroy inputs. Scientific discoveries allow for technological change as a supply shock.

The "Yes" camp also views mistaken government fiscal and monetary policies as demand shocks that trigger unemployment and inflation. A tax increase is a negative demand shock that can cause a recession. Increased government spending is a positive demand shock that increases inflation if the economy is already at potential GDP. Government does not intend to cause economic problems, but it is difficult to time policy decisions, and unintentional policy mistakes can cause business cycles. For the "Yes" camp, government is part of the problem, not part of the solution.

NOTE
For the "Yes — Markets Self-Adjust" camp, the origins of shocks are external to the economy.

Rational Expectations

The "Yes" camp sees individuals and businesses as making logical, rational choices, based on the best information available. Like Mr. Spock, the Vulcan of *Star Trek*, even investment choices with limited information are made coolly and efficiently. The "Yes" camp downplays changing expectations as a source of demand shocks. Investors, for the "Yes" camp, are clear-thinking, steady calculators of profits and losses.

▶ Spock, a character from *Star Trek*, is famous for his ability to make cool, unemotional decisions. The "Yes — Markets Self-Adjust" camp believes people — business investors and consumers — make Spock-like economic decisions.

NOTE

For the "Yes — Markets Self-Adjust" camp, price adjustments in markets work to quickly restore long-run macroeconomic equilibrium and a match between short-run aggregate supply and aggregate demand.

▲ This woman adjusts a thermostat to keep the temperature inside where she wants it to be, regardless of the weather outside. According to the "Yes — Markets Self-Adjust" camp, price mechanisms in markets work like a thermostat, keeping the economy where it should be, regardless of external shocks.

NOTE

For the "No — Markets Fail Often" camp, the origins of shocks are internal to the economy.

Market Price Responses to Business Cycles   When external shocks or government policy mistakes trigger contractions or expansions, the "Yes" camp argues that price adjustments in separate markets — input, output, international trade, and loanable funds markets — all work together to quickly restore the match between short-run aggregate supply and aggregate demand. Consider a recessionary gap example, when a negative demand shock causes real GDP to decrease below potential GDP, increasing unemployment and putting downward pressure on average prices.

With increasing unemployment, there is a surplus of labour. The wage rate falls, increasing business hiring. Similar price adjustments occur in all input markets, until all inputs are once again fully employed.

The international trade market also helps to increase production back to the level of potential GDP. Falling Canadian prices make our exports more competitive and attractive to R.O.W. Falling Canadian prices also mean consumers will substitute more domestically produced products and services in place of imports. Those additional net export sales increase aggregate quantity demanded and Canadian real GDP.

Finally, price adjustment in the loanable funds market provides a solution to the problem of saving for Say's Law. Additional savings are deposited in banks, increasing the supply of loanable funds. The interest rate — the price of loanable funds — falls, increasing consumer and especially business borrowing for investment spending. Increased spending offsets the increased saving, returning the economy to long-run equilibrium.

Price mechanisms in markets function like an economic thermostat. If the weather outside gets hotter or colder, a thermostat automatically adjusts the cooling or heating systems to maintain the indoor temperature right where it should be, at the perfect comfortable temperature. Price mechanisms in markets adjust to aggregate supply and demand shocks, bringing the economy back to potential GDP, full employment, and stable prices — right where it should be.

No — Markets Fail Often, So Hands-On

Following Keynes, the "No" camp emphasizes the short run, when the self-adjusting mechanisms of market economies can be slow and weak. Business cycles of boom and bust, long periods of unemployment, reduced living standards, and rising or falling prices occur regularly unless the government steps in.

Origins of Shocks and Business Cycles — "No" Camp   The "No — Markets Fail Often" camp believes that shocks to short-run aggregate supply and aggregate demand are largely *internally generated* as unintended byproducts of markets. Expectations, the role of money, and connections between different market economies in R.O.W. create shocks.

Because no one can foretell the future, investment plans are based on expectations, or informed guesses. The "No" camp sees investment decisions as based largely on a gut-level instinct to act, which Keynes called *animal spirits* — "a spontaneous urge to action rather than inaction."

◀ Professors George Akerlof and Robert Shiller (both Nobel Prize winners) returned to Keynes's ideas in their 2009 book explaining business cycles and the Global Financial Crisis.

Volatile Expectations and Money With few solid facts, investors look for guidance to what other investors are doing. This "herd mentality" causes boom and bust cycles like the Global Financial Crisis. When housing prices were rising and everyone was making money in the real estate market, it was easy to jump on the bandwagon and start investing. But without solid facts, when pessimism appears, it can easily spread, causing prices to fall quickly.

Fundamental uncertainty about the future, relying on the "herd" of other equally uncertain investors for guidance, and the postponable nature of investments all combine to make expectations and investment spending decisions very volatile. Quickly changeable expectations coming from inside the economy create fluctuating positive and negative aggregate demand shocks.

The "No — Markets Fail Often" camp also emphasizes the role of money put into savings in dealing with the fundamental uncertainty about the future. When consumers and businesses worry about the future, they save more from their incomes and earnings. Ironically, pessimistic expectations and higher savings can become a self-fulfilling prophecy, causing a negative demand shock and recession.

Market Price Responses to Business Cycles The "No — Markets Fail Often" camp does not have much faith in markets to quickly adjust to shocks. The adjustment stories for the "No" camp to a recessionary gap example are very different from the "Yes" camp for the input, output, international trade, and loanable funds markets.

In labour markets, wages don't fall often or easily. Economists describe these as *sticky wages*. It is much easier to raise wages than to cut them. There are many reasons for sticky wages. Union and other contracts can't be quickly changed. Workers resist having their wages and incomes reduced. Employers also resist wage cuts so as not to demoralize workers, hurt productivity, or lead employees to start looking elsewhere for jobs.

When prices don't adjust, quantities do. Unemployment is a quantity adjustment in labour markets. Workers and employers accept layoffs instead of lower wages in response to a negative demand shock.

The "No — Markets Fail Often" camp argues layoffs in labour markets mean less income for workers to spend, which decreases demand for products and services in output markets. Falling output prices from unsold goods may not be enough to restore sales in output markets. The "No" camp sees the *connections* between input and output markets as slowing market adjustments to a negative demand shock. It may take a long time to restore employment and output to the target level of potential GDP.

In international trade markets, the "No" camp worries about the destabilizing effects of fluctuating Canadian exports due to business cycles in R.O.W. These additional demand shocks from R.O.W. may be worse than the stabilizing role of price adjustments in export and import markets.

Finally, the "No — Markets Fail Often" camp argues that increased saving in the loanable funds market does *not* turn into increased investment spending. On its own, an increase in saving — the supply of loanable funds — puts pressure on interest rates to fall. But if the increase in saving is caused by more pessimistic expectations about the future, then business investment spending may *decrease*, not increase, even if interest rates fall. This is actually what happened during the Global Financial Crisis. For the "No" camp, expectations are more important than interest rates in influencing business investment spending.

... human decisions affecting the future ... cannot depend on strict mathematical expectation, since the basis for making such calculations does not exist; ... it is our innate urge to activity which makes the wheels go round, our rational selves ... calculating where we can, but often falling back for our motive on whim or sentiment or chance.

—*John Maynard Keynes, 1936*

NOTE
Adjustment problems in all markets fail to restore a match between short-run aggregate supply and aggregate demand for the "No — Markets Fail Often" camp.

With internally generated shocks regularly causing business cycles, and with weak or slow price adjustment mechanisms, the "No — Markets Fail Often" camp sees an obvious role for government in market economies: The thermostat needs adjusting and only government can do it. Government fiscal and monetary policies can be used to counter the shocks that have triggered recessionary or inflationary gaps. Government action is necessary to bring short-run aggregate supply, aggregate demand, and the economy back into balance to hit the macroeconomic performance targets.

Yes or No: How Do You Decide?

If I have done my job properly, you will find yourself agreeing with some of the arguments of both the "Yes — Markets Self-Adjust" and the "No — Markets Fail Often" camps. Both camps have insights about how economies work. However, this chapter does not contain enough evidence, especially data about the Canadian and other market economies, to allow you to come to an informed conclusion.

As you learn more in coming chapters, and in your own observations of the economy, you will be able to clarify your own opinions. It is easier to make judgments about individual arguments than to pass a single judgment on the whole "Yes–No" macroeconomic question. With those informed opinions, you will better understand how to think like a macroeconomist, make better personal economic choices, and be better able to choose among politicians whose economic policy choices will enhance your personal economic success.

Comparing Camps: Origins of Shocks and Business Cycles   Figure 8.18 is a good study device for reviewing the differences between the two camps regarding the origin of shocks and their effect on business cycles. It extends Figure 5.3 (on page 119) comparing the two camps on their answers to the fundamental macroeconomic question.

Figure 8.18 Origins of Shocks and Business Cycles

Answer to Fundamental Macroeconomic Question	Yes — Left Alone, Markets Self-Adjust (Say)	No — Left Alone, Markets Fail Often (Keynes)
Time focus	Long run	Short run
Origin of shocks	External to economy	Internal to economy
Most important shocks	Supply shocks	Demand shocks
Expectations	Rational; steady	Based on animal spirits, herd mentality; volatile
Price adjustments in response to business cycles	Work together to quickly restore long-run equilibrium — match between aggregate supply and demand	Adjustment problems in all markets fail to restore long-run equilibrium
Most important influence on business investment spending	Interest rates as cost of borrowing	Expectations of future profits
Saving and loanable funds market	Interest rate in loanable funds market adjusts so investment spending offsets saving, maintaining aggregate demand	Saving causes negative demand shock; falling sales and expectations decrease investment spending

1. Identify the origins of shocks causing business cycles for the "Yes — Markets Self-Adjust" camp.

2. Describe the role of *animal spirits* in the "No — Markets Fail Often" camp explanation of volatile expectations for investors.

3. Based on your current understanding of the "Yes" and "No" camps, which of their individual arguments do you find most convincing? If you had to pick, which camp would you support? Why?

MyEconLab

For answers to these Refresh Questions, visit MyEconLab.

Study Guide

CHAPTER 8 SUMMARY

8.1 Macroeconomic Performance Targets: Potential GDP and Long-Run Aggregate Supply

Long-run aggregate supply models the macroeconomic target outcomes of potential GDP and full employment with existing inputs.

- The full-employment output of an economy can be modelled as
  - points on a production possibilities frontier (*PPF*).
  - **long-run aggregate supply** — potential GDP — the quantity of real GDP supplied when all inputs are fully employed.
  - long-run aggregate supply curve (*LAS*) — vertical line at potential GDP; quantity of potential GDP does not change when the price level changes.

- Existing inputs
  - determine the position of the *PPF* and *LAS* curves.
  - are unused or unemployed at points inside a *PPF*.
  - are unused or unemployed at any quantity of real GDP less than potential GDP.

- Time periods for macroeconomic analysis are the
  - *long run* — a period of time long enough for all prices and wages to adjust to equilibrium; the economy is at potential GDP, the full employment outcome of coordinated smart choices.
  - *short run* — a period of time when some input prices do not change; all prices have *not* adjusted to clear all markets.

8.2 If You Plan and Build It . . . Aggregate Supply

Supply plans for existing inputs determine aggregate quantity supplied. Supply plans to increase the quantity and quality of inputs, together with supply shocks, change aggregate supply.

- Macroeconomic players — consumers, businesses, government — make two kinds of plans for supplying Canadian real GDP:
  - supply plans for existing inputs
  - supply plans to increase inputs

- Business supply plans for existing inputs with fixed input prices are similar to microeconomic choices about quantity supplied.
  - **Short-run aggregate supply** — quantity of real GDP macroeconomic players plan to supply at different price levels
  - **Law of short-run aggregate supply** — as the price level rises, aggregate quantity supplied of real GDP increases.
  - Changes in price level cause movement along an unchanged short-run aggregate supply curve (*SAS*).

- Supply plans to increase quantity or quality of inputs cause an **increase in aggregate supply** — increase in economy's capacity to produce real GDP.
  - Changes in the quantity or quality of inputs shift both the long-run aggregate supply curve (*LAS*) and short-run aggregate supply curve (*SAS*) in the same direction.
  - Both aggregate supply curves shift rightward for increase in inputs, leftward for decrease in inputs.

- Changes in input prices shift the short-run aggregate supply curve (*SAS*) but do not shift the long-run aggregate supply curve (*LAS*)
  - Rising input prices shift *SAS* leftward. Falling input prices shift *SAS* rightward.

- *Negative supply shocks* directly increase costs or reduce inputs, decreasing short-run aggregate supply and shifting *SAS* leftward.

- *Positive supply shocks* directly decrease costs or improve productivity, increasing short-run aggregate supply and shifting *SAS* rightward.

8.3 . . . Will They Come and Buy It? Aggregate Demand

Demand plans by macroeconomic players determine aggregate quantity demanded. Demand shocks — from changes in expectations, interest rates, government policy, GDP in R.O.W., exchange rates — change aggregate demand.

- All macroeconomic players — consumers, businesses, government, R.O.W. — make demand plans for spending, similar to microeconomic choices about quantity demanded.
  - All aggregate demand plans are in the short run.
  - **Aggregate demand** — quantity of real GDP macroeconomic players plan to demand at different price levels.
  - **Law of aggregate demand** — as the price level rises, aggregate quantity demanded of real GDP decreases.
- *Fallacy of composition* makes macroeconomic law of aggregate demand different from microeconomic law of demand.
  - When average prices rise for all Canadian products and services, the only substitutes are imports from R.O.W.
  - Decreased aggregated quantity demanded of Canadian real GDP is due to Canadians buying more imports, and R.O.W., buying fewer Canadian exports due to higher prices.
- Consumers plan to spend (C) a fraction of *disposable income* — earned income plus transfer payments less taxes — and save the rest.
  - Consumer spending is largest, most stable component of aggregate demand.
- Businesses plan investment spending (I) for new factories and equipment. Investment spending plans change quickly because they are easily postponed.
- Government spending plan (G) for products and services is set by the government budget.
  - Transfer payments are not part of G.
- R.O.W. spending plans (X) for Canadian exports:
  - must subtract imports (IM) from all other planned spending to get net exports ($X - IM$); the difference between what Canada exports and imports.
- Planned spending on aggregate demand = planned C + planned I + planned G + planned ($X - IM$).
- **Demand shocks** — changes in factors other than the price level that change aggregate demand and shift the aggregate demand curve (AD) — expectations, interest rates, government policy, GDP in R.O.W., and exchange rates.
  - Negative demand shocks decrease aggregate demand and shift AD leftward: more pessimistic expectations, higher interest rates, lower government spending or higher taxes, decreased GDP in R.O.W., higher value of Canadian dollar.
  - Positive demand shocks increase aggregate demand and shift AD rightward: more optimistic expectations, lower interest rates, higher government spending or lower taxes, increased GDP in R.O.W., lower value of Canadian dollar.

8.4 Hit or Miss the Macroeconomic Performance Targets? The Aggregate Supply and Aggregate Demand Model

The loanable funds market allows the economy to hit long-run equilibrium performance targets over time. Aggregate demand and aggregate supply shocks move the economy away from long-run equilibrium targets.

- In *macroeconomic equilibrium,* aggregate demand *matches* aggregate supply and there is no tendency for change.
  - Short-run equilibrium with existing inputs is the point where short-run aggregate supply (SAS) and aggregate demand (AD) intersect.
  - Long-run equilibrium with existing inputs is the point where SAS, AD, and LAS all intersect. The aggregate quantity supplied and aggregate quantity demanded of real GDP also equal potential GDP.
- To explain macroeconomic equilibrium over time with increasing inputs we must add the banking system.
  - **Market for loanable funds** — banks coordinate the supply of loanable funds (saving) with the demand for loanable funds (borrowing for investment spending). The interest rate is the price of loanable funds.
  - If banks loan out savings to business borrowers who use the money for investment spending on new factories and equipment, that spending replaces consumer saving. Short-run aggregate supply remains equal to aggregate demand.
  - Business investment spending also increases quantity and quality of inputs, so potential GDP and living standards increase over time. Full employment continues and average prices stay stable.
- Four *mismatches* between aggregate demand and aggregate supply move the economy away from long-run equilibrium targets.
  - *Negative demand shocks* cause a recessionary gap: falling average prices, decreased real GDP, and increased unemployment.
  - *Positive demand shocks* cause an inflationary gap: rising average prices, increased real GDP, and decreased unemployment.
  - *Negative supply shocks* cause stagflation: rising average prices, decreased real GDP, and increased unemployment.
  - *Positive supply shocks* cause falling average prices, increased real GDP, continued full unemployment.

8.5 Shocking Starts and Finishes: Origins and Responses to Business Cycles

The "Yes — Markets Self-Adjust" and "No — Markets Fail Often" camps disagree about the external/internal origins of shocks, about rational/volatile expectations, and about how quickly price adjustments restore the match between aggregate supply and aggregate demand.

- "Yes — Markets Self-Adjust" camp, so government should be hands-off.
  - Long-run focus.
  - Origins of shocks are external to economy — in nature, science, and mistaken government policies.
  - Emphasizes rational expectations of investors and logical choices.
  - When shocks occur, price adjustments in markets work to quickly restore match between aggregate supply and aggregate demand.
  - In labour market, unemployment causes wage rate to fall, increasing hiring of labour until full employment restored.

- "No — Markets Fail Often" camp, so government should be hands-on.
  - Short-run focus.
  - Origins of shocks are internal to economy — from changing expectations, role of money, and connections with R.O.W.
  - Emphasizes volatile expectations of investors based on fundamental uncertainty; changeable "herd mentality" of investors; postponable nature of investments; investment based on *animal spirits* — gut-level instinct to act.
  - When shocks occur, price adjustments are difficult and slow, so role for government to bring short-run aggregate supply and aggregate demand back into balance.
  - In labour market, wages are *sticky* (don't fall easily) even with unemployment — workers and employers accept layoffs instead of lower wages.

TRUE/FALSE

Circle the correct answer. Solutions to these questions are available at the end of the book and on MyEconLab. You can also visit the MyEconLab Study Plan to access additional questions that will help you master the concepts covered in this chapter.

You are skating on an outdoor ice rink when suddenly hockey superstar Sidney Crosby comes by and offers to teach you how to anticipate where the puck is going. After the lesson he notices your economics textbook in your gym bag and says,

> *I own a small hockey equipment business, and I would like to anticipate where the economy is going in order to make supply plans for my business. If I read an interesting story in the news, I'd like to send you a text message so you can confirm if my statement about the macro economy is true.*

Use this scenario to answer questions 1–15.

8.1 Long-Run Aggregate Supply

1. Points on the long-run aggregate supply curve (*LAS*) correspond to points inside the macro production possibilities frontier (*PPF*).   T   F

2. The *short run* is a period of time when some input prices, like rubber for hockey pucks, do not change.   T   F

8.2 Short-Run Aggregate Supply

3. An improved hockey stick technology increases the short-run and long-run aggregate supply of real GDP.   T   F

4. Rising input prices shift both the *SAS* and *LAS* curves rightward.   T   F

5. Rising average prices, including prices of ticket to hockey games, increases the aggregate quantity supplied of real GDP.   T   F

8.3 Aggregate Demand

6. Optimistic expectations about the Maple Leafs winning the Stanley Cup spread to the business sector and increase business investment spending. This increases aggregate quantity demanded.   T   F

7. Positive demand shocks shift the aggregate demand curve (*AD*) leftward.   T   F

8. An increase in business investment in new hockey rinks increases aggregate demand. T F

9. An increase in the value of the Canadian dollar relative to the U.S. dollar increases aggregate demand for Canadian GDP. T F

8.4 Aggregate Supply and Aggregate Demand

10. In long-run macroeconomic equilibrium, the *SAS*, *AD*, and *LAS* curves all intersect. T F

11. A negative supply shock like rising electricity prices (including for hockey rinks) increases unemployment in the short run. T F

12. All economists agree on descriptions of equilibrium and on the impact of demand and supply shocks. T F

8.5 Origins and Responses to Business Cycles

13. All economists agree that government expenditures quickly lead to steady growth in living standards, full employment, and stable prices. T F

14. In a recession, the "Yes — Markets Self-Adjust" camp believes that full employment is restored quickly because unemployment causes wages to fall and employment to increase. T F

15. In a recession, the "No — Markets Fail Often" camp believes that potential GDP is restored because surpluses of products and services cause prices to fall and sales to increase. T F

MULTIPLE CHOICE

Circle the best answer. Solutions to these questions are available at the end of the book and on MyEconLab. You can also visit the MyEconLab Study Plan to access similar questions that will help you master the concepts covered in this chapter.

8.1 Long-Run Aggregate Supply

1. The *long run* is a period of time
   a) greater than 1 year.
   b) greater than 10 years.
   c) when the economy is at potential GDP.
   d) when some input prices do not change.

2. Points inside the macroeconomic *PPF*
   a) represent unemployed inputs.
   b) correspond to quantities of real GDP less than potential GDP.
   c) represent short-run choices.
   d) are all of the above.

8.2 Short-Run Aggregate Supply

3. Business supply plans to increase inputs increase aggregate
   a) supply.
   b) demand.
   c) quantity supplied.
   d) quantity demanded.

4. Aggregate supply of real GDP increases if
   a) productivity increases.
   b) input prices increase.
   c) output prices increase.
   d) all of the above.

5. Suppose that, in the future, businesses only pay high wages to people with college and university degrees. If people plan ahead and start increasing their years of schooling, this increases aggregate
   a) quantity demanded.
   b) demand.
   c) quantity supplied.
   d) supply.

8.3 Aggregate Demand

6. If your income is $20 000, your taxes are $6000, and your transfer payments are $3000, then your disposable income is
   a) $11 000.
   b) $14 000.
   c) $17 000.
   d) $20 000.

7. Of all components of aggregate demand, investment spending is the
   a) largest component.
   b) most volatile, unpredictable component.
   c) component that is not postponable.
   d) least affected by interest rates and expectations.

8. Aggregate demand in Canada increases if
   a) China buys more Canadian oil.
   b) aggregate demand in India decreases.
   c) Canada buys more Porsches from Germany.
   d) the value of the Canadian dollar increases.

8.4 Aggregate Supply and Aggregate Demand

9. ING Direct was known for its slogan "save your money." Suppose a new competitor, BLING Direct, advertises with the slogan "spend your money." If BLING Direct's advertisement encourages households to spend more of their income, this will be a
   a) positive supply shock.
   b) negative supply shock.
   c) positive demand shock.
   d) negative demand shock.

10. In the Global Financial Crisis, changes in unemployment and inflation moved in the opposite directions — unemployment went up and inflation went down. This suggests the Global Financial Crisis was a result of a
   a) positive supply shock.
   b) negative supply shock.
   c) positive demand shock.
   d) negative demand shock.

11. Which shock causes stagflation?
   a) positive supply shock
   b) negative supply shock
   c) positive demand shock
   d) negative demand shock

12. When consumers save some of their income, what can save Say's Law?
   a) consumer spending
   b) consumer saving
   c) business investment spending based on borrowed funds
   d) Superman

8.5 Origins and Responses to Business Cycles

13. Why are wages "sticky"?
   a) Employment contracts can't be quickly changed.
   b) Workers resist having their wages reduced.
   c) Employers resist wage cuts because wage cuts hurt productivity.
   d) All of the above.

14. The "Yes — Markets Self-Adjust" camp of economists emphasizes
   a) animal spirits.
   b) that individuals and businesses make rational choices based on the best information available.
   c) that expectations are more important than interest rates.
   d) that shocks are generated from inside the economy.

15. Two businesses, Dunder and Mifflin, need to reduce input costs because of economic conditions. The boss of Dunder announces, "The bad news is that I need to lay off some of you, but the good news is that wages will remain the same for those of you that I don't lay off." The boss of Mifflin announces, "The bad news is that I need to reduce everyone's wages, but the good news is that no one will lose their job."
   a) Dunder's announcement resembles the Keynesian view that wages are sticky and do not fall much during a recession.
   b) Mifflin's announcement resembles the Keynesian view that wages are sticky and do not fall much during a recession.
   c) Dunder's announcement resembles the Keynesian view that jobs are sticky and do not fall much during a recession.
   d) Mifflin's announcement resembles the Keynesian view that jobs are sticky and do not fall much during a recession.

9

Money Is for Lunatics

Demanders and Suppliers of Money

LEARNING OBJECTIVES

After reading this chapter, you should be able to:

9.1 Explain three functions of money and why people give up interest on bonds to demand money.

9.2 Identify four forms of money, and describe how the Bank of Canada and chartered banks create money.

9.3 Relate bond prices and interest rates, and explain how money and loanable funds markets determine the interest rate.

9.4 Explain how money affccts real GDP, unemployment, and inflation through the domestic monetary transmission mechanism.

9.5 Differentiate the "Yes — Markets Self-Adjust" and "No — Markets Fail Often" positions on the effect of money on business cycles.

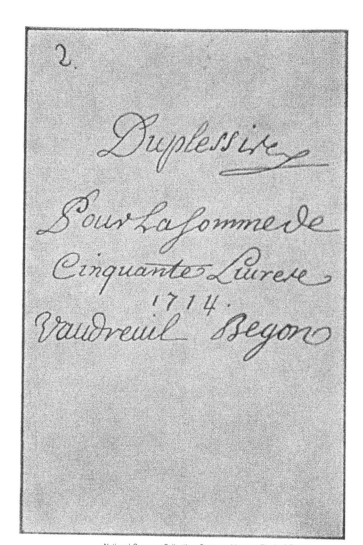

WHO WANTS MORE MONEY?

Okay, you can all put down your hands. From the title of this chapter, you are probably thinking that I am the lunatic here. Let me explain.

When you want to save money, there are a few options open to you. You can stash it — as cash — under your mattress, which pays no interest. Alternatively, you can save your money and earn interest on it. So why would you ever choose to hold cash and lose the interest? In this chapter, we will explain why people demand cash and voluntarily give up the possibility to earn interest.

"What is money?" is another question with unexpected answers. Historically, precious metals, jewels, beads, stones, and even furs have been used as money. Even the playing cards shown in the photo above once served as paper money back in 1685 in what is now Canada. Today, in our world of digital banking, cash is the least common form of money.

The interest rate is the price of money and is the answer to the question, "How much will you pay for money?" Demanders and suppliers of money and loanable funds markets all play a role in setting interest rates. And interest rates, in turn, affect business investment spending, real GDP, unemployment, and inflation.

And to tie it all together, we will answer the question, "Who supplies money?"

Get ready to enter the world of money, which is not crazy, but is full of surprising answers to many unusual questions.

9.1

Is It Smart to *Not* Want Money?
Demand for Money

Explain three functions of money and why people give up interest on bonds to demand money.

money anything acceptable as a means of paying for products and services

NOTE
As a medium of exchange, money solves the barter problem of the double coincidence of wants.

▲ Jill is trading some of her bread for some of Marie's wood. This form of trade, bartering, only works when the person who is selling what you want, wants what you're selling. Can you see the limitations of bartering for a large economy?

NOTE
As a unit of account, money functions as a standard unit for measuring prices.

There is a good reason why you all raised your hands about wanting more money. In a market economy like Canada's, money buys all of the products and services we want. Any business will accept your cash (or debit card) in exchange for what it is selling. That *acceptability* is the key to what we use as money. **Money** is anything acceptable as a means of paying for products and services.

But what makes money acceptable?

What Does Money Do?

Money serves three essential functions: as a medium of exchange, a unit of account, and a store of value.

Medium of Exchange   Markets are based on voluntary exchange. Barter is a simple exchange where two people directly trade one product for another, without the use of money. If Jill bakes bread and Marie chops wood, they can trade, or barter, bread for wood. In a barter world, Say's Law is always true. No one supplies — brings a product or service to market — unless she is demanding another product or service in exchange. Supply creates its own demand.

The problem with barter exchange is that you must find a trading partner who not only is selling what you want, but who also wants — is willing to accept — what you are selling. Economists call this problem the *double coincidence of wants*. If Jill is selling bread and wants wood, and Marie is selling wood but wants eggs instead of bread, there is no double coincidence of wants. No trade happens.

If all traders accept money in exchange for whatever they are selling, the problem of the double coincidence of wants is solved. Jill only needs to find buyers who want bread, and Marie only needs to find buyers who want wood. Once each exchanges her product for money, she can then buy whatever she wants from whomever she wants.

Money functions as a *medium of exchange*. Its acceptability by all traders as a means of payment overcomes the problem of the double coincidence of wants, and makes exchange or trade easier for all.

Unit of Account   The second function of money is providing a standard unit for measuring prices. In Canada, the standard unit is the Canadian dollar. All products and services are measured in dollars. A loaf of bread costs $4, a log of wood costs $0.40, a dozen eggs costs $2. These convenient and simple measurements seem so obvious we rarely think about them.

Instead of using money, prices can be measured in terms of any product. A loaf of bread could cost you 10 logs of wood, or you could pay half a loaf of bread for a dozen eggs. It would almost impossible to make smart choices in comparing what you must pay to buy a product or service when each is priced in terms of a different unit. Imagine trying to plan a budget! Using money as a unit of account eliminates this pricing problem.

With money, dollar prices act as a common denominator, allowing you to easily see the relative prices of all products and services. For example, a loaf of bread costs 10 times more than a log of wood or twice as much as a dozen eggs. You can easily figure out what you can afford to buy because everything is measured in dollars.

Store of Value   Money allows you to separate supply from demand. Once you have sold something of value on the market — usually your ability to work in the labour market in exchange for wages — money allows you to save some of your income for future spending. Money, as a store of value, functions as a time machine for moving the purchasing power of your money from the present to the future — you can earn it now and spend it later.

There are many reasons for storing value for the future. You may be saving for big purchases like a car or tuition. Because the future is uncertain, you may be saving as a precaution, so that you will have money if you become unemployed, or get ill and can't work. As you get older, you will save money for retirement, so that when you are no longer working you can still afford to eat and enjoy your free time!

Are There Three Functions of Money?   Economists have long been aware of these three functions of money. In a world where Say's Law holds true, aggregate supply and aggregate demand match, plans work out as expected, and all savings that are put into the loanable funds market earn interest. Those funds are then borrowed by businesses for investment spending. In this world of Say's Law, even without inflation, why would anyone store their wealth in the form of money? In *The General Theory of Employment*, Keynes said " . . . it is one of the recognised characteristics of money as a store of wealth that it is barren; whereas practically every other form of storing wealth yields some interest or profit. Why should anyone outside a lunatic asylum wish to use money as a store of wealth?"

If all savings can be safely and predictably invested to earn interest, why would anyone want money as a store of value?

NOTE
As a store of value, money functions as a time machine for moving purchasing power from the present to the future.

Jeff Rotman/Alamy

▲ Money's use as a store of value is demonstrated by these very old gold coins, found on a ship that sank in 1658. They are still valuable today. What conditions must be met for money to act as a store of value?

Why Hold Money?

There are sane reasons to hold some of your wealth as money, even if it means giving up earned interest.

Money or Bonds?   The true cost of any choice is the opportunity cost — the cost of the best alternative given up. The opportunity cost of choosing to hold money is the interest you could have earned by investing the money instead.

Let's take a simple example where there are only two choices for holding wealth: as money, which pays no interest, or as loanable funds, which do pay interest. Bonds are the most important loanable fund. A **bond** is a financial asset for which the borrower promises to repay the original value at a specific future date and to make fixed regular interest payments.

bond   financial asset for which borrower promises to repay the original value at a specific future date and to make fixed regular interest payments

When companies need cash, they often go to the loanable funds markets to borrow money. To do this, they issue bonds. For example, the Ford Motor Company, in order to get cash for new assembly-line robots, may issue many $10 000 bonds. Each bond promises to repay the borrowed $10 000 on January 1, 2025, and to make $500 interest payments on every January 1st until then. By using $10 000 of your savings to buy the bond from Ford, you are actually loaning Ford $10 000. In exchange, Ford gives you a piece of paper (the bond), which is a promise to repay your loan of $10 000 with a specific dollar amount of interest.

Corporations, governments, public utilities, and even cities issue bonds as a way of borrowing money. There are many other interest-paying assets in the loanable funds market, but I chose bonds for this example because they are the most important asset in the monetary system worldwide, and are used by the Bank of Canada and other central banks for influencing interest rates. Think of bonds as representing bonds, savings accounts, equities, and all forms of interest-paying loanable funds. For the examples that follow, we will consider loanable funds and bonds as the same thing.

NOTE
Bonds represent bonds, savings accounts, equities, and all other interest-paying loanable funds.

Liquidity

Why would you hold money rather than buy a Ford bond? By holding money you give up the $500 a year in interest.

All reasons for wanting to hold money and give up earned interest are summarized in one word — liquidity. **Liquidity** is the ease with which assets can be converted into the economy's medium of exchange. Money — which is by definition the medium of exchange — is the most liquid of all assets. No conversion is required to use money as a means for paying for products and services. Bonds are much less liquid. It may take days to sell your bonds to get your money.

liquidity ease with which assets can be converted into the economy's medium of exchange

What Money Can Buy and Bonds Can't

To illustrate the difference in liquidity, suppose you run out of milk at 10 o'clock at night and walk to the nearest corner store. If you pay with money, the owner readily accepts the $10 bill you offer for the bag of milk. If you try and pay with the bond ("Let me tear off a little corner of the bond for the milk, okay?"), the owner will call the police or the mental health authorities. Bonds are not liquid — not normally acceptable as a means of payment.

In deciding whether to hold your wealth in the form of money or bonds, there is a trade-off — interest or liquidity. Money pays no interest, but has liquidity. Bonds pay interest, but do not have much liquidity. The liquidity convenience of money has value, and that is worth paying for. The opportunity cost of that convenience — the cost of liquidity — is the interest you give up by not holding bonds.

NOTE
Money pays no interest, but has liquidity. Bonds pay interest, but do not have liquidity.

All macroeconomists agree that to get liquidity and the benefits of money as a medium of exchange and as a unit of account, people are willing to pay the opportunity cost — giving up interest they could have earned.

Why Hold Money to Store Value? What about the store of value function of money? You will hold enough of your wealth as money to be able to make your regular purchases, but will you also hold money (instead of bonds) as a store of value, that is, as savings? Here the "Yes — Markets Self-Adjust" and "No — Markets Fail Often" camps give different answers.

Let's look first at a "Yes — Markets Self-Adjust" scenario, where supply creates its own demand, and aggregate supply and aggregate demand match. Investors have rational expectations, and savings can be relatively safely and predictably invested to earn interest. In this scenario, there is not much demand for money as a store of value. People will hold more of their wealth as interest-paying bonds. Savings, which reduce aggregate demand, are put into bonds (loanable funds), which causes the interest rate to fall, increasing business investment spending. Ford buys new robots for its factories with the $10 000 you loaned the car-maker in exchange for its bond. The additional investment spending increases aggregate demand and offsets the saving, so the economy continues to operate at potential real GDP with full employment. Even with money and saving, supply continues to create its own demand.

Now compare this to a Keynesian "No — Markets Fail Often" scenario, where business cycles occur because there is a mismatch between aggregate supply and aggregate demand. When there is fundamental uncertainty about the future and volatile expectations, people hold more of their wealth as money. With the unpredictability of recessions, interest-earning bond investments are risky, not safe.

Think of the people, just before the Global Financial Crisis, who invested their savings in U.S. financial institutions that went bankrupt. The 158-year-old Lehman Brothers investment bank was the most publicized of these bankruptcies. All those who invested money in Lehman Brothers lost their savings. Similarly, when Chrysler and General Motors went briefly into bankruptcy in 2009, bondholders of those corporations lost much of their invested money — the money they loaned those businesses through buying their bonds.

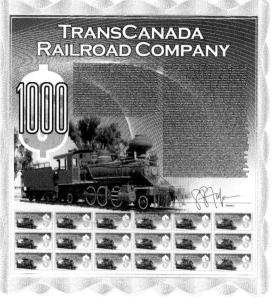

Anthony Leung

▲ This bond, from the TransCanada Railroad Company, is for $1000. Each coupon attached to the bond can be redeemed at a specific time for the interest payment. At the expiry date, the bond itself can be cashed in for its original value. Why are bonds sometimes be preferred to cash?

When investors worry about recessions, they hold more of their savings and wealth as money, even though money pays no interest. Earning no interest may be better than losing your savings with risky investments in the loanable funds market. During the Global Financial Crisis, most investors wished they had been holding money instead of equities and bonds whose value plunged by 40 percent during the trough of the business cycle. Investors (like Joseph Kennedy, father of U.S. president John F. Kennedy) who switched to cash before the stock market crash of 1929 that started the Great Depression became the wealthy elite of the 1930s.

In Keynes's world, holding money is like a security blanket, protecting the holder from unpredictable economic changes. The more worried investors are, the higher the interest rate they will demand to let go of the security blanket and move their wealth from money to loanable funds. Fear about the future causes interest rates to rise, which discourages investment spending by businesses and intensifies the recession. Pessimistic expectations can become self-fulfilling expectations — they help create the negative outcome investors are worrying about.

All economists agree that people need to be rewarded with interest payments in order to give up the benefits of the liquidity of money. The "No — Markets Fail Often" camp places more emphasis on the security of money as a store of value protecting you against future uncertainty.

> *Our desire to hold money is a barometer of our distrust of . . . the future. . . . The possession of money lulls our disquietude; and the premium which we require to make us part with money is the measure of the degree of our disquietude.*
>
> — *John Maynard Keynes*

Economics *Out There*

Canadians Sitting on a $1-Trillion Pile of Idle Cash

Economist Derek Holt of Scotia Capital Inc. reports that "risk-averse Canadian households are sitting on up to $1 trillion of cash and near-cash holdings, earning next to nothing" in interest.

Holt understands why households are so cautious, given the recent "financial shocks" of the Global Financial Crisis. But, he argues, households should be holding more of their savings in the form of financial assets like bonds that yield higher returns. Holt is implying that households are acting like lunatics by holding money and giving up earned interest!

As Keynes would predict, households are holding cash to avoid risk and to have the benefits of liquidity. By holding cash, households are betting that earning no interest will be better than losing their savings trying to gain higher interest though risky investments.

Source: "Families sitting on up to $1-trillion," Virginian Galt, found in *Globe and Mail* Update, September 28, 2009.

How Much Money to Hold?
Interest Rates and the Demand for Money

Money pays no interest, but has liquidity. Loanable funds pay interest, but do not have liquidity. How do you make a smart choice about *how much* of your wealth to hold as money, and *how much* as loanable funds?

Interest Rate as the Price of Money   The **interest rate** is the price of holding money: what you give up by not holding loanable funds. The interest rate is determined by demand and supply in both the money market and the loanable funds market. Money and loanable funds are intimately connected, as the definition of the interest rate shows.

interest rate   price of holding money: what you give up by not holding loanable funds

To illustrate how interest rates are determined, we will stick with the simple choice between money and bonds. First we will look at the demand for money. Then we will look at the supply of money, and finally at the interactions of demand and supply in the money and loanable funds markets.

Macroeconomic Demand for Money   According to the microeconomic law of demand, when the price of something rises, the quantity demanded decreases. The law of demand also applies to money. As the price of money — the interest rate — rises, the quantity demanded of money decreases. At higher interest rates people want to hold less money (and hold more of their assets as bonds). The **law of demand for money** works as long as other factors besides the interest rate do not change.

law of demand for money   as the price of money — the interest rate — rises, the quantity demanded of money decreases

Suppose the interest rate on bonds is very low — 1 percent per year. If you put $100 of your savings in a bond, at the end of the year you get back $101 — your original $100 plus $1 in interest. It makes almost no difference whether you hold your wealth in the form of money (which pays no interest) or bonds. Since your bond payoff is only $1, you might as well keep most of your wealth as money, to have the convenience of liquidity.

Now imagine that the interest rate on bonds is 100 percent per year, so each $100 investment yields $200 at the end of the year — your original $100 plus $100 in interest. By choosing bonds you double your assets! Then you might keep as much of your assets as possible in bonds, and hold the minimum quantity of money you need for purchases. There is an inverse relation between the interest rate and the quantity demanded of money. The lower the interest rate, the higher the quantity demanded of money. The higher the interest rate, the lower the quantity demanded of money.

If we total — aggregate — the demands for money of all individuals, we get the macroeconomic demand for money. The table of numbers in Figure 9.1 (on the next page) illustrates the inverse relation between the interest rate and the quantity demanded of money for the economy as a whole. For simplicity, the numbers are made up, but the pattern represents what the actual macroeconomic demand for money looks like. If you graph the combinations of interest rates and quantity demanded, you get the downward-sloping demand for money curve in Figure 9.1.

Figure 9.1 Demand for Money

Price (interest rate)	Quantity Demanded (billions of dollars)
2%	100
4%	90
6%	80
8%	70
10%	60

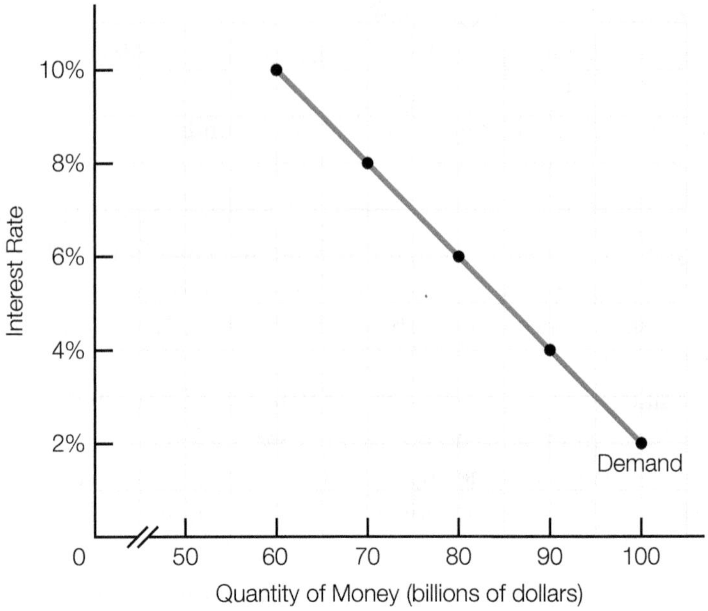

As the price of money — the interest rate — rises, the quantity demanded of money decreases. Money is like other products and services. As the price rises, people look for substitutes. Bonds are a substitute for holding wealth — an alternative to money. When something, even money, becomes more expensive, people economize on its use.

What Changes the Demand for Money? Real GDP and Average Price Level

In macroeconomics, as in microeconomics, we distinguish a change in quantity demanded from a change in demand. Only a change in the price of money — the interest rate — changes the *quantity demanded* of money. A change in other factors changes the *demand for money*.

Figure 9.1 assumes that all factors, other than the interest rate, influencing the demand for money remain unchanged. Two factors that can change the macroeconomic demand for money are real GDP and the average price level. A change in either factor shifts the money demand curve.

Real GDP   In the circular flow diagram (Figure 6.5, p. 139), real GDP always equals aggregate income. When real GDP increases, the economy has produced more stuff, and people have more income. When income increases, people buy more products and services, so they need more money to make those purchases. As a student struggling to make ends meet, think about how much cash you carry around in your wallet for your daily purchases. You need to pay transit fares, lunch at Mr. Sub, maybe money for the movies. Now think about what a wealthy entrepreneur carries around in her wallet. Enough cash to fill up the Mercedes with gas, to pay for lunch at expensive restaurants, to tip doormen and parking valets, and maybe for opera tickets. In general, as real GDP and income increase, the demand for money as a medium of exchange also increases.

Figure 9.2 shows the original demand for money and the new demand for money after real GDP increases. At any interest rate (column 1), with more real GDP and real income (column 3), the quantity demanded of money is greater than it was originally (column 2). An increase in real GDP increases the demand for money and shifts the money demand curve rightward. A decrease in real GDP decreases the demand for money and shifts the money demand curve leftward.

NOTE
An increase in real GDP increases the demand for money and shifts the money demand curve rightward. A decrease in real GDP decreases the demand for money and shifts the money demand curve leftward.

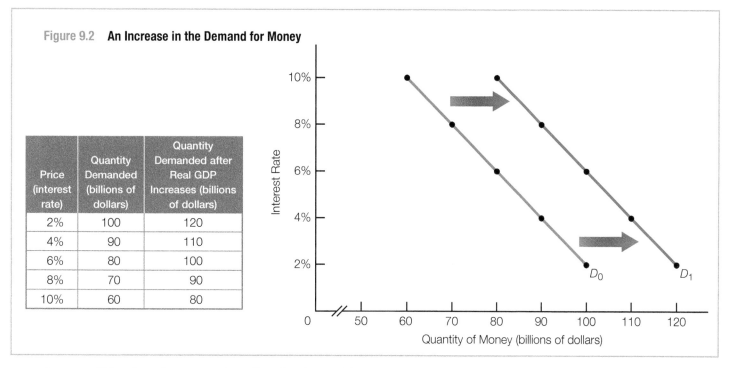

Figure 9.2   **An Increase in the Demand for Money**

Price (interest rate)	Quantity Demanded (billions of dollars)	Quantity Demanded after Real GDP Increases (billions of dollars)
2%	100	120
4%	90	110
6%	80	100
8%	70	90
10%	60	80

Average Price Level   Prices also affect the demand for money. An increase in the average price level — inflation — means you need to carry more dollars in your wallet to purchase the same products and services. If the price of milk rises from $6 to $7 a bag, and prices of all other products and services rise similarly, you need to carry more dollars to make the same purchases as before.

An increase in prices affects the demand for money in the same way as an increase in real GDP. The quantity demanded for money *after prices rise* would again look like column 3 in Figure 9.2. An increase in the average price level increases the demand for money and shifts the demand for money curve rightward. A decrease in the average price level — deflation — decreases the demand for money and shifts the demand for money curve leftward.

So it turns out that it's not always smart to demand more money. The next question is, who supplies the money people demand?

NOTE
An increase in the average price level increases the demand for money and shifts the money demand curve rightward. A decrease in the average price level decreases the demand for money and shifts the money demand curve leftward.

Refresh 9.1

MyEconLab

For answers to these Refresh
Questions, visit MyEconLab.

1. In your own words, explain the law of demand for money.

2. Explain liquidity and why it's a major factor in demanding money over bonds.

3. You have just won $5000 in the lottery. You go on a shopping spree with $4000 and save $1000. What benefits or worries will influence your decision to hold the $1000 as cash or to invest it in an interest-earning bond?

9.2

Legal Counterfeiting?
Supply of Money

Identify four forms of money and describe how the Bank of Canada and chartered banks create money.

Money! We all want it. We all work hard for it. But what is it? All the references to "cash in your wallet" sound so old-fashioned. What is money these days and where does it come from?

What's a Money?

Throughout history there have been only four basic forms of money: commodity money, convertible paper money, fiat money, and deposit money.

Commodity Money   A commodity is any product that can be sold. Commodity money is exactly what its name says — a commodity such as fur pelts, beads, cattle, or precious metals used as money. Commodity money has alternative uses. Gold and silver, for example, are used for jewellery and industrial purposes, as well as for coins. To be useful as a medium of exchange and as a unit of account, commodity money must be easy to carry, to measure, and to divide into fractions. That's why cattle and fur pelts are inferior forms of commodity money compared to coins (loonies, quarters, dimes, etc.). As a store of value, commodity money must not deteriorate over time. Coins also work well as a store of value. But imagine trying to use sticks of butter as money in a tropical climate. As your savings melted, your money would literally go down the drain.

The earliest known coins made from precious metals date back to 600 BCE. They were found by archaeologists in the Temple of Artemis in what is now Turkey. After that, coins quickly became the dominant form of commodity money.

Convertible Paper Money   Carrying around large bags of gold coins makes you an easy target for thieves. Merchants began to store, or deposit, their gold with goldsmiths, who had the best safes and security. The goldsmith issued the depositor a piece of paper — an "I owe you" or IOU — promising to return the gold when it was asked for. Soon these IOUs (one of the first text abbreviations!) began to circulate as money. As long as a seller trusted that the goldsmith would return, or convert, the paper into gold, he would accept the more convenient and easily hidden IOU as payment in place of the actual coins.

Many early national paper currencies — Canadian Dominion Notes introduced after Confederation and U.S. dollar notes — used to be convertible into gold. They were, in effect, IOUs from the government.

Fiat Money   The paper (now made out of plastic mylar!) dollar bill notes in your wallet are no longer convertible into gold or silver. They have value simply because the government decrees that they are valuable. Money that has no alternative uses and is valuable simply by governmental decree (a fiat) is called fiat money. The bills and the coins made from mylar and non-precious metals that we use are fiat money. Economists also refer to the government-issued bills and coins in circulation as **currency**.

Acceptability is the key characteristic of money. Currency — the bills and coin fiat money we use — is acceptable because we trust the government that issued it. If you look at any bill in your wallet, you will see that it is "signed" by the Governor of the Bank of Canada, who decrees that "Ce billet a cours légal — This note is legal tender." Similarly, the playing card money in the opening photograph of the chapter was also fiat money. Its acceptability depended on its being signed by Governor of New France, who was trusted.

Deposit Money   Most money today is deposit money. **Demand deposits** are balances in bank accounts that depositors can withdraw on demand by using a debit card or writing a cheque. Currency and demand deposits are today's most widely accepted means of paying for products and services. An exchange of money for products and services is only complete when the buyer transfers either currency or demand deposits to the seller. Debit cards and cheques are not themselves money. They are just a means of transferring demand deposits, which are money. Credit cards are definitely *not* money. When you pay using a credit card, Visa or MasterCard is giving you a temporary loan, which they use to pay the merchant. But the transaction is not complete until you transfer currency or demand deposits to the credit card company to pay off the loan.

▲ This dollar bill, issued by Canada when it was a Dominion, is convertible paper money. The word "dollar" comes from the German word *thaler*, a silver coin minted in Joachimsthal, Bohemia, in 1519. What might happen to this form of currency if people no longer trust the government that issued it?

currency   government-issued bills and coins

demand deposits   balances in bank accounts that depositors can withdraw on demand by using a debit card or writing a cheque

Economics *Out There*

Card Money in New France

In 1685, Jacques de Meulles, the Governor of New France, didn't have enough funds to pay his soldiers fighting the English. Typically, the government delayed paying merchants for products until a fresh supply of gold and silver coins arrived from France. But he could not delay paying his soldiers. De Meulles's clever solution was to issue paper money printed on playing cards.

In a letter to France dated September 24, 1685, de Meulles wrote,

"I have found myself this year in great straits with regard to the subsistence of the soldiers. You did not provide for funds, my Lord . . . . Money being extremely scarce . . . for the pay of the soldiers, it occurred to me to issue, instead of money, notes on cards, which I have cut in quarters . . . I have issued an ordinance by which I have obliged all the inhabitants to receive this money in payments, and to give it circulation, at the same time pledging myself, in my own name, to redeem the said notes."

These cards were widely accepted by merchants, given that they were backed by the government. Even though the cards were redeemable for gold, many were not redeemed and remained in circulation as money.

Playing card money was fiat money. It was valuable by the decree of the government, and functioned as a medium of exchange because of its acceptability by sellers, who trusted the government and obeyed the government decree.

Source: James Powell, *A History of the Canadian Dollar,* Bank of Canada, December 2005, pp 4–6.

▲ Chartered banks are private banks chartered under the *Bank Act* of 1992. They include Bank of Montreal, CIBC, Scotiabank, Royal Bank of Canada, TD Canada Trust, and 42 other Canadian- and foreign-owned banks. All banks in Canada are regulated by the government.

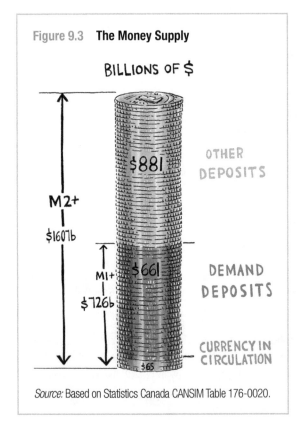

Figure 9.3 The Money Supply

BILLIONS OF $

OTHER DEPOSITS

M2+
$1607b

$881

M1+
$726b

$661

DEMAND DEPOSITS

CURRENCY IN CIRCULATION

$65

Source: Based on Statistics Canada CANSIM Table 176-0020.

central bank government institution responsible for supervising chartered banks and other financial institutions, and for regulating the supply of money

Measuring the Money Supply

Where does money come from? In Canada today, money consists of currency issued by the Bank of Canada and deposit money in *chartered banks*, credit unions, and similar financial institutions. Chartered banks — private banks chartered under the *Bank Act* of 1992 to receive deposits and makes loans — are the most important financial institutions for creating the supply of money. Banks creating money? Are you surprised? Read on.

M1+ and M2+   There are many ways to measure the supply of money in Canada. The official measures used by the Bank of Canada are called M1+ and M2+ (see Figure 9.3).

M1+ consists of currency in circulation plus demand deposits. In March 2014, there was $65 billion in currency and $661 billion in demand deposits. M1+ equaled $726 billion.

M2+ is a broader measure of the money supply. It includes all of M1+ plus all other deposits, like savings accounts and guaranteed investment certificates. M2+ was $1607 billion. These other deposits are not as liquid as demand deposits. They have restrictions or penalties for withdrawal on demand. But they are relatively easy to convert into money, which is why they are included in this broader measure of the money supply.

Notice that currency ($65 billion) is a small fraction of the money supply — about 9 percent of M1+ and 4 percent of M2+.

The Bank of Canada: Canada's Central Bank

A **central bank** is a government institution responsible for supervising chartered banks and other financial institutions, and for regulating the supply of money. Canada's central bank, the Bank of Canada, was created during the Great Depression by the 1935 *Bank of Canada Act*. The Bank of Canada's mandate is to control the quantity of money and interest rates to avoid inflation, business cycles, and unemployment.

The Bank of Canada plays five important roles in the Canadian economy: issuing currency, acting as banker to chartered banks, acting as a lender of last resort, acting as a banker to government, and conducting monetary policy.

Issuing Currency   The Bank of Canada is the only legal issuer of bills and coins. The Bank of Canada issues instructions to the Royal Mint, which is responsible for actually "making" the bills and coins.

Banker to Chartered Banks   Chartered private banks take deposits from consumer households and businesses and make loans. While you might have demand deposits in a chequing account at Scotiabank, Scotiabank and all other chartered banks have their own demand deposits in accounts at the Bank of Canada. These Bank of Canada deposits allow the chartered banks to make payments to each other. When you use your Scotiabank debit card to buy jeans from a merchant who has an account at the Bank of Montreal, Scotiabank transfers the money to the Bank of Montreal through their accounts at the Bank of Canada.

Lender of Last Resort   The Bank of Canada also is a **lender of last resort** to the financial system. When chartered banks are short of funds — for example, if borrowers go bankrupt and fail to repay loans owed to the bank — chartered banks can borrow from the Bank of Canada. This role helps maintain stability and liquidity in the financial system. During the Global Financial Crisis, the Bank of Canada, the U.S. Federal Reserve, and central banks around the world played crucial roles as lenders of last resort in preventing a breakdown of the financial system like that which occurred during the Great Depression.

lender of last resort   central bank's role of making loans to banks to preserve the stability of the financial system

Banker to Government   The Government of Canada has a demand deposit account at the Bank of Canada. The Bank of Canada manages the government's accounts, the government's reserves of foreign currency (like U.S. dollars), and the national debt (discussed in Chapter 12).

Conducting Monetary Policy   Monetary policy consists of changes in the supply of money and interest rates to achieve the macroeconomic outcomes of steady growth, full employment, and stable prices. The Bank of Canada is responsible for monetary policy, which we will discuss in detail in Chapter 11.

How Banks Create Money: Profits versus Prudence

The Bank of Canada is the only legal supplier of Canadian currency. But currency is only a small fraction of the supply of money. Most money takes the form of demand deposits, and those can be created legally by chartered banks.

Don't you wish you could create money? Me too. But a chartered bank's creation of money comes with risks.

▶

All Canadian currency — bills and coins — is produced by order of the Bank of Canada. The Bank placed the order to have these loonies manufactured by the Royal Canadian Mint. The Canadian Bank Note Company and BA International are the only institutions authorized to print Canadian bills, and they also receive printing orders from the Bank of Canada. When might the Bank of Canada order the printing or minting of more money?

Winnipeg Free Press/Ken Gigliotti/CP Images

An Offer You Can't Refuse To explore how banks create money, let's start with a simple story. Suppose someone gives you $1000 cash to hold. His "offer" is that it will be very unpleasant for you (you might lose a kneecap or other body part) if you don't return the money when he asks for it. He will be back sometime within 10 days. On any day there is a 1/10 chance he will ask you for the money. You have no choice but to hold the money in a form (cash) that you can give back.

Now suppose 100 people each give you $1000 on the same terms. Then on any day, what is the probability — the odds — of your having to give out the whole $100 000? It is $(1/10)^{100}$, which is a very, very, very, very small number. Those tiny odds of being asked for all of the money depends on the probabilities being independent — the likelihood of one person asking for her money is not influenced by whether any of the other people ask for their money. This will be important.

If you want to play it safe, the probability of being asked for more than $80 000 on any given day is even smaller. You would be quite safe holding $20 000 in reserve and loaning out $80 000 to other people and collecting interest. By making loans, you can profit from other peoples' money.

This simple story contains all of the main features of banking — deposits ($100 000), loans ($80 000), and reserves ($20 000).

Making Money by Making Money There is much historical truth to the simple story of goldsmiths becoming bankers. Goldsmiths had secure safes that attracted depositors. Goldsmiths issued paper IOUs for gold, and also acted like banks. Once the public trusted and accepted paper notes issued by goldsmiths — acceptability is the key to money — goldsmiths could issue notes that were not fully backed by gold.

Goldsmiths made loans, giving the borrower not gold but a paper note convertible into gold. In exchange, the borrower signed a contract to repay the loan plus interest at a future date. The borrower could use the goldsmith's note as money since it was accepted as a means of payment.

The value of the paper notes in circulation was greater than the value of gold in the safes. The goldsmiths were relying on (you could say "banking on") the very small probability that all depositors and borrowers would want to withdraw the gold at the same time. By making loans not backed by gold, the goldsmiths created money (acceptable paper notes) and made profits (interest) on the loans. For trust in the paper notes to continue, the goldsmiths had to hold enough gold in reserve so that when customers did show up with one of their paper notes and asked for the equivalent amount of gold, it was there.

Loans and Money Creation Go Together

Essentially, the chartered banks are the goldsmiths today, but without the gold. When you or any other depositor put money into a chartered bank, you get a credit on your chequing account balance. If you deposit $1000 cash, you can use your debit card to pay for products and services worth up to $1000. But the bank doesn't keep your cash in their vaults. They keep a very small fraction of your deposit in the form of cash reserves, and loan out the rest at interest. Like the goldsmiths, the banks are banking on the very small probability that depositors and borrowers would all want to withdraw their cash at the same time. This system of banking is called **fractional-reserve banking**.

Instead of issuing paper notes like goldsmiths, the bank creates a digital demand deposit credit in the borrower's chequing account equal to the amount of the loan. Since demand deposits are money — part of M1+ — the bank has created both a loan and money. When loans are paid off, there is a reduction in the quantity of both loans and money. In the Canadian monetary system, loan creation and money creation are two sides of the same coin. By loaning money, chartered banks are legally creating money, without counterfeiting.

fractional-reserve banking banks hold only a fraction of deposits as reserves

Look Ma, No Reserves!

While the Bank of Canada carefully supervises all banks and financial institutions, you will be surprised to know that chartered banks are not legally required to keep any cash reserves at all! Canadian banks actually hold less than 1 percent of the value of all demand deposits as cash!

Nonetheless, the Canadian banking system is one of the safest and most admired banking systems in the world. There are many reasons for this, but we will focus on just a few related to the basics of deposits and loans. First, most bank customers rarely demand cash. Think about the small proportion of bills or purchases that you pay for with currency. Second, in the rare event that customers want to withdraw more demand deposits or currency than the bank has, chartered banks can borrow from each other and from the Bank of Canada (the lender of last resort) to meet their customers' demands and maintain trust.

Probabilities and Bank Runs

Fractional-reserve banking, whether done by individuals, goldsmiths, merchants, or chartered banks, has risks. What happens when probabilities are *not* independent — when the likelihood of one person asking for her money *is* influenced by other people asking for their money? This is what happens when the public loses trust in a goldsmith or a bank. It is called a run on the bank. A **bank run** occurs when many depositors want to get their cash out at the same time. When this happens, banks can fail, or go bankrupt.

bank run many depositors withdraw cash all at once

Bank runs and bank failures were common during the 1800s, but are rare since the tightening of banking regulation and the *Bank of Canada Act*. The last bank failures in Canada, of four small banks, occurred in the late 1980s and the recession of 1991. While investors in the bank lost money, depositors were largely protected by deposit insurance from the Canadian banking system.

▲ This is the Northern Rock Bank in Cambridge, U.K., September 15, 2007. Fear of this bank's failure caused many depositors to try, all at the same time, to withdraw their savings. The bank closed its doors temporarily, received government guarantees, and remains in business still.

Bank Profits versus Prudence   The everyday risks of fractional-reserve banking and loans are that borrowers will default on their loans — not be able to pay back the bank. Banks try to protect against this risk by requiring *collateral* on loans — property pledged as security for repayment of the loan. When a bank loans you money for a car or mortgage on a house, the bank owns the car or the house, as collateral, until you pay off the loan. If you default on the loan, the bank sells the property to recover the value of the loan. Banks also charge higher interest payments on loans that they consider to be riskier.

With fractional-reserve banking and loans, there is a trade-off between profits and prudence or safety. Banks make profits by loaning money at interest. The more deposits that they turn into loans, the greater their potential profits. And higher risk loans earn the most interest.

But each loan creates an equivalent demand deposit. More loans mean more demand deposits created for borrowers' accounts. More demand deposits with unchanged reserves makes it riskier for banks to be able meet the demands of depositors for withdrawals. Prudence is necessary to maintain the trust of depositors and meet their needs for withdrawals, and more prudence means holding more reserves, making fewer loans, and earning lower profits. This is the tension in any banking system — between profits and prudence — and why banks are regulated around the world. Without regulation, more banks will be tempted to take risks in pursuit of profits that might lead to the failure of the bank if loans are not repaid. When banks fail, bank owners justifiably lose the money they have invested in the banking business. But innocent, trusting depositors, who did not make the risky loan decisions, also lose their money.

The Supply of Money

In our fractional-reserve banking system, the supply of money is determined by the Bank of Canada and by the chartered banks, through the demand deposits and matching loans they create. The Bank of Canada controls the supply of currency, and, as we will see in Chapter 11, influences the quantity of demand deposits that chartered banks choose to create.

In measuring the supply of money, currency is easy to count. Figure 9.4 gives you a picture of the harder-to-count demand deposits and loans created by the chartered banks. Deposits of $1474.1 billion are part of the money supply. Notice that currency reserves ($4.8 billion) are less than 1 percent of deposits. Liquid assets ($197.7 billion) consist of the lowest-risk Government of Canada Treasury bills (bonds) and commercial bills (bonds) that can quickly and easily be converted into reserves. These earn banks a low interest rate. Securities ($301.4 billion) are slightly riskier bonds, but earn banks higher interest rates. Loans ($2043.4 billion) to businesses and consumers (including credit card balances) are riskiest, and earn banks the highest interest rates.

NOTE
Banks face a trade-off between profits and prudence. A smaller fraction of reserves and higher-risk loans may make more bank profits, but at the cost of giving up safety and risking customers' deposits and trust.

Figure 9.4   Chartered Banks: Sources and Uses of Funds

	$ billion (April 2014)	Percentage of Deposits
Total Funds	2547.3	172.8
Sources		
Deposits	1474.1	100.0
Borrowing and own capital	1073.2	72.8
Uses		
Reserves	4.8	0.3
Liquid assets	197.7	13.4
Securities and other assets	301.4	20.5
Loans	2043.4	138.6

Source: Based on Statistics Canada, CANSIM Table 176-0011

The amounts for sources of funds and uses of funds are equal ($2547.3 billion). Having loaned out much of the deposited money, notice that bank currency reserves (0.3 percent) and liquid assets (13.4 percent) are only a fraction of deposits. That is fractional-reserve banking. Most deposits are not held in banks, but are loaned out to make profits for the banks.

Higher Interest Rates, More Loans, Increased Quantity of Money Supplied The total quantity of money supplied by both the Bank of Canada and the banking system (currency plus demand deposits, measured as M1+) depends on the quantity of loans and demand deposits that the banking system creates. When interest rates are higher, loans are more profitable, so banks make more loans and create more demand deposits. There is a positive relationship between interest rates and the quantity of money supplied (both go up or down together). If we use simple made-up numbers relating the interest rate and the quantity of money supplied, it would look like the table Figure 9.5. If you graph the combinations of interest rates and quantity supplied, you get the upward-sloping supply of money curve in Figure 9.5.

Figure 9.5 **Supply of Money**

Price (interest rate)	Quantity Supplied (billions of dollars)
2%	60
4%	70
6%	80
8%	90
10%	100

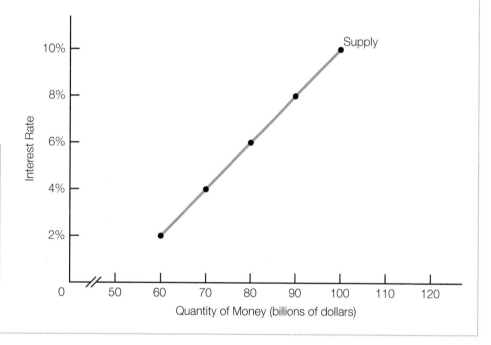

We will use money demand and money supply curves in the next section to illustrate how interest rates are determined.

Refresh 9.2

1. In your own words, define the two official measures of the money supply in Canada.

2. Explain how a chartered bank creates money.

3. Banks, like other businesses, operate to make profits. Are there reasons why banks should be subject to more government regulations than, for example, shoe stores or dollar stores? Explain your answer.

MyEconLab

For answers to these Refresh Questions, visit MyEconLab.

9.3

What Is the Price of Money? Interest Rates, Money, and Bonds

Relate bond prices and interest rates, and explain how money and loanable funds markets determine the interest rate.

"How much will you pay for more money?" That question might sound strange, because the price you pay for most products or services is stated in dollars — $2 for a cup of coffee, $15 for a movie. But asking how much will you pay for a dollar is not that crazy. Even money has a price.

The interest rate is the price of money in two ways:

- The interest rate is the price, or opportunity cost, of holding money — what you give up by not holding your wealth as bonds that pay interest.

- The interest rate is also the price you pay to borrow money. If the interest rate is 5 percent per year, to borrow $100 for a year you have to pay $105 back at the end of the year — the original $100 plus $5 in interest.

To see how the interest rate is determined, we will continue with the simple choice between two assets: money and bonds. The interest rate is determined by the interaction of the demand for money and the supply of money in both the money and loanable funds markets.

Before looking at that interaction, we must explain one other price — the price of bonds.

Opposites by Nature: Bond Prices and Interest Rates

Bonds are the most important type of loanable funds. Internationally traded bonds are worth US$18 trillion, and domestically traded bonds (like Canadian bonds owned by Canadian investors) are valued at an incredible US$50 trillion. Bonds can be issued for short (one month) or long (30 years) time periods. There is a bond market where bonds are bought and sold after being issued by businesses or governments. Because of the bond market's huge size, the bond market determines long-term (30-year) interest rates for all economies.

Bond prices change from the original value of the bond as economic conditions change, as you are about to see.

Let's take a simple example of a $10 000 bond issued by the Ford Motor Company for one year that promises to repay the $10 000 and a $500 payment at the end of the year. The original value of the bond is $10 000, and the current price of the bond on the bond market is also $10 000.

If the price of the bond is $10 000, the $500 payment amounts to 5 percent interest for the year. It is important to remember that *bonds specify a fixed dollar amount that they pay* in addition to repaying the original value. Bonds do *not* specify an interest rate in percent. The specific fixed dollar amount is very important.

NOTE
Bonds promise to pay back the original value plus a fixed dollar amount of money. Bonds do *not* promise a fixed percentage of interest.

When Interest Rates Change, So Do Bond Prices
Suppose you bought the bond for $10 000. You loaned Ford $10 000 and Ford gave you a piece of paper — the bond. You are happy to receive the $500 payment at the end of the year (which translates into an interest rate of 5 percent), and Ford is happy to pay you $500 for borrowing $10 000 of your money.

The next day, interest rates around the world rise to 10 percent. You can now get a bond that will pay you $1000 in interest on a $10 000 investment. All of a sudden, your Ford bond looks like a bad investment choice. You decide to sell your bond on the bond market, and use the money to buy a new bond that pays 10 percent interest.

Unfortunately, you will not find a buyer for your bond at the price of $10 000. Now that other bonds yield a $1000 return on $10 000 at the end of a year, why would anyone buy your bond yielding only a $500 return on $10 000 at the end of the year? With no buyers for your bond, the only way to sell it is to lower the price you are willing to accept. At what new price can you sell your bond — find a buyer — on the bond market?

The market price of your bond will fall until the fixed return it offers at the end of the year amounts to a 10 percent interest rate — the same rate of return investors can get on other bonds now for sale. The price for your Ford bond falls to approximately $9545. If someone buys your Ford bond for $9545, at the end of the year she receives from Ford $10 500. That difference is a gain of $955. In percentage terms, that's 10 percent.

Don't worry about the precise math in the calculations. That's what accountants, calculators, and accounting software are for. The important fact to remember is that *when interest rates rise, the market price of bonds falls*. This inverse relation between bond prices and interest rates is the most important feature of all bond markets. Bond prices and interest rates are instantly and inversely connected. If interest rates rise, bond prices fall. If interest rates fall, bond prices rise.

NOTE
Bond prices and interest rates are inversely related. When interest rates rise, bond prices fall. When bond prices fall, interest rates rise.

Why Bonds Are Risky and Less Liquid Than Money
This instant and inverse relationship between bond prices and interest rates is why bonds are a risky and non-liquid form of saving. If interest rates change after you buy a bond, the price at which you can sell the bond changes. When interest rates rise, the price of the bond falls. If you want to convert your bond back to money by selling it, you receive less money than what you paid for it. Your savings take an unexpected fall in value. Bonds are inferior to money as a store of value when interest rates rise.

When interest rates fall, the price of a bond you are holding rises. If you want to convert your bond back to money by selling it, you receive more money than what you paid for it. You make an extra, unexpected profit on your savings. Bonds are better than money as a store of value when interest rates fall.

If you hold a bond until its time period is up, you receive exactly what you were promised — the original value plus the fixed dollar amount payment. Changes in interest rates do not change the fixed dollar amounts bondholders receive. You receive both the original value and the fixed payments, as promised. The unexpected losses and gains come from selling bonds before their time period is up, something you might need to do for liquidity — because you need the money now to pay for products or services or to repay a debt.

Money Markets, Loanable Funds Markets, and Interest Rates

In the bond market example, I changed the interest rate from 5 percent to 10 percent without explanation. But what determines the interest rate? Why do interest rates change, and why does the interest rate settle at a specific number?

The economist's short answer to these questions about what determines the interest rate — the price of money — is that "interest rates are determined by the interaction of demand and supply in money markets and loanable funds markets." But that answer, while true, is pretty useless. We can point to anything that happens in an economy and say, in our best educated voice, "It is all determined by the laws of demand and supply." The longer and more useful answer combines the details about why people choose to demand money with supply of money decisions made by the Bank of Canada and chartered banks.

To answer the question of what determines the interest rate, Figure 9.6 combines the information in Figures 9.1 and 9.5 about the macroeconomic demand for and supply of money. These numbers represent the money market — the demand for, and supply of, money. But as we will see, these numbers make sense only if we bring the loanable funds market into the longer explanation.

Figure 9.6 Demand and Supply for Money

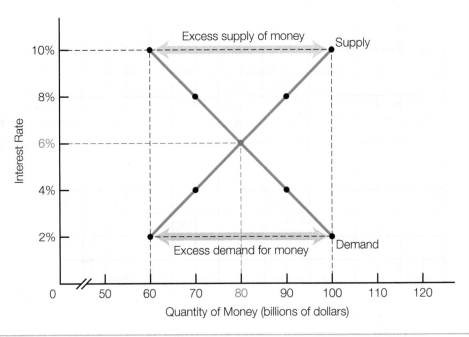

Price (interest rate)	Quantity Demanded (billions of dollars)	Quantity Supplied (billions of dollars)
2%	100	60
4%	90	70
6%	80	80
8%	70	90
10%	60	100

Plotting those combinations of price and quantity demanded, and then price and quantity supplied, gives the downward-sloping demand curve and the upward-sloping supply curve in the graph.

The interest rate will settle at 6 percent, the rate at which the quantity of money demanded ($80 billion) equals the quantity of money supplied ($80 billion). In this example, 6 percent is the equilibrium, or market-clearing, interest rate.

As in microeconomics (section 4.2), the best way to understand why prices — in this case the interest rate — settle at the particular number is to look at what happens in markets when prices have not settled.

Excess Demand for Money   What if the interest rate were 2 percent in the money market? Look at the first row of the table of numbers in Figure 9.6. At a 2 percent interest rate, people want to hold $100 billion worth of money — the quantity of money demanded is $100 billion. But the quantity of money supplied is only $60 billion. There is excess demand — the quantity demanded of money exceeds the quantity supplied of money.

Excess demand for money is a demand for more liquidity. People demand more money (and are willing to give up earned interest on loanable funds) for the convenience of money's liquidity. When you are holding assets in money or bonds, how do you "get more money?" If we rule out counterfeiting or stealing, you have to sell some of your bonds to get more money to hold.

The additional supply of bonds for sale on the loanable funds market causes bond prices to fall. A decrease in the price of bonds instantly causes interest rates to rise.

In our example, as long as the interest rate is below 6 percent, there is excess demand for money. People sell bonds, bond prices fall, and interest rates rise. The excess demand for money only disappears when the interest rate rises to 6 percent.

NOTE
When there is excess demand for money, people sell bonds to get more money. The increased supply of bonds causes bond prices to fall, and interest rates to rise.

Excess Supply of Money   What if the interest rate were 10 percent in the money market? Look at the last row of the table of numbers in Figure 9.6. At a 10 percent interest rate, people want to hold $60 billion worth of money — the quantity of money demanded is $60 billion. But the quantity of money supplied is $100 billion. There is excess supply — the quantity supplied of money exceeds the quantity demanded of money.

Excess supply of money means there is more liquidity available than people want. Remember, liquidity has an opportunity cost — the earned interest you give up by not holding bonds. If you hold assets in money or bonds, how do you "get rid of money"? You use some of your money to buy bonds.

The additional demand for bonds on the bond market causes bond prices to rise. An increase in the price of bonds instantly causes interest rates to fall.

As long as the interest rate is above 6 percent, there is an excess supply of money. People buy bonds, bond prices rise, and interest rates fall. The excess supply of money only disappears when the interest rate falls to 6 percent.

NOTE
When there is excess supply of money, people buy bonds to get rid of money. The increased demand for bonds causes bond prices to rise, and interest rates to fall.

A Multitude of Interest Rates

I always talk about "the" interest rate, as though there is only one. In fact, there are many interest rates on different financial assets, different forms of loanable funds. Interest rates vary depending on the time periods for repaying the original amount (long-term investments like 30-year bonds usually have higher interest rates than short-term investments), the riskiness of the investment, and how liquid the investment is (how easy is it to sell). There are also interest rates on mortgages, on consumer loans, on credit cards, and on savings accounts — there are many interest rates.

While there are many interest rates, they all tend to move together — to rise at the same time, and to fall at the same time. So the stories about how "the" interest rate is determined apply generally to all interest rates.

Refresh 9.3

MyEconLab

For answers to these Refresh
Questions, visit MyEconLab.

1. Explain two ways that the interest rate is the price of money.

2. Explain how interest rates and bond prices are related using an example. What characteristic of bonds causes this relationship?

3. If you have bought a bond as an investment, which way do you hope interest rates will move? Explain how you will profit from your investment if interest rates move in the direction you hope.

9.4 Does Money Make the Real World Go Around? Domestic Transmission Mechanism from Money to Real GDP

Explain how money affects real GDP, unemployment, and inflation through the domestic monetary transmission mechanism.

Money does not have inherent value — you can't eat it or wear it or live in it. But we all want more money because our society gives it value. Money's value comes from its liquidity — sellers will accept money in exchange for any product or service we want. Money gives us access to stuff that improves our personal standard of living.

But do the demand and supply of money — and the interest rates they determine — affect real GDP, the aggregate amount of stuff the economy produces? Is there any connection between money and the three macroeconomic outcomes that most influence everyone's economic well-being — real GDP per person, unemployment, and inflation?

Chapter 7 examined the answer for the third outcome, inflation. The quantity theory of money states that money can directly affect inflation. An increase in the supply of money can increase the average price level.

But what about the other two outcomes? Does money affect the amount of real GDP the economy produces? Does money affect the unemployment rate and therefore your job prospects? Let me ask these questions slightly differently: After moving from barter exchange to the advantages of a money economy, does money make any difference to the real, or non-price, outcomes of a market exchange economy — real GDP and unemployment?

Money and Aggregate Supply

Our material standard of living increases only when the economy produces more real GDP per person. Real GDP is the value, at *constant* prices, of all final products and services produced annually in Canada. Does money affect real GDP?

As a medium of exchange and unit of account, money overcomes the barter problems of the double coincidence of wants. With money, it is easier for Jill and Marie, or for Tim Hortons and Ford Motor Company, to specialize in producing products or services, and to be productive and efficient at what they do. There are gains from having people and businesses specialize in producing what they are best at, and then trading for other products and services. Mutually beneficial trades (Chapter 1) between individuals and businesses increase the production of real GDP beyond what a barter economy would produce.

But once we have a market economy with money, do *changes* in the demand or supply of money affect real GDP?

Money Does Not Directly Affect Aggregate Supply   There is no direct connection between changes in the money supply and changes in the aggregate supply of real GDP. Increases in aggregate supply come from increases in the quantity or quality of inputs, including technological change. Money is not an input into production like labour, capital (equipment), land and other natural resources, or entrepreneurship. And unlike technological change, changes in the money supply do not increase the quality of other inputs. Money does not directly increase (or decrease) aggregate supply or directly contribute to economic growth.

Money and Aggregate Demand

Changes in the demand or supply of money, however, do affect real GDP and unemployment through aggregate demand. Economists call the way money affects real GDP the *monetary transmission mechanism*. Money affects aggregate demand through two transmission mechanisms, domestic and international. The **domestic monetary transmission mechanism** works through the effect of interest rates on spending and aggregate demand. Chapter 10 looks at international transmission mechanisms that work through the effect of interest rates on the value of the Canadian dollar and net exports.

domestic monetary transmission mechanism   how money affects real GDP through interest rates, spending, and aggregate demand

Domestic Transmission Mechanism between Money and Real GDP
The key to the domestic monetary transmission mechanism is the effect of interest rates on consumer spending and business investment spending. Figure 9.7 illustrates the domestic transmission mechanism from the demand for and supply of money (at the top) to real GDP and inflation (at the bottom). The demand for money and the supply of money interact in money and loanable funds markets to determine the interest rate. The interest rate affects consumer spending (C) through the cost of consumer borrowing.

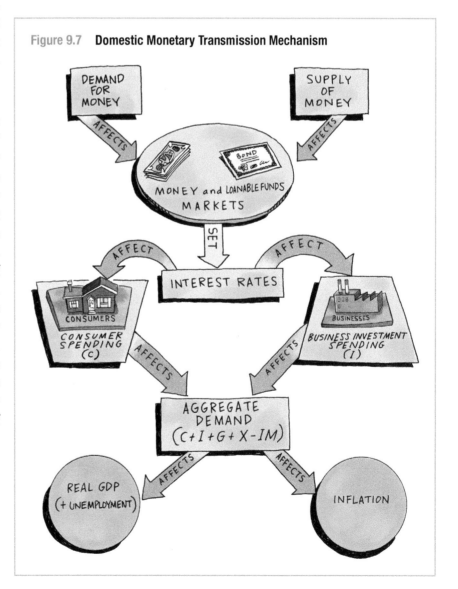

Figure 9.7   **Domestic Monetary Transmission Mechanism**

Think about what happens when interest rates fall and borrowing becomes cheaper. Spending on expensive consumer purchases that require loans, like houses financed with mortgages, cars with car loans, and major appliances on credit cards, is very interest-sensitive. Lower interest rates reduce the total cost of these purchases, so consumers buy more of them, spending more.

The interest rate also affects the cost of business borrowing. Business investment spending (I) is often financed by borrowing in loanable funds markets and is very interest-sensitive. Lower interest rates make investment spending cheaper, and businesses spend more on new factories and equipment.

NOTE
Lower interest rates are a positive aggregate demand shock, increasing aggregate demand, increasing real GDP, decreasing unemployment, and causing inflation.

Lower Interest Rates Are a Positive Aggregate Demand Shock   The net effect of lower interest rates is increased aggregate demand. Remember your mantra: Aggregate demand equals $C + I + G + X - IM$. Increases in C and I both increase aggregate demand. As Chapter 8 explained, a positive aggregate demand shock increases real GDP, decreases unemployment, and causes inflation (rising average prices). Lower interest rates can push the economy into the expansion phase of the business cycle as real GDP increases.

NOTE
Higher interest rates are a negative aggregate demand shock, decreasing aggregate demand, decreasing real GDP, increasing unemployment, and causing deflation.

Higher Interest Rates Are a Negative Aggregate Demand Shock   Higher interest rates work through a similar domestic transmission mechanism but with opposite effects. Higher interest rates increase the cost of borrowing, decrease C and I, and decrease aggregate demand. Higher interest rates are a negative aggregate demand shock and decrease real GDP, increase unemployment, and cause deflation (falling average prices). Higher interest rates can push the economy into the contraction phase of the business cycle as real GDP decreases.

Money affects aggregate demand through the domestic monetary transmission mechanism. The two main macroeconomic camps agree about this.

Refresh 9.4

MyEconLab

For answers to these Refresh Questions, visit MyEconLab.

1. What is the connection between money and aggregate supply? Explain your answer.

2. Explain how a rise (or fall) in interest rates affects your decision to buy (or not) a new car.

3. When interest rates rise and borrowing becomes more expensive, use Figure 9.7 to explain the monetary transmission mechanism from money demand and supply to real GDP.

"Yes, Markets Self-Adjust" and "No, Markets Fail Often" as Facebook Friends?
How Much Does Money Matter for Business Cycles?

All economists, including J. B. Say and the "Yes — Markets Self-Adjust" camp, and J. M. Keynes and the "No — Markets Fail Often" camp, agree on the advantages of money exchange over barter exchange. All agree that money affects prices and inflation (as explained by the quantity theory of money). And all agree that changes in the demand and supply of money indirectly affect real GDP and other key macroeconomic outcomes through interest rates and aggregate demand — the domestic monetary transmission mechanism. With all of these agreements, it seems like J. B. Say, J. M. Keynes, and their modern followers could be Facebook friends.

But there are still money questions on which the camps disagree. With the introduction of money to barter exchange, will supply still create its own demand? How much difference does the existence of money make in answering the fundamental macroeconomic question: "If left alone by government, do the price mechanisms of market economies adjust quickly to maintain steady growth in living standards and full employment (leaving out the agreed impact on prices)?"

In a barter economy, supply always creates its own demand, the economy is always in equilibrium, and no one is kicking himself. In a money economy, there can be mismatches between aggregate supply and demand, business cycles, and disappointed expectations.

The camps disagree about the difference money makes to two aspects of business cycles:

- How often do business cycles happen?
- How quickly do markets adjust back to potential GDP and full employment?

    Let's look at each camp's position on these two ways that money can matter.

How Much Does Money Matter?
"Yes — Markets Self-Adjust" Answer — "Not Much"

How much does the move from a barter economy to a money economy affect how often business cycles happen, and how quickly markets adjust? For J. B. Say and the "Yes — Markets Self-Adjust" camp, the answer is "not much."

Money Does Not Affect How Often Business Cycles Happen   Business cycles are triggered by demand or supply shocks that cause a mismatch between aggregate supply and demand. Say and his followers believe that most shocks to the economy come from forces outside the economy like scientific discoveries, technological change, and natural disasters. These aggregate supply shocks are the main source of business cycles for this camp. Adding money to the "real economy" of inputs, technology, and outputs doesn't affect aggregate supply, and doesn't create new shocks. Money, the "Yes — Markets Self-Adjust" camp states, does not significantly affect how often business cycles happen.

Money Helps Markets Adjust   When external supply shocks cause temporary mismatches between aggregate supply and demand, the "Yes — Markets Self-Adjust" camp believes that price adjustments in separate markets — input, output, international trade, and loanable funds markets — all work harmoniously to quickly restore the match between aggregate supply and aggregate demand.

Money, which makes savings possible, is the biggest aid helping the loanable funds market adjust. After suppliers sell products or services for money, they may save some money instead of demanding products and services. Savings are deposited in banks, increasing the supply of loanable funds. This causes the interest rate — the price of loanable funds — to fall. Falling interest rates encourage more consumer spending and business borrowing to finance more investment spending. Spending increases, offsetting the additional saving and restoring aggregate spending in output markets, making it equal to aggregate income earned in input markets.

Money allows saving to flow easily through the loanable funds market to encourage business borrowing for investment spending. The economy quickly ends up with a match of aggregate supply and aggregate demand — just like the barter outcome — at potential real GDP and full employment. Money, according to the "Yes — Markets Self-Adjust" camp, *helps* markets quickly adjust to equilibrium.

How Much Does Money Matter?
"No — Markets Fail Often" Answer — "A Lot"

How much does money affect how often business cycles happen, and how quickly markets adjust? For J. M. Keynes and the "No — Markets Fail Often" camp, the answer is "a lot." Money, as a store of value, is a fundamental change to the barter economy's match of aggregate supply and aggregate demand.

NO
MARKETS FAIL OFTEN
GOVERNMENT
HANDS-ON

Money Causes Business Cycles by Creating a Way Not to Spend Business cycles are triggered by demand or supply shocks. Keynes and his followers believe that most business cycles are caused by demand shocks that are internal to the economy. Volatile (quickly changeable) expectations are an internal demand shock for this camp, causing investment spending and aggregate demand to fluctuate. When expectations become pessimistic, *money gives consumers and businesses a way not to spend*, causing a negative demand shock. This is an important change from barter.

The banking system's ability to create loans and demand deposits is another money-based internal source of demand shocks. Crises in the financial sector cause banks to reduce loans and the supply of money, raising interest rates and decreasing spending, aggregate demand, real GDP, and employment. If optimistic banks create loans and money, as happened in the bubble leading up to the Global Financial Crisis, falling interest rates can increase spending, aggregate demand, real GDP, and employment. Money makes business cycles happen more often.

Money Slows Market Adjustments When there are internal demand shocks causing business cycles, the "No — Markets Fail Often" camp believes that adjustment problems in all markets fail to restore the match between aggregate supply and aggregate demand.

Money makes the biggest difference for the loanable funds market. When worried consumers and businesses stop spending and increase their saving, they may *not* put their saving into loanable funds markets, and businesses may postpone investment spending even if interest rates are low. Consumers and businesses hold money instead to calm their unease and reduce risk. The domestic monetary transmission mechanism — whereby falling interest rates in the loanable funds market increase spending and aggregate demand — gets blocked by money. It may take years for markets to adjust mismatches between aggregate supply and demand. Without government help, the economy falls short of potential real GDP and full employment.

Comparing Camps: How Much Money Matters for Business Cycles

I hope you now better understand how money helps explain some of the differences between the camps on the fundamental macroeconomic question: "If left alone by government, do the price mechanisms of market economies adjust quickly to maintain steady growth in living standards, full employment (and stable prices)?"

Figure 9.8 is a good study device for reviewing the differences between the two camps regarding money, business cycles, and market adjustments. It extends Figure 5.2's comparison of the two camps' answers to the fundamental macroeconomic question.

Figure 9.8 How Much Does Money Matter for Business Cycles and How Quickly Markets Adjust?

Question	Answers for Each Camp	
Compared to a barter economy, how does money affect:	Yes — Markets Self-Adjust	No — Markets Fail Often
How Often Business Cycles Happen?	**Money has no effect.** Money does not affect external supply shocks that are main source of business cycles.	**Money creates new shocks.** Money gives consumers and businesses a way not to spend, adding new internal demand shocks.
How Quickly Markets Adjust?	**Money helps loanable funds market quickly adjust economy back to equilibrium.**	**Money blocks domestic monetary transmission mechanism, slowing economy's adjustment to equilibrium.**

Refresh 9.5

MyEconLab

For answers to these Refresh Questions, visit MyEconLab.

1. List the agreements between all economists on the effect of money in the economy.

2. Explain either the "Yes — Markets Self-Adjust" or "No — Markets Fail Often" position on the effect of money on business cycles.

3. Which position seems closer to how you think about how much money matters for business cycles? Explain why.

Study Guide

9.1 Is It Smart to *Not* Want Money? Demand for Money

People demand money for its liquidity as a medium of exchange, unit of account, and store of value, and are often willing to give up interest on bonds in order to hold their wealth as money.

- **Money** — anything *acceptable* as a means of paying for products and services; money has three functions.
  - Medium of exchange — acceptability by all as a means of payment solves the barter problem of the double coincidence of wants.
  - Unit of account — standard unit for measuring prices.
  - Store of value — time machine for moving purchasing power from present to future; you can earn now and spend later.
- **Bond** — financial asset for which borrower promises to repay the original value at a specific future date, and to make fixed regular interest payments.
- Why hold wealth as money that pays no interest, rather than as bonds that pay interest?
  - Money provides **liquidity** — ease with which assets can be converted into the economy's medium of exchange.
  - Money is the most liquid asset — acceptable by sellers as a means of payment.
  - Money pays no interest, but has liquidity. Bonds pay interest, but do not have liquidity.
- Why hold money as a store of value?
  - For "Yes — Markets Self-Adjust" camp (Say's Law), people hold more wealth as interest-paying bonds, since savings can be safely invested in loanable funds (bonds).
  - For "No — Markets Fail Often" camp (markets fail to quickly adjust, Keynes's business cycles), people hold more wealth as money because fundamental uncertainty about future makes bond investments risky.
- **Interest rate** — price of holding money: what you give up by not holding bonds.
  - Determined by demand and supply in both money and loanable funds markets.

- **Law of demand for money** — as the price of money — the interest rate — rises, the quantity demanded of money decreases.
  - Increase in real GDP increases demand for money and shifts the money demand curve rightward; decrease in real GDP decreases demand for money and shifts money demand curve leftward.
  - Increase in average prices increases demand for money and shifts money demand curve rightward; decrease in average prices decreases demand for money and shifts money demand curve leftward.

9.2 Legal Counterfeiting? Supply of Money

In a fractional-reserve banking system, the supply of money — currency plus demand deposits — is created both by the Bank of Canada and by chartered banks making loans.

- Forms of money:
  - Commodity money — saleable product with alternative uses serving as money.
  - Convertible paper money — paper money that can be converted into gold on demand.
  - Fiat money — **currency** (government-issued bills and coins) with no alternative uses; valuable simply by government decree.
  - Deposit money — **demand deposits** — balances in bank accounts that depositors can withdraw on demand by using a debit card or writing a cheque.
- Supply of money in Canada consists of currency and deposit money.
  - M1+ = currency in circulation plus demand deposits.
  - M2+ = M1+ plus all other less liquid deposits.

- Bank of Canada is Canada's **central bank** — government institution responsible for supervising chartered banks and other financial institutions, and for regulating the supply of money; roles include:
  - Issuing currency.
  - Banker to chartered banks — chartered bank deposits at the Bank of Canada allow the chartered banks to make payments to each other.
  - **Lender of last resort** — making loans to banks to preserve the stability of the financial system.
  - Banker to government — managing government's accounts, foreign currency reserves, and the national debt.
  - Conducting monetary policy — changing the money supply and interest rates to achieve steady growth, full employment, and stable prices.
- Chartered banks can create money (demand deposits) because of **fractional-reserve banking** — banks hold only a fraction of deposits as reserves.
  - Banks create loans and money (demand deposits) together; when a bank makes a loan, it creates demand deposit credit in the borrower's chequing account equal to the amount of the loan.
  - With fractional-reserve banking, there is risk of a **bank run** — many depositors withdraw cash all at once so bank may not have enough cash reserves to pay all depositors.
- Banks face a trade-off between profits and prudence.
  - More potential profits by holding a smaller fraction of reserves, making more loans, and making higher-risk loans.
  - Trade-off is giving up safety and risking customers' deposits and trust.
- Supply of money is determined by the Bank of Canada and chartered banks.
  - Quantity of money supplied depends on the quantity of loans and demand deposits the banking system creates.
  - When interest rate rises, the quantity of money supplied increases. Higher interest rates makes loans more profitable, so banks loan more and create more demand deposits.

9.3 What Is the Price of Money? Interest Rates, Money, and Bonds

Bond prices and interest rates are inversely related and determined together in the money and loanable funds markets.

- The interest rate is the price of money in two ways:
  - Opportunity cost of holding money.
  - Cost of borrowing money.

- Bonds promise to pay back the original value plus a fixed dollar amount of money.
  - Bonds do *not* promise a fixed percentage of interest. When interest rates rise, the market price of a bond falls; When interest rates fall, the market price of a bond rises.
  - When holding a bond until its time period is up, you receive the promised, fixed dollar amount payments plus the original value.
- Bonds are riskier and less liquid than money as a store of value, because the market price of the bond changes.
- Interest rate is determined by the interaction of demand and supply in money and loanable funds markets.
  - At the equilibrium, or market-clearing, interest rate, the quantity of money demanded equals the quantity of money supplied.
  - At interest rates below the equilibrium rate, there is excess demand for money; people sell bonds to get more money; the increased supply of bonds causes falling bond prices and rising interest rates.
  - At interest rates above the equilibrium rate, there is excess supply of money; people buy bonds to get rid of money; the increased demand for bonds causes rising bond prices and falling interest rates.
- There are many interest rates on financial assets, but all tend to rise or fall together.

9.4 Does Money Make the Real World Go Around? Domestic Transmission Mechanism from Money to Real GDP

Money affects interest rates, domestic spending (consumption and business investment), and aggregate demand, which change real GDP, unemployment, and inflation.

- Money affects the key macroeconomic outcomes of increasing real GDP per person (economic growth), unemployment, and inflation.
  - Money affects inflation, according to quantity theory of money.
  - Money does *not* directly affect aggregate supply or economic growth.
- Money indirectly affects real GDP and unemployment through the **domestic monetary transmission mechanism** — how money affects real GDP through interest rates, spending, and aggregate demand.
  - When the interest rate falls, interest-sensitive purchases become cheaper so consumer spending (*C*) and business investment spending (*I*) increase increasing aggregate demand.
  - Lower interest rates are a positive demand shock, increasing aggregate demand, increasing real GDP, decreasing unemployment, and causing inflation.
  - Higher interest rates are a negative demand shock, decreasing aggregate demand, decreasing real GDP, increasing unemployment, and causing deflation.

9.5 "Yes — Markets Self-Adjust" and "No — Markets Fail Often" as Facebook Friends? How Much Does Money Matter for Business Cycles?

"Yes — Markets Self-Adjust" camp thinks money has no effect on business cycles and helps loanable funds markets adjust. "No — Markets Fail Often" camp thinks money creates new shocks and blocks the transmission mechanism, slowing market adjustments.

- Economists disagree on the question "How much does money matter for business cycles and how quickly markets adjust?

- "Yes — Markets Self-Adjust" answer — "not much."
  - Money does not affect external supply shocks that are main source of business cycles.
  - Money allows savings to flow easily through the loanable funds market to encourage business borrowing for investment spending.
  - Money helps markets quickly adjust to equilibrium.

- "No — Markets Fail Often" answer — "a lot."
  - Money gives people a way not to spend but to save, creating the possibility of financial crises, adding new internal demand shocks for business cycles.
  - Money blocks the domestic transmission mechanism so the loanable funds market does not match spending to saving.
  - Money slows markets' adjustments to equilibrium.

TRUE/FALSE

Circle the correct answer. Solutions to these questions are available at the end of the book and on MyEconLab. You can also visit the MyEconLab Study Plan to access additional questions that will help you master the concepts covered in this chapter.

You sign up for a speed dating event at your campus. It is obvious that your next speed date is obsessed with money: (1) Your speed date is wearing lots of gold dollar-sign jewellery; and (2) when the announcer asks everyone to make 15 statements about the thing they like most in life, your speed date chooses money as the topic. Use your knowledge of economics to determine whether your speed date's statements are true or false.

Use this scenario to answer questions 1–15.

9.1 Demand for Money

1. It is always smart to want to hold more money.   T   F

2. If interest rates rise, it is smarter to want to hold more money.   T   F

3. If average prices increase, the demand for money increases.   T   F

4. If I hold more of my wealth as money, this guarantees my purchasing power stays the same.   T   F

9.2 Supply of Money

5. If you withdraw $50 from your bank account and put it in your wallet, the money supply increases.   T   F

6. Coins and bills are a large fraction of the money supply.   T   F

7. The quantity of money supplied depends on the interest rate.   T   F

8. If I shift money from my chequing to savings accounts, M1+ decreases and M2+ increases.   T   F

9.3 Interest Rates, Money, and Bonds

9. Bonds are less risky than money as a store of value.   T   F

10. Bonds promise to pay back the original value plus a fixed dollar amount of money.   T   F

11. When the interest rate is above the equilibrium rate, people sell bonds to get more money.   T   F

9.4 Domestic Monetary Transmission Mechanism

12. Money does not directly affect aggregate supply.   T   F

13. Lower interest rates are a negative   T   F
aggregate demand shock.

9.5 Money and Business Cycles

14. Economists disagree about whether   T   F
money helps, or slows, the economy's
adjustment to equilibrium.

15. Economists all agree that money is   T   F
a major cause of business cycles.

MULTIPLE CHOICE

Circle the best answer. Solutions to these questions are available at the end of the book and on MyEconLab. You can also visit the MyEconLab Study Plan to access similar questions that will help you master the concepts covered in this chapter.

9.1 Demand for Money

1. If you sell your bonds in order to hold more of your wealth as money, you
   a) get liquidity and give up interest.
   b) give up liquidity and earn interest.
   c) get liquidity and earn interest.
   d) give up liquidity and give up interest.

2. The double coincidence of wants is
   a) buyers wanting the same thing.
   b) sellers wanting the same thing.
   c) buyers and sellers wanting nothing to do with each other.
   d) buyers and sellers each wanting what the other has.

3. Which function of money seems crazy to Keynes?
   a) medium of exchange
   b) unit of account
   c) store of value
   d) all of the above

4. The demand for money increases (the demand curve shifts rightward) when
   a) the quantity of money supplied decreases.
   b) real GDP decreases.
   c) average prices decrease.
   d) average prices increase.

9.2 Supply of Money

5. When you pay for lunch using your debit card, you are using
   a) commodity money.
   b) convertible paper money.
   c) fiat money.
   d) deposit money.

6. Which is most liquid?
   a) demand deposits
   b) real estate
   c) government bonds
   d) savings deposits

7. Which statement about how chartered banks use their funds is *true*?
   a) Loans to businesses and consumers are riskiest and earn banks the highest interest rates.
   b) Loans to businesses and consumers are riskiest and earn banks the lowest interest rates.
   c) Government of Canada Treasury bills are riskiest and earn banks the highest interest rates.
   d) Government of Canada Treasury bills are riskiest and earn banks the lowest interest rates.

8. The quantity of money supplied depends
   a) only on the Bank of Canada.
   b) only on the chartered banks.
   c) only on the money market.
   d) on the interest rate.

9.3 Interest Rates, Money, and Bonds

9. If interest rates fall, the market price of bonds
   a) falls. If you sell the bond you take an unexpected loss.
   b) falls. If you sell the bond you make an unexpected profit.
   c) rises. If you sell the bond you take an unexpected loss.
   d) rises. If you sell the bond you make an unexpected profit.

10. Excess demand for money
   a) occurs when interest rates are above the equilibrium rate.
   b) causes people to sell bonds.
   c) causes people to buy bonds.
   d) causes interest rates to fall.

9.4 Domestic Monetary Transmission Mechanism

11. Money can directly affect
   a) inflation.
   b) real GDP.
   c) unemployment.
   d) all of the above.

12. Money indirectly affects real GDP and unemployment through
   a) the domestic monetary transmission mechanism.
   b) interest rates.
   c) aggregate demand.
   d) all of the above.

13. Higher interest rates
   a) increase inflation.
   b) make business investment spending more expensive.
   c) are a positive aggregate demand shock.
   d) increase bond prices.

14. Lower interest rates are a
   a) positive aggregate supply shock.
   b) positive aggregate demand shock.
   c) negative aggregate supply shock.
   d) negative aggregate demand shock.

9.5 Money and Business Cycles

15. Both "Yes — Markets Self-Adjust" and "No — Markets Fail Often" camps agree that
   a) money affects prices and inflation.
   b) money exchange is better than barter exchange.
   c) the domestic monetary transmission mechanism indirectly affects real GDP.
   d) all of the above.

10 Trading Dollars for Dollars?

Exchange Rates and Payments with the Rest of the World

LEARNING OBJECTIVES

After reading this chapter, you should be able to:

10.1 Explain how demand and supply determine the value of the Canadian dollar.

10.2 Explain five forces causing exchange rate fluctuations.

10.3 Trace the effect of exchange rates on real GDP, unemployment, and inflation.

10.4 Describe how purchasing power parity and rate of return parity provide standards for exchange rates.

10.5 Describe the two main parts of the balance of payments account, and explain why they must add up to zero.

IF YOU HAVE EVER BEEN to the United States, you know that

the shopping experience is much different than in Canada. With a population 10 times larger than Canada's, there are more products to choose from and often lower prices, at least in U.S. dollars. In 2012, when the Canadian dollar rose to be equal in value to the U.S. dollar, Canadians crossed the border to shop in record numbers. It felt like everything in the United States was on sale.

What determines the value of the Canadian dollar? Why is it sometimes worth as little as 60 cents U.S. or as much as US$1.10? In this chapter you will learn what determines exchange rates, the price of one country's money in terms of another country's money. Exchange rates, like interest rates, are another price of money. You will learn why people trade Canadian dollars for U.S. dollars or for euros or Japanese yen.

Interest rates help determine the value of the Canadian dollar. When interest rates in Canada rise, the value of the Canadian dollar usually increases, which affects how much we pay for products imported from elsewhere and how expensive our exports are for the rest of the world to buy. By affecting the prices and quantities of net exports, the value of the Canadian dollar plays an important role in determining the key macroeconomic outcomes of real GDP, unemployment, and inflation. The Canadian dollar's value and net exports also affect the flows of moneys of different countries across international borders.

While a "high" value for the Canadian dollar is better for cross-border Canadian shoppers, is it better for the economy as a whole than a "low" dollar? And how do we know what counts as "high" or "low?" Another topic we will look at is the deeper forces, beyond demand and supply, that determine the value of the Canadian dollar. Interest rates appear yet again, but so do Big Macs. Big Macs as a deep force for understanding exchange rates? Yes! Read on.

10.1

Shuffling Off to Buffalo: Demand and Supply of Canadian Dollars

Explain how demand and supply determine the value of the Canadian dollar.

Unless you are fabulously wealthy, every purchase you make includes the question, "How much does it cost?" The answer to that question is usually an amount of money for each product or service: an Apple iPad costs $519, Ugg boots cost $299, movie tickets cost $15.

But buying money is different.

How Much Does That Dollar Cost?

exchange rate price at which one currency exchanges for another currency

The question, "How much does that dollar cost?" is not as silly as it sounds. It's really asking, "What's the exchange rate?" An **exchange rate** is the price at which one currency exchanges for another. When we say the Canadian dollar is worth 95 cents U.S., we are saying that the exchange rate of the Canadian dollar for the U.S. dollar is US$0.95. You need 95 cents U.S. to buy one Canadian dollar. With exchange rates, think of the Canadian dollar as the product for sale. The exchange rate is the price for buying Canadian dollars with another country's currency.

Every currency has more than one exchange rate. In 2014, for example, you could buy one Canadian dollar for 0.63 euros or 85 Japanese yen. These prices, or exchange rates, for the Canadian dollar — and for all other currencies — are determined in the **foreign exchange market**, a worldwide market for buying and selling currencies. Money, whether dollars, euros, yen, Chinese yuan, or Mexican pesos, is the only product for sale in the foreign exchange market. Each currency has its own demanders and suppliers.

foreign exchange market worldwide market where all countries' currencies are bought and sold in exchange for each other

The foreign exchange market (often abbreviated as *forex*) is the largest financial market in the world, with a trading volume of around US$5 trillion per day. It has multiple locations and trades are made digitally around the world at all hours of the day. About 86 percent of these trades involve the U.S. dollar, about 37 percent involve the euro, 16 percent the yen, 15 percent the British pound, 7 percent the Swiss franc, 7 percent the Australian dollar, and 4 percent the Canadian dollar.

We will focus on the market for Canadian dollars, which determines the exchange rates for Canadian currency. The principles behind the market for Canadian dollars are the same in the markets for U.S. dollars, euros, yen, and all other currencies.

Appreciation and Depreciation Exchange rates fluctuate (go up and down) constantly. Figure 10.1 shows the exchange rate for the Canadian dollar in terms of U.S. dollars since 1970. The exchange rate is on the vertical axis. Notice that the exchange rate fell from 1991 to 2002, rose dramatically from 2002 to 2007, stayed about equal in value to the U.S. dollar from 2010 to 2013, and then started falling.

◄

This electronic board at a U.S. currency exchange displays the cost of various currencies in U.S. dollars. The loonie, for example, is selling for over 96 cents U.S. Why isn't the U.S. dollar listed on the board?

Exchange Rates

		We Sell
AUSTRALIA		0.8264
BRAZIL		0.5263
CANADA		0.9677
CHINA		0.1417
Costa Rica		0.0023
Euro		1.4093
HONG KONG		0.1412
JAPAN		0.0094
MEXICO		0.1019
NEW ZEALAND		0.7284
S Korea		0.0012
SINGAPORE		0.6922
Sweden		0.1502
Switzerland		0.8837
TAHITI		0.0123
TAIWAN		0.0342
THAILAND		0.0303
UNITED KIN		

Karin Hildebrand Lau/Shutterstock

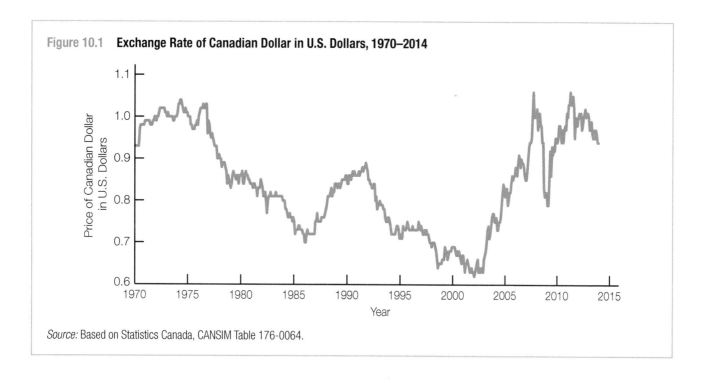

Figure 10.1 Exchange Rate of Canadian Dollar in U.S. Dollars, 1970–2014

Source: Based on Statistics Canada, CANSIM Table 176-0064.

A fall in the exchange rate is called a **currency depreciation**. The Canadian dollar depreciated against the U.S. dollar between 1991 and 2002, in 2008, and in 2014. A rise in the exchange rate is called a **currency appreciation**. The Canadian dollar appreciated against the U.S. dollar between 2002 and 2007, and between 2009 and 2010.

The foreign exchange market has buyers (demanders) and sellers (suppliers), like all other markets. But who demands Canadian dollars, and why? And who supplies Canadian dollars, and why? Here is a hint. If you are shuffling off to Buffalo, New York, or to Bellingham, Washington, for a cross-border shopping trip, you are demanding U.S. dollars *and* supplying Canadian dollars.

Identifying demanders and suppliers helps explain exchange rates and why they fluctuate so much.

currency depreciation fall in the exchange rate of one currency for another

currency appreciation rise in the exchange rate of one currency for another

Non-Canadians Demanding Canadian Dollars

Who goes to the worldwide foreign exchange market to demand Canadian dollars? If you live and work in Canada, you are paid in Canadian dollars. You don't need to go to the foreign exchange market to buy Canadian dollars. You can use the Canadian dollars you earn to buy any products or services for sale in Canada. The demanders of Canadian dollars on the foreign exchange market are largely non-Canadians from the rest of the world.

There are two main reasons why non-Canadians demand Canadian dollars on the foreign exchange market. The first is to buy Canadian exports and assets. The second is to speculate on the future value of the Canadian dollar.

NOTE
The demand for Canadian dollars is demand for Canadian exports and assets, and for speculating on the future value of the Canadian dollar.

Demand for Canadian Exports and Assets   A non-Canadian who wants to buy Canadian exports — products and services produced in Canada but sold to the rest of the world — must pay in Canadian dollars. Since non-Canadians do not earn Canadian dollars, they must exchange some of their country's currency for Canadian dollars. Similarly, a non-Canadian investor who wants to buy Canadian assets — bonds, stocks, businesses, or real estate — also must pay in Canadian dollars, again, exchanging their currency for those Canadian dollars.

Law of Demand for Canadian Dollars   The law of demand applies to Canadian dollars, just as it applies to iPads, boots, or any product or service — as the price of a product or service rises, the quantity demanded decreases. The exchange rate is the price of a Canadian dollar. So, the **law of demand for Canadian dollars** states that as the exchange rate rises, the quantity demanded of Canadian dollars decreases.

The table in Figure 10.2 illustrates the inverse relation (when one goes up, the other goes down) between the exchange rate and the quantity demanded of Canadian dollars in the foreign exchange market. For simplicity, the numbers are made up, but the pattern represents what the actual demand for Canadian dollars looks like. If you graph the combinations of exchange rates and quantity demanded, you get the downward-sloping demand for Canadian dollars curve in Figure 10.2.

The inverse relationship between the price of the Canadian dollar and the quantity demanded of Canadian dollars is caused by the export effect.

law of demand for Canadian dollars as the exchange rate rises, the quantity demanded of Canadian dollars decreases

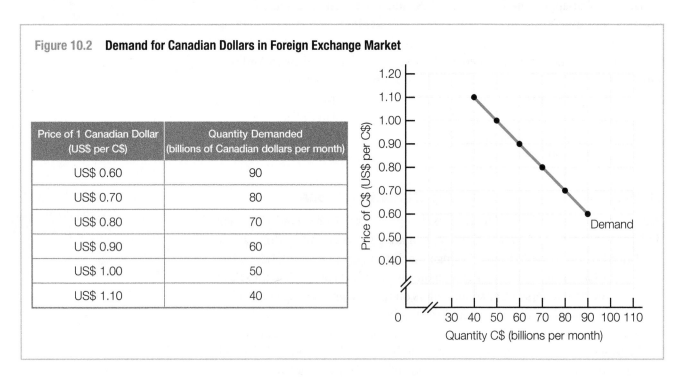

Figure 10.2   Demand for Canadian Dollars in Foreign Exchange Market

Price of 1 Canadian Dollar (US$ per C$)	Quantity Demanded (billions of Canadian dollars per month)
US$ 0.60	90
US$ 0.70	80
US$ 0.80	70
US$ 0.90	60
US$ 1.00	50
US$ 1.10	40

Export Effect Cross-border shopping is a two-way street. When the value of the Canadian dollar rises, U.S. products and services become cheaper for Canadians. For example, when the exchange rate is US$0.60 per Canadian dollar, a dress that costs $60 in the United States costs 100 Canadian dollars. But if the exchange rate appreciates to US$1.00 per Canadian dollar, the same US$60 dress falls in price to only C$60. For U.S. consumers, the price of the dress remains constant at US$60.

The opposite is true for U.S. consumers buying Canadian products or services. Look at Figure 10.3. Suppose a month's supply of Tim Hortons coffee costs C$100. This is the price Canadian consumers will pay no matter what happens to the exchange rate. When the exchange rate is US$0.60 per Canadian dollar (row one), the U.S. consumer pays only US$60 for the coffee. If the exchange rate rises to US$1.00 per

Figure 10.3	Price of Tim Hortons Coffee in Canada and United States	
Price of 1 Canadian Dollar (US$ per C$)	Price of Month's Supply of Tim Hortons Coffee in Canada (in C$)	Price of Month's Supply of Tim Hortons Coffee in U.S. (in US$)
US$ 0.60	C$ 100	US$ 60
US$ 1.00	C$ 100	US$ 100

Canadian dollar (row two), the same C$100 coffee rises in price to US$100. A higher value of the Canadian dollar makes Canadian exports, like Tim Hortons coffee, and Canadian assets such as bonds, stocks, businesses, and real estate, more expensive for people in the United States and the rest of the world.

As the exchange rate rises, the prices non-Canadians pay for Canadian exports and assets in U.S. dollars rises. Non-Canadians will *not* want to buy as many exports and assets. With fewer purchases by non-Canadians, the quantity demanded of Canadian dollars decreases.

Supplying Canadian Dollars to Non-Canadians

Who supplies Canadian dollars to the worldwide foreign exchange market? Consider this scenario: You are heading south for some cross-border shopping in the United States. That makes you a Canadian who wants U.S. dollars. You must supply Canadian dollars in exchange. Your demand for U.S. dollars is also a supply of Canadian dollars. In the unique world of the foreign exchange market, the demand for one currency is the supply of another.

There are two main reasons why Canadians supply Canadian dollars on the foreign exchange market: to buy imports and assets from the rest of the world and to speculate on the future value of the Canadian dollar.

NOTE
The demand for one currency is the supply of another currency.

▲ Each of these people is buying (demanding) foreign currency and paying for (supplying) it with their own domestic currency. Each demander is also a supplier on the foreign currency market.

Demand for Imports and Foreign Assets   A Canadian who wants to buy imports must pay in the currency of the country supplying them. The dress in Buffalo that costs US$60 must be paid for with U.S. dollars. If you stay at Hotel California, or go to a Red Wings hockey game in Detroit, you are "importing" (using) U.S. hotel or entertainment services that must be paid for with U.S. dollars. To get U.S. dollars, you must exchange some of your Canadian dollars. Similarly, a Canadian investor who wants to buy U.S. assets must pay in U.S. dollars, which she buys using Canadian money. When you convert Canadian dollars into U.S. dollars, you are both supplying Canadian dollars and demanding U.S. dollars at the same time.

Law of Supply for Canadian Dollars   The law of supply states that as the price of a product or service rises, the quantity supplied increases. The exchange rate is the price of the Canadian dollar. So the **law of supply for Canadian dollars** states that as the exchange rate rises, the quantity supplied of Canadian dollars increases.

law of supply for Canadian dollars
as the exchange rate rises, the quantity supplied of Canadian dollars increases

The table in Figure 10.4 illustrates the positive (both go up together) relationship between the exchange rate and the quantity supplied of Canadian dollars in the foreign exchange market. For simplicity, the numbers are made up, but the pattern represents what the actual relationship looks like. If you graph the combinations of exchange rates and quantity supplied, you get the upward-sloping supply of Canadian dollars curve in Figure 10.4.

Figure 10.4   Supply of Canadian Dollars in Foreign Exchange Market

Price of 1 Canadian Dollar (US$ per C$)	Quantity Supplied (billions of Canadian dollars per month)
US$ 0.60	30
US$ 0.70	40
US$ 0.80	50
US$ 0.90	60
US$ 1.00	70
US$ 1.10	80

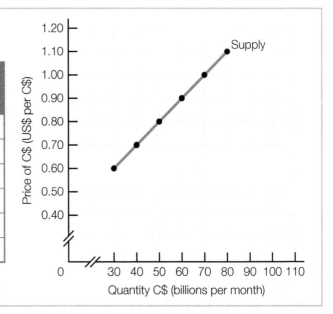

As the price of the Canadian dollar rises (appreciates), the quantity supplied of Canadian dollars increases.

Import Effect   The exchange rate and the quantity supplied move together because of the import effect. When the exchange rate is low, for example, US$0.60 per Canadian dollar, the dress that costs $60 in the United States costs $100 in Canada. If the exchange rate appreciates to US$1.00 per Canadian dollar, the same US$60 dress falls in price to only $60 Canadian. When the exchange rate rises (appreciates), U.S. products and services become less expensive for Canadians, so Canadians buy more of them. But in order to buy more U.S. products and services with U.S. dollars, Canadians must increase the quantity supplied of Canadian dollars. A rise in the exchange rate increases the quantity supplied of Canadian dollars in the foreign exchange market — the import effect.

The Prices of the Canadian Dollar: Foreign Exchange Rates

The exchange rate of the Canadian dollar is determined by the interaction of demand and supply in the foreign exchange market. The three columns in Figure 10.5 combine the previous numbers for the quantity demanded of Canadian dollars with the numbers for the quantity supplied.

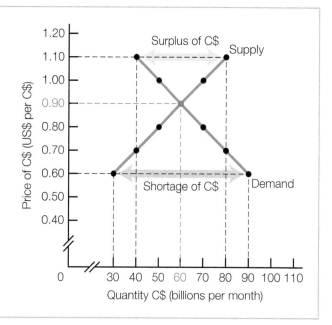

Figure 10.5 Foreign Exchange Market for Canadian Dollars

Price of 1 Canadian Dollar (US$ per C$)	Quantity Demanded (billions of Canadian dollars per month)	Quantity Supplied (billions of Canadian dollars per month)
US$ 0.60	90	30
US$ 0.70	80	40
US$ 0.80	70	50
US$ 0.90	60	60
US$ 1.00	50	70
US$ 1.10	40	80

Equilibrium Exchange Rate   The equilibrium, or market-clearing, exchange rate is at the intersection of the demand and supply curves. In our example, that exchange rate is US$0.90. When a Canadian dollar sells for US$0.90, the quantity demanded of Canadian dollars (60 billion) equals the quantity supplied of Canadian dollars (60 billion). There are no leftover demands or supplies — no shortages or surpluses.

The best way to understand why prices settle at the market-clearing exchange rate of US$0.90 is to look at what happens when prices have not settled.

Excess Demand for Canadian Dollars   What happens if the exchange rate is US$0.60 per Canadian dollar? The quantity demanded of Canadian dollars is $90 billion. But the quantity supplied of Canadian dollars is only $30 billion. There is excess demand — quantity demanded exceeds quantity supplied. There is a shortage of Canadian dollars.

As in any market with a shortage, competition among buyers (demanders) for the scarce Canadian dollars causes the price of a Canadian dollar to rise. As long as the exchange rate is below US$0.90, there is excess demand.

Excess Supply of Canadian Dollars   What happens if the exchange rate is US$1.10 per Canadian dollar? The quantity demanded of Canadian dollars is $40 billion. But the quantity supplied of Canadian dollars is $80 billion. There is excess supply — quantity supplied exceeds quantity demanded. There is a surplus of Canadian dollars.

As in any market with a surplus, competition among sellers (suppliers) to find customers for the Canadian dollars they can't get rid of causes the price of a Canadian dollar to fall. As long as the exchange rate is above US$0.90, there is excess supply.

A Multitude of Exchange Rates

In the foreign exchange market, the demand for one currency is the supply of another. The demand and supply for Canadian dollars is the same as the supply and demand for U.S. dollars. The same principle applies to all currency exchanges. The demand for Canadian dollars comes from people supplying currencies from other countries. The supply of Canadian dollars comes from Canadians demanding currencies of other countries. Because of the connections among all currencies in the currency market, exchange rates can be expressed in any currency.

NOTE

To find a reciprocal exchange rate for any two currencies, divide 1 by the other. For example, if 1 Canadian dollar = US$ 0.90, the reciprocal exchange rate is 1 U.S. dollar = 1/0.90 = C$1.11.

Reciprocal Exchange Rates   We have only described the price of one Canadian dollar in terms of the number of U.S. dollars it takes to buy it. We can also describe the price of one U.S. dollar in terms of the number of Canadian dollars it takes to buy it. These two exchange rates are mirror images of each other and are called *reciprocal exchange rates*. When the price of one Canadian dollar is US$0.90, then the price of one U.S. dollar is $1 \div 0.90 = 1.11$. It takes C$1.11 to buy one U.S. dollar. US$0.90 and C$1.11 are reciprocal rates.

The media in Canada usually report the exchange rate for the Canadian dollar in terms of U.S. dollars. But the media in the United States usually report the exchange rate for the U.S. dollar in terms of Canadian dollars. These two exchange rates are reciprocals, mirror images of each other. The relationship between any two currencies is always reciprocal.

NOTE

When the Canadian dollar appreciates against any currency, that currency depreciates against the Canadian dollar, and vice versa.

Because of these connections, when the Canadian dollar appreciates against any currency (for example, the Canadian dollar rises from US$0.60 to US$0.90), the reciprocal is a depreciation of that currency against the Canadian dollar. The U.S. dollar falls from C$1.67 to C$1.11.

Just as the demand for one currency is the supply of another currency, the appreciation of one currency is the depreciation of another.

Multiple Currencies and Exchange Rates   The exchange rate of the Canadian dollar in terms of U.S. dollars is the exchange rate you will see and hear most about in the media. But there are exchange rates between the Canadian dollar and every other currency, like the euro or yen. For each exchange rate, there is always a reciprocal in terms of Canadian dollars.

The exchange rates between any pair of currencies, and their reciprocals, are often presented in a table like Figure 10.6. This table contains exchange rates between the Canadian dollar, U.S. dollar, euro, and Japanese yen. Reading down any column, the currency at the top is expressed in terms of other currencies. The first column, for example, shows the exchange rates for the Canadian dollar in terms of U.S. dollars (US$0.9297), euros (0.6298 euros), and Japanese yen (84.67 yen).

Figure 10.6 Foreign Exchange Cross Rates*

	Canadian dollar	U.S. dollar	euro	Japanese yen
Canadian dollar	———	1.0880	1.4091	0.0104
U.S. dollar	0.9191	———	1.2952	0.0095
euro	0.7097	0.7721	———	0.0073
Japanese yen	96.59	105.09	136.11	———

*As of 7 September 2014

Reading across any row, you see the reciprocal exchange rates. The first row, for example, shows the exchange rate for each currency in terms of Canadian dollars. One U.S. dollar costs 1.0880 Canadian dollars, 1 euro costs 1.4091 Canadian dollars, and 1 yen costs 0.0104 Canadian dollars. These are the prices for each currency in terms of Canadian dollars.

The dashes (–) in the table are there because the exchange rate of any currency for itself is always one. No one buys Canadian dollars with Canadian dollars on the foreign exchange market, or U.S. dollars with U.S. dollars, so these number ones are omitted.

What all currencies share is that their exchange rates are determined by the forces of demand and supply in the foreign exchange market. In the next section, we examine what happens to exchange rates when demand and supply change.

Refresh 10.1

1. Explain why the title of the section, "How much does that dollar cost?" is not silly at all.

2. In your own words, explain what a reciprocal relationship is. Use an exchange rate between U.S. and Canadian dollars to demonstrate your answer.

3. When you cross the border to shop in the United States, explain how you are participating in the foreign exchange market.

MyEconLab

For answers to these Refresh Questions, visit MyEconLab.

10.2 Dancing with Dollars: Fluctuating Exchange Rates

Canadian cross-border shoppers dance to the beat of exchange rate fluctuations — buying more when the rate rises and less when the exchange rate falls. Exchange rate fluctuations set the pace for Canadian consumers' purchases of imports. But what causes the exchange rate to rise or fall? Why does the value of the Canadian dollar dance around so much on the foreign exchange market?

Exchange rates are like fantastic, connected dance partners who move quickly and effortlessly together. When one dance partner glides forward, the other glides backward. When demand for Canadian dollars increases, the supply of Canadian dollars decreases. For all currencies, changes in demand move with changes in supply. The demand for Canadian dollars is also the supply of U.S. dollars, and the supply of Canadian dollars is the demand for U.S. dollars. This is true for all currencies.

Forces Changing Demand and Supply   There are five economic forces that change demand and supply together and explain why exchange rates fluctuate:

- interest rate differentials
- inflation rate differentials
- Canadian real GDP changes
- changes in R.O.W. demands for Canadian exports and R.O.W. prices
- changes in expectations

▲ Think of exchange rate fluctuations like the distance that dance partners cover on the floor. Do they cover more distance (more fluctuations) when their steps are coordinated or uncoordinated?

Each of these forces changes *both* demand and supply in the foreign exchange market, shifting *both* the demand and supply curves. This is not like other demand and supply curves, where the forces changing demand differ from the forces changing supply. We will continue using the example of Canadian – U.S. dollar exchanges, but the explanations apply to exchange rates between any currencies.

Interest Rate Differentials

There are usually differences in interest rates in different countries as well as differences in inflation rates. Economists call these differences *differentials*.

In the foreign exchange market, money flows almost instantly to where the rate of return — the interest rate on an investment — is highest. When investors buy bonds, stocks, businesses, or real estate, they search worldwide for the highest rate of return. If they can earn a 5 percent return in Canada, they will not accept a 3 percent return in the United States. The difference between the two interest rates is called the **interest rate differential**. When interest rates rise in Canada relative to other countries, it is an increase in the Canadian interest rate differential.

interest rate differential   difference in interest rates between countries

Increase in Canadian Interest Rate Differential An increase in the Canadian interest rate differential makes Canadian assets more attractive to investors. Investors outside of Canada need Canadian dollars to buy those assets, increasing the demand for Canadian dollars in the foreign exchange market. Canadian investors also want to invest more in Canada and less in the United States, decreasing their demand for U.S. dollars, which decreases the supply of Canadian dollars. The increase in demand and decrease in supply of Canadian dollars *both* raise the price of the Canadian dollar. The Canadian dollar appreciates relative to the U.S. dollar and other currencies. An increase in the Canadian interest rate differential raises the exchange rate.

NOTE
An increase in the Canadian interest rate differential increases demand and decreases supply of Canadian dollars, so the Canadian dollar appreciates.

Figure 10.7 shows the effect on the exchange rate of an increase in demand and decrease in supply of Canadian dollars. When demand increases and supply decreases at the same time, the exchange rate rises quickly because the shifts of both curves push up the exchange rate, in this example from US$0.90 to US$1.00.

Figure 10.7 Increase in Demand and Decrease in Supply of Canadian Dollars in Foreign Exchange Market

Price of 1 Canadian Dollar (US$ per C$)	Quantity Demanded (billions of C$ per month)		Quantity Supplied (billions of C$ per month)	
	Original (D_0)	New (D_1)	Original (S_0)	New (S_1)
US$ 0.60	90 → 100		30 → 20	
US$ 0.70	80 → 90		40 → 30	
US$ 0.80	70 → 80		50 → 40	
US$ 0.90	60 → 70		60 → 50	
US$ 1.00	50 → 60		70 → 60	
US$ 1.10	40 → 50		80 → 70	

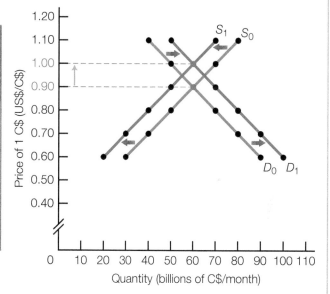

Decrease in Canadian Interest Rate Differential   A decrease in the Canadian interest rate differential lowers the exchange rate. This is illustrated in Figure 10.8.

Figure 10.8   Decrease in Demand and Increase in Supply of Canadian Dollars in Foreign Exchange Market

Price of 1 Canadian Dollar (US$ per C$)	Quantity Demanded (billions of C$ per month)		Quantity Supplied (billions of C$ per month)	
	Original (D_0)	New (D_2)	Original (S_0)	New (S_2)
US$ 0.60	90 → 80		30 → 40	
US$ 0.70	80 → 70		40 → 50	
US$ 0.80	70 → 60		50 → 60	
US$ 0.90	60 → 50		60 → 70	
US$ 1.00	50 → 40		70 → 80	
US$ 1.10	40 → 30		80 → 90	

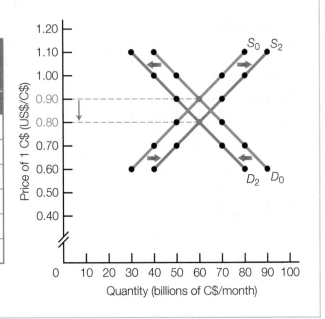

The demand for Canadian dollars decreases, the supply of Canadian dollars increases, and the value of the Canadian dollar falls. The Canadian dollar depreciates relative to the U.S. dollar and other currencies. When demand decreases and supply increases at the same time, the exchange rate falls quickly because the shifts of both curves push down the exchange rate, in this example from US$0.90 to US$0.80.

Inflation Rate Differentials

Prices of products and services also affect the exchange rate through imports and exports. The **inflation rate differential** is the difference in inflation rates between countries. The Canadian inflation rate differential increases when the inflation rate in Canada rises relative to inflation rates in the rest of the world.

inflation rate differential   difference in inflation rates between countries

Increase in Canadian Inflation Rate Differential   When the inflation rate in Canada is higher than inflation rates in other countries, Canadian products and services, including exports, become relatively more expensive for buyers in the rest of the world. The R.O.W. buys fewer Canadian exports and therefore demands fewer Canadian dollars. As the prices of Canadian products and services rise, imports from R.O.W. become relatively less expensive for Canadians. Canadians buy more, cheaper, imported products and services and need more U.S. dollars. The increased Canadian demand for U.S. dollars is also an increased supply of Canadian dollars. The decrease in demand and increase in supply of Canadian dollars *both* work to lower the price of the Canadian dollar, as shown in Figure 10.8. The Canadian dollar depreciates relative to the U.S. dollar and other currencies.

NOTE
An increase in the Canadian inflation rate differential decreases demand and increases supply of Canadian dollars, so the Canadian dollar depreciates.

An increased inflation rate differential also reduces the attractiveness of Canadian assets. Investors want the highest possible real return. The real interest rate on an investment equals the nominal interest rate minus the inflation rate. When inflation increases, the real interest rate on investments falls, making Canadian assets less attractive to investors. The demand for Canadian dollars decreases, the supply of Canadian dollars increases, and the price of the Canadian dollar falls.

NOTE
Real Interest Rate =
Nominal Interest Rate − Inflation Rate

Decrease in Canadian Inflation Rate Differential A decrease in the Canadian inflation rate differential increases demand and decreases supply of Canadian dollars, as illustrated in Figure 10.7. The Canadian dollar appreciates relative to the U.S. dollar and other currencies.

Canadian Real GDP Changes

Changes in Canadian real GDP affect imports and investors but with opposing effects on exchange rates.

Increasing Real GDP in Canada — Imports When real GDP increases in Canada, so does aggregate income. With increased income, Canadian consumers and businesses buy more of most products and services, including more imports. To buy more imports, consumers' demand for U.S. dollars increases. This increases the supply of Canadian dollars in the foreign exchange market. But this increased supply of Canadian dollars is *not* accompanied by a decreased demand for Canadian dollars. It's like one dancer taking a solo. The effect lowers the price of the Canadian dollar, although not as much as coordinated changes in demand and supply.

Increasing Real GDP in Canada — Investors Increasing real GDP is economic growth. Investors see economic growth as evidence of a strong Canadian economy, with profits to make from Canadian assets. Investors react to increasing real GDP like they do to an increased Canadian interest rate differential in Figure 10.7. Canadian assets become more attractive, increasing demand for Canadian dollars in the foreign exchange market to buy them. Higher Canadian profits also mean that Canadian investors will invest more in Canada, decreasing their demand for U.S. dollars. This decreases the supply of Canadian dollars in the foreign exchange market. These are two coordinated dance partners moving together. The increase in demand and decrease in supply of Canadian dollars both work to raise the price of the Canadian dollar — the exchange rate.

Of these two opposite effects — the import effect lowering the price of the Canadian dollar and the growth effect raising the price — the growth effect usually dominates. So when Canadian real GDP increases, the Canadian dollar appreciates relative to the U.S. dollar and other currencies. The next time the media report new data showing strong growth in Canadian real GDP, watch what happens to the exchange rate of the Canadian dollar.

NOTE
When Canadian real GDP increases, the Canadian dollar appreciates.

If investors are confident that the Canadian economy will be strong, they will be more likely to buy more Canadian assets, pushing up the dollar's value.

— Bank of Canada

Decreasing Real GDP in Canada   These forces work in reverse when there is a decrease in real GDP in Canada. Decreasing aggregate income decreases the amount of money Canadian consumers have, decreasing demand for imports. This decreases Canadians' demand for U.S. dollars, decreasing the supply of Canadian dollars in foreign exchange markets. The effect slightly raises the price of the Canadian dollar.

But a decrease in Canadian real GDP is evidence of economic contraction. Investors worry about future profits, and Canadian assets become less attractive. Since foreign investors are not buying Canadian assets, the demand for Canadian dollars decreases. Canadian investors now find U.S. assets relatively more attractive and so demand more U.S. dollars. This increases the supply of Canadian dollars. The decrease in demand and increase in supply of Canadian dollars both work to lower the price of the Canadian dollar.

The contraction effect usually dominates. So when Canadian real GDP decreases, the Canadian dollar depreciates relative to the U.S. dollar and other currencies.

R.O.W. and Canadian Exports

Two forces in the rest of the world have important effects on the value of the Canadian dollar:

* demand for Canadian exports
* world prices for Canadian resource exports

R.O.W. Demand for Canadian Exports   In order to buy more Canadian exports, R.O.W. buyers need more Canadian dollars. As the demand for Canadian exports increases, the demand for Canadian dollars increases. But there is no change in the supply of Canadian dollars. The effect raises the price of the Canadian dollar, although not as much as when there are coordinated changes in demand and supply. When the demand for Canadian exports increases, the Canadian dollar appreciates slightly relative to the U.S. dollar and other currencies.

World Prices for Canadian Resource Exports   Canada is a major exporter of oil, gold, potash, nickel, diamonds, and other resources. Resource prices are set in worldwide markets. There are no separate Canadian prices for these resources. When the world price of oil, for example, rises, non-Canadians will require more Canadian dollars to buy the now more expensive Canadian oil. Rising world prices for Canadian resource exports increases the demand for Canadian dollars. But this does not trigger a coordinated change in the supply of Canadian dollars. The effect raises the price of the Canadian dollar.

I hope you are feeling at least a little confused by this explanation. After all, in the explanation of inflation rate differentials, when prices of Canadian exports rise, demand for exports *decreases*, decreasing demand for Canadian dollars. With relatively cheaper imports available, the supply of Canadian dollars increases, to demand more U.S. dollars to buy U.S. imports. The Canadian dollar depreciates.

NOTE
When Canadian real GDP decreases, the Canadian dollar depreciates.

NOTE
Increased R.O.W. demand for Canadian exports causes the Canadian dollar to appreciate slightly.

NOTE
Rising world prices for Canadian resource exports causes the Canadian dollar to appreciate relative to non-resource producing currencies.

The crucial difference between these explanations is that resource prices are set worldwide, not in Canada alone. The differential inflation rate explanation is based on *differences* in prices and inflation rates. Most Canadian exports have different prices from substitute products produced in other countries. When Canadian exports become more expensive, buyers switch to cheaper substitutes elsewhere. But a change in the worldwide price of oil applies to *all* countries. There is no cheaper oil somewhere else. So buyers, paying higher prices, demand more Canadian dollars to buy Canadian oil. The Canadian dollar appreciates relative to the U.S. dollar.

The same upward pressure on exchange rates applies to all countries that are major exporters of resources. When oil prices rise, the Canadian dollar usually appreciates relative to the U.S. dollar, but not against currencies of other oil-exporting countries such as Mexico, Venezuela, or Russia. Their currencies also appreciate relative to the U.S. dollar. So with rising world oil prices, the Canadian dollar appreciates against the currencies of non–oil-exporting countries, but not against currencies of other oil-exporting counties.

Speculators and Changing Expectations

Most of the demand for and supply of foreign currencies, including the Canadian dollar, comes from speculators. Every day, foreign currencies worth about US$5 trillion are traded on the foreign exchange market. The daily trade in products and services is worth only about US$50 billion. That means speculative currency trading is 100 times more important than currency trading for buying products and services! Speculators try to make profits by buying low and selling high. They hope to buy Canadian dollars when the exchange rate is low and sell when the exchange rate is high. If a speculator bought US$1 million worth of Canadian dollars at a price of US$0.63, and sold at a price of US$0.93, she would make a profit of US$300 000! Many fortunes have been made, and lost, on the foreign exchange market.

Because speculators are the major players on the foreign exchange market, speculators' expectations about the future value of the Canadian dollar are the most important force behind fluctuating exchange rates.

Self-Fulfilling Expectations   When speculators expect a rise in the future price of the Canadian dollar, they buy Canadian dollars now in the hope of selling after the value of the dollar rises. The increase in speculative purchases of Canadian dollars increases the demand for Canadian dollars, raising the price of the Canadian dollar. The Canadian dollar appreciates relative to the U.S. dollar and other currencies.

As long as enough speculators have the same expectation of a rise in the price of the Canadian dollar, the actions they take — buying/demanding Canadian dollars — immediately raise the price of the Canadian dollar and make the expectation come true.

The same logic applies when most speculators expect a fall in the future price of the Canadian dollar. They sell Canadian dollars now, increasing the supply and immediately lowering the price of the Canadian dollar. The Canadian dollar depreciates relative to the U.S. dollar and other currencies.

Speculators Reinforce Exchange Rate Forces   Speculators also reinforce and speed up the effects of the other forces on exchange rates. Changes in interest rate differentials, inflation rate differentials, Canadian real GDP, R.O.W. demand for Canadian exports, and worldwide resource prices normally take months or years to affect exchange rates. But speculators learned the same economics lessons about exchange rates you are learning. For example, as soon as the Canadian interest rate differential increases, speculators immediately increase their demand for Canadian dollars, confident that the relative rise in Canadian interest rates will eventually raise the price of the Canadian dollar. If enough speculators act in the same way at the same time, their increased demand makes the expectation of a higher Canadian dollar come true instantly.

All speculators do not become instant millionaires. If an individual speculator bets a currency will appreciate, when most other speculators bet the currency will depreciate, the individual can lose a fortune of money. Speculation is very risky.

Think of Figure 10.9 as a checklist that speculators use to predict the future price of the Canadian dollar. It's also a good study device for reviewing the forces causing fluctuating exchange rates.

NOTE

Speculators' expectations of changes in exchange rates can be self-fulfilling, and reinforce the effects of other forces on the price of the Canadian dollar.

Figure 10.9   Forces Changing the Price of the Canadian Dollar

Canadian Dollar Appreciates (exchange rate rises)	Canadian Dollar Depreciates (exchange rate falls)
Canadian interest rates rise relative to other countries	Canadian interest rates fall relative to other countries
Canadian inflation rate falls relative to inflation rates in other countries	Canadian inflation rate rises relative to inflation rates in other countries
Real GDP in Canada increases	Real GDP in Canada decreases
R.O.W. demand for Canadian exports increases	R.O.W. demand for Canadian exports decreases
World prices for Canadian resource exports rise	World prices for Canadian resource exports fall
Expectation that Canadian dollar will appreciate	Expectation that Canadian dollar will depreciate

Refresh 10.2

MyEconLab

For answers to these Refresh Questions, visit MyEconLab.

1. In your own words, explain interest rate differentials and inflation rate differentials. List and define the five forces causing exchange rate fluctuations.

2. Explain why a demand for Canadian oil exports by buyers in the R.O.W. does not increase the supply of Canadian dollars in the foreign exchange market.

3. If you were a speculator on the foreign exchange market, what would be the key piece of information you would use in deciding whether to buy or sell Canadian dollars? Explain your choice.

How Exchange Rates Affect Your Life: International Transmission Mechanism

Once the foreign exchange market determines the price of the Canadian dollar, what effect do those fluctuating, dancing exchange rates have on the Canadian economy and on you? Exchange rates, by changing the prices we pay for imports, affect all of us as consumers. An appreciating Canadian dollar encourages shopping trips across the border or buying imports rather than Canadian products and services. But fluctuating exchange rates also affect key macroeconomic outcomes — real GDP, unemployment, and inflation.

The **international transmission mechanism** describes how foreign exchange rates affect — are transmitted to — real GDP, unemployment, and the price level. The key is the effect of exchange rates on exports and imports.

Figure 10.10 illustrates the international transmission mechanism from the demand and supply of Canadian dollars (at the top) to real GDP and inflation (at the bottom). The demand and supply of Canadian dollars interact in the foreign exchange market to determine the exchange rate. That is the story we have been telling up until now.

Trace the effect of exchange rates on real GDP, unemployment, and inflation.

international transmission mechanism how exchange rates affect real GDP, unemployment, and inflation

Figure 10.10 **International Transmission Mechanism**

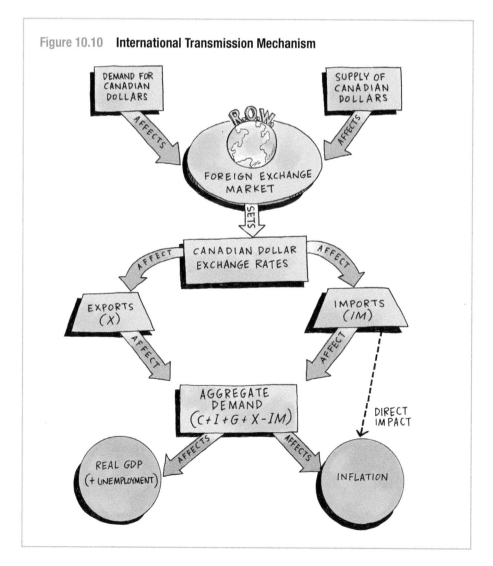

Impact on Net Exports

What happens to exports and imports in Figure 10.10 when the exchange rate of the Canadian dollar appreciates or depreciates?

NOTE

Appreciating Canadian dollar is a negative aggregate demand shock — decreases net exports; decreasing aggregate demand, decreasing real GDP, increasing unemployment, decreasing inflation.

Appreciating Canadian Dollar Is a Negative Aggregate Demand Shock A higher Canadian dollar makes Canadian exports more expensive for customers in the United States and the rest of the world. When non-Canadians must pay more of their own currencies for Canadian exports, they buy fewer exports. Exports (X) decrease, decreasing Canadian aggregate demand. Remember your mantra: Aggregate demand equals $C + I + G + X - IM$.

A higher Canadian dollar makes imports from the rest of the world cheaper for Canadian customers. Canadians buy more imports and fewer Canadian products and services. In calculating aggregate demand, imports (IM) are subtracted. So an increase in imports decreases aggregate demand.

Decreases in exports and increases in imports both decrease aggregate demand. As explained in Chapter 8, an appreciating, stronger Canadian dollar is a negative demand shock decreasing real GDP, increasing unemployment, and causing deflation (falling average prices). Look back at Figure 8.14 on page 224. An appreciating Canadian dollar can push the economy into a contraction.

Economics *Out There*

High Canadian Dollar Threatens *Twilight* Sequels and Economic Recovery

The first *Twilight* movies were filmed in British Columbia, but because of the rising value of the Canadian dollar, *Breaking Dawn*, the fourth film in the blockbuster series, was filmed in the United States. The rising loonie increased the cost of film services and the country lost an important Canadian export.

The decreasing sales of Canadian exports concerned the Bank of Canada, which noted that while "a recovery in economic activity is ... under way in Canada, ... heightened volatility and persistent strength in the Canadian dollar are working to slow growth and subdue inflation pressures."

The stronger Canadian dollar made exports like film services more expensive, decreasing exports, aggregate demand, and GDP. At the same time, imports were less expensive, which is why the Bank of Canada referred to subdued inflation pressures.

Sources: Based on Bank of Canada Monetary Policy Report Summary, October 2009; "Will Night Set on *Twilight's* B.C. Film Sets?" www.bclocalnews.com/entertainment/70572072.html. Accessed November 20, 2009.

Depreciating Canadian Dollar Is a Positive Aggregate Demand Shock A lower Canadian dollar makes Canadian exports cheaper for customers in the United States and the rest of the world. When Canadian exports become less expensive, non-Canadians buy more of them. Exports (X) increase, increasing aggregate demand — aggregate demand equals $C + I + G + X - IM$.

A lower Canadian dollar makes imports from the rest of the world more expensive for Canadian customers. Canadians buy fewer imports and more Canadian products and services. So a decrease in imports increases aggregate demand.

Increases in exports and decreases in imports both increase aggregate demand. This positive demand shock increases real GDP, decreases unemployment, and increases inflation (rising average prices). Look back at Figure 8.15 on page 225. An increase in real GDP due to increased net exports is sometimes called an *export-led boom*. A depreciating Canadian dollar can push the economy into an expansion.

NOTE
Depreciating Canadian dollar is a positive aggregate demand shock — increases net exports; increasing aggregate demand, increasing real GDP, decreasing unemployment, increasing inflation.

Economics *Out There*

Who Wins from a Falling Loonie?

The exchange rate for the Canadian dollar fell from a high of US$1.01 in 2013 to US$0.88 in early 2014. But, as John Greenwood states in his 2014 article, ". . . depending on what you do for a living," the falling value of the loonie can be a good thing. Yes, the depreciating dollar has been bad news for cross-border shoppers and travellers vacationing in the United States, but very good news for Canadian exporters.

According to Doug Porter, BMO Capital Markets chief economist, the falling loonie "is a blessing" for Canadian exporters and domestic tourism operators.

The "biggest winners" are businesses that sell their output in U.S. dollars while paying for their costs in Canadian dollars. They win both ways, sending their profit margins up.

Porter estimates that "a 10% drop" in the value of the Canadian dollar increases Canadian real GDP by "0.5 to 1.0 percentage points per year." This economic growth creates Canadian jobs.

Porter believes that the government and the Bank of Canada understand "what's in the interests of the country" overall and will not try to stop the falling loonie.

Source: "Why Canada's policy makers won't stand in the way of the falling loonie," John Greenwood, *National Post* 16 January 2014 http://business.financialpost.com/2014/01/16/why-canadas-policy-makers-wont-stand-in-the-way-of-the-falling-loonie/

Impact on Inflation

The rise or fall in price of Canadian exports to the rest of the world, measured in other currencies, affects inflation rates in those other countries. There is no effect on the Canadian inflation rate.

But when *imports* to Canada fall or rise in price, measured in Canadian dollars, there is a direct effect on the Canadian inflation rate. That effect appears at the bottom right of Figure 10.10 on page 291 in the dashed line from imports to inflation.

Appreciating Canadian Dollar Is Deflationary   When the exchange rate of the Canadian dollar rises, exports decrease and imports increase. The falling price of imports directly decreases the Canadian inflation rate. A decrease in the inflation rate is deflationary.

This direct decrease in inflation reinforces the indirect effect of decreased net exports on inflation. Decreasing net exports are a negative demand shock, decreasing aggregate demand, decreasing real GDP, increasing unemployment, and decreasing inflation.

NOTE

An appreciating Canadian dollar causes deflation; a depreciating Canadian dollar causes inflation.

Depreciating Canadian Dollar Is Inflationary   When the exchange rate of the Canadian dollar falls, exports increase and imports decrease. This rising price of imports directly increases Canadian inflation — the average level of all prices, including the prices of imports.

This direct increase in the inflation rate reinforces the indirect impact of increased net exports on inflation. Increasing net exports are a positive demand shock, increasing aggregate demand, increasing real GDP, decreasing unemployment, and increasing inflation.

Exchange Rates and You

You often hear arguments in the media about a "strong" or "weak" Canadian dollar. Since most people think of "strong" as "good" and "weak" as "bad," they conclude that a "strong" Canadian dollar — a higher exchange rate in terms of U.S. dollars — is desirable for Canadians. You now know the truth is not so simple. There are advantages and disadvantages to both higher and lower exchange rates.

When the Canadian dollar strengthens, or appreciates in value, imports are less expensive and cross-border shopping is better. But an appreciating Canadian dollar is a negative demand shock, hurting exporters hardest, decreasing real GDP, increasing unemployment, and decreasing inflation.

When the Canadian dollar weakens, or depreciates in value, imports are more expensive and cross-border shopping is worse for Canadians heading south. But a depreciating Canadian dollar is a positive demand shock, helping exporters, increasing real GDP, decreasing unemployment, and increasing inflation.

Refresh 10.3

MyEconLab

For answers to these Refresh Questions, visit MyEconLab.

1. In your own words, explain the connection between exchange rates and aggregate demand.

2. When the media refer to a "weak Canadian dollar," explain what they are telling us.

3. Do you support a higher or lower Canadian dollar measured against the U.S. dollar? Explain your choice.

Overvalued Compared to What? Purchasing Power Parity and Rate of Return Parity Anchors

There are advantages and disadvantages to the economy from the ups and downs of the Canadian dollar. There is no single exchange rate that is "best" for the performance of the macro economy.

Still, you often hear the media describe the Canadian dollar, or another country's currency, as "overvalued" or "undervalued." These descriptions are based on a point of reference or a standard. They imply that there is some "value" that is just right.

The two standards that economists and speculators use to predict where exchange rates will eventually settle are purchasing power parity and rate of return parity. Both standards depend on the law of one price.

Law of One Price

Once again, speculators play a key role. By buying low and selling high, speculators enforce the **law of one price**, which states that any time there are differences in the price of a product or service across markets, the actions of profit-seekers eliminate the differences and establish a single price.

law of one price profit seekers eliminate differences in prices of the same product or service across markets and establish a single price

Imagine this scenario: One carat diamonds are selling for US$1000 in South Africa but US$1500 in Canada. If you buy diamonds in South Africa, and sell them in Canada, you make US$500 per diamond. Buy low in South Africa — sell high in Canada. But as more people pursue these profits, demand for diamonds in South Africa increases, driving up prices there. The additional supply of diamonds in Canada drives prices down here. That US$500 price difference quickly disappears. As long as there is a difference in price, the profit-driven forces of demand and supply lead to a single price across both markets. The law of one price applies to all markets, including the foreign exchange market.

How Much for a Big Mac? Purchasing Power Parity

The law of one price causes prices to adjust between markets. The principle of purchasing power parity causes exchange rates to adjust between *countries*. Parity means equality. According to **purchasing power parity (PPP)**, exchange rates adjust so that money has equal real purchasing power in any country.

purchasing power parity (PPP) exchange rates adjust so that money has equal real purchasing power in any country

Let's look at examples where purchasing power parity exists and where it does not.

When Purchasing Power Parity Exists There are often two prices on book covers, such as US$8.00 in the United States, C$10.00 in Canada. The very same book is selling for two different prices. Or is it?

Suppose the price of the Canadian dollar — the exchange rate — in terms of U.S. dollars is US$0.80. If you buy the book in Canada, you pay C$10.00. If instead you cross the border to buy the book in the United States, you have to exchange your Canadian dollars for U.S. dollars. You get US$0.80 for each loonie. C$10.00 gets you US$8.00 (10.00 × 0.80 = 8.00). Your C$10.00 buys exactly the same book in Canada as it does in the United States after converting into U.S. dollars. In other words, your Canadian dollars have the same real purchasing power in both countries for that book. Ten dollars Canadian, at this exchange rate, buys the same book in Canada or in the United States.

The reciprocal exchange rate — the price of a U.S. dollar in terms of Canadian dollars — is 1 ÷ 0.80 or C$1.25 in this example.

The same parity applies if we start with an American. Instead of buying the book in the United States, he exchanges his 8 U.S. dollars for Canadian dollars, and gets C$10.00 (8.00 × 1.25 = 10.00) — the cost of the book in Canada. His US$8.00 has the same real purchasing power in both countries.

In this example, the exchange rate of C$1.00 = US$0.80 (and the reciprocal rate of US$1.00 = C$1.25) is the purchasing power parity (*PPP*) exchange rate. The *PPP* exchange rate equalizes the purchasing power of money on both sides of the border.

When Purchasing Power Parity Does Not Exist To see why purchasing power parity provides an anchor for fluctuating exchange rates, look at what happens to book buying when there are different exchange rates.

Suppose the exchange rate is C$1.00 = US$1.00. One Canadian dollar exchanges for one U.S. dollar. If you buy the book in Canada, you pay C$10.00. If, instead, you cross the border to buy the book in the United States, you exchange your 10 Canadian dollars for 10 U.S. dollars. You buy the book for US$8.00, and have US$2.00 left over to spend on anything else. Your purchasing power is greater in the United States.

The reciprocal exchange rate in this example is also one U.S. dollar for one Canadian dollar. Our American can buy the book for US$8.00 in the United States. If, instead, he crosses the border to buy in Canada, he exchanges his 8 U.S. dollars for 8 Canadian dollars. He doesn't have enough money to buy the book in Canada. His purchasing power also is greater in the United States.

Can you figure out what will happen to demand and supply for the Canadian dollar? Canadians, now wanting to shop in the United States, increase the supply of Canadian dollars in the foreign exchange market in order to demand more U.S. dollars. Americans decrease their demand for Canadian dollars. The combined increase in supply and decrease in demand for Canadian dollars forces down the price of the Canadian dollar (the exchange rate). As long as there is a difference in the purchasing power of money across the border, the exchange rate keeps falling. The pressure for a falling price of the Canadian dollar ends only when the Canadian dollar depreciates and again exchanges in this example for US$0.80.

▲ These book buyers discovered that the purchasing power of their currency changed when they crossed borders.

The exchange rate of US$1.00 for a Canadian dollar is higher than the purchasing power parity exchange rate of US$0.80. At the exchange rate of US$1.00, the Canadian dollar is *overvalued* relative to the *PPP* rate with the U.S. dollar.

The story works in reverse if the exchange rate is C$1.00 = US$0.50 (with the reciprocal rate of US$1.00 = C$2.00). If you buy the book in the United States, your C$10 would exchange for US$5. You could not afford to buy the book in the United States. Your purchasing power is greater in Canada. An American shopper would have the same experience. His purchasing power is greater in Canada. As Canadians and Americans decrease the supply and increase the demand for Canadian dollars, the Canadian dollar appreciates. The exchange rate of US$0.50 for a Canadian dollar is lower than the purchasing power parity exchange rate of US$0.80. At the exchange rate of US$0.50, the Canadian dollar is *undervalued* relative to the *PPP* rate with the U.S. dollar.

The purchasing power parity exchange rate serves as an anchor when the exchange rate fluctuates above or below it. When the exchange rate is different from the *PPP* rate, profit-seeking forces and the law of one price push the exchange rate back toward the *PPP* rate.

The Hamburger Standard   To calculate the purchasing power parity exchange rate among currencies, you must compare more than the price of a single book. Official calculations use a basket of products and services, much like the basket used to calculate the Consumer Price Index. The problem is that the basket of products and services consumed by a typical household differs among countries. The basket in Japan contains much more sushi and the basket in Canada may contain maple syrup! To get around these complications, economists use other methods to calculate *PPP*.

The Economist magazine publishes a simple and fun calculation of *PPP* called the *Big Mac Index*. *The Economist*'s "basket" is simply a McDonald's Big Mac, which has the advantage of being produced and sold in about 120 countries. Using the United States as the country of comparison, the Big Mac *PPP* is the exchange rate that makes hamburgers cost the same in the United States and other countries. For example, suppose a Big Mac costs US$4.00 in the United States, and 2 pounds in Britain. This makes the Big Mac *PPP* rate US$2.00 per British pound. The Big Mac *PPP* rate compares the number of U.S. dollars it takes to buy a Big Mac in the United States with the cost of a Big Mac in other countries.

Comparing actual exchange rates with the Big Mac *PPP* rate shows whether a currency is undervalued or overvalued relative to the Big Mac *PPP* rate in U.S. dollars. Figure 10.11 contains examples from *The Economist*'s calculations in July 2014, when a Big Mac cost US$4.80 in the United States. The Big Mac *PPP* and actual exchange rates (columns three and four) are expressed as the price of each country's currency in terms of U.S. dollars.

Figure 10.11 Big Mac Purchasing Power Parity Index

Country	Price of Big Mac in Local Currency	Big Mac *PPP* Rate (US$/local currency)	Actual Exchange Rate (US$/local currency)	Under (−) or Over (+) Valuation of Local Currency against US$
Canada	C$5.64	0.85 US$/C$	0.93 US$/C$	+9%
Japan	370 yen	0.013 US$/yen	0.010 US$/yen	−24%
Euro area	3.68 euros	1.30 US$/euro	1.35 US$/euro	+3%
Britain	2.89 pounds	1.67 US$/pound	1.69 US$/pound	+3%
Brazil	13.00 real	0.37 US$/real	0.45 US$/real	+22%
China	16.9 yuan	0.28 US$/yuan	0.16 US$/yuan	−43%

Source: "Big Mac Index," *The Economist*, February 4, 2009 and author's calculations.

Look at the row for Canada. At the Big Mac *PPP* rate of 0.85 US$/C$, the C$5.64 it takes to buy a Big Mac in Canada turns into US$4.80 and allows you to buy the same Big Mac in the United States. But the actual exchange rate is 0.93, 8 cents more. The Canadian dollar is overvalued by 9 percent (0.08 ÷ 0.85 = 0.09 = 9%) relative to the *PPP* rate for the U.S. dollar.

Notice that actual exchange rates are pretty close to Big Mac *PPP* rates for Canada, the Euro Area, and Britain. China's actual exchange rate is furthest from Big Mac *PPP* for reasons we will discuss shortly.

Limitations of Purchasing Power Parity   Most descriptions of a currency as overvalued or undervalued refer to purchasing power parity. *PPP* is a rough estimate of where we expect exchange rates to settle eventually.

There are major limitations to *PPP* as the anchor point for exchange rates. The *PPP* story assumes all products and services are traded easily and without cost across borders. In reality, there are many costs, including transportation and storage. As well, how many consumers cross borders (to the United States, let alone to Japan or China!) to get haircuts or buy books? Most importantly, the *PPP* story assumes demand and supply of dollars on the foreign exchange market are only to buy exports or imports. You now know that most demand and supply of currencies is for speculation.

Despite these limitations, purchasing power parity is the best available standard for predicting where exchange rates are likely to settle.

The purchasing power parity exchange rate is *not* necessarily the "best" rate for the Canadian macroeconomic outcomes of full employment, stable prices, and steady economic growth. Because of the trade-offs of a lower or higher exchange rate, there is no single "best" value for the Canadian dollar. There is no exchange rate like the natural rate of unemployment that economists consider to be the "best" rate for the performance of the macro economy.

NOTE
Purchasing power parity is the best available standard for predicting exchange rates, but it does not account for trading limitations and the major role of speculators in influencing exchange rates.

Money Flows Where Interest Rates Are Highest: Rate of Return Parity

The law of one price states that price differences across markets will be eliminated by the actions of profit-seekers, buying low and selling high. In the interconnected foreign exchange market, money flows almost instantly to the highest rate of return on investments — no matter what country it's in.

So why are there differences in rates of return across countries? In 2014, for example, the annual rate of return on bonds in Canada was 0.5 percent, while the annual rate of return on bonds of comparable risk in Japan was 2 percent. Why weren't these differences eliminated by the law of one price? Why didn't investment dollars flow out of Canada (decreasing demand for Canadian bonds, lowering bond prices) and into Japan (increasing demand for Japanese bonds, raising bond prices), raising Canadian interest rates and lowering Japanese interest rates until they were equal?

The answer, in words, is *exchange rate expectations*. The answer, in numbers, comes from this formula.

Rate of Return = Rate of Return − expected (depreciation [−] or appreciation [+])
in Japan   in Canada   of yen against C$

The formula is simpler than it looks. Let me explain. For Canadian investors to earn 2 percent in Japan, they must first convert Canadian dollars to Japanese yen to buy the Japanese bond. When they sell the Japanese bond at the end of the year, they must then convert the yen back into Canadian dollars. The difference between the 0.5 percent return in Canada and the 2 percent return in Japan reflects the expected depreciation of the yen against the Canadian dollar (1.5 percent). If these expectations come true, the Canadian investor earns 2 percent measured in yen, but then loses 1.5 percent when converting yen back into dollars. The net rate of return is 0.5 percent, the same rate as in Canada.

Plugging these numbers into the formula gives

2% return   = 0.5% return   − (−1.5% depreciation of
in Japan   in Canada   yen against C$)
2%   = 0.5%   + 1.5%

The same formula works in reverse. Japanese investors considering investing in Canada must first convert Japanese yen to Canadian dollars to buy the Canadian bond. When they sell the Canadian bond at the end of the year, they must then convert the Canadian dollars back into Japanese yen. The expected depreciation of the yen is an appreciation of the Canadian dollar. So when investors convert Canadian dollars back into Japanese yen, they gain 1.5 percent in addition to the 0.5 percent return on the Canadian bond. The net rate of return for Japanese investors buying a Canadian bond is 2 percent, the same rate as in Japan.

Rates of return on investments are equal across countries when expected depreciation or appreciation of exchange rates is accounted for. This is called **rate of return parity** or **interest rate parity**.

So the law of one price does apply to rates of return across countries. Instead of prices adjusting, exchange rates adjust, equalizing net rates of return.

rate of return parity (interest rate parity) rates of return on investments are equal across countries, accounting for the expected depreciation or appreciation of exchange rates

Would You Like Your Exchange Rate Floating or Fixed?

floating exchange rate determined by demand and supply in the foreign exchange market

The exchange rate for the Canadian dollar is a **floating exchange rate**, determined by demand and supply in the foreign exchange market. Most countries today have floating exchange rates that adjust, or float, with changes in demand or supply.

This was not always so. From the end of World War II to the early 1970s, most countries, including Canada, had **fixed exchange rates**, determined by governments or central banks.

fixed exchange rate determined by governments or central banks

Of the countries listed in Figure 10.11, China is the only one that currently fixes its exchange rate. This fixed rate is the reason why there is a such a large difference between the Big Mac *PPP* rate and the actual exchange rate for China. According to the Big Mac Index, the Chinese yuan is significantly *undervalued* relative to the U.S. dollar. This lower exchange rate is a directed policy of the Chinese government. Lower or depreciating exchange rates make a country's exports cheaper for customers in the rest of the world. The purposefully undervalued yuan is one reason behind China's strong sales of exports.

There are complex economic and political considerations, beyond the scope of this book, that affect all exchange rates, and why countries fix or allow their exchange rates to float. But a basic understanding of exchange rates is important because they affect the key macroeconomic outcomes of real GDP, unemployment, and inflation.

Refresh 10.4

MyEconLab

For answers to these Refresh Questions, visit MyEconLab.

1. In your own words, explain purchasing power parity and rate of return parity and how they provide standards for exchange rates.

2. Explain the statement "The Canadian dollar is overvalued compared to the U.S. dollar" to a friend who has not taken this economics course.

3. Why must you understand the principle of rate of return parity in order to invest profitably in another country?

10.5 Where Do All the Dollars Flow? International Balance of Payments

Describe the two main parts of the balance of payments accounts, and explain why they must add up to zero.

balance of payments accounts measure a country's international transactions

Exchange rates affect the flows of exports, imports, and investments across international borders. A country's **balance of payments accounts** measure all international transactions during a year.

There are two main parts to the balance of payments accounts: the current account and the financial account. Figure 10.12 shows Canada's balance of payments accounts for 2013. We'll look at each part separately.

Figure 10.12   Canada's Balance of Payments Accounts 2013 (billions of C$)

Current Account	
Exports of products and services	+566
Imports of products and services	−598
Net investment/labour/transfer income	− 28
Current Account Balance	**− 60**
Financial Account	
Canadian investments in R.O.W	− 71
R.O.W. investments in Canada	+129
Financial Account Balance	**+ 58**
Statistical Discrepancy	+ 2

Source: Based on Statistics Canada. Table 376-0101 - Balance of international payments, current account and capital account, annual (dollars), CANSIM (database).

Current Account:
Exports, Imports, and Interest and Transfer Payments

The *current account* measures Canada's yearly exports and imports of products and services. To understand the pluses and minuses in Figure 10.12, focus on the flows of money into (positive) and out of (negative) Canada.

When Canada exports Bombardier airplanes to Germany, the German buyer pays by exchanging euros for Canadian dollars in the foreign exchange market and then sending the Canadian dollars to Bombardier in Canada. When Canada sells exports to the rest of the world, Canadian dollars flow into Canada. Flows of money into Canada are positive numbers. In 2013, Canada exported products and services worth $566 billion, bringing that amount of money into Canada — products out, money in.

When Canadians import wine from France, we pay by exchanging Canadian dollars for euros in the foreign exchange market and then sending the euros to France. When Canadians buy imports from R.O.W., Canadian dollars flow out of Canada. Flows of money out of Canada are negative numbers. In 2013, Canada imported products and services worth $598 billion from R.O.W., sending that amount of money out of Canada — products in, money out.

The other, smaller item on the current account measures net flows of interest income on investments, and labour and transfers income between Canada and R.O.W. The –$28 billion in 2013 means $28 billion *more* in investment/labour transfer income flowed out of Canada than into Canada.

The current account balance of –$60 billion adds up these flows of money for exports, imports and net interest and transfer payments. The negative number means Canadians sent $60 billion more to R.O.W for imports (and income and transfers) than R.O.W. sent to Canada for our exports (and income and transfers). A negative balance is a deficit. Canada had a $60 billion current account deficit in 2013.

NOTE

Flows of Canadian dollars into Canada are positive numbers on the balance of payments accounts; flows of Canadian dollars out of Canada are negative numbers.

NOTE

There is a current account deficit (negative balance) when Canadian spending on imports from R.O.W. is greater than R.O.W. spending on Canadian exports (and net investment/labour/transfers).

Financial Account: Investments between Canada and R.O.W.

The *financial account* measures international investments in financial assets like bonds and direct investment in buying companies. When Canadians invest in R.O.W., money flows out of Canada into other countries. In 2013, Canadians invested $71 billion in R.O.W., which is a negative number because the money left Canada. When R.O.W invests in Canadian assets and companies, money flows into Canada. The R.O.W. invested $129 billion in Canada, which is a positive number because the money came into Canada.

NOTE
There is a financial account surplus (positive balance) when R.O.W. investments in Canada are greater than Canadian investments in R.O.W.

The financial account balance of +$58 billion comes from adding up these flows of international investments. The positive number means that the R.O.W. invested $58 billion *more* in Canada than Canadians invested in R.O.W. A positive balance is a surplus. Canada had a $58 billion financial account surplus in 2013.

Statistical Discrepancy

The financial account also has a statistical discrepancy category, to deal with errors and missing information. This category, while part of the actual balance of payments tables, is not something you need to know the details of.

Why International Payments Account Must Balance

All international transactions begin with an exchange in the foreign exchange market. When R.O.W. buys Canadian exports or invests in Canadian companies, they first buy enough Canadian dollars on the foreign exchange market to pay for those transactions. When Canadians buy imports or invest in companies from R.O.W., we first buy enough of each foreign currency to pay for those transactions. The demand for a different currency on the foreign exchange market is also a supply of your own currency.

Because demand for one currency is also the supply of another, the balance of payments accounts must add up to zero.

Current Account Balance	+	Financial Account Balance	+	Statistical Discrepancy	=	0

Plugging the numbers for 2013 for Canada into this formula shows

$$(-\$60\,\text{bil}) \quad + \quad (+\$58\,\text{bil}) \quad + \quad (+\$2\,\text{bil}) \quad = \quad 0$$

Why must these balances add up to zero? Let me explain using the 2013 numbers for Canada.

Current Account Deficit and Financial Account Surplus The current account deficit of $60 billion means that Canadians spent more on imports from R.O.W. than R.O.W. spent on Canadian exports. Where did Canadians get the extra $60 billion worth of foreign currency to pay for those imports? From the financial account surplus. The $58 billion financial account surplus means that R.O.W. invested more in Canada than Canadians invested in R.O.W. The R.O.W. effectively "loaned" Canadians the extra foreign currency necessary to finance our purchases of R.O.W. exports. The $2 billion statistical discrepancy completes the equality between the current account deficit and financial account surplus.

Current Account Surplus and Financial Account Deficit The adding up logic also works in reverse. A Canadian balance of payments surplus in the current account means R.O.W. spent more on Canadian exports than Canada spent on R.O.W. imports. Where does R.O.W. get the extra Canadian dollars to pay for those exports? From a financial account deficit. A financial account deficit means that Canada invests more in R.O.W. than R.O.W. invests in Canada. Canada effectively "loans" R.O.W. the extra Canadian dollars necessary to finance R.O.W. purchases of Canadian product and service exports.

Mirror Images The current account and financial account balances are mirror images of each other. When one balance is in deficit, the other is in surplus. The statistical discrepancy is used to allow for missing data and errors.

Why International Transactions and Exchange Rates Matter

The balance of payments accounts measure the flows of currencies across international borders. You now know why people demand and supply foreign currencies (for buying exports or assets from another country) and the important role of speculators. These demand and supply choices determine exchange rates, which in turn affect exports, imports, and aggregate demand. By affecting aggregate demand, exchange rates have a very real impact on our lives — on our standard of living (real GDP), unemployment, and inflation.

Refresh 10.5

1. In your own words, list and explain the two main parts to a country's balance of payments accounts.

2. Explain what a financial account surplus means.

3. Explain why a country's balance of payments accounts must be zero at the end of each year.

MyEconLab

For answers to these Refresh Questions, visit MyEconLab.

Study Guide

CHAPTER 10 SUMMARY

10.1 Shuffling Off to Buffalo: Demand and Supply of Canadian Dollars

The demand for products, services, and assets from other countries, which must be paid for in local currencies, are behind demand and supply on the foreign exchange market, determining exchange rates.

- **Exchange rate** — price at which one currency exchanges for another currency.
  - Exchange rate is the price of 1 Canadian dollar. An exchange rate of C$1.00 = US$0.95 means it takes 95 cents U.S. to buy 1 Canadian dollar.

- **Foreign exchange market** — worldwide market where all countries' currencies are bought and sold in exchange for each other.

- Exchange rates fluctuate (go up and down) constantly.
  - **Currency depreciation** — fall in the exchange rate of one currency for another.
  - **Currency appreciation** — rise in the exchange rate of one currency for another.

- Non-Canadians' demand for C$ is demand for Canadian exports and assets, and for speculating on the future value of the C$.

- **Law of demand for Canadian dollars** — as the exchange rate rises, the quantity demanded of C$ decreases.
  - Higher value of C$ makes Canadian exports and assets more expensive for non-Canadians, who buy less of them. With fewer sales to non-Canadians, the quantity demanded of C$ decreases.

- Canadians' supply of C$ is the demand for foreign currency to buy imports and assets from rest of the world, and for speculating on the future value of C$.

- The demand for one currency is the supply of another currency.

- **Law of supply for Canadian dollars** — as the exchange rate rises, the quantity supplied of C$ increases.
  - Higher value of C$ makes R.O.W. imports and assets less expensive for Canadians, who buy more of them. To buy more R.O.W. products and services, Canadians demand a greater quantity of foreign currency, so the quantity supplied of C$ increases.

- At the equilibrium exchange rate, quantity demanded and quantity supplied of C$ are equal.

- Americans demanding C$ supply US$ in exchange. Canadians demanding US$ supply C$ in exchange.
  - Reciprocal exchange rate = 1 ÷ other exchange rate. If C$1.00 = US$0.90, reciprocal exchange rate is US$1.00 = 1 ÷ 0.90 = C$1.11.
  - When C$ appreciates against any currency, that currency depreciates against C$, and vice versa.

10.2 Dancing with Dollars: Fluctuating Exchange Rates

Exchange rate fluctuations are caused by changes in interest rate differentials, inflation rate differentials, Canadian real GDP, R.O.W. demand for Canadian exports and world prices, and expectations by speculators.

- Each of the following five economic forces changes *both* demand and supply in the foreign exchange market, shifting *both* the demand and supply curves.

- **Interest rate differential** — difference in interest rates between countries.
  - Increase in Canadian interest rate differential increases demand and decreases supply of C$ — C$ appreciates.
  - Decrease in Canadian interest rate differential has opposite effect.

- **Inflation rate differential** — difference in inflation rates between countries.
  - Increase in Canadian inflation rate differential decreases demand and increases supply of C$ — C$ depreciates.
  - Decrease in Canadian inflation rate differential has opposite effect.
- Increasing *Canadian real GDP* has two opposite effects on the value of C$:
  - Increased imports cause a slight depreciation.
  - Increased investor confidence causes a strong appreciation.
  - Net effect is C$ appreciates.
  - Decreasing Canadian real GDP has opposite effects.
- Increasing *R.O.W. demand for Canadian exports* causes a slight appreciation of C$ (increases demand for C$).
  - Decreasing R.O.W. demand for Canadian exports has opposite effect.
- Rising *world prices for Canadian resource exports* causes C$ to appreciate relative to currencies of non–resource-producing countries (increases demand for C$).
  - Falling world prices for Canadian resource exports has opposite effect.
- Currency speculators are the most important force determining fluctuations of foreign exchange rates.
  - Expectations of a rise in the future price of the C$ causes a self-fulfilling appreciation of C$ (increases demand for C$).
  - Speculators reinforce effects of other forces on the price of the C$.

10.3 How Exchange Rates Affect Your Life: International Transmission Mechanisms

Exchange rates affect real GDP and inflation through the international transmission mechanism affecting net exports, aggregate demand, and the price level.

- **International transmission mechanism** — how exchange rates affect real GDP and inflation.
- Appreciating C$ is negative aggregate demand shock.
  - Decreases net exports (decreases exports and increases imports); decreasing aggregate demand, decreasing real GDP, increasing unemployment.
  - Decreases inflation.
  - Pushes the economy into a contraction.
- Depreciating C$ is positive aggregate demand shock.
  - Increases net exports (increases exports and decreases imports); increasing aggregate demand, increasing real GDP, decreasing unemployment.
  - Increases inflation.
  - Pushes the economy into expansion.

- Changing exchange rate for C$ affects the price of imports measured in C$ and the inflation rate.
  - Appreciating C$ causes deflation.
  - Depreciating C$ causes inflation.
- Advantages and disadvantages to both higher and lower exchange rates.
  - Appreciating C$ makes imports less expensive, but is a negative demand shock, hurting exporters, decreasing real GDP, increasing unemployment, and decreasing inflation.
  - Depreciating C$ makes imports more expensive, but is a positive demand shock, helping exporters, increasing real GDP, decreasing unemployment, and increasing inflation.

10.4 Overvalued Compared to What? Purchasing Power Parity and Rate of Return Anchors

The law of one price, purchasing power parity, and rate of return parity are the best available standards for predicting where exchange rates eventually settle, despite their limitations.

- Predictions where exchange rates settle are based on **law of one price** — profit seekers eliminate differences in prices of same product across markets and establish a single price.
- **Purchasing power parity** (*PPP*) — exchange rates adjust so that money has equal real purchasing power in any country.
  - When *PPP* exists, C$10 buys exactly same products in Canada — and when converted into US$ at *PPP* exchange rate — and in the United States.
  - When *PPP* does not exist, profit-seeking forces and law of one price push exchange rate toward *PPP* rate.
  - *PPP* does not account for trading limitations and the role of speculators influencing exchange rates.
- **Rate of return parity** (**interest rate parity**) — rates of return on investments are equal across countries, accounting for expected depreciation or appreciation of exchange rates.

Rate of Return in Japan	=	Rate of Return in Canada	−	expected (depreciation [−] or appreciation [+]) of yen against C$.

- Different systems for determining exchange rates.
  - **Floating exchange rate** — determined by demand and supply in foreign exchange market.
  - **Fixed exchange rate** — determined by governments or central banks.

10.5 Where Do All the Dollars Flow? International Balance of Payments

The two main parts of the balance of payments accounts — the current account and the financial account — must add up to zero.

- **Balance of payments accounts** — measure a country's international transactions. Parts are:
  - current account
  - financial account
  - statistical discrepancy
- Flows of C$ into Canada are positive numbers on balance of payments accounts; flows of C$ out of Canada are negative numbers.
- *Current account* measures flows from exports, imports, and net investment/labour/transfer income.
  - Canadian exports create positive inflow of C$ to Canada; imports create negative outflow of C$.
  - Current account deficit (negative balance) when Canadian spending on imports from R.O.W. is greater than R.O.W. spending on Canadian exports (and net investment/labour/transfers).
  - Current account surplus (positive balance) when R.O.W. spending on Canadian exports is greater than Canadian spending on imports from R.O.W. (and net investment/labour/transfers).
- *Financial account* measures international investments in financial assets like bonds and direct investment in buying companies.
  - Canadian investments in R.O.W. are negative outflow of C$ to R.O.W.; R.O.W. investments in Canada are positive inflow of C$.
  - Financial account deficit (negative balance) when Canadian investments in R.O.W. greater than R.O.W. investments in Canada.
  - Financial account surplus (positive balance) when R.O.W. investments in Canada are greater than Canadian investments in R.O.W.

- *Statistical discrepancy* for missing data and errors is not important for balance of payments accounts.
  - Inflow of international currencies is negative outflow of C$; outflow of international currencies is positive inflow of C$.

Current Account Balance	+	Financial Account Balance	+	Statistical Discrepancy	=	0

  - The balance of payments accounts must add to zero.
  - When there is a current account surplus there is a financial account deficit. If R.O.W. spends more on Canadian exports than Canadians spend on R.O.W. imports, where does R.O.W. get extra C$? From financial account deficit, with Canadians "loaning" R.O.W. extra C$ through investments.
  - When there is a current account deficit there is a financial account surplus. If Canada spends more on R.O.W. imports than R.O.W. spends on Canadian exports, where does Canada get extra foreign currency? From financial account surplus, with R.O.W. "loaning" Canada extra foreign currency through investments.

TRUE/FALSE

Circle the correct answer. Solutions to these questions are available at the end of the book and on MyEconLab. You can also visit the MyEconLab Study Plan to access additional questions that will help you master the concepts covered in this chapter.

You are sitting on the boat dock at a watersports resort reading this chapter when a famous Australian wakeboarder sits down beside you and says:

Sweet textbook, dude. I'm reading the same one. I'm studying the exchange rates chapter while training for the upcoming Pan American Games. But, when I was practising a toeside front flip, my textbook fell out of my backpack and the answers got wet and are unreadable. I'd be stoked if you told me if the answers are true or false.

Use this scenario to answer questions 1–15.

10.1 Demand and Supply of Canadian Dollars

1. When Australians pay for Canadian exports using Australian dollars, they supply Australian dollars and demand Canadian dollars.   T   F

2. An exchange rate of Australian $1.00 = C$0.95 means it takes 95 cents Australian to buy 1 Canadian dollar.   T   F

3. The Australian dollar buys more products and services in Canada if the value of the Canadian dollar increases from 95 cents Australian to 1 Australian dollar.   T   F

4. On December 24, 2013, US$1.00 = C$1.06, 1.00 euro = C$1.45. If American and Europeans were to convert their currency for Canadian dollars that day, the American selling U.S. dollars would get the most Canadian dollars.   T   F

10.2 Fluctuating Exchange Rates

5. The Canadian dollar depreciates against the Australian dollar if Canada's inflation rate is rising more than the inflation rate in Australia.   T   F

6. The Canadian dollar depreciates against the Australian dollar if Canada's interest rate is rising more than the interest rate in Australia.   T   F

7. The Canadian dollar appreciates against the Australian dollar if R.O.W. demand for Canadian products and services increases.   T   F

10.3 International Transmission Mechanism

8. A strong Canadian dollar is good for all Canadians.   T   F

9. A depreciating Canadian dollar increases inflation in Canada.   T   F

10.4 Purchasing Power Parity and Rate of Return Parity

10. When purchasing power parity holds, Australian $5.00 buys different quantities of the same products in Australia and Canada.   T   F

11. If the purchasing power parity exchange rate is C$1.00 = Australian $0.95, then Australians could pay for a C$100 hotel room in Quebec City with either 95 Australian dollars or 100 Canadian dollars.   T   F

12. Rate of return parity holds when the rates of return on Canadian and Australian investments are equal across the two countries, accounting for expected changes in exchange rates.   T   F

10.5 International Balance of Payments

13. The current account measures this year's investment flows among countries.   T   F

14. There is a current account deficit when Canadian spending on imports from R.O.W. is greater than R.O.W. spending on Canadian exports (and net investment/labour/transfers).   T   F

15. There is a financial account deficit when Canadian investments in R.O.W. are greater than R.O.W. investments in Canada.   T   F

Circle the best answer. Solutions to these questions are available at the end of the book and on MyEconLab. You can also visit the MyEconLab Study Plan to access similar questions that will help you master the concepts covered in this chapter.

10.1 Demand and Supply of Canadian Dollars

1. An exchange rate of C$1.00 = US$0.90 means
   a) 1 Canadian dollar is worth 90 cents U.S.
   b) 1 U.S. dollar is worth 1.11 cents Canadian.
   c) the price of one Canadian dollar is 90 cents U.S.
   d) all of the above.

2. If the exchange rate for the Canadian dollar falls, the quantity
   a) demanded of Canadian dollars decreases.
   b) demanded of Canadian dollars increases.
   c) supplied of Canadian dollars increases.
   d) supplied of U.S. dollars decreases.

3. If more Americans visit Canada and demand Canadian dollars,
   a) the Canadian exchange rate rises.
   b) the Canadian dollar appreciates against the U.S. dollar.
   c) the U.S. dollar depreciates against the Canadian dollar.
   d) all of the above.

4. The Canadian dollar appreciated relative to the U.S. dollar between May 2009 and October 2009. The value of the Canadian dollar remained constant relative to the euro over this period. This implies that the U.S. dollar
   a) remained constant relative to the Canadian dollar.
   b) appreciated relative to the Canadian dollar.
   c) appreciated relative to the euro.
   d) depreciated relative to the euro.

10.2 Fluctuating Exchange Rates

5. The Canadian dollar depreciates if
   a) the Canadian interest rate differential increases.
   b) the Canadian inflation rate differential increases.
   c) world prices for Canadian resource exports rise.
   d) speculators expect a rise in the future price of the Canadian dollar.

6. The effect of increased Canadian real GDP on the Canadian dollar exchange rate is to
   a) increase imports, which causes a slight depreciation.
   b) increase investor confidence, which causes a strong appreciation.
   c) cause a net appreciation the Canadian dollar.
   d) all of the above.

7. If the Bank of Canada informs speculators that it will not let the value of the Canadian dollar rise any more, then
   a) speculators will react by buying more Canadian dollars.
   b) the demand for Canadian dollars decreases.
   c) the demand for Canadian dollars increases.
   d) the Canadian exchange rate appreciates.

10.3 International Transmission Mechanism

8. Changes in exchange rates affect real GDP and inflation through
   a) the domestic monetary transmission mechanism.
   b) international transmission mechanisms.
   c) purchasing power parity.
   d) interest rate parity.

9. A falling exchange rate for the Canadian dollar
   a) decreases inflation in Canada.
   b) decreases exports.
   c) increases real GDP in Canada.
   d) all of the above.

10.4 Purchasing Power Parity and Rate of Return Parity

10. Suppose C$1.00 = US$1.00 and C$1.00 = 0.67 euro. Purchasing power parity holds when the same McDonald's burger, fries, and drink combo sells for
    a) C$10, US$10, and 10 euros.
    b) C$10, US$10, and 6.70 euros.
    c) C$10, US$10, and 15 euros.
    d) C$10, US$20, and 10 euros.

11. Purchasing power parity
    a) is the best available standard for judging exchange rates.
    b) does not account for trading limitations.
    c) does not account for the role of speculators in influencing exchange rates.
    d) is all of the above.

12. In 2009, the rate of return on bonds in Canada was 3 percent, while the rate of return on bonds of comparable risk in Japan was 7 percent. If the Japanese investor buys a Canadian bond, then she expects the Japanese yen to
    a) appreciate against the C$ by 4 percent.
    b) depreciate against the C$ by 4 percent.
    c) appreciate against the C$ by 3 percent.
    d) depreciate against the C$ by 3 percent.

10.5 International Balance of Payments

13. **When a Canadian invests in an Italian bicycle company, this is a**
   a)   positive entry on the current account.
   b)   negative entry on the current account.
   c)   positive entry on the financial account.
   d)   negative entry on the financial account.

14. **If Canada has a current account surplus on the balance of payments, then to pay for the extra Canadian exports,**
   a)   R.O.W. is loaning Canada extra C$.
   b)   R.O.W. is loaning Canada extra foreign currency.
   c)   Canada is loaning R.O.W. extra C$.
   d)   Canada is loaning R.O.W. extra foreign currency.

15. **If the statistical discrepancy is zero, then any**
   a)   deficit on the current account equals the surplus on the financial account.
   b)   surplus on the current account equals the surplus on the financial account.
   c)   deficit on the current account means Canada invests more in R.O.W. than the R.O.W. invests in Canada.
   d)   surplus on the current account means the R.O.W. invests more in Canada than Canada invests in the R.O.W.

11 Steering Blindly?

Monetary Policy and the Bank of Canada

LEARNING OBJECTIVES

After reading this chapter, you should be able to:

11.1 Identify the objectives of monetary policy.

11.2 Explain how the Bank of Canada uses open market operations to change target interest rates.

11.3 Trace the effects of interest rate changes on aggregate demand, inflation, real GDP, and unemployment.

11.4 Explain what blocks monetary transmission mechanisms, and how quantitative easing can overcome a balance sheet recession.

11.5 Explain how inflation rate targeting by an independent central bank anchors expectations, helps market economies function, and gets economists to agree.

IMAGINE DRIVING DOWN a winding mountain road, the

kind that makes you wish you owned a beautiful sports car. You have to brake and accelerate through every curve, with rocks on one side and a sheer drop on the other. With the right car and the right skills, the drive could be exhilarating.

Now imagine that every time you hit the gas pedal or the brakes, there is a 30-second delay before your car responds. You need to anticipate every curve far in advance. It probably wouldn't take long before you plunged off the road.

That is the challenge facing the Bank of Canada. In this chapter, you will learn how the Bank of Canada uses monetary policy to steer the economy toward full employment, stable prices, and steady economic growth. It changes interest rates and the money supply to try to keep the economy safely on the road to potential GDP with stable prices. But interest rate changes take 18 to 24 months to have an effect on the economy! Like putting on the brakes and having to wait 30 seconds before your car slows down!

Because it is difficult to get the timing of monetary policy just right, you might expect many disagreements from backseat drivers about the best way to steer the economy. But interestingly, most economists agree that the Bank of Canada's driving is pretty good.

The Governor of the Bank of Canada is not elected. Still, as a citizen you should understand how the Bank's policy choices affect your standard of living, your prospects for finding a job, and the cost of living. Wrong policy choices can send the economy over a cliff into cycles of bust and boom. And knowing how the Bank of Canada is likely to act will help you make smart financial choices.

11.1 What Do Central Banks Do?
Bank of Canada's Objectives and Targets

Identify the objectives of monetary policy.

Canada's economy is not run on the barter system. In our monetary-based economy, supply doesn't necessarily create its own demand. Business cycles, like the Great Depression and the Global Financial Crisis, occur when there are mismatches between aggregate supply and aggregate demand. In an attempt to end economic suffering and private bank failures, Parliament created the Bank of Canada. According to the 1935 *Bank of Canada Act*:

> it is desirable to establish a central bank in Canada to regulate credit and currency in the best interests of the economic life of the nation, to control and protect the external value of the national monetary unit and to mitigate by its influence fluctuations in the general level of production, trade, prices and employment, so far as may be possible within the scope of monetary action, and generally to promote the economic and financial welfare of Canada.

The Bank of Canada's job is to control the quantity of money and interest rates to avoid inflation, business cycles, and unemployment. Notice also the reference to "control and protect" the value of the Canadian dollar. The financial sector, interest rates, and exchange rates are all connected, as we have seen in Chapters 9 and 10. Those connections are also important for how the Bank of Canada does its job.

The Governor of the Bank of Canada — the driver at the wheel — currently is Stephen S. Poloz. His seven-year term as Governor began in June 2013.

> *The goal of Canadian monetary policy is to contribute to solid economic performance and rising living standards for all Canadians by keeping inflation low and stable.*
>
> — Bank of Canada
> 1999 Annual Report

Bank of Canada Head Office. ca. 1938/Associated Screen News/Bank of Canada Archives PC300.5-62

▲ Shown here on Wellington Street in Ottawa just after it opened for business in March 1935, the Bank of Canada was established by an act of Parliament. Considering the events that led to the decision to create the Bank of Canada, is the Bank still relevant today?

THE CANADIAN PRESS / Adrian Wyld

▲ Mr. Poloz, when testifying before the Senate Committee on Banking, Trade and Commerce, noted the difficulties in setting monetary policy. He told the committee, "Monetary policy formulation is more a process of risk management than one of engineering."

The Bank of Canada's Job

Chapter 9 identified four roles the Bank of Canada plays in the Canadian economy: issuing currency, acting as banker to banks, acting as a banker to government, and conducting monetary policy. In this chapter, we will focus on the Bank of Canada's responsibility for **monetary policy** — adjusting the supply of money and interest rates to achieve steady growth, full employment, and price stability. **Price stability** means the inflation rate is low enough that it does not significantly affect people's economic decisions.

Since 1991, the Government of Canada and the Bank of Canada have also agreed to two specific objectives for monetary policy:

- to contain the annual rate of inflation between 1 percent and 3 percent, as measured by increases in the Consumer Price Index (CPI). This is called the **inflation-control target**.

- to use monetary policy to achieve the 2 percent midpoint of that range.

The Bank of Canada aims for a 2 percent inflation rate target as measured by the CPI, but also pays close attention to the core CPI (see section 7.3), which excludes products and services with the most volatile prices from the CPI calculation. The core inflation rate — which the Bank of Canada calls its *operational guide* — provides a better measure of the long-run, underlying trend of inflation.

Notice that these two specific objectives focus entirely on the inflation rate, and do not mention steady growth in living standards, full employment, or the value of the Canadian dollar. As the original Phillips Curve demonstrates, there can be trade-offs between inflation and unemployment, so lower inflation may mean higher unemployment. This is a source of controversy about inflation-control targeting that we will return to later.

No matter what objectives the Bank of Canada focuses on, interest rates are its most important monetary policy tool for achieving them.

monetary policy   adjusting the supply of money and interest rates to achieve steady growth, full employment, and price stability

price stability   inflation rate is low enough that it does not significantly affect people's economic decisions

inflation-control target   range of inflation rates set by a central bank as a monetary policy objective

Refresh 11.1

1. In your own words, explain what the Bank of Canada's objectives are. Include a definition of monetary policy in your answer.

2. Explain why the Bank of Canada uses both the CPI and the core CPI in making monetary policy decisions.

3. The inflation rate is one of the Bank of Canada's main policy objectives. Explain why this objective is very important to you personally.

MyEconLab

For answers to these Refresh Questions, visit MyEconLab.

11.2 Target Shooting: Open Market Operations

The interest rate plays the central role in maintaining Say's Law in a monetary economy. Adjustments in the interest rate — the price of money — can help the economy stay on the road of steady growth in living standards, full employment, and stable prices.

Interest Rate as a Driving Force

In our monetary economy, Say's Law — supply creates its own demand — can break down if consumers stop shopping and start saving. Without enough spending, businesses find products sitting on shelves, and lay off workers. The economy plunges off the road into the bust of a recession. But if banks take those savings and lend them to businesses that increase their investment spending, Say's Law can be saved. It is still possible that all income earned by suppliers in input markets is spent to create an equal demand for products and services in output markets.

Banks, supervised by the Bank of Canada, are a key driver determining whether or not market economies adjust quickly to maintain steady growth in living standards, full employment, and stable prices.

Interest rates affect how much we, as consumers, homeowners, and business people, can afford to borrow and buy. When interest rates are lower, we can afford to borrow more and spend more, and we save less. When interest rates are higher, we can't afford to borrow, so we spend less and save more. If savings flowing into the banking system cause interest rates to fall, encouraging businesses and consumers to borrow and spend more, this restores the match between aggregate supply and aggregate demand. The right interest rate can keep the economy on the road toward potential GDP.

Interest rates are determined in money and loanable funds markets *and by central banks*. As part of the loanable funds markets, bond markets determine long-run interest rates, such as rates for 25-year mortgages and 10- to 30-year government bonds. Central banks cannot influence long-run interest rates, but they can influence short-run interest rates.

"I DON'T UNDERSTAND HOW HIGH INTEREST RATES AND THE NATIONAL DEFICIT AFFECT MY ALLOWANCE."

▲ This cartoon shows that when people have to pay high interest rates, they have less to spend — even on their kid's allowance — reducing aggregate demand. *Source:* www.CartoonStock.com

overnight rate the interest rate banks charge each other for one-day loans — the main monetary policy tool

In aiming for its 2 percent target rate of inflation, the Bank of Canada focuses on the **overnight rate** — the interest rate that chartered banks charge each other for one-day loans. That's about as short run as it gets! The overnight rate then determines *all other* interest rates that banks charge their customers. The overnight rate directly affects rates on lines of credit, rates for consumer and car loans, and rates for variable mortgages.

Every Picture Tells a Story: Bank of Canada Homepage

To see how the Bank of Canada influences short-run interest rates, go to its excellent website — www.bankofcanada.ca. Figure 11.1 is a 2014 screen shot from the website. You can see the importance of the inflation-control target and the overnight rate. These key indicators always appear on the Bank of Canada homepage.

At the top of the screen is the inflation-control target range of +1 to +3 percent, with the midpoint target of +2 percent. The most recent inflation rate (between August 2013 and August 2014) was 2.1 percent, shown in the box below the target range.

Next down the page is the Bank of Canada's operational guide — the core CPI — also with a target range of +1 to +3 percent. The most recent core inflation rate was also +2.1 percent, close to the middle of the target range.

The Bank of Canada's target for the overnight rate was 1.00 percent. This is the interest rate we will examine next.

Finally, at the bottom, is the exchange rate for the Canadian dollar in terms of U.S. dollars. Putting the exchange rate on the Bank of Canada's homepage reflects the important connection between interest rates (which the Bank of Canada helps determine) and exchange rates (which the Bank of Canada does not try to determine). In setting interest rates, the Bank of Canada is keenly aware of their effect on the value of the Canadian dollar, which in turn affects net exports, real GDP, employment, and inflation.

Moving Targets: Open Market Operations

The Bank of Canada's specific objective is to keep inflation at the target rate of 2 percent per year. The Bank also wants full employment and steady growth in real GDP and living standards. This complete set of objectives amounts to driving the Canadian economy on the road to potential GDP at the ideal speed, avoiding the booms and busts of business cycles on either side of the road. The Bank of Canada uses monetary policy to steer the economy. The steering method is changing the target for the overnight rate, which in turn changes most other interest rates. Changes in interest rates affect the economy. They speed it up or slow it down the same way that stepping on the gas or hitting the brakes changes the speed of your car.

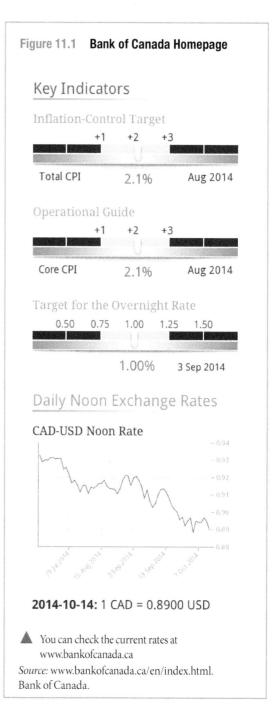

Figure 11.1   Bank of Canada Homepage

Key Indicators

Inflation-Control Target

Total CPI   2.1%   Aug 2014

Operational Guide

Core CPI   2.1%   Aug 2014

Target for the Overnight Rate

1.00%   3 Sep 2014

Daily Noon Exchange Rates

CAD-USD Noon Rate

2014-10-14: 1 CAD = 0.8900 USD

▲ You can check the current rates at www.bankofcanada.ca

Source: www.bankofcanada.ca/en/index.html. Bank of Canada.

NOTE
In a recessionary gap, the Bank of Canada lowers interest rates to increase aggregate demand and accelerate the economy.

NOTE
In an inflationary gap, the Bank of Canada raises interest rates to decrease aggregate demand to slow down the economy.

open market operations buying or selling government bonds on the bond market by the Bank of Canada

Accelerating with Lower Interest Rates When the economy slows down, inflation falls below the target, real GDP falls below potential GDP, and unemployment increases. This is a recessionary gap. To get the economy back up to speed, the Bank of Canada steps on the gas by lowering interest rates. Lower interest rates increase borrowing and spending, decrease saving, and cause the value of Canadian dollar to fall, increasing net exports. Aggregate demand increases and the economy speeds up. The inflation rate rises, real GDP increases, and unemployment decreases.

Braking with Higher Interest Rates When the economy is speeding too fast, inflation rises above the target, real GDP rises above potential GDP, and unemployment decreases below the natural rate. This is an inflationary gap. To slow down the economy, the Bank of Canada steps on the brakes by raising interest rates. Higher interest rates decrease borrowing and spending, increase saving, and cause the value of Canadian dollar to rise, decreasing net exports. Aggregate demand decreases and the economy slows down. The inflation rate falls, the growth in real GDP decreases, and unemployment increases.

Predicting the Future with Aggregate Supply and Aggregate Demand The Bank of Canada's steering job for monetary policy sounds relatively simple, until you remember that it can't wait to see if the economy is actually slowing down or speeding up before acting. The impact on the economy of lower or higher interest rates takes up to 24 months. The Bank of Canada has to predict the impact of a change in interest rates on the economy, and especially on the inflation rate, two years in advance!

There is no crystal ball foretelling the future, so the Bank hires economists to estimate what they think will happen to the economy. The economists use the aggregate supply and aggregate demand model (Chapter 8) to make predictions that the Bank of Canada uses to decide whether to raise, lower, or hold interest rates steady.

Moving Targets Eight Dates a Year The Bank of Canada sets eight fixed dates each year when it announces whether or not it will change the target for the overnight rate and, therefore, other interest rates.

The Bank of Canada changes the target overnight rate through **open market operations** — buying or selling Government of Canada bonds and Treasury bills (a Treasury bill is a short-term government bond) on the bond market. The bond market, as part of the loanable funds market, is open to the public — any individual or bank can buy or sell bonds.

When the Bank of Canada buys or sells bonds, it affects the loanable funds markets and the supply of money in money markets. The loanable funds markets and money markets are interconnected (see Chapter 9), so we can tell the story of open market operations from either perspective.

Changing the Money Supply to Change Interest Rates

This is the story from the money supply perspective. The money supply — M1+ — consists of currency in circulation and demand deposits. The Bank of Canada changes the money supply using open market operations to influence the quantity of demand deposits — which make up 90 percent of the money supply that chartered banks choose to create.

Buying Bonds to Increase the Money Supply When the Bank of Canada wants to lower interest rates to accelerate the economy, it buys bonds, which increases the money supply.

When the Bank of Canada buys a bond from you or from a chartered bank, it effectively pays with cash. That cash deposit increases bank reserves. As Chapter 9 showed, banks make profits by loaning out excess reserves. With new reserves, chartered banks make new loans (and matching demand deposits) that people can spend. This increase in demand deposits is an increase in the money supply.

To see the effect on interest rates, let's return to the example from Chapter 9. Figure 11.2 shows the initial demand and supply for money (same as Figure 9.6), which shows the initial demand and supply for money before the Bank of Canada's open market operation.

NOTE

To lower interest rates and accelerate the economy, the Bank of Canada buys bonds, which increases the money supply.

Figure 11.2 **Initial Demand and Supply in the Money Market**

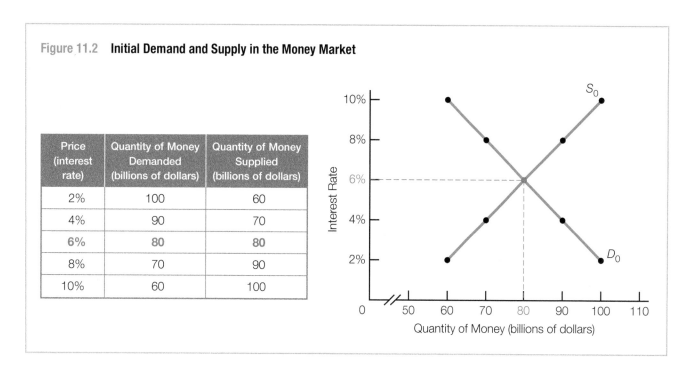

Price (interest rate)	Quantity of Money Demanded (billions of dollars)	Quantity of Money Supplied (billions of dollars)
2%	100	60
4%	90	70
6%	80	80
8%	70	90
10%	60	100

The equilibrium, market-clearing interest rate is 6 percent, the rate at which the quantity of money demanded ($80 billion) equals the quantity of money supplied ($80 billion).

When the Bank of Canada buys bonds and pays with cash, chartered bank reserves increase. Suppose the chartered banks then create $20 billion in new loans, with matching demand deposits, at every interest rate. With the increase in demand deposits, the supply of money (M1+) increases, shifting the money supply curve rightward to S_1. The unchanged demand and the new supply of money in the money market are shown in Figure 11.3.

Figure 11.3   Demand and Supply in the Money Market after Bank of Canada Buys Bonds

Price (interest rate)	Quantity of Money Demanded (billions of dollars)	Quantity of Money Supplied (billions of dollars)
2%	100	80
4%	90	90
6%	80	100
8%	70	110
10%	60	120

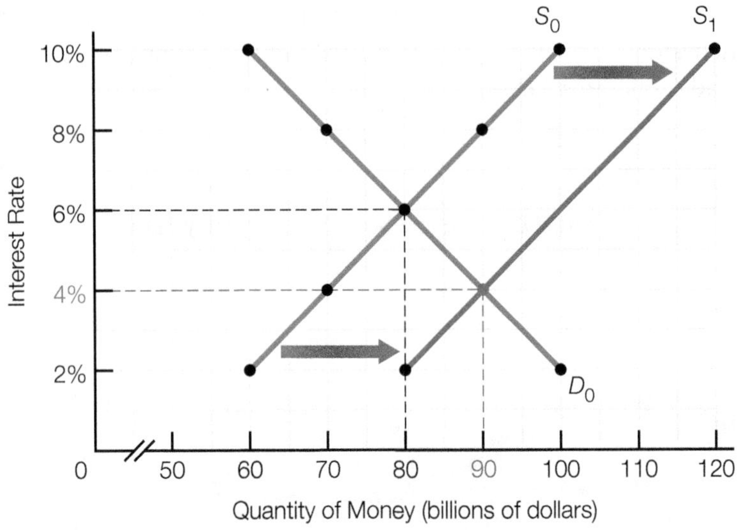

The equilibrium, market-clearing interest rate falls to 4 percent — the new rate at which the quantity of money demanded ($90 billion) equals the quantity of money supplied ($90 billion).

Remember, the interest rate is the price of money. Since the Bank of Canada's open market operation has increased the supply of money, the price of money — the interest rate — falls.

Selling Bonds to Decrease the Money Supply   The same story works in reverse when the Bank of Canada wants to raise interest rates to slow the economy down. It sells bonds to decrease the money supply.

NOTE
To raise interest rates and slow down the economy, the Bank of Canada sells bonds, which decreases the money supply.

When the Bank of Canada sells a bond, it must be paid. As a result, cash reserves leave the chartered banking system and go to the Bank of Canada. With fewer reserves, chartered banks reduce the quantity of loans (and matching demand deposits) that they make. Suppose the chartered banks reduce loans, with matching demand deposits, by $20 billion at every interest rate. With the decrease in demand deposits, the supply of money (M1+) decreases, shifting the money supply curve leftward to S_2. The unchanged demand and the new lower supply of money in the money market are shown in Figure 11.4.

Figure 11.4 Demand and Supply in the Money Market after Bank of Canada Sells Bonds

Price (interest rate)	Quantity of Money Demanded (billions of dollars)	Quantity of Money Supplied (billions of dollars)
2%	100	40
4%	90	50
6%	80	60
8%	70	70
10%	60	80

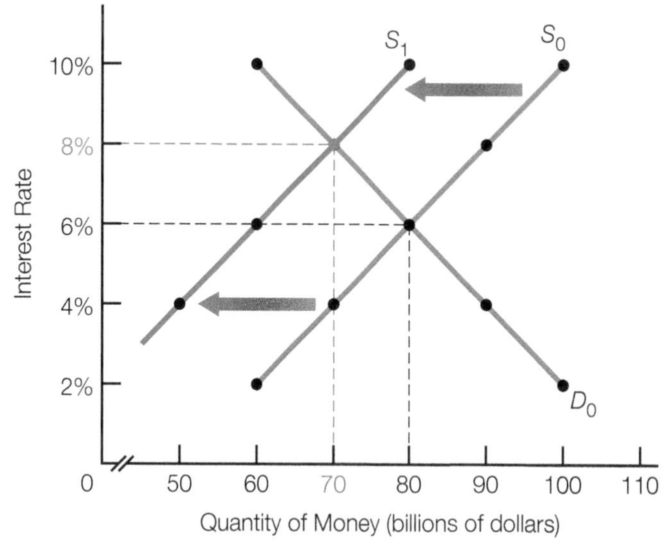

The equilibrium, market-clearing interest rate rises to 8 percent — the new rate at which the quantity of money demanded ($70 billion) equals the quantity of money supplied ($70 billion).

Changing Bond Prices to Change Interest Rates

Here is the same story from the bond market perspective. The Bank of Canada is a major player in the bond market. When the Bank of Canada buys bonds, it causes a big increase in the demand for bonds. When the Bank of Canada sells bonds, it causes a big increase in the supply of bonds.

Buying Bonds Increases the Price of Bonds When the Bank of Canada buys large quantities of bonds on the bond market, the demand for bonds increases. This causes the price of bonds to rise. Bond prices and interest rates are inversely related. (To recall why, review section 9.3.) A rise in the price of bonds decreases the interest rate on bonds. By buying bonds, the Banks of Canada drives the interest rate down. In the example in Figure 11.3, the interest rate falls from 6 percent to 4 percent.

NOTE
When the Bank of Canada buys bonds, the increased demand for bonds raises bond prices and lowers interest rates.

Selling Bonds Decreases the Price of Bonds   When the Bank of Canada sells large quantities of bonds on the bond market, the supply of bonds increases. This causes the price of bonds to fall. Bond prices and interest rates are inversely related. A fall in the price of bonds increases the interest rate on bonds. By selling bonds, the Bank of Canada drives the interest rate up. In the example in Figure 11.4, the interest rate rises from 6 percent to 8 percent.

NOTE
When the Bank of Canada sells bonds, the increased supply of bonds lowers bond prices and raises interest rates.

Interest Rates Move Together (Mostly)

The Bank of Canada conducts open market operations, buying or selling bonds, to change the overnight rate. Most other interest rates change at the same time.

prime rate   the interest rate on loans to lowest-risk corporate borrowers

The overnight rate only affects banks. But the **prime rate**, the interest rate that banks charge to their best, lowest-risk corporate borrowers, equals the overnight rate plus 2 percent. In August 2014, when the overnight loans rate was 1 percent, the prime lending rate was 3 percent.

Other short-run interest rates for consumer loans, variable rate mortgages, savings accounts, and short-term bonds also change with changes to the overnight rate.

Figure 11.5 shows the values for four interest rates in Canada between 1979 and 2013. The overnight rate, the prime rate, and the rate on three-month government Treasury bills (the most common short-term bond) all move up and down together. The fourth, the 10-year government bond rate, is not directly linked to the over night rate.

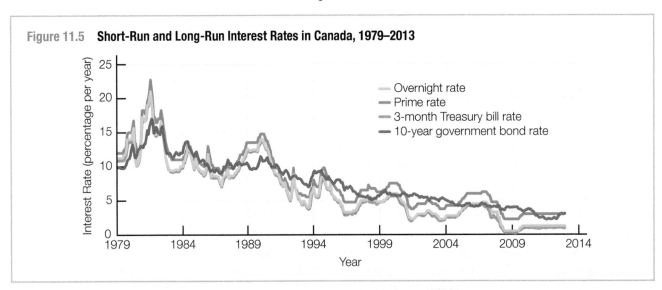

Figure 11.5   **Short-Run and Long-Run Interest Rates in Canada, 1979–2013**

The interest rate in Figure 11.5 for long-run 10-year government bonds (in red) is different. Long-run interest rates, for government and corporate bonds of 10–30 years, tend to be higher than short-run rates because longer-run bonds are riskier. The longer the time to pay back the loan, the more that can go wrong. Investors require a greater reward for forgoing liquidity for so long. Long-run interest rates also do not fluctuate as much as short-run interest rates, because expectations about the long run are not as volatile as short-run expectations. Long-run rates are set in the bond market, not by central banks.

Now that you understand how the Bank of Canada uses monetary policy to change interest rates, let's look more closely at how interest rates can help maintain Say's Law and affect the key macroeconomic outcomes of inflation, real GDP, and unemployment.

1. In your words, define the overnight rate. What is the relationship between the overnight rate, the prime rate, and other interest rates?

2. Tell the bond market story that explains how the Bank of Canada uses open market operations to lower or raise interest rates. Point form is fine.

3. How might the overnight rate affect your decision to make a big purchase on credit now or to wait?

MyEconLab

For answers to these Refresh Questions, visit MyEconLab.

Driving with the Bank of Canada: Transmission Mechanisms

11.3

Trace the effects of interest rate changes on aggregate demand, inflation, real GDP, and unemployment.

When you step on the gas while driving a car, power from the engine travels through the transmission to turn the wheels to make the car go faster. When the Bank of Canada wants to accelerate the economy, it uses open market operations to lower interest rates. The effects of lower interest rates travel through increased spending to increase aggregate demand.

While cars have different gas and brake pedals, the brake for monetary policy is just the accelerator in reverse. To slow the economy down, the Bank of Canada uses open market operations to raise interest rates. The effects of higher interest rates travel through decreased spending to decrease aggregate demand.

Turning the Wheels of Aggregate Demand

The effects of monetary policy work through *aggregate demand* to speed up or slow down the economy.

Remember your mantra from Chapters 6 and 8. Planned spending on aggregate demand equals $C + I + G + X - IM$. Aggregate demand is the sum of planned consumer spending (C), business investment spending (I), government spending on products and services (G), and net exports ($X - IM$). To see exactly where interest rates affect aggregate demand, let's return to Figure 6.7, which is reproduced on the next page as Figure 11.6.

The paths in Figure 11.6 are like a winding mountain road, full of turns and twists, tracing the flows of income through input markets (on the right) and spending through output markets (in the middle). Two main paths transmit the effects of interest rates to aggregate demand.

Domestic Effects of Interest Rates   The domestic path, within Canada, is highlighted in red. It starts with the banking system, where the Bank of Canada sets short-run interest rates. Interest rates affect business borrowing (at the bottom) and consumer borrowing (at the top), and then business investment spending (I) and consumer spending (C) (see Chapter 9).

▲ This economist is using his own special mantra to gain peace and harmony. It's the mantra you should also learn by heart to better understand economic harmony.

International Effects of Interest Rates   The international path, from the rest of the world (R.O.W), is highlighted in blue. It also starts with the banking system, where the Bank of Canada sets short-run interest rates. Interest rates affect the value of the Canadian dollar, which is not shown on this diagram. As explained in Chapter 10, changes in the exchange rate affect the prices that the rest of the world pays for Canadian exports (X) and the prices that Canadians pay for imports (IM).

Looking Inside the Transmissions   Figure 11.6 is missing many of the details from both the domestic and international transmission of the effects of interest rates. Fortunately, Chapters 9 and 10 already have detailed diagrams of the missing links in the transmission mechanisms. Let's return to those diagrams to complete the explanation of how the effects of monetary policy are transmitted to the wheels of aggregate demand.

Figure 11.6   Enlarged GDP Circular Flow of Income and Spending ($) with Banking System

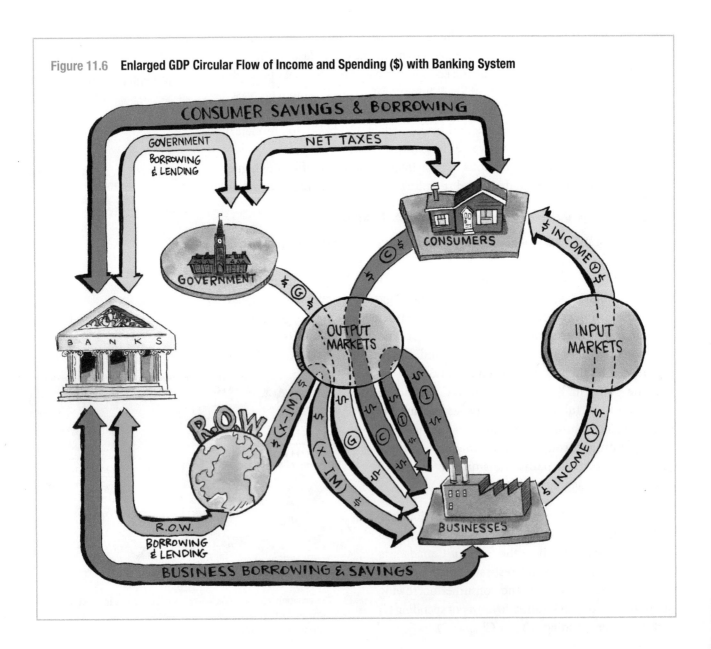

Domestic Monetary Transmission Mechanism: Borrowing and Spending

The details of the domestic monetary transmission mechanism are shown in Figure 11.7, which is the same as Figure 9.7 but with the Bank of Canada added at the top.

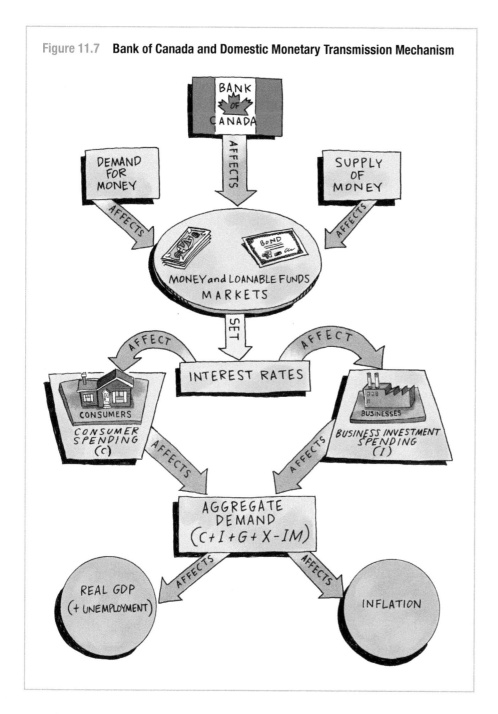

Figure 11.7 Bank of Canada and Domestic Monetary Transmission Mechanism

The Bank of Canada uses open market operations to intervene in the money and loanable funds markets to steer short-run interest rates to match its target rate.

Lower interest rates reduce the cost of interest-sensitive purchases that require loans (houses, cars, major appliances), so consumers spend more (*C*). Business investment spending (*I*) is heavily financed by borrowing and therefore very interest sensitive. Lower interest rates make investment spending cheaper, so businesses spend more on new factories and equipment.

Lower Interest Rates Are a Positive Aggregate Demand Shock The domestic effect of lower interest rates increases aggregate demand and accelerates the economy. Remember your mantra: Aggregate demand equals $C + I + G + X - IM$. Increases in *C* and *I* both increase aggregate demand. A positive demand shock causes increased real GDP, decreased unemployment, and rising inflation (Chapter 8).

Higher Interest Rates Are a Negative Aggregate Demand Shock Higher interest rates increase the cost of borrowing, decreasing *C* and *I*, and decreasing aggregate demand. Higher interest rates are a negative demand shock and cause decreased real GDP, increased unemployment, and decreasing inflation or deflation (Chapter 8).

We must add the effects of the international transmission mechanism to these domestic effects to get the net effect of monetary policy.

International Transmission Mechanisms: Exchange Rate Effects

The foreign exchange market, which determines the value of the Canadian dollar, is not on Figures 11.6 or 11.7. When the Bank of Canada uses open market operations to change short-run interest rates, the Canadian interest rate differential with the rest of the world changes. A fall in interest rates decreases the Canadian interest rate differential. This causes the Canadian dollar to depreciate on the foreign exchange market. A rise in interest rates increases the Canadian interest rate differential, causing the Canadian dollar to appreciate on the foreign exchange market.

The value of the Canadian dollar, in turn, affects the cost of exports for the R.O.W., and imports for Canadians. For example, if the Bank of Canada lowers the target interest rate, the Canadian dollar depreciates in value. A lower Canadian dollar makes Canadian exports cheaper for customers in the rest of the world. When Canadian exports become less expensive, non-Canadians buy more of them. A lower Canadian dollar makes imports from the rest of the world more expensive for Canadian customers. Canadians then buy fewer imports and more Canadian products and services.

The details of the international transmission mechanisms are in Figure 11.8, which is the same as Figure 10.10 but with the Bank of Canada added at the top.

Figure 11.8 **Bank of Canada and International Transmission Mechanisms**

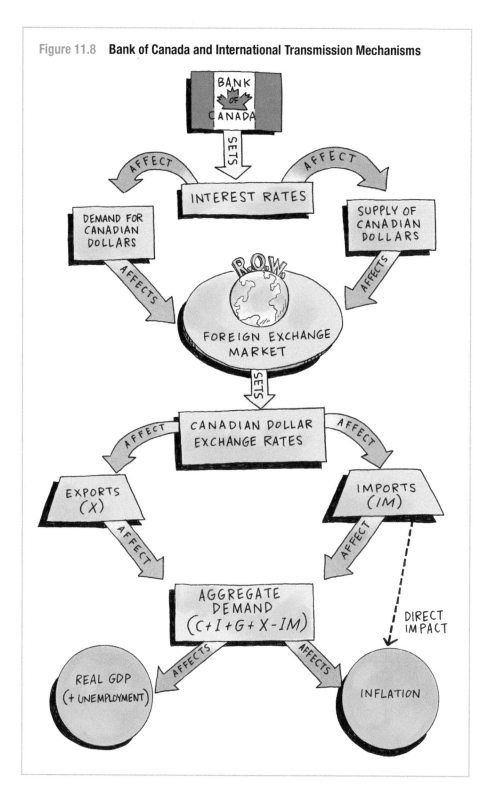

Depreciating Canadian Dollar Is a Positive Aggregate Demand Shock The international effect of lower interest rates, just like the domestic effect, increases aggregate demand and accelerates the economy. Both the increase in exports (X) and the decrease in imports (IM) increase aggregate demand. Remember your mantra: Aggregate demand equals $C + I + G + X - IM$. This increase in net exports ($X - IM$) is a positive aggregate demand shock, causing increased real GDP, decreased unemployment, and rising inflation.

Appreciating Canadian Dollar Is a Negative Aggregate Demand Shock

Higher interest rates increase the Canadian interest rate differential, causing the Canadian dollar to appreciate on the foreign exchange market. The higher exchange rate makes exports (X) more expensive for the R.O.W. and imports (IM) cheaper for Canadians. Net exports (X − IM) decrease, decreasing aggregate demand. The appreciating Canadian dollar is a negative demand shock, causing decreased real GDP, increased unemployment, and decreasing inflation or deflation.

NOTE

Depreciating Canadian dollar is a positive aggregate demand shock.

Appreciating Canadian dollar is a negative aggregate demand shock.

All Together Now: Reinforcing Transmission Mechanisms

The domestic and international transmission mechanisms both work in the same direction, reinforcing each other.

Lowering Interest Rates to Increase Aggregate Demand   Open market operations by the Bank of Canada to lower interest rates increase aggregate demand. This is an appropriate monetary policy for an economy that is predicted to be in a recessionary gap 18 to 24 months in the future. If the predicted inflation rate is below the Bank of Canada's target inflation rate of 2 percent, and real GDP is predicted to be below potential GDP with cyclical unemployment, then lower interest rates help steer the economy toward potential GDP, full employment, and stable prices.

Figure 11.9 shows the aggregate demand effects of monetary policy to lower interest rates. Suppose the economy is in a short-run equilibrium where aggregate demand (AD_0) intersects short-run aggregate supply (SAS_0) at a real GDP of $1400 billion. Potential GDP, shown by the long-run aggregate supply curve (LAS_0), is $1500 billion. The economy is in a recessionary gap, with real GDP $100 billion below potential GDP.

When the Bank of Canada lowers interest rates, this causes a positive demand shock. Aggregate demand shifts rightward to AD_1. The new equilibrium is at the intersection of AD_1, SAS_0, and LAS_0. As real GDP increases to potential GDP of $1500 billion, unemployment decreases. Average prices rise from 110 to 120, increasing the inflation rate.

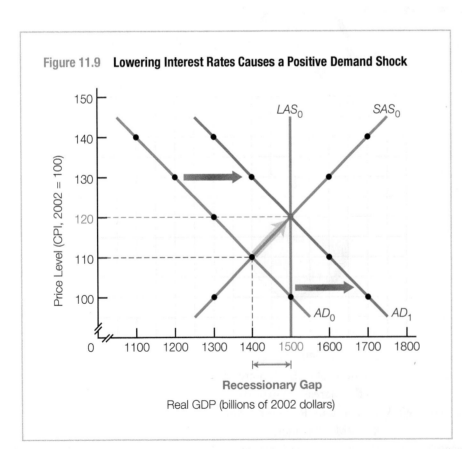

Figure 11.9   Lowering Interest Rates Causes a Positive Demand Shock

Raising Interest Rates to Decrease Aggregate Demand   Open market operations by the Bank of Canada to raise interest rates decrease aggregate demand. This is an appropriate monetary policy for an economy that is predicted to be in an inflationary gap 18–24 months in the future. If the predicted inflation rate is above the Bank of Canada's target inflation rate of 2 percent, and real GDP is predicted to be above potential GDP with an unemployment rate below the natural rate of unemployment, then higher interest rates help steer the economy toward potential GDP, full employment, and stable prices.

Figure 11.10 shows the aggregate demand effects of monetary policy to raise interest rates. Suppose the economy is in a short-run equilibrium where aggregate demand (AD_0) intersects short-run aggregate supply (SAS_0) at a real GDP of $1600 billion. Potential GDP, shown by the long-run aggregate supply curve (LAS_0), is $1500 billion. The economy is in an inflationary gap, with real GDP $100 billion above potential GDP.

When the Bank of Canada raises interest rates, this causes a negative demand shock. Aggregate demand shifts leftward to AD_1. The new equilibrium is at the intersection of AD_1, SAS_0, and LAS_0. As real GDP decreases back to potential GDP of $1500 billion, unemployment increases back to the natural rate. Average prices fall from 130 to 120, decreasing the inflation rate.

The time lags inherent in the transmission mechanism make it difficult to conduct monetary policy. In particular, these long time lags mean that central banks must be forward-looking in their policy decisions.

— Bank of Canada

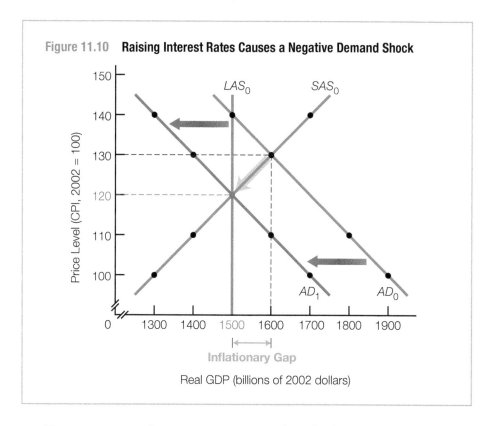

Figure 11.10   Raising Interest Rates Causes a Negative Demand Shock

Figure 11.11 on the next page is a good study device summarizing the combined effects of monetary policy from domestic and international transmission mechanisms.

Figure 11.11　Transmission Effects of Monetary Policy

	Monetary Policy	
	Lower Interest Rates	Raise Interest Rates
Output Gap	**Recessionary Gap**	**Inflationary Gap**
Impact on Economy		
Business Investment (I) and Consumption (C)	Increase	Decrease
Exchange Rate	Depreciates	Appreciates
Net Exports ($X - IM$)	Increase	Decrease
Aggregate Demand	Positive Demand Shock	Negative Demand Shock
Unemployment	Decreases	Increases
Inflation	Increases	Decreases

> *Central bankers are often accused of fighting demons that are not present. The problem is that if central bankers delayed their policy response until inflation actually appeared in the data, it would be too late to have the desired impact. Being forward-looking means anticipating where the demons will surface and acting in a pre-emptive manner.*
>
> — *Professor Christopher Ragan, McGill University*

Not a Popularity Contest　When the Bank of Canada's predictions are right, monetary policy keeps the economy moving steadily on the road to potential GDP and the policy objectives of price stability, growth in living standards, and full employment.

Monetary policy is not always politically popular. Consumers and businesses are usually pleased when the Bank of Canada lowers interest rates to fight a recession. But when economic growth speeds up, with more jobs, more profits, and more income, the Bank of Canada raises interest rates — raising the cost of mortgages, car loans, and business borrowing. People complain, especially because they can't see any inflation in the present. But the Bank of Canada is concerned that, 18 to 24 months in the future, continuing growth will cause inflation to rise beyond the target range. One central banker describes his job as "taking away the punch bowl just when the party is getting started." Not a popular move. But successful monetary policy is about moderation — accelerating the economy when it is slowing, and braking the economy when it is speeding up.

Refresh 11.3

MyEconLab

For answers to these Refresh Questions, visit MyEconLab.

1. In point form, show how a Bank of Canada open market operation selling bonds affects interest rates, domestic aggregate demand, real GDP, unemployment, and inflation.

2. What is the connection between the value of the Canadian dollar (the exchange rate) and monetary policy's impact on the Canadian economy?

3. Who benefits when the Bank of Canada lowers interest rates? Who benefits when interest rates rise? Explain how each policy could directly affect your life and your consumer decisions.

Transmission Breakdowns: Balance Sheet Recessions and Monetary Policy 11.4

Monetary policy succeeds when consumers and businesses respond to changing interest rates with changing spending patterns, and banks adjust loans and demand deposits when reserves change. But the macroeconomic players don't always cooperate, and monetary policy can break down, as it did during the Global Financial Crisis.

When the U.S. real estate bubble burst in 2008, the value of mortgage-backed securities plunged. Investors and banks, holding suddenly almost worthless assets, were forced to sell other assets to meet their debts. Panicked selling led to bank failures, business bankruptcies, and plunging stock market values. Real GDP started falling, and unemployment rose to over 10 percent in the United States and in Canada. The Global Financial Crisis had begun.

Recessions are often triggered by a decrease in business investment spending, falling net exports, or rising interest rates. Not the Global Financial Crisis. The recession of 2008–2009 is also referred to as a *balance sheet recession* — a contraction caused by the collapse of asset prices. A balance sheet — for businesses, banks, or individuals — shows assets on one side (what you own or earn) and debts or liabilities on the other side (what you owe or spend). When the value of the assets you own falls, you need to cut back on what you spend or owe to restore balance. This is a problem for monetary policy.

Central banks around the world, including the U.S. Federal Reserve and the Bank of Canada, responded to the Global Financial Crisis as you would expect from reading this chapter. With a recessionary gap opening, they used open market operations to buy bonds and lower the target interest rate, hoping generally lower interest rates would stimulate borrowing, spending, and aggregate demand.

When the Bank of Canada changes its interest rate target, it almost always does so slowly, 25 basis points (a basis point is one-hundredth of 1 percent, so 25 basis points is 0.25 percent) at a time, and on only eight dates a year. Bankers have a justifiable reputation for being conservative in all ways — wearing conservative dark blue suits and taking conservative, moderate actions. Slow and steady, the bankers say, wins the race and keeps the economics car running smoothly and safely.

Stepping on the Gas?

The Global Financial Crisis led the Bank of Canada to dramatically change its driving habits. The threatened collapse of the banking system was so serious, and fears of repeating the Great Depression of the 1930s were so real, that central bankers abandoned their conservatism and stepped on the accelerator as hard as they could.

From a target overnight rate of 4 percent at the start of 2008, the Bank of Canada began aggressively cutting interest rates. There were unusually large 50 basis point cuts in March 2008, April 2008, and October 2008, lowering the overnight rate to 2.5 percent. Just two weeks later in October (breaking the eight-dates-a-year tradition) the Bank of Canada cut another 25 basis points, followed by an unprecedented 75 basis-point cut in December 2008, bringing the overnight rate down to 1.5 percent. These actions were the equivalent of a conservative banker wearing a pink polka dot suit!

In the first four months of 2009, the Bank of Canada cut another 125 basis points, dropping the overnight rate almost to zero — to 0.25 percent. The Bank of Canada kept the overnight rate at 0.25 percent until mid-2010.

Explain what blocks monetary transmission mechanisms, and how quantitative easing can overcome a balance sheet recession.

NOTE
In a balance sheet recession, individuals and businesses focus on paying down debt and are reluctant to borrow or spend. Even when monetary policy lowers interest rates, the economy remains in recession.

Almost Free Money   The corresponding prime rate — the lowest rate charged to businesses or consumers — beginning in April 2009 was 2.25 percent. The prime rate, set 200 basis points above the overnight rate, is a nominal interest rate — it is not adjusted for inflation. The realized real interest rate (see section 7.3) adjusts the nominal interest rate to remove the effects of inflation.

$$\text{Real Interest Rate} = \text{Nominal Interest Rate} - \text{Inflation Rate}$$

With a nominal prime interest rate of 2.25 percent and an inflation rate of about 2 percent, that meant that from mid-2009 to mid-2010, the real interest rate was 0.25 percent, close to zero.

$$\text{Real Interest Rate} = 2.25 \text{ percent} - 2 \text{ percent}$$

$$\text{Real Interest Rate} = 0.25 \text{ percent}$$

The real rate of interest — what you give up in purchasing power to "buy" money — is more important than the nominal rate of interest for making smart saving and investing decisions. Since the interest rate is the price of money, borrowing money was almost free for about a year!

Despite almost free money, consumer and business borrowing and spending did not increase as the Bank of Canada had hoped. The Bank of Canada stepped hard on the gas, but power was not transmitted to the wheels of aggregate demand. What accounts for this transmission breakdown?

Paying Down Debt Instead of Spending: Consumers and Businesses

2009 was a bad year for balance sheets and economies around the world, including Canada's.

Consumers   Many consumers were unemployed in 2009, and those lucky enough to have work were worried about losing their jobs. Plunging stock market and asset prices wiped out much of the value of people's assets — savings, pensions, and retirement accounts. Even though you could borrow money and spend it for almost nothing, there were hardly any borrowers.

Pessimistic *expectations* about the future were more important than lower interest rates for determining consumers' spending and saving choices. Instead of responding to lower interest rates by saving less and borrowing and spending more, as the Bank of Canada had hoped, consumers did just the opposite. Households cut back on their spending and starting paying off their debts (reducing liabilities) and saving more (increasing assets).

Businesses   Businesses reacted similarly. Business investment decisions depend on the cost of borrowing, but also on expectations about future profitability. In the depths of the Global Financial Crisis, pessimistic expectations had more effect than cheaper money. With fewer valuable assets on their balance sheets, business investment spending decreased, rather than increasing with lower interest rates as the Bank of Canada hoped.

Money as a Store of Value   Both consumers and businesses used money as a store of value during the Global Financial Crisis. With fundamental uncertainty about the future and pessimistic expectations, consumers, businesses, and investors chose the safety of money over both business investment spending and investing in bonds. As Keynes said (Chapter 9), "our desire to hold money is a barometer of our distrust of…the future. … The possession of money lulls our disquietude." Money provides a way to *not* spend, blocking the transmission mechanisms. The loanable funds market, where businesses borrow to finance investment spending, failed to match spending to savings. With pessimistic expectations, consumers and businesses poured their assets into money, blocking the domestic monetary transmission mechanism.

Government was the only macroeconomic player who spent a lot during the Global Financial Crisis. We will discuss government spending in Chapter 12.

Piling Up Reserves Instead of Lending: Banks

The Bank of Canada's monetary policy — buying bonds from individuals and banks — pumped lots of cash into chartered banks' reserves. In pursuing profits, banks would normally use the new reserves to make more loans, create more demand deposits, and increase the money supply.

But banks were also suffering from falling asset prices, desperately trying to repair their balance sheets by increasing assets. Banks held on to new cash reserves to protect against the growing number of borrowers who were going bankrupt and defaulting on — not paying back — their loans. Chartered banks did not increase their lending as the Bank of Canada hoped. They kept the extra cash reserves as assets. Banks chose prudence over profits. Pessimistic expectations about loan repayments and economic conditions had more effect than the attraction of potential profits from new loans.

Banks in Canada and the United States hesitated to lend money, except to the most creditworthy customers. In the U.S., banks refused to renew mortgages, even for homeowners who had never missed a mortgage payment and had perfect credit histories.

Ironically, in the U.S. housing boom that led up to the 2008–2009 recession, banks chose profits over prudence, lending money even to those who were not credit-worthy (sub-prime mortgages). Those loose lending practices helped create the housing bubble that triggered the Global Financial Crisis. After the housing bubble burst, banks chose prudence over profits, and the restrictive lending practices, which limited spending, made the recession deeper and longer lasting. The banking system contributed to the cycle of boom and bust.

Flooding the System with Money: Quantitative Easing and the Quantity Theory of Money

When the usual monetary policy tools of open market operations did not restore spending during the Global Financial Crisis, central banks did not give up. The U.S Federal Reserve Bank (the "Fed"), headed by then Chairman Ben Bernanke (*Time Magazine's* Person of the Year — see Economics Out There on page 333), implemented an additional, more controversial policy tool.

It is this flight into cash that makes interest-rate policy such an uncertain agent of recovery…. That is why Keynes did not think that cutting the central bank's interest rate would necessarily — and certainly not quickly — [stimulate spending]. This was his main argument for the use of government [spending] to fight a depression.

— Robert Skidelsky (Keynes's biographer)

Quantitative Easing

Quantitative Easing   Bernanke decided to use a more powerful tool from his monetary policy toolbox — quantitative easing. **Quantitative easing** floods the financial system with money by having the central bank buy high-risk bonds, mortgages, and assets directly from banks. By eliminating these liabilities from bank balance sheets and replacing them with cash assets, banks are in a better position to make new loans and new demand deposits, and increase the quantity of money. Quantitative easing succeeded in stabilizing the banking system and had some success increasing lending. But this tool carries risks of inflation further on down the road.

Quantitative easing is similar to open market operations where the central bank buys bonds and pays with cash, which increases bank reserves. The difference is that the central bank is not buying government bonds, but riskier, private commercial assets directly from banks. This increases cash reserves in the banking system, allowing banks to increase loans, demand deposits, and the quantity of money. It produces the same result as open market bond purchases, but the central bank assumes more risk than with government bond purchases.

When coming to the aid of banks with troubled balance sheets, central banks around the world, including the U.S. Federal Reserve and the Bank of Canada, played the role of lender of last resort (see section 9.2). The Bank of Canada's policy as lender of last resort states: "In conditions of severe and unusual stress on the financial system…the Bank has authority to provide liquidity through outright purchases of securities issued by any Canadian or foreign entities, including non-financial firms." The Bank of Canada used quantitative easing to provide cash (liquidity) to chartered banks to help avoid runs on banks and other difficulties in order "to avoid damaging the interests of unsecured creditors" — innocent depositors like you or me.

Inflation Risks   The quantity theory of money (see section 7.4) is the key to understanding the inflation risks from quantitative easing or open market operations.

The quantity theory of money states that an increase in the quantity of money causes an equal percentage increase in the inflation rate. The quantity theory is represented as

$$M \times V = P \times Q$$

> *Inflation is always and everywhere a monetary phenomenon.*
>
> — *Milton Friedman,*
> *1976 Nobel Prize in Economics*

where M is the quantity of money, V is the velocity of money, P is the price level measured by the Consumer Price Index, and Q is real GDP.

If (and these are big ifs) velocity (V) is constant and *if* real GDP (Q) is constant at potential GDP, then any increase in the money supply (M) causes an equal percentage increase in the inflation rate (P). Or looking at it from the other direction — if there is an increase in the inflation rate, there must be an accompanying increase in the quantity of money.

Simply put, the quantity theory of money says, "printing money causes inflation." When central banks buy bonds in open market operations and pay with cash, it is similar to printing money. Chartered banks get additional reserves, and can create new loans and demand deposits — part of M1+ — which are money.

If (I said *if* would be an important word) the economy were at potential GDP instead of in a deep recession, then these monetary policies would be inflationary. But when real GDP is below potential GDP, increases in the money supply can lower interest rates and stimulate borrowing and spending. Some of the increase in the money supply on the left side of the equal sign increases real GDP (Q) on the right side of the equal sign, rather than increasing the price level (P). Monetary policy can help real GDP grow.

The tricky part is what happens when the economy approaches potential GDP. At that point, any additional money in the banking system will be inflationary. Central banks know that there will come a time when they have to step on the brake ("take away the punch bowl just when the party is getting started"), selling previously purchased bonds and assets.

When chartered banks buy back those bonds and assets from the central bank with cash, reserves leave the banking system and go to the central bank. The decrease in reserves decreases the money supply and raises interest rates, slowing the economy and reducing the risk of inflation. The timing of the monetary "brake" is crucial. If the central bank steps on the brake too soon, it risks halting the recovery. If it waits too long, it risks inflation. Paul Masson, a professor at University of Toronto and former advisor at the Bank of Canada says, "I am not confident, given the lags in monetary policy, that they can exactly get it right."

The risk of getting it wrong can be seen in Zimbabwe (Chapter 5, page 121). There, the central bank printed money recklessly on behalf of the government to finance government spending, and the result was hyperinflation.

Economics *Out There*

Ben Bernanke is *Time Magazine*'s 2009 Person of the Year

Mark Wilson/Getty Images

▲ Ben Bernanke, former Chairman of the U.S. Federal Reserve Bank, is given credit by many for preventing the Global Financial Crisis from causing a new Great Depression.

Ben Bernanke's leadership as Chairman of the U.S. Federal Reserve Bank is widely credited with saving the world from depression. That accomplishment earned him *Time Magazine*'s 2009 Award as Person of the Year.

In an interview, Bernanke said, "We came very, very close to a depression...The markets were in anaphylactic shock. I'm not happy with where we are, but it's a lot better than where we could be."

Many central banks followed Bernanke's lead in implementing the innovative policy of quantitative easing. Mervyn King, Governor of the Bank of England, described the policy this way: "People always talk about central banks taking away the punch bowl, but when demand was falling so rapidly, Ben had to put the punch bowl on the table and say, 'Let's party!'"

Bernanke, an economics professor at Princeton University, had studied the monetary policy blunders of the Great Depression, and "was determined not be the Fed Chairman who presided over Depression 2.0."

The story that captivated Bernanke as a child was about a town with many shoe factories that closed during the Depression, leaving the community so poor that its children went barefoot. "I kept asking, 'Why didn't they just open the factories and make the kids shoes?'" he recalls.

Bernanke has devoted his career to questions like that: the same question that is posed at the start of Chapter 5 of this book — "Are your smart choices smart for all?".

Source: http://www.time.com/time/specials/packages/article/0,28804,1946375_1947251_1947520,00.html

Driving with an Unpredictable Transmission: Timing Is Everything

Even when all is going well, the timing of monetary policy — when to step on the accelerator or the brake — is difficult because central banks have to predict the impact up to two years in advance.

But when macroeconomic players resist borrowing, spending, and lending, and instead choose the security of money and savings, monetary policy becomes even more challenging. Balance sheet recessions cause transmission problems for monetary policy, making it harder to steer the economy toward recovery.

Facing falling asset values on their balances sheets, consumers, businesses, and banks make individually smart choices to resist borrowing, spending, and lending. But those individual smart choices did not add up to smart choices for the economy as a whole.

Refresh 11.4

MyEconLab

For answers to these Refresh Questions, visit MyEconLab.

1. Explain how consumers, businesses, and banks can block the monetary transmission mechanism.

2. Why might quantitative easing lead to inflation?

3. In a balance sheet recession, explain how the individual smart choices made by consumers, businesses, and banks do not necessarily add up to smart choices for the economy as a whole.

11.5 Who's Driving? Anchoring Inflation Expectations

Explain how inflation rate targeting by an independent central bank anchors expectations, helps market economies function, and gets economists to agree.

The Governor of the Bank of Canada has more power to influence economic outcomes than almost any other Canadian. In a democracy like Canada's, it is unusual for an unelected official to be that powerful. The relationship between the Bank of Canada and our elected Parliament contains a classic Canadian compromise between government authority to act and accountability to voters. And speaking of compromises, the "Yes — Markets Self-Adjust, so Hands-Off" and "No — Markets Fail Often, so Hands-On" camps largely agree on the need for a central bank to prevent runaway inflation expectations and to help markets operate well.

Is the Bank or the Government of Canada Driving?

The Bank of Canada's inflation control target range is 1 to 3 percent. This specific policy objective is set by agreement between the Government of Canada and the Bank of Canada. But the Bank of Canada *alone* sets the monetary policy for achieving that target. The Minister of Finance — for the government — and the Governor of the Bank of Canada jointly decide on the destination of Canada's economic car, but the Governor gets to drive.

If the government and the Governor cannot agree on the policy objectives, the government can legally direct the Bank to accept the government's directions, forcing the Governor to resign. Investors and markets like predictability, so governments do not like to quarrel publicly with a Governor of the Bank of Canada. A disagreement over monetary policy would cause stock market values to fall and investors to lose confidence in the stability of the financial system. "Who is in charge?" they would ask. This gives the Bank of Canada considerable independence, even though it is ultimately accountable to Parliament: a classic Canadian compromise between authority to act and accountability to the voters.

The Coyne Affair   The only Governor forced to resign was James Coyne in 1961. Coyne was appointed Governor of the Bank of Canada in 1955. In 1957, he was confronted by a new finance minister after John Diefenbaker was elected prime minister. When the new finance minister and Coyne disagreed about monetary policy objectives, Coyne was forced to resign in what has come to be known as the "Coyne Affair." Coyne's successor, Louis Rasminsky, put the current agreement in place for government–Bank relations.

Independence Matters   The independence of our central bank has important advantages. The hyperinflation in Zimbabwe, like hyperinflations that have occurred elsewhere in the world, is usually a result of the government controlling the central bank and ordering it to print money to finance government spending. That kind of government influence cannot happen in Canada.

NOTE
The Bank of Canada has considerable independence, but ultimately is accountable to Parliament.

The independence of the Bank of Canada prevents government influences on monetary policy decisions that are clearly not in the best interests of the country.

Inflation–Unemployment Trade-offs and Expectations

Inflation rate targeting is now the only specific objective agreed to by the Government of Canada and the Bank of Canada. Now, when the Bank of Canada mentions the broader objectives in the 1935 *Bank of Canada Act* like "solid economic performance" and "rising living standards," it states that those objectives will be achieved by "keeping inflation low and stable."

There is no longer much controversy over this single-minded focus on inflation targeting, even though the original Phillips Curve suggests lower inflation is often tied to higher unemployment.

Central banks in other countries do not have this single focus on inflation. The U.S. *Federal Reserve Act* lists the Fed's (U.S. central bank) specific objectives as "maximum employment, stable prices, and moderate long-term interest rates."

But by focusing only on inflation-rate targeting since 1991, the Bank of Canada has succeeded not only in keeping inflation within the target range, but in promoting rising living standards and movement toward full employment. There are two important reasons behind the Bank's success. First, the target anchors expectations about inflation — everyone knows what to expect. Second, the target improves the predictability of prices, making smart choices easier for all macroeconomic players.

Speeding Is Easier than Braking, So Anchor Expectations   The original Philips Curve trade-off between inflation and unemployment works as long as people's expectations of inflation do not change. Using monetary policy to lower interest rates and accelerate aggregate demand, a central bank can steer toward lower unemployment and higher inflation. But once higher inflation occurs, the gas pedal can stick to the floor — runaway inflation — because of changing expectations.

If people begin expecting inflation, it creates a self-fulfilling prophecy. Consider this scenario: You are expecting the inflation rate next year to be 4 percent, and your employment contract is up for renewal. How much of a raise will you ask for?

If you are like most people, you will be thinking, "The cost of living next year will be 4 percent higher. Unless I get at least a 4 percent raise, my income won't keep pace with the rising cost of living. My standard of living will go down. I'd better ask for at least a 4 percent raise."

Once expectations of inflation begin, many people think the same way. Businesses expect higher prices for inputs, and set output prices higher to protect their profits. Banks expect inflation, and increase nominal interest rates on loans to protect the real rate of interest they will receive. When workers, businesses, and banks expect inflation, they reasonably try to protect themselves by pushing up wages, prices of output, and interest rates. This creates self-fulfilling expectations — by reacting to the expectation of inflation we may help cause it.

Once inflation begins, expectations of higher inflation rates keep rising, creating a vicious cycle that, if not broken, runs the risk of spiralling out of control. Dramatically higher oil prices in the 1970s caused a negative supply shock (see section 8.4). Most central banks, including the Bank of Canada, mistook the resulting contraction for a negative demand shock. They increased the money supply and lowered interest rates, trying to increase aggregate demand. But the decrease in aggregate supply from rising input prices combined with increased aggregate demand from expansionary monetary policy created rising prices. This led to greater expectations of continued inflation, which led to higher inflation in the 1980s. Once inflation expectations rose and central banks allowed the quantity of money to increase, higher rates of inflation were associated with higher levels of unemployment. The simple trade-off between higher inflation and lower unemployment that the original Phillips Curve showed for the 1950s and early 1960s no longer existed. Look back at Figure 7.12 on p. 192.

VICIOUS CYCLE

I EXPECT INFLATION NEXT YEAR.

I DEMAND A WAGE RAISE TO COMPENSATE FOR MY EXPECTATIONS OF INFLATION.

BUSINESSES RAISE PRICES OF PRODUCTS/SERVICES TO COVER INCREASED WAGE COSTS.

HIGHER PRICES OF PRODUCTS/SERVICES PROVE TO ME THAT PRICES ARE RISING AND MIGHT CONTINUE RISING.

▲ Expectations of inflation can help cause inflation.

In order to break inflation expectations, a former Governor of the Bank of Canada, Gerald Bouey, and former Federal Reserve Chairman Paul Volcker decreased the money supply and raised interest rates dramatically. The prime lending rate in Canada peaked at over 19 percent in 1981. The result was a severe recession. Figure 11.12 shows that this succeeded in bringing down actual inflation (as the quantity theory of money predicts), and expectations of inflation also fell. Notice also that since inflation targeting by the Bank of Canada began in 1991, inflation has stayed within the target range of 1 to 3 percent.

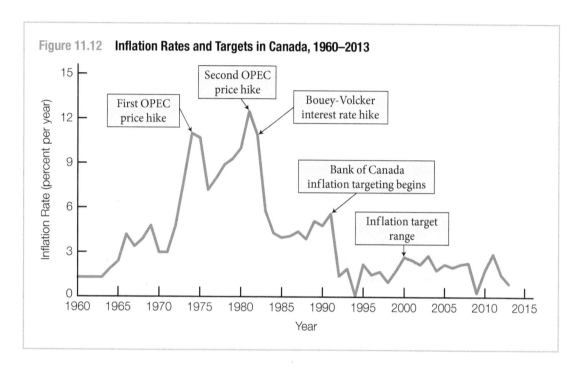

Figure 11.12 **Inflation Rates and Targets in Canada, 1960–2013**

Once inflation expectations start, people and businesses do not like settling for raises that are lower than the expected inflation rate. Inflation expectations go up quickly and easily, but breaking (and braking) inflation expectations is slow and painful. It takes a long period of recession, with unemployment and depressed business sales, before everyone begins accepting more slowly rising wages and prices. For this reason, most economists and policymakers now agree that it is important to keep inflation rates low, stable, and predictable. An inflation target range accomplishes this by anchoring inflation expectations.

High Inflation Is Unpredictable, Causing Not-Smart Choices High inflation is usually volatile. At higher inflation rates, the speed of price rises becomes unpredictable.

Unpredictable prices are a serious problem for businesses. Producing for output markets takes time. Businesses must first buy inputs, produce products, and then transport them to output markets for sale. Businesses make commitments today for products and services that only come to market in the future. If your business is not sure of a steady supply of inputs at predictable prices, your costs are unpredictable and therefore so are your profits. It is hard to set your own output price, and to know what demand will be like if your customers are paying more for all other products and services.

NOTE
Inflation expectations go up quickly and easily, but come down slowly and painfully.

With unpredictable inflation, when you observe rising market prices, you don't know if the prices reflect increased demand for your output (a good thing) or general inflation (not so good). It is hard to make smart business decisions. Unpredictability creates risk, discourages business investment, and interferes with normal price movements — signals for smart choices — in a market economy. The costs of uncertainty associated with high and unpredictable inflation are important reasons to keep inflation rates low, stable, and predictable.

"Yes, Hands-Off" and "No, Hands-On" Agree! Markets Need a Central Bank

It has been a while since I asked the fundamental macroeconomic question:

> If left alone by government, do the price mechanisms of market economies adjust quickly to maintain steady growth in living standards, full employment, and stable prices?

Normally, there are two answers. The "Yes" camp says markets self-adjust, so government should keep hands off. The "No" camp says markets fail often, so there is a hands-on role for government. But, when it comes to the Bank of Canada's role, there are more agreements between camps than disagreements.

Both camps agree on the need for a government-like player like the Bank of Canada for a market economy to function properly. Both camps see three of the four roles of the Bank of Canada — issuing currency, acting as banker to banks, and acting as a banker to government — largely as the government's role of setting the rules of the road. To gain the benefits of a monetary economy, we must have a banking system with a central bank that controls the rules of the road.

Banks around the world are regulated through rules because they face a trade-off between profits and prudence. Without regulation, banks are tempted to take risks in pursuit of higher and faster profits that might lead to more bank failures. When banks fail, not only do bank owners lose money, but innocent, trusting depositors, who were not involved in the risky loan decisions, also lose their money. The Bank of Canada, by protecting the prudence of the banking system, is protecting investors and depositors.

One of the lessons of the Global Financial Crisis is the need for more government oversight of the financial system, with clearer rules of the road and protection for innocent depositors. While chartered banks are already regulated, many other major financial institutions, for example, the investment banks that created sub-prime mortgage-backed securities, are not.

The Bank of Canada also protects the value of money by keeping inflation low and stable, allowing all markets, not just financial markets, to operate smoothly. Predictable prices mean all macroeconomic players can make smart choices in whatever markets they trade.

On the fourth role of the Bank of Canada — conducting monetary policy — there are some disagreements between the two camps, but there is also a growing consensus around inflation target rules as a compromise.

"Yes, Hands-Off": Rules for Monetary Policy The "Yes — Markets Self-Adjust" believers in Say's Law favour a hands-off role for government. They believe that government failure is more likely than market failure. They support an independent central bank to keep monetary policy out of the hands of government politicians, including finance ministers. To keep the independent central bank as hands-off as possible, the "Yes" camp supports fixed rules for monetary policy, like targets, that leave no discretionary choices for central bankers.

Besides believing that markets quickly adjust to any external shocks, the "Yes, Hands-Off" camp points to the long delays before monetary policy has an effect. Those delays increase the chances that policymakers will get the timing wrong and do more harm than good with discretionary monetary policy. Suppose the central bank, expecting a recession, steps on the gas and lowers interest rates. If the economy is expanding by the time the economic car finally speeds up, the expansionary policy steers the car off the cliff into an inflationary boom that eventually turns into a bust. Better, the "Yes, Hands-Off" camp says, to leave the driving to the flexibility of markets.

Finally, the "Yes, Hands-Off" camp believes that the strongest argument for a hands-off monetary policy is the need to anchor inflationary expectations. Without target rules, politicians may be tempted to allow a higher inflation rate to get lower unemployment. Macroeconomic players would lose confidence in a stable and predictable inflation rate. Once prices start rising, the gas pedal can stick to the floor because of changing expectations, leading to runaway inflation.

"No, Hands-On": Discretion for Monetary Policy The "No — Markets Fail Often" followers of Keynes favour a hands-on role for government. They believe that market failure is more likely than government failure. They are more willing to give government the discretion to set and conduct monetary policy to counter internally generated business cycles.

The "No, Hands-On" camp points to the uncertainty of transmission breakdowns in monetary policy — that a fixed rule for stepping on the interest rate gas or brake will not always produce the same response in the economic car. There needs to be an active driver ready to take the wheel and steer — to make decisions.

Finally, the "No, Hands-On" camp points to the short-run trade-off between inflation and unemployment, arguing that sometimes the cost of keeping inflation low may have too high an opportunity cost — high unemployment, lost production, and economic suffering. Democratically elected politicians, the "No, Hands-On" camp says, should decide on that trade-off.

Economics *Out There*

Should the Bank of Canada Worry about Inflation or Deflation?

While the central bank's inflation target anchors inflationary expectations, deflation has been a bigger risk than inflation since the Global Financial Crisis. Inflation rates have been around 1 percent, at the bottom of the Bank of Canada's inflation target range, and unemployment has remained stubbornly high. Glen Hodgson, Chief Economist of the Conference Board of Canada, argues that "deflation is very dangerous. It depresses aggregate demand and can suck the energy out of an ... economy for decades." With deflation, average prices keep falling. Consumers hold off on buying products and services since they will be cheaper tomorrow. Sales drop and businesses cut back production and employment. Wages fall as the economy contracts and

unemployment increases. Should the Bank of Canada raise its inflation target?

A higher inflation target may avoid the problems of deflation and increase employment, but at the risk of unleashing inflationary expectations. The existing inflation target will contain inflationary expectations, but at the risk of deflation and prolonged unemployment. As Hodgson says "The advantages of a 2-percent inflation anchor ... need to be weighed against the ... risks of deflation ...., raising the inflation target ... may be a reasonable and responsible policy compromise." As always, there is a policy trade-off.

Inflationary expectations? Deflation? The Bank of Canada must keep both in sight when setting its target inflation rate.

Sources: Based on http://www.theglobeandmail.com/report-on-business/economy/economy-lab/is-the-bank-of-canadas-2-per-cent-inflation-target-too-low/article16238207/; http://www.conferenceboard.ca/press/speech_oped/14-01-08/is_the_bank_of_canada_s_2-per-cent_inflation_target_too_low.aspx

Shake Hands Despite these disagreements, there is a growing consensus among economists and politicians that the inflation control targeting is an effective compromise between the hands-off emphasis on rules and the hands-on emphasis on government discretion. Since the Bank of Canada adopted inflation targeting, the practice has spread to central banks in Israel, Scandinavia, Spain, Australia, and elsewhere. Mark Carney, the former governor of the Bank of Canada, who is now the governor of the Bank of England, is implementing inflation targeting there, and the U.S. Federal Reserve is also moving toward inflation targeting.

There are three reasons behind the growing consensus in Canada. First, the government and the Bank of Canada *jointly* set the inflation control target, while the largely independent Bank of Canada *alone* conducts the monetary policy to achieve that target. This compromise combines accountability to voters (favoured by the hands-on camp) with a minimum role for government politicians in conducting monetary policy (favoured by the hands-off camp).

Second, the inflation control target is a fixed rule (favoured by the "Yes, Hands-Off" camp), but has the effect of stabilizing business cycles (favoured by the "No, Hands-On" camp). With an inflation control target, the Bank of Canada automatically takes policy actions to counter an inflationary boom (by raising interest rates to step on the brakes) or a recessionary bust (by lowering interest rates to step on the accelerator).

Both camps recognize that business cycles happen, but disagree on whether the causes are external ("Yes, Hands-Off") or internal ("No, Hands-On") to market economies. Both see a role for monetary policy adjustments in avoiding cycles of boom and bust and keeping the economy on the road to steady growth in living standards, full employment, and stable prices.

Third, both camps agree that inflationary expectations can ruin the short-run trade-off between inflation and unemployment. Some hands-on followers of Keynes want lower unemployment in the short run at the expense of higher inflation. But most of the "No, Hands-On" camp thinks that the short-run benefits of lower unemployment are not enough to outweigh the long-run costs of having to crush unleashed inflation expectations — a long, painful period of recession and high unemployment. Both camps agree on the value of an inflation control target in anchoring inflation expectations.

These unusual agreements between those advocating a hands-off and a hands-on role for government disappear in the next chapter on fiscal policy.

Refresh 11.5

1. What is the relationship between the Bank of Canada and the Government of Canada?

2. Explain why the Bank of Canada's focus on the inflation rate target has benefits beyond price stability. Include the concept of inflation expectations in your answer.

3. Look back at Figure 7.12 (Phillips Curve in Canada, 1946–2013) on page 192. Explain why the points from 1973 to 1983 don't fit the original Phillips Curve.

MyEconLab

For answers to these Refresh Questions, visit MyEconLab.

Study Guide

11.1 What Do Central Banks Do?
Bank of Canada's Objectives and Targets

The Bank of Canada changes the money supply and interest rates, aiming for an inflation control target that achieves steady growth, full employment, and stable prices.

- Bank of Canada is responsible for **monetary policy** — adjusting the supply of money and interest rates to achieve steady growth, full employment, and price stability.

  - **Price stability** means inflation rate is low enough to not significantly affects peoples' decisions.

- **Inflation-control target** — range of inflation rates set by a central bank as a monetary policy objective.

  - Bank of Canada's target is an annual inflation rate of 1 to 3 percent as measured by the CPI.

  - Monetary policy aims for the 2 percent midpoint of that range.

  - Bank of Canada uses core CPI as an operational guide about underlying inflation trends.

11.2 Target Shooting:
Open Market Operations

The Bank of Canada uses open market operations to change interest rates. Buying bonds increases the money supply and raises bond prices, lowering interest rates. Selling bonds decreases the money supply and lowers bond prices, raising interest rates.

- Interest rates are determined in the money and loanable funds markets and central banks influence short-run interest rates (but not long-term interest rates).

  - Bank of Canada's main policy tool is the **overnight rate** — the interest rate banks charge each other for one-day loans.

  - Overnight rate determines all other short-term interest rates.

- Lower interest rates mean more borrowing and spending, less saving. Higher interest rates mean less borrowing and spending, more saving.

  - In a recessionary gap, the Bank of Canada lowers interest rates to increase aggregate demand and accelerate the economy.

  - In an inflationary gap, the Bank of Canada raises interest rates to decrease aggregate demand and slow down the economy.

- Bank of Canada changes the target interest rate through **open market operations** — buying or selling government bonds on bond market.

  - The money market and bond market are interconnected, so open market operations can be explained from either perspective.

- From the money market perspective, the Bank of Canada changes the money supply using open market operations to influence quantity of demand deposits (part of M1+).

  - To lower interest rates and accelerate the economy, the Bank of Canada buys bonds, increasing bank reserves, loans, demand deposits, and the money supply.

  - To raise interest rates and slow down economy, the Bank of Canada sells bonds to decrease bank reserves, loans, demand deposits, and the money supply.

- From a bond market perspective, the Bank of Canada changes the money supply using open market operations to influence bond prices and therefore interest rates.

  - When the Bank of Canada buys bonds, demand for bonds increases, raising bond prices and lowering interest rates.

  - When the Bank of Canada sells bonds, supply of bonds increases, lowering bond prices and raising interest rates.

- When the Bank of Canada changes the overnight rate, most other interest rates change in same direction.

  - **Prime rate** — the interest rate on loans to lowest-risk corporate borrowers.

11.3 Driving with the Bank of Canada: Transmission Mechanisms

Monetary policy affects aggregate demand by reinforcing domestic and international transmission mechanisms connecting interest rates, exchange rates, and spending.

- Open market operations and interest rates affect aggregate demand ($C + I + G + X - IM$) through
  - domestic monetary transmission mechanism.
  - international transmission mechanisms.
- Domestic monetary transmission mechanism
  - Lower interest rates cause a positive aggregate demand shock, increasing consumption (C) and business investment spending (I).
  - Higher interest rates cause a negative aggregate demand shock, decreasing consumption (C) and business investment spending (I).
- International transmission mechanisms work through impact of interest rates on the exchange rate.
  - Lower interest rate causes a depreciating Canadian dollar; a positive demand shock increasing net exports ($X - IM$), increasing inflation.
  - Higher interest rate causes an appreciating Canadian dollar; a negative demand shock decreasing net exports ($X - IM$), decreasing inflation.
- Domestic and international transmission mechanisms reinforce each other — use monetary policy to
  - correct a recessionary gap with lower interest rates — aggregate demand increases, unemployment decreases, inflation increases.
  - correct an inflationary gap with higher interest rates — aggregate demand decreases, unemployment increases to natural rate, inflation decreases.
- Monetary policy is about moderation — accelerating when the economy is slowing, braking when the economy is speeding up.

11.4 Transmission Breakdowns: Balance Sheet Recessions and Monetary Policy

In a balance sheet recession, individuals and businesses focus on paying down debt and do not want to borrow or spend. Even when monetary policy lowers interest rates, the economy remains in recession.

- Recessions often start with decreasing business investment spending, falling net exports, or rising interest rates.
  - The Global Financial Crisis instead started with falling asset prices.
- A basis point is one-hundredth of 1 percent. 1 percent = 100 basis points.

- A balance sheet shows assets on one side (what you own or earn) and debts or liabilities on the other side (what you owe or spend).
  - The Global Financial Crisis was a balance sheet recession — falling asset prices led individuals and businesses to cut spending, save, and pay down debt.
  - There were transmission breakdowns for monetary policy. Low interest rates did not increase spending and aggregate demand.
- Transmission breakdowns are caused by
  - consumers — saving more, paying off debts, spending less.
  - businesses — pessimistic expectations decrease business investment spending even with lower interest rates.
  - money as a store of value — giving individuals and businesses a way not to spend.
  - banks — holding on to cash reserves and *not* making new loans, demand deposits, or increasing the money supply.
- To counteract transmission breakdowns, central banks used **quantitative easing** — flooding the financial system with money by buying high-risk bonds, mortgages, and assets from banks. These liabilities on bank balance sheets are replaced with cash assets, enabling banks to make new loans, new demand deposits, and increase the quantity of money.
- Risk of flooding financial system with money is inflation.
  - Quantity theory of money predicts increasing the money supply when the economy approaches potential GDP will cause inflation.
  - Central banks have a difficult timing problem of applying the monetary "brake" of higher interest rates before inflation starts, but not too soon to stop economic recovery.
- Balance sheet recessions cause transmission problems for monetary policy, making it harder to steer the economy toward recovery.

11.5 Who's Driving? Anchoring Inflation Expectations

Inflation rate targeting by an independent central bank anchors inflation expectations, helps price signals work, and combines a hands-off emphasis on rules and hands-on emphasis on government discretion.

- Inflation-control target is set jointly by the Government of Canada and the Bank of Canada.
  - The Bank of Canada alone is responsible for monetary policy to achieve the target.
  - The Bank of Canada has considerable independence, but ultimately is responsible to Parliament.

- Bank of Canada focused only on inflation rate targeting since 1991.
  - Inflation stayed within the target range.
  - Steered economy toward rising living standards, full employment.
- Advantages of inflation rate targeting
  - Anchoring expectations about inflation
  - Improving predictability of prices
- Original Phillips Curve trade-off between inflation and unemployment works when expectations of inflation do not change.
  - Once inflation starts, changing expectations can be self-fulfilling — by reacting to an expectation of inflation we may cause it.
  - Changing inflation expectations, combined with increases in the money supply, eliminated original Phillips Curve's trade-off between higher inflation and lower unemployment.
  - Inflation expectations go up quickly and easily, but come down slowly and painfully.
- Unpredictable prices — due to inflation — create risk, discourage business investment, and interfere with price signals for smart choices.

- "Yes, Hands-Off" and "No, Hands-On" camps agree that markets need a central bank.
  - Banks are regulated because of the trade-off between profits and prudence.
  - Some disagreements between camps on monetary policy.
- "Yes — Markets Self-Adjust" camp favours hands-off rules for monetary policy, likes targets, with no discretion for central bankers and no opportunity for politicians to influence monetary policy.
  - Believes government failure is more likely than market failure.
- "No — Markets Fail Often" camp favours hands-on government discretion for monetary policy to correct transmission breakdown, allowing democratically elected politicians to set policy.
  - Believes market failure is more likely than government failure.
- Both camps agree that inflation control targets are an effective compromise between hands-off emphasis on rules and hands-on emphasis on government discretion.

TRUE/FALSE

Circle the correct answer. Solutions to these questions are available at the end of the book and on MyEconLab. You can also visit the MyEconLab Study Plan to access additional questions that will help you master the concepts covered in this chapter.

You accidentally schedule a driving lesson for the night before your test on monetary policy. Fortunately, your driving instructor, Lindsay, has an economics degree and offers to quiz you on monetary policy during the lesson. She says:

Steering the economy through monetary policy is similar to steering a car through a winding mountain road. If you can recognize a true or false statement on monetary policy as well as you steer this car, you will do great on your test tomorrow. Tell me if the following statements are true or false.

Use this scenario to answer questions 1–15.

11.1 Bank of Canada's Job

1. The prime minister is the driver at   T   F
   the wheel for Canadian monetary policy.

2. The Bank of Canada uses monetary policy   T   F
   to steer the economy toward stable prices,
   steady economic growth, and full employment.

11.2 Open Market Operations

3. The Bank of Canada's tool for steering   T   F
   the economy is the inflation rate.

4. The Bank of Canada tries to keep   T   F
   inflation rates between 1 percent and
   3 percent in order to steer the economy
   on the right track.

5. The Bank of Canada's main objective is   T   F
   to drive the Canadian economy on the
   road to potential GDP at the ideal speed,
   avoiding the booms and busts of business
   cycles on either side of the road.

6. When the economy is slowing down,   T   F
   the Bank of Canada steps on the gas by
   lowering interest rates.

7. When the economy is speeding too fast,   T   F
   the government pulls the Bank of Canada
   over and tells it to lower interest rates.

11.3 Transmission Mechanisms

8. When the central bank steps on the gas,   T   F
   the effects of lower interest rates travel
   through the transmission mechanisms to
   increase spending and aggregate demand.

9. While cars have different pedals for the   T   F
gas and brake, monetary policy has one pedal
(interest rates) that can be lowered or raised.

10. It is politically popular when the Bank of   T   F
Canada puts on the brakes by raising interest rates.

11.4   Transmission Breakdowns

11. The timing of the monetary "brake" is   T   F
crucial. If the central bank steps on the brake
too soon, it risks halting the recovery. If it waits
too long, it risks inflation.

12. Balance sheet recessions cause transmission   T   F
problems for monetary policy, making it
harder to steer the economy toward recovery.

11.5   Anchoring Inflation Expectations

13. The Minister of Finance for the government   T   F
and the Governor of the Bank of Canada
jointly decide on the destination of Canada's
economic car, but the Governor gets to drive.

14. Inflation expectations are like driving cars   T   F
uphill — they go up slowly and painfully,
but come down quickly and easily.

15. The "Yes — Markets Self-Adjust, so Hands-Off"   T   F
and "No — Markets Fail Often, so Hands-On"
camps largely disagree about inflation
control targets.

MULTIPLE CHOICE

Circle the best answer. Solutions to these questions are available at the end of the book and on MyEconLab. You can also visit the MyEconLab Study Plan to access similar questions that will help you master the concepts covered in this chapter.

11.1   Bank of Canada's Job

1. The price stability goal of the Bank of Canada is to keep the
   a) unemployment rate low at any cost.
   b) inflation rate low at any cost.
   c) inflation rate low enough to not significantly affect decisions.
   d) inflation rate at zero to not significantly affect decisions.

2. The Bank of Canada's inflation-control target is the
   a) CPI.
   b) core CPI.
   c) CPI, with core CPI as an operational guide.
   d) core CPI, with CPI as an operational guide.

11.2   Open Market Operations

3. The CPI inflation rate was 0.7 percent in November 2013 and 1.3 percent in July 2013. The CPI inflation rate was
   a) in the target range in both November and July.
   b) below the target range in both November and July.
   c) in the target range in November but not July.
   d) in the target range in July but not November.

4. Many central bank governors failed to anticipate the Global Financial Crisis, and wish they had responded sooner. Ben Bernanke said, "I'm not one of those people who look at this as some kind of video game… This is all very real to me." Suppose monetary policy was as simple as pushing a button on a video game. The button that should have been pushed sooner would
   a) increase the inflation rate.
   b) raise the overnight interest rate.
   c) lower the overnight interest rate.
   d) turn off the video game.

5. Vanessa has a bad credit rating. When she goes to the bank for a loan, the interest rate the bank will give her is
   a) the target rate.
   b) the prime rate.
   c) between the target rate and the prime rate.
   d) above the prime rate.

6. When the Bank of Canada buys bonds, the
   a) increased demand for bonds raises bond prices and interest rates.
   b) increased demand for bonds raises bond prices and lowers interest rates.
   c) increased supply of bonds lowers bond prices and raises interest rates.
   d) decreased supply of bonds lowers bond prices and lowers interest rates.

11.3 Transmission Mechanisms

7. Which statement describes the effect of monetary policy to accelerate the economy?

a) Selling bonds decreases the money supply, raising interest rates, decreasing aggregate demand.

b) Selling bonds decreases the money supply, lowering interest rates, increasing aggregate demand.

c) Buying bonds raises the price of bonds, lowering interest rates, increasing aggregate demand.

d) Buying bonds raises the price of bonds, lowering interest rates, decreasing aggregate demand.

8. The Bank of Canada will increase interest rates today if

a) the economy is currently in an inflationary gap.

b) the economy is currently in a recessionary gap.

c) it expects a recessionary gap 18–24 months into the future.

d) it expects an inflationary gap 18–24 months into the future.

9. During a recessionary gap, the Bank of Canada should

a) drink out of the punch bowl.

b) take away the punch bowl.

c) add punch to the punch bowl.

d) catch demons swimming in the punch bowl.

10. Monetary policy to speed up the economy

a) lowers interest rates and causes a depreciating exchange rate.

b) lowers interest rates and causes an appreciating exchange rate.

c) raises interest rates and causes a depreciating exchange rate.

d) raises interest rates and causes an appreciating exchange rate.

11.4 Transmission Breakdowns

11. If real GDP is less than potential GDP, an increase in the quantity of money leads to a(n)

a) increase in both real GDP and the price level.

b) increase in real GDP and a decrease the price level.

c) increase in real GDP and no change in the price level.

d) decrease in both real GDP and the price level.

12. Which statement best describes the Bank of Canada's policy dress code before and during the Global Financial Crisis?

a) "Pink polka dot suits" before and during the Global Financial Crisis.

b) "Conservative blue ties" before and during the Global Financial Crisis.

c) "Pink polka dot suits" before, "conservative blue ties" during the Global Financial Crisis.

d) "Conservative blue ties" before, "Pink polka dot suits" during the Global Financial Crisis.

13. Which statement best describes the banking system's choices before and during the Global Financial Crisis?

a) "Profits over prudence" before and during the Global Financial Crisis.

b) "Profits over prudence" before, "prudence over profits" during the Global Financial Crisis.

c) "Prudence over profits" before, "profits over prudence" during the Global Financial Crisis.

d) "Prudence over profits" before and during the Global Financial Crisis.

11.5 Anchoring Inflation Expectations

14. The "No — Markets Fail Often" camp favours

a) a central bank run by politicians.

b) fixed rules for monetary policy.

c) a role for government in setting monetary policy.

d) all of the above.

15. Canada has

a) an inflation-control target jointly decided by government and the Bank of Canada.

b) a central bank that independently achieves the target.

c) no government discretion for achieving the target.

d) all of the above.

12 Spending Others' Money

Fiscal Policy, Deficits, and National Debt

NO ONE LIKES BEING IN DEBT. When governments —

federal, provincial, or municipal — spend more than they collect in taxes, their budgets are not balanced. They run deficits. Debt starts piling up. Many citizens disapprove, saying, "Get your financial house in order! Avoid debt. Don't spend more than you've got." But is going into debt always a bad choice?

Most consumers and businesses regularly make smart choices that involve debt. People with a mortgage or car payments are in debt. Businesses regularly issue bonds to borrow money for building new factories. If debt can be smart for individuals and businesses, can it be smart for governments?

When spending collapsed during the Global Financial Crisis, the only macroeconomic player who kept spending steadily was government. Government financed this spending by going into debt. Was this financially irresponsible, or did government spending and debt save the market economy from depression?

In this chapter, you will learn about government spending, its multiplied impact on the economy, and the differences between deficits and debts. The Canadian government had a budget deficit of $18.9 billion in 2013. That means it had to borrow that much money in 2013 to pay for its spending. As well, by 2013, the government already had a debt of over $602 billion. Is that a cause for alarm, or for celebration of smart choices? You will learn how to analyze the heated mix of economics and politics fuelling most debates about government spending and debt from politicians seeking your votes.

Should the government leave the economy alone, or step in to try to correct market failures? Hands-off or hands-on? This chapter will help you make up your own mind about the role that government should play in a market economy.

12.1 Spenders of Last Resort: Aggregate Demand Policies for Stabilizing Business Cycles

Use the concepts of injections and leakages to explain the multiplied impact of aggregate demand fiscal policies.

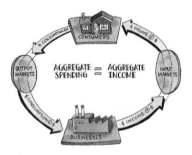

▲ The simple GDP circular flow diagram does not include money coming in (injected) from spending by government, businesses, or R.O.W. on exports.

Monetary policy is about money. But what is fiscal policy? *Fiscal* comes from the Latin word *fisc* — the public treasury of Rome. In the time of the Roman Empire, the emperor controlled the public treasury — the *fisc*. Today, governments control the public treasury, and fiscal policy is about the changes governments make to purchases, transfers, and taxes in trying to achieve the key macroeconomic outcomes of steady growth, full employment, and stable prices.

Fiscal policy works through aggregate demand, speeding up or slowing down an economy facing recessionary or inflationary gaps.

Aggregate demand is the sum of planned consumer spending (*C*), business investment spending (*I*), government spending on products and services (*G*), and net exports (*X* − *IM*).

$$\text{Aggregate Demand} = C + I + G + X - IM$$

To see where fiscal policy affects aggregate demand, let's return yet again to Figure 6.7, which is reproduced as Figure 12.1. In the simple GDP circular flow above, all spending is done by consumers. In Figure 12.1, government purchases (*G*), business investment spending (*I*), and exports (*X*) are all *additional* injections of spending. Injections are important for understanding the impact of fiscal policy.

Figure 12.1   Enlarged GDP Circular Flow of Income and Spending with Banking System

Virtuous and Vicious Circles: Multiplier Effects

There are two main paths that transmit the effects of fiscal policy to aggregate demand in Figure 12.1 — government purchases and net taxes.

Government Purchases as Injections

The government purchases path is highlighted in red. Government purchases of products and services in output markets include such things as building highways or hiring the services of accounting firms.

Government purchases are an example of what economists call injections into the circular flow. An **injection** is spending in the circular flow that does not start with consumers. Government purchases (G), business investment spending (I), and exports (X) are injections.

Net Taxes as Leakages

The net taxes path of fiscal policy is highlighted in blue in Figure 12.1. Net taxes combine taxes paid by consumers to government, minus transfer payments (Employment Insurance, Canada Pension) consumers receive from government. Because taxes are greater than transfers (people pay government more than they get), the flow of net taxes is from consumers to government.

Net taxes are an example of what economists call leakages from the circular flow. A **leakage** is spending that leaks out of (leaves) the circular flow through taxes, savings, and imports.

Round and Round the Circle

Injections and leakages, money flowing into and out of the circular flow, are key to understanding the multiplied impact of fiscal policy on aggregate demand and GDP. Let's start with government purchases — an injection — and look at what happens in Figure 12.1.

Suppose the government spends $100 million to buy a new bridge: G goes up by $100 million. That means aggregate demand, which equals $C + I + G + X - IM$, goes up by the $100 million injection in this first round of spending. Here is the surprise — the full effect on aggregate demand is *more than* $100 million. To see how, let's follow the circle.

The initial effect is that the bridge-building business (businesses are at the bottom of the circle) gets $100 million. Following the circle up to the right, that means incomes of everyone working for the business — workers, owners, suppliers — goes up by $100 million. What do people do with that additional income? The government takes some of the income as taxes — a leakage out of the circular flow (the net taxes flow from consumers to government at the top). People save some — another leakage out of the circular flow (the consumer saving and borrowing flow at the very top). Some of that new spending is on imports — the final leakage (the net export flow between businesses and R.O.W.). But even after all of those leakages, there will be some new spending in output markets on Canadian products and services.

injection spending in the circular flow that does not start with consumers: G (government spending), I (business investment spending), X (exports)

leakage spending that leaks out of the circular flow through taxes, savings, and imports

Javier Soriano/Getty Images

▲ The Vancouver 2010 Winter Olympics were predicted to have a huge multiplier effect for the B.C. economy. The impact of the increased tourism, new buildings, and improved infrastructure was estimated to add $6 to $10 billion in new spending in the province before 2015. It is because of such multiplier effects that cities willingly pay millions of dollars for the rights to host the Games.

Suppose leakages are 50 percent of additional income. Out of every dollar Canadians receive in income, 50 cents goes to leakages (taxes, saving, imports) and 50 cents is spent on Canadian products and services. That means that businesses in Canada will receive $50 million in this second round of spending. The story, and the flow around the circle, repeats. There will again be leakages in taxes, savings, and imports from this $50 million in new income, but 50 percent of the income will again turn into new spending on Canadian products and services. In the third round of spending, businesses in Canada will receive $25 million. The circles of spending and income continue getting smaller and smaller, and eventually fade away. Figure 12.2 shows the cumulative effect of all of the rounds of spending. In this example, the $100 million injection of government spending increases aggregate demand by $200 million after all of the rounds of spending are finished.

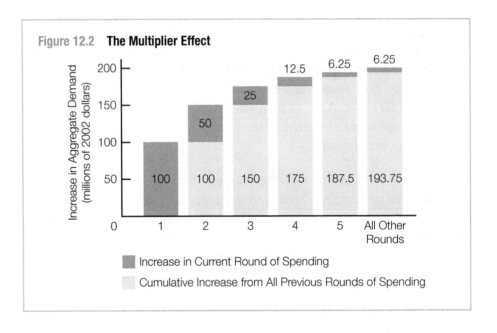

Figure 12.2   The Multiplier Effect

The effect of the initial $100 million injection of government spending is multiplied by going around and around the circular flow. Economists call this the **multiplier effect** — a spending injection has a multiplied effect on aggregate demand.

The multiplier effect also works in reverse. A reduction in government spending, business investment spending, or R.O.W. spending on Canadian exports has a multiplied impact reducing aggregate demand.

multiplier effect a spending injection has a multiplied effect on aggregate demand

◀ The multiplier effects of an increase in injections are like the expanding ripples from a stone dropped into water. The ripples expanding outward are like the cumulative effects on spending from an initial injection.

Leakages and the Multiplier Effect   The size of the multiplier effect depends on leakages out of the circular flow. There is a simple formula for calculating the size of the multiplier effect.

$$\text{Size of Multiplier Effect} \; = \; \frac{1}{\text{\% of leakages from additional income}}$$

In our simple example, where leakages (taxes, saving, imports) are 50 percent (0.50) of additional income,

$$\text{Size of Multiplier Effect} \; = \; \frac{1}{0.50} = 2$$

The larger the percentage of leakages — taxes, saving, imports — the less money gets spent on Canadian products and services in each round of spending. More leakages mean a smaller multiplier effect; fewer leakages mean a larger multiplier effect.

How Big Are Multiplier Effects?   Changes in government spending on products and services or in net taxes have multiplied effects on aggregate demand and real GDP. How big are the effects of these fiscal policy tools that governments can use? Estimates vary, but many place the size of the multiplier effect for government spending around two. A $100 million injection of new spending increases real GDP by about $200 million after all rounds of spending finish.

Tax and Transfer Multipliers   There is a similar multiplier effect from changes in taxes or government transfers. A tax cut or an increase in transfer payments reduces leakages. This leaves consumers with more money to spend. The new spending has a multiplied effect, increasing aggregate demand.

In reverse, an increase in taxes or decrease in transfers is an increase in leakages, leaving consumers with less money to spend. The reduced spending has a multiplied effect, decreasing aggregate demand.

The multiplier effect in not as big for tax and transfer changes as it is for government spending. For example, when consumers get a $100 million tax cut, they don't spend all $100 million on Canadian products and services. They save some of the $100 million and spend some on imports. Because the initial round of new consumer spending is less than $100 million, the multiplier impact is less than for a government injection of $100 million.

Multipliers and Aggregate Demand An increase in government spending or a decrease in taxes is a positive aggregate demand shock, shifting the aggregate demand curve rightward. The size of the rightward shift depends on the size of the multiplier effect. Figure 12.3 shows a $100 million increase in government spending, which shifts the aggregate demand curve rightward by $200 million — the multiplied effect of the initial increase in income.

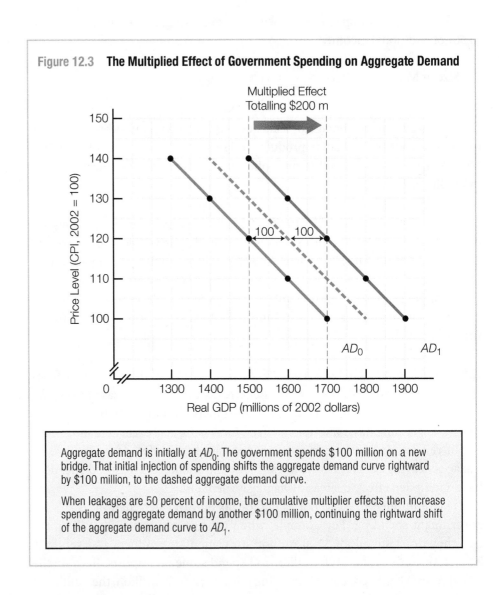

Figure 12.3 **The Multiplied Effect of Government Spending on Aggregate Demand**

Aggregate demand is initially at AD_0. The government spends $100 million on a new bridge. That initial injection of spending shifts the aggregate demand curve rightward by $100 million, to the dashed aggregate demand curve.

When leakages are 50 percent of income, the cumulative multiplier effects then increase spending and aggregate demand by another $100 million, continuing the rightward shift of the aggregate demand curve to AD_1.

A decrease in government spending or an increase in taxes is a negative aggregate demand shock, shifting the aggregate demand curve leftward by the multiplied effect of the initial decrease in income.

Other Injections:
Multiplier Effects and Business Cycles

Multiplier effects don't flow just from government. Any change in injections — from business investment spending or exports — also has a multiplied effect on aggregate demand. Many Canadian business cycles, both recessions and expansions, are triggered by changes in investment spending or exports.

NOTE

Any change in injections — G, I, or X — has a multiplied effect on aggregate demand and on real GDP.

Business Investment Spending   Business investment spending is the most volatile part of aggregate demand — it fluctuates up and down with changes in interest rates and expectations of future profits. Businesses can easily postpone spending on new factories or additional machinery. When business investment spending decreases, there is a multiplied decrease in aggregate demand and real GDP. A collapse in investment spending between 1929 and 1933 was an important cause of the Great Depression. Investment spending dropped almost 80 percent, from $1.4 billion to $0.3 billion. The reverse is also true. Expansions are often triggered by increases in business investment spending that increase aggregate demand with a multiplied impact on GDP.

Export-Led Busts and Booms
Canada is a trading nation. Thirty percent of Canadian GDP comes from export sales, and 80 percent of our exports are sold to the United States. When the Global Financial Crisis started in the United States, it spread to Canada through fast-falling U.S. demand for Canadian exports, especially automobiles. In reverse, growing demands from the rest of the world for Canadian exports — especially commodities like oil and other resources — trigger many expansions. Economic growth driven by the multiplied effects of increasing exports is called *export-led growth*.

▲ Canada exports products ranging from oil and lumber to wheat and gold, but Canada also exports art and entertainment. Cirque du Soleil, a modern circus combining circus acts and street-type entertainment, seen here performing in England in 2012, was founded in Quebec in 1984 and currently has over 20 travelling shows performing around the world.

Filling the Gaps:
Fiscal Policy and Aggregate Demand

Multiplier effects improve the effectiveness of fiscal policy as a tool for changing aggregate demand to counter business cycles. There are two types of fiscal policy.

Expansionary fiscal policy increases aggregate demand by increasing government spending, decreasing taxes, or increasing transfers. The multiplied impact of expansionary fiscal policy shifts the aggregate demand curve rightward — a positive aggregate demand shock.

Contractionary fiscal policy decreases aggregate demand by decreasing government spending, increasing taxes, or decreasing transfers. The multiplied impact of contractionary fiscal policy shifts the aggregate demand curve leftward — a negative aggregate demand shock.

expansionary fiscal policy   increases aggregate demand by increasing government spending, decreasing taxes, or increasing transfers; shifts the aggregate demand curve rightward — a positive aggregate demand shock

contractionary fiscal policy decreases aggregate demand by decreasing government spending, increasing taxes, or decreasing transfers; shifts the aggregate demand curve leftward — a negative aggregate demand shock

Recessionary Gaps and Expansionary Fiscal Policy   Figure 12.4 shows an economy initially in a short-run equilibrium where aggregated demand (AD_0) intersects short-run aggregate supply (SAS_0) at a real GDP of $1400 billion. Potential GDP, shown by the long-run aggregate supply curve (LAS_0), is $1500 billion. The economy has a recessionary gap, with real GDP $100 billion below potential GDP, and the unemployment rate is above the natural rate. Inflation is falling or stable — not a concern.

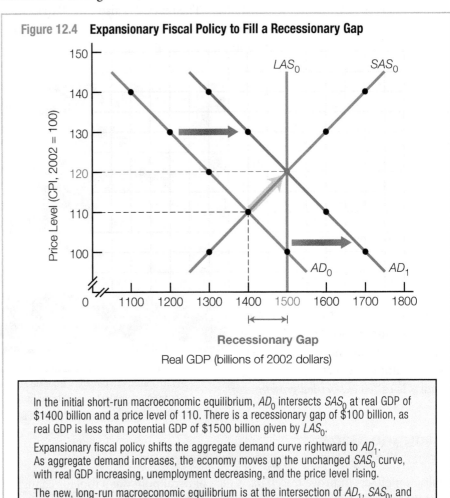

Figure 12.4   **Expansionary Fiscal Policy to Fill a Recessionary Gap**

In the initial short-run macroeconomic equilibrium, AD_0 intersects SAS_0 at real GDP of $1400 billion and a price level of 110. There is a recessionary gap of $100 billion, as real GDP is less than potential GDP of $1500 billion given by LAS_0.

Expansionary fiscal policy shifts the aggregate demand curve rightward to AD_1. As aggregate demand increases, the economy moves up the unchanged SAS_0 curve, with real GDP increasing, unemployment decreasing, and the price level rising.

The new, long-run macroeconomic equilibrium is at the intersection of AD_1, SAS_0, and LAS_0. Real GDP is $1500 billion, the price level rises to 120, and unemployment is at the natural rate since the economy is at potential GDP.

NOTE
Fiscal policies to increase government spending, cut taxes, or increase transfers are positive aggregate demand shocks for countering a recessionary gap.

To increase aggregate demand, governments can increase spending, cut taxes, or increase transfer payments. Expansionary fiscal policy is a positive aggregate demand shock, shifting the aggregate demand curve rightward from AD_0 to AD_1, increasing real GDP, decreasing unemployment, and increasing inflation. The new equilibrium is at the intersection of AD_1, SAS_0, and LAS_0.

That is what governments in Canada did during the Global Financial Crisis in 2009. Consumers were spending less and saving more. Businesses, facing poor sales and banks' unwillingness to lend money, cut back production and investment spending. Exports to the United States and the rest of the world fell. Governments became the "spenders of last resort," spending when other macroeconomic players were not. Governments increased spending and cut taxes as positive demand shocks in their expansionary fiscal policy to fight the recession.

Inflationary Gaps and Contractionary Fiscal Policy Figure 12.5 shows an economy initially in a short-run equilibrium where aggregated demand (AD_0) intersects short-run aggregate supply (SAS_0) at a real GDP of $1600 billion. Potential GDP, shown by the long-run aggregate supply curve (LAS_0), is $1500 billion. The economy has an inflationary gap, with real GDP $100 billion above potential GDP, and the unemployment rate is below the natural rate. Unemployment is not a problem since there are shortages of workers and rising wages, not shortages of jobs.

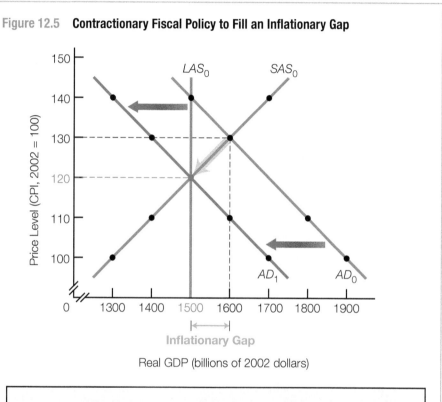

Figure 12.5 Contractionary Fiscal Policy to Fill an Inflationary Gap

In the initial short-run macroeconomic equilibrium, AD_0 intersects SAS_0 at real GDP of $1600 billion and a price level of 130. There is an inflationary gap of $100 billion, as real GDP is greater than potential GDP of $1500 billion.

Contractionary fiscal policy shifts the aggregate demand curve leftward to AD_1. As aggregate demand decreases, the economy moves down the unchanged SAS_0 curve, with real GDP decreasing, unemployment increasing, and the price level falling.

The new, long-run macroeconomic equilibrium is at the intersection of AD_1, SAS_0, and LAS_0. Real GDP is $1500 billion, the price level falls to 120, and unemployment is at the natural rate since the economy is at potential GDP.

To decrease aggregate demand, governments can decrease spending, raise taxes, or decrease transfer payments. Contractionary fiscal policy is a negative aggregate demand shock, shifting the aggregate demand curve leftward from AD_0 to AD_1, decreasing real GDP, increasing unemployment, and decreasing inflation. The new equilibrium is at the intersection of AD_1, SAS_0, and LAS_0. Real GDP is $1500 billion and the price level falls to 120, decreasing the inflation rate. Unemployment is at the natural rate.

Multiplier Effects and Real GDP   Any change in injections has a multiplied effect on aggregate demand. The aggregate demand curve shifts rightward when injections increase and shifts leftward when injections decrease. The multiplier effects of an injection *on equilibrium real GDP* depends on how close the economy is to potential GDP (*LAS*). When the economy is in recession and far below potential GDP, more of the increase in aggregate demand increases real GDP. When the economy is at or above potential GDP, more of the increase in aggregate demand drives up prices instead of increasing real GDP. A recent study measuring the effects of fiscal policy found that the size of multipliers for expansionary fiscal policy range from about 2.5 during recessions to close to zero when the economy is at full employment.

Hands-Off and Hands-On Choices for Demand-Side Fiscal Policies

The two camps agree that fiscal policy affects aggregate demand, real GDP, unemployment, and inflation. But they disagree about how to use fiscal policy.

Hands-Off   The "Yes — Markets Self-Adjust" camp believes that government should keep its hands off of the economy whenever possible. If fiscal policy is necessary to accelerate the economy, the hands-off position favours tax cuts instead of increased government spending. This puts more money in the hands of private individuals and businesses, who should make their own smart choices about how to best spend their money. The "Yes — Markets Self-Adjust" camp believes that government spending is subject to political influence and is not always spent where it is needed.

If fiscal policy is necessary to slow down the economy, the hands-off position favours reduced government spending instead of tax increases. This keeps money in the hands of private individuals and businesses, and reduces the amount of what they believe is unnecessary government spending.

Hands-On   The "No — Markets Fail Often" camp sees an essential hands-on role for government to correct those failures. All forms of fiscal policy are acceptable, especially when monetary policy is ineffective due to transmission breakdowns (section 11.4). The hands-on position often favours government spending over tax cuts. Government spending is more effective, since consumers and businesses may save the money from tax cuts rather than spend it, causing transmission breakdowns.

If fiscal policy is necessary to slow the economy down, the hands-on position favours tax increases over reduced government spending. This preserves the government's ability to stabilize the economy. They argue that democratically elected politicians are the right people to choose how to spend taxpayers' money, and want spending plans to pay attention to equity among different groups in Canada, rather than just aiming for the most efficient expenditure of funds.

Multipliers at Work Multiplier effects help explain the ups and downs of business cycles, as well as fiscal policies for counteracting those cycles. Fiscal policies, working through aggregate demand shocks — positive and negative — are tools that can keep the economy on the road to potential GDP, full employment, and stable prices.

Refresh 12.1

1. In your own words, explain the multiplier effect of government or business spending. Include the concepts of injections and leakages in your answer.

2. In terms of fiscal policy choices, which position — hands-off or hands-on — is closer to your beliefs? Explain.

3. Politicians in your area want to spend millions of tax dollars to build a stadium to bring a professional sports team to your community. Do you support that decision? Explain your position.

MyEconLab

For answers to these Refresh Questions, visit MyEconLab.

Building Foundations: Aggregate Supply Policies for Promoting Growth

12.2

Identify three aggregate supply fiscal policies for growth, and explain the controversy over supply-sider incentive effects.

Fiscal policies for aggregate demand can counter the bust and boom of business cycles, keeping the economy moving steadily on the road toward potential GDP, full employment, and stable prices. Government spending, tax, and transfer changes attempt to *match aggregate demand and aggregate supply at potential GDP*.

The other key macroeconomic outcome — steady growth in living standards — calls for a different kind of fiscal policy. Economic growth (see section 10.2) expands the economy's capacity to produce products and services — an *increase in potential GDP*. Economic growth happens when increases in the quantity and quality of inputs — labour, capital, land, and entrepreneurship — increase (long-run and short-run) aggregate supply.

Increases in aggregate supply, not adjustments to aggregate demand, produce economic growth. Increases in the quality of inputs, including technological change, increase productivity — each person produces more. Living standards rise when economic growth increases potential GDP per person.

Figure 12.6 (same as Figure 8.17) shows the economic growth from a positive supply shock — an increase in the quantity or quality of inputs.

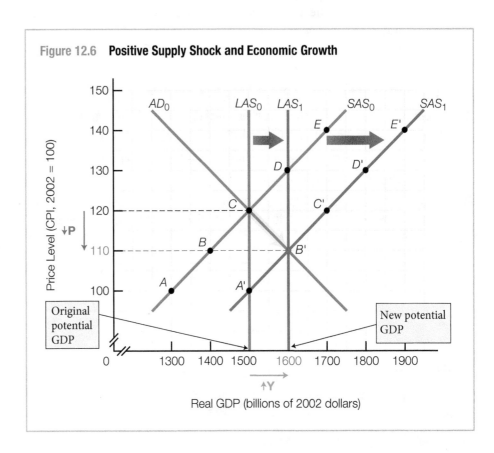

Figure 12.6   **Positive Supply Shock and Economic Growth**

Starting at point C (where AD_0, SAS_0, and LAS_0 intersect), increases in inputs increase potential GDP and shift rightward both the long-run aggregate supply curve (LAS_1) and short-run aggregate supply curve (SAS_1). The new equilibrium is at point B'. As long as the increase in potential GDP is greater than the increase in the population, living standards rise.

Investing in the Future: Policies for Economic Growth

When aggregate supply increases, economic growth raises living standards by increasing potential GDP per person. Fiscal policies targeting aggregate supply aim for three outcomes — stimulate saving and capital investment, encourage research and development, and improve education and training.

Stimulate Saving and Capital Investment   Government uses tax incentives as a fiscal policy tool to stimulate saving and increase the quantity of capital available. Government tax exemptions for interest earned in Tax-Free Savings Accounts (TFSAs) and Registered Retirement Savings Plans (RRSPs) reward saving and increase the supply of loanable funds. This makes it easier and cheaper for businesses to borrow to finance new factories or new machinery, and promote economic growth.

Productivity isn't everything, but in the long run it is almost everything. A country's ability to improve its standard of living over time depends almost entirely on its ability to raise output per worker.

— *Paul Krugman*
2008 Nobel Prize winner in Economics

NOTE
Tax incentives can stimulate saving, increase the quantity of capital, and promote economic growth.

Encourage Research and Development   Most productivity-improving technological change begins with research and development to improve ways of making existing products and services, and to develop new and better products and services. Government uses targeted government spending and tax incentives as fiscal policy to encourage research and development. The government funds the National Science and Engineering Research Council (NSERC), which subsidizes basic scientific research in universities. The government also provides tax incentives to businesses to encourage research and development.

NOTE
Government spending and tax incentives for research and development promote economic growth.

Improve Education and Training   *Human capital* — the quality of labour inputs — increases through education and training. Education, training, and work experience increase your earning potential. Businesses are willing to pay higher wages to workers with more human capital because they are more productive. Government can spend to directly provide education (as it does for kindergarten to grade 12), and it can provide subsidies to schools (as it does to colleges and universities) and to students (bursaries and grants). There are also tax incentives to improve education and training.

NOTE
Government-financed education and training that increase human capital promote economic growth.

To Save or To Spend?
Hands-Off and Hands-On Supply-Side Differences

Both the "Yes — Markets Self-Adjust — Hands-Off" and "No — Markets Fail Often — Hands-On" camps agree that fiscal policy can affect aggregate supply and promote economic growth. But they disagree about the effects of saving on economic growth.

All economists agree that fiscal policies to encourage saving and capital investment will *eventually* increase aggregate supply and potential GDP.

But remember your mantra: Aggregate demand = $C + I + G + X - IM$. It is the sum of planned consumer spending (C), business investment spending (I), government spending on products and services (G), and net exports ($X - IM$). An increase in saving means a decrease in consumer spending. There is a trade-off between increased aggregate supply in the future — through business investment spending — and reduced aggregate demand in the present due to lower consumer spending. Every choice has an opportunity cost!

Save!   The "Yes — Hands-Off" camp strongly supports fiscal policies to encourage saving and capital investment. They believe that as saving flows into the loanable funds market, interest rates quickly fall, encouraging more consumer spending and especially business borrowing to finance more investment spending (I). These spending increases quickly offset the additional saving, restoring aggregate demand to match aggregate supply. The long-run benefits of increased aggregate supply for economic growth, the "Yes — Hands-Off" camp argues, outweigh any short-run mismatches between aggregate demand and aggregate supply.

Spend! The "No — Hands-On" camp is less enthusiastic about government fiscal policies to encourage saving and capital investment. They worry that when businesses see reduced consumer spending, they will postpone investment spending. Even if saving causes interest rates to fall in the loanable funds market, more pessimistic expectations about sales and profits outweigh the lower costs of borrowing.

While the "No — Hands-On" camp sees long-run benefits of increased saving for aggregate supply and economic growth, they are concerned that short-run decreases in aggregate demand may cause a recession because markets fail to quickly adjust. These short-run adjustment costs might outweigh the long-run benefits of economic growth. Keynes, the original hands-on economist, said, "In the long run, we are all dead."

Long-Run or Short-Run? The two camps agree that government policies to stimulate saving can eventually promote economic growth in the long run. But the camps place different emphasis on the importance of the long run ("Yes — Hands-Off" camp) and the short run ("No — Hands-On" camp).

Supply-Siders and Voodoo Economics: Incentive Effects

Suppose your boss lets you decide how many hours to work this week. She asks, "How many hours will you work if I pay you $15 an hour?" After you answer, she asks, "How many hours will you work if I pay you $20 an hour?" If you are like most people, you will work more hours at $20 an hour than at $15 an hour. The higher wage is an *incentive* for you to supply a greater quantity of labour. That is the law of supply (section 3.3).

A tax cut gives the same incentive as a wage increase. Your take-home pay, after the government deducts income tax, is always less than what your boss pays you. If the government cuts your income taxes, your take-home pay rises, just as if you had a raise.

Tax cuts have supply-side effects. If the government cuts taxes on labour as well as on capital investments, the quantities of labour and capital inputs supplied to markets could increase, and then aggregate supply increases. Through incentive effects, called **supply-side effects**, a tax cut can increase aggregate supply and potential GDP.

supply-side effects the incentive effects of taxes on aggregate supply

All economists believe that tax cuts have incentive effects causing a small increase in aggregate supply — shifting both the *LAS* and *SAS* curves rightward. The supply-side effects are small because most people already work as many hours as they can, and don't get much choice from their bosses over how long to work. More take-home pay may encourage a few more hours per week, but not many more.

Supply-Siders Economists and politicians who believe that there are *powerful* supply-side incentive effects to tax cuts are called *supply-siders*. There is no empirical evidence to support supply-siders' claims that tax cuts have large effects on aggregate supply. Tax cuts certainly affect the economy, but most of that effect is through increased spending and aggregate demand, as we discussed in section 12.1.

NOTE
Supply-siders believe that tax cuts have powerful incentive effects, and claim that tax cuts will increase, not decrease, government tax revenues.

Are you wondering why I am explaining an idea that almost all economists reject as an exaggeration? It is important to know about supply-side effects because many politicians are supply-siders. Politicians who favour a hands-off role for government often use supply-sider arguments to support tax cuts.

The false argument they present goes like this: Tax cuts will *increase*, not decrease, government tax revenues. How is that possible? If tax cuts have powerful incentive effects, people will work many more hours and incomes will go up dramatically. Even though a lower tax rate means that the government gets a smaller portion from every dollar people earn, people are earning so many more dollars from longer hours worked that the total amount of taxes collected increases. Government tax revenues increase instead of decrease.

Laffer Curve This idea was proposed by an advisor to U.S. President Ronald Reagan named Arthur Laffer. He explained his idea using the graph in Figure 12.7 known as the *Laffer Curve*.

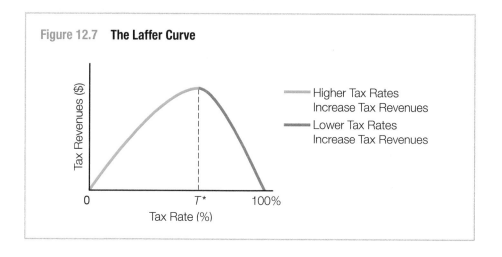

Figure 12.7 **The Laffer Curve**

The horizontal axis measures the income tax rate, from zero to 100 percent. The vertical axis measures the total tax revenues that will be collected for each tax rate. At a zero tax rate there will be zero tax revenues. And at a 100 percent tax rate, there will also be zero tax revenues because no one has any incentive to work if the government takes everything. In between these extremes, as the tax rate rises from zero, tax revenues increase (the upward-sloping green part of the curve). Eventually, at tax rate T^*, tax revenues are at a maximum. As rates rise beyond T^*, the disincentive effects of further tax increases discourage work. People work so much less that their reduced incomes, even when taxed at a higher rate, produce decreasing tax revenues (the downward-sloping red part of the curve).

Laffer convinced President Reagan that the U.S. economy was at a tax rate above T^* in the red range. If that were true, a cut in the tax rate would increase tax revenues. President Reagan — a pioneering hands-off supply-sider — cut taxes in the 1980s expecting increases in tax revenues. Instead, tax revenues decreased. With tax revenues falling short of government spending, the U.S. government went heavily into debt. During Reagan's presidency, the U.S. national debt (a concept coming in section 12.4) skyrocketed from US$700 billon to US$3 trillion. In Canada, former Ontario Premier Mike Harris was also a supply-sider whose tax cuts decreased tax revenues, despite claiming that revenues would increase.

Almost every country in the world (France with a tax rate of 75 percent on high incomes might be an exception) has a tax rate in the green range below the rate T^*. That means a tax cut decreases, not increases, tax revenues, which is what happened in the United States and Canada.

▶
Former British Prime Minister Thatcher and former American President Reagan believed strongly in supply-side economics. Both cut taxes drastically expecting government revenues to increase. But as most economists predicted, revenues decreased, and their governments ran huge deficits.

Tom Hanley/Alamy

Too Good to Be True Supply-sider arguments appeal to politicians who promise tax cuts — which voters like — while not reducing government services or going into debt. If supply-side effects were that powerful, tax cuts would have no opportunity cost! But you know that every choice has an opportunity cost. Any claim that a choice has no opportunity cost is too good to be true. No matter what politicians and voters want to believe, it would take magic to make the supply-sider argument true. That's why economists often refer to supply-sider arguments as "voodoo economics."

Refresh 12.2

MyEconLab

For answers to these Refresh Questions, visit MyEconLab.

1. In your own words, explain how fiscal policy can increase aggregate supply.

2. Why do most economists believe that cutting taxes (supply-side incentive) will not increase tax revenues?

3. Explain how saving can help economic growth. Explain how saving can hurt economic growth. Which effect do you think is more important? Explain your answer.

Are Deficits Always Bad?
Government Budget Surpluses and Deficits

Working, going to school, paying living expenses — I'm sure you know all about budgets. The word *budget* comes from the Latin word *bulga* — a pouch or wallet and its contents. The English word *budget* first applied only to governments! In the mid-1700s, the British Chancellor of the Exchequer (the Minister of Finance) presented his annual statement to Parliament and was said "to open the budget." The word applied to individuals and businesses only in the late 1800s. Today, a budget is a plan of income and spending — money flowing into and out of your wallet.

In a government budget, incomes come mainly from tax revenues, and governments spend on products and services and on transfer payments. Fiscal policy — changes in government spending, taxes, and transfers — affects governments' budgets.

The language of budgets applies to governments, individuals, and businesses. But governments are different from individuals and businesses in many important ways.

Living on $264 Billion a Year: Government Budgets, Revenues, and Spending

Every month you have income coming into your wallet, and spending going out. If your income and spending match, you have a *balanced budget.* If you are like most students, your spending is more than your income, so you have a *deficit* — an amount by which your spending exceeds your income for the month. You have to finance (get money to cover) your deficit by going into *debt* — borrowing from student loans, credit cards, or family. If you are lucky enough to have a month when your income is greater than your expenses, you have a *surplus* — an amount by which your income exceeds your spending for the month. You can use the surplus money to treat yourself (splurge for an extra movie?), to save, or to pay off some of your debts. Government budgets are similar.

Government Revenues   Government income is called revenue. It comes from many sources, including personal income taxes, corporate taxes, Employment Insurance premiums paid by workers and employers, GST/HST, and other, non-tax areas. Figure 12.8 shows the sources of government revenue. The income taxes you and I pay make up the bulk (49 percent) of government revenues.

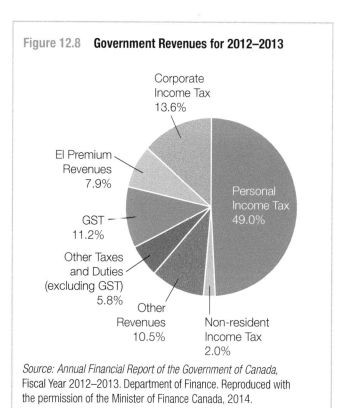

Figure 12.8   **Government Revenues for 2012–2013**

Corporate Income Tax 13.6%

El Premium Revenues 7.9%

GST 11.2%

Other Taxes and Duties (excluding GST) 5.8%

Other Revenues 10.5%

Non-resident Income Tax 2.0%

Personal Income Tax 49.0%

Source: Annual Financial Report of the Government of Canada, Fiscal Year 2012–2013. Department of Finance. Reproduced with the permission of the Minister of Finance Canada, 2014.

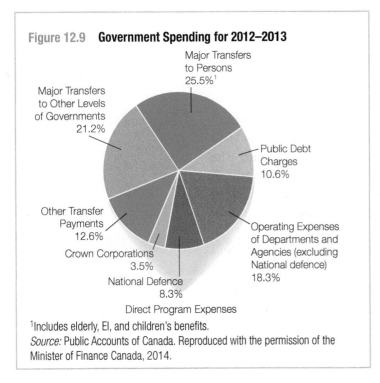

Figure 12.9   Government Spending for 2012–2013

Major Transfers to Persons 25.5%[1]

Major Transfers to Other Levels of Governments 21.2%

Public Debt Charges 10.6%

Other Transfer Payments 12.6%

Crown Corporations 3.5%

National Defence 8.3%

Operating Expenses of Departments and Agencies (excluding National defence) 18.3%

Direct Program Expenses

[1]Includes elderly, EI, and children's benefits.

Source: Public Accounts of Canada. Reproduced with the permission of the Minister of Finance Canada, 2014.

Government Spending   Government spends on purchases of products and services, transfer payments to businesses and individuals (like Employment Insurance benefits), and interest payments on the national debt (like your interest payments on a credit card balance). Figure 12.9 shows that we pay 11 percent of our taxes on interest payments (public debt charges) on the accumulated government debt. The largest expenditure is on direct program spending, which includes health care.

Balancing the Budget   In comparing revenues and spending, the yearly balance of the government budget, like your monthly budget, has three scenarios.

- **Balanced budget** — revenues equal spending
- **Budget deficit** — revenues less than spending
- **Budget surplus** — revenues greater than spending

balanced budget
revenues = spending

budget deficit
revenues < spending

budget surplus
revenues > spending

Figure 12.10 shows the year-end position of the Government of Canada's budget for selected years between 1987–88 and 2012–13. For each year, there are three numbers — revenues, spending, and the resulting deficit or surplus. A deficit is represented by a negative number, a surplus by a positive number.

Figure 12.10   Government of Canada Budgets, Selected Years, 1992–2014 (billions of $)

Year	1992–93	1997–98	2007–08	2009–10	2012–13
Revenues	124.5	160.9	242.4	218.6	256.6
Spending	163.5	157.9	232.8	274.2	275.6
Deficit (–) or Surplus (+)	–39.0	+3.0	+9.6	–55.6	–18.9

Source: Department of Finance, Federal Government Public Accounts. Table 1 Fiscal Transactions. http://www.fin.gc.ca/frt-trf/2009/frt0901-eng.asp; Budget 2014, Table 4.2.4 Summary Statement of Transactions. Totals may not add due to rounding.

On the bottom line (pun intended) of the last three columns, notice that the federal budget went from a surplus of $9.6 billion in 2007–08 to a deficit of $55.6 billion in 2009–10. The move from a budget surplus to a large deficit happened as the Canadian economy went into recession during the Global Financial Crisis. As the economy has recovered from the Global Financial Crisis, the deficit has fallen to $18.9 billion. The connections between increasing deficits and economic recession, and decreasing deficits and economy recovery, is not accidental.

Automatic Weapons for Stabilizing Business Cycles

The fiscal policy tools described so far require the government to make decisions to act. To correct a recessionary gap, Parliament cuts taxes or increases spending. To correct an inflationary gap, Parliament raises taxes or decreases spending. But there are other fiscal policy tools that work automatically with changes in the business cycle. No government decisions are necessary.

Automatic Stabilizers   Existing taxes and transfer programs are also fiscal policy tools for fighting business cycles. When a negative demand shock causes the economy to contract, real GDP decreases. Government tax revenues automatically fall, returning some money to the other macroeconomic players to spend. Transfer payments automatically increase, in programs like Employment Insurance, supporting consumer spending (C) and aggregate demand. These tax and transfer adjustments that happen automatically during business cycles are called **automatic stabilizers**. They help counteract changes to real GDP and steer the economy back toward potential GDP without requiring explicit government decisions.

automatic stabilizers   tax and transfer adjustments that counteract changes to real GDP without explicit government decisions

Automatic stabilizers work in both directions. When a positive demand shock causes the economy to expand beyond potential GDP, tax revenues increase and transfer payments decrease. The resulting decrease in aggregate demand pushes the economy back down toward potential GDP.

Automatic stabilizers work like the thermostat in your house, reacting to the weather outside. When it's colder outside, the heat goes on. When it's warmer, the heat goes off. The temperature inside your house stays stable, despite the fluctuating temperatures outside.

▲ This woman is adjusting the thermostat to keep the temperature inside where she wants it. The temperature inside is automatically controlled for her comfort regardless of the weather outside. Automatic stabilizers work like a thermostat, keeping the economy closer to potential GDP regardless of external shocks.

NOTE
Since automatic stabilizers were
introduced after the Great Depression,
business cycles in Canada have been
less frequent, and contractions have
been less severe.

Smoothing Business Cycles   Most automatic stabilizers did not exist during the Great Depression. Income taxes and transfer programs like Employment Insurance, welfare payments, Canada Pension Plan, and health care were introduced after the Great Depression. Because of automatic stabilizers, business cycles in Canada have been less frequent, and the contractions have been less severe. Automatic stabilizers do their job, helping "steady" the key macroeconomic outcome of steady growth.

But every choice, including the choice to introduce automatic stabilizers, has an opportunity cost. Increases in government budget deficits and accumulated debt since the Global Financial Crisis reflect that opportunity cost.

Automatic Deficits and Surpluses   Automatic stabilizers create automatic deficits and surpluses. Suppose the economy starts at potential GDP and the government budget is balanced. A negative aggregate demand shock pushes the economy into a recession. As automatic stabilizers start working, tax revenues decrease and spending on transfer payments increases. A budget deficit is automatically created as the stabilizers do their job.

Alternatively, start again at potential GDP with a balanced government budget. This time, a positive aggregate demand shock pushes the economy into an expansion. As automatic stabilizers start working, tax revenues increase and spending on transfer payments decreases. A budget surplus is automatically created.

cyclical deficits and surpluses
created only as a result of
automatic stabilizers
counteracting business cycles

The deficits and surpluses created only as a result of automatic stabilizers counteracting the business cycle are called **cyclical deficits** and **cyclical surpluses**.

Balanced Budgets Can Be Bad   Once there are automatic stabilizers, balancing the budget can be dangerous for an economy. Most individuals try to balance their budgets, and believe that governments should do the same. But look what happens if governments always follow this advice.

If a negative aggregate demand shock pushes the economy into a recession, automatic stabilizers start working and create a cyclical deficit. If the government tries to balance the budget, it has to either increase revenues or decrease spending. Increasing revenues means raising taxes on consumers or businesses, which decreases consumer spending (C) or business investment spending (I). Decreasing government spending means reducing government purchases of products and services (G) or reducing transfer payments, which in turn decrease consumer spending (C).

NOTE
Government's attempt to balance
the budget during a recession
decreases aggregate demand, make
recessions worse.

Remember your mantra: Aggregate demand $= C + I + G + X - IM$. The government's attempt to balance the budget during a recession decreases aggregate demand (decreasing C, I, and G). This negative demand shock *makes the recession even worse.*

Before Keynes introduced his views on macroeconomics, governments followed the advice to act like financially responsible individuals and balance their budgets. Even without many automatic stabilizers in place, governments raised taxes and decreased spending. These fiscal policies, while well-intentioned, helped make the Great Depression worse.

In 2009, facing the Global Financial Crisis, governments around the world followed Keynes's advice, cutting taxes and increasing spending. Deficits in Canada and most countries increased dramatically, as governments acted as "spenders of last resort." Economists from both the hands-off and hands-on camps give credit to this deficit-financed government spending for helping to prevent another Great Depression.

Economics *Out There*

Europe's "Austerians" Need a Lesson on Multipliers and Macroeconomics

When governments around the world used expansionary fiscal policy to counter the Global Financial Crisis and rescue national banking systems, budget deficits skyrocketed, especially in Europe. Many policymakers, including those at the International Monetary Fund (IMF), became alarmed, and argued that governments must reduce their deficits. These "austerians" — supporters of fiscal austerity — insisted that governments cut spending and increase taxes. They believed that balanced budgets would restore confidence, business investment, and stimulate the depressed economies.

Many countries had IMF loans, and felt pressure to follow the austerian advice. Governments cut spending, laid off public servants, and stopped buying from the private sector. Decreased spending means decreases incomes in the circular flow. This is a negative demand shock, with multiplier effects. A cut in government spending causes an even larger decrease in GDP.

After years of austerity policies and little improvement in the European economies, the IMF Chief Economist, Olivier Blanchard, made a remarkable admission of their mistake. We "significantly underestimated the increase in unemployment and the decline in domestic demand" from austerity policies. The IMF discovered that the multiplier for government spending was about 1.5, much larger than they had believed. That means every $1 cut in government spending reduced GDP by $1.50.

As Professor Christopher Ragan notes, it is sad that so many European governments "have forgotten or never understood" basic macroeconomic concepts like the circular flow and multipliers, and "millions of their countrymen are now paying the economic price."

Sources: Based on Neil Irwin, "An Amazing Mea Culpa from the IMF's Chief Economist on Austerity," *Washington Post*, 3 January 2013; Christopher Ragan, "Why Europe's 'Austerians' Need a Lesson in Macroeconomics," *Globe and Mail*, 16 July 2013.

Why Spend Other People's Money?　Budget surpluses can also be a problem. If a positive aggregate demand shock pushes the economy into an expansion, automatic stabilizers start working and create a cyclical surplus. While you or I are happy with a personal budget surplus, the government surplus is money coming from taxpayers' pockets. Why should the government collect taxes it doesn't need?

If the government tries to balance the budget, it has to either decrease revenues or increase spending. Decreasing revenues means cutting taxes on consumers or businesses, which will increase consumer spending (C) and business investment spending (I). Increasing government spending means increasing government purchases of products and services (G) or increasing transfer payments, which in turn increases consumer spending (C).

Government attempts to reduce the surplus to balance the budget during an expansion increase aggregate demand (increasing C, I, and G). This positive demand shock *accelerates the expansion beyond potential GDP and increases the risk of inflation.*

NOTE
Government's attempt to balance the budget during an expansion increases aggregate demand, increasing the risk of inflation.

Deficits and Surpluses: Cyclical versus Structural

Balanced budgets can be bad fiscal policy, but not always. When the government *always* applies the advice to balance budgets to the aggregate economy, the results are destabilizing — worsening both recessions and inflationary expansions. This is an example of the fallacy of composition — what is true for one individual (micro) is not necessarily true for the economy as a whole (macro).

That does not mean that economists favour unlimited government deficits or surpluses. There are other deficits, different from cyclical deficits, that do seriously concern economists. Most economist favour a policy for government to balance the budget over the business cycle (section 12.5 examines the differences between the "Yes" and "No" camps).

NOTE
With a balanced budget over the business cycles, cyclical surpluses during expansions offset cyclical deficits during contractions.

Good Balanced Budgets over the Business Cycle   What does it mean to balance the budget over the business cycle? The phases of a business cycle (section 6.3) include an expansion and a contraction. A "good" balanced budget will have a surplus during the expansion and a deficit during the contraction. If the positive amount of the surplus equals the negative amount of the deficit, then the budget is balanced over the business cycle. The money in the government's wallet will be the same at the end of the cycle as it was at the beginning.

This fiscal policy has the benefits of automatic stabilizers, while keeping government from spending more or less than it collects in taxes. The government can live within its means, like a financially responsible individual, and still help steer the economy.

structural deficits and surpluses
budget deficits and surpluses occurring at potential GDP

Structural Deficits (and Surpluses) at Potential GDP   The deficits (and surpluses) that most concern economists are not cyclical but structural. A **structural deficit** occurs when governments spend more than their revenues *even while the economy is at potential GDP and growing steadily*. Structural deficits are not caused by business cycles. They are built into the structure of government taxes, transfers, and spending programs.

A **structural surplus** occurs when there is a government budget surplus even while the economy is at potential GDP and growing steadily.

There are problems with both structural deficits and structural surpluses. Structural deficits are ongoing. Even when the economy is at full employment, the government has to borrow money. There are no offsetting surpluses. As deficits accumulate, the government must go deeper into debt. The Government of Canada had continuous structural deficits for 20 years between 1975 and 1995. Total deficits (cyclical deficits plus structural deficits) ranged from roughly $6 billion to $39 billion *every year*. As a result, Canada's accumulated debt increased, from about $34 billion in 1975–1976 to $554 billion in 1995–1996. Think about the interest payments on a debt of $554 billion borrowed dollars! And every Canadian has to help pay for it through taxes!

Structural surpluses also accumulate over time, raising the question of why government keeps collecting taxpayers' money that it is not spending. From 2006 until the Global Financial Crisis, Canada's Conservative government had deliberately small structural surpluses. They used those structural surpluses to start paying down the accumulated debt from past deficits.

But we are getting ahead of the story. To fully understand these issues, we have to examine Canada's national debt — and that's next.

1. In your own words, explain how automatic stabilizers work. In your explanation, include the terms "surplus" and "deficit."

2. What do economists mean when they say, "balance the budget over the business cycle?"

3. How might a structural governmental deficit directly affect you?

MyEconLab

For answers to these Refresh Questions, visit MyEconLab.

We Owe How Much?!
From Deficits to the National Debt

12.4

Explain the difference between deficits and debts, and identify five arguments about the national debt.

What is the difference between a deficit and a debt — two often confused words?

Suppose you start the year with no debt. You don't owe anyone money, and you have a zero balance on your credit card. In January, you earn $2000, but spend $2500. You have a deficit of $500 for January — the amount by which your income for the month (money flowing into your wallet) is less than your spending (money flowing out of your wallet). You put the $500 on your credit card, so now you have a debt of $500.

February is an expensive month. You earn $2000 but spend $3000. Your deficit for the month is $1000, and you pay for it by putting another $1000 on your credit card. At the end of February your credit card balance — your debt — is now $1500, the sum of your accumulated deficits.

Deficits and debts have different time dimensions. Deficits (and surpluses) are a *flow*, while debt is a *stock* (see Chapter 6).

Deficits Are a Flow   A *flow* is an amount per unit of time. Your income is a flow. To say your income is $2000 makes no sense, unless we know if it is $2000 a week, $2000 a month, or $2000 a year. The number is meaningful only when there is a time dimension. Deficits (and surpluses) are flows. They must be measured for a specified time dimension. In the example above, you had *monthly* deficits for January ($500) and February ($1000). For government, deficits and surpluses are usually measured *annually* — per year.

Debt Is a Stock   Debt is a *stock* — a fixed amount at a moment in time. In our example, your debt on February 28 was $1500, the total amount you owed at that moment in time. Canada's national debt on March 31, 2013, was $602.4 billion — the amount the nation owed at that moment in time.

▲ Credit and debit cards make shopping and spending easy. Problems start when you cannot pay enough back at the end of the month to even cover the interest charges. Then deficit spending can become crippling debt.

Marie C Fields/Shutterstock

Counting to $600 Billion and Beyond: Measuring the National Debt

national debt (public debt) total amount owed by government equals (sum of past deficits) − (sum of past surpluses)

The **national debt** (also called the **public debt**) is the sum of past government budget deficits minus the sum of past budget surpluses. The national debt goes back to the creation of Canada. In 1867, the national debt was $76 million, measured in 1867 prices. The national debt in 2013 was $602.4 billion, measured in 2013 prices. The national debt in any year is measured in the nominal prices of that year.

Because prices change from year to year, and the economy is changing, it is difficult to compare the national debt from year to year. The most meaningful measure of the national debt is the national debt as a percentage of GDP. This ratio eliminates complications of price changes and economic growth. Figure 12.11 shows Canada's national debt as a percentage of GDP between 1926 and 2013.

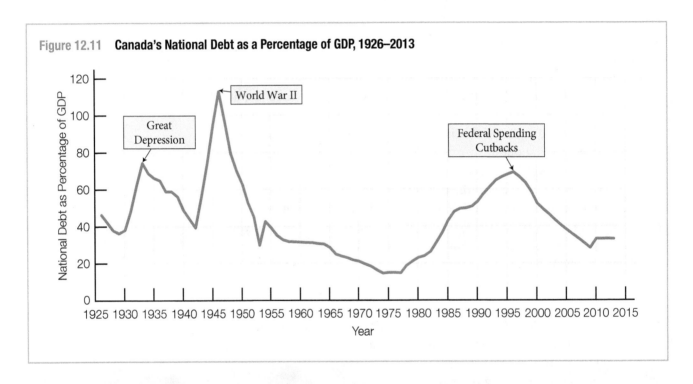

Figure 12.11   Canada's National Debt as a Percentage of GDP, 1926–2013

The first two major spikes in the ratio of national debt to GDP were due to the Great Depression (when tax revenues fell and government spending increased) and World War II (due to government spending on the war effort). The big spike from the late 1970s until the mid-1990s was different. This increase was due to a long string of peacetime budget deficits, which kept adding to the accumulated national debt. Then, starting in 1996, the federal government cut spending dramatically, especially transfer payments to provincial governments. From 1997 to 2008, annual budget surpluses reduced both the amount of the national debt and the ratio of the national debt to GDP.

The 2013 ratio of national debt to GDP for Canada was 33 percent. This was much lower than the 2013 ratio for the United States (87 percent), the United Kingdom (85 percent), France (87 percent), Germany (56 percent), Italy (110 percent), or Japan (140 percent).

What's in a Number? There are many numbers to consider when examining the national debt. Government debt as a percentage of GDP (33 percent), where Canada currently does well relative to other countries, is one number. That number is also much lower than Canada's ratio during the Great Depression (74 percent) or World War II (113 percent).

The amount of the national debt is another number. The national debt reached a new peak of $562.9 billion in 1997 (in 1997 prices). It was $463.7 billion in 2009 (in 2009 prices), but then rose as a result of the Global Financial Crisis to $602.4 billion in 2013.

You often see calculations of the national debt as a dollar amount per Canadian. That number is the national debt divided by the population. For 2013 that number was $17 043 per person. In effect you and I and every other person in Canada "owed" $17 043. If I had that balance owing on my credit card, I would be worried! Should we, as citizens, be concerned about these numbers for the national debt? What do the numbers mean?

Bad Debt or Good Debt?
Myths and Problems about the National Debt

Is the national debt a problem, or does it reflect the government's wise use of fiscal policy to help correct past problems of business cycles? There are many arguments about the national debt. Some are based on false assumptions and can be rejected as myths. But reasonable differences remain between the "Yes — Markets Self-Adjust — Hands-Off" and "No — Market Fail Often — Hands-On" camps, and among politicians, about whether the national debt is a problem, and what, if anything, should be done about it.

Let's examine five common arguments criticizing the national debt to see if they are based on myths and should be ignored, or are genuine problems and must be considered.

1. Will Canada Go Bankrupt? If you or I don't repay our debts — pay off that credit card balance — we may go bankrupt, our credit rating will suffer, and it will be difficult to borrow money in the future. Is Canada at risk of bankruptcy and a negative credit rating because since 1867 the country has never paid off the national debt?

This argument is largely a myth. The Government of Canada never has to pay back the national debt — it can simply refinance it. Here's why.

The argument that Canada must pay back the national debt is based on the idea that what is true for an individual must be true for the government. If an 80-year-old man walks into the bank with a small down payment and asks for a 25-year mortgage, the banker will laugh and say no. There is not much chance of the man living long enough to repay the loan.

While the man is mortal and will die, the Government of Canada is effectively immortal. Politicians running the federal government come and go, but the country of Canada, its government, and the institutions of Parliament remain. They have remained intact since Confederation and are expected to continue to do so.

NOTE
The Government of Canada never has to pay back the national debt — it can simply refinance it.

The national debt is financed mostly by government bonds that have a 30-year maturity. Every year, some of those bonds come due and must be repaid. The Government of Canada repays them by issuing a new set of 30-year bonds and uses that newly borrowed money to pay off the old bonds. This is called refinancing the debt. Old debt is paid off with new debt. The only significant cost is the interest that must continue to be paid — a problem we will examine shortly. With refinancing, the national debt can stay in place indefinitely without repayment — as long as the bondholders trust the Canadian government will pay all bonds and interest payments that come due. That trust can disappear for countries that borrow too much, with expensive consequences.

Following an economic crisis and deadly rioting, Argentina defaulted on its national debt in 2002. Since then, it has been difficult for Argentina to borrow money. Only Venezuela has been willing to lend Argentina money, but at high interest rates — 15 percent! More than 10 years later, Argentina is still suffering the consequences of its actions.

2. Burden for Future Generations
By borrowing money today, is the Government of Canada imposing a burden on future generations, who must either repay the debt or at least pay the interest? The argument that the debt must be repaid is a myth, but what about the burden of interest payments?

There is undoubtedly interest to be paid. A key question is, who receives the interest payments? About 80 percent of the national debt is held by Canadians. That means the interest payments are mainly going to Canadians. So most interest payments are more of a redistribution of money than a burden on taxpayers. The taxes collected from all Canadians go, in part, to pay interest received by Canadian government bondholders. If more of the Canadian government bonds were held by non-Canadians, this argument would become more important. As it stands now, the interest payments on the national debt are not a serious problem for future generations.

3. Debt Is Always Bad
"Governments should live within their means, like responsible individuals, and not go into debt." This argument is based on a myth, because most individual consumers and businesses regularly make smart choices that involve going into debt. People taking on a mortgage or a car lease are going into debt. Businesses regularly issue bonds and go into debt to build new factories. Debt is a smart choice if the expected future profits or benefits from spending the borrowed money are greater than the interest costs on the loan.

For government, debt can be a smart choice if the positive impact on the economy of the spending financed by debt is greater than the interest cost. If the debt is used to finance infrastructure — such as roads, bridges, public transit, education, or communications networks — that improve productivity, lower costs, and provide positive externalities to the economy, most economists see a smart choice. And these improvements mostly benefit future generations. But if the debt is used simply to finance consumption, spent by politicians trying to win votes before an election, most economists see that as a problem.

What about debt-financed government spending to prevent a recession? The "Yes — Hands-Off" camp might disapprove, while the "No — Hands-On" camp clearly approves. So government debt can be a problem, but it can also be a smart choice. See Economics Out There (page 376) for one unusual "Yes — Hands-Off" camp argument against government debt.

4. Interest Payments Create Self-Perpetuating Debt With a balance on your credit card, you have to make a minimum payment every month. If you don't pay at least the interest owing on your debt, then you have to borrow more to pay the interest, which increases your debt. The balance on your credit card grows. The next month you have to pay interest on this larger balance. It is easy to get caught in this vicious cycle. You may never get out of debt.

Figure 12.12 shows an example of a person paying $50 each month on her credit card balance. Her original balance was $5000. The credit card company charges 2 percent interest per month (don't you wish?). After four payments, she has paid $200 but now owes $5202 — she is deeper in debt in month four than she was in month one.

Figure 12.12 Self-Perpetuating Debt on a Credit Card

Month	Balance	Payment	Balance after Payment	Interest	Month End Balance
1	$5000	$50	$5000 − $50 = $4950	$4950 × 2% = $99	$4950 + $99 = $5049
2	$5049	$50	$5049 − $50 = $4999	$4999 × 2% = $99.98	$4999 + $99.98 = $5098.98
3	$5098.98	$50	$5098.98 − $50 = $5048.98	$5048.98 × 2% = $100.98	$5048.98 + $100.98 = $5149.96
4	$5149.96	$50	$5149.96 − $50 = $5099.96	$5099.96 × 2% = $102	$5099.96 + $102 = $5201.96

The Government of Canada faced a similar situation between the mid-1970s and mid-1990s. Persistent yearly deficits increased the national debt, which increased interest payments. Larger interest payments lead to larger yearly deficits. At the end of 1996, interest payments on the national debt reached $42.4 billion for the year — too high to be sustained.

The opportunity cost of spending that much money on interest alone was extraordinary. To put that number in perspective, interest payments on the national debt in 1996 took 36 cents of every dollar the government collected in revenues. That left only 64 cents of every tax dollar to spend on all government programs. The $42.4 billion interest bill was more money than the government spent that year on all transfers to Canadians, including Employment Insurance, Canada Pension Plan, Old Age Security, and national defence *combined*. That interest bill on the national debt represented 30 percent of all government spending. In 1996, the government, recognizing the national debt as a problem, began paying it down. By 2013, public debt charges had fallen to 11 percent of all government spending (see Figure 12.9, page 366).

NOTE
There is a problem when interest payments create self-perpetuating debt. There is a vicious cycle when yearly deficits increase national debt, increasing interest payments, increasing yearly deficits, etc.

Economics *Out There*

Why Bother?

Robert Barro — a prominent hands-off economist at Harvard University — argues that any government spending financed by going into debt will have no impact on the economy, so why bother?

He argues that consumers, with rational expectations, will expect higher taxes in the future to pay for the interest on the debt. So to save for future taxes, consumers cut back spending now and offset any government spending. The result is government debt without any impact on economy.

The argument — called Ricardian equivalence — was first suggested almost 200 years ago by David Ricardo, an English economist and member of Parliament. Government "stimulus spending is doomed to failure because taxpayers tend to save their stimulus dollars rather than spend them."

Source: Heather Schoffield, "The Ricardian Equivalence Makes a Comeback," *The Globe and Mail*, Report on Business, July 6, 2009.

---

crowding out tendency for government debt-financed fiscal policy to decrease private investment spending by raising interest rates

5. Crowding Out and Crowding In When governments finance the national debt by selling bonds, this increases the supply of bonds, drives down bond prices, and raises interest rates. Higher interest rates make it more expensive for consumers and businesses to borrow. The reduction in business investment spending caused by debt-financed higher interest rates is called **crowding out**. High government borrowing raises interest rates, which in turn reduces (crowds out) some private investment.

On the other hand, if debt-financed government fiscal policy succeeds in increasing real GDP and expanding economic growth, the improvement in business *expectations* of profitability may increase private investment. This positive impact of debt-financed fiscal policy on expectations and business investment spending is called **crowding in**.

crowding in tendency for government debt-financed fiscal policy to increase private investment spending by improving expectations

Myth or Truth? Some, but not all, of the arguments about the national debt are based on myths. How do such myths survive? The answer has to do with the explosive mix of economics and politics that fuels most debates about government deficits and debts and the proper hands-off or hands-on role for government in a market economy. And that is our final topic in this chapter.

Refresh 12.4

MyEconLab

For answers to these Refresh Questions, visit MyEconLab.

1. In your own words, explain the difference between deficits and debts. In your answer, use the terms *flow* and *stock*.

2. Which of the following macroeconomic outcomes are flows and which are stocks: real GDP, unemployment rate, inflation rate, money supply? Explain.

3. Which of the arguments about the problems of the national debt seems most convincing to you? Why?

---

376 CHAPTER 12 SPENDING OTHERS' MONEY

Are Deficits Like Potato Chips? Hands-Off or Hands-On Role for Government?

Distinguish between normative and positive, and between economic and political, arguments about fiscal policy.

Politicians disagree on fiscal policy, deficits, debt, and whether government should play a hands-off or hands-on role in the economy. Their arguments often mix economics with politics, and confuse personal value judgments with statements of fact. One argument, discussed below, compares deficits to potato chips! How can you, as a citizen, analyze those arguments to make your own informed choice about the role of government in a market economy?

Economists, as well as politicians, disagree on the proper role of government in managing our economy. There is no single right answer. But fiscal policy has a powerful impact on the key macroeconomic outcomes of steady growth, full employment, and stable prices. Your vote — whether for a hands-off or a hands-on politician — influences the direction of future economic policy in Canada, and therefore your own future well-being.

Politics

Governments around the world play very different roles in their respective countries. Those different roles are based on different political philosophies. Let's look at one set of differences — between the United States and Canada.

The United States was created through a revolution against British government interference. Their founding political principles emphasized "life, liberty, and the pursuit of happiness." The focus was on the individual's right to pursue her own destiny, free from government restrictions. The United States has hands-off origins.

Canada, created by an act of government, has founding political principles that stress "peace, order, and good government." Canada, as a civil society, stresses government's responsibility to promote and protect the public good. Canada has hands-on origins.

Today, citizens in both countries are attracted to both hands-off and hands-on approaches for government.

NOTE
The United States — created through a revolution against British government interference — has hands-off political origins.

Canada — created by an act of government — has hands-on political origins.

Loaded Words   The words used in arguments about the proper role for government often reveal the speaker's point of view.

For those supporting a hands-off role, the word *government* is often paired with words like *intervene*, *interfere*, and *mistake*. For example, "the government should not *intervene* . . . ," "that is government *interference* . . . ," or "it is a *mistake* for government to . . . ." These words show the speaker believes that government has no legitimate business in taking action, and if government does act, it usually gets it wrong.

For those supporting a hands-on role, the word *government* is often paired with words like *act*, *participate*, and *responsibility*. For example, "the government needs to *act* to . . . ," "this initiative requires government *participation*," or "the government has a *responsibility* to . . . ."

Look for these words when listening to a politician's arguments. They are clues to the politician's views on the proper role of government.

Opinions and Facts: Normative and Positive Statements

There is no right or wrong answer to the question, "What role should government play in our economy?" You might answer, "Government should play a hands-off role," and your sister might answer, "Government should play a hands-on role." The answer depends on your political values, and people have different values or opinions. These *normative statements* involve value judgments or opinions. Normative statements often use the word *should* and cannot be evaluated as true or false by checking the facts.

Positive statements are about what *is*, rather than about what should be. Positive statements *can* be evaluated as true or false by checking the facts. An example of a positive statement is "The Chinese government plays a much larger role in Chinese society than does the Canadian government in Canadian society." We can identify and measure all of the actions taken by the Chinese government and compare them to the actions taken by the Canadian government. If there are more in China, the statement is true. If there are fewer, the statement is false.

In contrast, the statement, "The government in Canada *should* play a larger role like the government in China" is a normative statement — an opinion. Notice the word *should*?

When you hear claims from politicians, or economists, identify if the statement is normative or positive. If it is a normative statement, you can agree or disagree. If it is a positive statement, look for the facts behind the claim to evaluate if it is true or false.

Economics

Economists also make both normative and positive statements, and it is important to distinguish between them. Economists pride themselves on their positive statements, so let's start with those.

Positive Statements   Here are some examples of positive statements in this chapter:

- Tax incentives stimulate saving, increase the quantity of capital, and promote economic growth.
- Tax cuts increase government tax revenues.
- The national debt does not have to be repaid, only refinanced.
- Automatic stabilizers create government budget deficits when the economy goes into a recession.

I am not claiming that any of these statements is actually true or false. But you can evaluate a positive statement as true or false by checking the facts. Some of the statements are true, and some are false. Most economists evaluate the claim by supply-siders that "tax cuts increase government tax revenues" as false because the facts show that when taxes were cut, revenues decreased, not increased. But the claim is still a positive statement — *capable* of being evaluated as true or false by checking the facts.

Normative Statements   Here are examples of normative statements from this chapter. Since they are opinion-based, you have to make up your own mind whether you agree with them or not.

* Government should use tax incentives to encourage saving and promote economic growth.
* Government should increase spending to counteract recessions.
* Government should pay down the national debt.
* Government should balance the budget over the business cycle.

Let's look at the different possible responses to these normative statements. Tax incentives encourage saving, but the hands-off and hands-on camps disagree about trade-offs. As saving increases, there is a cost of reduced aggregate demand in the present, but benefits in the future of increased economic growth.

On government spending to counteract recessions, the hands-off and hands-on camps disagree on whether spending or tax cuts are better policy. Even if the camps could agree on the need to counteract recessions with government policy (they don't!), the choice between tax cuts (less government) and spending (more government) depends on hands-off versus hands-on views on the proper role of government.

Paying down the national debt reduces future interest payments on the debt. But every policy has an opportunity cost. The money could instead be spent on improving infrastructure in the present, which would promote growth in the future. There are no right or wrong choices here, only trade-offs.

While most economists agree that governments should balance the budget over the business cycle, when politicians go to act on that advice, there may be problems, as you will see in the next section.

Mixing It Up: Politics and Economics

Arguments from politicians about fiscal policy, deficits, and debt often combine politics and economics, creating additional problems in evaluating what you hear. There are two main mix-ups.

Will Politicians Follow Economists' Advice?   "Bet you can't eat just one," was an advertising slogan for potato chips. Most economists see the value in government deficits during economic contractions as long as they are offset by government surpluses during expansions, resulting in a balanced budget over the business cycle. But there is a potato chip argument — combining politics and economics — against running *any* deficits.

Politicians, not economists, decide on government tax, transfer, and spending programs. More government spending and tax cuts can make economic sense in a contraction, but it is hard for politicians to stop spending and raise taxes — both politically unpopular — when the contraction ends. Deficits are too politically tasty to trust politicians to stop at just one. So policy advice that makes economic sense — balance the budget over the business cycle — might be reasonably rejected because it doesn't make political sense.

Deficits are like potato chips, you just can't stop at one, or two, or three, or four, or five.

— Saskatchewan premier Brad Wall, 2007

Are You Hearing a Political or Economic Argument?

You will hear politicians argue against the national debt, claiming that governments must act like responsible individuals and never go into debt, or that Canada will go bankrupt when we have to pay back the debt. These sound like economic arguments about debt. But you have seen that some parallels between individuals and governments are false. Responsible individuals and businesses regularly go into debt, and the national debt does not have to be paid back, only refinanced. So these statements are really political, hands-off arguments against a larger role for government, disguised as an economic argument about the national debt.

Hands-Off or Hands-On?
Your Choice

Arguments over fiscal policy are often the main event for fights between the "Yes — Markets Self-Adjust" camp so hands-off, and the "No — Markets Fail Often" camp so hands-on. Disagreement over taxes versus government spending, and over deficits, surpluses, and the national debt are often heated. But the arguments often mix politics and economics in misleading ways. Sort out the positive from the normative statements, and the economic arguments from the political arguments, so that you can make informed choices as a citizen about hands-off and hands-on roles for government fiscal policy and your own future.

Refresh 12.5

MyEconLab

For answers to these Refresh Questions, visit MyEconLab.

1. Choose two words each that you would use to best describe the hands-on and hands-off approaches to government.

2. In your own words, describe the difference between a normative and positive statement.

3. On fiscal policy, what position would you vote for, hands-off or hands-on? Explain your answer.

Study Guide

12.1 Spenders of Last Resort: Aggregate Demand Policies for Stabilizing Business Cycles

Fiscal policies — changes in government spending, taxes, and transfers — act as aggregate demand shocks, have multiplied impact on aggregate demand, and can counter output gaps.

- *Fiscal policy* — changes in government purchases, taxes, and transfers to achieve macroeconomic outcomes of steady growth, full employment, and stable prices.

- The circular flow transmits the effects of fiscal policy.
  - **Injection** — spending in the circular flow that does not start with consumers: *G* (government spending), *I* (business investment spending), *X* (exports).
  - **Leakage** — spending that leaks out of the circular flow through taxes, saving, and imports.

- **Multiplier effect** — a spending injection has a multiplied effect on aggregate demand.

- There is a multiplied increase in aggregate demand from
  - increased government spending
  - tax cuts
  - increased transfers

- There is a multiplied decrease in aggregate demand from
  - decreased government spending
  - tax increase
  - decreased transfers

- Size of multiplier effects depends on leakages out of circular flow.
  - $\text{Size of Multiplier Effect} = \dfrac{1}{\text{\% of leakages from additional income}}$
  - More leakages = smaller multiplier
  - Fewer leakages = larger multiplier
  - The multiplier effect for tax and transfer changes is not as big as for government spending.

- Any change in injections — *G, I, X* — is an aggregate demand shock, shifting the aggregate demand curve rightward (increase in injections) or leftward (decrease in injections) by a multiplied effect of the initial injection.

- **Expansionary fiscal policy** — increases aggregate demand by increasing government spending, decreasing taxes, or increasing transfers
  - shifts the aggregate demand curve rightward — a positive aggregate demand shock
  - counters a recessionary gap

- **Contractionary fiscal policy** — decreases aggregate demand by decreasing government spending, increasing taxes, or decreasing transfers
  - shifts the aggregate demand curve leftward — a negative aggregate demand shock
  - counters an inflationary gap

- Multiplier effects of an injection on equilibrium real GDP depend on how close the economy is to potential GDP.
  - When the economy is below potential GDP, more of the increase in aggregate demand increases real GDP.
  - When the economy is at or above potential GDP, more of the increase in aggregate demand drives up prices.

- Hands-off camp favours tax cuts to accelerate the economy; spending reductions to slow down the economy.

- Hands-on camp favours government spending to accelerate the economy; tax increases to slow down the economy.

12.2 Building Foundations: Aggregate Supply Policies for Promoting Growth

Fiscal policies targeting aggregate supply — tax incentives, support for R&D, education, training — promote economic growth, but hands-off and hands-on camps differ in emphasizing long-run or short-run effects.

- Government policies to promote economic growth include spending and tax incentives
  - to stimulate saving and increase the quantity of capital.
  - for research and development.
  - for education and training that increase human capital.

- Fiscal spending and tax policies can increase the quantity and quality of inputs, increasing (long-run and short-run) aggregate supply and potential GDP per person.

- Fiscal policies that encourage saving can decrease aggregate demand in the present.
  - Hands-off camp believes long-run benefits of increased aggregate supply outweigh short-run mismatches between reduced aggregate demand and aggregate supply.
  - Hands-on camp worried that short-run costs of decreased aggregate demand and recession outweigh long-run benefits of economic growth.
- **Supply-side effects** — incentive effects of taxes on aggregate supply.
- *Supply-siders* believe tax cuts have powerful incentive effects and will increase, not decrease, government tax revenues.
  - *Laffer Curve* — a graph showing that as the tax rate increases, tax revenues increase, reach a maximum, and then decrease.
  - Evidence shows that tax cuts reduce revenue.
  - Supply-sider arguments appeal to politicians who promise tax cuts — which voters like — without having to reduce government services or go into debt.

12.3 Are Deficits Always Bad?
Government Budget Surpluses and Deficits

Automatic stabilizers create cyclical budget deficits and surpluses while keeping the economy close to potential GDP. Structural deficits and surpluses at potential GDP are more problematic.

- Government budget scenarios:
  - **Balanced budget** — revenues = spending
  - **Budget deficit** — revenues < spending
  - **Budget surplus** — revenues > spending
- **Automatic stabilizers** — tax and transfer adjustments that counteract changes to real GDP without explicit government decisions.
  - During contractions, tax revenues fall, transfer payments increase, supporting spending and aggregate demand, but causing automatic budget deficit.
  - During expansions, tax revenues rise, transfer payments decrease, reducing spending and aggregate demand, but causing automatic budget surplus.
- Automatic stabilizers work like a thermostat, keeping the economy close to potential GDP.
  - Since automatic stabilizers were introduced, business cycles are less frequent, and contractions less severe.

- **Cyclical deficits and surpluses** — created only as a result of automatic stabilizers counteracting business cycles.
- With automatic stabilizers, government attempts to balance the budget during:
  - recessions decrease aggregate demand, make recessions worse.
  - expansions increase aggregate demand, increase the risk of inflation.
- With a balanced budget over the business cycle, cyclical surpluses during expansions offset cyclical deficits during contractions.
- Economists are most concerned with **structural deficits and surpluses** — budget deficits and surpluses at potential GDP.

12.4 We Owe How Much?!
From Deficits to the National Debt

Deficits are a flow while debt is a stock. Of five common arguments about national debt, some are myths, some are potential problems.

- Deficits and debt have different time dimensions.
  - Deficits and surpluses are *flows*.
  - Debt is a *stock*.
- **National debt (public debt)** — total amount owed by government = (sum of past deficits) – (sum of past surpluses)
- Five common arguments about whether national debt is a problem or reflects wise government use of fiscal policy are:
  1. Will Canada go bankrupt?
     - Largely a myth.
     - Government of Canada never has to pay back the national debt — it can simply refinance it.
     - Governments that do not pay debts find it difficult to borrow on the international bond market.
  2. Burden for future generations.
     - Depends on who receives interest payments on the national debt — Canadians or non-Canadians.
  3. Debt is always bad.
     - Myth — consumers with mortgages or car leases, businesses issuing bonds to build factories, make smart choices to go into debt.
     - Government debt can be a smart choice if the positive impact on the economy of spending financed by debt is greater than the interest cost.
     - Government debt can be a not-smart choice if spending financed by debt is for consumption only.

4. Interest payments create self-perpetuating debt.
   – Potential problem of the national debt.
   – Canada had yearly deficits between mid-1970s and mid-1990s, which increased national debt and increased interest payments, thereby increasing yearly deficits. This vicious cycle broke in 1996.

5. Crowding out and crowding in.
   – Potential problem and benefit of the national debt.
   – **Crowding out** — tendency for government debt-financed fiscal policy to decrease private investment spending by raising interest rates.
   – **Crowding in** — tendency for government debt-financed fiscal policy to increase private investment spending by improving expectations.

12.5 Are Deficits Like Potato Chips? Hands-Off or Hands-On Role for Government?

Sort out economic arguments from political arguments so that you can make informed choices as a citizen about hands-off and hands-on roles for government fiscal policy and your own future.

- Political philosophies differ among countries.
  – United States — created through a revolution against British government interference — has hands-off origins.
  – Canada — created by an act of government — has hands-on origins.

- Words used in arguments about proper role for government often reveal the speaker's point of view.
  – Hands-off words used with *government*: *intervene, interfere, mistake.*
  – Hands-on words used with *government*: *act, participate, responsibility.*

- Arguments from politicians about fiscal policy, deficits, and debt often mix up politics and economics.
  – Political hands-off arguments against government are often disguised as arguments against the national debt.

TRUE/FALSE

Circle the correct answer. Solutions to these questions are available at the end of the book and on MyEconLab. You can also visit the MyEconLab Study Plan to access additional questions that will help you master the concepts covered in this chapter.

Suppose that after watching the YouTube video "Fear the Boom and Bust: A Hayek vs. Keynes Rap Anthem" (https://www.youtube.com/watch?v=d0nERTFo-Sk) a few of your classmates are inspired to start a musical group called the "Yo camp." They chose the name "Yo camp" because some group members favour the "Yes" camp of economists and some favour the "No" camp. The songwriter asks you to check if the lyrics of the song on fiscal policy are accurate, because you are the best economics student in the class.

Use this scenario to answer questions 1–15. Five of the questions include lyrics based on popular rap songs — see if you can identify which ones!

12.1 Demand Policies for Stabilization

1. If instead of spending money you watch a TV show, you cause a leakage, which exits the circular flow.   T   F

2. In my 'hood we believe in the economist camp spelled N-O! This camp favours tax cuts when the economy is slow.   T   F

3. In recessions, economists like fiscal policies increasing real GDP! But all economists favour tax increases to slow the economy.   T   F

4. The multiplier effect drives higher the economy's health. Government purchases have a large impact on the economy's wealth.   T   F

12.2 Supply Policies for Growth

5. If governments reduced the tax rate you and I pay, They'd make more money because we'd work more hours per day.   T   F

6. Go Shorty, it's your birthday, yeah you can find me at the club, I ain't into "voodoo economics" so only supply-siders can come give me a hug.   T   F

7. As Keynes once said, in the long run we're all dead, which suggests don't spend and save your money instead.   T   F

8. Government spending and tax incentives   T   F
encourage R&D. The R&D knowledge
that benefits others is a positive externality.

12.3 Budget Surpluses and Deficits

9. I like big tax cuts and I cannot lie, but it   T   F
raises the deficit, which you can't deny.

10. When a contracting economy gets   T   F
that shrinking feeling, it automatically
gets government spending healing.

11. Automatic stabilizers work like a   T   F
thermostat for the economy. They
drop spending when the economy's hot;
they drop GDP when it's not.

12.4 National Debt

12. As anyone from the "Yes" or "No"   T   F
camp should know, debt is always bad,
deficits are a stock, and debt is a flow.

13. If you asked economists David Ricardo and   T   F
Robert Barro, they'd agree that to finance
spending, governments should borrow.

12.5 Government Hands-Off or Hands-On?

14. I'm not into making a positive statement,   T   F
so here's what they call a normative statement:
If you invest your savings in an RRSP,
in the long run it's better for you and me.

15. When the economy grows older, it will   T   F
be stronger. They call Canada's founding
origins freedom, just like the United States.

MULTIPLE CHOICE

Circle the best answer. Solutions to these questions are available at the end of the book and on MyEconLab. You can also visit the MyEconLab Study Plan to access similar questions that will help you master the concepts covered in this chapter.

12.1 Demand Policies for Stabilization

1. Fiscal policy is changes in
   a) government purchases.
   b) taxes.
   c) transfers.
   d) all of the above.

2. Which of the following statements about
   multipliers is *false*?
   a) Changes in injections have a multiplied
      effect on aggregate demand.
   b) With more leakages, you get a bigger multiplier.
   c) The multiplier effect for tax changes is smaller
      than for government purchases.
   d) The multiplier effect for transfer changes is
      smaller than for government purchases.

3. Leakages are spending that leaks out
   of the circular flow through
   a) taxes.
   b) savings.
   c) imports.
   d) all of the above.

12.2 Supply Policies for Growth

4. Which of the following fiscal policies is *least*
   likely to increase aggregate supply and
   potential GDP?
   a) Tax incentives for saving accounts
   b) Tax incentives for research and development
   c) Tax incentives for education and training
   d) Fiscal policies for aggregate demand

5. If government reduces tuition fees for
   post-secondary students, this
   a) increases the quality of labour inputs.
   b) decreases the quality of labour inputs.
   c) increases the quantity of labour inputs.
   d) decreases the quantity of labour inputs.

6. Supply-siders believe people respond
   to a lower income tax rate by
   a) stopping work so they stop paying taxes.
   b) working fewer hours and paying less total taxes.
   c) working more hours and paying
      the same total taxes.
   d) working more hours and paying more total taxes.

7. Fiscal policies that encourage savings and capital investment can
   a) decrease both aggregate supply and aggregate demand.
   b) decrease aggregate supply and increase aggregate demand.
   c) increase aggregate supply and decrease aggregate demand.
   d) increase both aggregate supply and aggregate demand.

12.3 Budget Surpluses and Deficits

8. If a country with $50 billion in debt then had revenues of $5 billion and spending of $4 billion, debt at the end of the year is
   a) $49 billion.
   b) $50 billion.
   c) $51 billion.
   d) $54 billion.

9. The deficits or surpluses that most concern economists are
   a) structural surpluses.
   b) structural deficits.
   c) cyclical surpluses.
   d) cyclical deficits.

10. During an expansion,
   a) both tax revenues and government spending decrease.
   b) tax revenues decrease and government spending increases.
   c) tax revenues increase and government spending decreases.
   d) both tax revenues and government spending increase.

12.4 National Debt

11. Which of the following is a genuine problem with the national debt?
   a) Debt is always bad.
   b) The national debt is a burden for future generations.
   c) Interest payments on the national debt can create self-perpetuating debt.
   d) Canada will go bankrupt because of debt.

12. Crowding out is the tendency for government debt-financed fiscal policy to decrease private investment spending by
   a) raising interest rates.
   b) lowering interest rates.
   c) improving expectations.
   d) reducing expectations.

12.5 Government Hands-Off or Hands-On?

13. The founding political principles of
   a) Canada have hands-on origins; United States have hands-on origins.
   b) Canada have hands-off origins; United States have hands-off origins.
   c) Canada have hands-on origins; United States have hands-off origins.
   d) Canada have hands-off origins; United States have hands-on origins.

14. Most economists agree that the government budget should
   a) always be in deficit.
   b) always be in surplus.
   c) always be in balance.
   d) balance over the business cycle.

15. Which of the following statements is normative?
   a) Tax incentives stimulate savings, increase the quantity of capital, and promote economic growth.
   b) Tax cuts will increase government tax revenues.
   c) Governments should pay down the national debt.
   d) The national debt does not have to be repaid, only refinanced.

13

Are Sweatshops All Bad?

Globalization and Trade Policy

LEARNING OBJECTIVES

After reading this chapter, you should be able to:

13.1 Describe how comparative advantage, specialization, and trade improve living standards.

13.2 Explain how competition creates winners, losers, and opponents to trade, and analyze three forms of protectionism.

13.3 Explain the pace of globalization and how to evaluate if sweatshop workers are better off with international trade.

13.4 Evaluate the hands-off and hands-on arguments about the role for government in the globalization debate.

SCPhotos/Alamy

GLOBALIZATION IS CHANGING the world, but

people do not agree whether the changes are for better or for worse. Controversies over the virtues and evils of trade go back centuries. Today, communication technology and transportation improvements have lowered the costs of international trade and sped up the process of globalization. Your technical support call may be answered by someone in Bangalore, India, and a steelworker in Hamilton, Ontario, may have lost a job to a factory worker in Shanghai, China.

Economists and free-trade supporters argue that specialization and trade raise living standards. Supporters point to once-struggling countries like Japan, South Korea, Taiwan — and now China and India — whose standards of living continue to rise with international trade. Critics point to sweatshops in third-world countries as one serious negative outcome of globalized trade. Other critics see globalization as just another way that developed countries in the West are using weaker countries as a source of cheap labour and raw materials.

In this chapter, you will learn about comparative advantage — the concept behind all pro-trade arguments — and how it applies not just to international trade, but also to your personal smart choices about jobs and "trading" in local markets for your everyday needs. You will also explore some of the arguments against globalization, including those of the Nobel Prize–winning economist Joseph Stiglitz.

The controversies over trade and globalization return us to the question of the role for government in the global economy. There are new issues about whether government should help those threatened from international competition through direct protection, or with a social safety net, or not at all. What it comes back to is the need for you — as a citizen of Canada and the world — to understand the issues and to make up your own mind.

13.1 Why Don't You Cook Breakfast? Gains from Trade

Describe how comparative advantage, specialization, and trade improve living standards.

> *What is prudence in the conduct of every family can scarce be folly in that of a great kingdom. If a foreign country can supply us with a commodity cheaper than we ourselves can make it, better buy it of them with some part of the produce of our own industry, employed in a way in which we have some advantage.*
>
> —Adam Smith
>
> *The Wealth of Nations, 1776*

What did you have for breakfast today? Did you have cereal and orange juice at home, or did you buy coffee and a bagel at Tim Hortons on the way to school? Either way, you made a choice — to make breakfast for yourself, or to buy it from a business. This is the most basic choice you and everyone else makes in trying to do the best you can: Do you yourself produce the products and services you want, or do you earn money at a job and then buy (or trade money for) products and services made by others?

In today's Canadian economy, most of us earn money by specializing in a particular occupation. We use (trade) that money to buy what we want. This specialization and trade replaced the self-sufficiency of people living in Canada two hundred years ago. Back then, most aboriginal peoples and pioneers made for themselves most of what they needed — hunting and growing their own food, making clothes from animal hides, and building shelters from available resources.

Voluntary Trade   What happened to lead us all away from self-sufficiency toward specializing and trading? The simple economic answer is that specializing and trading make us better off. Our standard of living in terms of material products and services is much higher with specialization and trade than it was in the past.

Trade is a key to our prosperity. Trade makes all of us better off. Why? Trade is voluntary. Any time two people make a voluntary trade, each person feels that what they get is of greater value than what they give up. If there weren't mutual benefits, the trade wouldn't happen. It's simple self-interest at work.

If You Trade, Should Canada?

Countries face the same basic choice as individuals. Should Canada try to be self-sufficient, producing everything Canadians want, or should Canada specialize in producing some products and services and trade for the rest? Economists from Adam Smith to today argue that the gains from trade make both individuals and countries better off.

Specialization and trade is widespread in Canada and other countries. Figure 13.1 shows the importance of international trade — trade between countries — for the GDP of selected countries in 2012. Remember your mantra: $GDP = C + I + G + X - IM$. Each green bar represents exports (X) as a percentage of GDP for that country. Each red bar represents imports (IM) as a percentage of each country's GDP.

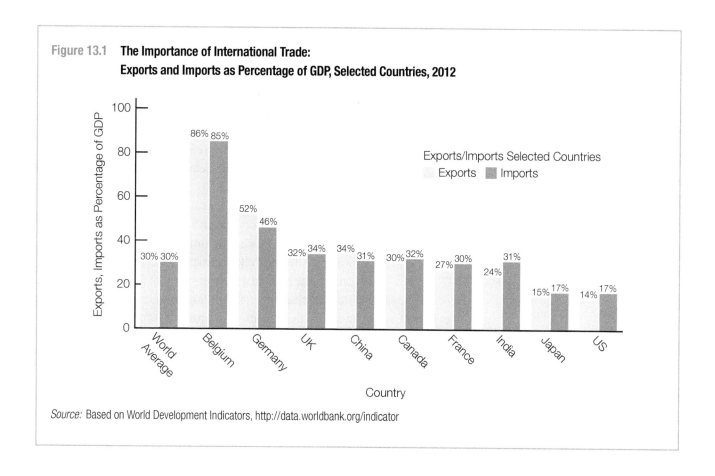

Figure 13.1   The Importance of International Trade:
Exports and Imports as Percentage of GDP, Selected Countries, 2012

Source: Based on World Development Indicators, http://data.worldbank.org/indicator

Canada Is a Trading Nation   If you look at Canada in Figure 13.1, exports are 30 percent of GDP. Almost one out of every three dollars earned by Canadians comes from the sale of exports to the rest of the world. Imports, which do not contribute to Canadian GDP but do contribute to GDP in the rest of the world, are 32 percent of Canadian GDP. Notice how much more important international trade is to the Canadian economy than it is to the U.S. or Japanese economies. Even though the United States and Japan sell a much greater *quantity* of exports than Canada, their domestic economies are much larger. So exports as a *percentage of GDP* are smaller for the United States and Japan than for Canada. Canada is a trading nation, and our standard of living depends significantly on international trade.

Furthermore, 80 percent of our international trade is with one country — the United States. Much is at stake in our trade relations with the United States because a significant portion of Canadian GDP depends on trade with the United States. And because U.S. GDP is ten times bigger than Canada's, Canada's trade with the United States is much more important to us than the United States' trade with Canada is to them.

Since trade is voluntary, both Canada and the United States must believe they are better off as a result of international trade. How does that happen? Where do the mutually beneficial gains from trade come from?

Jill produces all of her own wood and bread. Would she be better off if she traded some of her wood for bread?

Bake or Chop?

Opportunity cost is the key to the mutual benefits from trade. To illustrate, let's return to our simple, imaginary example of two early Canadians who are each self-sufficient in producing food and shelter (section 1.2). While this example is simple, it contains the basic argument behind every pro-trade position you will ever hear supporting "free trade" or globalization.

Jill grows her own wheat to make bread, and chops her own wood for fire and shelter. If she spends an entire month producing only bread, she can make 50 loaves. Alternatively, if she spends all her time chopping wood, she can cut 100 logs.

Since Jill is self-sufficient, that means she can consume only what she produces herself, so she must divide her time and produce some bread and some wood. The table in Figure 13.2 shows different possible combinations (A – F) of bread and wood she can produce, depending on how she divides up her time during the month. From these production possibilities, Jill chooses to produce possibility D, 20 loaves of bread and 60 logs of wood. We will get to the graph in a moment.

Figure 13.2 Jill's Production Possibilities

Possibility	Bread (loaves per month)	Wood (logs per month)
A	50	0
B	40	20
C	30	40
D	20	60
E	10	80
F	0	100

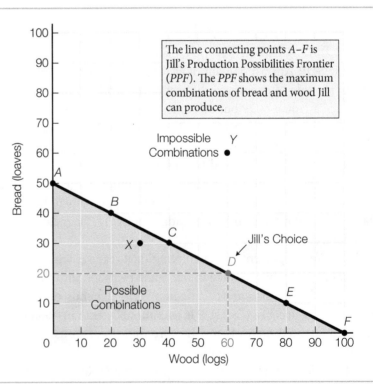

The line connecting points A–F is Jill's Production Possibilities Frontier (PPF). The PPF shows the maximum combinations of bread and wood Jill can produce.

Marie, Jill's nearest neighbour, also grows her own wheat to make bread, and chops her own wood for fire and shelter. The table in Figure 13.3 shows the possible monthly combinations of bread and wood she can produce, depending on how she divides up her time.

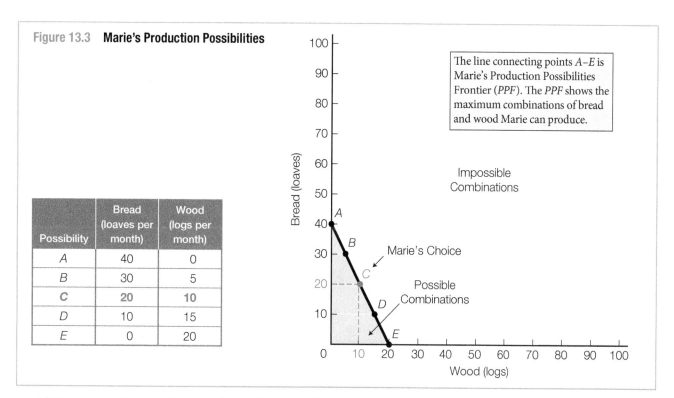

Figure 13.3 **Marie's Production Possibilities**

Possibility	Bread (loaves per month)	Wood (logs per month)
A	40	0
B	30	5
C	20	10
D	10	15
E	0	20

The line connecting points *A–E* is Marie's Production Possibilities Frontier (*PPF*). The *PPF* shows the maximum combinations of bread and wood Marie can produce.

Impossible Combinations

Marie's Choice

Possible Combinations

If Marie spends an entire month producing only bread, she can make 40 loaves (possibility *A*). Alternatively, if she spends all her time chopping wood, she can cut only 20 logs (possibility *E*). Since Marie is also self-sufficient, and can consume only what she produces herself, she divides her time and produces some bread and some wood. From these production possibilities, Marie chooses to produce possibility *C*, 20 loaves of bread and 10 logs of wood.

Production Possibilities Frontier The graphs in Figures 13.2 and 13.3 show the production possibilities frontier (*PPF*) of each pioneer.

Look first at Jill's *PPF* in the graph in Figure 13.2. When you connect the points representing her possible combinations of wood and bread, you get the straight black line that is Jill's production possibilities frontier. The points on Jill's *PPF* show the *maximum* combinations of bread and wood she can produce if she uses all of her time, tools, and other inputs. Jill chose combination *D*, *20 loaves and 60 logs*.

Jill could also choose not to work so hard and produce less. She could choose to produce any combination of bread and wood *inside* her production possibilities frontier. For example, she could decide to produce the combination of 30 loaves and 30 logs (possibility *X*). The shaded area inside her *PPF* represents all of her "possible combinations." These combinations are possible, but are not maximum.

Combinations of bread and wood *outside* of Jill's *PPF* are impossible for her to produce. Jill, like all of us, faces the problem of scarcity. She has limited time and energy, and can't produce everything she might want. A combination of 60 loaves of bread and 60 logs of wood (possibility *Y*) might make Jill happier, but that combination is impossible for her to produce.

Similarly, Marie's *PPF* in the graph in Figure 13.3 shows the maximum possible combinations of bread and wood she can produce. Marie chose combination *C*. Her other possible production combinations are inside her *PPF*. Impossible combinations are outside her *PPF*. Marie has fewer possible combinations of bread and wood production than Jill.

Deal or No Deal? Opportunity Cost Rules

Can trade make both Jill and Marie better off? It doesn't look promising, especially for Jill. She is a better bread maker than Marie (50 loaves versus 40 loaves) *and* a better wood chopper (100 logs versus 20 logs). Jill has an **absolute advantage** — the ability to produce a product or service at a *lower absolute cost* than another producer — over Marie in both bread production and wood production. That is, Jill is more productive as a bread maker and as a wood chopper. If we were to measure dollar costs (which I have left out to keep the example as simple as possible), absolute advantage would mean Jill could produce both bread and wood at lower absolute dollar costs than Marie could.

If you are not keen on history, then in place of Jill and Marie, think China and Canada. If China can produce everything at lower cost than Canada, can there be mutually beneficial gains from trade for both countries? What's the benefit for China? Won't all Canadians end up unemployed?

Comparative Advantage But mutually beneficial gains from trade do not depend on absolute advantage. They depend on **comparative advantage** — the ability to produce a product or service at a *lower opportunity cost* than another producer. To figure out comparative advantage, we need to calculate *opportunity costs* for Jill and Marie.

Opportunity costs are always calculated by comparing two alternative possibilities — two choices. Comparing possibilities *A* and *F* in the table or graph in Figure 13.2, Jill can produce 50 loaves of bread and zero wood or 100 logs of wood and zero bread. If she chooses to bake 50 loaves of bread, the opportunity cost is 100 logs of wood. If she instead chooses to chop 100 logs of wood, the opportunity cost is 50 loaves of bread. Opportunity cost is the value of the path — the choice — *not taken.*

To compare opportunity costs, it is easier if we measure them per unit of the product chosen. Here is a simple, useful formula for finding opportunity cost:

$$\text{Opportunity cost} = \frac{\text{Give Up}}{\text{Get}}$$

So Jill's opportunity cost of producing more bread is

$$\frac{\text{Opportunity cost of}}{\text{additional bread}} = \frac{100 \text{ logs of wood}}{50 \text{ loaves of bread}} = \frac{2 \text{ logs of wood}}{1 \text{ loaf of bread}}$$

Jill must give up 2 logs of wood to get each additional loaf of bread.

What is Jill's opportunity cost of producing more wood?

$$\frac{\text{Opportunity cost of}}{\text{additional wood}} = \frac{50 \text{ loaves of bread}}{100 \text{ logs of wood}} = \frac{\frac{1}{2} \text{ loaf of bread}}{1 \text{ log of wood}}$$

Jill must give up ½ loaf of bread to get each additional log of wood.

If you calculate opportunity costs for Marie (compare possibilities *A* and *E* in Figure 13.3) her opportunity cost of getting an additional loaf of bread is giving up ½ log of wood, and her opportunity cost of getting an additional log of wood is giving up 2 loaves of bread. These opportunity cost calculations are summarized in Figure 13.4. Since comparative advantage is defined as lowest opportunity cost (not lowest absolute cost), you can see that Marie has a comparative advantage in bread-making (give up ½ log of wood versus 2 logs of wood), while Jill has a comparative advantage in wood-chopping (give up ½ loaf of bread versus 2 loaves of bread).

absolute advantage the ability to produce a product or service at a lower absolute cost than another producer

comparative advantage the ability to produce a product or service at a lower opportunity cost than another producer

Figure 13.4 tells the story of Jill and Marie's specialization and trade.

Figure 13.4	Opportunity Costs for Jill and Marie	
	Opportunity Cost of 1 Additional	
	Loaf of Bread	Log of Wood
Jill	Gives up 2 logs of wood	Gives up ½ loaf of bread
Marie	Gives up ½ log of wood	Gives up 2 loaves of bread
Comparative Advantage	Marie has comparative advantage (lower opportunity cost) in bread-making	Jill has comparative advantage (lower opportunity cost) in wood-chopping

Smart Deals

Here's the payoff to these calculations. Instead of each pioneer being self-sufficient, and producing everything she needs herself, look what happens if our pioneers specialize in producing what each is best at, and then trading.

According to comparative advantage, Jill should specialize in only chopping wood, and Marie should specialize in only making bread. In this way, Jill will produce 100 logs of wood and no bread, and Marie will produce 40 loaves of bread and no wood.

They agree on a trade of 20 logs of wood for 20 loaves of bread. Jill, the specialized woodchopper, is "exporting" wood and "importing" bread. Marie, the specialized baker, is "exporting" bread and "importing" wood.

The ratio at which they exchange wood for bread — one log of wood trades for one loaf of bread in this example — is called the **terms of trade**. In general, the terms of trade are the quantity of exports required to pay for one unit of imports.

terms of trade quantity of exports required to pay for one unit of imports

After specializing and trading, here are the outcomes:

- Jill ends up with 20 loaves of bread (0 produced plus 20 imported) and 80 logs of wood (100 produced minus 20 exported);
- Marie ends up with 20 loaves of bread (40 produced minus 20 exported) and 20 logs of wood (0 produced plus 20 imported).

Figure 13.5 tells the story of Jill and Marie's specialization and trade.

Figure 13.5 **Mutually Beneficial Gains from Trade**

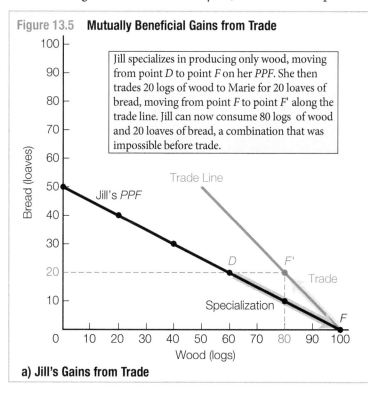

Jill specializes in producing only wood, moving from point D to point F on her PPF. She then trades 20 logs of wood to Marie for 20 loaves of bread, moving from point F to point F' along the trade line. Jill can now consume 80 logs of wood and 20 loaves of bread, a combination that was impossible before trade.

a) Jill's Gains from Trade

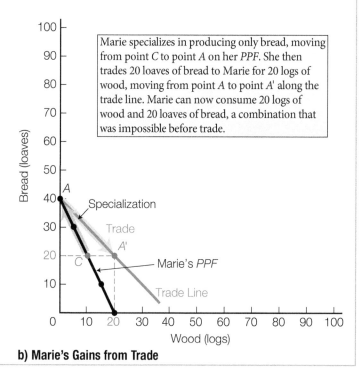

Marie specializes in producing only bread, moving from point C to point A on her PPF. She then trades 20 loaves of bread to Marie for 20 logs of wood, moving from point A to point A' along the trade line. Marie can now consume 20 logs of wood and 20 loaves of bread, a combination that was impossible before trade.

b) Marie's Gains from Trade

Jill (Figure 13.5a) starts out at point D on her *PPF* (20 loaves and 60 logs). Choosing to specialize in only chopping wood, she moves down along her production possibilities frontier to point F, producing 100 logs of wood and no bread.

Marie (Figure 13.5b) starts out at point C on her *PPF* (20 loaves and 10 logs). Choosing to specialize in only baking bread, she moves up along her production possibilities frontier to point A, producing 40 loaves of bread and no wood.

Trade occurs along the blue Trade Lines, which reflect the terms of trade. As either Jill or Marie moves along the Trade Lines to exchange wood for bread, 1 log of wood trades for 1 loaf of bread.

Jill moves from her point F (100 logs, 0 loaves) to the new point F' along the Trade Line, trading 20 logs of wood for 20 loaves of bread. She ends up with 80 logs of wood and 20 loaves of bread.

Marie moves from her point A (40 loaves, 0 logs) along the Trade Line to the new point A', trading 20 loaves of bread for 20 logs of wood. She ends up with 20 loaves and 20 logs.

Achieving the Impossible   Check it out. *After trading, Jill and Marie are both better off than when they were each self-sufficient.* Before trade, the best Jill could produce with 20 loaves of bread was 60 logs of wood (point D). After trade, Jill has the same amount of bread and more wood. Before trade, the best Marie could produce with 20 loaves of bread was just 10 logs of wood (point C). After trade, Marie has the same amount of bread and more wood.

Jill and Marie each reach a combination of wood and bread that was impossible before trade. After specialization and trade, each can now consume a combination of wood and bread that is outside of her production possibilities frontier. Voluntary trade is not a zero-sum game, where one person's gain is the other's loss. Both traders gain.

What is remarkable is that these *gains from trade,* which improve both Jill's and Marie's standard of living (with more wood they can stay warmer or build better houses), *happen without anyone working harder, or without any improvement in technology or new inputs.* Both are better off because they have made smart decisions to specialize and trade, rather than each trying to produce only what each will consume. Both can have toast for breakfast (bread roasted over a fire), even though each produced only part of what was necessary to make the breakfast.

Notice also that there are gains for both Jill and Marie, even though Jill can produce more bread and wood than Marie can. Despite Jill's absolute advantage in producing everything at lower cost, there are still differences in opportunity costs, or comparative advantage. *Comparative advantage is the key to mutually beneficial gains from trade.* The trade can be between individuals, or between countries. That is why China trades with Canada, even though China can produce most things more cheaply than Canada can. There are still differences in comparative advantage based on opportunity costs. Trade allows us all to work smarter and live better.

Terms of Trade

NOTE

For a trade to have mutual benefits, terms of trade must be between each trader's local opportunity costs.

For a trade to have mutual benefits, the terms of trade must be somewhere between each trader's opportunity costs. Jill's own opportunity cost of producing a loaf of bread is two logs. Jill is importing bread, "paying" only one log for each loaf of bread, so for her the imported bread is a bargain. Marie's own opportunity cost of producing a log is two loaves of bread. Marie is importing wood, "paying" only one loaf of bread for each log, so for her the imported wood is a bargain. Both traders gain.

In this simple example, the gains from trade are split evenly between the traders — the ratio of 1 to 1 (1 loaf for 1 log) is halfway between the ratios of 2 to 1 and 1 to 2.

Gains from trade are not always split evenly. Different terms of trade will split the gains differently, with more of the gains going to Jill and less to Marie, or vice versa. But for the trade to occur voluntarily, the terms of trade must be somewhere between the opportunity costs that each trader (or country) faces locally. Exactly where the terms of trade settle in international markets can mean one country gains more than the other. This is one source of controversy we will soon examine. But as long as trade happens voluntarily, both countries still get some gain.

Technology and Competition   Gains from trade are a big part of rising living standards, even without anyone working harder, any improvement in technology, or any new resources. But competition and technological advances also contribute to rising living standards. Those forces not only create more gains and winners from trade, but also create losers. The losers from new competition and new technologies are behind the story of why not everyone welcomes international trade.

Refresh 13.1

1. Explain the difference between absolute advantage and comparative advantage.

2. How is the concept of personal gain reflected in voluntary trade?

3. The best auto mechanic in town (who charges $120 per hour) is also a better typist than her office manager (who earns $20 per hour). Should the mechanic do her own typing?
   [*Hint*: The best alternative employment for the office manager is another office job that also pays $20 per hour.]

MyEconLab

For answers to these Refresh Questions, visit MyEconLab.

What's So Wonderful about Free Trade? Protectionism and Trade

13.2

Explain how competition creates winners, losers, and opponents to trade, and analyze three forms of protectionism.

If voluntary trade brings mutual benefits, why do so many people and politicians oppose "free trade"? Arguments to "buy Canadian," or to "protect Canadian businesses and jobs" by taxing or excluding inexpensive imports are arguments against free trade. Complaints against the "outsourcing of Canadian jobs to non-Canadians," or calls for government to compensate domestic producers "harmed by foreign competition" are calls for government to take a hands-on role in international trade. Economists usually come down on the side of free trade. What do they see that's different from the critics of free trade?

Creative Destruction on a Global Scale

In addition to mutually beneficial gains, freer trade increases competition. This creates opponents to freer trade.

The completion of the Canadian Pacific Railway in 1885 connected previously separate markets in Halifax, Montreal, Toronto, Winnipeg, the prairies, and Vancouver. This trans-Canada railway brought lower transportation costs, allowing farmers and businesses anywhere in Canada to sell across the county, opening up new possibilities for specialization and trade. Many more Jills and Maries could now easily specialize and gain the advantages of trading in a large national market.

But newly connected markets also bring new competition. Grain farmers in Quebec faced competition from prairie farmers who produced wheat more cheaply. Even with the added transportation costs, grain from Saskatchewan was cheaper in Montreal than Quebec-grown grain. Textile businesses in Winnipeg faced new competition from lower-cost, higher-volume factories in Toronto. Increased trade and specialization increased competition in every market across Canada.

Creative Destruction   Connections to new markets bring connections to new competitors. A local producer may have been a big fish in her small, local pond. But increased trade has her now swimming in bigger ponds with bigger fish. Some fish, and some businesses, don't survive.

Businesses compete in markets by figuring out new ways to beat their rivals. Businesses do this through cutting costs, developing new technologies of production, inventing new products, exploiting economies of large-scale production, or finding new or cheaper sources for raw materials and resources.

Over time, these competitive innovations, which result from the endless quest for profits, make businesses and labour more productive and improve living standards and product choices for consumers. This is Schumpeter's process of *creative destruction*, described in section 6.3. Adam Smith's invisible hand channels the restless energy of profit-seeking self-interest into the public good of rising living standards. That is the positive, creative part of creative destruction.

The gains from specialization, trade, competition, and innovation also have a down side — destruction of less productive, higher-cost, and less popular products and businesses. Nineteenth-century Quebec wheat farmers and Manitoba textile companies went out of business in the face of new, more productive Canadian competition. Many twenty-first century auto workers in Ontario lost their jobs to robotic assembly lines in South Korea. These failed businesses and lost jobs are the opportunity costs of the gains from trade.

The jobs lost through trade, competition, and innovation come under the Chapter 7 definition of *structural unemployment* — unemployment due to technological change or international competition that makes workers' skills obsolete in Canada.

On the whole, consumers and businesses in Canada benefit from specialization, trade, and increased competition. Productivity and overall living standards improve. That is why we are so much better off than Canadians were 200 years ago. But trade creates winners and losers. The losers pay a high price for the changes brought on by increased specialization and trade.

> *Free trade, one of the greatest blessings which a government can confer on a people, is in almost every country unpopular.*
> —*Thomas Macaulay*
> *British MP, 1824*

Winners and Losers from International Trade

When new international markets open up through trade — connecting Canada to other countries — who wins and who loses within Canada? The main winners are Canadian consumers and businesses and workers in export industries. The main losers are businesses and workers in import-competing industries.

Winners   Consumers gain from lower prices and greater product variety that result from new imports. If imports sell successfully in Canada, there is a comparative advantage to the country selling to Canadians.

Canadian export businesses gain from access to new markets and new customers. If Canadian exports sell successfully in the rest of the world, there is a comparative advantage to those Canadian businesses. Export businesses have more sales, more profits, and hire more workers. Workers in exporting businesses gain from more jobs and higher wages.

Losers   Canadian businesses that cannot successfully compete with the new imports lose. These domestic businesses face increased competition and lower prices, as businesses in the rest of the world have a comparative advantage in selling to Canadian customers. Workers in import-competing businesses also lose, as jobs disappear and wages fall with shrinking sales in Canada.

No Competition in My Backyard! Protectionism

Those who lose from international trade, facing threats to their businesses and jobs, look for help to elected politicians — the government. Workers and businesses in Canadian import-competing industries look for protection from the bigger fish that appear when Canadian markets get connected to international markets. Government protection of their economic interests takes three main forms: tariffs, import quotas, and domestic subsidies.

▲ Worldwide international exports of products and services increased over 15% between 2009 and 2012. About 40 percent of these products and services are delivered via containers on large ships like the one shown here.

Tariffs   A **tariff** is a tax applied to a product or service imported into a country. The Canadian business importing the product must pay the tariff to the Canadian government. That tariff is a business cost, which is passed on to consumers, increasing the price of the product.

tariff   tax applied to imports

Tariffs are attractive to governments for three reasons. First, tariffs raise revenues for the government to spend. Second, tariffs win votes and campaign donations for politicians from businesses and workers in import-competing industries. Third, because tariffs are a tax on non-Canadians who don't vote, there is little political damage from raising tariffs. While tariffs raise the price paid by Canadian consumers for the taxed imports, the tariff is not identified at the cash register. Consumers and voters usually do not blame the government for the higher import prices.

Figure 13.6 shows the history of tariffs in Canada since Confederation in 1867. The vertical axis measures the average tariff rate as a percentage of the value of imports.

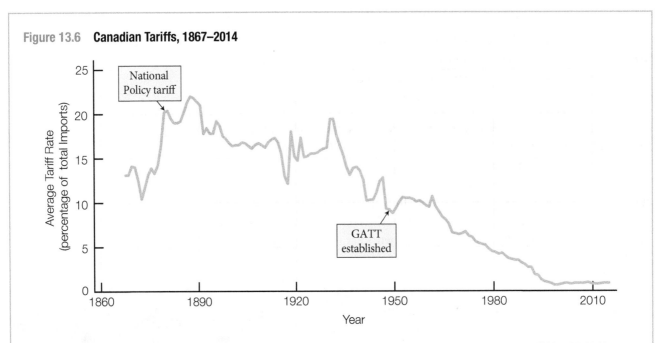

Figure 13.6   **Canadian Tariffs, 1867–2014**

National Policy tariff

GATT established

Source: Based on *Historical Statistics of Canada*, 2nd ed., Series G485; Statistics Canada, Table 380-0034, series v499996, Table 380-0017, series v646958.

WorldFoto/Alamy

▲ About 160 countries, including Canada, belong to the World Trade Organization (WTO) — www.wto.org — that describes itself as "the only international organization dealing with the global rules of trade between nations." Its main function is to ensure that trade flows smoothly, predictably, and freely. These protesters strongly disagree with the decisions the WTO is making. They believe the WTO should not interfere with a country's internal politics.

import quota limit on the quantity of a product or service that can be imported

Tariffs increased significantly after Confederation, and stayed relatively high until the 1930s. In 1947, the international General Agreement on Tariffs and Trade (GATT) began an ongoing process of reducing tariffs around the world. GATT turned into the World Trade Organization (WTO). Today, most tariffs in Canada have disappeared.

Where tariffs still apply, they protect domestic producers competing with imports. Because consumers pay a higher price — including the tariff — for the imported products, competing domestic producers win from higher prices and profits. Canadian consumers lose from higher prices.

Import Quotas   While tariffs raise the *price* of imports, quotas limit the *quantity* of products or services that can be imported into Canada during a year. For example, Canada imposes **import quotas** on meat, eggs, dairy products, and steel.

With reduced supply and restricted competition, higher prices for imported products means the quantity sold in Canada is less than with freer trade. But the quantity sold by Canadian producers increases. With quotas, Canadian import-competing industries win. There are higher prices and profits for the businesses and more jobs and higher wages for workers. Canadian consumers again lose from higher prices.

Domestic Subsidies   The most common and controversial form of protectionism today is **subsidies to domestic producers**. A subsidy is a government payment to domestic producers of products or services that are threatened by international competition. Many governments, especially in Europe and the United States, give subsidies for agricultural products like cotton and grain. Canada gives large subsidies to protect the dairy industry. The businesses and workers being subsidized are winners while consumers lose by paying higher prices.

subsidies to domestic producers
government payment to domestic
producers of products or services

The Politics of Trade Policy

Why do governments often respond to domestic producers' requests for protection from international competition? The answer is not obvious, since the higher prices and reduced variety of products hurt far more Canadians — especially consumers — than the small number of businesses and workers helped in import-competing industries. But the unequal distribution of the gains and losses creates political pressures for government to help those who lose from international trade.

Domestic Trade Politics   A large number of consumers gain from freer international trade, but the gain for each consumer is small. Each of us, as consumers, benefits from slightly lower prices of imported products and services. The slightly higher prices caused by protectionism are not easily noticed. Even if consumers realized, for example, they were paying five percent more for a product because of tariffs, quotas, or subsidies, most would not feel strongly enough to pressure politicians.

The impact for the small number of businesses and workers who lose from freer international trade is very large. Many such businesses and workers in import-competing industries could lose their lifetime investments and their jobs. Facing great losses, those affected put as much political pressure as possible on politicians for tariffs, quotas, or subsidies. They often succeed in getting government to protect them from the increased competition and creative destruction of international trade.

The protection that government puts in place makes Canadians as a whole worse off — without the gains of rising living standards from increased competition and creative destruction. The hands-off camp argues that protectionist policies are a government failure that is a bigger problem than market failure.

Competition from any new market, even within Canada, threatens existing industries. There is even pressure on provincial governments to provide protection against Canadian businesses and workers in other provinces. Many provinces require government purchases to come only from businesses within the province, and government jobs to go only to provincial residents.

In 1994, the Canadian provinces signed the Agreement on Internal Trade to prevent provinces from erecting new trade barriers and to reduce existing ones. Nonetheless, some Canadian businesses claim that trade between provinces is still more difficult than trade between Canada and the United States!

NOTE
A large number of consumers gain from freer international trade, but the gain for each consumer is small. A small number of businesses and workers in import-competing industries lose from freer trade, but the loss for each is large. The unequal distribution of the gains and losses creates political pressures for protectionism to help those who lose from international trade.

YES
MARKETS SELF-ADJUST
GOVERNMENT
HANDS-OFF

NOTE
Political pressure in many countries from import-competing industries is a barrier to international trade negotiations.

International Trade Politics   The unequal distribution of gains and losses also affects international trade politics between counties. Through decades of negotiations between developed and developing countries, the WTO has tried to reduce protectionist policies and promote freer international trade. Such trade potentially benefits far more people than it harms. But the barrier is political pressure in many countries from import-competing industries protecting themselves from competition.

Developed countries — especially the United States and some countries in Europe — want freer access to markets in the developing countries of Africa, Asia, and South America for the products and services they export. The list includes pharmaceuticals, intellectual property (patents on drugs that cannot be undersold by cheaper generic drugs), copyright on movies and music (not allowing pirated DVDs), and patents on inventions and technology so they cannot simply be copied. But the United States and European countries don't want to remove domestic protectionist measures — especially domestic subsidies — from their agricultural and textile industries. The developing countries, which produce cotton, grains, and textiles, want access to those protected markets. Canada, while generally supportive of freer trade, is reluctant to remove subsidies to Canadian producers of dairy products, poultry, eggs, and wheat.

The political influence in many countries of the affected, protected industries is the barrier to international trade negotiations.

Arguments for Protectionism?

The politics of protectionism helps explain why there are opponents to freer trade. There are two common arguments for protectionism that sound believable, but that fail to incorporate comparative advantage. There are also some valid, but limited, arguments for protectionism. Let's examine them.

Saving Canadian Jobs   One argument states that tariffs, quotas, and subsidies can save jobs in Canadian import-competing industries. But freer trade creates jobs in Canadian export industries. Imports also create jobs in Canada for those businesses that sell and service the imports.

While eliminating tariffs, quotas, and subsidies will cost jobs in Canadian import-competing industries, freer trade creates more jobs than are lost as was seen in the NAFTA agreement discussed next.

Necessary to Compete with Cheap Foreign Labour   When Canada entered into the North American Free Trade Agreement (NAFTA) in 1994, many tariffs and quotas were eliminated among Canada, the United States, and Mexico. Many people predicted a "giant sucking sound" from jobs draining out of Canada and the United States into Mexico, because wages for labour were so much lower there. That did not happen.

Low-skill, low-wage jobs requiring little education did move to Mexico. But the evidence suggests that the total number of jobs in Canada has increased because of greater exports to expanded North American markets. The mistake in this argument about competing with cheap foreign labour is the focus on absolute cost and absolute advantage, instead of comparative advantage. While Mexico has a comparative advantage for some products, Canada has a comparative advantage for others. Mexico too has benefited from the mutual gains from trade.

Valid, Limited Protectionism Arguments Freer trade leads to increased specialization and reliance on other countries to supply products and services. While there are gains from trade, there are also risks from that reliance.

Canada does not want to rely entirely on another country for strategic products like military equipment, energy, and other essentials. In the event of a war, what if your only suppliers of strategic products are your enemies? To avoid that risk, governments protect strategic domestic industries.

Another non-economic risk of freer trade is the threat to a country's cultural identity. Canada's reliance on U.S. trade brings with it exposure to the culture of a country that is ten times larger. In the name of protecting Canada's cultural identity, the government restricts imported content of radio and television programs, restricts broadcast licences to domestic providers, and subsidizes the production of Canadian culture in the form of domestic books, movies, music, and other media.

Trade Wars:
Powerful Argument against Protectionism

Supporters of tariffs, quotas, and subsidies rarely mention one of the most important arguments against protectionism — the risk of retaliation by other countries. Protectionist policy can trigger a trade war.

In an attempt to protect U.S. jobs and businesses during the Great Depression, the U.S. government introduced many tariffs. Other countries quickly retaliated with their own tariffs, and international trade collapsed, contributing to the length and severity of the Great Depression.

This is an example of the fallacy of composition at work. One country may temporarily make itself better off through tariffs, but when all countries do the same, then all end up worse off.

Aqua/Shutterstock

▲ In response to the Global Financial Crisis in 2009 the U.S. introduced laws requiring state and local governments to buy products and services only from U.S. producers, even if the costs were higher than from Canadian producers. Canada protested, and worked out a trade deal where Canadian producers could compete for U.S. government contracts, and U.S. producers could compete for Canadian government contracts.

Refresh 13.2

1. In your own words, explain who might be the winners and losers from freer international trade.

2. Explain the process of creative destruction. In your answer, include how this process is both positive and negative.

3. Present a counterargument to those who say they want to protect Canadian jobs by demanding government protection for their industry from cheaper imports.

MyEconLab

For answers to these Refresh Questions, visit MyEconLab.

13.3 Globalization and Its Discontents
Is Free Trade the Problem?

Explain the pace of globalization and how to evaluate if sweatshop workers are better off with international trade.

There are other opponents of expanded international trade beyond businesses and workers in import-competing industries. Some social activists, human rights organizations, and anti-market groups worry about what they see as the harmful consequences of international trade. At a student demonstration against free trade, one passionate activist asked the crowd,

> "Who made your T-shirt? . . . Was it a child in Vietnam? Or a young girl from India earning 18 cents per hour? . . . Did you know that she lives 12 to a room? . . . That she is forced to work 90 hours each week, without overtime pay? . . . That she lives not only in poverty, but also in filth and sickness, all in the name of Nike's profits?"

Anti-globalization critics view uncontrolled international trade as the cause of many undesirable problems in developing countries: low wages, poverty, poor working conditions, farmers who can no longer make a living, high-priced drugs from Western pharmaceutical companies, environmental damage, and local governments undermined by international organizations. These critics view the competition from expanded international trade as a "race to the bottom" that will result in low wages, low standards for working conditions, greater pollution, and lower taxes (especially on corporations) in every country, both developing and developed.

Many anti-globalization protestors target two international organizations — the World Bank and the International Monetary Fund (IMF).

The World Bank and International Monetary Fund

At the end of World War II, the same 1947 international conference that created GATT also created the World Bank and the International Monetary Fund (IMF). These international organizations — currently with 188 member nations — were created as the world struggled to recover from the devastation of war. Their mission was to support countries' economic growth and development through trade.

The World Bank is not a traditional bank. Its name is an abbreviation for two related institutions — the International Bank for Reconstruction and Development (IBRD) and the International Development Agency (IDA). The World Bank describes its mission as "inclusive and sustainable globalization." The IRBD focuses on reducing poverty in middle-income countries, while the IDA focuses on the world's poorest countries. The World Bank does act like a bank in loaning money at low interest or no interest to countries for economic development projects.

The IMF describes its mission as fostering global monetary cooperation, securing financial stability, facilitating international trade, promoting high employment and sustainable economic growth, and reducing poverty.

You are probably wondering why anti-globalization protestors target these organizations, whose missions do not seem to match the criticisms. The story behind the protests comes from the policies that the World Bank and IMF use to achieve their missions.

Hands-Off Policies for Developing Countries Economists and policymakers at the World Bank and the IMF believe that free-trade policies based on comparative advantage are best for helping developing countries achieve rising standards of living. Specialization, trade, competition, and connected international markets will, they argue, create a tide of wealth that will eventually lift up all countries. These free-trade policies come directly from the hands-off camp's answer, "Yes — Markets Self-Adjust" to the fundamental macroeconomic question:

> If left alone by government, do the price mechanisms of market economies adjust quickly to maintain steady growth in living standards, full employment and stable prices?

Using this hands-off view of the role of government, policymakers at the World Bank and IMF set "free market" conditions on loans and assistance to developing countries, especially during the 1990s. Those conditions require governments to enforce contracts and property rights — cracking down on pirated software, DVDs, and low-cost copies of expensive pharmaceutical drugs. Other hands-off conditions include removing regulations from labour markets, eliminating protectionist tariffs and quotas to allow imports from developed countries, lowering taxes on businesses to encourage private investment, and privatizing state-run industries — returning those industries to private businesses.

Economists usually support freer trade and a prominent role for markets. But these hands-off views were especially strong during the 1990s. That decade saw the collapse of state communism in East Germany and the USSR, and the failure of their notoriously inefficient state-run industries. There was also widespread corruption among many governments of developing countries. Hands-on policies do not succeed if governments cannot be trusted to spend loan money on the people and projects that need it most. Government failure seemed a bigger problem than market failure. Much evidence supported a hands-off position.

Joseph Stiglitz Changes the Debate Economists often dismiss protestors opposing free trade and free markets as misguided do-gooders who do not understand the concept of comparative advantage. But the globalization debate changed when a prominent economist added his voice to those of the protesters.

Joseph Stiglitz, a professor at Columbia University, served on the Council of Economic Advisors under U.S. President Bill Clinton. In 1997, Stiglitz became chief economist at the World Bank. He left the World Bank after three years, and was awarded the Nobel Prize in Economics in 2001. As an insider at the World Bank, and winner of the most prestigious prize an economist can get, Stiglitz's criticisms counted. He published an influential, bestselling book in 2002 with the title of this section — *Globalization and Its Discontents*.

Stiglitz's criticisms of the strongly hands-off policies of the World Bank and the IMF, and the responses from other pro-trade economists (see Economics Out There, p. 404) helped to reconcile the apparent contradiction between pro-trade arguments that gains for trade are the key to rising living standards, and the anti-globalization accusations that global trade causes so much harm.

▲ Joseph Stiglitz, a Nobel Prize–winning economist, was the chief economist at the World Bank from 1997 to 2000. His arguments against a strictly hands-off position for world monetary institutions supported the anti-globalization critics.

Economics *Out There*

What Is Globalization?

In order to understand the debate triggered by World Bank and IMF policies, protestors, and Stiglitz's book, it is helpful to first establish some facts about globalization.

Controversy swirls around the consequences of globalization — is globalization a force for good or for evil? Does globalization bring rising living standards or a descent into poverty? Before trying to reconcile pro- and anti-globalization arguments in the next section, let's start with a simple definition. **Economic globalization** is the integration of economic activities across borders, and through markets. When markets in one country are connected to markets in other countries, economic activities are connected, or integrated. The technical support for your computer may come from a business in India. The potash used by factories in the Czech Republic to make glass may come from Saskatchewan. The T-shirt you wear may be made from cotton grown in Texas but woven into cloth in Shanghai.

economic globalization integration of economic activities, across borders, through markets

Why Is Globalization Happening?   The reason for the spread of integrated economic activity across borders is the same as it was for Jill and Marie. Voluntary trade is motivated by self-interest, profits from innovation, and mutually beneficial gains. Connections to bigger ponds in international markets provide new opportunities for gains, but also new competitors and new threats of creative destruction. There are winners and losers from globalization, just as there are winners and losers from trade within a country.

Self-interest is always a motive for expanded trade. The pace of globalization is speeding up due to falling costs for both transportation and communications technologies. It is quickly becoming cheaper and easier to connect markets among countries, in the same way that railroads did across Canada.

Globalization is also speeding up from the elimination of government barriers to trade. Free-trade agreements among countries, decreasing tariffs, quotas, and domestic subsidies combined with efforts of the WTO, World Bank, and IMF to reduce protectionist policies impeding trade all speed globalization.

Globalization itself — the integration of economic activities, across borders, through markets — is neither good nor bad. But the consequences of globalization for different groups can be good or bad.

Sweatshops versus Farms   The new markets and opportunities from globalization may not look good to us, even though the participants see them as major improvements in their lives. When we hear of the low pay and working conditions in sweatshops, our first thoughts — like those of the activist quoted at the start — may be that these workers are being exploited in the interest of corporate profits.

But that does not explain why millions of young Chinese women voluntarily choose low-wage factory jobs over life on the farm in rural China. One woman, Liang Ying, who fled to the Shenzhen factory zone in southern China, felt almost anything was better than life on the family rubber farm:

> "Every morning, from 4 a.m. to 7 a.m. you have to cut through the bark of 400 rubber trees in total darkness. It has to be done before daybreak, otherwise the sunshine will evaporate the rubber juice. If you were me, what would you prefer, the factory or the farm?"

In evaluating sweatshop jobs, always ask a key question about opportunity cost. Are workers' lives better, or worse, compared to a situation without globalization, trade, and the factory jobs that follow? This is the same question behind the Jill and Marie example — are they better off with specialization and trade, or better off being self-sufficient? Behind the law of supply (section 3.1) is the basic idea that to hire labour (or any other input), businesses must pay at least the value of the best alternative use of the worker's time.

When workers voluntarily choose the sweatshop over the farm, it is because, from their perspective, factory jobs make them better off. What looks like poverty to us, and is poverty by Western standards, is a rising standard of living for the workers measured by their standards.

People in the West may regard low-paying jobs at Nike as exploitation, but for many people in the developing world, working in a factory is a far better option than staying down on the farm and growing rice.

— Joseph Stiglitz
2001 Nobel Prize in Economics

NOTE
Economists ask the opportunity cost question about sweatshops — are workers lives better or worse compared to a situation without globalization, trade, and the factory jobs that follow?

Sweatshops throughout History   The story of workers migrating from farms to factory jobs is not new. In the original English cotton factories of the late 1700s, people with few opportunities moved from farms to the original sweatshops in cities. While the working conditions and pay were terrible, they were better than the alternative.

The same pattern repeated in the U.S. cotton industry in New Hampshire and Massachusetts in the 1800s, where many French Canadians worked. The pattern continued in the Japanese textile industry in the 1920s and in Korea and Taiwan in the 1970s and 1980s. In all of these countries, standards of living and working conditions improved over time. Some of those improvements came from governments playing a hands-on role, and some happened when the government took a hands-off position.

As globalization connected the original British textile industry to new markets and new competitors, less competitive textile industries in older countries declined. Creative destruction created winners and losers. But since overall standards of living have continued to rise in the countries whose textile industries ultimately lost out to new competitors — first England, then the United States, Japan, South Korea, and Taiwan — new and better-paying jobs were created in other export industries where the countries had a comparative advantage.

Winners and Losers from Globalization   Globalization continues this pattern today. While specialization and trade bring mutually beneficial gains to countries, there are individual groups within a country who win and who lose.

Jamaica, for example, reduced trade barriers to milk imports in 1992. Local dairy farmers were losers, having to compete with cheaper imports of milk powder. Jamaican milk production dropped significantly. But poor children, who could get imported milk more cheaply, were winners.

With a better understanding of what globalization is, can we reconcile the apparent contradiction between pro-trade arguments (that gains for trade are the key to rising living standards), and the anti-globalization accusations that global trade causes harm in so many ways? That is our final topic.

Refresh 13.3

MyEconLab

For answers to these Refresh Questions, visit MyEconLab.

1. In your own words, define economic globalization. Provide one example where globalization has affected you.

2. Identify several forces that speed up globalization, and several that slow it down.

3. What argument would you make to counter the claim that all sweatshop workers are exploited by big business?

13.4 Hands-Off or Hands-On Again? Governments and Global Markets

Evaluate the hands-off and hands-on arguments about the role for government in the globalization debate.

Is globalization a force for good or for evil? Does globalization bring rising living standards or a descent into poverty? The answers to these questions lead back to the fundamental macroeconomic question. But this time, the context is not within a country, but across connected countries. Should governments in the global economy be hands-off or hands-on?

Hands-On for Stiglitz

One of Stiglitz's valuable contributions to the globalization debate is to make explicit the importance of the hands-off versus hands-on question.

Although a great believer in markets, Stiglitz's own position is hands-on, favouring an "important, if limited, role for government to play." He contrasts his hands-on position with the free-market, free-trade policies supported by the World Bank and the IMF in the 1990s — the hands-off position criticized by anti-globalization protestors.

> "The IMF's policies . . . based on the . . . presumption that markets, by themselves, lead to efficient outcomes, failed to allow for desirable government interventions in the market, measures which can guide economic growth and make everyone better off. What was at issue . . . is . . . conceptions of the role of the government . . . "*

Social Safety Nets   The hands-on position believes government in all countries has a responsibility to maintain a social safety net to support the welfare of citizens left behind by trade and markets — especially by labour markets that determine incomes. Specialization, trade, and creative destruction — whether within a country or between countries — always creates winners and losers. In Canada, there are many government programs to assist those who lose from expanded trade. There are Employment Insurance benefits for the unemployed, job retraining programs, social assistance payments, and health-care benefits that do not depend upon a person having a job.

Most poor, developing countries do not have a social safety net, so the competitive forces of creative destruction can lead to poverty and misery as jobs disappear in import-competing industries. Social safety net programs cost money that governments in poor countries may not have. But even if those governments wanted to create such programs, the strong hands-off policies of the World Bank and the IMF in the 1990s restricted their ability to operate or finance — through higher taxes — social safety net programs. The strong hands-off policies for labour markets also discouraged government regulation of working conditions. Bureaucrats and policymakers at the World Bank and IMF, rather than local governments, influenced decisions about local social programs.

Opening the Door to Trouble   Stiglitz's book appeared to validate many concerns of anti-globalization critics. But his hands-on policy choice, like any choice, has an opportunity cost. And the opportunity cost of allowing the government in developing countries to act hands-on brings us to the arguments presented by the hands-off position.

NOTE
The hands-on position believes government has a responsibility to maintain a social safety net to support citizens left behind by trade and markets.

*www.amazon.ca/Globalization-Its-Discontents-Joseph-Stiglitz/dp/0393324397

Hands-Off for *The Economist* Magazine

Once governments take a hands-on role helping people and industries who lose from the creative destruction of market competition, the door opens for special-interest groups to ask the government to protect them from such competition.

Buried in Wool   Protectionism in global trade is not new. In England in the 1600s — before the rise of the cotton textile industry — virtually all clothes were made of wool from domestic sheep. The British East India Company connected to new markets in India, and began importing hand-spun calico cotton into England. The new fabric was cheap, light, washable, colourful, and was an instant hit with consumers. Of course, local wool sales suffered, and the wool industry persuaded Parliament to pass protectionist measures. All students and professors at the universities were required by law to wear only wool garments, and corpses could only be buried wrapped in wool!

A law in 1701 banned all imports of calico cotton (a quota of zero!). The wool industry thought it had won, but the innovative profit-seeking forces of creative destruction led English entrepreneurs to set up industrial cotton factories in England that eventually crushed the sales and political influence of the wool industry.

In hindsight, such protectionist measures look ridiculous. But the motivation for protectionism is exactly the same today as it was then.

Whose Side Are They On?   *The Economist* magazine has been reporting from England on global economic stories, including stories on the cotton industry, since 1843. *The Economist* supports free markets and globalization, and generally opposes government "interference" in economic or social activity.

As part of the debate over globalization, *The Economist* published the following editorial. What is striking is the support it seems to give to the anti-globalization critics.

> Rich countries' trade rules, especially in farming and textiles, still discriminate powerfully against poor countries. Rich countries' subsidies encourage wasteful use of energy and natural resources, and harm the environment. . . . rich countries' protection of intellectual property discriminates unfairly against the developing world. And without a doubt, rich countries' approach to financial regulation offers implicit subsidies to their banks and encourages reckless lending; it results, time and again, in financial crises in rich and poor countries alike.
>
> All these policies owe much to the fact that corporate interests exercise undue influence over government policy. [Critics] are right to deplore this. But undue influence is hardly new in democratic politics; it has not been created by globalisation forcing governments to bow down. . . . If allowed to, all governments are happy to seek political advantage by granting preferences.

The Economist's argument is that the harm that poor countries suffer is not caused by market forces but by government action.

NOTE

The Economist's hands-off position on globalization is that the harm poor countries suffer is not caused by market forces, but by governments giving in to political pressure for protectionism.

Here is one example. Some of the poorest countries in the world are in Africa. The cotton-growing industry in West Africa, where the climate is ideal for growing cotton, is poverty-stricken. The problem is that the U.S government pays Texas farmers a domestic subsidy for growing cotton of up to 19 cents on a 59 cent pound of cotton. If Texas farmers had to produce without that subsidy, West African cotton would be competitive on world markets. But with the subsidy to U.S. farmers, the world price of cotton is less than what it takes for the West African farmers to make a living.

Practice What You Preach   Some of the opposition to the free-trade policies of the World Bank, IMF, and WTO stems from what from anti-globalization critics and governments of poor countries see as the hypocrisy of Western trade proposals. In recent WTO negotiations, richer Western countries pushed for reduced tariffs, quotas, and subsidies on products they export, but continued to protect their own industries — especially agriculture and textiles — where import competition from poorer developing countries threatens their domestic industries. This was noted by *The Economist* in the editorial on page 408.

To be fair, poorer developing countries did the same during the negotiations. They pushed for expanded access to Western markets for products they export, while still trying to protect their domestic industries from Western import competition.

Terms of Trade   This is a power struggle between governments of rich and poor countries, which explains the standoff of the current WTO negotiations. The terms of trade — quantity of exports required to pay for one unit of imports — are largely determined by prices in international markets. But the power struggle over tariffs and subsidies strongly influences the terms of trade.

Stiglitz argues that an earlier, 1995 round of WTO negotiations produced an agreement that *lowered* the prices the poorest countries in the world received for their exports relative to what they paid for their imports. Some of the poorest countries actually were *worse off* as a result of this agreement.

Shake Hands?

Specialization and trade — whether within a country or across the globe — always creates winners and losers. The competitive forces of creative destruction generally cause rising standards of living, but can also cause poverty and misery as jobs disappear in import-competing industries. Both the hands-on and hands-off positions recognize these unfortunate outcomes as the side effects of specialization, trade, and economic growth.

Limited Role for Government? Stiglitz's hands-on position sees an important, but limited, role for government. Government, particularly in developing countries, should maintain a social safety net to support the economic welfare of citizens left behind by trade and markets — especially labour markets that determine incomes.

The hands-off position sees many unfortunate globalization outcomes resulting not from trade, but from government interference in markets. Tariffs, quotas, and domestic subsidies — responses to political pressure from industries and workers harmed by competing imports — create unfair terms of trade and disadvantage industries and workers in the poorest countries.

Markets Failure or Government Failure? As a citizen of Canada and the world, you must decide the globalization and trade policies you will support. There are no right or easy choices, only trade-offs.

If you think it is important for all governments to help losers from expanded trade in import-competing industries — in Canada or abroad — the risk is that governments will also give in to political pressure and introduce protectionist policies that slow the expansion of trade and economic growth. If you support this hands-on position, you are betting that market failure is worse than government failure. The failure of markets to produce rising standards of living for all, full employment, and stable prices is more likely and costly than government failing by giving in to political pressure from special interests for market protection.

If you think the markets are best left alone to produce economic growth that eventually benefits all, the risk is that losers from expanded trade in import-competing industries end up in poverty and misery. If you support this hands-off position, you are betting that government failure is worse than market failure. The failure of government, that comes from introducing protectionist policies that are not in society's best interests, is more likely and costly than markets failing in the form of falling living standards for those in import-competing industries.

Figure 13.7 summarizes the trade-offs for the hands-off and hands-on positions on government's role in trade policy.

Figure 13.7   Government and Global Markets: Hands-Off or Hands-On?

	Camp	
	Hands-Off (Yes—Left Alone, Markets Self-Adjust)	Hands-On (No—Left Alone, Markets Fail Often)
Role of government	None	Limited to maintaining social safety net supporting those left behind by trade and markets
Risk of chosen role for government	Losers in import-competing businesses get no assistance in adjusting	Government gives in to political pressure for protectionism
Which failure is worse?	Government failure is worse than market failure	Market failure is worse than government failure

Travels of a T-Shirt Pietra Rivoli, a business school professor at Georgetown University, witnessed the student demonstration against free trade reported on page 402. In response, she decided to travel the world, following the globally integrated production path of a T-shirt. She bought the T-shirt in Florida. It was made from Texas cotton and manufactured in China. She wanted to determine whether the accusations of the student activist about the harmful effects of globalization were justified.

In the conclusion of the book about her travels (see Economics Out There, on the next page) she asked what she should say to the student activist demonstrating against free trade who was

> so concerned about the evils of the race to the bottom, so concerned about where and how her T-shirt was produced? I would tell her to appreciate what markets and trade had accomplished for all of the sisters in time who have been liberated by life in a sweatshop, and that she should be careful about dooming anyone to life on the farm. I would tell her that the poor suffer more from exclusion from politics than from the perils of the market, and that if she has activist energy left over it should be focused on including people in politics rather than shielding them from markets.

Rivoli's travels led her to conclude that the harmful outcomes we see from globalized trade have less to do with market forces, and more to do with governments protecting domestic industries and workers. Those tariffs, quotas, and domestic subsidies, she argues, force prices below subsistence levels for producers in poorer countries. The resulting unfavourable terms of trade and poverty are due to government protectionist policies.

Her advice is to become politically involved to protect the interests of foreign workers, but not by opposing free trade. Instead, she suggests opposing protectionist policies while supporting safety net policies in all countries. It is a combination of hands-off and hands-on.

Economics *Out There*

Travels of a T-Shirt in the Global Economy

Many of the stories about textiles in this chapter can be found in the easy-to-read and fascinating book by Pietra Rivoli, *The Travels of a T-Shirt in the Global Economy: An Economist Examines the Markets, Power, and Politics of World Trade* (with Updates on Economics Issues and Main Characters) (2014).

The original version was published in 2009, but the author updated the story in 2014. Professor Rivoli follows up on what has become of the people she originally interviewed, like Liang Ying, who escaped from a rural rubber farm to the Shenzhen factory zone in southern China.

Your Hand at the Ballot Box   The globalization debate includes many points of view. You have read arguments by the World Bank and IMF, *The Economist*, and Professors Stiglitz and Rivoli. It is possible that the suggestion of Professor Rivoli combining hands-off and hands-on policies is achievable — if government failure is less likely than market failure. It is also possible that her suggestion will make things worse — if the government failure she fears is more likely than market failure.

Governments respond to political pressure. If you care about globalization, you will have to decide on your own position when voting for elected politicians — the people who set policy and influence trade negotiations.

Refresh 13.4

MyEconLab

For answers to these Refresh Questions, visit MyEconLab.

1. In point form, summarize either the hands-on or hands-off arguments on freer global trade.

2. Present a case for either the hands-on or hands-off argument for increasing freer global trade.

3. Now that you have finished all macroeconomic chapters, how would you answer the fundamental macroeconomic question, "If left alone by government, do price mechanisms of market economies adjust quickly to maintain steady growth in living standards, full employment, and stable prices?" Explain your choice.

Study Guide

13.1 Why Don't You Cook Breakfast? Gains from Trade

Opportunity cost and comparative advantage are key to understanding why specializing and trading makes us all better off.

- With voluntary trade, each person (or country) feels that what they get is of greater value than what they give up.

- Canada is a trading nation — 30 percent of Canadian GDP is from selling exports to the rest of the world.

- **Absolute advantage** — ability to produce a product or service at a lower absolute cost than another producer.

- **Comparative advantage** — ability to produce a product or service at a lower opportunity cost than another producer.

- $\text{Opportunity Cost} = \dfrac{\text{Give Up}}{\text{Get}}$

- Comparative advantage is the key to mutually beneficial gains from trade. Trade makes individuals (or countries) better off when each specializes in products and services in which each has comparative advantage (lower opportunity cost) and then trades for other products and services.

- Even if one individual (or country) has an *absolute* advantage in producing everything at lower cost, differences in *comparative* advantage allow mutually beneficial gains from specializing and trading.

- **Terms of trade** — quantity of exports required to pay for one unit of imports.
  - For mutual benefits, terms of trade must be between each trader's local opportunity costs.
  - Different terms of trade will split the gains differently.

13.2 What's So Wonderful about Free Trade? Protectionism and Trade

Freer trade creates winners and losers from the competitive process of creative destruction. Concentrated losses in import-competing industries create political pressure for protectionism despite overall gains.

- Freer trade increases competition, creating opponents to freer trade.
  - Connections to new markets bring new competitors.

- In the process of *creative destruction*, gains from specialization, trade, competition, and innovation destroy less productive, higher-cost, and less popular products and businesses.
  - Gains are increased productivity and higher living standards for consumers and businesses on the whole.
  - Job losses in form of *structural unemployment* — technological change or international competition — make some workers' skills obsolete in Canada.

- Trade that opens new international markets creates winners and losers in Canada.
  - Winners — Canadian consumers (lower prices, greater product variety), Canadian exporters (increased sales, greater profits), Canadian workers in exporting industries (more jobs, higher wages).
  - Losers — Canadian businesses in import-competing industries (decreased sales, lower prices, profits), Canadian workers in import-competing industries (fewer jobs, lower wages).

- Government responses to protect losers from freer trade include:
  - **tariff** — tax applied to imports, raising the price of products to consumers.
  - **import quota**—limit on the quantity of a product or service that can be imported.
  - **subsidies to domestic producers**—government payment to domestic producers of products or services.

- Unequal distribution of gains and losses produces political pressure for protectionism to help the losers.
  - Number of consumers who gain from free trade is large, but the gain for each consumer is small.
  - Number of businesses and workers in import-competing industries who lose from free trade is small, but the loss for each is large.

- Protectionism leaves Canadians as a whole worse off.
  - Hands-off camp sees protectionist policies as a government failure that is a bigger problem than market failure.

- Political pressure from import-competing industries in countries is a barrier in international trade negotiations.

- Freer trade costs jobs in Canadian import-competing industries, but creates more jobs than are lost.

- Protecting national security and cultural identity are valid, limited arguments for protectionism.

- Protectionism creates risk of retaliation, triggering trade wars that make all countries worse off.

13.3 Globalization and Its Discontents: Is Free Trade the Problem?

While anti-globalization critics view sweatshops as the outcome of globalization and free-market policies, economists ask whether workers are better off or worse off with international trade.

- Anti-globalization groups view international trade as causing problems in developing countries and target the World Bank and the International Monetary Fund (IMF).

- Economists and policymakers at World Bank and IMF, especially during 1990s, attached "free market" hands-off conditions to assistance to developing countries.

- **Economic globalization** — integration of economic activities, across borders, through markets.
  - Speeding up due to falling transportation and communication costs, and elimination of government barriers to trade.

- Sweatshops — a historical consequence of globalization going back 200 years — provide low-wage jobs, often under poor working conditions.
  - Anti-globalization critics view sweatshops as exploitation for corporate profits.
  - Economists ask the opportunity cost question — are workers lives better off, or worse off, compared to a situation without globalization and trade.

13.4 Hands-Off or Hands-On Again? Governments and Global Markets

On the role of government in global markets, the hands-off position views government failure as worse than market failure; the hands-on position views market failure as worse than government failure.

- In contrast to the hand-off policies of the World Bank and IMF, Stiglitz and hands-on economists support a limited role for government.
  - Support a social safety net to support those left behind by trade and markets

- *The Economist* magazine and hands-off economists worry that opening the door to government will result in protectionist policies.
  - Argue that when poor countries suffer from globalization, it is caused by government protectionist policies, not by market forces.

- In trade negotiations at the World Trade Organization (WTO), power struggles over tariffs and subsidies between rich and poor countries affect the terms of trade — how gains are divided.

- As a citizen of Canada and the world, you can take a position on globalization.
  - Hands-off position — markets best left alone to produce economic growth that eventually benefits all; risk is losers in import-competing industries get no assistance in adjusting; believe government failure is worse than market failure
  - Hands-on position — government should help losers from expanded trade in import-competing industries; risk is the government gives into political pressure for protectionism; believe market failure is worse than government failure

TRUE/FALSE

Circle the correct answer. Solutions to these questions are available at the end of the book and on MyEconLab. You can also visit the MyEconLab Study Plan to access additional questions that will help you master the concepts covered in this chapter.

You and your friend Ursula have been studying together for the macro exam that's coming up soon. You are invited to stay for dinner. At the table, her great-grandfather, who is close to 100 years old, suddenly announces, "The trouble with the world today is young people buy too many things from other countries — that's the problem! When I was young, if I needed something, I made it myself." You and Ursula roll your eyes. You both know that's not true, so you suggest a game of true or false. You invite the other dinner guests to discuss the following statements on globalization and trade. What answers should they give?

Use this scenario to answer questions 1–15.

13.1 Gains from Trade

1. The concepts of comparative advantage, specialization, and trade are consistent with Ursula's great-grandfather's belief in self-sufficiency. T F

2. Voluntary trade implies that self–interest is at work. T F

3. Canadian exports are a smaller percentage of Canada's GDP than exports are for U.S. GDP. T F

4. Ursula and her great-grandfather will be willing to trade apples for oranges if their terms of trade are between each trader's local opportunity costs.　　T　F

5. The variety of foods such as tuna, coffee, tea, and the many different fruits being served for dinner at Ursula's home are examples of the gains from trade and specialization.　　T　F

13.2 Protectionism and Trade

6. Ursula's great-grandfather, like most consumers, is an economic winner when new international trade markets open up for Canada.　　T　F

7. Ursula's great-grandfather was a technician in a factory that made vacuum-tube radios in the 1950s. When new technology emerged, his company changed over to produce transistor-type radios. This is a positive outcome of creative destruction.　　T　F

8. Tariffs raise the price of imports into Canada, raise money for the government, and allow older, less competitive businesses to keep operating. Tariffs therefore are completely beneficial for a country.　　T　F

9. Political pressure for protectionism occurs because freer trade results in big losses for some businesses and workers, and small gains for each consumer.　　T　F

10. When it comes to products or services that protect our national security, many economists agree with Ursula's great-grandfather's idea of "making it ourselves."　　T　F

13.3 Globalization and Sweatshops

11. Most hands-off and hands-on policymakers agree on the need for freer trade. They disagree on how it is implemented.　　T　F

12. Globalization forces workers in developing countries to choose lower-paying jobs in sweatshops over higher-paying farm jobs.　　T　F

13.4 Governments and Global Markets

13. Being invited for a "free" dinner at Ursula's house is an example of a government social safety net.　　T　F

14. Rivoli, in her book *Travels of a T-Shirt*, argues that globalization can improve the economic lives of most people if countries develop social safety nets and oppose protectionist policies.　　T　F

15. Your vote can influence how Canada responds to globalization and international trade.　　T　F

MULTIPLE CHOICE

Circle the best answer. Solutions to these questions are available at the end of the book and on MyEconLab. You can also visit the MyEconLab Study Plan to access similar questions that will help you master the concepts covered in this chapter.

13.1 Gains from Trade

1. An easy way to calculate opportunity cost is to use the formula

　a)　$\dfrac{\text{Give Up}}{\text{Get}}$

　b)　$\dfrac{\text{Get}}{\text{Give Up}}$

　c)　Give Up – Get

　d)　Get – Give Up

2. Voluntary trade improves standards of living by moving us from self-sufficiency to

　a)　making our own breakfast.

　b)　calculating the opportunity costs for any change.

　c)　specializing and trading.

　d)　transferring mutual benefits.

3. An absolute advantage in producing a product or service means you have

　a)　higher absolute costs than your competitor.

　b)　lower opportunity costs than your competitor.

　c)　lower absolute costs than your competitor.

　d)　higher opportunity costs than your competitor.

4. A comparative advantage in the production of any product or service means you have

　a)　greater absolute costs than your competitor.

　b)　lower opportunity costs than your competitor.

　c)　lower absolute costs than your competitor.

　d)　greater opportunity costs than your competitor.

13.2 Protectionism and Trade

5. **Mutually beneficial gains from trade come from**
   a) absolute advantage.
   b) comparative advantage.
   c) self-sufficiency.
   d) the United States.

6. **All of the following are forms of protectionism *except***
   a) tariffs.
   b) terms of trade.
   c) import quotas.
   d) domestic subsidies.

7. **For a voluntary trade to have mutual benefits, the terms of trade must**
   a) be between each trader's local opportunity costs.
   b) be greater than each trader's local opportunity costs.
   c) be less than each trader's local opportunity costs.
   d) divide the gains equally.

8. **Jobs lost through competition and innovation are part of**
   a) creative trading.
   b) cyclical employment.
   c) frictional unemployment.
   d) structural unemployment.

9. **Creative destruction**
   a) ruins most economies.
   b) creates more jobs than it destroys.
   c) makes it harder to import products and services.
   d) eliminates gains from trade.

10. **Creative destruction occurs when**
    a) one country has an absolute advantage over its trading partners.
    b) the United States stops trading with Canada.
    c) businesses and workers agree on a new profit structure.
    d) new technologies or greater international competition arise.

11. **When new international markets open up for Canadian businesses, usually**
    a) everybody wins.
    b) nobody wins.
    c) consumers win.
    d) consumers lose.

13.3 Globalization and Sweatshops

12. **Economic globalization is the integration of**
    a) banks, businesses, and labour.
    b) economic activities in developed countries.
    c) markets in developing nations.
    d) economic activities through markets a cross borders.

13. **When economists evaluate sweatshops, they ask the question, "Are sweatshop**
    a) workers' wages too low?"
    b) workers exploited for corporate profits?"
    c) workers' lives better than a situation without the sweatshop jobs?"
    d) workers' lives better than the lives of workers in the developed world?"

13.4 Governments and Global Markets

14. **In the debate surrounding globalization, the hands-on camp believes**
    a) government should provide social safety nets.
    b) government failure is worse than market failure.
    c) businesses should provide social safety nets.
    d) sweatshops should all be shut down.

15. **The forces that encourage creative destruction also cause**
    a) rising standards of living.
    b) some job loss.
    c) some job creation.
    d) all of the above.

SUMMING UP

You and I have finished our last trip around the enlarged GDP circular flow. But this "map," together with the aggregate demand and aggregate supply model, will continue to be your best guides to thinking like a macroeconomist for the rest of your life.

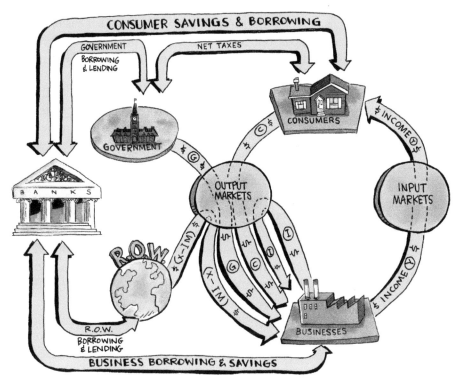

We looked at the five macroeconomic players — consumers, businesses, government, Bank of Canada and the banking system, and the rest of the world (R.O.W.) — whose combined choices create the macroeconomic outcomes we see around us.

To think like a macroeconomist, to understand how the economy as a whole works, and how well it performs, the key is focus on the *connections* between input markets and output markets. The role of banks and money, and the effect of expectations on decisions, are also key. These areas usually determine the success or breakdown of macroeconomic performance.

When the economy performs well, as Say's Law and the "Yes — Markets Self-Adjust" camp predict, markets work well to coordinate individuals' choices and support economic growth. The whole economy is equal to the sum of the (smart) parts. Government can keep its hands-off.

When the economy falters, as Keynes and the "No — Markets Fail Often" camp predict it will without government policy assistance, these areas usually create the breakdowns and economic growth stalls. Smart choices for you do not turn into smart choices for all. Government must be hands-on.

Why Learn to Think Like an Economist?

The purpose of learning to think like a macroeconomist to help you make up your own mind about the fundamental macroeconomic question:

If left alone by government, do the price mechanisms of market economies adjust quickly to maintain steady growth in living standards, full employment, and stable prices?

More simply, if left alone, do markets quickly self-adjust?

By now, I hope you have come up with your own answer. Remember, economists and politicians disagree about the answers — there is no single right answer. Furthermore, most economists and most politicians do not fit entirely into one camp or the other. The extreme answers of these camps are meant to sharpen your thinking — like a macroeconomist — and make it easier for you to figure out your own position. Most likely, your position will be some combination of the "Hands-off" and "Hands-on" positions, depending on the particular economic issue or policy.

As the textbook's cover suggests, your life is filled with choices that are connected to the choices that others make. With your new-gained knowledge of

macroeconomics, you will be better able to understand the world around you, make smarter choices for personal success, and make smarter choices as a citizen. As a citizen, you vote for governments that make policy decisions that influence our economy's performance — living standards, unemployment, and inflation. Politicians will ask you to support policies based on either a hands-off or hands-on view of the market economy. Those policies could make the difference between steady growth in living standards and prolonged recession — in other words, your economic future.

Choose wisely.

The only way for me to know how close I've come to achieving the goal of helping you choose wisely is to hear from you. Let me know what works for you in this book — and, more importantly, what doesn't. You can write to me at **avicohen@yorku.ca**. In future editions I will acknowledge by name all students who help improve *Macroeconomics for Life: Smart Choices for All?*

Professor Avi J. Cohen
Department of Economics
York University
University of Toronto

Glossary

A

absolute advantage: the ability to produce a product or service at a lower absolute cost than another producer (p. 9, p. 392)

aggregate demand: quantity of real GDP macroeconomic players plan to demand at different price levels (p. 211)

automatic stabilizers: tax and transfer adjustments that counteract changes to real GDP without explicit government decisions (p. 367)

B

balance of payments accounts: measure a country's international transactions (p. 300)

balanced budget: revenues = spending (p. 366)

bank run: many depositors withdraw cash all at once (p. 255)

bond: financial asset for which borrower promises to repay the original value at a specific future date, and to make fixed regular interest payments (p. 243)

budget deficit: revenues < spending (p. 366)

budget surplus: revenues > spending (p. 366)

business cycles: ups and downs of overall economic activity, measured as fluctuations of real GDP around potential GDP (p. 156)

C

central bank: government institution responsible for supervising chartered banks and other financial institutions, and for regulating the supply of money (p. 252)

comparative advantage: the ability to produce a product or service at lower opportunity cost than another producer (p. 10, p. 392)

comparative statics: comparing two equilibrium outcomes to isolate the effect of changing one factor at a time (p. 95)

complements: products or services used together to satisfy the same want (p. 42)

Consumer Price Index (CPI): measure of the average prices of fixed shopping basket of products and services (p. 177)

consumer surplus: the difference between the amount a consumer is willing and able to pay, and the price actually paid (p. 97)

contraction: period during which real GDP decreases (p. 156)

contractionary fiscal policy: decreases aggregate demand by decreasing government spending, increasing taxes, or decreasing transfers; shifts the aggregate demand curve leftward — a negative aggregate demand shock (p. 355)

core inflation rate: inflation rate excluding volatile categories (p. 180)

cost-push inflation: rising average prices caused by decreases in supply (p. 193)

creative destruction: competitive business innovations generate profits for winners, improving living standards for all, but destroy less productive or less desirable products and production methods (p. 154)

crowding in: tendency for government debt-financed fiscal policy to increase private investment spending by improving expectations (p. 376)

crowding out: tendency for government debt-financed fiscal policy to decrease private investment spending by raising interest rates (p. 376)

currency: government-issued bills and coins (p. 251)

currency appreciation: rise in the exchange rate of one currency for another (p. 277)

currency depreciation: fall in the exchange rate of one currency for another (p. 277)

cyclical deficits and surpluses: created only as a result of automatic stabilizers counteracting business cycles (p. 368)

cyclical unemployment: due to fluctuations in economic activity over the business cycle (p. 174)

D

deadweight loss: the decrease in total surplus compared to an economically efficient outcome (p. 101)

decrease in demand: decrease in consumers' willingness and ability to pay (p. 40)

decrease in supply: decrease in business's willingness to produce; leftward shift of supply curve (p. 68)

deflation: persistent fall in the average price level and a rise in the value of money (p. 183)

demand: consumers' willingness and ability to pay for a particular product or service (p. 29)

demand curve: shows the relationship between price and quantity demanded, other things remaining the same (p. 35)

demand deposits: balances in bank accounts that depositors can withdraw on demand by using a debit card or writing a cheque (p. 251)

demand-pull inflation: rising average prices caused by increases in demand (p. 191)

demand shocks: changes in factors other than the price level that change aggregate demand and shift the aggregate demand curve (p. 215)

discouraged workers: want to work but have given up actively searching for jobs (p. 171)

disposable income: aggregate income minus net taxes (p. 142)

domestic monetary transmission mechanism: how money affects real GDP through interest rates, spending, and aggregate demand (p. 263)

E

economic globalization: integration of economic activities, across borders, through markets (p. 404)

economic growth: expansion of economy's capacity to produce products and services; increase in potential GDP per person (p. 146)

economic growth rate: annual percentage change in real GDP per person (p. 150)

economics: how individuals, businesses, and governments make the best possible choices to get what they want, and how those choices interact in markets (p. 4)

efficient market outcome: consumers buy only products and services where marginal benefit is greater than marginal cost; products and services produced at lowest cost, with price just covering all opportunity costs of production (p. 101)

equilibrium price: the price that equalizes quantity demanded and quantity supplied, balancing the forces of competition and cooperation so that there is no tendency for change (p. 85)

excess demand (or shortage): quantity demanded exceeds quantity supplied (p. 82)

excess supply (or surplus): quantity supplied exceeds quantity demanded (p. 83)

exchange rate: price at which one currency exchanges for another currency (p. 276)

expansion: period during which real GDP increases (p. 156)

expansionary fiscal policy: increases aggregate demand by increasing government spending, decreasing taxes, or increasing transfers; shifts the aggregate demand curve rightward — a positive aggregate demand shock (p. 355)

F

fallacy of composition: what is true for one is not true for all; the whole is greater than the sum of the individual parts (p. 110)

fiscal policy: changes in government purchases and taxes/transfers to achieve macroeconomic outcomes of steady growth, full employment, and stable prices (p. 122)

fixed exchange rate: determined by governments or central banks (p. 300)

floating exchange rate: determined by demand and supply in the foreign exchange market (p. 300)

flow: amount per unit of time (p. 133)

foreign exchange market: worldwide market where all countries' currencies are bought and sold in exchange for each other (p. 276)

fractional-reserve banking: banks hold only a fraction of deposits as reserves (p. 255)

frictional unemployment: due to normal labour turnover and job search; healthy part of changing economy (p. 173)

full employment: there is only frictional, structural, and seasonal unemployment (p. 175)

G

globalization (economic): integration of economic activities, across borders, through markets (p. 404)

government failure: government policy fails to serve the public interest (p. 116)

gross domestic product (GDP): value of all final products and services produced annually in Canada (p. 141)

H

human capital: increased earning potential from work experience, on-the-job training, and education (p. 147)

I

implicit costs: hidden opportunity costs of what business owner could earn elsewhere with time and money invested (p. 20)

import quota: limit on the quantity of a product or service that can be imported (p. 398)

incentives: rewards and penalties for choices (p. 6)

increase in aggregate supply: increase in economy's capacity to produce real GDP caused by increases in quantity or quality of inputs (p. 205)

increase in demand: increase in consumers' willingness and ability to pay; rightward shift of demand curve (p. 40)

increase in supply: increase in businesses' willingness to produce; rightward shift of supply curve (p. 66)

inferior goods: products or services you buy less of when your income increases (p. 42)

inflation: a persistent rise in the average price level and a fall in the value of money (p. 177)

inflation-control target: range of inflation rates set by a central bank as a monetary policy objective (p. 313)

inflation rate: annual percentage change in the consumer price index (p. 178)

inflation rate differential: difference in inflation rates between countries (p. 286)

inflationary gap: real GDP above potential GDP (p. 157)

injection: spending in the circular flow that does not start with consumers; *G* (government spending), *I* (business investment spending), *X* (exports) (p. 351)

inputs: the productive resources — labour, natural resources, capital equipment, and entrepreneurial ability — used to produce products and services (p. 14)

interest rate: price of holding money: what you give up by not holding loanable funds (bonds) (p. 247)

interest rate differential: difference in interest rates between countries (p. 284)

interest rate parity (rate of return parity): rates of return on investments are equal across countries, accounting for expected depreciation or appreciation of exchange rates (p. 299)

international transmission mechanisms: how effects of exchange rates are transmitted to real GDP, unemployment, and inflation (p. 291)

investment spending: business purchases of new factories and equipment (p. 121)

L

labour force: employed + unemployed (p. 169)

labour force participation rate: percentage of working-age population in the labour force (employed or unemployed) (p. 169)

law of aggregate demand: as the price level rises, aggregate quantity demanded of real GDP decreases (p. 212)

law of demand: if the price of a product or service rises, quantity demanded decreases, other things remaining the same (p. 34)

law of demand for Canadian dollars: as the exchange rate rises, the quantity demanded of Canadian dollars decreases (p. 278)

law of demand for money: as the price of money — the interest rate — rises, the quantity demanded of money decreases (p. 247)

law of one price: profit seekers eliminate differences in prices of the same product or service across markets and establish a single price (p. 295)

law of short-run aggregate supply: as the price level rises, aggregate quantity supplied of real GDP increases (p. 205)

law of supply: if the price of a product or service rises, quantity supplied increases (p. 62)

law of supply for Canadian dollars: as the exchange rate rises, the quantity supplied of Canadian dollars increases (p. 280)

leakage: spending that leaks out of the circular flow through taxes, savings, and imports (p. 351)

lender of last resort: central bank's role of making loans to banks to preserve the stability of the financial system (p. 253)

liquidity: ease with which assets can be converted into the economy's medium of exchange (p. 244)

long-run aggregate supply: potential GDP — the quantity of real GDP supplied when all inputs are fully employed (p. 203)

M

macroeconomics: analyzes performance of the whole Canadian economy and global economy; the combined outcomes of all individual microeconomic choices (p. 18)

marginal benefits: the additional benefit from a choice, changing with circumstances (p. 20, p. 30)

marginal cost: additional opportunity cost of increasing quantity supplied, changing with circumstances (p. 52)

marginal opportunity costs: additional opportunity costs from the next choice (p. 20, p. 58)

market: the interactions between buyers and sellers (p. 78)

market-clearing price: the price that equalizes quantity demanded and quantity supplied (p. 85)

market demand: sum of demands of all individuals willing and able to buy a particular product or service (p. 34)

market failure: market outcomes are inefficient or inequitable and fail to serve the public interest (p. 115)

market for loanable funds: banks coordinate the supply of loanable funds (savings) with the demand for loanable funds (borrowing for investment spending). The interest rate is the price of loanable funds. (p. 221)

market supply: sum of supplies of all businesses willing to produce a particular product or service (p. 61)

microeconomics: analyzes choices that individuals in households, individual businesses, and governments make, and how those choices interact in markets (p. 18)

model: a simplified representation of the real world, focusing attention on what's important for understanding (p. 14)

monetary policy: adjusting the supply of money and interest rates to achieve steady growth, full employment, and stable prices (p. 313)

money: anything acceptable as a means of paying for products and services (p. 242)

multiplier effect: a spending injection has a multiplied impact on real GDP (p. 352)

N

national debt (public debt): total amount owed by government = (sum of past deficits) − (sum of past surpluses) (p. 372)

natural rate of unemployment: unemployment rate at full employment, when there is only frictional, structural, and seasonal unemployment (p. 175)

negative externalities (external costs): costs to society from your private choice that affect others, but that you do not pay (p. 21)

net taxes: taxes minus transfer payments (p. 142)

nominal GDP: value at current prices of all final products and services produced annually in a country (p. 132)

nominal interest rate: observed interest rate; equal to number of dollars received per year in interest as percentage of the number of dollars saved (p. 181)

normal goods: products or services you buy more of when your income increases (p. 42)

normative statements: about what you believe *should* be; involve value judgments (p. 17)

O

open market operations: buying or selling government bonds on the bond market by the Bank of Canada (p. 316)

opportunity cost: cost of best alternative given up (p. 5)

output gap: real GDP minus potential GDP (p. 157)

overnight rate: the interest rate banks charge each other for one day loans — main monetary policy tool (p. 314)

P

paradox of thrift: attempts to increase saving cause total savings to decrease because of falling employment and incomes (p. 111)

Phillips Curve: graph showing an inverse relation between unemployment and inflation (p. 189)

positive externalities (external benefits): benefits to society from your private choice that affect others, but that others do not pay you for (p. 21)

positive statements: about what is; can be evaluated as true or false by checking the facts (p. 17)

potential GDP: real GDP when all inputs — labour, capital, land/resources, and entrepreneurial ability — are fully employed (p. 144)

potential GDP per person: potential GDP divided by the population (p. 144)

preferences: your wants and their intensities (p. 28)

price stability: inflation is low enough that it does not significantly affect people's economic decisions (p. 313)

prime rate: the interest rate on loans to lowest-risk corporate borrowers (p. 320)

producer surplus: the difference between the amount a producer is willing to accept, and the price actually received (p. 97)

production possibilities frontier: maximum combinations of products or services that can be produced with existing inputs (p. 9)

productivity: measured as quantity of real GDP produced by an hour of labour (p. 153)

property rights: legally enforceable guarantees of ownership of physical, financial, and intellectual property (p. 79)

public debt (national debt): total amount owed by government = (sum of past deficits) − (sum of past surpluses) (p. 372)

purchasing power parity (*PPP*): exchange rates adjust so that money has equal real purchasing power in any country (p. 295)

Q

quantitative easing: a central bank tool of flooding the financial system with money by buying high-risk bonds, mortgages, and assets from banks. These liabilities on bank balance sheets are replaced with cash assets, enabling banks to make new loans (p. 332)

quantity demanded: amount you actually plan to buy at a given price (p. 33)

quantity supplied: quantity you actually plan to supply at a given price (p. 56)

quantity theory of money: increase in the quantity of money causes an equal percentage increase in the inflation rate (p. 188)

R

rate of return parity (interest rate parity): rates of return on investments are equal across countries, accounting for expected depreciation or appreciation of exchange rates (p. 299)

real GDP: value at constant prices of all final products and services produced annually in a country (p. 135)

real GDP per person: real GDP divided by population (p. 136)

real interest rate: nominal interest rate adjusted for effects of inflation (p. 181)

recession: two or more successive quarters of contraction of real GDP (p. 157)

recessionary gap: real GDP below potential GDP (p. 157)

Rule of 70: number of years it takes for initial amount to double is roughly 70 divided by annual percentage growth rate (p. 152)

S

Say's Law: supply creates its own demand (p. 113)

scarcity: the problem that arises from our limited money, time, and energy (p. 4)

seasonal unemployment: due to seasonal changes in weather (p. 174)

shortage (or excess demand): quantity demanded exceeds quantity supplied (p. 82)

short-run aggregate supply: quantity of real GDP macroeconomic players plan to supply at different price levels (p. 204)

stagflation: combination of recession (higher unemployment) and inflation (higher average prices) (p. 193)

stock: fixed amount at a moment in time (p. 149)

structural deficits and surpluses: budget deficits and surpluses occurring at potential GDP (p. 370)

structural unemployment: due to technological change or international competition that makes workers' skills obsolete; there is a mismatch between the skills workers have and the skills new jobs require (p. 173)

subsidies to domestic producers: government payment to domestic producers of products or services (p. 399)

substitutes: products or services used in place of each other to satisfy the same want (p. 41)

sunk costs: past expenses that cannot be recovered (p. 54)

supply: businesses' willingness to produce a particular product or service because price covers all opportunity costs (p. 55)

supply curve: shows relationship between price and quantity supplied, other things remaining the same (p. 62)

supply shocks: events directly affecting businesses' costs, prices, and supply (p. 192)

supply-side effects: the incentive effects of taxes on aggregate supply (p. 362)

surplus (or excess supply): quantity supplied exceeds quantity demanded (p. 83)

T

tariff: tax applied to imports (p. 397)

technological change: improvements in the quality of capital (p. 147)

terms of trade: quantity of exports required to pay for one unit of imports (p. 393)

total surplus: consumer surplus plus producer surplus (p. 99)

U

unemployed: not employed and actively seeking work (p. 168)

unemployment rate: percentage of people in labour force who are unemployed (p. 169)

V

value added: value of output minus the value of intermediate products and services bought from other businesses (p. 137)

velocity of money (*V*): number of times a unit of money changes hands during a year (p. 186)

Answers to the Study Guide Questions

CHAPTER 1

TRUE/FALSE

1. True. Definition of economics.
2. False. Even people who win the lottery can never satisfy all of their wants; they also face trade-offs and have to make smart choices.
3. False. The opportunity cost is the value of what you give up to take that path, action, or activity.
4. False. The grant covers the money cost of getting an apprenticeship but not the opportunity cost — the total value of what the individual gives up by taking an apprenticeship, which includes the money that the individual could have earned in a job.
5. False. Women have a larger incentive because the return on post-secondary education — the gap between incomes of post-secondary graduates and high-school graduates — is higher for women than for men.
6. False. If men held a comparative advantage in housework then traditional gender roles would be reversed (men would be doing the housework) because individuals should specialize in the activity where they have a comparative advantage.
7. False. Possible to produce but not maximum combinations.
8. False. Lower opportunity cost.
9. False. There are benefits for both people from trade.
10. True.
11. False. Economists must instead build models that assume all other things are unchanged.
12. True. The word *should* is a sign of a normative statement.
13. False. They are microeconomic choices.
14. True. Microeconomics focuses mostly on individual decisions.
15. False. They are the costs that affect others.

MULTIPLE CHOICE

1. **d)** We all have limited time, energy, and money.
2. **d)** Even Bill Gates faces the problem of scarcity.
3. **b)** Economics is about people (also in businesses and government) making choices.
4. **d)** All are scarce.
5. **a)** Paid tuition is the same for either choice.
6. **d)** See *Economics Out There* on p. 6.
7. **b)** Going to college means giving up *fewer* good jobs. With fewer good jobs in a weaker economy, the opportunity cost of going to school decreases.
8. **b)** Differences in opportunity costs key to gains from trade.
9. **a)** Formula on p. 10.
10. **c)** Chloe's opportunity cost of muffins (2 cookies per muffin) lower than Zabeen's (3 cookies per muffin).
11. **a)** Notice the word *should*.
12. **d)** See pp. 14–15.
13. **a)** Macroeconomic choice by government.
14. **c)** International exchange rates are a macroeconomic topic.
15. **b)** The past is the same no matter what choice you make now.

CHAPTER 2

TRUE/FALSE

1. False. Demand is a stronger word, meaning willing and able to pay.
2. True.
3. False. Also depends on your time and effort.
4. True. Marginal means additional.
5. True. Flat fee is not an additional cost.
6. False. Marginal benefit equals average benefit only in special circumstances. For example, if a basketball player with a shooting percentage of 50 percent successfully makes one out of her next two shots, then the additional points she adds are equal to the amount of points she usually (on average) adds.
7. True. Willingness to pay changes with circumstances.
8. False. Quantity demanded is a much more limited term than demand. Only a change in price changes quantity demanded. A change in any other influence on consumer choice changes demand.
9. True. Only a change in price changes quantity demanded.
10. True. Add up all individual demands at any price to get market demand.
11. False. Slope downward to the right.
12. True. For any quantity, maximum willing to pay is now less.

13. False, for normal goods. A decrease in income decreases demand. But true, for inferior goods.
14. False. As the holidays get nearer, people's willingness and ability to pay for certain products or services increases for any given price. Therefore, an increase in demand drives the rising prices.
15. False. Statement is true for normal goods, false for inferior goods.

MULTIPLE CHOICE

1. **d)** Definition of preferences.
2. **b)** *Give up* includes money, time, effort.
3. **d)** Intensities of your wants.
4. **c)** Each additional plate brings less satisfaction.
5. **d)** Marginal costs greater than marginal benefits.
6. **a)** Quantity demanded is not wants. Must be willing and able to pay.
7. **d)** Price depends on marginal benefits, not total benefits.
8. **c)** With switch to cheaper substitutes, quantity demanded decreases.
9. **d)** Rising price is movement along demand curve for garbage collection.
10. **b)** Definition of substitutes.
11. **a)** Buy less as income increases, switching to better food that was previously unaffordable.
12. **c)** Price changes quantity demanded, not demand.
13. **b)** Cars and tires are complements.
14. **d)** (a) for inferior goods, (b) for normal goods.
15. **d)** Price only affects quantity demanded. Change in income changes demand.

CHAPTER 3

TRUE/FALSE

1. False. Workers with fewer alternatives may accept lower wages.
2. True. Choose to produce when additional benefits are greater than additional opportunity costs.
3. True.
4. True. Forgone opportunity is now more valuable.
5. False. Rent payments are sunk costs not relevant to the decision of how much to produce.
6. False. Sunk costs are the same no matter what choice you make.
7. True. Not willing to supply if prices don't cover marginal opportunity costs.
8. False. Opportunity cost equals what you give up divided by what you get.
9. False. As you spend more time in any activity (working instead of relaxing), the marginal opportunity cost of that activity increases.
10. True. Opportunity cost is a short form of marginal opportunity cost.
11. False. Start with quantity and go up and over to price (marginal cost).

12. True. Shifts supply curve leftward.
13. False. Rise in price decreases market supply of the other product.
14. True. Higher expected future prices decreases supply today.
15. False. Increase in quantity supplied.

MULTIPLE CHOICE

1. **c)** The 30 minutes of studying you must give up become more valuable with an exam tomorrow.
2. **b)** $15 is the best forgone opportunity to make money.
3. **c)** Sunk costs are in the past, cannot be changed, and are not additional costs.
4. **b)** Previous money lost makes no difference to smart choice on next turn.
5. **c)** Tattoo remains whether he breaks up or not. (Are tattoos a sunk cost if they can be removed?)
6. **c)** Marginal cost is constant.
7. **d)** All describe a relationship between rising price and increasing quantity of hours supplied.
8. **a)** Law of supply.
9. **c)** If inputs *not* equally productive, opportunity cost increases.
10. **c)** Price changes quantity supplied.
11. **a)** Only (a) shifts supply curve rightward. (b), (c), (d) shift supply leftward.
12. **a)** Rightward shift in supply for (b), (c), (d).
13. **a)** Rightward shift of supply curve.
14. **b)** Other answers change demand.
15. **d)** Piercing and tattoos are related products produced.

CHAPTER 4

TRUE/FALSE

1. False. Transactions would not be voluntary and there would be no incentive to supply the product to consumers.
2. False. Price should cover all opportunity costs.
3. False. Price and quantity adjustments do not require the consumer or business to know anything about anyone's personal wants or production capabilities.
4. True. Surplus, with quantity supplied greater than quantity demanded.
5. True.
6. True. Definition of market-clearing price.
7. False. May not be willing or able to pay the equilibrium price.
8. True. Quantity demanded equals quantity supplied.
9. False. Increased supply causes equilibrium price to fall and quantity to increase.
10. False. Increase in demand and increase in supply increase market-clearing quantity, but effect on price uncertain.
11. False. Increased supply lowers the price of grey seals, reducing the cost of producing seal coat fur, resulting in a lower price.

12. True. Reduced qualifications increases supply.
13. False. Price minus marginal cost.
14. False. Decrease in total surplus compared to economically efficient outcome.
15. True. Maximum total surplus and zero deadweight loss.

MULTIPLE CHOICE

1. **d)** Definition.
2. **d)** Price must cover marginal opportunity cost of seller and be less than marginal benefit of buyer.
3. **c)** Government guarantees of property rights allow markets to function.
4. **d)** When prices change, so do smart choices and quantities.
5. **c)** Price adjustment.
6. **c)** Excess demand and frustrated buyers.
7. **d)** Market-clearing price.
8. **a)** No one is kicking himself about wanting to buy or sell more.
9. **a)** Draw rightward shift demand and leftward shift supply.
10. **d)** Draw leftward shift demand and rightward shift supply.
11. **c)** Falling price increases quantity demanded and decreases quantity supplied.
12. **b)** Exercise and reading books are substitute activities for a child's time.
13. **b)** Area under the marginal benefit curve and above the (market) price actually paid.
14. **b)** Consumer surplus plus producer surplus.
15. **c)** For any quantity greater than the equilibrium quantity, read up to marginal cost and marginal benefit curves.

CHAPTER 5

TRUE/FALSE

1. True. Working means input markets; products and services sold in output markets.
2. True. Government sets rules of the game and chooses where to interact.
3. False. Superstars at microeconomics may not be superstars at macroeconomics.
4. False. Fallacy of composition — individual superstars may not function as a superstar team. They might not be able to work effectively together.
5. True. Policy fails to serve the public interest.
6. True. Believe market failure more likely than government failure.
7. False. They prefer a hands-off approach believing that left alone, markets quickly self-adjust to produce desirable outcomes.
8. True. Hands-on camp believes in fallacy of composition.
9. False. If fewer products and services per person available, then standard of living of aliens is decreasing.
10. False. More workers looking for work, but unable to find work, is bad news.

11. True. Inflation is a rise in the average level of all prices.
12. False. To buy Canadian exports, aliens can convert their money into Canadian dollars.
13. True. Monetary policy affects interest rates, including mortgage interest rates.
14. False. Employers can choose from large pool of job applicants.
15. False. Macroeconomic thinking focuses on connections between markets.

MULTIPLE CHOICE

1. **b)** No inflation in either, and no government programs in Great Depression.
2. **d)** All made bad choices by assuming prices would always go up.
3. **b)** Unemployment increased.
4. **d)** Spending and GDP decrease, incomes decrease, so people can't save as much as they hoped to.
5. **c)** Definition.
6. **d)** No need for government policy.
7. **b)** Hands-off usually associated with political right.
8. **d)** Three key performance outcomes.
9. **b)** Different from financial investments in stocks.
10. **d)** All federal transfer payments to individuals.
11. **c)** Bank of Canada is largely independent of Government of Canada.
12. **d)** Lower unemployment improves all conditions for workers.
13. **a)** Increasing unemployment connected to decreasing GDP and growth.
14. **a)** Value of money falls with inflation.
15. **a)** Households are consumers when spending or saving.

CHAPTER 6

TRUE/FALSE

1. False. Part of the increase in nominal GDP is due to inflation.
2. False. The increase in real GDP was accompanied by population growth, so real GDP *per person* is not 20 times higher.
3. True. Real GDP per person is the best measure of material living standards.
4. False. According to Figure 6.1, since the 1960s, nominal GDP has risen faster than real GDP.
5. False. Only new production or value added in 2012 adds to 2012 GDP.
6. False. Consumption increases but net exports decrease by the same amount since Ferraris are imports.
7. True. See examples in text.
8. False. The invention of the cell phone, a technological change, increased the quality of capital.
9. False. Fertilizer is a capital input, so Fred increased the quality of capital.
10. True. Use the Rule of 70.

11. True. High point before the Global Financial Crisis.
12. True. Two consecutive quarters (or more) of decrease in real GDP is a recession.
13. True. Real GDP omits the underground economy.
14. False. GDP per person is the best measure of material standards of living, but doesn't account for many other factors affecting well-being.
15. False. Real GDP per person is an imperfect measure of well-being: does not include crime, pollution, and freedom

MULTIPLE CHOICE

1. **c)** Looks don't count, only production!
2. **a)** Current prices and current quantities.
3. **b)** Real GDP is constant, but real GDP per person and living standard decrease.
4. **d)** All definitions of GDP.
5. **d)** Must subtract all spending on imports by any domestic macroeconomic players.
6. **d)** Business investment spending is on factories and machines.
7. **d)** Definitions of potential GDP = full employment GDP.
8. **b)** $1000 \div $40\,000 = 0.025$ per person.
9. **c)** Financial assets not part of real GDP and measures of growth.
10. **c)** Getting more for less work.
11. **c)** Definition of recession.
12. **d)** Real GDP > potential GDP.
13. **c)** Voluntary, non-market work is not counted in GDP
14. **d)** Income that is illegal or unreported to tax authorities.
15. **b)** Market transactions are $400, but Moby earns and spends $200 per week.

CHAPTER 7

TRUE/FALSE

1. True. Temporary layoffs count as unemployed.
2. False. Unemployed last month but not in the labour force this month because he gave up searching.
3. True. V. J. went from unemployed to not in the labour force.
4. False. Number of employed stayed the same and number of unemployed decreased, so unemployment rate decreased. Last month it was 50% = unemployed ÷ labour force × 100 = 2 ÷ (2 + 2) × 100. This month it was 33% = 1 ÷ (1 + 2) × 100.
5. True. C. J. and V. J. would then count as unemployed.
6. True. Due to business cycle.
7. False. B. J. is cyclically unemployed, so no full employment.
8. False. There was no cyclical unemployment if A. J. and B. J. are employed, C. J. and V. J. are structurally unemployed, and D. J. is not in the labour force.

9. False. Stagflation, not stagnation, if prices are rising and output is decreasing.
10. False. It would overestimate A. J.'s true cost of living increase since A. J. does not consume the products and services rising in price so does not have an increase in his cost of living.
11. False. Real interest rate is zero equals nominal interest rate minus the inflation rate.
12. True. Increase in quantity of money causes equal percentage increase in inflation rate.
13. False. Velocity = 2 because $M \times V = 100$, and $M = 50$.
14. True. Inverse relation between unemployment rate and inflation rate.
15. False. With cost-push inflation, inflation and unemployment change in the same direction.

MULTIPLE CHOICE

1. **b)** Miguel is frictionally unemployed.
2. **d)** Working or searching for work, Salma is part of labour force.
3. **b)** (20 million ÷ 25 million) × 100 = 80 percent.
4. **d)** There is lower labour force participation and fewer students are working.
5. **d)** Those seeking work moved to Alberta.
6. **c)** Discouraged workers are officially not counted as unemployed.
7. **b)** Part of normal labour turnover and job search for that year.
8. **b)** Unemployment above the natural rate means cyclical unemployment.
9. **a)** (126 − 120) ÷ 120 × 100 = 5 percent, above the Bank of Canada's target range for inflation of 1 to 3 percent.
10. **d)** Not measured in the official calculation.
11. **d)** Inflation reduces purchasing power of money.
12. **b)** Definition of velocity.
13. **b)** Velocity fixed and real GDP = potential GDP.
14. **b)** Stagflation combines high unemployment and high inflation.
15. **b)** OPEC oil price shocks occurred in the 1970s.

CHAPTER 8

TRUE/FALSE

1. False. Correspond to points on the macro *PPF*.
2. True. Definition.
3. True. Technological change is an increase in quality of capital, shifting both *LAS* and *SAS* rightward.
4. False. Rising input prices — a negative supply shock — shift only *SAS* leftward.
5. True. Rising average prices cause movement up along *SAS* curve.
6. False. Optimistic expectations increase aggregate demand, shifting *AD* rightward.
7. False. Shift *AD* rightward.

8. True. Business investment (*I*) part of
$AD = C + I + G + X - IM$.
9. False. Appreciation of Canadian dollar makes Canadian exports more expensive and U.S. demands fewer.
10. True. Definition of long-run macroeconomic equilibrium.
11. True. Shifts *SAS* leftward, decreasing real GDP and increasing unemployment.
12. True. Differences are about origin of shocks.
13. False. The "Yes — Markets Self-Adjust" camp believes government can make things worse, as part of the problem, not the solution.
14. True. Labour markets self-adjust with flexible prices (wages).
15. False. "Yes — Markets Self-Adjust" (hands-on) camp believes this.

MULTIPLE CHOICE

1. **c)** Definition.
2. **d)** Real GDP = potential GDP at points on macro *PPF* in long-run.
3. **a)** Rightward shift of both *SAS* and *LAS*.
4. **a)** Increases in quality of inputs increase productivity and shift both *SAS* and *LAS* rightward.
5. **d)** More schooling increases the quality of inputs, increasing aggregate supply.
6. **c)** $17 000 = $20 000 − $6000 + $3000.
7. **b)** Investment spending is the most volatile, unpredictable component, affected by interest rates and expectations, and is postponeable.
8. **a)** Canadian exports of oil and aggregate demand both increase.
9. **c)** More disposable income increases planned consumption spending and aggregate demand.
10. **d)** Demand shocks cause unemployment and inflation to move in opposite directions.
11. **b)** Leftward shift of *SAS* decreases GDP and increases unemployment and inflation.
12. **c)** Businesses borrow from loanable funds markets where savings are deposited and invest in new equipment.
13. **d)** Both workers and employers can resist wage reductions, and contracts cannot be changed easily.
14. **b)** Other answers describe "No — Markets Fail Often" camp.
15. **a)** Wages (price of labour) don't adjust, so quantities (employment) do.

CHAPTER 9

TRUE/FALSE

1. False. Since money pays no interest but bonds pay interest, sometimes it is smarter to hold less money and more bonds.

2. False. Rising interest rates increase the opportunity cost of holding money, decreasing the quantity demanded of money.
3. True. Need more money to cover more expensive purchases.
4. False. Money's purchasing power will decrease with inflation.
5. False. Stays the same. This shifts money from one component of M1+ (demand deposits) to another (currency).
6. False. Currency is a small fraction of the money supply (4 percent of M2+).
7. True. Rise in the interest rate increase quantity of money supplied.
8. False. M1+ decreases, but since chequing and saving accounts are both part of M2+, no change in M2+.
9. False. Bonds are riskier because changes in the interest rate change the market price of bonds.
10. True. Bonds do not promise a fixed interest rate.
11. False. When interest rates are high, there is excess supply of money; people buy bonds to get rid of money.
12. True. Money affects aggregate demand.
13. False. Positive aggregate demand shock.
14. True. Camps disagree.
15. False. The "Yes — Markets Self-Adjust" camp believes external supply shocks, not money, are the main source of business cycles.

MULTIPLE CHOICE

1. **a)** Money provides liquidity and you give up interest earned on bonds.
2. **d)** The problem is finding a seller who has what you want and who wants what you are selling.
3. **c)** Store of value — why hold money, which pays no interest.
4. **d)** **(a)** does not change money demand; **(b)** and **(c)** cause leftward shift of demand for money.
5. **d)** Debit card transfers your deposit money to seller.
6. **a)** Demand deposits are the medium of exchange.
7. **a)** Loans are riskiest and earn banks the highest interest rates. Treasury bills are lower risk and earn lower interest rates.
8. **d)** **(a)**, **(b)**, and **(c)** are all true but not only source.
9. **d)** Interest rates and market price of bonds move in opposite directions; rises in market price create unexpected profit (buy low, sell high).
10. **b)** Excess demand causes people to sell bonds to get money, lowering bond prices and raising interest rates.
11. **a)** Quantity theory of money.
12. **d)** Interest rates affect aggregate demand through the domestic monetary transmission mechanism.
13. **b)** Higher cost of borrowing to finance new factories and equipment.
14. **b)** Cause rightward shift of aggregate demand curve.
15. **d)** Disagreements are about money's effect on business cycles and market adjustments.

CHAPTER 10

TRUE/FALSE

1. True. Must exchange Australian dollars to get Canadian dollars to pay for Canadian products and services.
2. False. It takes 95 cents Canadian to buy 1 Australian dollar.
3. False. The Australian dollar depreciates against the C$, buying fewer Canadian products and services.
4. False. The European gets the most Canadian dollars. Each euro is worth C$1.50 and each US$ is worth C$1.04.
5. True. Increase in the Canadian inflation rate differential decreases demand and increases supply of C$.
6. False. Increase in the Canadian interest rate differential increases demand and decreases supply of C$.
7. True. Increases demand for C$, causing slight appreciation of C$.
8. False. Higher exchange rate for the Canadian dollar has advantages (imports are less expensive and cross-border shopping is better) and disadvantages (fewer exports and lower real GDP).
9. True. Prices of imports more expensive in C$, raising the average price level.
10. False. $5 Australian buys exactly the same quantity of products in both Australia. and Canada.
11. True. C$100 = $95 Australian.
12. True. Definition.
13. False. Measures flows from exports, imports, and net investment/labour/transfer income.
14. True. More C$ flow out of Canada than into Canada.
15. True. Canadian investments in R.O.W. create a negative outflow of C$ to R.O.W.; R.O.W. investments in Canada create a positive inflow of C$.

MULTIPLE CHOICE

1. **d)** **(b)** is the reciprocal exchange rate.
2. **b)** Price and quantity demanded of a currency move in opposite directions, and price and quantity supplied move in the same direction.
3. **d)** Demand for C$ increases, so value of C$ appreciates against US$, which is equal to a depreciation of the US$ against the C$.
4. **d)** If the US$ depreciates against the C$ and the C$ remains constant against the Euro, then the US$ depreciates against the Euro.
5. **b)** Increase in the Canadian inflation rate differential decreases demand and increases supply of C$.
6. **d)** Increased real GDP increases imports and investor confidence, resulting in a net appreciation of C$.
7. **b)** Expectations of a fall in future price of C$ causes self-fulfilling depreciation of C$ (decreases demand for C$).
8. **b)** Effects of changes in exchange rates on real GPD and inflation happen through international transmission mechanisms.

9. **c)** Depreciating C$ is a positive aggregate demand shock, increases net exports and real GDP.
10. **b)** Purchasing power parity holds when C$10 has the same purchasing power when converted into US dollars (US$10) and European euros (6.7 euros).
11. **d)** All are aspects of purchasing power parity.
12. **b)** Rate of return in Japan (7%) = rate of return in Canada (3%) minus expected depreciation [− 4%] of yen against C$. 7% = 3% + 4%.
13. **d)** C$ flow out of Canada.
14. **c)** Canada is loaning R.O.W. extra C$, causing financial account deficit.
15. **a)** Current Account Balance + Financial Account Balance + Statistical Disrepancy = 0.

CHAPTER 11

TRUE/FALSE

1. False. The Governor of the Bank of Canada is the driver.
2. True. Goals of monetary policy.
3. False. Tool is the overnight interest rate.
4. True. Range of the inflation-control target.
5. False. Potential GDP is desirable, but the main objective is keeping the inflation rate between 1 percent and 3 percent.
6. True. Positive demand shock.
7. False. The Bank of Canada should step on the brakes by raising interest rates.
8. True. Lower interest rates increase aggregate demand through both domestic and international transmission mechanisms.
9. True. Increase or decrease interest rates.
10. False. It is politically unpopular higher interest rates decrease GDP and income.
11. True. Apply the monetary "brake" of higher interest rates before inflation starts, but not too soon to stop economic recovery.
12. True. Lower interest rates do not increase aggregate demand in a balance sheet recession.
13. True. Inflation-control target set jointly by Government of Canada and Bank of Canada, but Bank of Canada is responsible for monetary policy to achieve the target.
14. False. Inflation expectations go up easily but come down painfully.
15. False. Both camps agree that inflation control targets are an effective compromise between hands-off emphasis on rules and hands-on emphasis on government discretion.

MULTIPLE CHOICE

1. **c)** Keep inflation rate within target-control range so it does not significantly affect decisions.

2. **c)** CPI between 1 percent and 3 percent, but paying attention to underlying trends of core inflation rate.
3. **d)** The CPI inflation target range is 1–3 percent.
4. **c)** Lowering the overnight interest rate sooner may have increased spending and aggregate demand.
5. **d)** The interest rate for high-risk borrowers is above the prime rate.
6. **b)** This is an open market operation.
7. **c)** When the Bank of Canada buys bonds, the increased money supply lowers interest rates, increasing aggregate demand.
8. **d)** 18–24 months is the time lag for monetary policy to have an effect on the economy.
9. **c)** The Bank of Canada should add punch to the bowl (lower interest rates) if the economy is in a recessionary gap.
10. **a)** To speed up the economy, monetary policy lowers interest rates, causing the value of the Canadian dollar to decrease, increasing net exports and aggregate demand.
11. **a)** The price level and the level of real GDP respond to an increase in the money supply.
12. **d)** Bank of Canada policy was conservative before the Global Financial Crisis, but not conservative during the Global Financial Crisis.
13. **b)** The banks made questionable loans in pursuit of profits before the Global Financial Crisis, and hesitated to make loans during the Global Financial Crisis.
14. **c)** A limited role for government in monetary policy.
15. **d)** Inflation-control target set jointly by Government of Canada and Bank of Canada, but Bank of Canada alone is responsible for monetary policy to achieve the target.

CHAPTER 12

TRUE/FALSE

1. True. Saving is a leakage.
2. False. "No — Markets Fail Often" camp favours government spending to accelerate the economy.
3. False. To slow the economy, "Yes — Markets Self-Adjust" camp favours spending reductions; "No — Markets Fail Often" camp favours tax increases.
4. True. Government purchases have a multiplied effect on aggregate demand and real GDP.
5. False. Empirical evidence shows tax revenues decrease with cuts in the tax rate.
6. False. Those disagreeing with supply-sider arguments refer to "voodoo economics." Supply-siders would not want your hug.
7. False. Keynes, the original hands-on economist, believes short-run adjustment costs of savings outweigh long-run benefits for economic growth.
8. True. Knowledge has positive externalities for growth.
9. True. Tax cuts decrease government revenues.

10. True. Automatic stabilizers support spending and decrease taxes.
11. False. Automatic stabilizers drop transfers when the economy's hot and decrease taxes or increase transfers when it's not.
12. False. Debt is a stock and sometimes a smart choice. Deficits are a flow.
13. False. Ricardo and Barro agree that government spending financed by borrowing (debt) has no impact on the economy.
14. True. Normative because there are different judgements about what "better" means.
15. False. Founding principles for Canada are peace, order, and good government; for the United States they are life, liberty, and the pursuit of happiness.

MULTIPLE CHOICE

1. **d)** All affect aggregate demand.
2. **b)** The size of the multiplier effect depends on leakages out of the circular flow. Fewer leakages = larger multiplier.
3. **d)** All are income not spent on Canadian GDP.
4. **d)** Fiscal policies attempt to match aggregate demand and aggregate supply at potential GDP.
5. **a)** More students get educated, increasing the quality of labour inputs.
6. **d)** Supply-siders claim tax rate cuts increase total tax revenues.
7. **c)** There can be a trade-off between increased aggregate supply in the future — through business investment spending financed by more savings — and reduced aggregate demand in the present due to lower spending.
8. **a)** If revenue is $1 billion greater than spending, this surplus reduces debt by $1 billion (from $50 billion to $49 billion).
9. **b)** Structural deficits are the greatest concern because debt rises and so do interest payments.
10. **c)** Increase in real GDP automatically increases tax revenues. Decreases in unemployment automatically decrease transfer payments.
11. **c)** True when interest payments cause budget deficits, which, in turn, increase the national debt and interest payment.
12. **a)** If government sells bonds to finance debt, increased supply of bonds drives down bond prices and raises interest rates, so it is more expensive for businesses to borrow.
13. **c)** Canada was created by an act of British government; United States was created through revolution against government.
14. **d)** Most economists agree governments should run deficits in recessions and surpluses during expansions, balancing over the business cycle.
15. **c)** "Should" indicates a value judgement.

CHAPTER 13

TRUE/FALSE

1. False. Comparative advantage, specialization, and trade reduce self-sufficiency.
2. True. Trade only happens when both parties benefit.
3. False. Exports as a percentage of GDP are 30 percent for Canada and 14 percent for the United States.
4. True. For mutual benefits, terms of trade must be between each trader's local opportunity costs.
5. True. Allows access to products not produced at home.
6. True. Trade benefits consumers.
7. True. Better products, in this case without the job loss often accompanying creative destruction.
8. False. Tariffs hurt consumers by making imports more expensive, and protect some non-competitive businesses.
9. True. Unequal distribution of gains and losses produces political pressure for protectionism to help the losers.
10. True. National security and cultural identity are valid, limited arguments for protectionism.
11. True. Hands-on economists support a limited role for government in helping losers adjust to freer trade.
12. False. Workers make smart economic choices selecting highest-paying jobs. Sweatshop jobs pay more than farm jobs.
13. False. Social safety nets are government programs to assist citizens through difficult economic transitions. Employment Insurance is an example of a Canadian social safety net.
14. True. She argues trade is not the problem.
15. True. Politicians you vote for make trade policy.

MULTIPLE CHOICE

1. **a)** Definition of opportunity cost.
2. **c)** Specializing and trading creates more wealth for all.
3. **c)** You are able to produce a product or services at a lower cost than competitors.
4. **b)** Definition of comparative advantage.
5. **b)** Specializing where you have a comparative advantage makes trading mutually beneficial.
6. **b)** Terms of trade are the ratio at which traded products exchange.
7. **a)** Traders must do better with trade than they can do locally.
8. **d)** Structural unemployment is caused by jobs becoming obsolete due to new technologies or international competition.
9. **b)** Jobs gained through new businesses and higher productivity outweigh jobs lost in less competitive businesses.
10. **d)** New technology or international competition pressures old businesses to change or close.
11. **c)** Consumers gain from better, less expensive products and services, but businesses and workers in import-competing industries lose.
12. **d)** Markets become more connected and interdependent.
13. **c)** Economists ask the opportunity cost question, "Are workers' lives better off, or worse off, compared to a situation without globalization and trade?"
14. **a)** Hands-on camp believes in a limited role for government to protect workers who lose from trade.
15. **d)** Jobs are gained through new technologies and international competition but lost when out-dated businesses close.

Index

expected inflation rate, 181
  formula for, 178
  inflation rate target, 313, 334–341
  limitations of, 184–185
  monetary policy, 179
  official inflation rate, 185
inflation rate differential, 286–287
inflationary gap, 157, 176, 225, 226, 232, 316, 327,
  350, 357, 367
injection, 351, 354–355
input markets, 14–15
  circular flow model, 138
  connections between input and output markets,
    111–112, 231
inputs, 14, 60, 61
  change in prices, 207
  costs of, 53–54
  equilibrium over time with increasing inputs, 220–223
  incomes of, 138
  long-run equilibrium with existing inputs, 220
  price of, 67, 207
  short-run equilibrium with existing inputs, 220
  short-run supply plans with existing inputs, 204
interest, 244, 375
interest payments, 301
interest rate, 247, 314
  and aggregate demand, 216
  and bonds, 244, 258–260, 319–320
  and borrowing, 264
  and the Canadian dollar, 275
  and demand for money, 247–248
  domestic effects, 321
  effects of, 124
  expected real rate of interest, 181
  and falling value of money, 181
  higher interest rates, 316, 324, 327
  higher rates, 257
  international effects, 322
  and loanable funds markets, 260–261
  lower interest rates, 316, 324, 326
  market-clearing interest rate, 260, 317, 318, 319
  and money, 299
  and money markets, 260–261
  and money supply, 316–319
  moving together, 320
  multitude of interest rates, 261
  as negative aggregate demand shock, 264
  nominal interest rate, 181
  overnight rate, 314
  as positive aggregate demand shock, 264
  as price of money, 241, 248
  prime rate, 320

real interest rate, 181
short-run interest rates, 320, 321
interest rate differentials, 284–286
interest rate parity, 299
intermediate products, 133
international balance of payments, 300–303
International Bank for Reconstruction and Development
  (IBRD), 402
International Development Agency (IDA), 402
International Monetary Fund (IMF), 402–403, 409, 412
international trade. *See* trade
international trade markets, 231
international trade politics, 400
international transactions, 303
international transmission mechanism, 263, 291–294,
  324–326, 327
investment, and unpredictable prices, 182
investment plans, 216
investment postponed, 213
investment spending, 121, 140, 141, 213, 214, 216, 221,
  222, 224, 230, 245, 246, 263–264, 266, 321, 324, 330,
  331, 351, 352, 354, 355, 356, 361, 362, 368, 369, 376
investment spending choices, 143
investors, and real GDP, 287
invisible hand, 86, 107, 144, 203
involuntary part-time workers, 170

J

Japanese deflation, 184

K

Keynes, John Maynard, 113, 117, 193, 230, 243, 246, 265,
  266, 331, 369
  see also "No – Markets Fail Often" camp
Keynesian revolution, 113–114
keys to smart choices, 19–21
  additional benefits and costs, 20, 30
  additional benefits *vs.* opportunity costs, 20, 28, 56, 99
  implicit costs and externalities, 20–21
Krugman, Paul, 154

L

labour
  and economic growth, 147
  underutilization, 171
labour force, 169
  female labour force participation, 147, 169
  labour force participation rate, 147, 169
  not in the labour force, 168

producer surplus, **97,** 98
production possibilities, 390–391
production possibilities frontier (*PPF*)**, 9,** 57, 146, 202, 391
productivity, 153–155, 396
profits, 256
property rights, 79, 80
protectionism, 397–401, 408
prudence, 256
public debt, 372–376
purchasing power, 180
purchasing power parity (*PPP*)**, 295**–298

Q

quantitative easing, 332
quantity adjustments, 84
quantity demanded, 33–34, 211, 248
 changes in quantity demanded, 44–45
 decrease in, 90
 vs. demand, 38–39
 increase in, 90
quantity of real output, 188
quantity supplied, 55–**56,** 204, 257
 changes in quantity supplied, 65, 69
 decrease in, 89
 increase in, 88
quantity theory of money, 185–**188,** 332–333

R

rate of return parity, 299
rational expectations, 229
Reagan, Ronald, 363–364
real GDP, 135
 calculation of, 136
 comparisons, 184
 decreasing, 288
 and demand for money, 248–249
 and environmental damage, 159
 equilibrium real GDP, 358
 exchange rates, and real GDP changes, 287–288
 expansion, 156
 and fall in price level, 204
 and imports, 287
 increasing, 287
 investors and, 287
 and leisure, 159
 limitations as measure of well-being, 158–160
 money and, 262–264
 and multiplier effects, 358
 and non-market production, 158
 and political freedoms, 160

 and potential GDP, 175–176
 vs. potential GDP, 157
 and social justice, 160
 and underground economy, 159
real GDP per person, 136, 158, 160
real GDP per person growth rate, 150
real interest rate, 181
recession, 157, 329–334, 368
recessionary gap, 157, 175, 191, 224, 226, 230, 231, 316, 326, 329, 356, 367
reciprocal exchange rates, 282
regional differences in unemployment rate, 172
Registered Retirement Savings Plans (RRSPs), 360
related products, 41–42, 67–68
research and development, 361
reserves, 255, 331
resources, 148
rest of the world (R.O.W.), 122
 and Canadian exports, 288–289
 choices, 143
 circular flow, enlargement of, 139–141
 demand choices, 214
 elimination of Canadian choices from R.O.W. spending, 214
 exports and imports, 141
 GDP in, and aggregate demand, 217
 substitutions from, 212
right of the political spectrum, 117
Rivoli, Pietra, 411, 412
Robinson, Joan, 219
R.O.W. *See* rest of the world (R.O.W.)
Rule of 70, 152
rules of the game, 79

S

savers, and deflation, 183
saving jobs argument for protectionism, 400
savings, 245–246, 360, 361–362
Say, Jean-Baptiste, 113, 116, 265
 see also Say's Law
Say's Law, 113, 138, 149, 176, 193, 209, 220, 221–222, 223, 228, 229, 230, 242, 243, 314, 320, 339
 see also "Yes – Markets Self Adjust" camp
Say's Law with banks, 143
scarcity, 4
 and choice, 4, 5
 trade-off, 5
seasonal unemployment, 174, 175, 176
self-adjustment mechanisms, 112–114
 see also "No – Markets Fail Often" camp; "Yes – Markets Self Adjust" camp

self-fulfilling expectations, 182, 289

self-interest, 84

self-perpetuating debt, 375

sellers, 78, 83

shifting curves, 207

shocks
    demand shocks, 215–217, 223–226, 228
    origins of, 229, 230
    supply shocks, 192–193, 208–209, 226–227, 228, 229

short run, 203

short-run aggregate supply, 204
    law of short-run aggregate supply, 205
    negative supply shocks, 208
    positive supply shocks, 208–209
    rising input prices, 226
    short-run aggregate supply curve, 204–205
    and supply shocks, 208–209

short-run aggregate supply curve, 204–205, 207

short-run equilibrium, 223, 224, 225, 227, 327, 356, 357

short-run equilibrium with existing inputs, 220

shortage, 82, 84

smart choices
    additional benefits *vs.* opportunity costs, 56
    and demand. *See* demand
    keys to smart choices, 19–21
    marginal choices, 30–32
    trade-offs, 5

Smith, Adam, 86, 107, 113, 116, 144, 203, 388

smoothing business cycles, 368

social justice, 160

social safety nets, 407

South America, 400

specialization, 10–12, 387, 388, 393

speculative bubbles, 112

speculators, 289–290

spenders of last resort, 356, 369

spending
    aggregate spending, 138, 139, 141
    circular flow of income and spending, 138
    consumer spending, 139–140, 212, 216
    debt-financed government spending, 375
    deficit-financed government spending, 369
    domestic transmission mechanisms, 323–324
    government spending, 140, 213, 366, 369, 375
    investment spending, 121, 140, 213, 355
    vs. paying down debt, 330–331

stable prices, 149, 174, 221

stagflation, 193, 227

stagnation, 193

standard of living, 7, 12, 131, 149, 151, 153–155, 184, 221, 222–223, 359, 387, 396

statistical discrepancy category, 302

Statistics Canada, 168, 170, 185

sticky wages, 231

Stiglitz, Joseph, 403, 407, 409, 410, 412

stock, 149, 371

stock market bubble, 109, 114

stock markets, 108

store of value, 243, 331

structural deficit, 370

structural surplus, 370

structural unemployment, 173, 175, 176, 396

subsidies to domestic producers, 399

substitutes, 41
    availability of, 33, 35
    from R.O.W., 212
    switch to cheaper substitutes, 184
    weighing substitutes, 28–29

sunk costs, 54–55

supply, 55
    see also demand and supply
    aggregate supply. *See* aggregate supply
    changes in supply, 64–70, 70, 87, 90–91, 92–95, 207
    combined changes in demand and supply, 92–93
    creation of own demand, 209
    decrease in supply, 68, 90–91
    demand and supply choices, 53
    and the environment, 67
    excess supply, 83
    and expected future prices, 68
    increase in supply, 66, 90
    increasing marginal opportunity costs, 57–61
    law of supply, 61–63, 70, 204
    market supply, 61
    of money, 252, 256–257, 261, 316–319
    and number of businesses, 68
    and price of inputs, 67
    and prices of related products and services, 67–68
    quantity supplied, 55–56, 65, 69, 204, 207, 257
    supply plans to increase inputs, 205–207
    supply plans with existing inputs, 204
    and technology, 65–66

supply curve, 62–63
    as marginal cost curve, 97
    movement along, 69
    shifts along, 69

supply plans to increase inputs, 205–207

supply plans with existing inputs, 204

supply shocks, 192–193, 194, 208–209, 226–227, 228, 229, 266, 267, 360
    see also negative supply shocks; positive supply shocks

supply-side effects, 362–364

supply-siders, 363, 364

surplus, **83,** 84, 365–370
    cyclical surpluses, 368, 369, 370
    government budget surpluses, 365–370
    structural surplus, 370
sweatshops, 405–406

T

tariff, 397–398
tax avoidance, 159
tax exemptions, 360
Tax-Free Savings Accounts (TFSAs), 360
tax multiplier, 353
technological change, 147
technology
    and competition, 395
    and supply, 65–66
technology boom, 227
terms of trade, 393–395, 409
thinking like a macroeconomist, 123–125
thinking like an economist, 13–17
total surplus, 99, 100–101
trade
    absolute advantage, 9, 392
    comparative advantage, 10, 11, 12, 392, 393
    domestic trade politics, 399
    free trade, 395–401, 402–406
    gains from trade, 7–12, 388–395
    international trade markets, 231
    international trade politics, 400
    and living standards, 387
    mutual benefits from trade, 390–391
    and opportunity costs, 7, 392–393
    politics of trade policy, 399–400
    protectionism, 397–401, 408
    specialization, 11
    terms of trade, 393–395, 409
    voluntary trade, 7–9, 78, 79, 388
    winners and losers, 397
trade-off, 5
    exchange rates, 298
    government and global markets, 410
    interest *vs.* liquidity, 244
    and national debt, 379
    profits *vs.* prudence or safety, 256
    trade policy, government role in, 410
    unemployment and inflation tradeoffs, 189–194
trade wars, 401
training, 361
transfer multiplier, 353
transfer payments. *See* government
      transfer payments

transmission mechanisms, 321–328
    domestic monetary transmission mechanism, 262–264,
      323–324
    international transmission mechanism, 291–294,
      324–326
    reinforcement of, 326–328
trough, 156
trust, 79

U

uncertainty, 231
underground economy, 159
unemployed, 168
unemployment, 120
    in Canada, 170
    cyclical unemployment, 174, 175
    frictional unemployment, 173, 175, 176
    healthy unemployment, 173–174
    and inflation tradeoffs, 189–194
    natural rate of unemployment, 175–176
    as quantity adjustment in labour markets, 231
    recessionary gap, 157
    seasonal unemployment, 174, 175, 176
    stagflation, 193
    structural unemployment, 173, 175, 176, 396
    thinking like a macroeconomist, 123
    unhealthy unemployment, 174, 175
    zero percent cyclical unemployment, 175, 176
unemployment rate, 167, **169**
    associated with full employment, 175–176
    calculation of, 168–169
    Canada, 167, 170
    and discouraged workers, 171
    and involuntary part-time workers, 170
    limitations of, 170–172
    and regional differences, 172
unit of account, 242
United Nations Development Programme, 160
United States
    Canada, trade with, 389
    Federal Reserve, 109, 329, 331–332
    Federal Reserve Act, 335
    Global Financial Crisis. *See* Global
      Financial Crisis
    hands-off origins, 377
    housing boom, 331
    housing-price bubble, 108, 224
    mortgage-backed securities, 329
    real estate bubble burst, 329
    trade politics, 400
    trading relationship with, 122

unpredictable inflation, 337–338
unpredictable prices, 182, 337

V

vacation time, 159
value
    of final products and services, 138
    and nominal GDP, 132
value added, 137–138
velocity of money, 186, 188
vicious cycles, 351–354
Vietnam War, 179
virtuous cycles, 351–354
volatile expectations and money, 231
Volcker, Paul, 337
voluntary exchange, 7–9, 78, 79, 388
von Hayek, Friedrich, 116
voodoo economics, 362–364
vote, 124, 412

W

wage gap, 6
The Wealth of Nations (Smith), 86
willingness to pay, 32
willingness to work, 52–53
women in the labour force, 147, 169
work time per purchase, 153
World Bank, 402–403, 409, 412

World Trade Organization (WTO), 398, 400, 409
World War II, 372, 373

Y

"Yes – Markets Self Adjust" camp, 113, 116–117
    central banks, 338–341
    changes over time in macroeconomic equilibrium, 220
    debt-financed government spending, 375
    deciding on "Yes-No" macroeconomic question, 232
    demand-side fiscal policies, 358
    developing countries, 403
    fundamental macroeconomic question, 119
    government and global markets, 408–409, 410
    macroeconomic agreements, 118–119, 228, 338–341
    macroeconomic equilibrium, 228
    market failure *vs.* government failure, 115–116
    market price responses to business cycles, 230
    monetary policy, 339
    money, importance of, 265–266
    money as store of value, 245
    origins of shocks and business cycles, 229
    rational expectations, 229
    right of the political spectrum, 117
    savings, and economic growth, 361

Z

zero percent cyclical unemployment, 175, 176
Zimbabwe, 333